Twist and Go (automatic transmission) Scooters
Service and Repair Manual

by Phil Mather

Models covered in Data Section

(4082-296-1AG2)

Aprilia Leonardo 125, Rally 50, Sonic FT and GP, SR50 (94-99)

Gilera Ice 50, Runner 50, Runner FX125 and FXR180, Runner VX125 and VXR180/200, SKP50 (Stalker)

Honda FES125 Pantheon, FES250 Foresight, NES125 @125, SCV100 Lead, SES125 Dylan, SFX50, SGX50 Sky, SH50, SH125, SZX50 (X8R-S/X8R-X)

Malaguti F12 Phantom 50, F12 Spectrum 50, F15 Firefox 50, Madison 125 and 150

MBK Doodo 125, Mach G 50, Nitro 50 and 100, Ovetto 50 and 100, Rocket, Skyliner 125, Stunt 50, Thunder 125

Peugeot Elyseo 50/100/125, Elystar 125 and 150, Looxor 50/100/125/150, Ludix 50, Speedfight 50 and 100, Speedfight 2 50 and 100, Trekker 50 and 100, Vivacity 50 and 100, Zenith

Piaggio B125 (Beverly), Fly 50 and 125, Hexagon 125, Super Hexagon 125 and 180, Liberty 50 and 125, NRG MC^2, NRG MC^3, NRG Power, Skipper 125, Skipper ST125, Typhoon 50/80/125, X8 125, X9 125, Zip 50, Zip 50 SP, Zip 125

Suzuki AN125, AP50, AY50 Katana, AY50W Katana R, UH125 Burgman

Sym DD50 City Trek, Jet 50 and 100, Shark 50, Super Fancy and City Hopper

Vespa ET2 50, ET4 50, ET4 125, GT125 and 200; LX2 50, LX4 50, LX4 125

Yamaha CS50 JogR, CS50Z JogRR, CW/BW 50, EW50 Slider, NXC125 Cygnus, XN125 Teo's, XQ125 Maxster, YN50 and100 Neo's, YP125 Majesty, YP250 Majesty, YQ50 and 100 Aerox

© Haynes Publishing 2008

A book in the **Haynes Service and Repair Manual Series**

ABCDE
FGHIJ
KLM

ISBN 978-1-84425-625-9

British Library Cataloguing in Publication Data
A catalogue record for this book is available from the British Library.

Printed in the USA

Haynes Publishing
Sparkford, Yeovil, Somerset BA22 7JJ, England

Haynes North America, Inc
861 Lawrence Drive, Newbury Park, California 91320, USA

Haynes Publishing Nordiska AB
Box 1504, 751 45 UPPSALA, Sweden

LIVING WITH YOUR SCOOTER

MAINTENANCE

REPAIRS AND OVERHAUL

DATA

REFERENCE

Thanks are due to Piaggio VE SpA, Italy, and to Mitsui Machinery Sales (UK) Ltd for permission to reproduce artwork from their publications. We would also like to thank NGK Spark Plugs (UK) Ltd for supplying colour spark plug condition photos and Draper Tools for some of the workshop tools shown.

We are grateful to the manufacturers or importers who supplied material for the Data section at the end of this manual, particularly the UK importers for Sym, Malaguti, Peugeot, Gilera, Piaggio and Vespa. For anyone we have inadvertently omitted, please accept our apologies.

Special thanks are due to VE (UK) Ltd, suppliers of scooter parts and accessories to the trade, for help and advice given.

About this manual

The aim of this manual is to help you get the best value from your scooter. It can do so in several ways. It can help you decide what work must be done, even if you choose to have it done by a dealer; it provides information and procedures for routine maintenance and servicing; and it offers diagnostic and repair procedures to follow when trouble occurs.

We hope you use the manual to tackle the work yourself. For many simpler jobs, doing it yourself may be quicker than arranging an appointment to get the scooter into a dealer and making the trips to leave it and pick it up. More importantly, a lot of money can be saved by avoiding the expense the shop must pass on to you to cover its labour and overhead costs. An added benefit is the sense of satisfaction and accomplishment that you feel after doing the job yourself.

References to the left or right side of the scooter assume you are sitting on the seat, facing forward.

We take great pride in the accuracy of information given in this manual, but manufacturers often make alterations and design changes during the production run of a particular machine of which they do not inform us. No liability can be accepted by the authors or publishers for loss, damage or injury caused by any errors in, or omissions from, the information given.

Identification numbers and buying spare parts

Frame and engine numbers

The frame serial number, or VIN (Vehicle Identification Number) as it is often known, is stamped into the frame, and also appears on the identification plate. The engine number is stamped into the rear of the transmission casing. Both of these numbers should be recorded and kept in a safe place so they can be furnished to law enforcement officials in the event of a theft.

The frame and engine numbers should also be kept in a handy place (such as with your driving licence) so they are always available when purchasing or ordering parts for your scooter.

Each model type can be identified by its engine and frame number prefix.

Buying spare parts

When ordering new parts, it is essential to identify exactly the machine for which the parts are required. While in some cases it is sufficient to identify the machine by its title, eg, 'Gilera Runner' or 'Yamaha Neo's', any modifications made to components mean that it is usually essential to identify the scooter by its year of production, or better still by its frame or engine number prefix.

To be absolutely certain of receiving the correct part, not only is it essential to have the scooter engine or frame number prefix to hand, but it is also useful to take the old part for comparison (where possible). Note that where a modified component has superseded the original, a careful check must be made that there are no related parts which have also been modified and must be used to enable the new to be correctly refitted; where such a situation is found, purchase all the necessary parts and fit them, even if this means renewing apparently unworn items.

Purchase parts from an authorised dealer or someone who specialises in scooter parts; they are more likely to have the parts in stock or can order them quickly from the importer. Pattern parts are available for certain components; if used, ensure these are of recognised quality brands which will perform as well as the original.

Expendable items such as lubricants, spark plugs, some electrical components, bearings, bulbs and tyres can usually be obtained at lower prices from accessory shops, motor factors or from specialists advertising in the national motorcycle press.

The frame number is stamped into the frame . . .

. . . and also appears on the identification plate

The engine number is stamped into the rear of the transmission casing

Professional mechanics are trained in safe working procedures. However enthusiastic you may be about getting on with the job at hand, take the time to ensure that your safety is not put at risk. A moment's lack of attention can result in an accident, as can failure to observe simple precautions.

There will always be new ways of having accidents, and the following is not a comprehensive list of all dangers; it is intended rather to make you aware of the risks and to encourage a safe approach to all work you carry out on your bike.

Asbestos

● Certain friction, insulating, sealing and other products - such as brake pads, clutch linings, gaskets, etc. - contain asbestos. Extreme care must be taken to avoid inhalation of dust from such products since it is hazardous to health. If in doubt, assume that they do contain asbestos.

Fire

● Remember at all times that petrol is highly flammable. Never smoke or have any kind of naked flame around, when working on the vehicle. But the risk does not end there - a spark caused by an electrical short-circuit, by two metal surfaces contacting each other, by careless use of tools, or even by static electricity built up in your body under certain conditions, can ignite petrol vapour, which in a confined space is highly explosive. Never use petrol as a cleaning solvent. Use an approved safety solvent.

● Always disconnect the battery earth terminal before working on any part of the fuel or electrical system, and never risk spilling fuel on to a hot engine or exhaust.
● It is recommended that a fire extinguisher of a type suitable for fuel and electrical fires is kept handy in the garage or workplace at all times. Never try to extinguish a fuel or electrical fire with water.

Fumes

● Certain fumes are highly toxic and can quickly cause unconsciousness and even death if inhaled to any extent. Petrol vapour comes into this category, as do the vapours from certain solvents such as trichloroethylene. Any draining or pouring of such volatile fluids should be done in a well ventilated area.
● When using cleaning fluids and solvents, read the instructions carefully. Never use materials from unmarked containers - they may give off poisonous vapours.
● Never run the engine of a motor vehicle in an enclosed space such as a garage. Exhaust fumes contain carbon monoxide which is extremely poisonous; if you need to run the engine, always do so in the open air or at least have the rear of the vehicle outside the workplace.

The battery

● Never cause a spark, or allow a naked light near the vehicle's battery. It will normally be giving off a certain amount of hydrogen gas, which is highly explosive.

● Always disconnect the battery ground (earth) terminal before working on the fuel or electrical systems (except where noted).
● If possible, loosen the filler plugs or cover when charging the battery from an external source. Do not charge at an excessive rate or the battery may burst.
● Take care when topping up, cleaning or carrying the battery. The acid electrolyte, even when diluted, is very corrosive and should not be allowed to contact the eyes or skin. Always wear rubber gloves and goggles or a face shield. If you ever need to prepare electrolyte yourself, always add the acid slowly to the water; never add the water to the acid.

Electricity

● When using an electric power tool, inspection light etc., always ensure that the appliance is correctly connected to its plug and that, where necessary, it is properly grounded (earthed). Do not use such appliances in damp conditions and, again, beware of creating a spark or applying excessive heat in the vicinity of fuel or fuel vapour. Also ensure that the appliances meet national safety standards.
● A severe electric shock can result from touching certain parts of the electrical system, such as the spark plug wires (HT leads), when the engine is running or being cranked, particularly if components are damp or the insulation is defective. Where an electronic ignition system is used, the secondary (HT) voltage is much higher and could prove fatal.

Remember...

✗ **Don't** start the engine without first ascertaining that the transmission is in neutral.

✗ **Don't** suddenly remove the pressure cap from a hot cooling system - cover it with a cloth and release the pressure gradually first, or you may get scalded by escaping coolant.

✗ **Don't** attempt to drain oil until you are sure it has cooled sufficiently to avoid scalding you.

✗ **Don't** grasp any part of the engine or exhaust system without first ascertaining that it is cool enough not to burn you.

✗ **Don't** allow brake fluid or antifreeze to contact the machine's paintwork or plastic components.

✗ **Don't** siphon toxic liquids such as fuel, hydraulic fluid or antifreeze by mouth, or allow them to remain on your skin.

✗ **Don't** inhale dust - it may be injurious to health (see Asbestos heading).

✗ **Don't** allow any spilled oil or grease to remain on the floor - wipe it up right away, before someone slips on it.

✗ **Don't** use ill-fitting spanners or other tools which may slip and cause injury.

✗ **Don't** lift a heavy component which may

be beyond your capability - get assistance.

✗ **Don't** rush to finish a job or take unverified short cuts.

✗ **Don't** allow children or animals in or around an unattended vehicle.

✗ **Don't** inflate a tyre above the recommended pressure. Apart from overstressing the carcass, in extreme cases the tyre may blow off forcibly.

✔ **Do** ensure that the machine is supported securely at all times. This is especially important when the machine is blocked up to aid wheel or fork removal.

✔ **Do** take care when attempting to loosen a stubborn nut or bolt. It is generally better to pull on a spanner, rather than push, so that if you slip, you fall away from the machine rather than onto it.

✔ **Do** wear eye protection when using power tools such as drill, sander, bench grinder etc.

✔ **Do** use a barrier cream on your hands prior to undertaking dirty jobs - it will protect your skin from infection as well as making the dirt easier to remove afterwards; but make sure your hands aren't left slippery. Note that long-term contact with used engine oil can be a health hazard.

✔ **Do** keep loose clothing (cuffs, ties etc. and long hair) well out of the way of moving

mechanical parts.

✔ **Do** remove rings, wristwatch etc., before working on the vehicle - especially the electrical system.

✔ **Do** keep your work area tidy - it is only too easy to fall over articles left lying around.

✔ **Do** exercise caution when compressing springs for removal or installation. Ensure that the tension is applied and released in a controlled manner, using suitable tools which preclude the possibility of the spring escaping violently.

✔ **Do** ensure that any lifting tackle used has a safe working load rating adequate for the job.

✔ **Do** get someone to check periodically that all is well, when working alone on the vehicle.

✔ **Do** carry out work in a logical sequence and check that everything is correctly assembled and tightened afterwards.

✔ **Do** remember that your vehicle's safety affects that of yourself and others. If in doubt on any point, get professional advice.

● If in spite of following these precautions, you are unfortunate enough to injure yourself, seek medical attention as soon as possible.

Note: *The Daily (pre-ride) checks outlined in your owner's manual covers those items which should be inspected on a daily basis.*

Two-stroke engine oil level check

Before you start
✔ Make sure you have a supply of the correct oil available.
✔ Support the machine in an upright position whilst checking the level. Make sure it is on level ground.

The correct oil
● Keep the oil tank topped up with a good quality two-stroke oil suitable for injector systems. Certain scooters require a specific grade of two-stroke oil – see *Data* section at the end of this manual.

● Don't rely on the oil level warning light to tell you that the oil needs topping-up. Get into the habit of checking the oil level at the same time as you fill up with fuel.

● If the engine is run without oil, even for a short time, serious engine damage and engine seizure will occur. It is advised that a bottle of engine oil is carried in the storage compartment at all times.

Scooter care
● If you have to add oil frequently, you should check whether you have any oil leaks, and check the oil pump adjustment (see Chapter 1).

1 Remove the filler cap to check the oil level.

2 If the level is low, top-up with the recommended grade and type of oil, then refit the filler cap securely.

Four-stroke engine oil level check

Before you start
✔ Make sure you have a supply of the correct oil available.
✔ Support the machine in an upright position whilst checking the level. Make sure it is on level ground.

The correct oil
● Modern engines place great demands on their oil. It is very important to use the correct oil for your engine.
● Always top-up with a good quality oil of the specified type and viscosity – see *Data* section at the end of this manual.

● Check the oil level carefully. Make sure you know the correct level for your scooter.

Scooter care
● If you have to add oil frequently, you should check whether you have any oil leaks.

1 Either check the level through the sight glass . . .

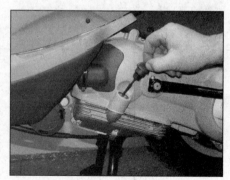

2 . . . or use the dipstick on the filler plug.

3 If the level is low, top-up with the recommended grade and type of oil, then refit the filler cap securely. Never overfill the oil.

Coolant level check (liquid-cooled engines)

 Warning: DO NOT leave open containers of coolant about, as it is poisonous.

Before you start

✔ Make sure you have a supply of coolant available (a mixture of 50% distilled water and 50% corrosion inhibited ethylene glycol antifreeze is needed).

✔ Always check the coolant level when the engine is cold.

✔ Support the machine in an upright position whilst checking the level. Make sure it is on level ground.

Scooter care

● Use only the specified coolant mixture. It is important that antifreeze is used in the system all year round, and not just in the winter. Do not top-up the system with water only, as the coolant will become too diluted.

● Make sure you know the correct level for your scooter – refer to your scooter handbook for details. If there are no minimum and maximum marks, top-up the coolant level to just below the bottom of the filler neck.

● Do not overfill the reservoir tank. Any surplus should be siphoned or drained off to prevent the possibility of it being expelled under pressure.

● If the coolant level falls steadily, check the system for leaks (see Chapter 1). If no leaks are found and the level continues to fall, it is recommended that the machine is taken to a scooter dealer for a pressure test.

1 On many scooters you will need to detach a body panel to view the coolant reservoir.

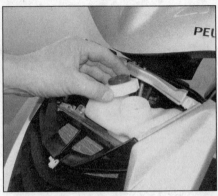

2 To top up, unscrew the filler cap and top up to the bottom of the filler neck or level marks.

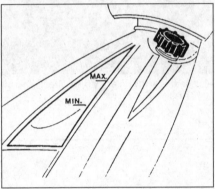

3 On other scooters the coolant reservoir has level marks on its side which are visible through slots in the body panel . . .

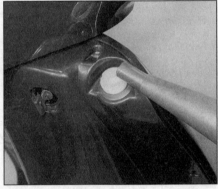

4 . . . and topping up is done via a filler cap at the top of the panel.

Suspension and steering checks

● Check that the front and rear suspension operates smoothly without binding.

● Check that the steering moves smoothly from lock-to-lock.

Fuel check

● This may seem obvious, but check that you have enough fuel to complete your journey.

Do not rely on the fuel gauge or warning light to tell you that the level in the tank is low before filling up.

● If you notice any fuel leaks you must rectify the cause immediately.

● Ensure you use the correct grade unleaded petrol, minimum 95 octane. Note that the use of unleaded petrol will increase spark plug life and have obvious benefits to the environment.

Brake fluid level check

⚠ **Warning:** *Brake hydraulic fluid can harm your eyes and damage painted surfaces, so use extreme caution when handling and pouring it and cover surrounding surfaces with rag. Do not use fluid that has been standing open for some time, as it absorbs moisture from the air which can cause a dangerous loss of braking effectiveness.*

Before you start

✔ Support the machine in an upright position on level ground and turn the handlebars until the hydraulic reservoir is as level as possible – remember to check both reservoirs if your scooter is equipped with front and rear disc brakes.
✔ Make sure you have a supply of DOT 4 hydraulic fluid.
✔ Access to the reservoir is restricted on most models by the upper handlebar cover. Remove the cover if the reservoir requires topping-up.
✔ Wrap a rag around the reservoir to prevent any hydraulic fluid coming into contact with painted or plastic surfaces.

Scooter care

● The fluid in the hydraulic reservoir will drop slightly as the brake pads wear down.
● If the reservoir requires repeated topping-up this is an indication of a fluid leak somewhere in the system, which should be investigated immediately.
● Check for signs of fluid leaks from the brake hoses and components – if found, rectify immediately.
● Check the operation of the brake before riding the machine; if there is evidence of air in the system (a spongy feel to the lever), it must be bled as described in Chapter 8.

1 The brake fluid level is visible through the sightglass in the reservoir body – it must be half way up the glass when the reservoir is level.

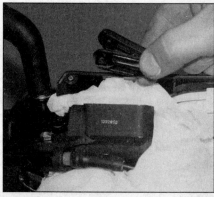

2 Remove the reservoir cap screws and remove the cover, the diaphragm plate and the diaphragm.

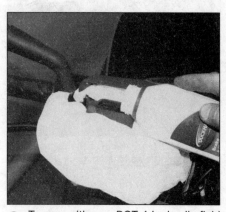

3 Top-up with new DOT 4 hydraulic fluid until the level is half way up the sightglass. Do not overfill and take care to avoid spills (see **Warning** above).

4 Ensure that the diaphragm is correctly seated before installing the plate and cover. Tighten the cover screws securely.

Legal and safety checks

Lighting and signalling

● Take a minute to check that the headlight, tail light, brake light, instrument lights and turn signals all work correctly.
● Check that the horn sounds when the switch is operated.
● A working speedometer graduated in mph is a statutory requirement in the UK.

Safety

● Check that the throttle twistgrip rotates smoothly and snaps shut when released, in all steering positions.
● Check that the stand return spring holds the stand securely up when retracted.
● Check that both brakes work correctly when applied and free off when released.

Tyre checks

The correct pressures

● The tyres must be checked when **cold**, not immediately after riding. Note that low tyre pressures may cause the tyre to slip on the rim or come off. High tyre pressures will cause abnormal tread wear and unsafe handling.
● Use an accurate pressure gauge.
● Proper air pressure will increase tyre life and provide maximum stability and ride comfort.
● Refer to the *Data* section at the end of this manual for the correct tyre pressures for your model.

Tyre care

● Check the tyres carefully for cuts, tears, embedded nails or other sharp objects and excessive wear. Operation of the scooter with excessively worn tyres is extremely hazardous, as traction and handling are directly affected.
● Check the condition of the tyre valve and ensure the dust cap is in place.
● Pick out any stones or nails which may have become embedded in the tyre tread. If left, they will eventually penetrate through the casing and cause a puncture.
● If tyre damage is apparent, or unexplained loss of pressure is experienced, seek the advice of a tyre fitting specialist without delay.

Tyre tread depth

● At the time of writing, for machines with an engine size greater than 50 cc, UK law requires that tread depth must be at least 1 mm over 3/4 of the tread breadth all the way around the tyre, with no bald patches. Many riders, however, consider 2 mm tread depth minimum to be a safer limit.
● For machines with an engine size not greater than 50 cc, UK law states that tread depth may be less than 1 mm if the tread pattern is clearly visible across the whole of the tread breadth all the way around the tyre.
● Many tyres now incorporate wear indicators in the tread. Identify the triangular pointer on the tyre sidewall to locate the indicator bar and renew the tyre if the tread has worn down to the bar.

1 Check the tyre pressures when the tyres are **cold** and keep them properly inflated.

2 Measure tread depth at the centre of the tyre using a tread depth gauge.

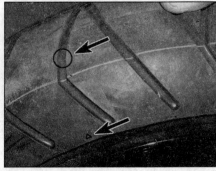

3 Tyre tread wear indicator bar and its location marking (usually either an arrow, a triangle or the letters TWI) on the sidewall (arrowed).

Chapter 1
Routine maintenance and servicing

Contents

Degrees of difficulty

Easy, suitable for novice with little experience	Fairly easy, suitable for beginner with some experience	Fairly difficult, suitable for competent DIY mechanic	Difficult, suitable for experienced DIY mechanic	Very difficult, suitable for expert DIY or professional 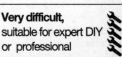

Specifications

Refer to the *Data* section at the end of this manual for servicing specifications.

1 Introduction

1 This Chapter is designed to help the home mechanic maintain his/her scooter for safety, economy, long life and peak performance.

2 Whenever you ride your scooter, and in some cases even when it is not in use, components wear and deteriorate. To counteract this process, every machine has a service schedule – relating to either a period of time or mileage – which stipulates when checks and adjustments should be made.

3 The majority of service items are common to all scooters, but some, like the radiator on a liquid-cooled model or the valves on a four-stroke engine, are specific to certain machines. The *Data* section at the end of this manual will help you identify the various systems on your scooter and their components, and provide you with the specifications necessary to ensure their continued reliable performance.

4 Deciding where to start or adopt a service schedule depends on several factors. If the warranty period on your scooter has just expired, and if it has been maintained according to the warranty standards, you will want to pick up routine maintenance as it coincides with the next mileage or calendar interval. If you have owned the machine for some time but have never performed any maintenance on it, then you may want to start at the nearest interval and include some additional procedures to ensure that nothing important is overlooked. If you have just had a major engine overhaul, then you will want to start the maintenance routine from the beginning as with a new machine. If you have a used scooter and have no knowledge of its history or maintenance record, it would be best to combine all the checks into one large initial service, and then settle into a regular routine schedule.

5 Don't worry if you haven't got a service schedule for your particular scooter; use the information in this Chapter to identify the service items on your machine – air filter, battery, brakes, etc – then create your own service schedule based on the examples we give. **Note:** *Certain maintenance information is sometimes printed on decals attached to the*

machine. If the information on the decals differs from that included here, use the information on the decal.
6 Before beginning any maintenance or repair, clean your scooter thoroughly, especially around the suspension, brakes, engine and transmission covers. Cleaning will help ensure that dirt does not contaminate the working parts and will allow you to detect wear and damage that could otherwise easily go unnoticed.
Note 1: *The 'Daily (pre-ride) checks' detailed at the beginning of this manual cover those*

items which should be inspected on a daily basis. Always perform the pre-ride inspection at every maintenance interval (in addition to the procedures listed).
Note 2: *The intervals listed below are the intervals generally recommended by manufacturers but are not specific to any make or model. The owner's handbook for your model may have different intervals to those shown. If available, always refer to the maintenance booklet supplied with the machine for the correct intervals.*

Routine maintenance and servicing procedures

2   Typical service items

Identifying service items

1 Use the accompanying list and the owner's handbook to identify the service items on your scooter and their locations **(see illustrations)**. The service items have been grouped under headings which identify the overall systems to which they belong. The headings also relate to the Chapters in this manual.
2 Not all the service items under each heading will require attention at the same time, but when you are working on a particular system it is useful to note all the parts that require servicing and check them at the same time. For example, when the drivebelt cover has been removed to inspect the variator and the condition of the belt, the general condition of the clutch and the kickstart mechanism can be checked. Also, if the belt has worn prematurely and is close to its service limit, a new one can be installed earlier than scheduled to prevent any damage caused by a broken belt.

Two-stroke engines
- [ ] *Engine oil level.*
- [ ] *Oil filter.*
- [ ] *Oil pump adjustment.*
- [ ] *Oil pump drivebelt.*
- [ ] *Cylinder head decarbonising.*

Four-stroke engines
- [ ] *Engine oil level.*
- [ ] *Engine oil change.*
- [ ] *Oil filter.*
- [ ] *Engine oil pressure.*
- [ ] *Valve clearances.*

Cooling system (air-cooled engines)
- [ ] *Cooling fan.*
- [ ] *Engine cowling.*

Cooling system (liquid-cooled engines)
- [ ] *Coolant.*
- [ ] *Radiator.*
- [ ] *Water pump.*
- [ ] *Hoses.*
- [ ] *Draining, flushing and refilling.*

Fuel and exhaust system
- [ ] *Air filters.*
- [ ] *Throttle cable.*
- [ ] *Carburettor.*
- [ ] *Fuel hose.*
- [ ] *Idle speed.*

Ignition system
- [ ] *Spark plug.*

Transmission
- [ ] *Drivebelt.*
- [ ] *Variator.*
- [ ] *Kickstart mechanism.*
- [ ] *Clutch pulley.*
- [ ] *Gearbox oil change.*
- [ ] *Gearbox oil level.*

Frame and suspension
- [ ] *Front suspension.*
- [ ] *Rear suspension.*
- [ ] *Stand.*
- [ ] *Steering head bearings.*

Brakes, wheels and tyres
- [ ] *Brake cable.*
- [ ] *Brake fluid (disc brake).*
- [ ] *Brake hose (disc brake).*
- [ ] *Brake levers.*
- [ ] *Brake pads (disc brake).*
- [ ] *Brake shoes and cam (drum brake).*
- [ ] *Wheel bearings.*
- [ ] *Tyre condition.*

Bodywork
- [ ] *Fasteners.*
- [ ] *Panel condition.*

Electrical systems
- [ ] *Battery.*
- [ ] *Headlight aim.*
- [ ] *Brake light.*
- [ ] *Horn.*
- [ ] *Speedometer cable.*

General
- [ ] *Nuts and bolts.*

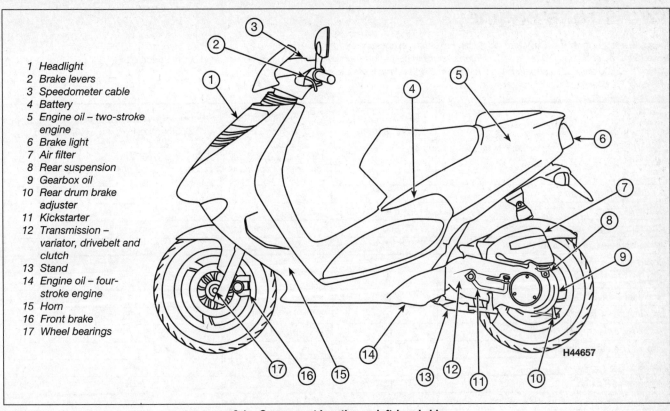

1 Headlight
2 Brake levers
3 Speedometer cable
4 Battery
5 Engine oil – two-stroke
   engine
6 Brake light
7 Air filter
8 Rear suspension
9 Gearbox oil
10 Rear drum brake
   adjuster
11 Kickstarter
12 Transmission –
   variator, drivebelt and
   clutch
13 Stand
14 Engine oil – four-
   stroke engine
15 Horn
16 Front brake
17 Wheel bearings

2.1a Component locations – left-hand side

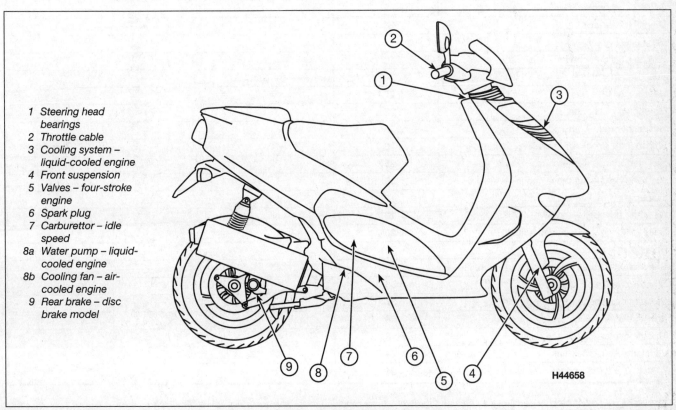

1 Steering head
   bearings
2 Throttle cable
3 Cooling system –
   liquid-cooled engine
4 Front suspension
5 Valves – four-stroke
   engine
6 Spark plug
7 Carburettor – idle
   speed
8a Water pump – liquid-
   cooled engine
8b Cooling fan – air-
   cooled engine
9 Rear brake – disc
   brake model

2.1b Component locations – right-hand side

Two-stroke engine

Note: *Always perform the 'Daily (pre-ride) checks' before every service interval – see the beginning of this Manual.*
Note: *Severe conditions are regarded as intensive urban use, short journeys with cold engine or use in dusty conditions.*
Note: *The 2500 mile tasks should be included with the 5000 mile service, etc.*

	Text section in this Chapter	Every 2500 miles (4000 km) or 12 months *1500 miles (2500 km) for severe conditions*	Every 5000 miles (8000 km) or 2 years *3000 miles (5000 km) for severe conditions*	Every 10,000 miles (16,000 km) or 3 years
Air filters – clean/renew	3	✓		
Battery – check	4	✓		
Body panels and fasteners – check	40	✓		
Brake cable – check and lubricate	7	✓		
Brake fluid – check	8	✓		✓*
Brake hose – check	9	✓		✓*
Brake lever pivots – lubricate	6	✓		
Brake pads – check	10	✓		
Brake shoes – check	11	✓		
Brake shoe cam – check and lubricate	12		✓	
Brake system – check	5	✓		
Carburettor – clean	15		✓	
Clutch pulley and bearing – check and lubricate	26		✓	
Cooling system – check	21	✓		✓**
Cylinder head – decarbonise	31		✓	
Drivebelt – check	22	✓		
Drivebelt – renew	23		✓	
Engine oil system – check	17	✓		
Engine oil filter – change	18		✓	
Fuel system – check	14	✓		
Gearbox oil level – check	27	✓		
Gearbox oil – change	28		✓	
Headlight, brake light and horn – check	33	✓		
Idle speed – check and adjust	16	✓		
Kickstart mechanism – check	25		✓	
Nuts and bolts – tightness check	39	✓		
Oil pump cable – check and adjust	19	✓		
Oil pump drivebelt – renew	20			✓
Spark plug – gap check and adjust	29	✓		
Spark plug – renew	30		✓	
Speedometer cable and drive gear – lubricate	36		✓	
Stand – check and lubricate	35	✓		
Steering head bearings – check and adjust	37		✓	
Suspension – check	38		✓	
Throttle cable – check and adjust	13	✓		
Variator pulley and rollers – check and lubricate	24	✓		
Wheels and tyres – check	34	✓		

* The brake fluid must be changed every 2 years and the brake hose renewed every 3 years, irrespective of mileage
** Drain and refill a liquid-cooled system with fresh coolant every 2 years, irrespective of mileage

Four-stroke engine

Note: *Always perform the 'Daily (pre-ride) checks' before every service interval – see the beginning of this Manual.*
Note: *Severe conditions are regarded as intensive urban use, short journeys with cold engine or use in dusty conditions.*
Note: *The 2500 mile tasks should be included with the 5000 mile service, etc.*

	Text section in this Chapter	Every 2500 miles (4000 km) or 12 months 1500 miles (2500 km) for severe conditions	Every 5000 miles (8000 km) or 2 years 3000 miles (5000 km) for severe conditions	Every 10,000 miles (16,000 km) or 3 years
Air filters – clean/renew	3	✓		
Battery – check	4	✓		
Body panels and fasteners – check	40	✓		
Brake cable – check and lubricate	7	✓		
Brake fluid – check	8	✓		✓*
Brake hose – check	9	✓		✓*
Brake lever pivots – lubricate	6	✓		
Brake pads – check	10	✓		
Brake shoes – check	11	✓		
Brake shoe cam – check and lubricate	12		✓	
Brake system – check	5	✓		
Carburettor – clean	15		✓	
Clutch pulley and bearing – check and lubricate	26		✓	
Cooling system – check	21	✓		✓**
Drivebelt – check	22	✓		
Drivebelt – renew	23		✓	
Engine oil system – check	17	✓		
Engine oil and filter – change	18	✓		
Fuel system – check	14	✓		
Gearbox oil level – check	27	✓		
Gearbox oil – change	28		✓	
Headlight, brake light and horn – check	33	✓		
Idle speed – check and adjust	16	✓		
Kickstart mechanism – check	25		✓	
Nuts and bolts – tightness check	39	✓		
Spark plug – gap check and adjust	29	✓		
Spark plug – renew	30		✓	
Speedometer cable and drive gear – lubricate	36		✓	
Stand – check and lubricate	35	✓		
Steering head bearings – check and adjust	37		✓	
Suspension – check	38		✓	
Throttle cable – check and adjust	13	✓		
Valve clearances – check and adjust	32			✓
Variator pulley and rollers – check and lubricate	24	✓		
Wheels and tyres – check	34	✓		

* The brake fluid must be changed every 2 years and the brake hose renewed every 3 years, irrespective of mileage
** Drain and refill a liquid-cooled system with fresh coolant every 2 years, irrespective of mileage

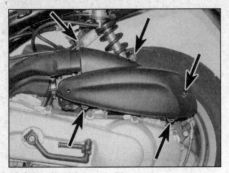

3.1a Undo the air filter cover screws (arrowed) . . .

3.1b . . . and remove the cover and filter element

3.1c A typical filter element panel

3 Air filters – clean and renewal

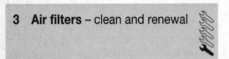

Caution: If the machine is continually ridden in continuously wet or dusty conditions, the filters should be checked more frequently.

Engine air filter

1 Remove the screws securing the air filter cover and detach the cover **(see illustration)**. Remove the filter element – note that some filter elements are fitted in a removable panel **(see illustrations)**.

2 Some manufacturers recommend that the filter element is renewed at every service interval – refer to your scooter handbook for details. However, foam filters can usually be cleaned and re-used if they are in good condition.

3 Wash the filter in hot soapy water, then blow dry using compressed air.

4 Soak the filter in dedicated air filter oil, or a mixture of petrol and 10% two-stroke oil or four-stroke engine oil, as recommended. Lay it on an absorbent surface and squeeze out the excess liquid, making sure you do not damage the filter by twisting it.

5 Allow the filter to dry for a while, then fit it back into the housing and install the cover and tighten the screws securely.

6 If the filter is excessively dirty and cannot be cleaned properly, or is torn or damaged in any way, renew it.

7 If the filter housing is fitted with a drain, undo the plug and release any trapped fluid **(see illustration)**.

Transmission air filter

8 Some scooters have a filter fitted to the belt drive housing. Remove the filter unit and lift out the filter element **(see illustrations)**. Clean and, if required, re-oil the element as described in Steps 3 to 5.

Secondary air system

9 A secondary air system is often fitted in conjunction with a catalytic converter exhaust system. The system sucks fresh air into the exhaust pipe to promote the burning of unburnt gases, reducing the emission of hydrocarbons into the atmosphere.

10 Remove any body panels as necessary to access the system components (see Chapter 9).

11 Undo the screws securing the housing cover and detach the cover, then lift out the reed valve and the filter element. Discard the cover O-ring or gasket if fitted as a new one must be used on reassembly.

12 Where fitted, lever the breather cap out of the drivebelt cover with a small screwdriver and carefully pull the filter element out of the cap.

13 Wash the filters in hot soapy water then blow them dry using compressed air. Never wring the filters dry as they may tear. If the filters are excessively dirty and cannot be cleaned properly, or are torn or damaged in any way, fit new ones.

14 To check the condition of the reed valve, hold it up to the light. The valve should be closed. If light can be seen around the edge of the reed a new valve should be fitted. Clean the reed carefully with a suitable solvent to remove any gum.

15 Install the components in the reverse order of disassembly, remembering to fit a new O-ring or gasket to the filter housing cover if required.

4 Battery – check

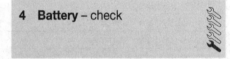

Caution: Be extremely careful when handling or working around the battery. The electrolyte is very caustic and an explosive gas (hydrogen) is given off when the battery is charging.

Conventional battery

1 Remove the battery access panel and partially lift the battery out of its holder. Check the electrolyte level which is visible through the translucent battery case – it should be

3.7 Undo the plug (arrowed) and drain the hose

3.8a Remove the belt drive housing filter unit . . .

3.8b . . . and lift out the filter element

4.1 Check the electrolyte level through the battery case

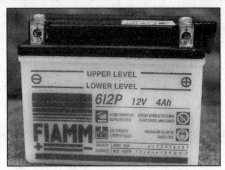

4.2 Top-up the battery to the upper mark with distilled water

occurs. If motor oil or light grease is being used, apply it sparingly as it may attract dirt (which could cause the controls to bind or wear at an accelerated rate). **Note:** *One of the best lubricants for the control lever pivots is a dry-film lubricant.*

between the UPPER and LOWER level marks **(see illustration)**.

2 If the electrolyte is low, disconnect the battery terminals (see Chapter 10) and move the battery to the work bench. Remove the cell caps and fill each cell to the upper level mark with distilled water **(see illustration)**. Do not use tap water (except in an emergency), and do not overfill. The cell holes are quite small, so it may help to use a clean plastic squeeze bottle with a small spout to add the water. Install the battery cell caps, tightening them securely, then install the battery (see Chapter 10).

Maintenance-free battery

3 On machines fitted with a sealed battery, no maintenance is required. **Note:** *Do not attempt to remove the battery caps to check the electrolyte level or battery specific gravity. Removal will damage the caps, resulting in electrolyte leakage and battery failure.* All that should be done is to check that the battery terminals are clean and tight and that the casing is not damaged. See Chapter 10 for further details.

5 Brake system – check

1 A routine check of the brake system will ensure that any problems are discovered and remedied before the rider's safety is jeopardised.
2 Check that the brake levers are not loose or

damaged, and that the lever action is smooth without excessive play. Renew any worn or damaged parts (see Chapter 8).
3 Make sure all brake fasteners are tight. Check the brake pads (disc brake) and brake shoes (drum brake) for wear (see Sections 10 and 11).
4 Where disc brakes are fitted, make sure the fluid level in the hydraulic reservoir is correct (see *Daily (pre-ride) checks*). Look for leaks at the hose connections and check for cracks and abrasions in the hoses and renew them if necessary (see Chapter 8). If the lever action is spongy, bleed the brakes (see Chapter 8).
5 Where drum brakes are fitted, check the cable for damage or stiff action (see Section 7).
6 Make sure the brake light operates when each brake lever is pulled in. The brake light switches are not adjustable. If they fail to operate properly, check them (see Chapter 10, Section 6).

6 Brake lever pivots – lubrication

1 The lever pivots should be lubricated periodically to reduce wear and ensure safe and trouble-free operation.
2 In order for the lubricant to be applied where it will do the most good, the lever should be removed (see Chapter 8). However, if chain or cable lubricant is being used, it can be applied to the pivot joint gaps and will work its way into the areas where friction

7 Brake cable – check, adjustment and lubrication

Check and adjustment

Drum brake

1 Check that there is no excessive freeplay in the handlebar lever before the brake takes effect **(see illustration)**. The wheel should spin freely when the brake is off, but the brake should come on before the lever is pulled back against the handlebar.
2 To reduce freeplay in the lever, turn the adjuster nut on the brake drum end of the cable clockwise; to increase freeplay, turn the adjuster nut anti-clockwise **(see illustration)**. If there is a locknut on the adjuster, tighten it securely on completion.
3 If the brake is binding without the lever being pulled, first check that the lever is moving freely (see Section 6). Next, disconnect the cable from the handlebar lever (see Chapter 8) and check that the inner cable slides smoothly in the outer cable. If the action is stiff, inspect along the length of the outer cable for splits and kinks, and the ends of the inner cable for frays, and renew either one if necessary (see Chapter 8).
4 If there are no signs of damage, lubricate the cable (see Step 9). If the cable is still stiff after lubrication, renew it (see Chapter 8).
5 If the handlebar lever and brake cable are in good condition, check the operation of the brake cam (see Section 12).

Disc brake

6 If the hydraulic master cylinder is activated by a cable from the handlebar lever, remove the front panel (see Chapter 9) and check that there is no freeplay in the cable. If there is, loosen the cable adjuster locknut and turn the adjuster anti-clockwise until all the slack is taken up, but make sure the lever arm is not activated and pressurising the system **(see illustration)**.

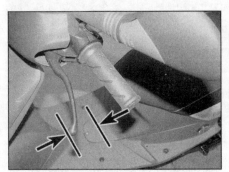

7.1 Measuring brake lever freeplay

7.2 Brake cable adjuster nut (arrowed)

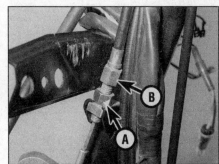

7.6 Loosen the locknut (A) and turn the adjuster (B) as required

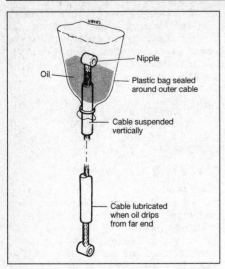

7.9 Lubricating a cable with a makeshift funnel and motor oil

7 If the brake is binding without the lever being pulled, turn the adjuster clockwise until the lever arm is at rest but make sure that no freeplay is created in the cable. Tighten the locknut securely on completion. To check the cable operation, follow the procedure in Step 3.

Lubrication

8 The cable should be lubricated periodically to ensure safe and trouble-free operation.
9 To lubricate the cable, disconnect it at its upper end and lubricate it with a pressure adapter, or using the set-up shown **(see illustration)**.
10 Reconnect the cable and adjust the handlebar lever freeplay.

8 Brake fluid – check

1 The fluid level in the hydraulic reservoir should be checked before riding the machine (see *Daily (pre-ride) checks*).
2 Brake fluid will degrade over a period of time. It should be changed every two years or whenever a new master cylinder or caliper is fitted. Refer to the brake bleeding and fluid change section in Chapter 8.

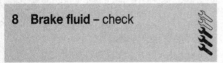

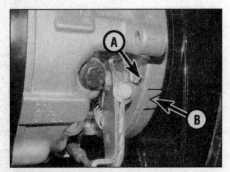

11.1 Wear indicator (A) and index mark (B)

9.1 Inspect the brake hose (A) and banjo fitting (B)

HAYNES HINT *Old brake fluid is invariably much darker in colour than new fluid, making it easy to see when all old fluid has been expelled from the system.*

9 Brake hose – check

1 Twist and flex the hose while looking for cracks, bulges and seeping fluid. Check extra carefully where the hose connects to the banjo fittings as this is a common area for hose failure **(see illustration)**.
2 Inspect the banjo fittings; if they are rusted, cracked or damaged, fit new hoses.
3 Inspect the banjo union connections for leaking fluid. If they leak when tightened securely, unscrew the banjo bolt and fit new washers (see Chapter 8).
4 Flexible hydraulic hose will deteriorate with age and should be renewed every three years regardless of its apparent condition (see Chapter 8).

10 Brake pads – wear check

1 The extent of friction material wear can normally be checked by looking at the underside of the caliper **(see illustration)**. If the

12.1 Typical brake shoe arrangement – note the brake cam (arrowed)

10.1 Check brake pad wear at the underside of the caliper

pads are dirty, or if you are in any doubt as to the amount of friction material remaining, remove the pads for inspection (see Chapter 8).
2 If the amount of friction material remaining on the pads is below the service limit, new pads must be fitted.

⚠ *Warning: Brake pads often wear at different rates. If there is any doubt about the condition of either of the pads in a caliper, remove the caliper and check. Brake failure will result if the friction material wears away completely.*

3 Refer to Chapter 8 for details of pad removal, inspection and renewal.

11 Brake shoes – wear check

1 Drum brakes are normally equipped with a wear indicator **(see illustration)**.
2 As the brake shoes wear and the cable is adjusted to compensate, the indicator moves closer to the index mark on the casing. To check the extent of brake wear, have an assistant apply the brake firmly; if the indicator aligns with the index mark, the brake shoes are worn to their limit and must be renewed (see Chapter 8, Section 9).
3 If there is no wear indicator, remove the wheel to check the amount of friction material remaining on the brake shoes (see Chapter 8, Section 9).
4 If the amount of friction material remaining on the shoes is below the service limit, new shoes must be fitted.

12 Brake shoe cam – check and lubrication

1 Remove the wheel; on front brakes, the brake shoes and brake cam are fitted to the backplate, on rear brakes the shoes and cam are fitted to the back of the gearbox casing **(see illustration)**.
2 Remove the brake shoes, then remove the brake arm and pull the brake cam out of the backplate or casing (see Chapter 8, Section 9).

3 Clean the shaft and cam and inspect the bearing surfaces for wear; renew the cam if necessary.
4 Apply some copper grease to the bearing surfaces of the cam and the shaft before reassembly.
Caution: Do not apply too much grease otherwise there is a risk of it contaminating the brake drum and shoe linings.

13 Throttle cable – check and adjustment

Twistgrip cable

1 Ensure the throttle twistgrip rotates easily from fully closed to fully open with the handlebars turned at various angles. The twistgrip should return automatically from fully open to fully closed when released.
2 If the throttle sticks, this is probably due to a cable fault. Remove the cable (see Chapter 4) and lubricate it following the procedure in Section 7.
3 With the throttle operating smoothly, check for a small amount of freeplay in the cable, measured in terms of the amount of twistgrip rotation before the throttle opens **(see illustration)**. Compare the amount of freeplay to the specifications in the *Data* section at the end of this manual.

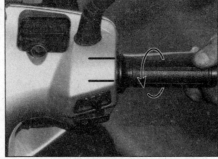

13.3 Throttle cable freeplay is measured in terms of twistgrip rotation

4 If there is insufficient or excessive freeplay, loosen the locknut on the cable adjuster, then turn the adjuster until the right amount of freeplay is evident, then retighten the locknut **(see illustration)**. If the adjuster has reached its limit, renew the cable (see Chapter 4).
5 Start the engine and check the idle speed. If the idle speed is too high, this could be due to incorrect adjustment of the cable. Loosen the locknut and turn the adjuster in – if the idle speed falls as you do, there is insufficient freeplay in the cable. Reset the adjuster (see Step 4). **Note:** *The idle speed should not change as the handlebars are turned. If it does, the throttle cable is routed incorrectly. Rectify the problem before riding the scooter (see Chapter 4).*

13.4 Adjusting the throttle cable freeplay

Oil pump cable (two-stroke engines)

Note: *Two-stroke engines are fitted with either a cable-controlled or centrifugal oil pump. A quick visual check will confirm which pump is fitted to your engine (see Section 17).*
6 There should be no freeplay in the cable from the splitter to the carburettor **(see illustration)**.
7 Remove the air filter housing (see Chapter 4) and pull back the boot on the cable adjuster on the top of the carburettor.
8 Screw the adjuster into the top of the carburettor to create a small amount of freeplay in the cable, then screw the adjuster out until the carburettor slide just begins to lift. Now turn the adjuster in a quarter turn **(see illustration)**. Refit the boot and the filter housing.
9 Check the adjustment of the oil pump cable (see Section 19).

14 Fuel system – check

> ⚠ *Warning: Petrol is extremely flammable, so take extra precautions when you work on any part of the fuel system. Don't smoke or allow open flames or bare light bulbs near the work area, and don't work in a garage where a natural gas-type appliance is present. If you spill any fuel on your skin, rinse it off immediately with soap*

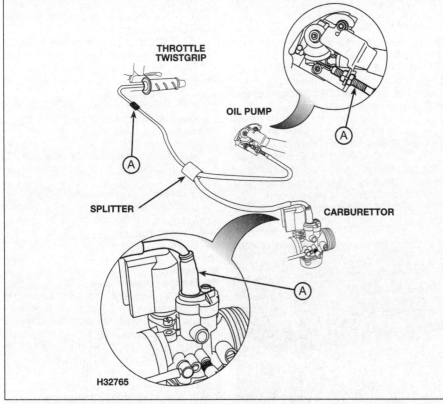

THROTTLE TWISTGRIP

OIL PUMP

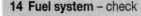

SPLITTER

CARBURETTOR

H32765

13.6 Cable arrangement for models fitted with a cable-operated oil pump
Location of cable adjusters (A)

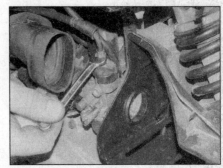

13.8 Adjusting the cable at the carburettor end

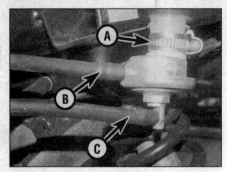

14.2 Fuel tap union clip (A), fuel hose (B) and vacuum hose (C)

15.2 Keep the carburettor body and throttle mechanism free from dirt. Note the idle speed adjuster (arrowed)

thousands of miles of satisfactory service. However, dirt particles and varnish will gradually accumulate inside the body, and the carburettor should be removed and disassembled periodically to avoid the jets becoming blocked (see Chapter 4).

4 If the scooter has not been used for a long period, a sticky residue may form in the carburettor, jamming the throttle slide. Disassemble the carburettor and clean the components with a suitable solvent or carburettor cleaner (see Chapter 4). *Note: If the carburettor is being disassembled, read through the entire procedure and make sure that you have obtained a new gasket set first.*

and water. When you perform any kind of work on the fuel system, wear safety glasses and have a fire extinguisher suitable for a Class B type fire (flammable liquids) on hand.

Check

1 Remove the body panels as necessary to access the fuel tank, tap or pump (as applicable to your scooter) and carburettor (see Chapter 9). Check the fuel tank, the tap or pump, and the fuel hose for signs of leaks, deterioration or damage; in particular check that there are no leaks from the fuel hose. Renew the fuel hose if it is cracked or deteriorated.

2 If a fuel tap is fitted to the tank, inspect the tap-to-tank union and ensure that the hose clip around the union is tight **(see illustration)**. If the union is leaking, remove the tap and check the condition of the fuel tap O-ring (see Chapter 4).

3 The fuel tap is vacuum-operated and should be closed when the engine is not running. Disconnect the hose from the tap to check that the valve inside is not leaking **(see illustration 14.2)**. If the valve is leaking, fit a new tap (see Chapter 4).

4 Cleaning or renewal of the fuel filter is advised after a particularly high mileage has been covered, or if fuel starvation is suspected (see Chapter 4).

5 Check that the fuel tank cap breather hole is clear. If the hole becomes blocked, fuel starvation will occur.

6 If your scooter is fitted with a fuel pump, ensure the fuel and vacuum hoses are securely attached to the pump and check the pump body for leaks. If you suspect that the pump is damaged or faulty, follow the procedure in Chapter 4 to test it.

7 If the carburettor gaskets are leaking, the carburettor should be disassembled and rebuilt using new gaskets and seals (see Chapter 4).

8 If the fuel gauge is believed to be faulty, check the operation of the sender (see Chapter 10).

15 Carburettor – clean

1 Remove the air filter housing (see Chapter 4) and the storage compartment (see Chapter 9) to access the carburettor.

2 The exterior of the carburettor and the throttle mechanism should be kept clean and free of road dirt **(see illustration)**. Wash it carefully with hot soapy water, ensuring no water enters the carburettor body, and dry it with compressed air. Clean away any grit with a small paint brush. Oil deposits can be removed with a rag soaked in a suitable solvent. Take care to ensure the idle speed setting is not disturbed during cleaning.

3 Provided the air filter element is kept clean (see Section 3) the carburettor will give many

16 Idle speed – check and adjustment

1 The idle speed (engine running with the throttle twistgrip closed) should be checked and adjusted when it is obviously too high or too low. Before adjusting the idle speed, make sure the throttle cable is correctly adjusted (see Section 13) and check the spark plug gap (see Section 29). On four-stroke engines, the valve clearances must be correct to achieve a satisfactory idle speed (see Section 32).

2 The engine should be at normal operating temperature, which is usually reached after 10 to 15 minutes of stop-and-go riding. Support the scooter on its centre stand with the rear wheel clear of the ground.

> ⚠️ *Warning: Do not allow exhaust gases to build-up in the work area; either perform the check outside or use an exhaust gas extraction system.*

3 Although most manufacturers specify idle speed in engine revolutions per minute (rpm), for scooters not fitted with a tachometer it is sufficient to ensure that at idle the engine speed is steady and does not falter, and that it is not so high that the automatic transmission engages.

4 The idle speed adjuster screw is located on the carburettor or adjacent to the carburettor – refer to your scooter handbook for details. With the engine running, turn the screw clockwise to increase idle speed, and anti-clockwise to decrease it **(see illustrations)**.

5 Snap the throttle open and shut a few times, then recheck the idle speed. If necessary, repeat the adjustment procedure.

6 If a smooth, steady idle can't be achieved, the fuel/air mixture may be incorrect (see Chapter 4) or the carburettor may need cleaning (see Section 15). If a satisfactory idle speed still cannot be achieved, have the ignition timing checked (see Chapter 5).

7 With the idle speed correctly adjusted, recheck the throttle cable freeplay (see Section 13).

16.4a Adjusting the idle speed with a screwdriver . . .

16.4b . . . or directly on the carburettor

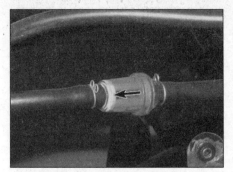

17.4 Two-stroke engine oil filter – arrow indicates direction of oil flow

17.5a Inspect the oil hose connections (arrowed) . . .

17.5b . . . and ensure they are secured by clips

17 Engine oil system – check

1 A routine check of the engine oil system will ensure that any problems are discovered and remedied before the engine is damaged.
2 Check the engine oil level (see *Daily (pre-ride) checks*).

Two-stroke engines

3 Check the operation of the oil level warning light in the instrument cluster. The light should come on temporarily when the ignition is first turned on as a check of the warning circuit, and then extinguish. If the light stays on the oil level is low and should be topped-up. If the light stays on when the tank is full, check the oil level warning circuit (see Chapter 10). If the light doesn't come on at all, check the bulb and oil level warning circuit (see Chapter 10, Section 8). **Note:** *On most scooters the oil level sensor is part of the safety circuit which prevents the engine starting if there is insufficient oil in the oil tank.*
4 If a filter is fitted in the hose from the oil tank to the pump, inspect the filter **(see illustration)**. Air bubbles should be bled from the filter by tilting it to allow the trapped air to rise through the hose into the oil tank. Check for sediment in the filter and renew the filter if necessary (see Section 18).
5 Check the condition of the oil inlet and outlet hoses. In particular check that there are no leaks from the hose connections to the oil tank, filter, oil pump and carburettor **(see illustration)**. Renew any hoses that are cracked or deteriorated and ensure they are properly secured by clips **(see illustration)**.
6 Two-stroke engines are fitted with either a cable-operated or centrifugal oil pump; the pump can be either mounted externally or inside part of the engine casing. On engines fitted with a cable-operated oil pump, check that the reference marks on the oil pump cam and pump body align with the throttle fully open. If the marks do not align, adjust the pump cable as necessary (see Section 19).

Four-stroke engines

7 Check the operation of the oil pressure

warning light in the instrument cluster. The light should come on when the ignition is turned on as a check of the warning circuit, and then extinguish when the engine is started.
8 If the light stays on, or comes on when the scooter is being ridden, stop the engine immediately. Check the oil level and top-up as necessary. If the level is correct, check for a fault in the oil pressure warning circuit. If the light doesn't come on at all, check the bulb and oil pressure warning circuit. **Note:** *If there is any doubt about the performance of the engine lubrication system, the oil pressure should be checked by a scooter dealer. Serious damage to the engine will result if there is a failure in the engine lubrication system.*

18 Engine oil and oil filter – change

Two-stroke engines

1 The oil filter should be changed at the specified service interval, or sooner if there is sediment in it.
2 Remove any body panels or the storage compartment as necessary to access the oil filter. Release the clips securing the inlet and outlet hoses to the filter and slide them along the hoses away from the filter **(see illustration 17.4)**. Detach the hoses and clamp them to prevent oil loss.

3 The oil filter body is marked with an arrow indicating the direction of oil flow. Connect the hoses to the filter unions, ensuring the arrow points towards the oil pump, then install the hose clips.
4 Ensure any trapped air is bled from the filter (see Section 17) before refitting the body panels.

Four-stroke engines

⚠️ **Warning: Be careful when draining the oil, as the exhaust pipe, the engine, and the oil itself can cause severe burns.**

5 Oil and filter changes are the single most important maintenance procedure you can perform on a four-stroke engine. The oil not only lubricates the internal parts of the engine, but it also acts as a coolant, a cleaner, a sealant, and a protector. Because of these demands, the oil takes a terrific amount of abuse and should be renewed at the specified service interval with oil of the recommended grade and type.
6 Before changing the oil, warm-up the engine so the oil will drain easily. Stop the engine and turn the ignition OFF. Support the scooter on its centre stand, and position a clean drain tray below the engine.
7 Unscrew the oil filler plug to vent the crankcase and to act as a reminder that there is no oil in the engine **(see illustration)**.
8 Unscrew the oil drain plug and allow the oil to flow into the drain tray **(see illustrations)**. Discard the sealing washer or O-ring on the drain plug as a new one must be used on reassembly. On some engines, a gauze

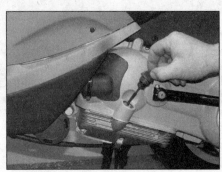

18.7 Unscrew the oil filler plug

18.8a Oil drain plug is situated on the underside . . .

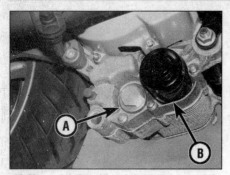

18.8b . . . or the side of the crankcase (A). Note the oil filter (B)

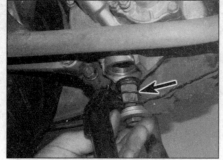

18.8c Where fitted, remove the strainer (arrowed)

18.9 Some engines have a separate oil strainer

strainer is fitted behind the drain plug; withdraw the strainer and clean it in solvent and remove any debris caught in the mesh **(see illustration)**. Check the gauze for splits or holes and renew it if necessary.

9 A separate oil strainer is fitted on some engines; unscrew the strainer plug and withdraw the strainer **(see illustration)**. Clean and check the strainer as described in Step 8. Install the strainer, fit a new sealing washer or O-ring to the plug as necessary, then install the plug and tighten it securely.

10 When the oil has completely drained, install the drain plug using a new sealing washer or O-ring. Tighten the plug to the specified torque, if available (see the *Data* section at the end of this manual). Avoid overtightening, as damage to the threads will result.

11 Now place the drain tray below the oil filter. On some engines the filter element is fitted inside a cover; unscrew the cover bolts, then remove the cover, the spring and the filter **(see illustrations)**. Tip any residual oil into the drain tray. Discard any O-rings on the cover and in the filter housing as new ones should be used. As required, fit the new housing O-ring, then install the new filter and fit the spring and the cover, again using a new O-ring **(see illustration 18.11b)**. Tighten the cover bolts securely.

12 Some engines have a spin-on type filter **(see illustration 18.8b)**. Unscrew the filter and tip any residual oil into the drain tray. Smear clean engine oil onto the seal of the new filter, then install the filter and tighten it securely by hand.

13 Refill the engine to the correct level using the recommended type and amount of oil (see the *Data* section at the end of this manual). Install the filler plug and tightening it by hand.

14 Start the engine and let it run for two or three minutes. Shut it off, wait five minutes, then check the oil level. If necessary, top-up the oil to the correct level (see *Daily (pre-ride) checks*). Check around the drain plug and the oil filter/strainer for leaks.

15 The old oil drained from the engine cannot

HAYNES HINT *Check the old oil carefully – if it is very metallic coloured, then the engine is experiencing wear from break-in (new engine) or from insufficient lubrication. If there are flakes or chips of metal in the oil, then something is drastically wrong internally and the engine will have to be disassembled for inspection and repair.*

be re-used and should be disposed of properly. Check with your local refuse disposal company, disposal facility or environmental agency to see whether they will accept the used oil for recycling. Don't pour used oil into drains or onto the ground.

OIL CARE
FOLLOW THE CODE

OIL BANK LINE
0800 66 33 66
www.oilbankline.org.uk

Note: It is antisocial and illegal to dump oil down the drain. To find the location of your local oil recycling bank, call this number free.

19 Oil pump cable (two-stroke engines) – check and adjustment

1 Where the oil pump is cable-controlled, the cable is connected to the throttle twistgrip via a splitter **(see illustration 13.6)**.

2 First ensure the throttle twistgrip rotates easily from fully closed to fully open with the handlebars turned at various angles, and

18.11a Unscrew the bolts (arrowed) . . .

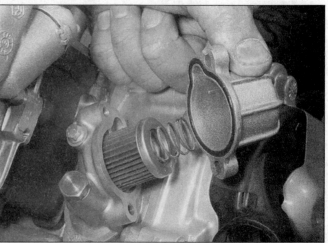

18.11b . . . and remove the cover, spring and filter

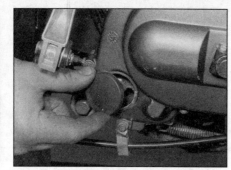

19.3a Externally-mounted oil pump. Note index marks (A) and adjuster locknuts (B)

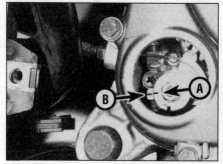

19.3b Remove the plug in the drivebelt cover . . .

19.3c . . . to access the internally-mounted pump. Note index marks (A) and (B)

check that the throttle cable freeplay is correct (see Section 13).

3 Remove any body panels or the storage compartment as necessary to access the oil pump. Where the pump is located inside the drivebelt cover, remove the inspection plug **(see illustrations)**.

4 At the pump end, the cable is connected to the pump cam. With the cable correctly adjusted, an index mark on the cam should align with a mark on the pump body, either with the throttle closed or with the throttle fully open – check with your scooter handbook for details **(see illustrations 19.3a and 19.3c)**. *Note: The oil pump cable will stretch slightly in use, so only a small amount of adjustment should be necessary to re-align the marks. As a guide, there should be no discernible freeplay in the pump cable with the throttle closed and the pump cam should turn as the throttle is opened. If the cable is over-adjusted (too tight), too much oil will be fed into the engine causing a fouled spark plug and a smoky exhaust. If there is any doubt about the adjustment of the pump cable consult a scooter dealer.*

5 If the marks are not aligned, loosen the cable adjuster locknut and turn the adjuster as required until the marks align, then retighten the locknut. If the adjuster has reached its limit of adjustment, renew the cable (see Chapter 4, Section 12).

20 Oil pump drivebelt (two-stroke engines) – renewal

1 On some engines, the oil pump is driven by a small belt from either the left or right-hand side of the crankshaft. To access the belt it is necessary to remove either the variator or the alternator.

2 Refer to you scooter handbook or check with a scooter dealer to confirm that belt renewal is a service item, then follow the appropriate procedure in Chapter 2A to renew the drivebelt.

21 Cooling system – check

Air-cooled engines

1 On air-cooled models, a fan mounted on the alternator rotor forces air into the engine cowling to cool the cylinder and cylinder head.

2 Check that the air intake in the fan cowling is unobstructed and that the sections of the engine cowling are fitted together correctly and secured with their mounting screws **(see illustration)**. *Note: If any sections of the engine cowling are missing the engine will not be properly cooled.*

21.2 Fan cowling (A) and engine cowling sections (B) and (C)

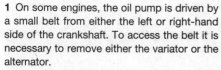

3 Remove the fan cowling and inspect the fan **(see illustration)**. If any of the vanes are broken, renew the fan. Check that the fan mounting bolts are tight; if the bolts are loose or if the bolt holes are worn oversize, the fan will run out of true and cause engine vibration. *Note: On some engines, the holes for the mounting bolts in the cooling fan are oversize and it is important to centralise the fan on the bolts before tightening them, otherwise the fan will run out of true and cause engine vibration. Use two shouldered bolts, or wrap a short length of electrical tape tightly around two bolts, and fit them in opposite holes to centralise the fan, then install two mounting bolts* **(see illustrations)**. *Remove the centralising bolts and install the remaining bolts.*

21.3a Check the fan for broken vanes and ensure the bolts (arrowed) are tight

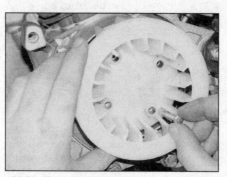

21.3b Use shouldered bolts to centralise the fan . . .

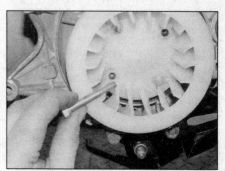

21.3c . . . then install the mounting bolts

21.5 Check the entire length of the coolant hoses between the engine and the radiator

25.1 Kickstart lever rest position

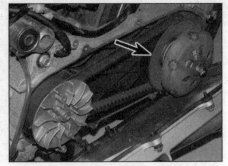

26.2 Check for play in the bearings of the clutch pulley hub (arrowed)

Liquid-cooled engines

 Warning: The engine must be cool before beginning this procedure.

4 Check the coolant level (see *Daily (pre-ride) checks*).

5 The entire cooling system should be checked for evidence of leaks. Remove any body panels as necessary and examine each coolant hose along its entire length **(see illustration)**. Look for cracks, abrasions and other damage. Squeeze the hoses at various points. They should feel firm, yet pliable, and return to their original shape when released. If they are hard or perished, renew them (see Chapter 3).

6 Check for evidence of leaks at each cooling system joint. Ensure that the hoses are pushed fully onto their unions and that the hose clips are tight. **Note:** *Check the tension of any hose spring clips and renew them if they are loose.*

7 Check the underside of the water pump for evidence of leaks (see Chapter 3).

8 Check the radiator for leaks and other damage. Leaks in the radiator leave tell-tale scale deposits or coolant stains on the outside of the core below the leak. If leaks are noted, remove the radiator (see Chapter 3) and have it repaired or renew it.

Caution: Do not use a liquid leak stopping compound to try to repair leaks.

9 Inspect the radiator fins for mud, dirt and insects which will impede the flow of air through the radiator. If the fins are dirty, remove the radiator (see Chapter 3) and clean it using water or low pressure compressed air directed through the fins from the back. If the fins are bent or distorted, straighten them carefully with a screwdriver. If the air flow is restricted by bent or damaged fins over more than 30% of the radiator's surface area, fit a new radiator.

10 Check the condition of the coolant in the reservoir. If it is rust-coloured or if accumulations of scale are visible, drain, flush and refill the system with new coolant (see Chapter 3).

11 Check the antifreeze content of the coolant with an antifreeze hydrometer. Sometimes coolant looks like it's in good

condition, but is too weak to offer adequate protection. If the hydrometer indicates a weak mixture, drain, flush and refill the system (see Chapter 3). **Note:** *The cooling system should be drained and refilled with fresh coolant every 2 years.*

12 Start the engine and let it reach normal operating temperature, then check for leaks again.

13 If the coolant level is consistently low, and no evidence of leaks can be found, have the entire system pressure-checked by a scooter dealer.

22 Drivebelt – check

1 Referring to Chapter 6, remove the drivebelt cover and inspect the belt. Some manufacturers specify service limits for drivebelt wear (see the *Data* section at the end of this manual).

2 If there is any doubt about the condition of the belt, renew it. In the event of premature belt wear, the cause should be investigated (see Chapter 6).

23 Drivebelt – renewal

1 The drivebelt must be renewed at the specified service interval, or earlier dependant on belt condition (see Chapter 6).

24 Variator pulley and rollers – check and lubricate

1 Referring to Chapter 6, remove the drive pulley and the variator. Disassemble the variator and check all components for wear as described. If applicable, grease the rollers and the roller tracks in the variator housing before reassembly. **Note:** *The self-locking variator*

centre nut and, where applicable, the variator housing O-ring, must be renewed on reassembly.

25 Kickstart gear and spindle bush – check

1 The kickstart lever should move smoothly and return to the rest position under the tension of the return spring **(see illustration)**. It is good practice to periodically check the operation of the kickstart to ensure it is in good working order.

2 Referring to Chapter 6, remove the drivebelt cover. Inspect the component parts of the kickstart mechanism for damage and wear and renew any parts as necessary. Lubricate the kickstart spindle with high-temperature grease before reassembly.

26 Clutch pulley and bearing – check and lubricate

1 Referring to Chapter 6, remove the drivebelt cover.

2 The outer half of the clutch pulley should slide outwards on the clutch hub, against the pressure of the clutch centre spring. Next, grasp the pulley assembly and check for play in the pulley hub bearings **(see illustration)**.

3 To dismantle the clutch and pulley assembly in order to check the condition of the clutch and to lubricate the pulley bearing surfaces, follow the procedure in Chapter 6. **Note:** *The self-locking clutch centre nut must be renewed on reassembly.*

27 Gearbox oil level – check

1 Some scooters are fitted with an integral gearbox filler cap and dipstick, while most have a filler plug which also acts as a level plug; the filler plug may be on the rear of the

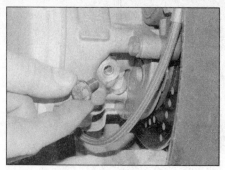

27.1a Gearbox oil level plug on the rear of the casing

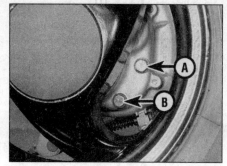

27.1b Oil level plug (A) and drain plug (B)

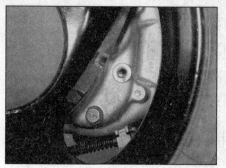

27.4 Gearbox oil should be level with the threads

gearbox casing or on the side facing the rear wheel **(see illustrations)**. On a few scooters, where the manufacturer does not require the oil level to be checked or the oil drained unless the gearbox is being overhauled, the filler plug is inside the belt drive casing.

2 The oil level should be checked either with the machine supported upright on level ground, or with it supported on its centre stand. It is important to clarify the correct procedure for your machine. On gearboxes fitted with a dipstick it is important to identify which mark on the dipstick is to be used and whether the dipstick should be screwed back into the casing or not when the level reading is being taken. Either refer to your scooter handbook or a scooter dealer for details.

⚠️ *Warning: It is important to have the right information for checking the gearbox oil level on your machine. Do not risk under-filling or over-filling the gearbox as a transmission seizure or dangerous oil leakage may result.*

3 Clean the area around the filler cap or plug and then unscrew the cap or plug from the gearbox casing. Discard the filler plug sealing washer as a new one should be used on reassembly. If you are using a dipstick, use a clean rag or paper towel to wipe off the oil.

4 On gearboxes with a level plug, the oil level should come up to the lower threads so that it is just visible on the threads **(see illustration)**. On gearboxes with a dipstick, insert the dipstick and then read the level on the stick in accordance with the manufacturer's recommendations.

5 If required, top the gearbox up with the recommended grade and type of oil (see the *Data* section at the end of this manual). Use a pump-type oil can or oil bottle to top-up gearboxes with a level plug **(see illustrations)**. Do not overfill.

6 Install the filler cap and tighten it securely by hand, or fit a new sealing washer to the level plug and tighten it securely.

7 If the oil level is very low, or oil is leaking from the gearbox, refer to Chapter 6 and inspect the condition of the case seals and gaskets and renew them if necessary.

28 Gearbox oil – change

1 If required to gain access to the gearbox drain plug, remove the rear wheel (see Chapter 8).

2 Position a clean drain tray below the

gearbox. Unscrew the filler cap or level plug (as applicable) to vent the case and to act as a reminder that there is no oil in it.

3 Unscrew the oil drain plug **(see illustration 27.1b)**, and allow the oil to flow into the drain tray. Discard the sealing washers on the drain and level plugs as new ones should be used.

4 When the oil has completely drained, fit the drain plug using a new sealing washer, and tighten it securely. Avoid overtightening, as damage to the casing will result. If available, tighten the drain plug to the specified torque setting (see the *Data* section at the end of this manual)

5 Refill the gearbox to the proper level using the recommended type and amount of oil (see Section 27). Install the filler cap and tighten it securely by hand, or fit a new sealing washer to the level plug and tighten it securely.

6 Check the oil level again after riding the scooter for a few minutes and, if necessary, add more oil. Check around the drain plug for leaks.

7 The old oil drained from the gearbox cannot be re-used and should be disposed of properly. Check with your local refuse disposal company, disposal facility or environmental agency to see whether they will accept the used oil for recycling. Don't pour used oil into drains or onto the ground.

27.5a Use a pump-type can to top up the oil . . .

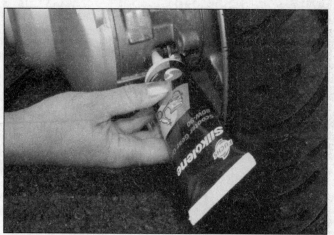

27.5b . . . or a bottle of specified gear oil

29 Spark plug gap – check and adjustment

⚠️ **Warning: Access to the spark plug is extremely restricted on some scooters. Ensure the engine and exhaust system are cool before attempting to remove the spark plug.**

1 Make sure your spark plug socket is the correct size before attempting to remove the plug – a suitable plug spanner is usually supplied in the scooter's tool kit.

2 As required, remove the engine access panel or side cover. Remove any access panel in the engine cowling **(see illustrations)**.

3 Pull off the spark plug cap, then ensure the spark plug socket is located correctly over the plug and unscrew the plug from the cylinder head.

4 Inspect the electrodes for wear. Both the centre and side electrode should have square edges and the side electrode should be of uniform thickness. Look for excessive deposits and evidence of a cracked or chipped insulator around the centre electrode. Compare your spark plug to the colour spark plug reading chart at the end of this manual. Check the condition of the threads and washer, and the ceramic insulator body for cracks and other damage.

5 If the electrodes are not excessively worn, and if the deposits can be easily removed with a wire brush, the plug can be regapped and re-used (if no cracks or chips are visible in the insulator). If in doubt concerning the condition of the plug, renew it, as the expense is minimal.

6 Cleaning a spark plug by sandblasting is permitted, provided you clean it with a high flash-point solvent afterwards.

7 Before installing the plug, make sure it is the correct type (see the *Data* section at the end of this manual). Check the gap between the electrodes **(see illustrations)**. Compare the gap to that specified and adjust as necessary. If the gap must be adjusted, bend the side electrode only and be very careful not to chip or crack the insulator nose **(see illustration)**.

29.2a Remove the engine access panel . . .

8 Make sure the washer is in place before installing the plug. Smear the plug threads with a little copper-based grease then thread it into the head by hand until it is finger-tight. Since the cylinder head is made of aluminium which is soft and easily damaged, ensure the plug threads are not crossed before tightening it securely with the spark plug socket. Reconnect the plug cap.

 HAYNES HiNT *A stripped plug thread in the cylinder head can be repaired with a thread insert.*

30 Spark plug – renewal

1 Remove the old spark plug as described in Section 29 and install a new one. Ensure the new plug is the correct type (see the *Data* section at the end of this manual). Check the gap between the electrodes and adjust it if necessary.

31 Cylinder head (two-stroke engines) – decarbonise

Note: *The use of modern, low ash engine oils specifically designed for use in two-stroke engines has considerably reduced the need to*

29.2b . . . or the spark plug panel in the engine cowling

decarbonise the engine. However, some manufacturers still recommend decarbonising as part of the routine service schedule, and if the machine is continually ridden on short journeys which do not allow the engine to reach and maintain its normal operating temperature, the cylinder head should be decarbonised more frequently.

1 Remove the cylinder head (see Chapter 2A).

2 Remove all accumulated carbon from inside the cylinder head using a blunt scraper. Small traces of carbon can be removed with very fine abrasive paper or a kitchen scourer.

Caution: The cylinder head and piston are made of aluminium which is relatively soft. Take great care not to gouge or score the surface when scraping.

3 Press the cylinder down against the crankcase to avoid breaking the cylinder base gasket seal, then turn the engine over until the piston is at the very top of its stroke. Smear grease all around the edge of the piston to trap any particles of carbon, then clean the piston crown, taking care not to score or gouge it or the cylinder bore. Finally, lower the piston and wipe away the grease and any remaining particles of carbon.

 HAYNES HiNT *Finish the piston crown and cylinder head off using a metal polish. A shiny surface is more resistant to the build-up of carbon deposits.*

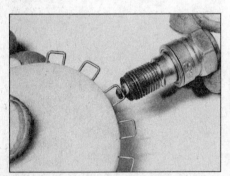

29.7a Using a wire type gauge to measure the spark plug electrode gap

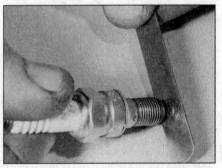

29.7b Using a feeler gauge to measure the spark plug electrode gap

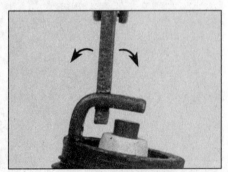

29.7c Adjust the electrode gap by bending the side electrode only

4 With the piston at the bottom of its stroke, check the exhaust port in the cylinder and scrape away any carbon. If the exhaust port is heavily coked, remove the exhaust system and clean the port and the exhaust pipe thoroughly (see Chapter 4).

5 Install the cylinder head (see Chapter 2A).

32 Valve clearances (four-stroke engines) – check and adjustment

1 The engine must be completely cold for this maintenance procedure, so let the machine sit overnight before beginning. Remove any body panels necessary to gain access to the alternator and cylinder head (see Chapter 9).

2 Remove the spark plug (see Section 29).

3 Remove the valve cover (see Chapter 2B). Discard the cover gasket or O-ring as a new one must be fitted on reassembly.

4 The valve clearances are checked with the piston at top dead centre (TDC) on its compression stroke (the valves are closed and a small clearance can be felt at each rocker arm). Turn the engine in the normal direction of rotation until the piston is at TDC; you can do this by rotating the crankshaft via the alternator rotor or the variator centre nut. **Note:** *On liquid-cooled engines with the water pump located on the alternator cover it should not be necessary to remove the water pump*

or disconnect the coolant hoses in order to displace the cover. If there is access, the position of the piston can be checked by inserting a screwdriver down the spark plug hole.

5 Look for timing marks on the camshaft sprocket and the camshaft holder or cylinder head **(see illustrations)**. Alternatively, look for timing marks on the alternator rotor and the crankcase **(see illustrations)**. With the piston at TDC on its compression stroke and the timing marks aligned, the valve clearances can be checked. **Note:** *On some engines with options for two or four valve heads there may be alternative timing marks.*

6 Insert a feeler gauge of the same thickness as the correct valve clearance between the rocker arm and stem of each valve (see the *Data* section at the end of this manual). The feeler gauge should be a firm sliding fit – you should feel a slight drag when the you pull the gauge out **(see illustration)**.

7 If the clearance is either too small or too large, loosen the locknut and turn the adjuster until a firm sliding fit is obtained, then tighten the locknut securely, making sure the adjuster does not turn as you do so **(see illustration)**. Recheck the clearances.

8 Apply some engine oil to the valve assemblies, rockers and camshaft before installing the valve cover and fit a new cover gasket or O-ring. Install the remaining components in the reverse order of removal.

33 Headlight, brake light and horn – check

Note: *An improperly adjusted headlight may cause problems for oncoming traffic or provide poor, unsafe illumination of the road ahead. Before adjusting the headlight aim, be sure to consult with local traffic laws and regulations – for UK models refer to MOT Test Checks in the Reference section.*

1 Before making any adjustment, check that the tyre pressures are correct and the suspension is adjusted as required. Make any adjustments to the headlight aim with the scooter on level ground, with the fuel tank half full and with an assistant sitting on the seat. If the machine is usually ridden with a passenger on the back, have a second assistant to do this.

2 All headlight units have provision for vertical (up and down) adjustment. The headlight adjuster screw will be located either at the front of the unit, adjacent to the light, accessible through a hole or grille, or behind a body panel. Alternatively an adjuster at the rear of the unit will be accessible through a hole in the kick panel or inside the glovebox. Refer to your scooter handbook for details.

3 Position the scooter as described in the *MOT Test Checks* in the Reference section. Switch the headlight main beam ON and turn

32.5a Check for camshaft sprocket timing mark (arrowed) . . .

32.5b . . . or a line on the camshaft sprocket (arrowed)

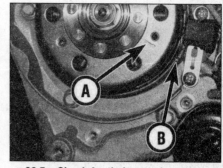

32.5c Check for timing marks on the alternator rotor (A) and crankcase (B) . . .

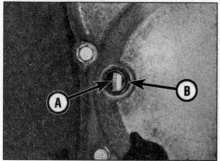

32.5d . . . or alternator rotor (A) and inside the inspection hole (B) in the engine side cover

32.6 Checking the valve clearance with a feeler gauge

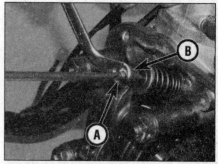

32.7 Hold the adjuster (A) while tightening the locknut (B)

36.1a Unscrew the knurled ring . . .

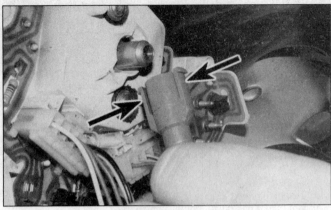

36.1b . . . or press the clips to release the speedometer cable

the adjuster screw to move the beam up or down as required.

4 The brake light should come on when either the front or rear brake levers are pulled in. If it does not, check the operation of the brake light switch and tail/brake light bulb (see Chapter 10). **Note:** *In most cases, check the operation of the brake light with the engine running.*

5 If the horn fails to work, check the operation of the handlebar switch and the horn itself (see Chapter 10). **Note:** *In most cases, check the operation of the horn with the engine running.*

34 Wheels and tyres – general check

Wheels

1 Wheels are virtually maintenance free, but they should be kept clean and corrosion-free and checked periodically for damage to the rims. Check cast wheels for cracks. Also check the wheel runout and alignment (see Chapter 8). Never attempt to repair damaged cast wheels; they must be renewed.

2 Wheel bearings will wear over a period of time and result in handling problems. Support the machine on its centre stand and check for any play in the bearings by pushing and pulling the wheel against the hub. Also rotate the wheel and check that it turns smoothly.

3 If any play is detected in the hub, or if the wheel does not rotate smoothly (and this is not due to brake or transmission drag), the wheel bearings must be inspected for wear or damage (see Chapter 8).

Tyres

4 Check the tyre condition and tread depth thoroughly – see *Daily (pre-ride) checks*. Check the valve rubber for signs of damage or deterioration and have it renewed if necessary. Also, make sure the valve stem cap is in place and tight.

35 Stand – check and lubrication

1 Since the stand pivots are exposed to the elements, they should be lubricated periodically to ensure safe and trouble-free operation.

2 In order for the lubricant to be applied where it will do the most good, the component should be disassembled. However, if chain or cable lubricant is being used, it can be applied to the pivot joint gaps and will usually work its way into the areas where friction occurs. If motor oil or light grease is being used, apply it sparingly as it may attract dirt (which could cause the controls to bind or wear at an accelerated rate).

3 The return spring must be capable of retracting the stand fully and holding it

retracted when the machine is in use. If spring has sagged or broken it must be renewed (see Chapter 7).

36 Speedometer cable and drive gear – lubrication

Note: *Some scooters are fitted with electronic speedometers. On these machines, only the drive gear needs lubricating. Do not attempt to disconnect the electrical wire from the drive housing.*

1 Displace the handlebar cover (see Chapter 9), then disconnect the speedometer cable from the underside of the instrument panel **(see illustrations)**.

2 Withdraw the inner cable from the outer cable and lubricate it with motor oil or cable lubricant. Do not lubricate the upper few inches of the cable as the lubricant may travel up into the instrument head.

3 On some scooters, the drive gear is contained within the hub (see Chapter 8). On some machines, the drive gear is sealed and requires no maintenance other than to check that the gear rotates smoothly when the hub is being overhauled. On others, the drive gear is retained by a plate. Loosen the bolt and withdraw the speedometer cable, then undo the bolt and remove the plate **(see illustrations)**. Pull out the drive gear and regrease it **(see illustration)**. Install the drive gear and cable in the reverse order of removal.

36.3a Loosen the retaining plate bolt . . .

36.3b . . . and withdraw the cable

36.3c Remove the drive gear and regrease it

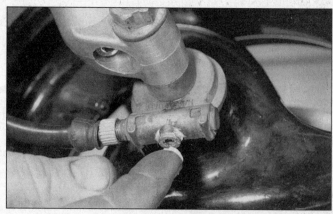

36.4a Remove the cap (arrowed) . . .

36.4b . . . and press some grease into the housing

4 Some scooters are fitted with a separate speedometer drive housing. Remove the cap from the housing and press some general purpose grease into it **(see illustrations)**. Refit the cap and tighten it securely.

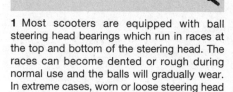

37 Steering head bearings – check

1 Most scooters are equipped with ball steering head bearings which run in races at the top and bottom of the steering head. The races can become dented or rough during normal use and the balls will gradually wear. In extreme cases, worn or loose steering head bearings can cause steering wobble – a condition that is potentially dangerous.
2 Place the scooter on the centrestand. Raise the front wheel off the ground either by having an assistant push down on the rear or by placing a support under the frame. **Note:** *Do not rest the weight of the machine on the bodywork; if necessary, remove the belly panel to expose the frame (see Chapter 9).*
3 Point the front wheel straight-ahead and slowly turn the handlebars from side-to-side. Any dents or roughness in the bearing races will be felt and the bars will not move smoothly and freely. If the bearings are damaged they must be renewed (see Chapter 7).
4 Next, grasp the front suspension and try to

37.4 Checking for play in the steering head bearings

move it forwards and backwards **(see illustration)**. Any freeplay in the steering head bearings will be felt as front-to-rear movement of the steering stem. **Note:** *On leading or trailing link front suspension, grasp the lower end of the suspension leg by the suspension arm pivot bolt for this test.* If play is felt in the bearings, follow the procedure described in Chapter 7 to adjust them.
5 Over a period of time the grease in the bearings will harden or may be washed out. Disassemble the steering head for regreasing of the bearings. Refer to Chapter 7 for details.

38 Suspension – check

1 The suspension components must be maintained in top operating condition to ensure rider safety. Loose, worn or damaged suspension parts decrease the scooter's stability and control.

Front suspension

2 While standing alongside the scooter, apply the front brake and push on the handlebars to compress the suspension several times. See if it moves up-and-down smoothly without binding. If binding is felt, the suspension should be disassembled and inspected (see Chapter 7).

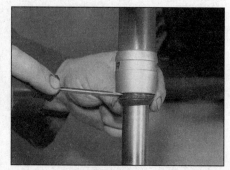

38.4 Lever off the seal and check for corrosion

3 On models with leading or trailing link suspension, inspect the shock for fluid leaks and corrosion on the damper rod. If the shock is faulty it should be renewed (see Chapter 7). Check that the shock mounting bolts are tight.
4 On models with telescopic forks, inspect the area around the dust seal for signs of grease or oil leaks, then carefully lever off the dust seal using a flat-bladed screwdriver and inspect the area behind it **(see illustration)**. If corrosion due to the ingress of water is evident, the seals must be renewed (see Chapter 7). The chromed finish on the forks is prone to corrosion and pitting, so it is advisable to keep them as clean as possible and to spray them regularly with a rust inhibitor, otherwise the seals will not last long. If corrosion and pitting is evident, tackle it as early as possible to prevent it getting worse.
5 Check the tightness of all suspension nuts and bolts to ensure none have worked loose.

Rear suspension

Note: *For scooters fitted with twin rear shocks, both shocks must be in good condition. If either is found to be faulty, renew the shocks as a pair.*
6 Inspect the rear shock for fluid leaks and corrosion on the damper rod. If a shock is faulty it should be renewed (see Chapter 7). Check that the shock mounting bolts are tight.
7 With the aid of an assistant to support the scooter, compress the rear suspension several times. It should move up-and-down freely without binding. If any binding is felt, the worn or faulty component must be identified and renewed. The problem could be due to either the shock absorber or the front pivot assembly.
8 Support the scooter so that the rear wheel is off the ground. Grab the engine/transmission unit at the rear and attempt to rock it from side-to-side – there should be no discernible freeplay felt between the engine and frame. If there is movement, inspect the tightness of the rear suspension mountings and the front engine mounting, referring to the torque settings specified in the *Data* section, then recheck for movement. If freeplay is felt,

disconnect the rear shock absorber lower mounting and displace the shock and check again – any freeplay in the front engine mounting should be more evident. If there is freeplay, inspect the mounting bolts and brackets for wear (see Chapter 7).

9 Reconnect the rear shock, then grasp the top of the rear wheel and pull it upwards – there should be no discernible freeplay before the shock absorber begins to compress. Any freeplay indicates a worn shock or shock mountings. The worn components must be renewed (see Chapter 7).

39 Nuts and bolts – tightness check

1 Since vibration tends to loosen fasteners, all nuts, bolts, screws, etc, should be periodically checked for proper tightness.

2 Pay particular attention to the following:
- Spark plug.
- Carburettor clamps.
- Gearbox oil filler and drain plugs (where fitted).
- Engine oil drain plug (four-stroke engines).
- Stand bolts.
- Engine mounting bolts.
- Suspension bolts.
- Wheel bolts.
- Handlebar clamp bolts.
- Brake caliper and disc mounting bolts (disc brakes).
- Brake hose banjo bolts (disc brakes).
- Exhaust system bolts/nuts.

3 If a torque wrench is available, use it along with the torque specifications given in the *Data* section at the end of this manual.

Chapter 2 Part A:
Two-stroke engines

Contents

Degrees of difficulty

Easy, suitable for novice with little experience		**Fairly easy,** suitable for beginner with some experience		**Fairly difficult,** suitable for competent DIY mechanic		**Difficult,** suitable for experienced DIY mechanic		**Very difficult,** suitable for expert DIY or professional

Specifications

Refer to the *Data* section at the end of this manual for servicing specifications.

1 General information

The engine is a single cylinder two-stroke, with either fan-assisted air cooling (see Chapter 1) or pumped liquid cooling (see Chapter 3). The crankshaft assembly is pressed together, incorporating the connecting rod. The piston runs on a needle roller bearing fitted in the small-end of the connecting rod. The crankshaft runs in caged ball main bearings.

The crankcase divides vertically – the left-hand crankcase is an integral part of the drivebelt casing and gearbox.

2 Operations possible with the engine in the frame

Most components and assemblies, with the obvious exception of the crankshaft assembly and its bearings, can be worked on without having to remove the engine/transmission unit from the frame. However, access to some components is severely restricted, and if a number of areas require attention at the same time, removal of the engine is recommended, as it is an easy task to undertake.

3 Major engine repair – general information

1 It is not always easy to determine if an engine should be completely overhauled, as a number of factors must be considered.

2 High mileage is not necessarily an indication that an overhaul is needed, while low mileage, on the other hand, does not preclude the need for an overhaul. Frequency of servicing is probably the single most important consideration. An engine that has regular and frequent maintenance will most likely give many miles of reliable service. Conversely, a neglected engine, or one which has not been run in properly, may require an overhaul very early in its life.

3 If the engine is making obvious knocking or rumbling noises, the connecting rod and/or main bearings are probably at fault.

4 Loss of power, rough running, excessive noise and high fuel consumption rates may also point to the need for an overhaul, especially if they are all present at the same time. If a complete service as detailed in Chapter 1 does not remedy the situation, major mechanical work is the only solution.

5 An engine overhaul generally involves restoring the internal parts to the specifications of a new engine. This may require fitting new piston rings and crankcase seals, or, after a high mileage, renewing the piston, cylinder and crankshaft assembly. The end result should be a like-new engine that will give as many trouble-free miles as the original.

6 Before beginning the engine overhaul, read through the related procedures to familiarise yourself with the scope and requirements of the job. Overhauling an engine is not all that difficult, but it is time-consuming. Check on the availability of parts and make sure that any necessary special tools and materials are obtained in advance.

7 Most work can be done with typical workshop hand tools, although manufacturers often produce a number of service tools for specific purposes such as disassembling the clutch and separating the crankcase halves. Precision measuring tools are required for inspecting parts to determine if they must be renewed. Alternatively, a dealer will handle the inspection of parts and offer advice concerning reconditioning and renewal. As a general rule, time is the primary cost of an overhaul so it does not pay to install worn or substandard parts.

8 As a final note, to ensure maximum life and minimum trouble from a rebuilt engine, everything must be assembled with care in a spotlessly clean environment.

4 Engine – removal and installation

Caution: The engine/transmission unit is not heavy, however removal and installation should be carried out with the aid of an assistant; personal injury or damage could occur if the engine falls or is dropped.

Removal

1 Support the scooter securely in an upright position. Work can be made easier by raising the machine to a suitable height on a hydraulic ramp or a suitable platform. Make sure it is secure and will not topple over.

2 Remove any body panels as necessary to access the engine (see Chapter 9).

3 Remove the exhaust system (see Chapter 4).

4 If the engine is dirty, particularly around its mountings, wash it thoroughly before starting any major dismantling work. This will make work much easier and rule out the possibility of dirt falling inside.

5 Disconnect the battery negative terminal (see Chapter 10) and pull the spark plug cap off the plug.

6 On liquid-cooled engines, disconnect the wire to the temperature sender on the cylinder head **(see illustration)**. Drain the cooling system and disconnect the coolant hoses from the unions on the water pump, cylinder and cylinder head (see Chapter 3). If fitted, undo the screw securing the carburettor heater union to the carburettor **(see illustration)**.

7 Trace the wiring from the alternator/ignition pulse generator coil and disconnect it at the connectors. Free the wiring from any clips or ties on the engine. Either remove the starter motor or disconnect the starter motor leads (see Chapter 10). If fitted, disconnect the earth (ground) wire between the frame and the engine.

8 If required, remove the air filter housing and the air intake duct (see Chapter 4).

9 Either remove the carburettor, leaving the throttle cable attached if required, or just disconnect the fuel hose and fuel tap vacuum hose from their unions on the carburettor and inlet manifold respectively, and disconnect the throttle cable (see Chapter 4). Where fitted, disconnect the automatic choke wiring connector.

10 Where fitted, disconnect the fuel pump vacuum hose from the engine.

11 Where fitted, detach the oil pump control cable from the pump pulley and detach the cable from its bracket (see Section 12).

12 Release the clip securing the hose from the oil tank to the union on the oil pump and detach the hose from the pump (see Section 12). Clamp the hose and secure it in an upright position to minimise oil loss. Wrap a clean plastic bag around the end to prevent dirt entering the system.

13 If required, remove the rear wheel (see Chapter 8). **Note:** *On machines where the centre stand is bolted to the underside of the engine unit, the rear wheel and stand provide a convenient support for the unit once it is removed from the scooter. However, it is useful to loosen the rear wheel nut at this point before disconnecting the rear brake.*

14 On models fitted with a drum rear brake, disconnect the brake cable from the brake arm (see Chapter 8). Undo any screws securing the cable to the underside of the drivebelt casing and detach the cable **(see illustration)**.

15 On models fitted with a disc rear brake, displace the brake caliper (see Chapter 8). Unclip the brake hose from the underside of the drivebelt casing **(see illustration 4.14)**.

16 Check that all wiring, cables and hoses are clear of the engine/transmission unit.

17 With the aid of an assistant, support the weight of the machine on the rear of the frame, then remove the bolt securing the rear shock absorber to the gearbox casing. If the rear wheel has been removed support the gearbox on a wood block to prevent damage to the casing. Undo the nut securing the upper end of the shock to the frame and remove the shock. **Note:** *On scooters fitted with twin rear shocks, remove both shocks.*

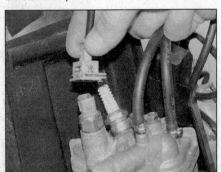

4.6a Disconnect the temperature sender wiring connector

4.6b Detach the carburettor heater union

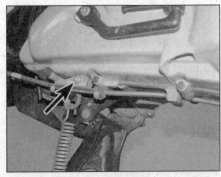

4.14 Undo the clip (arrowed) to detach the brake cable

4.18a Undo the nut (arrowed) . . .

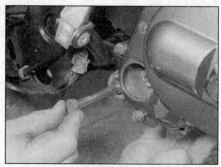

4.18b . . . and withdraw the bolt

4.18c Separate the engine unit from the frame

18 Remove the front engine mounting bolt **(see illustrations)**. Note that on some scooters the engine is supported by a bracket on the top of the engine/transmission unit. If the stand is fitted to the frame, manoeuvre the engine unit back and out of the frame. If the stand is bolted to the engine unit, lift the frame away **(see illustration)**.

19 If required, remove the stand (see Chapter 7) and the rear wheel (see Chapter 8).

Installation

20 Installation is the reverse of removal, noting the following:
● *Make sure no wires, cables or hoses become trapped between the engine and the frame when installing the engine.*
● *Tighten the front engine mounting bolt and shock absorber bolt to the torque settings specified in the Data section at the end of this manual.*
● *Make sure all wires, cables and hoses are correctly routed and connected, and secured by any clips or ties.*
● *On liquid-cooled engines, fill the cooling system (see Chapter 3).*
● *Bleed the oil pump (see Section 12) and check the adjustment of the oil pump cable where fitted (see Chapter 1).*
● *Check the operation of the rear brake before riding the machine (see Chapter 8).*

<table>
<tr><td>**5**</td><td>**Disassembly and reassembly** – general information</td></tr>
</table>

Disassembly

1 Before disassembling the engine, the external surfaces of the unit should be thoroughly cleaned and degreased. This will prevent contamination of the engine internals, and will also make working a lot easier and cleaner. A high flash-point solvent, such as paraffin can be used, or better still, a proprietary engine degreaser such as Gunk. Use an old paintbrush to work the solvent into the various recesses of the engine casings. Take care to exclude solvent or water from the electrical components and inlet and exhaust ports.

 Warning: The use of petrol (gasoline) as a cleaning agent should be avoided because of the risk of fire.

2 When clean and dry, arrange the unit on the workbench, leaving suitable clear area for working. Gather a selection of small containers and plastic bags so that parts can be grouped together in an easily identifiable manner. Some paper and a pen should be on hand to permit notes to be made and labels attached where necessary. A supply of clean rag is also required.

3 Before commencing work, read through the appropriate section so that some idea of the necessary procedure can be gained. When removing components it should be noted that great force is seldom required, unless specified. In many cases, a component's reluctance to be removed is indicative of an incorrect approach or removal method – if in any doubt, recheck with the text.

4 When disassembling the engine, keep 'mated' parts that have been in contact with each other during engine operation together. These 'mated' parts must be re-used or renewed as an assembly.

5 Complete engine disassembly should be done in the following general order with reference to the appropriate Sections (refer to Chapter 6 for details of transmission components disassembly):
● *Remove the cylinder head.*
● *Remove the cylinder.*
● *Remove the piston.*
● *Remove the alternator.*
● *Remove the variator (see Chapter 6).*

6.2a Unclip any wires or hoses . . .

● *Remove the starter motor (see Chapter 10).*
● *Remove the oil pump.*
● *Remove the water pump if fitted internally (see Chapter 3).*
● *Remove the reed valve (see Chapter 4).*
● *Separate the crankcase halves.*
● *Remove the crankshaft.*

Reassembly

6 Reassembly is accomplished by reversing the order of disassembly.

<table>
<tr><td>**6**</td><td>**Cylinder head** – removal, inspection and installation</td><td></td></tr>
</table>

Note: *This procedure can be carried out with the engine in the frame. If the engine has been removed, ignore the steps that do not apply.* **Caution: The engine must be completely cool before beginning this procedure or the cylinder head may become warped.**

Air-cooled engines
Removal

1 Remove the body panels as necessary to access the cylinder head (see Chapter 9).

2 Pull the spark plug cap off the spark plug. It will be necessary to remove the engine cowling, or part of the cowling, to access the cylinder head. On some engines, the cooling fan cowling forms part of the engine cowling. Check around the cowling and disconnect any wires or hoses clipped to it, then undo the bolts securing the cowling and remove it, noting how it fits **(see illustrations)**.

6.2b . . . then undo the cowling fixing bolts (arrowed)

6.3a Undo the cylinder head nuts . . .

6.3b . . . or the cylinder head bolts

Note: *Some cowlings are clipped together – take care not to damage the fixing lugs when separating them.* Remove any spacers for the cowling bolts for safekeeping if they are loose.
3 Remove the spark plug, then unscrew the cylinder head bolts, or cylinder head nuts, evenly and a little at a time in a criss-cross sequence until they are all loose and remove them, together with any washers **(see illustrations)**.
Note: *Some cylinder heads are secured by long bolts which pass down through the cylinder and screw into the crankcase, others are secures by nuts on long studs. In both cases, once the cylinder head is loose care must be taken not to break the cylinder base gasket seal otherwise a new base gasket will have to be fitted before refitting the head (see Section 7).*
4 Lift the head off the cylinder. If the head is stuck, tap around the joint face between the head and cylinder with a soft-faced mallet to free it. Do not attempt to free the head by inserting a screwdriver between the head and cylinder – you'll damage the sealing surfaces.
5 If fitted, remove the cylinder head gasket and discard it as a new one must be used on reassembly.

Inspection

6 Refer to Chapter 1 and decarbonise the cylinder head.
7 Inspect the head very carefully for cracks and other damage. If cracks are found, a new head will be required.
8 Inspect the threads in the spark plug hole.

Damaged or worn threads can be reclaimed using a thread insert (see *Tools and Workshop Tips* in the *Reference* section). Most scooter dealers and small engineering firms offer a service of this kind.
9 Check the mating surfaces on the cylinder head and cylinder for signs of leaks, which could indicate that the head is warped.
10 Using a precision straight-edge and a feeler gauge, check the head mating surface for warpage. **Note:** *Clean all traces of old gasket material from the cylinder head and cylinder with a suitable solvent. Take care not to scratch or gouge the soft aluminium.* Lay the straight-edge across the surface and try to slip the feeler gauge under it on either side of the combustion chamber. If the feeler gauge can be inserted between the straight-edge and the cylinder head, the head is warped and must be either machined or, if warpage is excessive, renewed. Check vertically, horizontally and diagonally across the head, making four checks in all **(see illustration)**. If there is any doubt about the condition of the head consult a scooter dealer or specialist engineer.

Installation

11 Installation is the reverse of removal, noting the following:
● *Ensure both cylinder head and cylinder mating surfaces are clean.*
● *Lubricate the cylinder bore with the specified type of two-stroke oil.*

● *Install the new head gasket if required.* **Note:** *The gasket may be marked to identify which side should face up when it is in place, or there may be a raised section around the inner edge of the gasket. If so, fit the gasket with the raised section uppermost.*
● *Tighten the cylinder head fixings evenly and a little at a time in a criss-cross pattern to the torque setting specified in the Data section.*
● *Ensure the engine cowling is correctly secured.*

Liquid-cooled engines
Removal

12 Remove the body panels as necessary to access the cylinder head (see Chapter 9). Remove any heat shield that may prevent access to the head.
13 Disconnect the battery negative terminal (see Chapter 10). Pull the spark plug cap off the plug and disconnect the wire to the temperature sender on the cylinder head **(see illustration 4.6a)**.
14 Drain the cooling system and disconnect the coolant hoses from the unions on the cylinder head **(see illustration)**. If fitted, disconnect the carburettor heater hoses **(see illustration 4.6b)**.
15 On some engines, the thermostat housing is mounted on the top of the cylinder head; if required, undo the bolts and remove the housing, then lift out the thermostat **(see illustration)**.

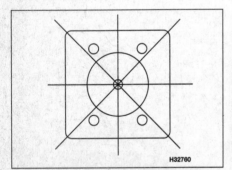

6.10 Check the cylinder head for warpage with a straight-edge

6.14 Disconnect the coolant hoses from the cylinder head

6.15 Remove the thermostat housing if required

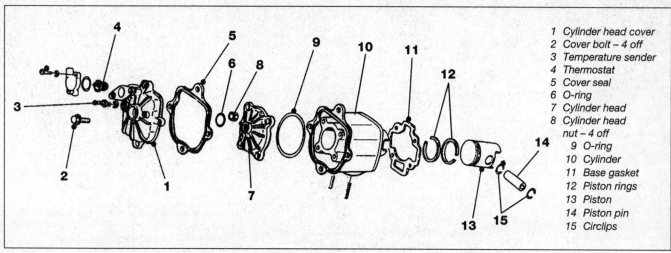

1 Cylinder head cover
2 Cover bolt – 4 off
3 Temperature sender
4 Thermostat
5 Cover seal
6 O-ring
7 Cylinder head
8 Cylinder head
   nut – 4 off
9 O-ring
10 Cylinder
11 Base gasket
12 Piston rings
13 Piston
14 Piston pin
15 Circlips

6.16 Liquid-cooled engine with separate cylinder head cover

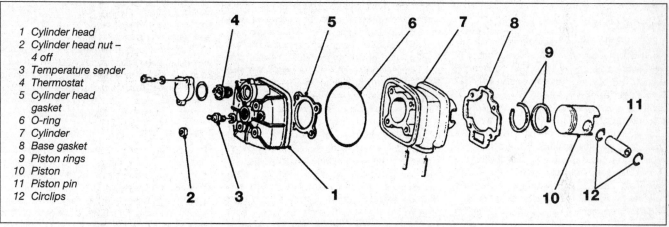

1 Cylinder head
2 Cylinder head nut –
   4 off
3 Temperature sender
4 Thermostat
5 Cylinder head
   gasket
6 O-ring
7 Cylinder
8 Base gasket
9 Piston rings
10 Piston
11 Piston pin
12 Circlips

6.17 Components of a conventional liquid-cooled engine

16 Some engines are fitted with a separate cylinder head cover which forms part of the engine cooling water jacket **(see illustration)**. Undo the bolts and remove the cover. Discard any gasket or O-ring as a new one must be used on reassembly.

17 Follow Steps 3 and 4 and remove the cylinder head. Discard any gasket or O-ring as new ones must be used **(see illustration)**.

18 If the thermostat is fitted inside the cylinder head, lift out the thermostat **(see illustration)**.

Inspection

19 Follow Steps 6 to 10 to decarbonise and check the cylinder head. If the thermostat is fitted inside the cylinder head, ensure that the thermostat bypass passage is clear **(see illustration)**. Check the condition of the thermostat (see Chapter 3).

Installation

20 Installation is the reverse of removal, noting the following:
● *Ensure both cylinder head and cylinder mating surfaces are clean.*
● *Lubricate the cylinder bore with the specified type of two-stroke oil.*
● *Assemble the components with new gaskets and O-rings.*
● *Tighten the cylinder head, and head cover where fitted, fixings evenly and a little at a time in a criss-cross pattern to the torque setting specified in the Data section.*
● *Ensure the thermostat and coolant system hoses are fitted correctly (see Chapter 3).*
● *Refill the cooling system (see Chapter 1).*

6.18 Where fitted, lift out the thermostat

6.19 Thermostat bypass passage must be clear

7.1 Detach the coolant hose (arrowed) from the cylinder

7.2 Support the piston as the cylinder is lifted off

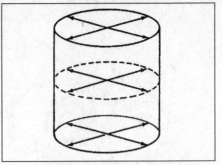

7.6 Measure the cylinder bore in the directions shown

7 Cylinder –
removal, inspection and installation

Note: *This procedure can be carried out with the engine in the frame.*

Removal

1 Remove the exhaust system (see Chapter 4) and the cylinder head (see Section 6). On liquid-cooled engines, where applicable, detach the coolant hose from the cylinder **(see illustration)**.

2 Lift the cylinder up off the crankcase, supporting the piston as it becomes accessible to prevent it hitting the crankcase opening **(see illustration)**. If the cylinder is stuck, tap around the joint face between the cylinder and the crankcase with a soft-faced mallet to free it. Don't attempt to free the cylinder by inserting a screwdriver between it and the crankcase – you'll damage the sealing surfaces. When the cylinder is removed, stuff a clean rag into the crankcase opening around the piston to prevent anything falling inside.

3 Remove the cylinder base gasket and discard it, as a new one must be fitted on reassembly.

4 Scrape off any carbon deposits that may have formed in the exhaust port, then wash the cylinder with a suitable solvent and dry it thoroughly. Compressed air will speed the drying process and ensure that all holes and recesses are clean.

Inspection

5 Check the cylinder bore carefully for scratches and score marks.

6 If available, use a telescoping gauge and micrometer to measure the diameter of the cylinder bore to assess the amount of wear, taper and ovality (see *Tools and Workshop Tips* in the *Reference* section). Measure near the top (but below the level of the top piston ring at TDC), centre and bottom (but above the level of the bottom ring at BDC) of the bore both parallel to and across the crankshaft axis **(see illustration)**. Calculate any differences between the measurements taken to determine any taper or ovality in the bore.

7 Now measure an unworn part of the cylinder bore (below the level of the bottom ring at BDC) and compare the result to the previous measurements to determine overall wear.

8 If the bore is tapered, oval, or worn excessively, or badly scratched, scuffed or scored, the cylinder and piston will have to be renewed. **Note:** *If no service limit specifications (see Data section) are available to assess cylinder wear, calculate the piston-to-bore clearance to determine whether the cylinder is useable (see Section 8).*

9 If there is any doubt about the serviceability of the cylinder, consult a scooter dealer. **Note:** *On some engines, the surface of the cylinder has a wear-resistant coating which, when damaged or worn through, requires a new cylinder. On others, the cylinder can be rebored and an oversize piston fitted (see Data section). Oversize pistons are not necessarily marked as*

such; in many cases the only way to determine if a cylinder has been rebored is to measure an unworn area of the bore and compare the result with the specifications in the Data section. Most manufacturers mark cylinders and pistons with a size code during production; the size code (usually a letter) is stamped into the cylinder gasket surface and the top of the piston (see illustration). It is important that new parts have matching codes.

10 If applicable, inspect the cylinder head bolt threads in the crankcase (see Section 13). If the head is secured by studs, check that they are tight. If any are loose, remove them and clean their threads. Apply a suitable permanent thread locking compound and tighten them securely.

Installation

Note: *On some engines, cylinder base gaskets are available in a range of thicknesses; the appropriate thickness depends on the height of the piston crown at TDC in relation to the cylinder top gasket surface. Consult a scooter dealer for details. In these instances, the correct gasket thickness must be calculated before reassembly (see Steps 17 to 21).*

11 Check that the mating surfaces of the cylinder and crankcase are clean, then remove any rag from the crankcase opening. Lay the new base gasket in place on the crankcase making sure it is the correct way round **(see illustration)**.

12 Check that the piston rings are correctly positioned so that the ring locating pins in the piston grooves are between the ring ends **(see illustration)**.

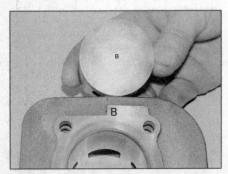

7.9 Cylinders and pistons are size-coded and should always match

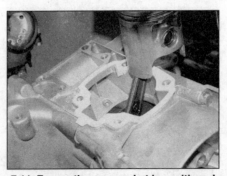

7.11 Ensure the new gasket is positioned correctly on the crankcase

7.12 Ring locating pins (arrowed) must be between the ring ends

7.13 Position the cylinder over the top of the piston . . .

7.14 . . . then carefully feed the piston into the cylinder

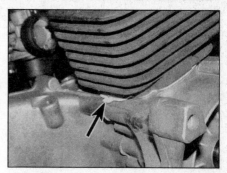

7.15 Check that the cylinder base gasket (arrowed) has not been displaced

13 Lubricate the cylinder bore, piston and piston rings, and the connecting rod big and small ends, with the specified type of two-stroke oil, then locate the cylinder over the top of the piston **(see illustration)**.

14 Ensure the piston enters the bore squarely and does not get cocked sideways. Carefully compress and feed each ring into the bore as the cylinder is lowered, taking care that the rings do not rotate out of position **(see illustration)**. Do not use force if the cylinder appears to be stuck as the piston and/or rings will be damaged.

15 When the piston is correctly installed in the cylinder, check that the base gasket has not been displaced, then press the cylinder down onto the gasket **(see illustration)**.

16 Install the remaining components in the reverse order of removal.

Cylinder base gasket thickness

17 To measure the height of the piston crown at TDC in relation to the cylinder top gasket surface you will require a dial gauge and a mounting plate **(see illustration)**.

18 Assemble the cylinder on the piston as described in Steps 12 to 14, but without a base gasket, and press the cylinder down onto the crankcase.

19 Set the dial gauge in the mounting plate, and with the mounting plate feet and gauge tip resting against the cylinder top gasket surface, zero the gauge. Rotate the crankshaft so that the piston is part way down the bore.

20 Clamp the mounting plate diagonally across the cylinder using the cylinder fixings and tighten them to ensure that the cylinder is held firmly against the crankcase.

21 Rotate the crankshaft via the alternator rotor nut so the piston rises to the top of its stroke (TDC). At this point read off the dial gauge **(see illustration 7.17)**. The reading represents the distance between the cylinder top gasket surface and the top of the piston crown. Use this measurement, together with the manufacturer's information, to identify the appropriate gasket thickness.

 8 Piston – removal, inspection and installation

Note: *This procedure can be carried out with the engine in the frame.*

Removal

1 Remove the cylinder and stuff a clean rag into the crankcase opening around the piston to prevent anything falling inside (see Section 7).

2 The piston top should be marked with an

arrow which faces towards the exhaust. If this is not visible, mark the piston accordingly so that it can be installed the correct way round. Note that the arrow may not be visible until the carbon deposits have been scraped off and the piston cleaned.

3 Carefully prise the circlip out from one side of the piston using needle-nose pliers or a small flat-bladed screwdriver inserted into the notch **(see illustration)**. Check for burring around the circlip groove and remove any with a very fine file or penknife blade, then push the piston pin out from the other side and remove the piston from the connecting rod **(see illustration)**. Use a socket extension to push the piston pin out if required. Remove the other circlip and discard them both, as new ones must be used on reassembly.

> **HAYNES HINT**
> *To prevent the circlip from flying away or from dropping into the crankcase, pass a rod or screwdriver, with a greater diameter than the gap between the circlip ends, through the piston pin. This will trap the circlip if it springs out.*

> **HAYNES HINT**
> *If the piston pin is a tight fit in the piston bosses, heat the piston gently with a hot air gun – this will expand the alloy piston sufficiently to release its grip on the pin.*

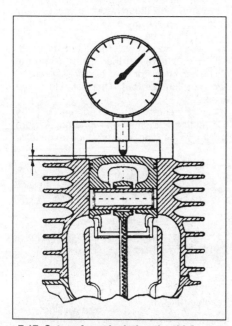

7.17 Set-up for calculating the thickness of the cylinder base gasket

8.3a Remove the circlip . . .

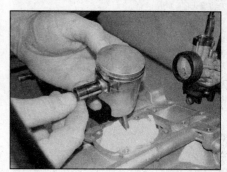

8.3b . . . then push out the piston pin

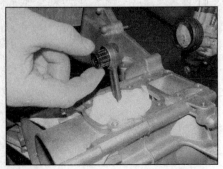

8.4 Remove the small-end bearing

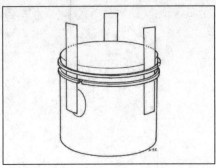

8.5 Remove the piston rings carefully

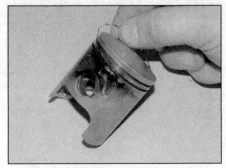

8.6 Expander fitted behind the second ring

4 The connecting rod small-end bearing is a loose fit in the rod; remove it for safekeeping, noting which way round it fits **(see illustration)**.

5 Before the inspection process can be carried out, the piston rings must be removed and the piston must be cleaned. **Note:** *If the cylinder is being renewed or rebored, piston inspection can be overlooked as a new one will be fitted.* The piston rings can be removed by hand; using your thumbs, ease the ends of each ring apart and carefully lift it off the piston, taking care not to expand it any more than is necessary **(see illustration)**. Do not nick or gouge the piston in the process.

6 Note which way up each ring fits and in which groove, as they must be installed in their original positions if being re-used. The upper surface of each ring should be marked at one end (see Section 9). Some pistons have an expander fitted behind the second ring **(see illustration)**. **Note:** *It is good practice to renew the piston rings when an engine is being overhauled. Ensure that the piston and bore are serviceable before purchasing new rings.*

7 Clean all traces of carbon from the top of the piston. A hand-held wire brush or a piece of fine emery cloth can be used once most of the deposits have been scraped away. Do not, under any circumstances, use a wire brush mounted in a drill motor; the piston material is soft and is easily damaged.

8 Use a piston ring groove cleaning tool to remove any carbon deposits from the ring grooves. If a tool is not available, a piece broken off an old ring will do the job. Be very

careful to remove only the carbon deposits. Do not remove any metal and do not nick or gouge the sides of the ring grooves.

9 Once the carbon has been removed, clean the piston with a suitable solvent and dry it thoroughly. If the identification previously marked on the piston is cleaned off, be sure to re-mark it correctly.

Inspection

10 Inspect the piston for cracks around the skirt, at the pin bosses and at the ring lands. Check that the circlip grooves are not damaged. Normal piston wear appears as even, vertical wear on the thrust surfaces of the piston and slight looseness of the top ring in its groove. If the skirt is scored or scuffed, the engine may have been suffering from overheating and/or abnormal combustion, resulting in excessively high operating temperatures.

11 A hole in the top of the piston, in one extreme, or burned areas around the edge of the piston crown, indicate that pre-ignition or knocking under load have occurred. If you find evidence of any problems the cause must be corrected or the damage will occur again. Refer to Chapter 4 for carburation checks and Chapter 5 for ignition checks.

12 Check the piston-to-bore clearance by measuring the cylinder bore (see Section 7) and the piston diameter. Measure the piston approximately 25 mm down from the bottom of the lower piston ring groove and at 90° to the piston pin axis **(see illustration)**. **Note:** *The precise point of measurement differs between manufacturers and engines, but the*

aim is to measure the piston in an area where it is worn. Subtract the piston diameter from the bore diameter to obtain the clearance. If it is greater than the specified figure, check whether it is the bore or piston that is worn the most (see *Data* section at the end of this manual). If the bore is good, install a new piston and rings. **Note:** *Oversize pistons fitted in a rebored cylinder are not necessarily marked as such; in many cases the only way to determine if a cylinder has been rebored is to measure an unworn area of the bore and compare the result with the specifications in the* Data *section. Most manufacturers mark cylinders and pistons with a size code during production; the size code (usually a letter) is stamped into the cylinder gasket surface and the top of the piston (see illustration 7.9).* It is important that new parts have matching codes. It is essential to supply the size code and any rebore specifications when purchasing a new piston.

13 Use a micrometer to measure the piston pin in the middle, where it runs in the small-end bearing, and at each end where it runs in the piston **(see illustration)**. If there is any difference in the measurements the pin is worn and must be renewed.

14 If the piston pin is good, lubricate it with clean two-stroke oil, then insert it into the piston and check for any freeplay between the two **(see illustration)**. There should be no freeplay.

15 Next, check the condition of the connecting rod small-end bearing. A worn small-end bearing will produce a metallic

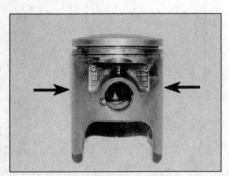

8.12 Measure the piston at 90° to the piston pin axis

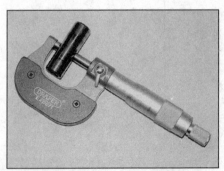

8.13 Measuring the piston pin where it runs in the small-end bearing

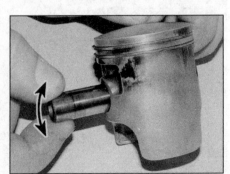

8.14 Check for freeplay between the piston and the piston pin

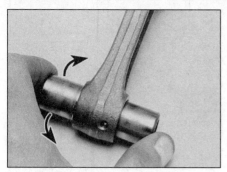

8.15 Rock the piston pin back-and-forth to check for freeplay

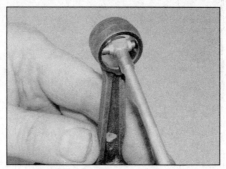

8.16 Measuring the internal diameter of the connecting rod small-end

rattle, most audible when the engine is under load, and increasing as engine speed rises. This should not be confused with big-end bearing wear, which produces a pronounced knocking noise. Inspect the bearing rollers for flat spots and pitting. Install the bearing in the connecting rod, then slide the piston pin into the bearing and check for freeplay **(see illustration)**. There should be only slightly discernible freeplay between the piston pin, the bearing and the connecting rod.

16 If there is freeplay, measure the internal diameter of the connecting rod small-end **(see illustration)**. Take several measurements; if there is any difference between the measurements, the small end is worn and either a new connecting rod or crankshaft assembly will have to be fitted (see Section 14). Consult a scooter dealer about the availability of parts. **Note:** *If a new rod is available, fitting it is a specialist task which should be left to a scooter dealer or automotive engineer. If a new rod is fitted, the big-end bearing should be renewed at the same time.*

17 If the small-end is good, fit a new small-end bearing. **Note:** *On some engines, a mark on the connecting rod indicates the matching size code of the small end bearing – the bearing will have the same mark or will be colour-coded. Refer to these marks when purchasing a new bearing.*

Installation

18 Install the piston rings (see Section 9).
19 Lubricate the piston pin, the piston pin bore in the piston and the small-end bearing

with the specified two-stroke oil and install the bearing in the connecting rod.
20 Install a new circlip in one side of the piston, line up the piston on the connecting rod, making sure the arrow on the piston top faces towards the exhaust, and insert the piston pin from the other side. Secure the pin with the other new circlip. When installing the circlips, compress them only just enough to fit them in the piston, and make sure they are properly seated in their grooves with the open end away from the removal notch.
21 Install the cylinder (see Section 7).

9 Piston rings – inspection and installation

1 New piston rings should be fitted whenever an engine is being overhauled. It is important that you get new rings of the correct size for your piston so ensure that any information relating to piston size, including rebore size, and size-coding is available when purchasing new parts.
2 Before fitting the new rings onto the piston, the ring end gaps must be checked. Insert the top ring into the bottom of the cylinder bore and square it up by pushing it in with the top of the piston. The ring should be about 15 to 20 mm from the bottom edge of the cylinder. To measure the end gap, slip a feeler gauge between the ends of the ring and compare the measurement to the specification in the *Data* section at the end of this manual **(see illustration)**.

3 If the gap is larger or smaller than specified, check to make sure that you have the correct rings before proceeding. If the gap is larger than specified it is likely the cylinder bore is worn. If the gap is too small the ring ends may come into contact with each other during engine operation, causing serious damage.
4 Repeat the procedure for the other ring.
5 Once the ring end gaps have been checked, the rings can be installed on the piston. First identify the ring locating pin in each piston ring groove – the ring must be positioned so that the pin is in between the ends of the ring **(see illustration 7.12)**.
6 If the piston has an expander fitted behind the lower ring, fit that first, ensuring that the ends of the expander do not overlap the ring locating pin **(see illustration 8.6)**.
7 The upper surface of each ring should be marked at one end; make sure you fit the rings the right way up. Install the lower ring first. Do not expand the ring any more than is necessary to slide it into place and check that the locating pin is between the ends of the ring **(see illustration)**.
8 Install the top ring. Always ensure that the ring end gaps are positioned each side of the locating pins before fitting the piston into the cylinder.

10 Alternator – removal and installation

Note: *This procedure can be carried out with the engine in the frame. If the engine has been removed, ignore the steps that do not apply.*

Removal

1 Remove the body panels as necessary to access the alternator (see Chapter 9). If required, remove the exhaust system (see Chapter 4).
2 On air-cooled engines, unclip any wiring or hoses from the fan cowling, then undo the bolts securing the fan cowling and remove it **(see illustration)**. Note that on some models the fan cowling is clipped to the engine cowling – take care not to damage the fixing lugs when separating them. Remove any spacers for the cowling bolts for safekeeping if they are loose. Undo the bolts securing the

9.2 Measuring installed ring end gap

9.7 Using a thin blade to install the piston ring

10.2 Remove the fan cowling

10.3 Water pump is driven by dampers on the alternator rotor

10.4 Lift off the side cover and alternator stator

10.5 Hold the rotor and undo the centre nut (arrowed)

10.6 Using a strap wrench to hold the rotor

cooling fan to the alternator rotor and remove the fan (see Chapter 1, Section 21).

3 On liquid-cooled engines where the water pump is mounted on the outside of the alternator cover, first drain the coolant and disconnect all the coolant hoses from the pump

(see Chapter 3). Undo the cover mounting bolts and lift off the cover. Depending on the tools available for removing the alternator rotor, it may be necessary to unscrew the pump drive dampers (see illustration).

4 On some engines the alternator is located behind the right-hand engine side cover. **Note:** *If the water pump is mounted on the outside of the engine side cover, first drain the coolant and disconnect all the coolant hoses from the pump (see Chapter 3).* Trace the wiring from the cover and disconnect it at the connector, then undo the cover bolts and lift off the cover (see illustration). Discard the gasket as a new one must be fitted and remove the cover dowels for safekeeping if they are loose. If applicable, remove the starter pinion assembly (see Section 11).

5 To remove the rotor centre nut it is necessary to stop the rotor from turning; some manufacturers produce a service tool for this

purpose. If the rotor face is accessible, you can make up a tool which engages the slots or holes (see illustration). **Note:** *Take great care not to damage the coils of the alternator when locating any tools through the rotor.*

TOOL TIP *A rotor holding tool can easily be made using two strips of steel bolted together in the middle, with a bolt through each end which locates into the slots or holes in the rotor. Do not allow the bolts to extend too far through the rotor otherwise the coils could be damaged.*

6 If the alternator stator is located in the engine side cover, the rotor can be held with a strap wrench (see illustration).

7 With the rotor securely held, unscrew the centre nut.

8 To remove the rotor from the shaft it is necessary to use a puller – either a manufacturer's service tool or a commercially available puller (see illustrations). To use the service tool, first screw the body of the tool all the way into the threads provided in the rotor. Hold the tool steady with a spanner on its flats and tighten the centre bolt, exerting steady pressure to draw the rotor off the crankshaft. To use a puller, engage the puller legs either in the slots in the rotor or thread them into the threaded holes in the rotor, then tighten the centre bolt exerting steady pressure to draw the rotor off the crankshaft. Remove the Woodruff key from the shaft for safekeeping, noting how it fits (see illustrations).

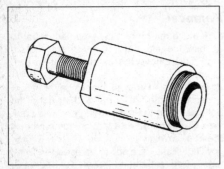

10.8a Typical service tool for removing the rotor

10.8b Using a screw-in type puller

10.8c Using a two-legged puller

10.8d Remove the Woodruff key for safekeeping

10.8e Note the alignment of the key (A) and the slot in the rotor (B)

10.10a Undo the stator screws (A) and the pulse generator coil screws (B) . . .

10.10b . . . and remove the assembly noting how the wiring fits

10.10c Note the position of the pulse generator (A) and the wiring grommet (B)

9 In most cases, the alternator stator coils and ignition pulse generator coil are wired together and have to be removed as an assembly. If not already done, trace the wiring back from the alternator and pulse generator, and disconnect it at the connectors. Free the wiring from any clips or guides and feed it through to the alternator.

10 Undo the screws securing the stator and the pulse generator and lift them off together **(see illustration)**. Where fitted, draw any rubber wiring boot out of the crankcase or engine side cover and carefully pull the wiring away, noting how it fits **(see illustrations)**.

Installation

11 Installation is the reverse of removal, noting the following:
- *Ensure the wiring is correctly routed before installing the stator and pulse generator.*
- *Make sure that no metal objects have attached themselves to the magnets on the inside of the rotor.*
- *Clean the tapered end of the crankshaft and the corresponding mating surface on the inside of the rotor with a suitable solvent.*
- *Fit the Woodruff key into its slot in the shaft, then install the rotor.*
- *Tighten the rotor centre nut to the torque setting specified in the Data section at the end of this manual.*
- *Secure the wiring with any clips or ties.*
- *If applicable, refill the cooling system and bleed it (see Chapter 3).*

11 Starter pinion assembly and starter clutch – removal, inspection and installation

Note 1: *Two different set-ups are used to transfer the starter motor drive to the engine – a sliding pinion assembly or a starter (one-way) clutch. The sliding pinion assembly engages with the driven gear on the variator pulley, or a driven gear on the crankshaft behind the variator. The starter clutch is located either on the back of the alternator rotor or on the crankshaft behind the variator. Note the point at which the starter motor shaft enters the engine case to locate the appropriate assembly.*

Note 2: *This procedure can be carried out with the engine in the frame.*

Starter pinion assembly

Removal

1 Note the position of the starter motor, then remove the drivebelt cover (see Chapter 6) and locate the pinion assembly adjacent to the variator pulley **(see illustration)**.

2 Where necessary, undo the bolts securing the starter pinion outer support and remove the support.

3 Withdraw the starter pinion assembly **(see illustration)**.

Inspection

4 Some pinion assemblies are fitted with a rubber boot. If the boot shows signs of

damage or deterioration, remove it. If a new boot is available, fit it on reassembly.

5 Check the starter pinion assembly for any signs of damage or wear, particularly for chipped or broken teeth on either of the pinions **(see illustration)**. Check the corresponding teeth on the starter motor pinion and the variator driven gear.

6 Rotate the outer pinion and check that it moves smoothly up-and-down the shaft, and that it returns easily to its rest position.

7 The starter pinion assembly is supplied as a complete unit; if any of the component parts is worn or damaged, the unit will have to be renewed.

8 Most manufacturers recommend that the starter pinion mechanism should not be lubricated as any excess grease may contaminate the drivebelt and cause it to slip. However, a smear of grease should be applied to both ends of the pinion shaft before reassembly.

Installation

9 Installation is the reverse of removal. Ensure the inner pinion engages with the starter motor shaft **(see illustration 11.1)**.

Starter (one-way) clutch

Removal

10 Note the position of the starter motor, then remove either the alternator cover (see Section 10) or the drivebelt cover (see Chapter 6).

11 The operation of the starter clutch can be

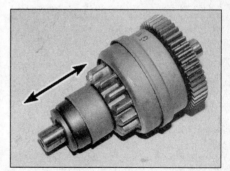

11.1 Starter pinion assembly is driven by the starter motor shaft (arrowed)

11.3 Remove the pinion assembly, noting how it fits

11.5 Check the pinion teeth. Outer pinion should move smoothly on shaft

11.13 Starter idler gear (A) and driven gear (B)

11.14 Examine the idler gear teeth for wear and damage

11.15 Gear should rotate freely in one direction only

11.16a Withdraw the gear from the clutch

11.16b Undo the bolts to remove the starter clutch from the alternator rotor

11.17 Check the condition of the clutch sprags – they should be flat on one side

checked while it is in place. Check that the starter driven gear is able to rotate freely in the opposite direction to engine rotation, but locks when rotated in the other direction **(see illustration 11.13)**. If not, the starter clutch is faulty and should be removed for inspection.

Removal

12 Remove the variator (see Chapter 6) or the alternator rotor (see Section 10) as appropriate. If the starter clutch is mounted on the crankshaft behind the variator, slide the clutch assembly off the shaft.
13 Remove the idler gear, noting how it fits **(see illustration)**.

Inspection

14 Inspect the teeth on the idler gear and renew it if any are chipped or worn **(see illustration)**. Check the idler shaft and bearing surfaces for signs of wear or damage, and renew it if necessary. Inspect the teeth of the driven gear.
15 Hold the starter clutch assembly or the alternator rotor, as appropriate, and check that the starter driven gear rotates freely in one direction and locks in the other direction **(see illustration)**. If it doesn't, the starter clutch is faulty and should be renewed. If individual components are available, follow Steps 16 and 17 and check the condition of the one-way mechanism. If there is any doubt about the condition of the starter clutch, have it tested by a scooter dealer.
16 Slowly rotate the driven gear and withdraw it from the clutch **(see illustration)**. If the starter clutch is on the back of the alternator rotor, use a strap wrench to hold

the rotor and undo the clutch mounting bolts **(see illustration)**.
17 Inspect the hub of the driven gear for wear and scoring. Inspect the clutch one-way mechanism; if a ring of sprags is used, the individual sprags should be smooth and free to rotate in their cage **(see illustration)**; if individual sprags are spring-loaded, check that the spring plungers are free to move.

Installation

18 Installation is the reverse of removal, noting the following:
● *Apply a drop of thread locking compound to the clutch mounting bolts.*
● *Lubricate the driven gear hub with clean engine oil.*
● *Rotate the driven gear to install it in the starter clutch.*
● *Ensure the idler gear engages with the pinion on the starter motor shaft.*

12 Oil pump – removal, inspection, installation and bleeding

Note 1: *Generally the oil pump is located on the outside of the crankcase, either in front or behind the cylinder, or inside the engine unit either behind the variator or behind the alternator rotor. Externally-mounted pumps are generally driven via a shaft and worm gear on the crankshaft and the rate of oil delivery is either cable-controlled (from the throttle twistgrip via a cable splitter – see Chapter 1) or automatic (centrifugal pump). Internally-*

mounted pumps are generally either belt- or gear-driven and rate of oil delivery is either cable-controlled or automatic.
Note 2: *This procedure can be carried out with the engine in the frame. If the engine has been removed, ignore the steps that do not apply.*

Externally-mounted pump

Removal

1 Remove the body panels as necessary to access the oil pump (see Chapter 9). If required, remove the exhaust system (see Chapter 4).
Note: *On some engines, the externally-mounted pump is located behind a cover on the side of the crankcase; the pump is driven by an extension of the water pump driveshaft. Remove the cover to access the pump.*
2 On engines fitted with a cable-operated pump, detach the cable from the pump pulley, then unscrew the bolts securing the cable bracket and remove the bracket with the cable attached **(see illustration)**.

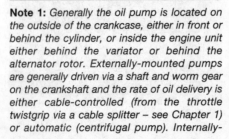

12.2 Remove the oil pump cable and bracket

12.3 Detach the oil hoses (arrowed) from the pump unions

12.5 Remove the wave washer

12.12a Fit a new pump body O-ring

3 On all models, release the clip securing the oil inlet hose from the oil tank to the union on the pump and detach the hose **(see illustration)**. Clamp the hose and secure it in an upright position to minimise oil loss. Release the clip securing the oil outlet hose to the union on the pump and detach the hose. Wrap clean plastic bags around the hose ends to prevent dirt entering the system. **Note:** *On some engines, the inlet and outlet hoses are protected from the exhaust pipe by a heat-proof sheath. Remove the sheath if necessary but don't forget to refit it on reassembly.*

4 On models fitted with a centrifugal pump (without cable operation), unscrew the pump mounting bolts and remove the bolts.

5 Withdraw the pump from the crankcase and remove the wave washer **(see illustration)**. Note how the tab on the back of the pump locates in the slot in the pump driveshaft.

6 Stuff a clean rag into the crankcase opening to prevent dirt falling inside.

7 Remove the O-ring from the pump body and discard it as a new one must be fitted on reassembly.

8 If fitted, remove the two nuts from the underside of the pump mounting on the crankcase for safekeeping.

9 Ensure no dirt enters the pump body and clean it using a suitable solvent, then dry the pump thoroughly.

Inspection

10 Check the pump body for obvious signs of damage especially around the mounting bolt holes. Turn the pump drive by hand and check that the pump rotates smoothly. Where fitted, check that the cable pulley turns freely and returns to rest under pressure of the return spring.

11 No individual internal components are available for the pump. If it is damaged or, if after bleeding the operation of the pump is suspect, renew it.

Installation

12 Installation is the reverse of removal, noting the following:

● *Fit a new O-ring on the pump body and lubricate it with a smear of grease (see illustration).*
● *Install the wave washer, then install the pump.*
● *Ensure the tab on the back of the pump engages with the slot in the driveshaft (see illustration).*
● *Ensure the hoses are secured to the pump unions with clips.*
● *Bleed the pump (see Step 24).*
● *On models fitted with a cable-operated pump, check the operation of the cable (see Chapter 1).*

Caution: Accurate cable adjustment is important to ensure that the oil pump delivers the correct amount of oil to the engine and is correctly synchronised with the throttle.

Internally-mounted pump

Removal

13 Trace the oil inlet hose from the oil tank to the engine unit and remove either the drivebelt cover or the alternator cover. Remove either the variator (see Chapter 6) or the alternator rotor (see Section 10) as applicable.

14 Undo the screws securing the oil pump, then withdraw the pump **(see illustration)**. Where fitted, slide the rubber grommet securing the hoses out of its cutout in the crankcase.

15 If the pump is belt-driven, note how the drive tab on the back of the pump locates in the slot in the driven pulley. If the pump is being removed rather than just being displaced for belt renewal, detach the cable from the pump pulley noting how it fits.

16 Release the clip securing the oil inlet hose from the oil tank to the union on the pump and detach the hose **(see illustration)**. Clamp the hose to minimise oil loss. Release the clip securing the oil outlet hose to the union on the pump and detach the hose. Wrap clean plastic bags around the hose ends to prevent dirt entering the system.

17 Ensure no dirt enters the pump body and clean it using a suitable solvent, then dry the pump thoroughly.

18 To remove the pump drivebelt, first undo the screw securing the belt cover, where fitted, then remove the cover and the plate

12.12b Ensure tab (A) locates in slot (B)

12.14 Remove the pump from the crankcase

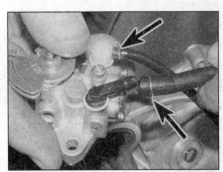

12.16 Detach the oil hoses from the pump

12.18a Remove the pump drivebelt cover

12.18b Remove the belt . . .

12.18c . . . then slide off the drive pulley

behind it noting how they fit **(see illustration)**. If a spacer is fitted to the crankshaft, slide it off. Slip the belt off the pulleys, then slide off the drive pulley noting which way round it fits **(see illustrations)**.

19 Remove the pump driven pulley and the thrustwasher behind it **(see illustration)**. On engines where the water pump is located inside the crankcase halves, note how the oil pump drive locates on the water pump shaft.

20 To remove the pump drive gear, use circlip pliers to remove the circlip, then slide the gear off the shaft. If the drive gear, or drive pulley, is retained by a ring nut, hold the crankshaft to prevent it turning, then use a peg spanner or punch to undo the ring nut. Note the drive pin in the shaft and remove it for safekeeping if it is loose.

Inspection

21 Follow Steps 10 and 11 to check the condition of the pump. If the pump is gear driven, check the condition of the pump drive and driven gears and renew them if necessary.

22 If the pump is belt-driven, check along the length of the pump drivebelt for splits, cracks or broken teeth and renew the belt if necessary. The belt should be renewed regardless of its condition at the service interval specified in Chapter 1, or during the course of dismantling.

Installation

23 Installation is the reverse of removal, noting the following:

- *Slide the drive pulley onto the crankshaft with the shoulder innermost.*
- *Install the thrustwasher between the crankcase and the driven pulley.*
- *Where fitted, secure the pump drivegear with a new circlip.*
- *Where fitted, fit a new O-ring on the pump body and lubricate it with a smear of grease.*
- *Ensure the hoses are secured to the pump unions with clips.*
- *Bleed the pump (see Step 24).*
- *On models fitted with a cable-operated pump, check the operation of the cable (see Chapter 1).*

Caution: Accurate cable adjustment is important to ensure that the oil pump delivers the correct amount of oil to the engine and is correctly synchronised with the throttle.

Bleeding

24 Bleeding the pump is the process of removing air from it and allowing it to be filled with oil. First ensure that the inlet hose from the oil tank and the oil filter are completely filled with oil. If necessary, detach the hose from the pump and wait until oil flows from the hose, then reconnect it.

25 Loosen the bleed screw on the pump and wait until oil, without any air mixed with it, flows out the hole, then tighten the screw **(see illustrations)**.

26 Ensure the ignition switch is OFF.

Disconnect the oil outlet hose from the carburettor and crank the engine with the kickstarter until oil, without any air mixed with it, flows out the hose, then reconnect the hose and secure it with the clip. Alternatively, fill an auxiliary fuel tank with a 2% (50:1) petrol/two-stroke oil mix and connect it to the carburettor. Disconnect the oil outlet hose from the carburettor, start the engine and run it until oil, without any air mixed with it, flows out the hose, then reconnect the hose and secure it with the clip.

> **Warning: Never run the engine without an oil supply or crank the engine on the electric starter without an oil supply. Never crank the engine with the ignition ON and the spark plug cap disconnected from the spark plug as the ignition system may be damaged.**

13 Crankcase halves and main bearings

Note: *To separate the crankcase halves, the engine unit must be removed from the frame.*

Separation

1 Follow the procedure in Section 4 and remove the engine from the frame.

2 Before the crankcase halves can be

12.19 Remove the pump driven pulley

12.25a Bleed screw on cable-operated pump

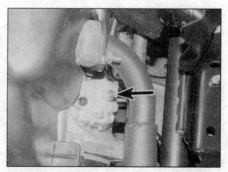

12.25b Bleed screw on centrifugal pump

13.3 Loosen the crankcase bolts evenly in a criss-cross sequence

13.4 Drawing the right-hand crankcase half off the crankshaft

separated the following components must be removed:

● *Alternator (see Section 10).*
● *Variator (see Chapter 6).*
● *Cylinder head (see Section 6).*
● *Cylinder (see Section 7).*
● *Piston (see Section 8).*
● *Starter motor (see Chapter 10).*
● *Oil pump (see Section 12).*
● *Water pump (see Chapter 3).*
● *Reed valve (see Chapter 4).*

3 Tape some rag around the connecting rod to prevent it knocking against the cases, then loosen the crankcase bolts evenly, a little at a time and in a criss-cross sequence until they are all finger-tight, then remove them **(see illustration)**. **Note:** *Ensure that all the crankcase bolts have been removed before attempting to separate the cases.*

> **HAYNES HINT**
> *Make a cardboard template of the crankcase and punch a hole for each bolt location. This will ensure all bolts are installed correctly on reassembly – this is important as some bolts may be of different lengths.*

4 Remove the right-hand crankcase half from the left-hand half by drawing it off the right-hand end of the crankshaft. The cases will be a tight fit on the crankshaft and most manufacturers produce a service tool to facilitate this procedure. Alternatively, use the

set-up shown, ensuring equal pressure is applied on both sides of the puller arrangement at all times **(see illustration)**. If the puller is placed across the end of the crankshaft, thread the old alternator centre nut on first to protect the threads. **Note:** *If the crankcase halves do not separate easily, first ensure all fasteners have been removed. Apply steady pressure with the tools described and heat the bearing housings with a hot air gun. Do not try and separate the halves by levering against the mating surfaces as they are easily scored and will not seal correctly afterwards. Do not strike the ends of the crankshaft with a hammer as damage to the end threads or the shaft itself will result.*

5 Now press the crankshaft assembly out of the left-hand crankcase half – again, a service tool will be available. Alternatively, use the set-up shown **(see illustration)**. Thread the old variator nut onto the end of the crankshaft to protect the threads and make sure the crankshaft assembly is supported to prevent it dropping if it suddenly comes free.

6 If fitted, remove the crankcase gasket and discard it as a new one must be used on reassembly.

7 Remove the dowels from either crankcase half for safekeeping if they are loose.

8 On engines where the oil pump is driven off the crankshaft, remove the pump driveshaft and the shaft bush. If necessary, heat the crankcase around the bush while applying pressure to the shaft.

9 On engines where the water pump is located inside the crankcase halves, remove the circlip from the outer end of the pump shaft, then press the shaft and its bearings out of the crankcase. Check the condition of the bearings and renew them if necessary (see *Tools and Workshop Tips* in the *Reference* section. The pump seal is located in the crankcase – have a new seal fitted by a scooter dealer or automotive engineer.

10 Note the position of the crankshaft oil seals and measure any inset before removing them **(see illustration)**. Note which way round the seals are fitted. Remove the seals by tapping them gently on one side and then pulling them out with pliers **(see illustration)**. Discard the seals, as new ones must be fitted on reassembly.

11 The main bearings will either remain in place in the crankcase halves during disassembly or come out with the crankshaft assembly (see Section 14). If the main bearings have failed, excessive rumbling and vibration will be felt when the engine is running. Sometimes this may cause the oil seals to fail, resulting in a loss of compression and poor running. Check the condition of the bearings (see *Tools and Workshop Tips* in the *Reference* section) and only remove them if they are unserviceable. Always renew both main bearings at the same time, never individually.

12 To remove the bearings from the cases, heat the bearing housings with a hot air gun and tap them out using a bearing driver or

13.5 Pressing the crankshaft out of the left-hand crankcase half

13.10a Measuring crankshaft oil seal inset

13.10b Tap the seals with a punch to displace them

13.12 Driving a main bearing out of the crankcase

13.18 Inspect the mounting bushes (A) and the main bearing housings (B)

13.22 Tap the bearing onto the crankshaft – do not use excessive force

suitable socket **(see illustration)**. Note which way round the bearings are fitted. If the bearings are stuck on the crankshaft, they must be removed with an external bearing puller to avoid damaging the crankshaft assembly. **Note:** *On some engines the main bearings are fitted in the crankcases prior to assembly, on others they are fitted to the crankshaft. Consult a scooter dealer for details before installing new bearings.*

13 If required, remove the transmission assembly from the left-hand crankcase half (see Chapter 6).

Inspection

14 Remove all traces of old gasket from the crankcase mating surfaces, taking care not to nick or gouge the soft aluminium if a scraper is used. Wash all the components in a suitable solvent and dry them with compressed air.

Caution: Be very careful not to damage the crankcase mating surfaces which may result in loss of crankcase pressure causing poor engine performance. Check both crankcase halves very carefully for cracks and damaged threads.

15 Small cracks or holes in aluminium castings can be repaired with an epoxy resin adhesive as a temporary measure. Permanent repairs can only be effected by welding, and only a specialist in this process is in a position to advise on the economy or practical aspect of such a repair. On some engines, the crankcase halves can be renewed individually, on others the two halves are only available together as a matching set – consult a scooter dealer for details.

16 Damaged threads can be economically

reclaimed by using a thread insert (see *Tools and Workshop Tips* in the *Reference* section). Most scooter dealers and small engineering firms offer a service of this kind. Sheared screws can usually be removed with screw extractors (see *Tools and Workshop Tips* in the *Reference* section). If you are in any doubt about removing a sheared screw, consult a scooter dealer or automotive engineer.

17 Always wash the crankcases thoroughly after any repair work to ensure no dirt or metal swarf is trapped inside when the engine is rebuilt.

18 Inspect the engine mounting bushes **(see illustration)**. If they show signs of deterioration renew them all at the same time. To remove a bush, first note its position in the casing. Heat the casing with a hot air gun, then support the casing and drive the bush out with a hammer and a suitably-sized socket. Alternatively, use two suitably-sized sockets to press the bush out in the jaws of a vice. Clean the bush housing with steel wool to remove any corrosion, then reheat the casing and fit the new bush. **Note:** *Always support the casing when removing or fitting bushes to avoid breaking the casing.*

19 If the main bearings came out with the crankshaft assembly, or if they have been removed from the cases for renewal, inspect the bearing housings **(see illustration 13.18)**. If a bearing outer race has spun in its housing, the inside of the housing will be damaged. A bearing locking compound can be used to fix the outer race in place on reassembly if the damage is not too severe. **Note:** *If a bearing has spun in its housing the bearing itself is likely to be damaged internally and should be renewed.*

20 Inspect the crankshaft assembly and bearings (see Section 14).

Reassembly

21 If the main bearings are to be fitted into the crankcase halves, heat the bearing housings with a hot air gun, then install them using a bearing driver or suitable socket which bears onto the outer race only.

22 If the main bearings are to be fitted onto the crankshaft, heat them first in an oil bath to around 100°C, then press them onto the shaft using a suitable length of tube that just fits over the shaft and bears onto the inner race only **(see illustration)**. If the bearings are difficult to fit they are not hot enough.

⚠️ *Warning: This must be done very carefully to avoid the risk of personal injury.*

23 Fit the new crankshaft oil seals into the crankcase halves and drive them to the previously measured inset using a seal driver or socket (see Step 10). Ensure the seals are fitted the right way round and that they enter the cases squarely **(see illustration)**.

24 On engines where the water pump is located inside the crankcase halves, ensure the pump components are fitted before joining the cases (see Step 9).

25 Fit the crankshaft assembly into the left-hand crankcase half first, ensuring that the connecting rod is aligned with the crankcase mouth. Lubricate the shaft, seal and bearing with the specified two-stroke oil and tape some rag around the connecting rod to prevent it knocking against the cases. If the main bearing is in the crankcase half, pull the assembly into

13.23 Ensure the new oil seals are installed correctly

13.25a Pulling the crankshaft into the case with a service tool . . .

13.25b . . . and with a home-made tool

13.26 Install the crankcase dowels (A) and gasket (B)

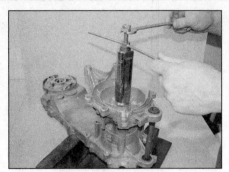

13.27 Installing the right-hand crankcase half

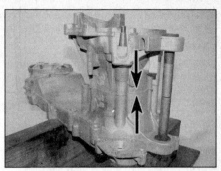

13.28a Ensure crankcase halves are seated on the gasket

13.28b Position of main bearings can be checked through oilways (arrowed)

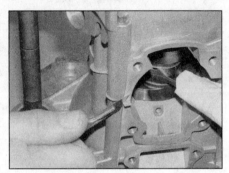

13.30 Trim off any excess gasket

place either with a service tool or using the set-up shown **(see illustrations)**. If the main bearing is on the crankshaft, heat the bearing housing in the crankcase with a hot air gun before fitting the crank assembly. **Note:** *Avoid applying direct heat onto the crankshaft oil seal.* If required, a freeze spray can be used on the bearing itself to aid installation. Ensure the bearing is fitted fully into its housing.

26 If applicable, allow the case to cool, then wipe the mating surfaces of both crankcase halves with a rag soaked in a suitable solvent and fit the dowels. Fit the crankcase gasket or apply a small amount of suitable sealant to the mating surface of the left-hand case as required **(see illustration)**.

27 Now fit the right-hand crankcase half. Lubricate the shaft, seal and bearing with the specified two-stroke oil. If the main bearing is in the crankcase half, press the crankcase half into place, either with a service tool or with the

set-up used in Step 25 **(see illustration)**. If necessary, place a thick washer over the centre of the right-hand crankcase to protect the aluminium. If the main bearing is on the crankshaft, heat the bearing housing with a hot air gun before fitting the crankcase half and, if required, use a freeze spay on the bearing. **Note:** *Avoid applying direct heat onto the crankshaft oil seal.*

28 Check that the crankcase halves are seated all the way round and that the main bearings are pressed fully into their housings **(see illustrations)**. If the casings are not correctly seated, heat the bearing housings while applying firm pressure with the assembly tools used previously. **Note:** *Do not attempt to pull the crankcase halves together using the crankcase bolts as the casing will crack and be ruined.*

29 Clean the threads of the crankcase bolts and install them finger-tight, then tighten them

evenly a little at a time in a criss-cross sequence to the torque setting specified in the *Data* section. Support the connecting rod and rotate the crankshaft by hand – if there are any signs of undue stiffness, tight or rough spots, or of any other problem, the fault must be rectified before proceeding further.

30 If necessary, trim the crankcase gasket flush with the mating surface for the cylinder **(see illustration)**.

31 Where fitted, lubricate the oil pump driveshaft and install the shaft and the shaft bush; tap the bush into its seat with a hammer and suitable-sized socket **(see illustrations)**. Rotate the crankshaft to ensure the oil pump drivegears are correctly engaged.

32 Install the remaining components in the reverse order of removal.

14 Crankshaft assembly and big-end bearing

1 To access the crankshaft and the big-end bearing, the crankcase must be split into two parts (see Section 13).

2 The crankshaft assembly should give many thousands of miles of service. The most likely problems to occur will be a worn small or big-end bearing due to poor lubrication **(see illustration)**. A worn big-end bearing will produce a pronounced knocking noise, most audible when the engine is under load, and increasing as engine speed rises. This should not be confused with small-end bearing wear,

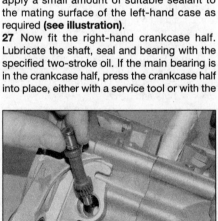

13.31a Install the oil pump shaft . . .

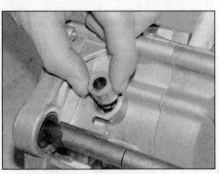

13.31b . . . and shaft bush

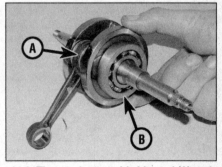

14.2 The crank assembly big-end (A) and main bearings (B)

which produces a lighter, metallic rattle (see Section 8).

Inspection

3 To assess the condition of the big-end bearing, hold the crankshaft assembly firmly and push and pull on the connecting rod, checking for any up-and-down freeplay between the two **(see illustration)**. If any freeplay is noted, the bearing is worn and either the bearing or the crankshaft assembly will have to be renewed. **Note:** *A small amount of big-end side clearance (side-to-side movement) is acceptable on the connecting rod.* Consult a scooter dealer about the availability of parts. **Note:** *If a new bearing is available, fitting it is a specialist task which should be left to a scooter dealer or automotive engineer.*

4 Inspect the crankshaft where it passes through the main bearings for wear and scoring. The shaft should be a press fit in the bearings; if it is worn or damaged a new assembly will have to be fitted. Evidence of extreme heat, such as discoloration or blueing, indicates that lubrication failure has occurred. Be sure to check the oil pump and bearing oil ways before reassembling the engine.

5 If available, place the crankshaft assembly on V-blocks and check the runout at the main bearing journals (B and C) and at either end (A and D) using a dial gauge **(see illustration)**. If the crankshaft is out-of-true it will cause excessive engine vibration. If there is any doubt about the condition of the crankshaft have it checked by a scooter dealer or automotive engineer. **Note:** *The crankshaft assembly is pressed together and is easily damaged if it is dropped.*

6 Inspect the threads on each end of the crankshaft and ensure that the retaining nuts for the alternator rotor and the variator are a good fit **(see illustration)**. Inspect the splines for the variator pulley on the left-hand end of the shaft. Inspect the taper and the slot in the right-hand end of the shaft for the alternator Woodruff key **(see illustration)**. Damage or wear that prevents the rotor from being fitted securely will require a new crankshaft assembly.

7 Where applicable, inspect the oil pump drivegear teeth on the crankshaft and on the pump driveshaft for damage or wear (see

14.3 Any freeplay indicates a worn big-end bearing

illustration). Inspect the ends of pump driveshaft where it runs in its bearings. Renew any components that are worn or damaged.

Reassembly

8 Follow the procedure in Section 13 to install the crankshaft assembly.

15 Initial start-up after overhaul

1 Make sure the oil tank is at least partly full and the pump is correctly adjusted (see Chapter 1) and bled of air (see Section 12).

2 On liquid-cooled models, make sure the coolant level is correct (see *Daily (pre-ride) checks*).

3 Make sure there is fuel in the tank.

4 With the ignition OFF, operate the kickstart to check that the engine turns over easily.

5 Turn the ignition ON, start the engine and allow it to run at a slow idle until it reaches operating temperature. Do not be alarmed if there is a little smoke from the exhaust – this will be due to the oil used to lubricate the engine components during assembly and should subside after a while.

6 If the engine proves reluctant to start, remove the spark plug and check that it has not become wet and oily. If it has, clean it and try again. If the engine refuses to start, go through the fault finding charts at the end of this manual to identify the problem.

7 Check carefully for fuel and oil leaks and make sure the transmission and controls,

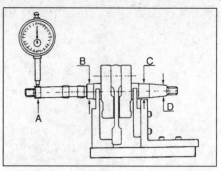

14.5 Check crankshaft runout at points A, B, C and D

especially the brakes, function properly before road testing the machine. Refer to Section 16 for the recommended running-in procedure.

8 Upon completion of the road test, and after the engine has cooled-down completely, check for air bubbles in the engine oil inlet and outlet hoses (see Section 12). On liquid-cooled models, check the coolant level (see *Daily (pre-ride) checks*).

16 Recommended running-in procedure

1 Treat the engine gently for the first few miles to allow any new parts to bed-in.

2 If a new piston, cylinder or crankshaft assembly has been fitted, the engine will have to be run-in as when new. This means a restraining hand on the throttle until at least 300 miles (500 km) have been covered. There's no point in keeping to any set speed limit – the main idea is to keep from labouring the engine and to gradually increase performance up to the 600 mile (1000 km) mark. Make sure that the throttle position is varied to vary engine speed, and use full throttle only for short bursts. Experience is the best guide, since it's easy to tell when an engine is running freely.

3 Pay particular attention to the *Daily (pre-ride) checks* at the beginning of this manual and investigate the cause of any oil or, on liquid-cooled models, coolant loss immediately. Check the tightness of all relevant nuts and bolts.

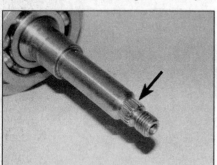

14.6a Inspect the shaft end threads and the variator pulley splines (arrowed)

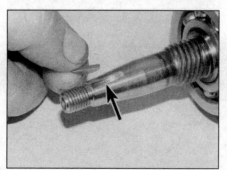

14.6b Inspect the shaft taper and slot (arrowed) for the Woodruff key

14.7 Inspect the oil pump drivegear teeth

Chapter 2 Part B:
Four-stroke engines

Contents

Specifications

Refer to the *Data* section at the end of this manual for servicing specifications.

Degrees of difficulty

| Easy, suitable for novice with little experience | | Fairly easy, suitable for beginner with some experience | | Fairly difficult, suitable for competent DIY mechanic | | Difficult, suitable for experienced DIY mechanic | | Very difficult, suitable for expert DIY or professional | |

---

1 General information

The engine is a single cylinder, overhead-camshaft four-stroke, with either fan-assisted air cooling (see Chapter 1) or pumped liquid cooling (see Chapter 3). The camshaft is chain-driven off the crankshaft and operates the valves via rocker arms.

The crankshaft assembly is pressed together, incorporating the connecting rod.

The crankcase divides vertically – the left-hand crankcase is an integral part of the drivebelt casing and gearbox.

2 Operations possible with the engine in the frame

Most components and assemblies, with the obvious exception of the crankshaft assembly and its bearings, can be worked on without having to remove the engine/transmission unit from the frame. However, access to some components is severely restricted, and if a number of areas require attention at the same time, removal of the engine is recommended, as it is an easy task to undertake.

3 Major engine repair – general information

1 It is not always easy to determine if an engine should be completely overhauled, as a number of factors must be considered.
2 High mileage is not necessarily an indication that an overhaul is needed, while

low mileage, on the other hand, does not preclude the need for an overhaul. Frequency of servicing is probably the single most important consideration. An engine that has regular and frequent oil and filter changes, as well as other required maintenance, will most likely give many miles of reliable service. Conversely, a neglected engine, or one which has not been run-in properly, may require an overhaul very early in its life.

3 Exhaust smoke and excessive oil consumption are both indications that the piston rings and/or valve guide oil seals are in need of attention.

4 If the engine is making obvious knocking or rumbling noises, the connecting rod and/or main bearings are probably at fault.

5 Loss of power, rough running, excessive noise and high fuel consumption rates may also point to the need for an overhaul, especially if they are all present at the same time. If a complete service as detailed in Chapter 1 does not remedy the situation, major mechanical work is the only solution.

6 An engine overhaul generally involves restoring the internal parts to the specifications of a new engine. The piston and piston rings are renewed and the cylinder is rebored. The valve seats are reground and new valve springs are fitted. If the connecting rod bearings are worn a new crankshaft assembly is fitted and, where possible, the main bearings in the crankcase are renewed. The end result should be a like-new engine that will give as many trouble-free miles as the original.

7 Before beginning the engine overhaul, read through the related procedures to familiarise yourself with the scope and requirements of the job. Overhauling an engine is not all that difficult, but it is time-consuming. Check on the availability of parts and make sure that any necessary special tools and materials are obtained in advance.

8 Most work can be done with typical workshop hand tools, although precision measuring tools are required for inspecting parts to determine if they must be renewed. Often a dealer will handle the inspection of parts and offer advice concerning reconditioning and renewal. As a general rule, time is the primary cost of an overhaul so it does not pay to install worn or substandard parts.

9 As a final note, to ensure maximum life and minimum trouble from a rebuilt engine, everything must be assembled with care in a spotlessly clean environment.

4 Engine – removal and installation

Caution: The engine/transmission unit is not heavy, however removal and installation should be carried out with the aid of an assistant; personal injury or damage could occur if the engine falls or is dropped.

Removal

1 The procedure for removing the four-stroke engine is the same as for two-stroke models. If required, drain the engine oil (see Chapter 1). Note: There is no external oil feed or external oil pump on four-stroke engines.

2 Refer to Chapter 2A, Section 4, for the rest of the procedure.

Installation

3 Installation is the reverse of the procedure in Chapter 2A. Note that if the engine oil was drained, or if any oil has been lost during overhaul, the engine must be filled with the specified quantity of oil (see Data section at the end of this manual) and the oil level checked as described in Daily (pre-ride) checks.

5 Disassembly and reassembly – general information

Disassembly

1 Before disassembling the engine, the external surfaces of the unit should be thoroughly cleaned and degreased. This will prevent contamination of the engine internals, and will also make working a lot easier and cleaner. A high flash-point solvent, such as paraffin, can be used, or better still, a proprietary engine degreaser such as Gunk. Use old paintbrushes and toothbrushes to work the solvent into the various recesses of the engine casings. Take care to exclude solvent or water from the electrical components and intake and exhaust ports.

⚠ Warning: The use of petrol (gasoline) as a cleaning agent should be avoided because of the risk of fire.

2 When clean and dry, arrange the unit on the workbench, leaving suitable clear area for working. Gather a selection of small containers and plastic bags so that parts can be grouped together in an easily identifiable manner. Some paper and a pen should be on hand to permit notes to be made and labels attached where necessary. A supply of clean rag is also required.

3 Before commencing work, read through the appropriate section so that some idea of the necessary procedure can be gained. When removing components it should be noted that great force is seldom required, unless specified. In many cases, a component's reluctance to be removed is indicative of an incorrect approach or removal method – if in any doubt, recheck with the text.

4 When disassembling the engine, keep 'mated' parts that have been in contact with each other during engine operation together. These 'mated' parts must be re-used or renewed as an assembly.

5 Complete engine disassembly should be done in the following general order with reference to the appropriate Sections (refer to Chapter 6 for details of transmission components disassembly):
● Remove the valve cover.
● Remove the camshaft and rockers.
● Remove the cylinder head.
● Remove the cylinder.
● Remove the piston.
● Remove the alternator.
● Remove the starter motor (see Chapter 10).
● Remove the water pump if fitted internally (see Chapter 3).
● Remove the oil pump.
● Separate the crankcase halves.
● Remove the crankshaft.

Reassembly

6 Reassembly is accomplished by reversing the order of disassembly.

6 Valve cover – removal and installation

Note: This procedure can be carried out with the engine in the frame. If the engine has been removed, ignore the steps that do not apply.

Removal

1 Remove the body panels as necessary to access the cylinder head (see Chapter 9).

2 On some air-cooled engines, the engine cowling covers the valve cover – pull the cap off the spark plug, then remove the screws securing the engine cowling and remove it. Note that it may also be necessary to remove the fan cowling to access the valve cover. Note: Some cowlings are clipped together – take care not to damage the fixing lugs when separating them.

3 Loosen the clips securing any breather hose or PAIR valve hose to the valve cover and detach the hoses (see illustration).

4 Unscrew the bolts securing the valve cover

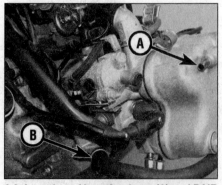

6.3 Location of breather hose (A) and PAIR valve hose (B)

and remove them, together with any washers, then lift the cover off **(see illustration)**. If the cover is stuck, tap around the joint face between the cover and the cylinder head with a soft-faced mallet to free it. Do not try to lever the cover off as this may damage the sealing surfaces.

5 Remove the gasket and discard it, as a new one must be used. Note that on some engines the gasket incorporates a camshaft end cap.

Installation

6 Clean the mating surfaces of the cylinder head and the valve cover with a suitable solvent to remove any traces of old gasket or sealant.

7 Lay the new gasket onto the valve cover, making sure it fits correctly into the groove **(see illustration)**. If a camshaft end cap is used, apply a suitable sealant around the edge of the cap before installing it.

8 Position the valve cover on the cylinder head, making sure the gasket stays in place. Install the cover bolts with their washers, if fitted, then tighten the bolts evenly and in a criss-cross sequence to the torque setting specified in the *Data* section.

9 Install the remaining components in the reverse order of removal.

6.4 Lift off the valve cover – note the gasket (arrowed)

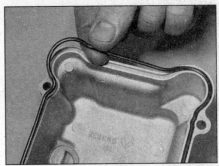

6.7 Fit a new gasket into the groove

washers where fitted, and remove the cooler and pipes.

5 If required, unscrew the banjo bolt securing each pipe to the cooler and detach the pipes. Discard the pipe sealing washers as new ones must be used.

Installation

6 Installation is the reverse of removal, noting the following:
● *Always use new sealing washers on the pipe unions.*
● *Tighten the banjo bolts securely.*
● *Fill the engine with oil (see Chapter 1) and check the oil level (see Daily (pre-ride) checks).*

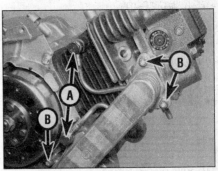

7.4 Oil pipe banjo bolts (A) and cooler mounting bolts (B)

securing the engine cowling and remove the cowling.

4 Undo the tensioner cap bolt **(see illustration)**. Note any sealing washer or O-ring fitted to the bolt and discard it, as a new one must be fitted.

5 On some tensioners, the cap bolt retains a spring in the tensioner body; withdraw the spring, then unscrew the tensioner mounting bolts and withdraw the tensioner from the cylinder **(see illustrations)**. On others, the tensioner is a sealed unit; to release the tensioner plunger before removing the tensioner, insert a small flat-bladed screwdriver into the end of the tensioner so that it engages the slotted plunger, then turn the screwdriver clockwise to retract the plunger. Hold the screwdriver in this position while undoing the tensioner mounting bolts

---

7 Oil cooler and pipes – removal and installation

Note: *This procedure can be carried out with the engine in the frame. If the engine has been removed, ignore the steps that do not apply.*

Removal

1 Remove the body panels as necessary to access the oil cooler (see Chapter 9).
2 Drain the engine oil (see Chapter 1).
3 On air-cooled engines, remove the screws securing the engine cowling and remove the cowling.
4 Unscrew the banjo bolt securing each pipe union to the engine **(see illustration)**. Now unscrew the cooler mounting bolts, noting the

---

8 Cam chain tensioner – removal, inspection and installation

Note: *This procedure can be carried out with the engine in the frame. If the engine has been removed, ignore the steps that do not apply.*

Removal

1 Remove the body panels as necessary to access the engine (see Chapter 9).
2 If necessary, displace the carburettor to access the cam chain tensioner (see Chapter 4).
3 On air-cooled engines, remove the screws

8.4 Cam chain tensioner cap bolt (arrowed)

8.5a Remove the cap bolt and spring . . .

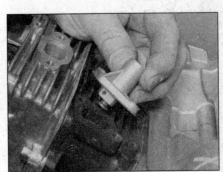

8.5b . . . then withdraw the tensioner

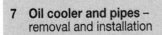

8.5c Use a small screwdriver to retract the plunger . . .

8.5d . . . while the tensioner is removed

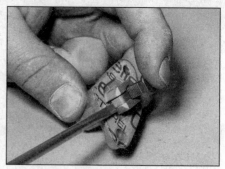

8.8 Release the ratchet and check the operation of the plunger

and withdraw the tensioner from the cylinder **(see illustrations)**. Release the screwdriver – the plunger will be released, but it can easily be reset for installation.

6 Remove the gasket from the base of the tensioner or from the cylinder and discard it, as a new one must be used.

Inspection

7 Examine the tensioner components for signs of wear or damage.

8 Release the ratchet mechanism from the tensioner plunger and check that the plunger moves freely in and out of the tensioner body **(see illustration)**.

9 Individual components are generally not available – if the tensioner or any of its components are worn or damaged, or if the plunger is seized in the body, a new tensioner must be fitted.

Installation

10 Turn the engine in the normal direction of rotation using the kickstarter or a spanner on the alternator rotor nut. This removes all the slack between the crankshaft and the camshaft in the front run of the chain and transfers it to the back run where it will be taken up by the tensioner.

11 Fit a new gasket on the tensioner body.

12 If the spring has been removed from the tensioner, release the ratchet mechanism and press the tensioner plunger all the way into the tensioner body **(see illustration 8.8)**. Install the tensioner in the cylinder and tighten the bolts. Fit a new sealing washer on the cap bolt, then install the spring and tighten the bolt securely.

13 If the tensioner is a sealed unit, retract the plunger as before with a small screwdriver, then hold it in this position while the tensioner is installed and the mounting bolts are tightened. The plunger should extend when the screwdriver is withdrawn. Fit a new washer or O-ring to the cap bolt and tighten the bolt securely.

14 It is advisable to remove the valve cover (see Section 6) and check that the cam chain is tensioned. If it is slack, the tensioner plunger did not release. Remove the tensioner and check the operation of the plunger again.

15 Install the remaining components in the reverse order of removal.

9 Cam chain, blades and sprockets – removal, inspection and installation

Note 1: *This procedure can be carried out with the engine in the frame, although on some scooters access to the top of the engine is extremely restricted.*

Note 2: *The general procedure for removing the cam chain, blades and sprockets is the same for all engines. However, since the positioning of the cam chain differs according to manufacturer, it will be necessary to remove components from the left- or right-hand side of the engine as applicable.*

Removal

1 Remove the valve cover (see Section 6).

2 On some engines, the camshaft is supported in a journal on the outside of the

9.3a If fitted, remove the oil seal holder. . .

9.3b . . . and lever out the seal

camshaft sprocket. On these engines, follow the procedure below to displace the sprocket and chain from the camshaft, but note that the camshaft itself must be removed in order to remove the sprocket and chain from the engine (see Section 10).

3 If the cam chain and, in some cases, the tensioner blade is being removed, access will be required to the crankcase and the crankshaft. If the cam chain is on the left-hand side of the engine, refer to the procedure in Chapter 6 and remove the variator. If the left-hand crankcase oil seal is fitted in a holder behind the variator, remove the holder and the seal **(see illustrations)**. If the oil pump is driven by a chain from the left-hand side of the crankshaft, remove the oil pump driven sprocket, drive chain and drive sprocket (see Section 18). If the cam chain is on the right-hand side of the engine, remove the alternator (see Section 16). If the oil pump drive is on the right-hand side, remove the oil pump driven sprocket, drive chain and drive sprocket (see Section 18).

4 If not already done, remove the spark plug.

5 Turn the crankshaft in the normal direction of rotation, using a spanner on the alternator rotor nut, until the piston is at top dead centre (TDC) on the compression stroke (all valves are closed and a small clearance can be felt at each rocker arm).

6 Look for timing marks on the camshaft sprocket and the camshaft holder or cylinder head, or alternatively, look for timing marks on the alternator rotor and the crankcase to confirm the position of the piston (see Chapter 1, Section 32). Note the alignment of the timing marks.

7 Remove the cam chain tensioner (see Section 8).

8 If an automatic decompressor mechanism is fitted to the camshaft sprocket, follow the procedure in Steps 18 to 26 to remove, inspect and install the mechanism.

9 If the camshaft is supported in a journal on the outside of the camshaft sprocket, undo the bolts securing the journal and remove it. Remove any dowels for safekeeping if they are loose.

10 Unscrew the bolt(s) securing the camshaft sprocket to the camshaft. To prevent the sprocket from turning, hold the alternator or use a suitable holding tool fitted into the

9.10 Hold the sprocket and undo the sprocket bolts

9.11 Draw the sprocket off the shaft and out of the chain

hole(s) in the sprocket **(see illustration)**. **Note:** *Some manufacturers recommend that new bolts and washers are used on reassembly – check with a scooter dealer.*

11 Draw the sprocket off the end of the camshaft, noting how it locates on the shaft, and disengage it from the camchain **(see illustration)**. Where fitted, remove the sprocket spacer for safekeeping.

12 Mark the chain with paint so that if it is to be re-used it can be fitted the same way round. Where fitted, remove the thrustwasher from the end of the crankshaft, then lower the cam chain down its tunnel, slip it off the sprocket on the crankshaft, and draw it out of the engine **(see illustrations)**. On some engines the sprocket is a sliding fit on the shaft; remove the sprocket, noting how it fits **(see illustration)**.

13 If required, undo the bolt securing the cam chain tensioner blade and withdraw the blade, noting which way round it fits **(see illustration)**. The guide blade can be removed when the cylinder head has been removed (see Section 11).

Inspection

14 Check the sprockets for wear and damaged teeth, renewing them if necessary. If the sprocket teeth are worn, the chain is also worn and should be renewed. If the sprocket is a press-fit on the crankshaft, pull it off with a bearing puller. If access is limited, it may be necessary to remove the crankshaft assembly

from the crankcases (see Sections 19 and 20).
15 Check the chain tensioner blade and guide blade for wear or damage and renew them if necessary. Check the operation of the cam chain tensioner (see Section 8).
16 Where fitted, check the components of the automatic decompressor mechanism (see Step 22)

Installation

17 Installation is the reverse of removal, noting the following:
● *Ensure the tensioner blade and guide blade are fitted the correct way round.*
● *Ensure any spacers and thrustwashers are installed correctly.*
● *Ensure the piston is at TDC on the compression stroke and that all the timing marks align as described in Step 6.*
● *Ensure any slack in the chain is in the back run where it will be taken up by the tensioner.*
● *Use new bolts and washers to secure the camshaft sprocket if recommended by the manufacturer.*
Caution: After installing the cam chain tensioner, turn the crankshaft and check that all the timing marks still align correctly. If the timing marks are not aligned exactly as described, the valve timing will be incorrect and the valves may strike the piston, causing extensive damage to the engine.

9.12a Remove the crankshaft thrustwasher where fitted

9.12b Lower the camchain down the tunnel . . .

9.12c . . . and draw it out of the engine

9.12d Note how the sprocket locates on the pin (arrowed)

9.13 The tensioner blade is secured by a pivot bolt (arrowed)

9.18a Undo the centre bolt . . .

9.18b . . . and remove the cover

Automatic decompressor mechanism

Removal

18 Undo the camshaft sprocket centre bolt and lift off the decompressor mechanism cover **(see illustrations)**. Hold the alternator to prevent the sprocket from turning.

19 Undo the decompressor mechanism bolt, then hold the bob weight return spring and withdraw the bolt and static weight **(see illustrations)**.

20 Lift off the bob weight – note the nylon bush on the back of the weight and how it locates in the slot in the cam chain sprocket **(see illustration)**. Remove the bush for safekeeping.

21 Lift the sprocket and its backing plate off the end of the camshaft, then disengage it from the camchain **(see illustration)**.

Inspection

22 Inspect the components of the decompressor mechanism. Check the nylon bush for wear and flat spots and renew it if necessary. Temporarily assemble the mechanism on the camshaft (see below) and check its operation – check the spring tension and ensure the bob weight does not bind on the cover.

Installation

23 Check that the piston is at TDC on the compression stroke (see Step 6). Install the camshaft sprocket backing plate on the end of the camshaft **(see illustration)**. Slip the camshaft sprocket into the top of the chain, then take up the slack in the lower run of the chain and fit the sprocket onto the camshaft, aligning the timing mark on the sprocket with the index mark on the camshaft holder (see

illustration). **Note:** *To prevent the backing plate falling off the end of the camshaft while the sprocket is being installed, pass the blade of a small screwdriver through the centre of the sprocket, the backing plate and the camshaft.*

24 Apply some silicone grease to the nylon bush and fit it onto the back of the cam timing bob weight, then install the bob weight – ensure the bush locates in the slot in the cam chain sprocket **(see illustration 9.20)**.

25 Lift the bob weight return spring and install the static weight, ensuring that the spring is located over the top of the static weight. Tighten the decompressor mechanism bolt to the specified torque setting. Check the operation of the mechanism – the bob weight should move freely on its spindle and return to the rest position under the tension of the spring.

26 Install the decompressor mechanism cover, aligning the small hole in the cover with the head of the mechanism bolt. Fit the camshaft sprocket centre bolt and tighten it securely. Hold the alternator to prevent the sprocket from turning.

10 Camshaft and rockers –
removal, inspection and installation

Note: *This procedure can be carried out with the engine in the frame, although on some scooters access to the top of the engine is extremely restricted.*

9.19a Undo the automatic decompressor mechanism bolt . . .

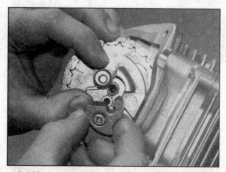

9.19b . . . and remove the static weight

9.20 Note how the bush (arrowed) locates in the slot

9.21 Disengage the sprocket from the camchain

9.23a Install the camshaft sprocket backing plate . . .

9.23b . . . and the camshaft sprocket

Removal

1 Remove the valve cover (see Section 6). Where fitted, remove the rubber insulating pad from the top of the camshaft holder for safekeeping, noting how it fits **(see illustration)**.

2 Remove the cam chain tensioner (see Section 8).

3 Where possible, remove the camshaft sprocket (see Section 9), then secure the cam chain using a cable tie to prevent it dropping into the engine. If the camshaft is supported in a journal on the outside of the camshaft sprocket, remove the journal, then displace the sprocket and lift off the chain (see Section 9).

4 Stuff a clean rag into the cam chain tunnel to prevent anything falling into the engine. Mark the end of the camshaft so that it can be refitted in the same position (TDC, all valves closed) **(see illustration)**.

5 On some engines, the camshaft and rockers are located in a separate holder. If the holder is retained by long studs that also secure the cylinder head and cylinder to the crankcases, check to see if the head is also secured by any smaller bolts, and if so, undo them first **(see illustration)**. Now unscrew the camshaft holder nuts or bolts, evenly and a little at a time in a criss-cross pattern, until they are all loose and remove them. Lift off the camshaft holder **(see illustration)**. If the camshaft remains in the cylinder head, lift it out and remove the sprocket, then detach the

10.1 Remove the rubber pad (where fitted)

10.4 Mark the end of the camshaft to aid reassembly

chain; secure the chain to prevent it dropping into the engine. If the camshaft is in the camshaft holder, remove the retaining plate or circlip and withdraw the camshaft from the holder **(see illustrations)**. Note that the bearings may come out with the camshaft.

6 If the camshaft housing is an integral part of the cylinder head, remove the retaining plate or circlip and withdraw the camshaft **(see illustrations)**. Note that the bearings, where fitted, may come out with the camshaft.

7 Mark the rocker arms so that they can be installed in their original positions. On some engines, the rocker shafts are retained in the camshaft housing by the camshaft housing bolts; once the housing has been removed, withdraw the shafts carefully and remove the rockers, noting the position of any thrustwashers on the shafts. On other

engines, the shafts are retained by a stopper bolt or circlip; remove the bolt or circlip, as applicable, and withdraw the shafts. Assemble the rockers and any thrustwashers on their shafts in the correct order so that they can be installed in their original positions. **Note:** *On some engines the rockers are located on one shaft, on others the intake and exhaust valve rockers have separate shafts. On engines with four-valve heads, the rockers are forked so that they bear on two valves simultaneously.*

Inspection

8 Clean all of the components with a suitable solvent and dry them.

9 Inspect the camshaft lobes for heat discoloration (blue appearance), score marks, chipped areas, flat spots and spalling.

10.5a Camshaft holder is retained by four nuts (A), but smaller bolts (B) must be loosened first

10.5b Lift off the camshaft holder

10.5c Remove the circlip . . .

10.5d . . . and withdraw the camshaft

10.6a Remove the retaining plate . . .

10.6b . . . and withdraw the camshaft

10.9 Measuring the camshaft lobe height with a micrometer

10.12 Inspect the contact surfaces (arrowed) on the rocker arms for wear and pitting

Measure each camshaft lobe height with a micrometer and compare the results with the specifications in the *Data* section at the end of this manual **(see illustration)**. If damage is noted or wear is excessive, the camshaft must be renewed.

10 Check the condition of the camshaft bearings and renew them if necessary (see *Tools and Workshop Tips* in the Reference section). If the bearing is on the camshaft it must be removed using a suitable bearing puller to avoid damaging the shaft. If the bearing is in the housing or cylinder head, it may be possible to remove it with a bearing driver or suitable socket that bears on the outer race only. Alternatively, a puller will be required. **Note:** *Take great care when removing the bearings to avoid damaging other components. If necessary, consult a scooter dealer or specialist engineer.*

11 If the camshaft runs directly in the cylinder head, inspect the bearing surfaces of the head and camshaft holder and the corresponding journals on the camshaft. Look for score marks, scratches and spalling. If damage is noted the relevant parts must be renewed.

12 Blow through the oil passages in the rocker arms with compressed air, if available. Inspect the face of the rocker arm and the contact area between the adjuster screw and the valve stem for pits and spalling **(see illustration)**. Where fitted, check the articulated tip of the adjuster screw for wear; the tip should move freely, but not be loose.

Check the rocker shaft for wear; if available, use a micrometer to measure the diameter of the shaft in several places; any difference in the measurements is an indication of wear. Assemble the rocker arm on its shaft – it should be a sliding fit with no discernible freeplay. Renew any components that are worn or damaged.

Installation

13 Installation is the reverse of removal, noting the following:
- *Ensure the piston is at TDC on the compression stroke before you start.*
- *Lubricate the shafts, bearing surfaces and bearings with clean engine oil before installation.*
- *It is good practice to use new circlips, where fitted.*
- *Tighten the main cylinder head fixings before any smaller bolts.*
- *Tighten the cylinder head fixings a little at a time in a criss-cross sequence to the torque setting specified in the Data section.*
- *Check the valve clearances (see Chapter 1).*

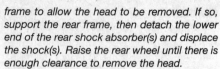

11 Cylinder head – removal and installation

Note: *On most scooters, this procedure can be carried out with the engine in the frame. However, in some cases there is insufficient clearance between the cylinder head and the*

frame to allow the head to be removed. If so, support the rear frame, then detach the lower end of the rear shock absorber(s) and displace the shock(s). Raise the rear wheel until there is enough clearance to remove the head. **Caution: The engine must be completely cool before beginning this procedure or the cylinder head may become warped.**

Removal

1 If fitted, remove the oil cooler (see Section 7).

2 Remove the carburettor and exhaust system (see Chapter 4).

3 On liquid-cooled engines, drain the cooling system (see Chapter 3). Detach the coolant hoses from the unions on the cylinder head, noting where they fit. Disconnect the coolant temperature sensor wiring connector. If required, remove the thermostat housing (see Chapter 3).

4 Remove the camshaft and rockers (see Section 10). **Note:** *On some engines it is possible to remove the cylinder head with the camshaft and rockers in place, but in practice the camshaft and rockers must be removed in order to service the valves. The fixings for the camshaft holder may also secure the cylinder head.*

5 Check to see which bolts secure the cylinder head; on some engines, in addition to the main internal fixings, the head is also secured by smaller, external bolts. Undo the smaller bolts first, then undo the main nuts or bolts, evenly and a little at a time in a criss-cross pattern, until they are all loose and remove them **(see illustrations)**.

6 Lift the cylinder head off carefully, feeding the cam chain down through the tunnel in the head **(see illustration)**. If the head is stuck, tap around the joint face between the head and the cylinder with a soft-faced mallet to free it. Do not try to lever the head off as this may damage the sealing surfaces. **Note:** *Avoid lifting the cylinder off the crankcase when the head is removed, otherwise a new cylinder base gasket will have to be fitted (see Section 13).*

7 Remove the old cylinder head gasket and discard it, as a new one must be fitted on reassembly; note any dowels in the head or

11.5a Undo the smaller bolts (arrowed) first . . .

11.5b . . . then undo the main nuts (arrowed)

11.6 Lift off the cylinder head

11.7a Discard the old cylinder head gasket

11.7b Note the position of dowels (arrowed) in the head . . .

11.7c . . . or the cylinder

cylinder and remove them for safekeeping if they are loose **(see illustrations)**.

8 Secure the cam chain to prevent it dropping into the engine.

9 Inspect the cylinder head gasket and the mating surfaces on the cylinder head and cylinder for signs of leaks, which could indicate that the head is warped. Refer to Section 12 and check the head mating surface for warpage.

10 Clean all traces of old gasket material from the cylinder head and cylinder with a suitable solvent. Take care not to scratch or gouge the soft aluminium. Be careful not to let any of the gasket material fall into the crankcase, the cylinder bore or the oil or coolant passages.

Installation

11 Installation is the reverse of removal, noting the following:

● *Lubricate the cylinder bore with clean engine oil.*
● *Install a new head gasket – never re-use the old gasket.*
● *Ensure the oil and coolant holes in the gasket align with the cylinder.*
● *Tighten the main cylinder head fixings first before the smaller, external bolts.*
● *Tighten the main cylinder head fixings evenly and a little at a time in a criss-cross pattern to the torque setting specified in the Data section.*
● *On liquid-cooled engines, refill the cooling system.*

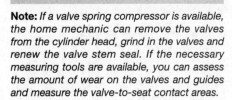

12 Cylinder head and valves – disassembly, inspection and reassembly

Note: *If a valve spring compressor is available, the home mechanic can remove the valves from the cylinder head, grind in the valves and renew the valve stem seal. If the necessary measuring tools are available, you can assess the amount of wear on the valves and guides and measure the valve-to-seat contact areas.*

Disassembly

1 Before you start, arrange to label and store the valves and their related components so that they can be returned to their original locations without getting mixed up **(see illustration)**.

2 If not already done, clean all traces of old gasket material from the cylinder head with a suitable solvent. Take care not to scratch or gouge the soft aluminium. On liquid-cooled engines, if the thermostat is fitted in the cylinder head, remove the thermostat (see Chapter 3).

3 Compress the valve spring on the first valve with a spring compressor, making sure it is correctly located onto each end of the valve assembly **(see illustration)**. On the underside of the head, make sure the plate on the compressor only contacts the valve and not the soft aluminium of the head – if the plate is too big for the valve, use a spacer between them. Do not compress the spring any more

than is absolutely necessary to release the collets.

4 Remove the collets, using either needle-nose pliers, a magnet or a screwdriver with a dab of grease on it. Carefully release the valve spring compressor and remove the spring retainer, noting which way up it fits, the spring, the spring seat, and the valve from the head. If the valve binds in the guide (won't pull through), push it back into the head and deburr the area around the collet groove with a very fine file **(see illustration)**. **Note:** *On some engines, two springs are fitted to each valve.*

5 Once the valve has been removed, pull the valve stem oil seal off the top of the valve guide with pliers and discard it, as a new one must be used on reassembly **(see illustration)**.

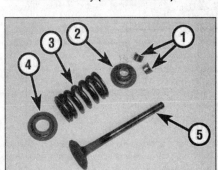

12.1 Valve components

1 Collets	4 Spring seat
2 Spring retainer	5 Valve
3 Valve spring	

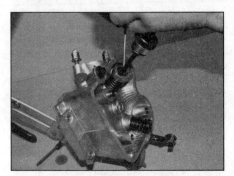

12.3 Compress the valve spring carefully and remove the collets

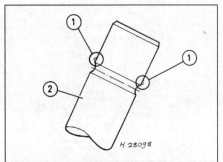

12.4 If the vale stem (2) won't pull through the guide, deburr the area (1) above the collet groove

12.5 Pull off the old valve stem oil seal (arrowed)

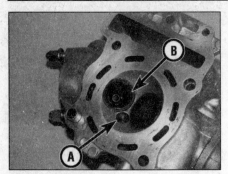

12.10 Check the head for cracks. Inspect the spark plug hole (A) and the valve seats (B)

12.12 Check the cylinder head for warpage in the directions shown

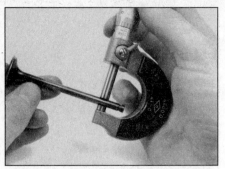

12.14a Measuring the valve stem diameter with a micrometer

6 Repeat the procedure for the remaining valve(s). Remember to keep the parts for each valve together and in order so they can be reinstalled in the correct location.

7 Next, clean the cylinder head with solvent and dry it thoroughly. Compressed air will speed the drying process and ensure that all holes and recessed areas are clean.

8 Clean the valve springs, collets, retainers and spring seats with solvent. Work on the parts from one valve at a time so as not to mix them up.

9 Scrape off any carbon deposits that may have formed on the valve, then use a motorised wire brush to remove deposits from the valve heads and stems. Again, make sure the valves do not get mixed up.

Inspection

10 Inspect the head very carefully for cracks and other damage **(see illustration)**. If cracks are found, a new head will be required.

11 Inspect the threads in the spark plug hole. Damaged or worn threads can be reclaimed using a thread insert (see *Tools and Workshop Tips* in the *Reference* section). Most scooter dealers and small engineering firms offer a service of this kind.

12 Using a precision straight-edge and a feeler gauge, check the head mating surface for warpage. Lay the straight-edge across the surface and try to slip the feeler gauge under it on either side of the combustion chamber. If the feeler gauge can be inserted between the straight-edge and the cylinder head, the head is warped and must be either machined or, if

warpage is excessive, renewed. Check vertically, horizontally and diagonally across the head, making four checks in all **(see illustration)**. If there is any doubt about the condition of the head consult a scooter dealer or specialist engineer.

13 Examine the valve seats in the combustion chamber. If they are deeply pitted, cracked or burned, it may be possible to have them repaired and recut by a specialist engineer, otherwise a new head will be required. The valve seats should be a uniform width all the way round **(see illustration 12.10)**.

14 If available, use a micrometer to measure the valve stem diameter in several places **(see illustration)**. Any difference in the measurements is an indication of wear. Inspect the valve face for cracks, pits and burned spots. Check the valve stem and the collet groove area for cracks **(see illustration)**. Rotate the valve and check for any obvious indication that it is bent. Check the end of the stem for pitting and excessive wear. If any of the above conditions are found, fit a new valve. If the stem end is pitted or worn, also check the contact area of the adjuster screw in the rocker arm.

15 Insert a known good valve into its guide – it should be a sliding fit with no discernible freeplay. If there is freeplay, the guide is probably worn. Have the guides checked by a scooter dealer or specialist engineer. If new valve guides are available, have them installed by a specialist who will also recut the valve seats. If new guides are not available, a

specialist engineer may be able to bore out the old ones and fit sleeves in them. Otherwise a new cylinder head will have to be fitted. **Note:** *Carbon build-up inside the guide is an indication of wear.*

16 Check the end of each valve spring for wear and pitting. Stand the spring upright on a flat surface and check it for bend by placing a square against it **(see illustration)**. If the spring is worn, or the bend is excessive, it must be renewed. Some manufacturers specify a service limit for the spring free length (consult a scooter dealer), but it is good practice to fit new springs when the head has been disassembled for valve servicing. Always fit new valve springs as a set.

17 Check the spring retainers and collets for obvious wear and cracks. Any questionable parts should not be re-used, as extensive damage will occur in the event of failure during engine operation.

Reassembly

18 Unless the valve seats have been recut, before installing the valves in the head they should be ground-in (lapped) to ensure a positive seal between the valves and seats. This procedure requires coarse and fine valve grinding compound and a valve grinding tool. If a grinding tool is not available, a piece of rubber or plastic hose can be slipped over the valve stem (after the valve has been installed in the guide) and used to turn the valve.

19 Apply a small amount of coarse grinding compound to the valve face, then slip the valve into the guide **(see illustration)**.

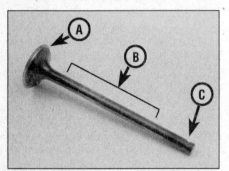

12.14b Check the valve face (A), stem (B) and collet groove (C) for signs of wear and damage

12.16 Check the valve springs for bending

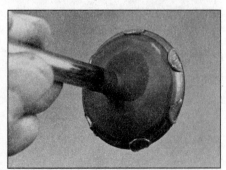

12.19 Apply the grinding compound sparingly, in small dabs, to the valve face only

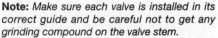

12.20a Rotate the grinding tool back and forth between the palms of your hands

12.20b The valve face and seat should show a uniform unbroken ring

12.25 A small dab of grease helps to keep the collets in place during installation

Note: *Make sure each valve is installed in its correct guide and be careful not to get any grinding compound on the valve stem.*

20 Attach the grinding tool (or hose) to the valve and rotate the tool between the palms of your hands. Use a back-and-forth motion (as though rubbing your hands together) rather than a circular motion (ie, so that the valve rotates alternately clockwise and anti-clockwise rather than in one direction only) **(see illustration)**. Lift the valve off the seat and turn it at regular intervals to distribute the grinding compound properly. Continue the grinding procedure until the valve face and seat contact areas are of uniform width and unbroken around the circumference **(see illustration)**.

21 Carefully remove the valve from the guide and wipe off all traces of grinding compound. Use solvent to clean the valve and wipe the seat area thoroughly with a solvent-soaked cloth.

22 Repeat the procedure with fine valve grinding compound, then repeat the entire procedure for the other valve(s).

HAYNES HiNT *Check for proper sealing of each valve by pouring a small amount of solvent into the valve port while holding the valve shut. If the solvent leaks past the valve into the combustion chamber the valve grinding operation should be repeated.*

23 Working on one valve at a time, lay the spring seat in place in the cylinder head, then install a new valve stem seal onto the guide. Use an appropriate size deep socket to push the seal over the end of the valve guide until it is felt to clip into place. Don't twist or cock it, or it will not seal properly against the valve stem. Also, don't remove it again or it will be damaged.

24 Lubricate the valve stem with molybdenum disulphide grease, then install it into its guide, rotating it slowly to avoid damaging the seal. Check that the valve moves up and down freely in the guide. Next, install the spring, with its closer-wound coils facing down into the cylinder head, followed by the spring retainer, with its shouldered side facing down so that it fits into the top of the spring. **Note:** *On some engines, two springs are fitted to each valve.*

25 Apply a small amount of grease to the collets to hold them in place as the pressure is released from the spring. Compress the spring with the valve spring compressor and install the collets **(see illustration)**. When compressing the spring, depress it only as far as is absolutely necessary to slip the collets into place. Make certain that the collets are securely locked in their retaining grooves.

26 Repeat the procedure for the remaining valve(s).

27 Support the cylinder head on blocks so the valves can't contact the workbench top, then very gently tap each of the valve stems with a soft-faced hammer. This will help seat the collets in their grooves.

13 Cylinder – removal, inspection and installation

Note: *On most scooters, this procedure can be carried out with the engine in the frame. However, in some cases there is insufficient clearance between the cylinder and the frame to allow the cylinder to be removed. If so, support the rear frame, then detach the lower end of the rear shock absorber(s) and displace the shock(s). Raise the rear wheel until there is enough clearance to remove the cylinder.*

Removal

1 Remove the cylinder head (see Section 11).

2 On liquid-cooled engines, where applicable, detach the coolant hose from the cylinder (see Chapter 3).

3 Note the location of the cam chain guide blade, then lift out the blade **(see illustration)**.

4 Where fitted, undo the bolt(s) securing the cylinder to the crankcase **(see illustration)**.

5 Lift the cylinder up off the crankcase, supporting the piston as it becomes accessible to prevent it hitting the crankcase opening **(see illustration)**. If the cylinder is stuck, tap around the joint face between the cylinder and the crankcase with a soft-faced mallet to free it. Don't attempt to free the cylinder by inserting a screwdriver between it and the crankcase – you'll damage the sealing surfaces. When the cylinder is removed, stuff a clean rag into the crankcase opening around the piston to prevent anything falling inside.

13.3 Lift out the cam chain guide blade

13.4 Bolt (arrowed) secures the cylinder to the crankcase

13.5 Support the piston as the cylinder is removed

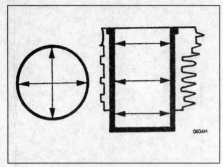

13.8 Measure the cylinder bore in the directions shown

6 Remove the cylinder base gasket and discard it, as new one must be fitted on reassembly.

Inspection

7 Check the cylinder bore carefully for scratches and score marks.

8 If available, use a telescoping gauge and micrometer to measure the diameter of the cylinder bore to assess the amount of wear, taper and ovality (see *Tools and Workshop Tips* in the *Reference* section). Measure near the top (but below the level of the top piston ring at TDC), centre and bottom (but above the level of the bottom ring at BDC) of the bore both parallel to and across the crankshaft axis **(see illustration)**. Calculate any differences between the measurements to determine any taper or ovality in the bore.

9 Now measure an unworn part of the cylinder bore (below the level of the bottom ring at BDC) and compare the result to the previous measurements to determine overall wear.

10 If the bore is tapered, oval, or worn excessively, or badly scratched, scuffed or scored, the cylinder and piston will have to be renewed. **Note:** *If no service limit specifications (see Data section) are available to assess cylinder wear, calculate the piston-to-bore clearance to determine whether the cylinder is useable (see Section 14). Alternatively, check for a lip around the (unworn) top edge of the cylinder bore as a rough indication of wear.*

11 If there is any doubt about the serviceability of the cylinder, consult a scooter

13.24 Zero the gauge against the cylinder top gasket surface

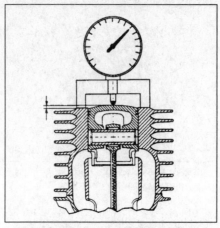

13.21 Set-up for checking the cylinder surface-to-piston crown relationship

dealer. **Note:** *On some engines, the surface of the cylinder has a wear-resistant coating which, when damaged or worn through, requires a new cylinder. On others, the cylinder can be rebored and an oversize piston fitted (see Data section). Oversize pistons are not necessarily marked as such; in many cases the only way to determine if a cylinder has been rebored is to measure an unworn area of the bore and compare the result with the specifications in the Data section. Some manufacturers mark cylinders and pistons with a size code during production; the size code (usually a letter) is stamped into the cylinder gasket surface and the top of the piston. It is important that new parts have matching codes.*

12 Where fitted, check that all the cylinder head studs are tight in the crankcase halves. If any are loose, remove them and clean their threads. Apply a suitable permanent thread locking compound and tighten them securely.

Installation

Note: *On some engines, cylinder base gaskets are available in a range of thicknesses; the appropriate thickness depends on the height of the piston crown at TDC in relation to the cylinder top gasket surface. Consult a scooter dealer for details. In these instances, the correct gasket thickness must be calculated before reassembly (see Steps 21 to 25).*

13.25 Measuring the piston height at TDC

13 Check that the mating surfaces of the cylinder and crankcase are clean, then remove any rag from the crankcase opening. Lay the new base gasket in place on the crankcase making sure it is the correct way round.

14 If required, install a piston ring clamp onto the piston to ease its entry into the bore as the cylinder is lowered. This is not essential if the cylinder has a good lead-in enabling the piston rings to be hand-fed into the bore. If possible, have an assistant to support the cylinder while this is done. Check that the piston ring end gaps are positioned as described in Section 15.

15 Lubricate the cylinder bore, piston and piston rings, and the connecting rod big- and small-ends, with the clean engine oil, then lower the cylinder down until the piston crown fits into the bore.

16 Gently push down on the cylinder, making sure the piston enters the bore squarely and does not get cocked sideways. If a piston ring clamp is not being used, carefully compress and feed each ring into the bore as the cylinder is lowered. If necessary, use a soft mallet to gently tap the cylinder down, but do not use force if it appears to be stuck as the piston and/or rings will be damaged. If a clamp is used, remove it once the piston is in the bore.

17 When the piston is correctly installed in the cylinder, check that the base gasket has not been displaced, then press the cylinder down onto the base gasket.

18 Install the cylinder bolt(s) finger-tight only at this stage (see Step 4).

19 Install the cam chain guide blade, then install the cylinder head (see Section 11).

20 Tighten the cylinder bolt(s) and, on liquid-cooled engines, install the coolant hose on the cylinder and secure it with the clip.

Cylinder base gasket thickness

21 To measure the height of the piston crown at TDC in relation to the cylinder top gasket surface you will require a dial gauge and a mounting plate **(see illustration)**.

22 Assemble the cylinder on the piston as described in Steps 13 to 16, but without a base gasket, and press the cylinder down onto the crankcase.

23 Clamp the mounting plate across the top of the cylinder using the cylinder fixings and tighten them to ensure that the cylinder is held firmly against the crankcase. Rotate the crankshaft so that the piston is part way down the bore.

24 Set the dial gauge on the mounting plate, and with the gauge tip resting against the cylinder top gasket surface, zero the gauge **(see illustration)**.

25 Now rest the gauge tip against the top of the piston. Rotate the crankshaft via the alternator rotor nut so the piston rises to the top of its stroke (TDC). At this point read off the dial gauge **(see illustration)**. The reading represents the distance between the cylinder

14.2 Mark the top of the piston

14.3a Prise out the circlip . . .

14.3b . . . then push out the piston pin

top gasket surface and the top of the piston crown. Use this measurement, together with the manufacturer's information, to identify the appropriate gasket thickness.

14 Piston – removal, inspection and installation

Note: *This procedure can be carried out with the engine in the frame.*

Removal

1 Remove the cylinder and stuff a clean rag into the crankcase opening around the piston to prevent anything falling inside (see Section 13).

2 The top of the piston should be marked with an arrow or lettering (eg, IN on the intake side, nearest the carburettor) to show which way round it should be fitted. If no mark is visible, scratch one lightly on the top of the piston **(see illustration)**. Note that the manufacturer's mark may not be visible until the carbon deposits have been scraped off and the piston cleaned.

3 Carefully prise out the circlip on one side of the piston using needle-nose pliers or a small flat-bladed screwdriver inserted into the notch **(see illustration)**. Check for burring around the circlip groove and remove any with a very fine file or penknife blade, then push the piston pin out from the other side and remove the piston from the connecting rod **(see illustration)**. Use a socket extension to push the piston pin out if required. Remove the other circlip and discard them both, as new ones must be used on reassembly.

4 Before the inspection process can be carried out, the piston rings must be removed and the piston must be cleaned. **Note:** *If the*

> **HAYNES HiNT**
> *To prevent the circlip from flying away or from dropping into the crankcase, pass a rod or screwdriver, with a greater diameter than the gap between the circlip ends, through the piston pin. This will trap the circlip if it springs out.*

> **HAYNES HiNT**
> *If the piston pin is a tight fit in the piston bosses, heat the piston gently with a hot air gun – this will expand the alloy piston sufficiently to release its grip on the pin.*

cylinder is being rebored, piston inspection can be overlooked as a new one will be fitted. The piston rings can be removed by hand; using your thumbs, ease the ends of each ring apart and carefully lift it off the piston, taking care not to expand it any more than is necessary **(see illustration)**. Do not nick or gouge the piston in the process.

5 Note which way up each ring fits and in which groove, as they must be installed in their original positions if being re-used. The upper surface of each ring should be marked at one end (see Section 15). Some pistons are fitted with a three-piece third (oil control) ring; there will be an upper and lower side rail and a central rail spacer. **Note:** *It is good practice to renew the piston rings when an engine is being overhauled. Ensure that the piston and bore are serviceable before purchasing new rings.*

6 Clean all traces of carbon from the top of the piston. A hand-held wire brush or a piece of fine emery cloth can be used once most of the deposits have been scraped away. Do not, under any circumstances, use a wire brush mounted in a drill motor; the piston material is soft and is easily damaged.

7 Use a piston ring groove cleaning tool to remove any carbon deposits from the ring

grooves. If a tool is not available, a piece broken off an old ring will do the job. Be very careful to remove only the carbon deposits. Do not remove any metal and do not nick or gouge the sides of the ring grooves.

8 Once the carbon has been removed, clean the piston with a suitable solvent and dry it thoroughly. If the identification previously marked on the piston is cleaned off, be sure to re-mark it correctly **(see illustration)**.

Inspection

9 Inspect the piston for cracks around the skirt, at the pin bosses and at the ring lands. Check that the circlip grooves are not damaged. Normal piston wear appears as even, vertical wear on the thrust surfaces of the piston and slight looseness of the top ring in its groove. If the skirt is scored or scuffed, the engine may have been suffering from overheating and/or abnormal combustion, which caused excessively high operating temperatures.

10 A hole in the top of the piston, in one extreme, or burned areas around the edge of the piston crown, indicate that pre-ignition or knocking under load have occurred. If you find evidence of any problems the cause must be corrected or the damage will occur again. Refer to Chapter 4 for carburation checks and Chapter 5 for ignition checks.

11 Check the piston-to-bore clearance by measuring the cylinder bore (see Section 13) and the piston diameter. Measure the piston approximately 25 mm down from the bottom of the lower piston ring groove and at 90° to

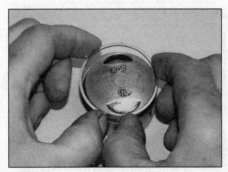

14.4 Remove the piston rings carefully

14.8 Manufacturer's mark on piston crown

14.11 Measuring the piston diameter with a micrometer

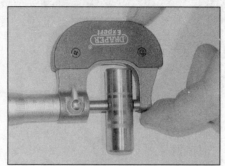

14.12 Measuring the diameter of the piston pin

14.13 Checking for freeplay between the piston and piston pin

the piston pin axis **(see illustration)**. **Note:** *The precise point of measurement differs between manufacturers and engines, but the aim is to measure the piston in an area where it is worn.* Subtract the piston diameter from the bore diameter to obtain the clearance. If it is greater than the specified figure, check whether it is the bore or piston that is worn the most (see *Data* section at the end of this manual). If the bore is good, install a new piston and rings. **Note:** *Oversize pistons fitted in a rebored cylinder are not necessarily marked as such; in many cases the only way to determine if a cylinder has been rebored is to measure an unworn area of the bore and compare the result with the specifications in the Data section. Some manufacturers mark cylinders and pistons with a size code during production; the size code (usually a letter) is stamped into the cylinder gasket surface and the top of the piston. It is important that new parts have matching codes. It is essential to supply the size code and any rebore specifications when purchasing a new piston.*

12 Use a micrometer to measure the piston pin in the middle, where it runs in the small-end bearing, and at each end where it runs in the piston **(see illustration)**. If there is any difference in the measurements the pin is worn and must be renewed.

13 If the piston pin is good, lubricate it with clean engine oil, then insert it into the piston and check for any freeplay between the two **(see illustration)**. There should be no freeplay.

14 Next, check the condition of the connecting rod small-end. A worn small-end

will produce a metallic rattle, most audible when the engine is under load, and increasing as engine speed rises. This should not be confused with big-end bearing wear, which produces a pronounced knocking noise. Lubricate the piston pin with clean engine oil, then slide it into the small-end and check for freeplay **(see illustration)**. There should only be slightly discernible freeplay between the piston pin and the connecting rod.

15 If there is freeplay, measure the internal diameter of the connecting rod small-end **(see illustration)**. Take several measurements; if there is any difference between the measurements, the small end is worn and either a new connecting rod or crankshaft assembly will have to be fitted (see Section 20). Consult a scooter dealer about the availability of parts. **Note:** *If a new rod is available, fitting it is a specialist task which should be left to a scooter dealer or automotive engineer. If a new rod is fitted, the big-end bearing should be renewed at the same time.*

16 If the small-end is good, fit a new piston pin. **Note:** *On some engines, the piston pin and small-end are marked with a size code during production; look for identification marks or colours on the components and refer to them when ordering new parts.*

Installation

17 Install the piston rings (see Section 15).
18 Lubricate the piston pin, the piston pin bore in the piston and the connecting-rod small-end with clean engine oil.
19 Install a new circlip in one side of the

piston, then line up the piston on the connecting rod, making sure it is the right way round (see Step 2), and insert the piston pin from the other side. Secure the pin with the other new circlip. When installing the circlips, compress them only just enough to fit them in the piston, and make sure they are properly seated in their grooves with the open end away from the removal notch.
20 Install the cylinder (see Section 13).

15 Piston rings –
inspection and installation

1 New piston rings should be fitted whenever an engine is being overhauled. It is important that you get new rings of the correct size for your piston so ensure that any information relating to piston size, including rebore size, and size coding is available when purchasing new parts.

2 Before fitting the new rings onto the piston, the ring end gaps must be checked. Insert the top ring into the bottom of the cylinder bore and square it up by pushing it in with the top of the piston. The ring should be about 15 to 20 mm from the bottom edge of the cylinder. To measure the end gap, slip a feeler gauge between the ends of the ring and compare the measurement to the specification in the *Data* section at the end of this manual **(see illustration)**.

3 If the gap is larger or smaller than specified, check to make sure that you have the correct rings before proceeding. If the gap is larger

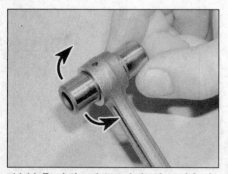

14.14 Rock the piston pin back-and-forth in the small-end to check for wear

14.15 Measuring the internal diameter of the connecting rod small-end

15.2 Measuring the installed piston ring end gap

15.6a Fit the oil ring expander first . . .

15.6b . . . then the lower side rail

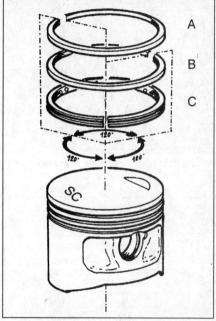

15.8a If a one-piece oil control ring is used, position the end gaps at 120° intervals

A First (top) compression ring
B Second (middle) compression ring
C Oil control ring

than specified it is likely the cylinder bore is worn. If the gap is too small the ring ends may come into contact with each other during engine operation, causing serious damage.

4 Repeat the procedure for the other two rings. **Note:** *If the piston is fitted with a three-piece third (oil control) ring, check the end gap on the upper and lower side rails only. The ends of the central rail spacer should contact each other when it is fitted on the piston.*

5 Once the ring end gaps have been checked, the rings can be installed on the piston. Do not expand the rings any more than is necessary to slide them into place. **Note:** *A ring installation tool can be used on the two compression rings, and on a one-piece oil control ring, if desired, but not on the side rails of a three-piece oil control ring.*

6 The oil control ring (lowest on the piston) is installed first. If a three-piece ring is used, fit the rail spacer into the groove, then install the lower side rail **(see illustrations)**. Place one end of the side rail into the groove between the spacer and the lower ring land. Hold it firmly in place, then slide a finger around the piston while pushing the rail into the groove. Install the upper side rail the same way. Ensure the ends of the spacer touch but do not overlap, then check that both side rails turn smoothly in the ring groove.

7 Next install the 2nd compression ring, noting that there is usually a marking or letter near the gap to denote the upper surface of

the ring. Finally install the top ring into its groove.

8 Once the rings are correctly installed, check they move freely without snagging, then stagger their end gaps before fitting the piston into the cylinder **(see illustrations)**.

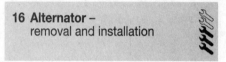

16 Alternator – removal and installation

Note: *This procedure can be carried out with the engine in the frame. If the engine has been removed, ignore the steps that do not apply.*

Removal

1 Remove the body panels as necessary to access the alternator (see Chapter 9). If required, remove the exhaust system (see Chapter 4).

2 On some air-cooled engines, the alternator is located behind the fan cowling. Unclip any wiring or hoses from the fan cowling, then undo the bolts securing the fan cowling and remove it **(see illustration)**. Note that on some models the fan cowling is clipped to the engine cowling – take care not to damage the fixing lugs when separating them. Remove any spacers for the cowling bolts for safekeeping if they are loose. Undo the bolts securing the cooling fan to the alternator rotor and remove the fan (see Chapter 1, Section 21).

3 On liquid-cooled engines where the water

pump is mounted on the outside of the alternator cover, first drain the coolant and disconnect all the coolant hoses from the pump (see Chapter 3). Undo the cover mounting bolts and lift off the cover. Depending on the tools available for removing the alternator rotor, it may be necessary to unscrew the pump drive dampers **(see illustration)**.

4 On some engines the alternator is located behind the right-hand engine side cover. **Note:** *If the water pump is mounted on the outside of the engine side cover, first drain the coolant and disconnect all the coolant hoses from the pump (see Chapter 3).* Drain the engine oil (see Chapter 1). Trace the wiring from the cover and disconnect it at the

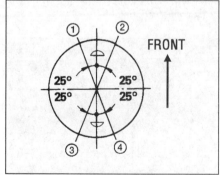

15.8b If a three-piece oil control ring is used, position the end gaps as shown – top ring (1), oil ring lower side rail (2), oil ring upper side rail (3), second ring (4)

16.2 Where necessary, remove the fan cowling

16.3 Water pump is driven by dampers on the alternator rotor

16.4 Lift off the side cover and alternator stator

16.5 Hold the rotor and undo the centre nut (arrowed)

16.6 Using a strap wrench to hold the rotor

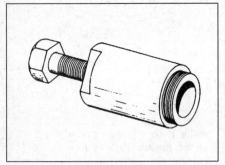

16.8a Typical service tool for removing the rotor

16.8b Using a screw-in type puller

16.8c Using a two-legged puller

connector, then undo the cover bolts and lift off the cover **(see illustration)**. Discard the gasket, as a new one must be fitted, and remove the cover dowels for safekeeping if they are loose. If applicable, remove the starter pinion assembly (see Section 17).

5 To remove the rotor centre nut it is necessary to stop the rotor from turning; some manufacturers produce a service tool for this

HAYNES HINT *A rotor holding tool can easily be made using two strips of steel bolted together in the middle, with a bolt through each end which locates into the slots or holes in the rotor. Do not allow the bolts to extend too far through the rotor otherwise the coils could be damaged.*

purpose. If the rotor face is accessible, you can make up a tool which engages the slots or holes **(see illustration)**. Note: *Take great care not to damage the coils of the alternator when locating any tools through the rotor.*

6 If the alternator stator is located in the engine side cover, the rotor can be held with a strap wrench **(see illustration)**.

7 With the rotor securely held, unscrew the centre nut.

8 To remove the rotor from the shaft it is necessary to use a puller – either a manufacturer's service tool or a commercially available puller **(see illustrations)**. To use the service tool, first screw the body of the tool all the way into the threads provided in the rotor. Hold the tool steady with a spanner on its flats and tighten the centre bolt, exerting steady pressure to draw the rotor off the crankshaft. To use a puller, engage the puller legs either

in the slots in the rotor or thread them into the threaded holes in the rotor, then tighten the centre bolt exerting steady pressure to draw the rotor off the crankshaft. Remove the Woodruff key from the shaft for safekeeping, noting how it fits **(see illustrations)**.

9 In most cases, the alternator stator coils and ignition pulse generator coil are wired together and have to be removed as an assembly. If not already done, trace the wiring back from the alternator and pulse generator and disconnect it at the connectors. Free the wiring from any clips or guides and feed it through to the alternator.

10 Undo the screws securing the stator and the pulse generator and lift them off together. Where fitted, draw any rubber wiring boot out of the crankcase or engine side cover and carefully pull the wiring away, noting how it fits **(see illustrations)**.

16.8d Remove the Woodruff key for safekeeping

16.8e Note the alignment of the key (A) and the slot in the rotor (B)

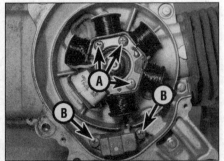

16.10a Undo the stator screws (A) and the pulse generator coil screws (B) . . .

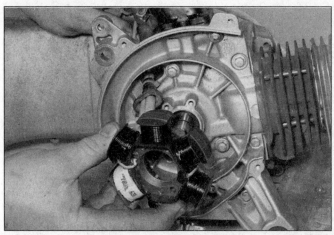

16.10b ... and remove the assembly noting how the wiring fits

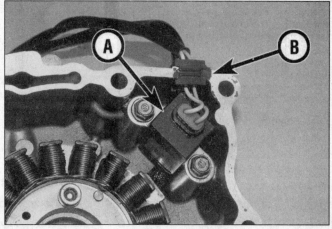

16.10c Note the position of the pulse generator (A) and the wiring grommet (B)

Installation

11 Installation is the reverse of removal, noting the following:
● Ensure the wiring is correctly routed before installing the stator and pulse generator.
● Make sure that no metal objects have attached themselves to the magnets on the inside of the rotor.
● Clean the tapered end of the crankshaft and the corresponding mating surface on the inside of the rotor with a suitable solvent.
● Fit the Woodruff key into its slot in the shaft, then install the rotor.
● Tighten the rotor centre nut to the torque setting specified in the Data section at the end of this manual.
● Secure the wiring with any clips or ties.
● If applicable, fill the engine with the correct type and quantity of oil (see Chapter 1).
● If applicable, refill the cooling system and bleed it (see Chapter 3).

17 Starter pinion assembly and starter clutch – removal, inspection and installation

Note: This procedure can be carried out with the engine in the frame.
1 The procedure for removal, inspection and installation of either the starter pinion assembly or the starter (one-way) clutch is the same as for two-stroke engines (see Chapter 2A, Section 17). Note that details for removal of the alternator on four-stroke engines are given in Section 16.

18 Oil pump – removal, inspection and installation

Note 1: Generally, the oil pump is located inside the engine unit and is chain-driven from either the left- or right-hand side of the

crankshaft. On some engines, the pump drive sprocket is integral with the crankshaft.
Note 2: This procedure can be carried out with the engine in the frame.

Removal

1 Remove either the variator (see Chapter 6) or the alternator rotor (see Section 16) as applicable.
2 If the pump drive sprocket is located on the crankshaft behind the variator, remove the cover (see illustration).
3 If the pump is located in a separate sump, remove the sump cover and discard the

gasket, as a new one must be fitted on reassembly (see illustration). Note: On some engines, the lubrication system incorporates an oil pressure relief valve. If the valve is located in the sump, remove it for safekeeping, noting how it fits. If the valve is fitted with an O-ring, discard it and fit a new one on reassembly.
4 Where fitted, remove the screws securing the pump drive chain cover and remove the cover (see illustrations).
5 Mark the chain so that it can be fitted the same way round.
6 On some pumps, the pump sprocket is

18.2 Undo the screws (arrowed) and remove the cover

18.3 Undo the bolts (arrowed) and remove the sump cover

18.4a Undo the screws (arrowed) ...

18.4b ... securing the pump drive chain cover

18.7a Remove the circlip . . .

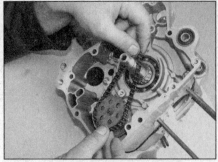

18.7b . . . and lift off the sprocket and chain

18.8a Undo the sprocket bolt . . .

18.8b . . . then remove the sprocket . . .

18.8c . . . and lift off the chain

retained by the chain cover. Withdraw the chain and sprockets from the engine as an assembly, then remove the dowel and thrustwasher from the pump shaft.

7 If the pump sprocket is retained by a circlip, use circlip pliers to remove the circlip, then withdraw the chain and sprocket(s) **(see illustrations)**.

8 If the sprocket is retained by a bolt, insert a pin punch or screwdriver through one of the holes in the sprocket and locate it against part of the casing to prevent the sprocket turning, then unscrew the bolt **(see illustration)**. Withdraw the chain and sprocket(s) **(see illustrations)**.

9 Where fitted, undo the pump retaining bolts, then withdraw the pump from the engine. If a gasket is fitted behind the pump, discard it, as a new one must be fitted.

Inspection

10 Check the pump body for obvious signs of damage especially around the mounting

bolt holes. Turn the pump shaft by hand and check that the pump rotates smoothly. Some pumps cannot be disassembled for inspection – if the operation of the pump is suspect, renew it.

11 Remove the screws securing the cover to the pump body, then remove cover **(see illustrations)**. Note any reference marks on the pump rotors; even if the rotors are not marked, it is essential that they are reassembled the correct way round. Lift out the inner and outer rotor and the pump shaft **(see illustration)**. Note the location of any drive pin in the shaft. **Note:** *On some pumps, the rotors are secured by a circlip – use a new circlip on reassembly.*

12 Clean the pump components with a suitable solvent and dry them with compressed air, if available. Inspect the pump body, rotors and shaft for scoring and wear. If any damage, scoring, uneven or excessive wear is evident, renew the pump (individual components are not available).

13 If the pump is good, reassemble all the components in the correct order and lubricate them with clean engine oil.

14 Fit the cover and tighten the screws securely, then rotate the pump shaft by hand to check that the rotors turn smoothly and freely.

15 Inspect the pump drive chain and sprockets for wear or damage, and renew them as a set if necessary. If the drive sprocket is not a sliding fit on the crankshaft, check to see if it is a press-fit or an integral part of the shaft. If the sprocket is a press-fit and needs to be renewed, measure its position from the end of the shaft, then pull it off with a bearing puller (see *Tools and Workshop Tips* in the *Reference* section). Heat the new sprocket in an oil bath to around 100°C, then press it onto the shaft using a suitable length of tube that just fits over the shaft. Ensure that the sprocket is installed at the correct distance from the end of the shaft.

Installation

16 Installation is the reverse of removal, noting the following:

● *If required, fit a new gasket to the pump.*
● *Where fitted, secure the pump drive gear with a new circlip.*
● *Ensure the chain is fitted the correct way round.*
● *Where fitted, ensure the oil pressure relief valve is correctly installed.*
● *Fit a new gasket to the sump.*
● *If applicable, fill the engine with the correct type and quantity of oil (see Chapter 1).*

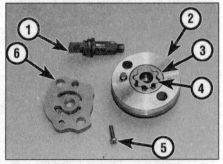

18.11c Oil pump components

1 Pump shaft	4 Inner rotor
2 Pump body	5 Body screw
3 Outer rotor	6 Cover

18.11a Remove the screws . . .

18.11b . . . and lift off the cover

19.3 Undo the crankcase bolts evenly in a criss-cross sequence

19 Crankcase halves and main bearings

Note: *To separate the crankcase halves, the engine must be removed from the frame.*

Separation

1 Follow the procedure in Section 4 and remove the engine from the frame.
2 Before the crankcase halves can be separated the following components must be removed:
● Camchain, blades and sprockets (see Section 9).
● Cylinder head (Section 11).
● Cylinder (Section 13).
● Alternator rotor (Section 16).
● Variator (Chapter 6).
● Starter motor (Chapter 10).
● Oil pump (Section 18).
3 Tape some rag around the connecting rod to prevent it knocking against the cases, then loosen the crankcase bolts evenly, a little at a time and in a criss-cross sequence until they are all finger-tight, then remove them **(see illustration). Note:** *Ensure that all the crankcase bolts have been removed before attempting to separate the cases.*

 HAYNES HINT *Make a cardboard template of the crankcase and punch a hole for each bolt location. This will ensure all bolts are installed correctly on reassembly – this is important as some bolts may be of different lengths.*

19.8 Measuring crankshaft oil seal inset

19.6 Drawing the right-hand crankcase half off the crankshaft

4 On some engines, the crankshaft is secured against the right-hand main bearing by a large nut. Lock the crankshaft by passing a bar through the connecting rod small-end and resting it on two pieces of wood to protect the cylinder gasket surface, then undo the nut.
5 If the crankshaft oil seals are fitted to the outside of the crankcases, remove the oil seals. Note that on some engines the seals are held in a fixing plate; undo the bolts and remove the plate, do not try to remove the seal from the plate.
6 Remove the right-hand crankcase half from the left-hand half by drawing it off the right-hand end of the crankshaft. On most engines, the cases will be a tight fit on the crankshaft and most manufacturers produce a service tool to facilitate this procedure. Alternatively, use the set-up shown, ensuring equal pressure is applied on both sides of the puller arrangement at all times **(see illustration).** If the puller is placed across the end of the crankshaft, thread the old alternator centre nut on first to protect the threads. **Note:** *If the crankcase halves do not separate easily, first ensure all fasteners have been removed. Apply steady pressure with the tools described and heat the bearing housings with a hot air gun. Do not try and separate the halves by levering against the mating surfaces as they are easily scored and will not seal correctly afterwards. Do not strike the ends of the crankshaft with a hammer as damage to the end threads or the shaft itself will result.*
7 Now press the crankshaft assembly out of the left-hand crankcase half – again, a service tool will be available. Alternatively, use the

19.10 Checking the main bearing on the crankshaft

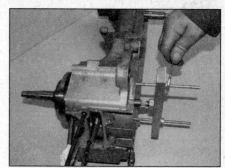

19.7 Pressing the crankshaft out of the left-hand crankcase half

set-up shown **(see illustration).** Thread the old variator nut onto the end of the crankshaft to protect the threads and make sure the crankshaft assembly is supported to prevent it dropping if it suddenly comes free.
8 Note the position of the crankshaft oil seals (if not already removed) and measure any inset before removing them **(see illustration).** Note which way round the seals are fitted. Lever the seals out carefully with a large, flat-bladed screwdriver and a piece of wood, taking care not to damage the crankcase. Discard the seals, as new ones must be fitted on reassembly.
9 Remove any dowels from either crankcase half for safekeeping if they are loose.
10 The main bearings will either remain in place in the crankcase halves during disassembly or come out with the crankshaft assembly **(see illustration).** If the main bearings have failed, excessive rumbling and vibration will be felt when the engine is running. Check the condition of the bearings (see *Tools and Workshop Tips* in the *Reference* section) and only remove them if they are unserviceable. Always renew both main bearings at the same time, never individually. Note that on some engines, plain (non-roller) main bearings are fitted in the crankcases. These bearings are generally not renewable, and if they are worn new crankcases will have to be fitted. Check the availability of new parts with a scooter dealer.
11 To remove the bearings from the cases, heat the bearing housings with a hot air gun and tap them out using a bearing driver or suitable socket **(see illustration).** Note which way round the bearings are fitted. If the

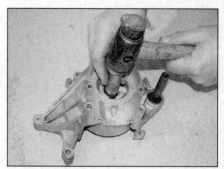

19.11 Driving a main bearing out of the crankcase

19.19a Installing the crankshaft assembly in the left-hand crankcase half

19.19b Check the location of the crankshaft bearing (arrowed)

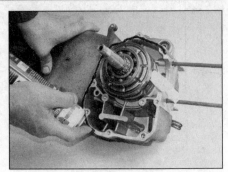

19.20 Apply sealant to the crankcase mating surface

bearings are stuck on the crankshaft, they must be removed with an external bearing puller to avoid damaging the crankshaft assembly. **Note:** *On some engines the main bearings are fitted in the crankcases prior to assembly, on others they are fitted to the crankshaft. Consult a scooter dealer for details before installing new bearings.*

12 If required, remove the transmission assembly from the left-hand crankcase half (see Chapter 6).

Inspection

13 Remove all traces of old sealant from the crankcase mating surfaces with a suitable solvent. Take care not to nick or gouge the soft aluminium. Wash the cases in a suitable solvent and dry them with compressed air.

14 The procedure for inspecting the crankcase halves and repairing minor damage is the same as for two-stroke engines (see Chapter 2A, Section 13).

15 Inspect the crankshaft assembly and bearings (see Section 20).

Reassembly

16 If the main bearings are to be fitted into the crankcase halves, heat the bearing housings with a hot air gun, then install them using a bearing driver or suitable socket which bears onto the outer race only.

17 If the main bearings are to be fitted onto the crankshaft, heat them first in an oil bath to around 100°C, then press them onto the shaft using a suitable length of tube that just fits over the shaft and bears onto the inner race

only. If the bearings are difficult to fit they are not hot enough.

⚠️ *Warning: This must be done very carefully to avoid the risk of personal injury.*

18 Fit the new crankshaft oil seals into the crankcase halves and drive them to the previously-measured inset using a seal driver or socket (see Step 8). Ensure the seals are fitted the right way round and that they enter the cases squarely.

19 Fit the crankshaft assembly into the left-hand crankcase half first, ensuring that the connecting rod is aligned with the crankcase mouth. Lubricate the shaft, seal and bearing with clean engine oil and tape some rag around the connecting rod to prevent it knocking against the cases. If the main bearing is in the crankcase half, pull the assembly into place either with a service tool or using the set-up shown **(see illustration)**. If the main bearing is on the crankshaft, heat the bearing housing in the crankcase with a hot air gun before fitting the crank assembly. **Note:** *Avoid applying direct heat onto the crankshaft oil seal.* If required, a freeze spray can be used on the bearing itself to aid installation. Ensure the bearing is installed fully into its housing **(see illustration)**.

20 If applicable, allow the case to cool, then wipe the mating surfaces of both crankcase halves with a rag soaked in a suitable solvent and fit the dowels. Apply a small amount of suitable sealant to the mating surface of the left-hand case **(see illustration)**.

21 Now fit the right-hand crankcase half.

Lubricate the shaft, seal and bearing with clean engine oil. If the main bearing is in the crankcase half, press the crankcase half into place, either with a service tool or with the set-up shown **(see illustration)**. If the main bearing is on the crankshaft, heat the bearing housing with a hot air gun before fitting the crankcase half and, if required, use a freeze spray on the bearing. **Note:** *Avoid applying direct heat onto the crankshaft oil seal.*

22 Check that the crankcase halves are seated all the way round **(see illustration)**. If the casings are not correctly seated, heat the bearing housings while applying firm pressure with the assembly tools used previously. **Note:** *Do not attempt to pull the crankcase halves together using the crankcase bolts as the casing will crack and be ruined.*

23 Clean the threads of the crankcase bolts and install them finger-tight, then tighten them evenly a little at a time in a criss-cross sequence to the torque setting specified in the *Data* section. Support the connecting rod and rotate the crankshaft by hand – if there are any signs of undue stiffness, tight or rough spots, or of any other problem, the fault must be rectified before proceeding further.

24 Where fitted, install the crankshaft nut (see Step 4). The nut should be tightened to a specific torque setting – check with a scooter dealer for details.

25 On engines where the crankshaft oil seals are fitted to the outside of the crankcases (see Step 5), lubricate the new seals with clean engine oil and install them in the cases.

26 Install the remaining components in the reverse order of removal.

20 Crankshaft assembly and big-end bearing

1 To access the crankshaft and the big-end bearing, the crankcase must be split into two parts (see Section 19).

2 The crankshaft assembly should give many thousands of miles of service. The most likely problems to occur will be a worn small or big-end bearing due to poor lubrication. A worn big-end bearing will produce a pronounced knocking noise, most audible when the engine

19.21 Installing the right-hand crankcase half

19.22 Ensure the crankcase halves are correctly seated

is under load, and increasing as engine speed rises. This should not be confused with small-end bearing wear, which produces a lighter, metallic rattle (see Section 14).

Inspection

3 To assess the condition of the big-end bearing, hold the crankshaft assembly firmly and push-and-pull on the connecting rod, checking for any up-and-down freeplay between the two **(see illustration)**. If any freeplay is noted, the bearing is worn and either the bearing or the crankshaft assembly will have to be renewed. **Note:** *A small amount of big-end side clearance (side-to-side movement) is acceptable on the connecting rod.* Consult a scooter dealer about the availability of parts. **Note:** *If a new bearing is available, fitting it is a specialist task which should be left to a scooter dealer or automotive engineer.*

4 Inspect the crankshaft where it passes through the main bearings for wear and scoring – if required, remove the bearings carefully with a bearing puller to avoid damaging the shaft **(see illustration)**. The shaft should be a press-fit in the bearings; if it is worn or damaged a new assembly will have to be fitted. Evidence of extreme heat, such as discoloration or blueing, indicates that lubrication failure has occurred. Be sure to check the oil pump and bearing oilways in the crankcases before reassembling the engine.

5 If available, place the crankshaft assembly on V-blocks and check the runout at the main bearing journals (B and C) and at either end (A and D) using a dial gauge **(see illustration)**. **Note:** *The main bearings will have to be removed for this check.* If the crankshaft is out-of-true it will cause excessive engine vibration. If there is any doubt about the condition of the crankshaft have it checked by a scooter dealer or automotive engineer. **Note:** *The crankshaft assembly is pressed together and is easily damaged if it is dropped.*

6 Inspect the threads on each end of the crankshaft and ensure that the retaining nuts for the alternator rotor and the variator are a good fit. Inspect the splines for the variator pulley on the left-hand end of the shaft. Inspect the taper and the slot in the right-hand end of the shaft for the alternator Woodruff key **(see illustration)**. Damage or wear that prevents the rotor from being fitted securely will require a new crankshaft assembly.

7 Where applicable, inspect the oil pump and/or the camshaft drive sprocket teeth on the crankshaft for damage or wear **(see illustration 20.6)**. If the sprocket is integral with the shaft, a new crankshaft assembly will have to be fitted. If the sprocket is a press-fit and needs to be renewed, measure its position from the end of the shaft, then pull it off with a bearing puller **(see illustration 20.4)**. Heat the new sprocket in an oil bath to around 100°C, then press it onto the shaft using a suitable length of tube that just fits over the shaft. Ensure that the sprocket is

20.3 Check for up-and-down play in the big-end bearing

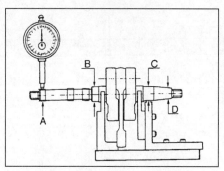

20.5 Support the crankshaft on V-blocks and check the runout at points A, B, C and D

20.4 Removing a main bearing using a bearing puller

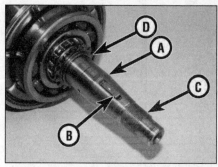

20.6 Inspect the crankshaft taper (A), location of the Woodruff key (B), thread (C) and sprocket teeth (D)

installed at the correct distance from the end of the shaft.

Reassembly

8 Follow the procedure in Section 19 to install the crankshaft assembly.

21 Initial start-up after overhaul

1 Make sure the engine oil level is correct (see *Daily (pre-ride) checks*).
2 On liquid-cooled models, make sure the coolant level is correct (see *Daily (pre-ride) checks*).
3 Make sure there is fuel in the tank.
4 With the ignition OFF, operate the kickstart a couple of times to check that the engine turns over easily.
5 Turn the ignition ON, start the engine and allow it to run at a slow idle until it reaches operating temperature. Do not be alarmed if there is a little smoke from the exhaust – this will be due to the oil used to lubricate the piston and bore during assembly and should subside after a while.
6 If the engine proves reluctant to start, remove the spark plug and check that it has not become wet and oily. If it has, clean it and try again. If the engine refuses to start, go through the fault finding charts at the end of this manual to identify the problem.
7 Check carefully for fuel and oil leaks and make sure the transmission and controls,

especially the brakes, function properly before road testing the machine. Refer to Section 22 for the recommended running-in procedure.
8 Upon completion of the road test, and after the engine has cooled down completely, recheck the valve clearances (see Chapter 1). Check the engine oil level and, on liquid-cooled models, check the coolant level (see *Daily (pre-ride) checks*).

22 Recommended running-in procedure

1 Treat the engine gently for the first few miles to allow any new parts to bed-in.
2 If a new piston, cylinder or crankshaft assembly has been fitted, the engine will have to be run-in as when new. This means a restraining hand on the throttle until at least 300 miles (500 km) have been covered. There's no point in keeping to any set speed limit – the main idea is to keep from labouring the engine and to gradually increase performance up to the 600 mile (1000 km) mark. Make sure that the throttle position is varied to vary engine speed, and use full throttle only for short bursts. Experience is the best guide, since it's easy to tell when an engine is running freely.
3 Pay particular attention to the *Daily (pre-ride) checks* at the beginning of this manual and investigate the cause of any oil or, on liquid-cooled models, coolant loss immediately. Check the tightness of all relevant nuts and bolts.

Chapter 3
Cooling system (liquid-cooled engines)

Contents

Degrees of difficulty

Easy, suitable for novice with little experience	**Fairly easy,** suitable for beginner with some experience	**Fairly difficult,** suitable for competent DIY mechanic	**Difficult,** suitable for experienced DIY mechanic	**Very difficult,** suitable for expert DIY or professional

Specifications

Refer to the *Data* section at the end of this manual for servicing specifications.

1 General information

The cooling system uses a water/antifreeze coolant to carry excess energy away from the engine in the form of heat. The coolant is contained within a water jacket inside the cylinder and cylinder head which is connected to the radiator and the water pump by the coolant hoses.

Coolant heated by the engine is circulated by thermo-syphonic action, and the action of the pump, to the radiator. It flows across the radiator core, where it is cooled by the passing air, then through the water pump and back to the engine where the cycle is repeated.

A thermostat is fitted in the cylinder head to prevent the coolant flowing to the radiator when the engine is cold, therefore accelerating the speed at which the engine reaches normal operating temperature. A coolant temperature sender mounted in the cylinder head is connected to the temperature gauge on the instrument panel.

 Warning: Do not remove the reservoir cap when the engine is hot. Scalding hot coolant and steam may be blown out under pressure, which could cause serious injury.

 Warning: Do not allow antifreeze to come in contact with your skin or painted or plastic surfaces of the scooter. Rinse off any spills immediately with plenty of water. Antifreeze is highly toxic if ingested. Never leave antifreeze lying around in an open container or in puddles on the floor; children and pets are attracted by its sweet smell and may drink it. Check with the local authorities about disposing of used antifreeze. Many communities will have collection centres which will see that antifreeze is disposed of safely. Antifreeze is also combustible, so don't store it near open flames.

Caution: At all times use the specified type of antifreeze, and always mix it with distilled water in the correct proportion. The antifreeze contains corrosion inhibitors which are essential to avoid damage to the cooling system. A lack of these inhibitors could lead to a build-up of corrosion which would block the coolant passages, resulting in overheating and severe engine damage. Distilled water must be used as opposed to tap water to avoid a build-up of scale which would also block the passages.

2 Draining, flushing and refilling

2.3a Drain the cooling system into a suitable container

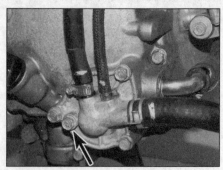

2.3b Water pump drain bolt (arrowed)

⚠ *Warning: Allow the engine to cool completely before performing this maintenance operation. Also, don't allow antifreeze to come into contact with your skin or the painted or plastic surfaces of the scooter. Rinse off spills immediately with plenty of water.*

Draining

1 Remove any body panels as necessary to access the hose connection either to the water pump or, if more easily accessible, the bottom of the radiator, and the coolant system filler cap (see Chapter 9). **Note:** *On some systems, the filler cap is on the radiator, on others it is on the coolant reservoir; refer to your scooter handbook for details.*

2 Remove the filler cap. If you hear a hissing sound as you unscrew it (indicating there is still pressure in the system), wait until it stops.

3 To drain the coolant, first loosen the clip securing the coolant hose either to the union on the water pump or the bottom of the radiator. Position a suitable container beneath the hose, then detach it and allow the coolant to drain from the system **(see illustration)**. Note that some water pumps are fitted with a drain bolt **(see illustration)**; if applicable, undo the bolt to drain the system without disturbing the coolant hoses. Retain the old sealing washer for use while flushing the system.

4 Where fitted, check that the coolant has drained from the coolant reservoir. If

necessary, detach the hose from the bottom of the reservoir and drain the coolant **(see illustration)**.

Flushing

5 Flush the system with clean tap water by inserting a garden hose in the filler neck. Allow the water to run through the system until it is clear and flows cleanly out of either the detached hose or the drain hole. If there is a lot of rust in the water, remove the radiator and have it professionally cleaned (see Section 8). If the drain hole appears to be clogged with sediment, remove the pump cover and clean the inside of the pump (see Section 9). If necessary, remove the coolant reservoir and rinse the inside with clean water, then refit it.

6 As applicable, attach the coolant hoses and secure them with the clips, and install the drain bolt using the old sealing washer.

7 Fill the system with clean water mixed with a flushing compound. **Note:** *Make sure the flushing compound is compatible with aluminium components and follow the manufacturer's instructions carefully.* If the system is fitted with a bleed valve, loosen the valve to release any trapped air, then tighten it securely **(see illustration)**. Alternatively, rock the scooter from side-to-side and bleed any trapped air out through the filler neck. Install the filler cap.

8 If necessary, fill the coolant reservoir separately with clean water.

9 Start the engine and allow it to reach normal operating temperature. Let it run for about five minutes.

10 Stop the engine. Let it cool for a while, then remove the filler cap (see Step 2) and drain the system (see Step 3).

11 Reconnect the coolant hoses and the drain bolt as applicable, then fill the system with clean water only and repeat the procedure in Steps 7 to 10. Where fitted, check that the water has drained from the coolant reservoir.

Refilling

12 Ensure all the hoses are correctly attached and secured with their clips. If applicable, fit a new sealing washer onto the drain bolt and tighten the bolt securely.

13 Fill the system with the proper coolant mixture (see the *Data* section at the end of this manual). **Note:** *Pour the coolant in slowly to minimise the amount of air entering the system.* Release any trapped air as described in Step 7. If necessary, top-up the coolant reservoir. Install the filler cap.

14 Start the engine and allow it to idle for 2 to 3 minutes. Flick the throttle twistgrip part open 3 or 4 times, so that the engine speed rises, then stop the engine. Release any trapped air (see Step 7) and check the system for leaks.

⚠ *Warning: Make sure that the machine is on its centre stand and that the rear wheel is off the ground before bleeding the cooling system. If necessary, place a support under the stand to prevent the rear wheel contacting the ground.*

15 Let the engine cool and check the coolant level (see *Daily (pre-ride) checks*), then install the body panels (see Chapter 9).

16 Do not dispose of the old coolant by pouring it down the drain. Pour it into a heavy plastic container, cap it tightly and take it into an authorised disposal site or garage – see **Warning** in Section 1.

3 Pressure cap

1 Where fitted, the pressure cap is designed to retain a specific working pressure within the cooling system and, in extreme cases, to

2.4 Detach the hose (arrowed) to drain the reservoir

2.7 Release any trapped air through the bleed valve (arrowed)

3.1 Some systems are fitted with a pressure cap

4.2 Temperature sender wiring connector

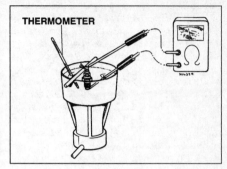

4.5 Set-up for testing the temperature gauge sender

release pressure before it becomes a danger **(see illustration)**.

2 If, after checking the cooling system (see Chapter 1), problems such as overheating or loss of coolant still occur, have the cap opening pressure checked by a scooter dealer with the special tester required for the job. If the cap is defective, renew it.

4 Temperature gauge and sender

Temperature gauge

Check

1 The circuit consists of the sender mounted in the cylinder head or thermostat housing and the gauge or warning light in the instrument panel. If the system malfunctions, first check the coolant level (see *Daily (pre-ride) checks*). If the level is correct, check that the battery is fully-charged and that the fuse is good (see Chapter 10). If a warning light is fitted, check the condition of the bulb.

2 If the gauge or warning light is still not working, disconnect the wire from the sender and connect it to earth (ground) with a jumper wire **(see illustration)**. Turn the ignition switch ON; the temperature gauge needle should swing over to the H on the gauge or the bulb should illuminate. If the gauge or warning light work as described, check the operation of the sender (see Steps 4 to 6). **Note:** *It is possible for a faulty gauge or light to register a reading in this check, but not when connected to the sender. Only renew the sender if it fails the checks described below.*

Caution: If the needle moves, turn the ignition OFF immediately to avoid damaging the gauge.

3 If the gauge or warning light is still not working, the fault lies in the wiring or the gauge itself. Check all the relevant wiring and wiring connectors; if all appears to be well, the gauge is defective and must be renewed. **Note:** *On some scooters the temperature gauge is an integral part of the instrument cluster and cannot be renewed as a separate item.*

Temperature gauge sender

Check

4 Disconnect the battery negative (-ve) lead, then disconnect the sender wiring connector **(see illustration 4.2)**. Using a multimeter or continuity tester, check for continuity between the sender body and earth (ground). There should be continuity. If there is no continuity, check that the sender mounting is secure, then recheck the operation of the gauge.

5 Remove the sender (see Steps 7 and 8 below). Fill a small heatproof container with coolant and place it on a stove. Using a multimeter set to the ohms scale, connect the positive (+ve) probe to the terminal on the sender and the negative (-ve) probe to the sender body. Using some wire or other support, suspend the sender in the coolant so that just the sensing portion and the threads are submerged **(see illustration)**. Also place a thermometer capable of reading temperatures up to approximately 120°C in the coolant so that its bulb is close to the sensor. **Note:** *None of the components should be allowed to directly touch the container.*

6 Check the resistance of the sender at approximately 20°C and keep the coolant temperature constant at 20°C for 3 minutes before continuing the test. Then increase the heat gradually, stirring the coolant gently. As the temperature of the coolant rises, the resistance of the sender should fall. Check that the correct resistance is obtained at the temperatures specified in the *Data* section at the end of this manual. If the meter readings obtained are different, or they are obtained at different temperatures, then the sender is faulty and must be renewed.

 Warning: This must be done very carefully to avoid the risk of personal injury.

Renewal

 Warning: The engine must be completely cool before carrying out this procedure.

7 Disconnect the battery negative (-ve) lead and drain the cooling system (see Section 2).

8 Disconnect the sender wiring connector **(see illustration 4.2)**. Unscrew the sender and remove it.

9 Apply a smear of a suitable non-permanent sealant to the threads of the new sender, then install it into the cylinder head or thermostat housing and tighten it securely. Connect the sender wiring.

10 Refill the cooling system (see Section 2) and reconnect the battery negative (-ve) lead.

5 Cooling fan and switch

Cooling fan

Note: *Where fitted, the cooling fan is located either on the front or the back of the radiator.*

Check

1 If the engine is overheating and the cooling fan isn't coming on, first check the cooling fan circuit fuse (see Chapter 10) and then the fan switch as described in Steps 8 and 9 below.

2 If the fan does not come on (and the fan switch is good), the fault lies in either the fan motor or the relevant wiring. Test all the wiring and connections as described in Chapter 10.

3 To test the fan motor, disconnect the fan wiring connector **(see illustration)**. Using a 12 volt battery and two jumper wires, connect the battery positive (+ve) lead to the positive wire terminal and the battery negative (-ve) lead to the earth (ground) wire terminal on the fan motor side of the connector. Once connected the fan should operate. If it does not, and the wiring is all good, then the fan motor is faulty and must be renewed

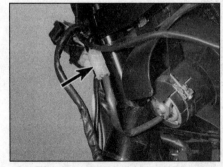

5.3 Disconnect the fan wiring connector (arrowed)

5.5 Fan assembly is mounted on the radiator

Renewal

Warning: The engine must be completely cool before carrying out this procedure.

4 Disconnect the battery negative (-ve) lead.
5 If required, remove the radiator (see Section 8). Ensure the wiring for the fan and the fan switch is free from any ties. Remove the screws securing the fan assembly to the radiator and lift it off, noting how it fits (see illustration).
6 Installation is the reverse of removal.

Cooling fan switch

Check

7 If the engine is overheating and the cooling fan isn't coming on, first check the cooling fan circuit fuse (see Chapter 10). If the fuse is blown, check the fan circuit for a short to earth.
8 If the fuse is good, disconnect the wiring

5.8 Disconnect the fan wiring connector (arrowed)

connectors from the fan switch on the radiator (see illustration). Using a jumper wire, connect the wiring connector terminals together. The fan should come on when the ignition is turned ON. If it does, the fan switch is confirmed faulty and must be renewed. If it does not come on, the fan motor should be tested (see Step 3).
9 If the fan motor is on all the time, even when the engine is cold, disconnect the switch wiring connectors and keep them apart. The fan should stop. If it does, the fan switch is defective and must be renewed. If it keeps running, check the wiring between the switch and the fan motor for a short to earth.

Renewal

Warning: The engine must be completely cool before carrying out this procedure.

10 Disconnect the battery negative (-ve)

lead. Drain the cooling system (see Section 2).
11 Disconnect the wiring connectors from the fan switch on the radiator. Unscrew the switch and withdraw it from the radiator. Discard the seal or O-ring as a new one must be used.
12 Apply a suitable sealant to the switch threads, then install the switch using a new seal and tighten it securely. Take care not to overtighten the switch as the radiator could be damaged.
13 Reconnect the switch wiring and refill the cooling system (see Section 2). Reconnect the battery (-ve) lead.

6 Thermostat

Warning: The engine must be completely cool before carrying out this procedure.

Removal

1 The thermostat is automatic in operation and should give many years service without requiring attention. In the event of a failure, the thermostat valve will probably jam open, in which case the engine will take much longer to reach its normal operating temperature, resulting in increased fuel consumption. If the valve jams shut, the coolant will be unable to circulate and the engine will overheat with the risk of seizure. In either case, if the thermostat is found to be faulty, a new unit should be fitted immediately.
2 Generally, the thermostat is located in a housing on the cylinder head or alongside the cylinder head (see illustrations). On some two-stroke engines, the thermostat is located inside the cylinder head (see illustration 6.4c). A visual check should identify the location of the thermostat.
3 Drain the cooling system (see Section 2). Loosen the clips securing any coolant hoses to the thermostat housing cover and detach the hoses. Where fitted, disconnect the temperature sender wiring connector.
4 Undo the bolts securing the thermostat housing cover, then lift out the thermostat, noting how it fits (see illustrations). Note the

6.2a Thermostat housing on cylinder head

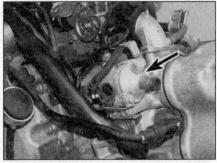

6.2b Separate thermostat housing assembly

6.4a Note how the thermostat fits . . .

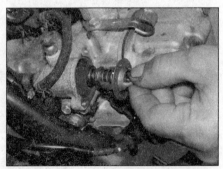

6.4b . . . before removing it

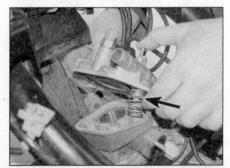

6.4c Remove the cylinder head with the thermostat assembly (arrowed) . . .

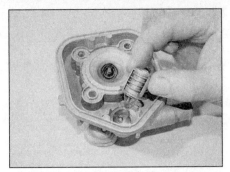

6.4d . . . then lift out the thermostat

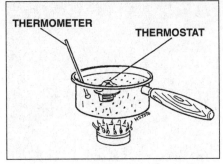

6.6 Set-up for testing the thermostat

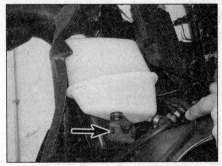

7.4 Note how the reservoir locates on its mounting (arrow)

position of any cover gasket or O-ring. If required, refer to Chapter 2A to remove the cylinder head, then lift out the thermostat (see illustrations). Note the position of any spring or O-ring.

5 Examine the thermostat visually before carrying out the test. If it remains in the open position at room temperature (20°C approximately), it should be renewed.

6 Fill a small, heatproof container with cold water and place it on a stove. Using a piece of wire, suspend the thermostat in the water (see illustration). Heat the water and see whether the thermostat opens. Opening temperatures vary between 70 and 80°C and the thermostat valve should open between 3 to 5 mm approximately. If the valve has not opened by the time the water starts to boil, the thermostat is faulty and must be renewed.

7 Where fitted, inspect the thermostat spring and renew it if it is corroded or damaged (see Step 4).

Installation

8 Installation is the reverse of removal, noting the following:

● Ensure any air bleed hole in the thermostat is at the top.
● Fit new gaskets and O-rings.
● Ensure the coolant hoses are secured with the clips.
● Refill the cooling system and bleed it (see Section 2).

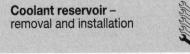

7 Coolant reservoir – removal and installation

 Warning: Ensure that the engine is cold before working on the coolant reservoir.

Removal

1 Generally, the coolant reservoir is located next to the radiator; remove any body panels as necessary to access the reservoir (see Chapter 9).

2 Remove the reservoir cap, then detach the hose from the bottom of the reservoir and drain the coolant into a suitable container (see Section 2).

3 Where fitted, detach the upper hose from the reservoir.

4 Undo the reservoir mounting bolts and lift it off; note any rubber bushes on the reservoir mounting (see illustration).

Installation

5 Installation is the reverse of removal, noting the following:

● Renew the reservoir mounting bushes if they are worn or damaged.
● Ensure the hose(s) are correctly installed and secured with their clips.
● Refill the reservoir with the proper coolant mixture (see Daily (pre-ride) checks).

8 Radiator – removal and installation

 Warning: Ensure that the engine is cold before working on the radiator.

Removal

1 Remove any body panels as necessary to access the radiator and the radiator hose connections (see Chapter 9).

2 Drain the cooling system (see Section 2).

3 Where fitted, disconnect the wiring from the cooling fan and the fan switch and release the wiring from any ties (see Section 5).

4 Loosen the clips securing the coolant hoses to the radiator and detach the hoses (see illustration).

 HAYNES HINT If a radiator hose is corroded in place on its union, cut the hose with a sharp knife then slit it lengthways and peel it off the union. Whilst this means renewing the hose, it is preferable to buying a new radiator.

Caution: The radiator unions are fragile. Do not use excessive force when attempting to remove the hoses.

5 Where fitted, loosen the clips securing the coolant reservoir hoses to the radiator and

detach the hoses; if necessary, remove the reservoir (see Section 7).

6 Undo the radiator mounting bolts and remove the radiator (see illustration 8.4). Note the position of any washers and rubber bushes.

7 Check the radiator for signs of damage and clear any dirt or debris that might obstruct air flow and inhibit cooling (see Chapter 1, Section 21).

Installation

8 Installation is the reverse of removal, noting the following:

● Renew the radiator mounting bushes if they are worn or damaged.
● Ensure the hoses are in good condition (see Chapter 1, Section 21).
● Ensure the hoses are correctly installed and secured with their clips.
● Refill the cooling system and bleed it (see Section 2).

9 Water pump – removal and installation

Note: A variety of pump designs are used; the pump may be mounted in the alternator cover, on the outside of the crankcase, inside the engine side cover, or in the crankcase. Trace the main coolant hoses to determine the location of the pump. On some two-stroke engines the pump can only be removed after the crankcase halves have been separated (see Chapter 2A).

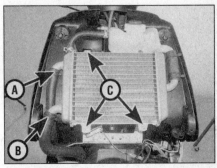

8.4 Radiator coolant hoses (A) and (B) and mounting bolts (C)

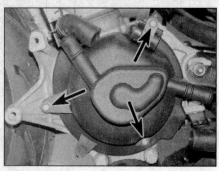

9.5a Undo the alternator cover mounting bolts

9.5b Water pump is driven by dampers on the alternator rotor . . .

9.5c . . . which engage in holes in the back of the pump

1 An internal seal prevents leakage of coolant from the pump; if the seal fails, coolant will either drain out of the bottom of the pump housing or the crankcase, depending on the location of the pump.

2 Leaks leave tell-tale scale deposits or coolant stains. Ensure the coolant is leaking from inside the pump and not from a hose connection or damaged hose. If the pump is leaking, a new seal must be fitted or the pump must be renewed. **Note:** *If a new internal seal is available, fitting it is a specialist task which should be left to a scooter dealer or automotive engineer.*

Mounted on alternator cover
Removal and installation

3 Drain the coolant and detach both the hoses from the pump (see Section 2).

4 Where fitted, undo the pump cover mounting screws and remove them. Remove the cover and discard the O-ring, as a new one must be used. **Note:** *On some scooters, the pump is integral with the alternator cover; if the pump seal or bearing fails a new cover must be fitted.*

5 Undo the alternator cover mounting bolts, noting the position of any hose guides secured by the bolts **(see illustration)**. Lift the cover away from the engine, noting how the pump drive dampers are attached to the alternator rotor and how the dampers locate into the back of the pump **(see illustrations)**.

6 If required, hold the alternator rotor to prevent it turning and unscrew the dampers. Renew the damper rubbers as a set if they are worn.

7 The pump impeller is a press-fit in the pump bearings. The remove the impeller, support the alternator cover upside down on the work surface with sufficient clearance below it to allow the impeller to be driven out. **Note:** *Take great care not to damage the sealing surface of the alternator cover. Use a soft drift (preferably aluminium or brass) to carefully drive the impeller out.*

8 Check the condition of the bearings in the alternator cover and renew them if necessary (see *Tools and Workshop Tips* in the *Reference* section). **Note:** *It may be necessary to remove the pump seals before the bearings can be removed; if available, have new seals and bearings fitted by a scooter dealer or automotive engineer.*

9 Installation is the reverse of removal, noting the following:
- *Make sure the drive dampers fit correctly into the back of the pump.*
- *Ensure the coolant hoses are pushed fully onto the pump unions and secured with the clips.*
- *Refill the cooling system and bleed it (see Section 2).*

Mounted on engine side cover
Removal and installation

10 Drain the coolant and, if required, detach the hoses, including the carburettor heater hose, from the pump **(see illustration)**.

11 Undo the pump cover bolts and lift off the cover **(see illustration)**. Discard the cover O-ring as a new one must be fitted. Clean any sediment out of the cover.

12 Hold the pump impeller with pipe grips to prevent it turning, then undo the impeller nut **(see illustrations)**.

⚠ *Warning: The impeller nut may have a left-hand thread (undoes clockwise). Check before you undo the nut to avoid damaging the thread.*

13 On four-stroke engines, drain the engine oil (see Chapter 1).

14 Trace any wiring from the engine side cover and disconnect it at the connector, then undo the cover bolts and lift it off. Note how the pump shaft locates in the drive from the oil

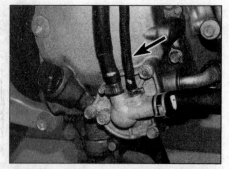

9.10 Side cover mounted pump – note the carburettor heater hose (arrowed)

9.11 Lift off the pump cover

9.12a Hold the pump impeller with grips . . .

9.12b . . . then undo the impeller centre nut (arrowed)

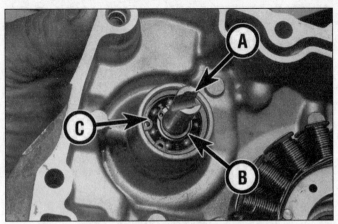

9.14 Oil pump shaft locates in slot (A). Note the water pump shaft circlip (B) and bearing circlip (C)

9.21 Discard the pump body O-ring (arrowed)

pump **(see illustration)**. Discard the engine cover gasket, as a new one must be fitted, and remove the cover dowels for safekeeping if they are loose.

15 The pump shaft and bearing are secured in the engine cover by circlips **(see illustration 9.14)**. Use circlip pliers to remove them, then pull out the shaft and bearing.

16 Check the condition of the bearing and renew it if necessary (see *Tools and Workshop Tips* in the *Reference* section).

17 The pump seal and an oil seal are located in the engine cover – have then both renewed by a scooter dealer or automotive engineer.

18 Installation is the reverse of removal, noting the following:
● Where removed, fit new circlips.
● Fit a new engine side cover gasket.
● Ensure the pump shaft locates correctly in the drive from the oil pump.
● Fit a new pump cover O-ring.
● Ensure the coolant hoses are pushed fully onto the pump unions and secured with the clips.
● Refill the cooling system and bleed it (see Section 2).
● If applicable, fill the engine with the correct type and quantity of oil (see Chapter 1).

Mounted on external crankcase

Removal and installation

19 Drain the coolant and detach the hose(s) from the pump (see Section 2).

20 On four-stroke engines, drain the engine oil (see Chapter 1).

21 Undo the pump mounting bolts and withdraw the pump from the crankcase. Note how the pump shaft locates in the drive from the oil pump. Discard the pump body O-ring as a new one must be fitted **(see illustration)**.

22 Undo the pump cover screws and remove the cover. Discard the cover O-ring, as a new one must be fitted **(see illustration)**. Clean any sediment out of the cover.

23 The pump shaft is secured by a circlip; ease the circlip off with a small screwdriver, then pull the shaft and impeller out of the

pump body, noting any sealing ring fitted behind the impeller **(see illustration)**. The impeller is integral with the shaft.

24 The pump seal and an oil seal are located in the pump body – have then both renewed by a scooter dealer or automotive engineer. Check the condition of the pump bearing and, if necessary, have it renewed at the same time.

25 Installation is the reverse of removal, noting the following:
● Fit a new sealing ring behind the pump impeller.
● Fit a new circlip to the pump shaft.
● Fit new O-rings to the pump body and pump cover.
● Ensure the pump shaft locates correctly in the drive from the oil pump.
● Ensure the coolant hoses are pushed fully onto the pump unions and secured with the clips.
● Refill the cooling system and bleed it (see Section 2).
● If applicable, fill the engine with the correct type and quantity of oil (see Chapter 1).

Mounted on internal crankcase

Removal and installation

26 On this type of water pump the seal is installed directly into the crankcase, so unless the engine has been removed from the frame

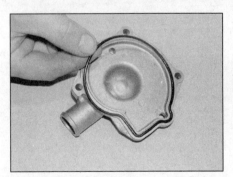

9.22 Remove the pump cover and O-ring

as part of an overhaul, it may be practical to have the entire procedure undertaken by a scooter dealer.

27 Before the seal can be renewed, the following components have to be removed:
● Alternator rotor (see Chapter 2A or 2B).
● If applicable, the oil pump.
● Water pump cover.

28 The pump shaft is driven by a belt from the crankshaft; the crankshaft pulley is located behind the alternator. To remove the pump shaft, first hold the pump shaft pulley to prevent it turning, then undo the pump rotor nut and pull off the rotor. Withdraw the pump shaft, together with the pulley and belt, from the crankcase.

29 The pump drive pulley is retained by a circlip or ring nut (see Chapter 2A, Section 12).

30 Check the condition of the pump bearing and renew it if necessary.

10 Coolant hoses –
   removal and installation

Removal

1 Before removing a hose, drain the coolant (see Section 2).

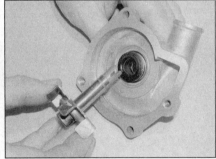

9.23 Pull the impeller out of the pump body

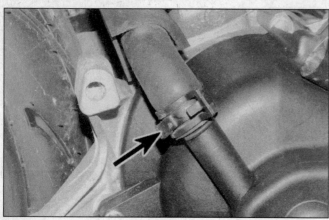

10.2a Loosen the hose clip (arrowed) and slide it back along the hose . . .

10.2b . . . then pull the hose off the union (arrowed)

10.5 Work the hose on all the way to the index mark

2 Loosen the hose clip, then slide it back along the hose clear of the union. Pull the hose off its union **(see illustrations)**.

3 If a hose proves stubborn, release it by rotating it on its union before working it off. If all else fails, slit the hose with a sharp knife at the union (see *Haynes Hint* in Section 8).
Caution: The radiator unions are fragile. Do not use excessive force when attempting to remove the hoses.

4 Check the condition of the hose clips; if they are corroded or have lost their tension, renew them.

Installation

5 Slide the clips onto the hose first, then work the hose all the way onto its union up to the index mark **(see illustration)**.

 HAYNES HiNT *Haynes Hint: If the hose is difficult to push on its union, it can be softened by soaking it in very hot water, or alternatively a little soapy water can be used as a lubricant.*

6 Rotate the hose on its unions to settle it in position before sliding the clips into place and tightening them securely.

7 Refill the cooling system and bleed it correctly (see Section 2).

Chapter 4
Fuel and exhaust systems

Contents

Degrees of difficulty

Easy, suitable for novice with little experience	**Fairly easy,** suitable for beginner with some experience	**Fairly difficult,** suitable for competent DIY mechanic	**Difficult,** suitable for experienced DIY mechanic	**Very difficult,** suitable for expert DIY or professional

Specifications

Refer to the *Data* section at the end of this manual for servicing specifications.

1 General information and precautions

The fuel system consists of the fuel tank, fuel tap with filter, carburettor, fuel hoses and control cables. On some scooters, either due to the position of the fuel tank or the use of a fuel header tank in the system, a fuel pump is fitted.

The fuel tap is automatic in operation and is opened by engine vacuum. Generally, the fuel filter is fitted inside the fuel tank and is part of the tap. On some models, an additional fuel filter is fitted in the fuel line.

For cold starting, an electrically-operated automatic choke is fitted in the carburettor. Some models also have an electrically-operated carburettor heater.

Air is drawn into the carburettors via an air filter which is housed above the transmission casing. **Note:** *On two-stroke engines, lubricating oil is mixed with the fuel in the intake manifold. See Chapter 2A for details of the oil pump.*

Several fuel system service procedures are considered routine maintenance items and for that reason are included in Chapter 1.

Precautions

 Warning: Petrol is extremely flammable, so take extra precautions when you work on any part of the fuel system. Don't smoke or allow open flames or bare light bulbs near the work area, and don't work in a garage where a natural gas-type appliance is present. If you spill any fuel on your skin, rinse it off immediately with soap and water. When you perform any kind of work on the fuel system, wear safety glasses and have a fire extinguisher suitable for a class B type fire (flammable liquids) on hand.

2.2a Detach the fuel hose from the carburettor . . .

2.2b . . . and the vacuum hose from the manifold . . .

2.2c . . . or the carburettor

- *Always perform service procedures in a well-ventilated area to prevent a build-up of fumes.*
- *Never work in a building containing a gas appliance with a pilot light, or any other form of naked flame. Ensure that there are no naked light bulbs or any sources of flame or sparks nearby.*
- *Do not smoke (or allow anyone else to smoke) while in the vicinity of petrol or of components containing it. Remember the possible presence of vapour from these sources and move well clear before smoking.*
- *Check all electrical equipment belonging to the house, garage or workshop where work is being undertaken (see the Safety first! section of this manual). Remember that certain electrical appliances such as drills, cutters, etc, create sparks in the normal course of operation and must not be used near petrol or any component containing it. Again, remember the possible presence of fumes before using electrical equipment.*
- *Always mop up any spilt fuel and safely dispose of the rag used.*
- *Any stored fuel that is drained off during servicing work must be kept in sealed containers that are suitable for holding petrol, and clearly marked as such; the containers themselves should be kept in a safe place.*

- *Read the Safety first! section of this manual carefully before starting work.*

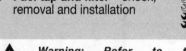

2 Fuel tap and filter – check, removal and installation

⚠ **Warning: Refer to the precautions given in Section 1 before starting work.**

Fuel tap

Note: *Some scooters do not have a separate fuel tap – instead the tap function is controlled by the fuel pump, which will only allow fuel to flow when the engine is turning over. See Section 13 for fuel pump check and renewal. On these machines, the fuel filter is fitted to the fuel supply hose (see Steps 10 to 14).*

Check

1 Where fitted, the fuel tap is located on the underside of the fuel tank. Remove any body panels as required for access (see Chapter 9). The tap is automatic, operated by a vacuum created when the engine is running which opens a diaphragm inside the tap. If the tap is faulty, it must be renewed – it is a sealed unit for which no individual components are available. The most likely problem is a hole or split in the tap diaphragm.

2 To check the tap, detach the fuel hose from the carburettor and place the open end in a small container **(see illustration)**. Detach the vacuum hose from the inlet manifold or carburettor, according to model **(see illustrations)**, and apply a vacuum to it (suck on the hose end) – if you are not sure which hose is which on your model, trace the hoses from the tap. Fuel should flow from the tap and into the container **(see illustration)** – if it doesn't, the diaphragm is probably split.

3 Before renewing the tap, check that the vacuum hose is securely attached, and that there are no splits or cracks in the hose. If in doubt, attach a spare hose to the vacuum union on the tap and again apply a vacuum. If fuel still does not flow, remove the tap and fit a new one.

Removal

4 The tap should not be removed unnecessarily from the tank otherwise the O-ring or filter may be damaged.

5 Before removing the tap, connect a drain hose to the fuel hose union and insert its end in a container suitable and large enough for storing the petrol. Detach the vacuum hose from the inlet manifold and apply a vacuum to it, to allow the tank to drain.

6 Loosen the clamp securing the tap and withdraw the tap assembly **(see illustration)**.

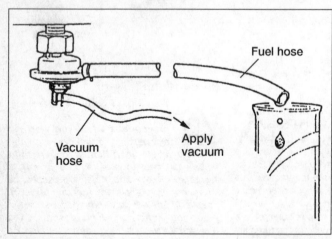

2.2d Place the fuel hose in a container and apply suction to the vacuum hose

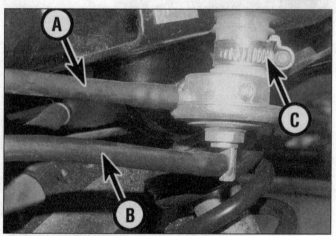

2.6 Fuel hose (A), vacuum hose (B) and retaining clip (C)

2.11 Check the condition of the in-line fuel filter

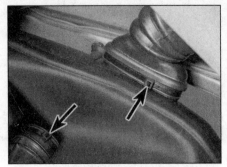

3.1a Release the ties securing the air ducts . . .

3.1b . . . and clips securing the hoses

Check the condition of the O-ring. If it is in good condition it can be re-used, though it is better to use a new one. If it is in any way deteriorated or damaged it must be renewed.
7 Clean the gauze filter to remove all traces of dirt and fuel sediment. Check the gauze for holes. If any are found, a new tap should be fitted as the filter is not available individually.

Installation

8 Install the fuel tap into the tank, preferably using a new O-ring, and tighten the clamp securely.
9 Fit the fuel and vacuum hoses onto their respective unions and secure them with their clips.

In-line filter

10 Remove any body panels as required for access (see Chapter 9).
11 Check the filter for signs of sediment or a clogged element **(see illustration)**.
12 To remove the filter, first clamp the fuel hoses to prevent leaks, then loosen the clips securing the fuel hoses to each end of the filter and detach the hoses. If the filter is fitted in a bracket, note which way up it fits.
13 The filter is a sealed unit. If it is dirty or clogged, fit a new one.
14 Installation is the reverse of removal, making sure the filter is the correct way up – there should be an arrow marked on the body indicating direction of fuel flow. Renew the clips on the fuel hoses if the old ones are

sprained or corroded. Remember to remove the clamps from the fuel hoses.

3 Air filter housing – removal and installation

Removal

1 Where applicable, remove the body panels to access the filter housing, which is located above the drivebelt cover on the left-hand side of the scooter. Release the clips or cut the plastic ties securing the air inlet and outlet ducts and, where fitted, the breather hose, and detach them from the housing **(see illustrations)**.
2 Where fitted, release the idle speed adjuster from its clip on the front of the housing.
3 Where fitted, release the air temperature sensor hose from the housing **(see illustration)**
4 Remove the bolts securing the air filter housing to the engine unit and manoeuvre the housing away, noting how it fits **(see illustrations)**.

Installation

5 Installation is the reverse of removal. Use new plastic cable ties to secure the air inlet and outlet ducts where the originals were cut free.

4 Idle fuel/air mixture adjustment – general information

Warning: Adjustment of the pilot screw is made with the engine running. To prevent accidents caused by the rear wheel contacting the ground, ensure that the scooter is on its centre stand and if necessary place a support under the scooter to prevent the rear wheel contacting the ground.

1 Idle fuel/air mixture is set using the pilot screw **(see illustration 8.1 or 9.1)**. Adjustment of the pilot screw is not normally necessary and should only be performed if the engine is running roughly, stalls continually, or if a new pilot screw has been fitted.
2 If the pilot screw is removed during a carburettor overhaul, record its current setting by turning the screw it in until it seats lightly, counting the number of turns necessary to achieve this, then unscrew it fully. On installation, turn the screw in until it seats lightly, then back it out the number of turns you've recorded. If fitting a new pilot screw, turn the screw in until it seats, then back it out the number of turns specified in the *Data* section at the end of this manual.
3 Pilot screw adjustment must be made with the engine running and at normal working

3.3 Detach the hose for the air temperature sensor (arrowed)

3.4a Undo the fixings . . .

3.4b . . . for the air filter housing

5.2a Automatic choke unit (arrowed) on
slide type carburettor . . .

5.2b . . . and on CV type carburettor

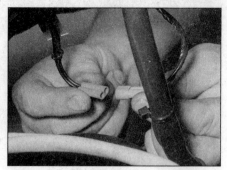

5.2c Disconnect the choke wiring at the
connector

temperature. Stop the engine and screw the pilot screw in until it seats lightly, then back it out the number of turns specified in the *Data* section. Start the engine and set the idle speed to the specified amount (see Chapter 1).

4 Now try turning the pilot screw inwards by no more than a small amount, noting its effect on the idle speed, then repeat the process, this time turning the screw outwards.

5 The pilot screw should be set in the position which gives the most consistent, even idle speed without the automatic transmission engaging, and so that the engine does not stall when the twistgrip is opened. **Note:** *It will not be possible to achieve an even idle speed if the spark plug needs adjustment or if the air filter element is dirty. On four-stroke engines ensure the valve clearances are correctly set.*

6 Once a satisfactory pilot screw setting has been achieved, further adjustments to the idle speed can be made with the idle speed adjuster screw (see Chapter 1).

7 If it is not possible to achieve a satisfactory idle speed after adjusting the pilot screw, take the machine to a scooter dealer and have the fuel/air mixture adjusted with the aid of an exhaust gas analyser.

possible signs that the automatic choke is not working properly.

2 The resistance of the choke should be checked with a multimeter after the engine has been warmed to normal operating temperature and then allowed to cool for ten minutes. Remove the engine access panel (see Chapter 9) and trace the wiring from the automatic choke unit on the carburettor and disconnect it at the connectors **(see illustrations)**.

3 Measure the resistance between the terminals on the choke unit side of the connector with the multimeter set to the ohms scale. If the result is not as specified in the *Data* section at the end of this manual, renew the choke unit (see Section 8 or Section 9).

4 To check that the plunger is not seized in the choke body, first remove the choke unit from the carburettor (see Section 8 or Section 9). Measure the protrusion of the plunger from the body **(see illustration)**. Next, use jumper wires to connect a good 12V battery to the choke unit terminals and measure the protrusion again after 5 minutes. If the measurement has not increased by approximately 3 to 6 mm (depending on the type of carburettor) the unit is faulty and should be renewed.

that carburettor maintenance may be required.

2 Keep in mind that many so-called carburettor problems can often be traced to mechanical faults within the engine or ignition system malfunctions. Try to establish for certain that the carburettor is in need of maintenance before beginning a major overhaul.

3 Check the fuel tap and filter, the fuel and vacuum hoses, the fuel pump (where fitted), the intake manifold joints, the air filter, the ignition system and the spark plug before assuming that a carburettor overhaul is required.

4 Most carburettor problems are caused by dirt particles, varnish and other deposits which build up in and eventually block the fuel jets and air passages inside the carburettor. Also, in time, gaskets and O-rings deteriorate and cause fuel and air leaks which lead to poor performance.

5 When overhauling the carburettor, disassemble it completely and clean the parts thoroughly with a carburettor cleaning solvent. If available, blow through the fuel jets and air passages with compressed air to ensure they are clear. Once the cleaning process is complete, reassemble the carburettor using new gaskets and O-rings.

6 Before disassembling the carburettor, make sure you have the correct carburettor gasket set, some carburettor cleaner, a supply of clean rags, some means of blowing out the carburettor passages and a clean place to work.

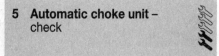

5 Automatic choke unit – check

1 Poor starting or poor engine performance and an increase in fuel consumption are

6 Carburettor overhaul – general information

1 Poor engine performance, difficult starting, stalling, flooding and backfiring are all signs

7 Carburettor – removal and installation

  Warning: *Refer to the precautions given in Section 1 before starting work.*

Removal

1 Remove the body panels as required on your scooter to access the carburettor (see Chapter 9). Where fitted, remove the carburettor cover, noting how it fits **(see illustration)**.

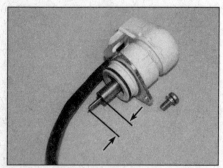

5.4 Measure the protrusion of the plunger
from the body

7.1 Remove the cover (arrowed) noting
how it fits

7.2 Release the clip (arrowed) and detach the air duct

7.3 Disconnect the carburettor heater hoses (arrowed)

7.4a Remove the screw . . .

2 Remove the air filter housing (see Section 3). Where fitted, release the clip or cut the tie securing the air intake duct and detach it from the carburettor **(see illustration)**.

3 Trace the wiring from the automatic choke unit and disconnect it at the connector. Where fitted, trace the wiring from the carburettor heater and disconnect it at the connector. Free the wiring from any clips or ties. Where fitted on liquid-cooled engines, undo the bolt securing the heater union to the carburettor or disconnect the heater hoses **(see illustration)**.

4 If the throttle cable is attached to a slide inside the carburettor (see Section 8), undo the carburettor top cover, then lift off the cover and withdraw the throttle slide assembly **(see illustrations)**. Secure the cable where the slide assembly will not be damaged. To detach the slide assembly from the cable, see Section 8.

5 If the throttle cable is attached to a pulley on the outside of the carburettor, first detach the outer cable from its bracket, then detach the cable end from the pulley **(see illustration)**.

6 If the idle speed adjuster is mounted adjacent to the carburettor, release the

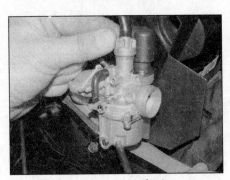

7.4b . . . or unscrew the top . . .

adjuster from its clip and feed it through to the carburettor.

7 Release the clips securing the fuel hose and vacuum hose, and oil hose on two-stroke engines, noting which fits where (see Section 2). Be prepared to catch any residue fuel in a suitable container. The fuel and oil hoses should be clamped to prevent leaks using any of the methods shown (see *Tools and Workshop Tips* in the *Reference* section). Where fitted, the breather and drain hoses can usually be left attached and withdrawn with the carburettor, as their lower ends are not secured. Note their routing as they are withdrawn. **Note:** *If the vacuum and oil hoses*

7.4c . . . then withdraw the throttle slide assembly

are connected to the intake manifold they can be left attached if the carburettor is being removed without it.

8 Loosen the drain screw and drain all the fuel from the carburettor into a suitable container **(see illustration)**. Discard the drain screw O-ring, as a new one must be used. On installation, fit the new O-ring and tighten the drain screw securely. **Note:** *If a cleaning solvent is going to be used, fit the new O-ring after the cleaning process.*

9 Either loosen the clamp or undo the bolts securing the carburettor to the inlet manifold on the engine and remove the carburettor, or undo the bolts securing the manifold to the

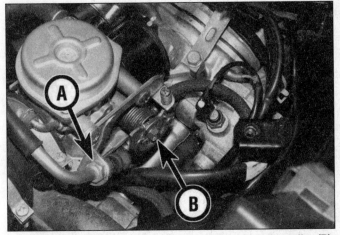

7.5 Detach the cable from the bracket (A) and then the pulley (B)

7.8 Carburettor drain screw (arrowed)

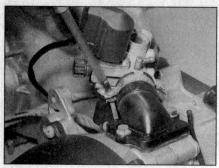

7.9a Loosen the carburettor clamp . . .

7.9b . . . undo the carburettor bolts . . .

7.9c . . . or remove the manifold bolts

engine and remove it and the carburettor together **(see illustrations)**. Discard the manifold gasket or O-ring and fit a new one on reassembly.
Caution: Stuff clean rag into the intake after removing the carburettor to prevent anything from falling inside.

Installation

10 Installation is the reverse of removal, noting the following:
● *Make sure the carburettor is fully engaged with the intake manifold and the clamp is securely tightened.*
● *Make sure all hoses are correctly routed and secured and not trapped or kinked.*
● *Check the throttle cable adjustment (see Chapter 1).*
● *On liquid-cooled models, top-up the cooling system if necessary.*
● *Check the idle speed and adjust as necessary (see Chapter 1).*

8 Slide carburettor – overhaul

Warning: Refer to the precautions given in Section 1 before starting work.

Note: *Carburettor design differs for two-stroke and four-stroke engines. Two-stroke engines use a slide type carburettor, whereas four-stroke engines generally use a constant-vacuum (CV) type – refer to the specifications in the Data section at the end of this manual to ensure that you follow the correct procedure either in this Section or Section 9.*

Disassembly

1 Remove the carburettor (see Section 7). Take care when removing components to note their exact locations and any springs or O-rings that may be fitted **(see illustration)**.
2 Where fitted, remove the cover on the automatic choke unit, then remove the clamp securing the unit in the carburettor **(see illustrations)**. Withdraw the choke unit, noting how it fits **(see illustration)**.

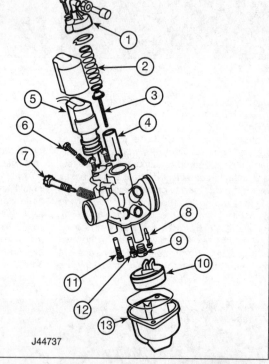

8.1 Slide-type carburettor components

1 Top cover
2 Slide spring
3 Needle
4 Slide
5 Automatic choke unit
6 Pilot screw
7 Idle speed adjuster screw
8 Float needle valve
9 Main jet
10 Float
11 Starter jet
12 Pilot jet
13 Float chamber

J44737

8.2a Remove the choke unit cover . . .

8.2b . . . then undo the clamp screws (arrowed) . . .

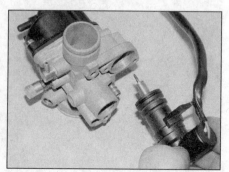

8.2c . . . and pull out the choke unit

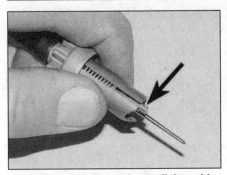

8.3a Compress the spring until the cable end (arrowed) is free . . .

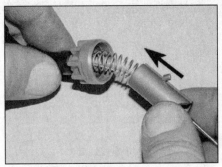

8.3b . . . then slot it up through the slide . . .

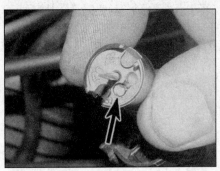

8.3c . . . or through the hole (arrowed) in the bottom of the slide

3 To remove the throttle slide assembly from the cable if the top cover and slide assembly have already been removed from the carburettor, first compress the slide spring. Either slot the cable end up through the side of the slide and detach the slide, or slot the cable end out of its recess and through the hole in the bottom of the slide **(see illustrations)**.

4 On some carburettors, the needle is retained by a spring clip – remove the clip, noting how it fits **(see illustration)**. Lift the needle out of the slide.

5 Remove the spring and, where fitted, the spring seat from the cable, then pull the carburettor top cover off the cable **(see illustrations)**.

6 If the carburettor top cover is still in place, unscrew the cover retaining screws, then lift off the cover and withdraw the slide assembly (see Section 7). Unhook the spring retaining the slide assembly, then twist the needle holder and withdraw it from the slide.

7 Undo the screws securing the float chamber to the base of the carburettor and remove it – discard the gasket, as a new one must be used **(see illustrations)**.

8 Using a pair of thin-nose pliers, carefully withdraw the float pin **(see illustration)**. Note: *The float pin may be retained by a small screw.* If necessary, displace the pin using a small punch or a nail. Remove the float and

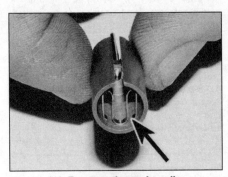

8.4 Remove the spring clip, where fitted

8.5a Remove the spring seat (arrowed) . . .

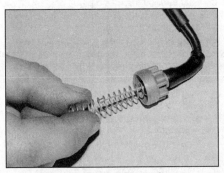

8.5b . . . then pull the spring . . .

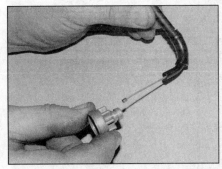

8.5c . . . and carburettor top cover off the cable

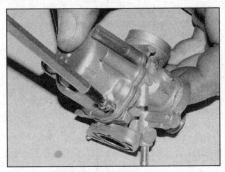

8.7a Undo the float chamber screws

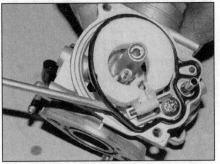

8.7b Lift out the float chamber gasket

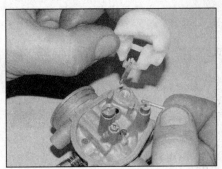

8.8a Remove the float pin and lift out the float

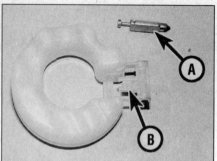

8.8b Note how the float needle valve (A) fits onto the tab (B)

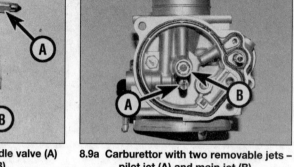

8.9a Carburettor with two removable jets – pilot jet (A) and main jet (B)

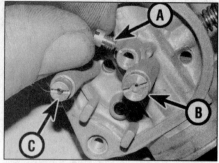

8.9b Carburettor with three removable jets – pilot jet (A), main jet (B) and starter jet (C)

unhook the float needle valve, noting how it fits onto the tab on the float (see illustration).
9 Some carburettors are fitted with two removable jets (pilot jet and main jet), some have three removable jets (pilot jet, main jet and starter jet) (see illustrations). Note the location of the jets, then unscrew them. The main jet screws into the base of the atomiser; if the atomiser is slotted, unscrew it if required. Note: The jets will be marked with an identification number or code; check the jets against the specifications in the Data section at the end of this manual.
10 The pilot screw can be removed if required, but note that its setting will be disturbed (see Haynes Hint). Unscrew and remove the pilot screw along with its spring and O-ring, where fitted.

HAYNES HINT
To record the pilot screw's current setting, turn the screw in until it seats lightly, counting the number of turns necessary to achieve this, then unscrew it fully. On installation, turn the screw in until it seats, then back it out the number of turns you've recorded.

Cleaning

Caution: Use only a petroleum-based solvent for carburettor cleaning. Don't use caustic cleaners.
11 Use carburettor cleaning solvent to loosen and dissolve the varnish and other deposits on the carburettor body and float chamber; use a nylon-bristled brush to remove the stubborn deposits. Dry the components with compressed air. Note: Avoid soaking the carburettor body in solvent if any O-ring seals remain inside.
12 If available, use compressed air to blow out all the fuel jets and the air passages in the carburettor body, not forgetting the passages in the carburettor intake.
Caution: Never clean the jets or passages with a piece of wire or a drill bit, as they will be enlarged, causing the fuel and air metering rates to be upset.

Inspection

13 If removed, check the tapered portion of the pilot screw and the spring for wear or

damage. Fit a new O-ring and renew the screw or spring if necessary.
14 Check the carburettor body, float chamber and top cover for cracks, distorted sealing surfaces and other damage. If any defects are found, renew the faulty component, although a new carburettor will probably be necessary.
15 Insert the throttle slide in the carburettor body and check that it moves up-and-down smoothly. Check the surface of the slide for wear. If it's worn or scored excessively or doesn't move smoothly, renew the components as necessary.
16 Where fitted, check that the clip is correctly positioned on the needle (see Data section). If necessary, remove the clip and check the needle for straightness by rolling it on a flat surface such as a piece of glass. Fit a new needle if it's bent or if the tip is worn. Refit the clip for safekeeping.
17 Inspect the tip of the float needle valve. If it has grooves or scratches in it, or is in any way worn, it must be renewed. If the valve seat is damaged, check the availability of new parts, otherwise a new carburettor body will have to be fitted. Note: On scooters with a pumped and pressurised fuel system, a worn or incorrectly-sized carburettor float needle valve seat will not be able to shut off the fuel supply sufficiently to prevent carburettor flooding and excessive use of fuel.
18 Check the float for damage. This will usually be apparent by the presence of fuel inside the float. If the float is damaged, it must be renewed.
19 Inspect the automatic choke unit plunger and needle for signs of wear and renew the unit if necessary (see illustration 5.4). To check the operation of the choke unit see Section 5.

Reassembly

Note: When reassembling the carburettor, be sure to use new O-rings and gaskets. Do not overtighten the carburettor jets and screws as they are easily damaged.
20 If removed, install the pilot screw, spring and O-ring; adjust the screw to the setting as noted on removal (see Step 10).
21 If removed, install the atomiser. Screw the main jet into the end of the atomiser.

22 Install the pilot jet and, if applicable, the starter jet.
23 Hook the float needle valve onto the float tab, then position the float assembly in the carburettor, making sure the needle valve enters its seat. Install the float pin, making sure it is secure. If necessary, the carburettor float height should be checked at this point (see Section 10).
24 Fit a new gasket onto the float chamber, making sure it is seated properly in its groove, then install the chamber onto the carburettor and tighten the screws securely. If necessary, the carburettor fuel height should be checked at this point (see Section 10).
25 Install the choke unit and secure it with the clamp and screws. Install the choke unit cover, if fitted.
26 If the carburettor top cover was removed as described in Step 6, install the needle holder in the slide and twist the holder to lock it in place. Secure the slide assembly to the cover with the spring, then install the slide assembly and the cover and tighten the cover screws securely.
27 Install the carburettor (see Section 7).
28 If applicable, install the needle in the throttle slide (see Step 4). Reverse the procedure in Steps 3 and 5 to install the throttle slide assembly onto the cable, then fit the carburettor top cover.

9 Constant-vacuum (CV) carburettor – overhaul

⚠ Warning: Refer to the precautions given in Section 1 before proceeding.
Note: Carburettor design differs for two-stroke and four-stroke engines. Two-stroke engines use a slide type carburettor, whereas four-stroke engines generally use a constant-vacuum (CV) type – refer to the specifications in the Data section at the end of this manual to ensure that you follow the correct procedure either in this Section or Section 8.

Disassembly

1 Remove the carburettor (see Section 7). Take care when removing components

to note their exact locations and any springs or O-rings that may be fitted **(see illustration)**.

2 Where fitted, remove the cover on the automatic choke unit, then remove the clamp securing the choke in the carburettor. Withdraw the choke, noting how it fits **(see illustration)**. On some carburettors, it is possible to undo the screws securing the choke unit mounting and remove it. Discard the gasket, as a new one must be fitted. If required, undo the screw securing the accelerator pump lever and remove the lever and return spring.

3 Unscrew and remove the top cover retaining screws, then lift off the cover and remove the spring from inside the piston **(see illustrations)**. Carefully peel the diaphragm away from its sealing groove in the carburettor and withdraw the diaphragm and piston assembly **(see illustration)**. Note how the tab on the diaphragm fits in the recess in the carburettor body.

Caution: Do not use a sharp instrument to displace the diaphragm as it is easily damaged.

4 On some carburettors it is necessary to unscrew the needle retainer, otherwise lift out the needle retainer, noting any spring or washer fitted underneath, then push the needle up from the bottom of the piston and withdraw it from the top **(see illustrations)**.

5 Remove the screws securing the float chamber to the base of the carburettor and

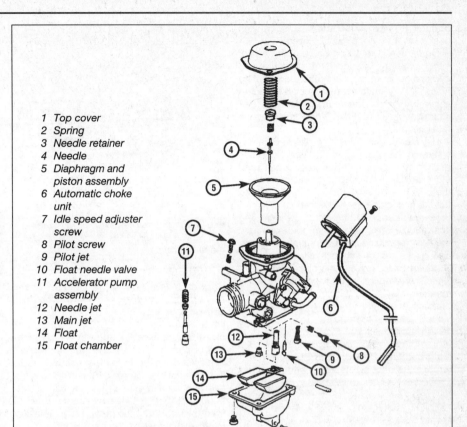

1 Top cover
2 Spring
3 Needle retainer
4 Needle
5 Diaphragm and piston assembly
6 Automatic choke unit
7 Idle speed adjuster screw
8 Pilot screw
9 Pilot jet
10 Float needle valve
11 Accelerator pump assembly
12 Needle jet
13 Main jet
14 Float
15 Float chamber

9.1 Constant vacuum (CV) type carburettor components

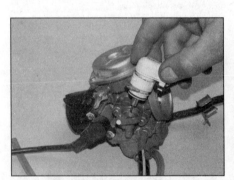

9.2 Withdraw the choke unit

9.3a Undo the top cover retaining screws (arrowed)

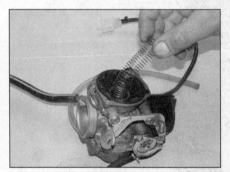

9.3b Lift out the spring

9.3c Lift out the diaphragm and piston assembly

9.4a Location of the needle retainer (arrowed)

9.4b Push the needle up from the bottom

remove it (see illustration). Discard the gasket, as a new one must be used.

6 On carburettors with an accelerator pump, either withdraw the accelerator pump spring and plunger from the carburettor body, noting how it fits, or unscrew the accelerator pump assembly from the float chamber (see illustration). Discard the O-ring as a new one must be fitted.

7 Using a pair of thin-nose pliers, carefully withdraw the float pin; if necessary, displace the pin using a small punch or a nail (see illustration). Remove the float and unhook the float needle valve, noting how it fits onto the tab on the float (see illustration).

8 Where fitted, undo the screw securing the float needle valve seat clamp, then withdraw the valve seat (see illustrations). Discard the O-ring as a new one should be used.

9 Where fitted, remove the plastic jet cover. Unscrew the pilot jet and the main jet (see illustrations). The main jet screws into the base of the needle jet; if the needle jet is slotted, unscrew it if required.

10 The pilot screw can be removed if required, but note that its setting will be disturbed (see *Haynes Hint*). Unscrew and remove the pilot screw along with its spring

HAYNES HiNT *To record the pilot screw's current setting, turn the screw in until it seats lightly, counting the number of turns necessary to achieve this, then unscrew it fully. On installation, turn the screw in until it seats, then back it out the number of turns you've recorded.*

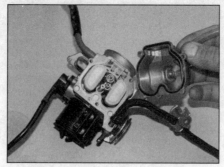
9.5 Remove the float chamber

9.6 Withdraw the accelerator pump assembly

and O-ring, where fitted. **Note:** *Do not remove the screws securing the throttle butterfly to the throttle shaft.*

Cleaning

Caution: Use only a petroleum-based solvent for carburettor cleaning. Don't use caustic cleaners.

11 Follow Steps 11 and 12 in Section 8 to clean the carburettor body and jets. If the carburettor has an accelerator pump, pay particular attention to the fuel passage in the float chamber. On some carburettors, the fuel passage is fitted with a one-way valve; blow through the fuel passage with compressed air from the bottom of the pump piston housing. **Note:** *Avoid soaking the carburettor body in solvent if any O-ring seals remain inside.*

Caution: Never clean the jets or passages with a piece of wire or a drill bit, as they will be enlarged, causing the fuel and air metering rates to be upset.

Inspection

12 If removed, check the tapered portion of the pilot screw and the spring for wear or damage. Fit a new O-ring and renew the screw or spring if necessary.

13 Check the carburettor body, float chamber and top cover for cracks, distorted sealing surfaces and other damage. If any defects are found, renew the faulty component, although renewal of the entire carburettor will probably be necessary.

14 Inspect the piston diaphragm for splits, holes and general deterioration. Holding it up to a light will help to reveal problems of this nature. Insert the piston in the carburettor body and check that the piston moves up-and-down smoothly. Check the surface of the piston for wear. If it's worn or scored excessively or doesn't move smoothly, renew the components as necessary.

15 Where fitted, check that the clip is

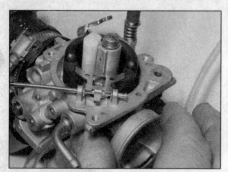
9.7a Displace the float pin

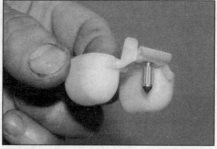
9.7b Note how the needle valve fits on the float tab

9.8a Remove the clamp screw (arrowed) . . .

9.8b . . . and withdraw the valve seat

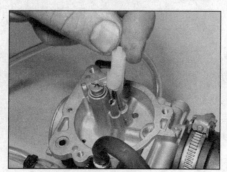
9.9a Remove the jet cover . . .

9.9b . . . then unscrew the main jet (A) and the pilot jet (B)

9.27 Insert the needle into the piston

9.28 Ensure the diaphragm and the tab (arrowed) are correctly seated

9.29 Ensure the spring locates correctly inside the cover

correctly positioned on the needle (see *Data* section). If necessary, remove the clip and check the needle for straightness by rolling it on a flat surface such as a piece of glass. Fit a new needle if it's bent or if the tip is worn. Refit the clip for safekeeping.

16 Inspect the tip of the float needle valve. If it has grooves or scratches in it, or is in any way worn, it must be renewed. If the valve seat is damaged, check the availability of new parts, otherwise a new carburettor body will have to be fitted. **Note:** *On scooters with a pumped and pressurised fuel system, a worn or incorrectly-sized carburettor float needle valve seat will not be able to shut off the fuel supply sufficiently to prevent carburettor flooding and excessive use of fuel.*

17 Operate the throttle shaft to make sure the throttle butterfly valve opens and closes smoothly. If it doesn't, cleaning the throttle linkage may help. Otherwise, renew the carburettor.

18 Check the float for damage. This will usually be apparent by the presence of fuel inside the float. If the float is damaged, it must be renewed.

19 Inspect the automatic choke unit plunger and needle for signs of wear and renew the unit if necessary. To check the operation of the choke unit see Section 5.

20 Inspect the accelerator pump piston and its seat in the float chamber for signs of wear. Ensure that the spring and the rubber boot are not damaged or deformed and renew them if necessary.

Reassembly

Note: *When reassembling the carburettor, be sure to use new O-rings and seals. Do not overtighten the carburettor jets and screws as they are easily damaged.*

21 If removed, install the pilot screw, spring and O-ring; adjust the screw to the setting as noted on removal (see Step 10).

22 If removed, install the needle jet.

23 Install the main jet and the pilot jet; install the plastic jet cover where fitted.

24 If removed, install the float needle valve seat using a new O-ring, then fit the clamp and tighten the screw.

25 Hook the float needle valve onto the float tab, then position the float assembly in the carburettor, making sure the needle valve enters its seat. Install the pin, making sure it is secure. If

necessary, the carburettor float height should be checked at this point (see Section 10).

26 On carburettors with an accelerator pump, either install the accelerator pump spring and plunger in the carburettor body, or fit a new O-ring to the accelerator pump assembly, then screw the assembly into the float chamber (see Step 6). Fit a new gasket onto the float chamber, making sure it is seated properly in its groove, then install the chamber onto the carburettor and tighten the screws securely. If necessary, the carburettor fuel height should be checked at this point (see Section 10).

27 Check that the clip is correctly positioned on the needle, then insert the needle into the piston **(see illustration)**. If applicable, install the spring and spring seat, then fit needle retainer.

28 Insert the piston assembly into the carburettor body and push it down lightly, ensuring the needle is correctly aligned with the needle jet. Align the tab on the diaphragm with the recess in the carburettor body, then press the diaphragm outer edge into its groove, making sure it is correctly seated **(see illustration)**. Check the diaphragm is not creased, and that the piston moves smoothly up-and-down in its bore.

29 Install the spring into the piston and fit the top cover to the carburettor, making sure the spring locates over the raised section on the inside of the cover, then tighten the cover screws securely **(see illustration)**.

30 Where fitted, install the choke unit mounting with a new gasket.

31 Install the automatic choke unit and secure it with its clamp. If fitted, install the choke unit cover.

32 If removed, install the accelerator pump lever and return spring and secure them with the screw.

33 Install the carburettor (see Section 7).

10 Fuel level and float height – check

1 If the carburettor floods when the scooter is in use, and the float needle valve and the valve seat are good, the fuel or float height should be checked and the result compared to the specification in the *Data* section at the end of this manual.

Fuel level check

2 If not already done, remove the carburettor (see Section 7).

3 Support the carburettor upright in a vice and connect a length of clear fuel hose to the drain union on the base of the float chamber. Secure the hose up against the side of the carburettor and mark it level with the float chamber-to-carburettor body joint, or the level mark on the side of the carburettor body **(see illustration)**.

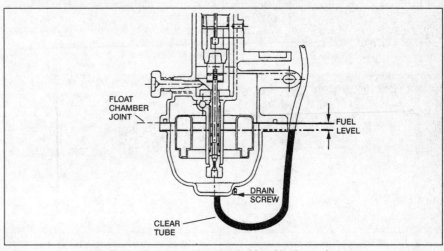

10.3 Set-up for measuring the fuel level in the carburettor

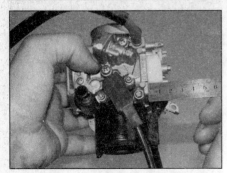

10.7 Measuring the carburettor float height

4 Carefully pour a small amount of fuel into the carburettor via the fuel hose union, then undo the drain screw in the bottom of the float chamber enough to allow fuel to flow into the clear hose. Continue pouring fuel into the carburettor until the float needle valve shuts off the supply, at which point the level in the clear hose should be at the specified height in relation to the mark (see *Data* section at the end of this manual).

5 If the fuel level is incorrect, remove the float chamber and check the float tab for wear or damage (see Section 8 or 9). If the float tab is metal it can be adjusted carefully to correct the fuel height, otherwise a new float will have to be fitted.

Float height check

6 If not already done, remove the carburettor (see Section 7). Remove the float chamber (see Section 8 or 9).

7 Angle the carburettor so that the float needle valve is resting against the valve seat and measure the distance between the float chamber gasket face and the bottom of the float **(see illustration)**.

8 Compare the result with the measurement in the *Data* section. **Note:** *On some carburettors, it is sufficient that the bottom straight-edge of the float should be parallel with the gasket face.*

9 If the float height is incorrect, check the float tab for wear or damage (see Section 8 or 9). If the float tab is metal it can be adjusted carefully to correct the fuel height, otherwise a new float will have to be fitted.

11 Reed valve (two-stroke engines) – removal, inspection and installation

Removal

1 Remove the carburettor, along with the intake manifold (see Section 7).

2 Withdraw the reed valve from the crankcase, noting which way round it fits **(see illustration)**.

3 Discard any seals or gaskets, as new ones must be fitted.

Inspection

4 Check the reed valve body closely for cracks, distortion and any other damage, particularly around the mating surfaces between the crankcase and the intake manifold – a good seal must be maintained between the components, otherwise crankcase pressure and therefore engine performance will be affected.

5 Check the reeds for cracks, distortion and any other damage. Check also that there are no dirt particles trapped between the reeds and their seats. The reeds should sit flat against the valve body so that a good seal is obtained when the crankcase is under pressure **(see illustration)**. After prolonged use, the reeds tend to become bent and will not therefore seal properly, in which case the assembly should be renewed. A good way to check is to hold the valve up to the light – if light is visible between the reeds and the body they are not sealing properly. If the engine is difficult to start or idles erratically, this could be the problem.

6 Check that the stopper plate retaining screws are tight; do not disassemble the reed valve unnecessarily as individual components are not available.

Installation

7 Installation is the reverse of removal, noting the following:
● *Ensure all mating surfaces are clean and perfectly smooth.*
● *Use new gaskets.*

12 Throttle cable and twistgrip – removal and installation

> ⚠ **Warning: Refer to the precautions given in Section 1 before proceeding.**

Note: *All four-stroke engines and two-stroke engines fitted with centrifugal oil pumps (see Chapter 2A) are fitted with one-piece throttle cables. Two-stroke engines with cable-controlled oil pumps are fitted with three-piece cables.*

One-piece cable

Removal

1 Remove the upper or front handlebar cover, the engine access panel and any body panels as required on your scooter to access the cable (see Chapter 9). Where fitted, remove the carburettor cover, noting how it fits **(see illustration 7.1)**.

2 Disconnect the cable from the twistgrip (see Steps 20 to 23).

3 If necessary, release the cable from the grommet where it passes through the handlebar cover **(see illustration)**.

4 Detach the cable from the throttle slide (see Section 8) or the carburettor pulley (see Section 9).

5 Ensure the cable is free from any clips or guides, then withdraw it from the machine, noting the correct routing.

> **HAYNES HiNT**
> *When fitting a new cable, tape the lower end of the new cable to the upper end of the old cable before removing it from the machine. Slowly pull the lower end of the old cable out, guiding the new cable down into position. Using this method will ensure the cable is routed correctly.*

Installation

6 Installation is the reverse of removal, noting the following:
● *Lubricate the upper end of the cable with grease before fitting it into the twistgrip.*
● *Ensure the cable is correctly routed and clipped into place.*

11.2 Lift off the reed valve and gasket – note the tabs (arrowed) for positioning

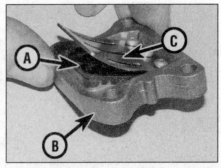

11.5 Reeds (A), valve body (B) and stopper plate (C)

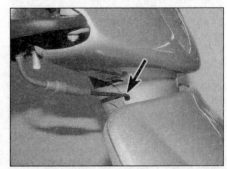

12.3 Release the cable from the grommet (arrowed)

12.13 Unscrew the locknut (arrowed) and detach the cable

12.17a Pull off the cable covers . . .

12.17b . . . then press in the tabs . . .

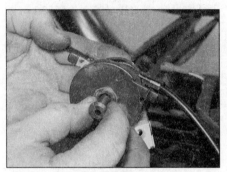

12.17c . . . and remove the peg and cover

12.17d Draw out the outer cables . . .

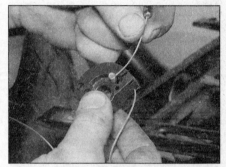

12.17e . . . then lift out the cam and detach the inner cable ends

● *Adjust the cable freeplay (see Chapter 1).*
● *Check the cable operation before riding the scooter.*

Three-piece cable

Removal

7 The throttle cable consists of three sections – the main cable from the twistgrip goes into a splitter, with separate cables from this going to the carburettor and oil pump (see Chapter 1, Section 13).
8 If a cable problem is diagnosed, check the availability of new parts – on some scooters it is possible to renew individual cables rather than the whole assembly.
9 Remove the upper or front handlebar cover, the engine access panel and any body panels as required on your scooter to access the cables (see Chapter 9). Where fitted, remove the carburettor cover, noting how it fits **(see illustration 7.1)**.
10 Disconnect the cable from the twistgrip (see Steps 20 to 23).
11 If necessary, release the cable from the grommet where it passes through the handlebar cover **(see illustration 12.3)**.
12 Either detach the cable from the throttle slide assembly and the carburettor top cover (see Section 8) or the carburettor pulley (see Section 9).
13 If required, to access the cable at the oil pump, remove the plug in the engine case or the pump cover on the engine side cover (see Chapter 1, Section 19). Loosen the cable adjuster locknut, then detach the cable end from the pump pulley and detach the outer

cable from its bracket or the engine case **(see illustration)**.
14 If the complete cable assembly is being removed, ensure the cables are free from any clips or guides, then withdraw the assembly from the machine, noting the correct routing.

> **HAYNES HINT** *When fitting a new cable, tape the lower end of the new cable to the upper end of the old cable before removing it from the machine. Slowly pull the lower end of the old cable out, guiding the new cable down into position. Using this method will ensure the cable is routed correctly.*

15 If an individual cable is being removed, first detach the cable from the twistgrip, carburettor or oil pump as applicable, then

12.18a Detach the splitter (arrowed) from the frame . . .

detach the cable from the splitter as follows.
16 Two types of cable splitter are used. One operates with the throttle cable pulling on a pivoted cam, while the other operates with the throttle cable pulling on a slider.
17 On models with the cam type splitter, first remove the screw securing the splitter to its mounting and draw the cable covers off the splitter. Depress the tabs on the bottom of the peg securing the splitter cover, then draw the peg out of the splitter and remove the cover **(see illustrations)**. Draw the outer cables out of their sockets, then lift the cam off its pivot and detach the cable ends from the cam as required, noting their relative positions **(see illustrations)**.
18 On models with the slider type splitter, first detach the splitter holder from the frame and draw the covers off the splitter housing **(see illustrations)**. Remove the cap from the splitter and pull the slider out of the housing with the

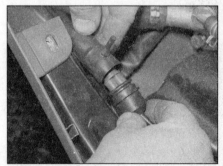

12.18b . . . then pull off the covers

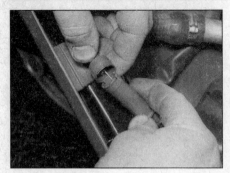

12.18c Remove the cap . . .

12.18d . . . and pull out the slider

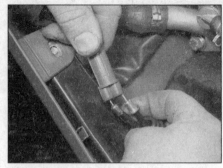

12.18e Detach the cables from the splitter

throttle cable **(see illustrations)**. Detach the cable(s) from the splitter as required, noting their relative positions **(see illustration)**.
Caution: Before removing a cable, make a careful note of its routing to ensure correct installation.

Installation

19 Installation is the reverse of removal, noting the following:
- *Lubricate the cable ends with grease.*
- *Ensure the cables are correctly routed and clipped into place – they must not interfere with any other component and should not be kinked or bent sharply.*
- *Adjust the cable freeplay and check the oil pump setting (see Chapter 1).*
- *Check the cable operation before riding the scooter.*

Throttle twistgrip

20 Two types of twistgrip are used. Some scooters have a motorcycle type twistgrip, where the end of the inner cable fits into a socket in the twistgrip. Others have a sliding type twistgrip, where the end of the inner cable is secured in a slider with a screw. The slider runs in a spiral track inside the twistgrip.
21 To access the cable at the twistgrip, first remove the upper or front handlebar cover (see Chapter 9).
22 On models with a motorcycle type twistgrip, loosen the cable adjuster locknut and thread the adjuster fully in to slacken the cable **(see illustration)**. Either pull back the twistgrip rubber, then remove the screws securing the cover plate and remove the plate, or undo the

twistgrip housing screws and separate the two halves of the housing **(see illustrations)**. Detach the cable end from its socket, then remove the cable from the housing, noting how it fits.
23 On models with a sliding twistgrip, loosen

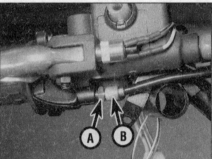
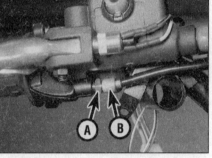

12.22a Loosen the locknut (A) and thread the adjuster (B) fully in

12.22c . . . then detach the cable end (arrowed) from its socket

the screw securing the end of the cable in the slider, then draw the cable out **(see illustrations)**. Note the distance from the end of the cable where the screw located as an aid for correctly setting the new cable.

12.22b Undo the screws (arrowed) and remove the plate . . .

12.22d Undo the screws (arrowed) and split the housing . . .

12.22e . . . then detach the cable end (arrowed)

12.23a Loosen the cable clamp screw (arrowed) . . .

12.23b . . . and pull out the cable

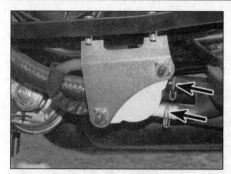

13.3 Location of fuel pump – note the clips (arrowed) securing the hoses

13.5 Check the vacuum hose (arrowed) from the crankcase

14.3a Undo the two nuts (arrowed) . . .

13 Fuel pump – check and renewal

 Warning: Refer to the precautions given in Section 1 before proceeding.

Check

1 When the engine is running, the alternating vacuum and pressure in the crankcase opens and closes a diaphragm in the pump. Generally, the pump supplies fuel direct to the carburettor, but on some scooters the pump supplies fuel to a header tank which ensures an immediate supply of fuel to the carburettor when the scooter has been standing unused.

2 The most likely cause of pump failure will be a split in the pump diaphragm.

3 Generally, the fuel pump is mounted on the frame alongside the fuel tank (see illustration). Remove the body panels as required on your scooter to access the pump (see Chapter 9).

4 To check whether the pump is operating, release the clip securing the fuel supply hose to the carburettor, or header tank as applicable, and detach the hose. Place the open end in a container suitable for storing petrol. Turn the engine over on the starter motor and check whether fuel flows from the hose into the container. If fuel flows, the pump is working correctly.

5 If no fuel flows from the pump, first check that this is not due to a blocked filter or fuel hose, or due to a split in the vacuum hose from the crankcase, before renewing the pump (see illustration). Check all the hoses for splits, cracks and kinks, and check that they are securely connected on each end by a good clip. Check that any air vent for the fuel tank is not blocked. If the filter and hoses are good, renew the pump.

Renewal

6 Release the clips securing the fuel and vacuum hoses and detach them from the pump, noting which fits where. Be prepared to catch any residue fuel in a suitable container. The fuel hoses should be clamped to prevent fuel leaks using any of the methods shown in Tools and Workshop Tips in the Reference section.

7 Undo the pump fixings and remove the pump, noting which way up it fits.

8 Install the new pump, making sure the hoses are correctly attached and secured with the clips. If the old clips are corroded or deformed, fit new ones.

14 Exhaust system – removal and installation

 Warning: If the engine has been running the exhaust system will be very hot. Allow the system to cool before carrying out any work.

Note: Some scooters are fitted with a one-piece exhaust system. Follow the procedure for removing the complete system.

Downpipe removal

1 Remove the body panels as required on your scooter to access the exhaust system and cylinder head (see Chapter 9).

2 On two-stroke machines fitted with a secondary air system (see Chapter 1, Section 3), loosen the clip securing the air hose to the extension on the exhaust downpipe and disconnect the hose.

HAYNES HINT *Exhaust system fixings tend to become corroded and seized. It is advisable to spray them with penetrating oil before attempting to loosen them.*

3 Undo the nuts securing the downpipe to the exhaust port in the cylinder or cylinder head, and the fixings securing the downpipe to the silencer and remove the downpipe (see illustrations). Note: On systems where the downpipe fits inside the silencer and is secured by a clamp it is necessary to remove the silencer first (see Step 5).

4 Remove the gasket from the exhaust port and from the downpipe-to-silencer joint and discard them, as new ones must be used (see illustrations).

Silencer removal

5 Undo the fixing securing the silencer to the downpipe (see illustration 14.3b) and the

14.3b . . . and the two bolts (arrowed)

14.4a Remove the gasket from the exhaust port . . .

14.4b . . . and the pipe-to-silencer joint

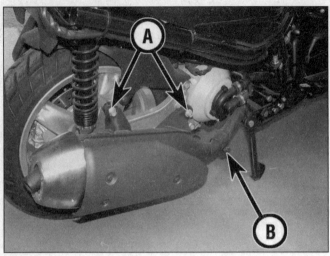

14.5 Silencer is secured to the frame (A) and to the downpipe (B)

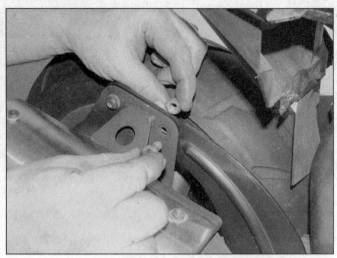

14.7a Undo the bolts securing the silencer . . .

bolts securing the silencer, or silencer bracket, to the engine or frame, and remove the silencer **(see illustration)**. Where fitted, remove the gasket from the silencer-to-downpipe joint and discard it, as a new one must be used.

Complete system removal

6 Follow Steps 1 to 3 to access the exhaust system and disconnect the exhaust pipe from the cylinder or cylinder head. Where fitted, disconnect the secondary air system.
7 Loosen the bolts securing the silencer, or silencer bracket, then support the exhaust system and remove the bolts. Lift the system off the scooter **(see illustrations)**.
8 Remove the gasket from the exhaust port and discard it, as a new one must be used **(see illustration 14.4a)**.
9 The exhaust system of restricted 50 cc two-stroke machines is fitted with a resonator tube

(see illustration). If your scooter has been de-restricted and the resonator tube has been removed, check around the welded patch on the exhaust for gas leaks. De-restricting requires a number of modifications to the engine and should only be undertaken by a scooter dealer.

Installation

10 Installation is the reverse of removal, noting the following:
● *Clean the exhaust port studs and lubricate them with a suitable copper-based grease before reassembly.*
● *Clean the jointing surfaces of the exhaust port and the pipe.*
● *Use new gaskets.*
● *Smear the port gasket with grease to hold it in place while fitting the exhaust system.*

14.7b . . . or silencer bracket . . .

● *Leave all fixings finger tight until the system has been installed and correctly aligned, then tighten the exhaust port nuts first.*
● *Run the engine and check that there are no exhaust gas leaks.*

14.7c . . . and lift off the complete system

14.9 Resonator tube on restricted 50cc exhaust system

16.2a Slacken the clip on the reed valve housing hose . . .

16.2b . . . then remove the two screws . . .

16.2c . . . and detach the housing from the filter surround

15 Catalytic converter

1 To minimise the amount of engine exhaust pollutants escaping into the atmosphere, certain models have a simple open-loop catalytic converter fitted in the exhaust system.
2 The catalytic converter has no link with the fuel and ignition systems, and requires no routine maintenance. However the following points should be noted:

l *Always use unleaded fuel – the use of leaded fuel will destroy the converter.*
l *Do not use any fuel or oil additives.*
l *Keep the fuel and ignition systems in good order – if the fuel/air mixture is suspected of being incorrect, have it checked by a dealer equipped with an exhaust gas analyser.*
l *When the exhaust system is removed from the scooter handle it with care to avoid damaging the catalytic converter.*
l *No attempt should be made to clean the catalytic converter or decarbonise the exhaust system.*

3 The catalytic converter works in conjunction with the secondary air system which promotes the burning of any excess fuel present in the exhaust gases.

16 Secondary air system

1 Many models have an air induction system fitted, often in conjunction with a catalytic converter, to reduce the harmful element of the exhaust gas CO content. Filtered air is fed into the exhaust port to promote the burning of any unburned particles of the exhaust gas, turning it into relatively harmless carbon dioxide and water vapour. The system varies between two- and four-stroke engines.

Two-stroke engines

2 Air is usually drawn from the atmosphere through a foam filter which forms part of the reed valve housing **(see illustrations)**. Negative pressure in the exhaust header pipe draws the fresh air through the filter and reed valve and into the exhaust port. The system is virtually maintenance free, but due to the oily

16.2d Separate the reed valve from its housing . . .

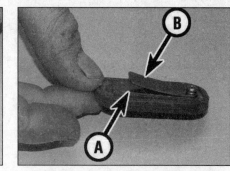

16.2e . . . and check the position of the reed (A) and its stopper plate (B)

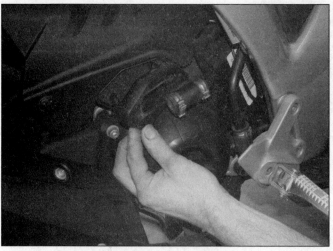

16.2f Unclip the filter lid . . .

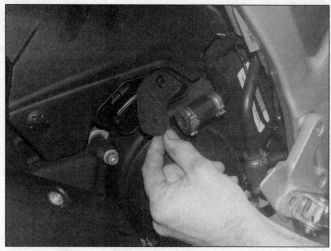

16.2g . . . and carefully extract the foam filter

16.3a Vacuum hose connection (A) to the diaphragm housing on the control unit (B)

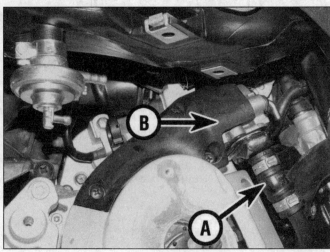

16.3b The air pipe (A) connects to the reed valve housing on the control unit (B) . . .

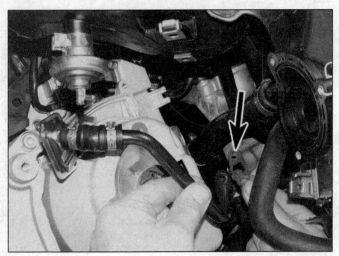

16.3c . . . and to the cylinder head (arrowed)

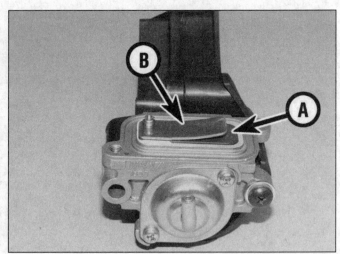

16.3d Control unit showing reed valve (A) and stopper plate (B)

nature of the exhaust gases, the components may require periodic cleaning.

Four-stroke engines

3 Air is drawn from the main air filter housing into a control valve. The control valve is usually opened by vacuum via a hose from the intake tract although can be opened electrically via the ignition control unit (see illustrations). The control valve opens when there is negative pressure in the exhaust system and allows fresh air to flow into the exhaust port. Reed valves located either on the engine's valve cover or combined with the control valve, prevent the return flow of exhaust gases (see illustration).

4 Unlike the two-stroke system, which is of a more oily nature, the system components on a four-stroke engine do not require regular maintenance.

Chapter 5
Ignition systems

Contents

Degrees of difficulty

| **Easy,** suitable for novice with little experience | | **Fairly easy,** suitable for beginner with some experience | | **Fairly difficult,** suitable for competent DIY mechanic | | **Difficult,** suitable for experienced DIY mechanic | | **Very difficult,** suitable for expert DIY or professional | |

Specifications

Refer to the *Data* section at the end of this manual for servicing specifications.

1 General information

All scooters covered by this manual are fitted with a fully-transistorised electronic ignition system. The components which make up the system are the alternator source coil, ignition trigger, pick-up coil, ignition control unit (ICU), HT coil and spark plug **(see illustration overleaf)**.

The ignition trigger, which is on the outside surface of the alternator rotor, operates the pick-up coil as the crankshaft rotates, sending a signal to the ICU which in turn supplies the HT coil with the power necessary to produce a spark at the plug. The alternator source coil produces the power for the ignition system when the engine is running, and on most machines the battery provides the power for initial starting.

In the typical ignition circuit shown overleaf, the solid black wires show the connection between the ignition system components described above. The role of the ignition switch is to complete the power feed to the starter motor circuit when in the ON position (see the circuit diagram on page 10.8) and to divert residual alternator source coil output to earth when turned to the OFF position. The hatched black wires illustrate the ignition switch function.

On some scooters the HT coil is integral with the ignition control unit (see Section 3).

The ICU incorporates an ignition advance system controlled by signals from the pick-up coil. This varies the timing of the ignition spark depending on engine speed. Although the ignition timing can be checked on most machines (see Section 7), there is no provision for adjusting the timing.

Depending upon the model specification, most ignition systems incorporate a safety circuit which prevents the engine from being started unless one of the brake levers is pulled in and/or the side stand is up (refer to your scooter handbook for details). For security, many scooters are fitted with an ignition immobiliser (see Section 4).

Due to their lack of mechanical parts, the components of the ignition system are totally maintenance-free. If ignition system troubles occur, and the faulty component can be isolated by a series of checks, the only cure is to renew it. Keep in mind that most electrical parts, once purchased, cannot be returned. To avoid unnecessary expense, make sure the faulty component has been positively identified before buying a new one.

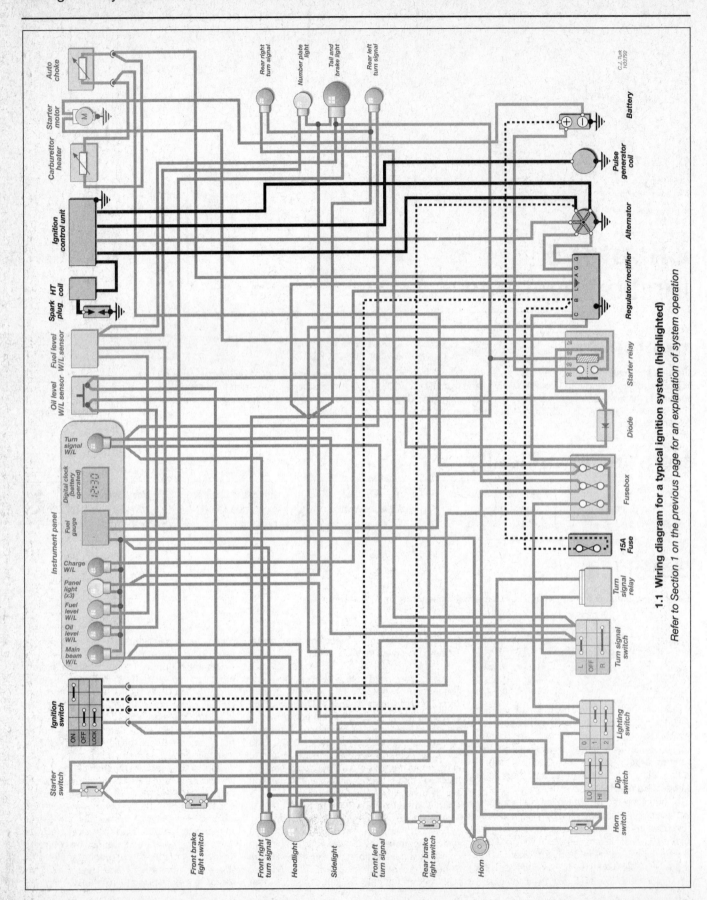

1.1 Wiring diagram for a typical ignition system (highlighted)

Refer to Section 1 on the previous page for an explanation of system operation

2.2 Earth the spark plug and operate the starter

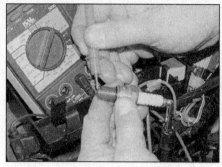

2.4 Measuring the resistance of the spark plug

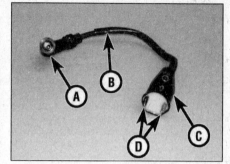

3.2 Spark plug cap (A), HT lead (B), coil (C) and primary circuit wiring terminals (D)

2 Ignition system – check

Warning: The energy levels in electronic systems can be very high. On no account should the ignition be switched on whilst the plug or plug cap is being held – shocks from the HT circuit can be most unpleasant. Secondly, it is vital that the engine is not turned over with the plug cap removed, and that the plug is soundly earthed when the system is checked for sparking. The ignition system components can be seriously damaged if the HT circuit becomes isolated.

1 As no means of adjustment is available, any failure of the system can be traced to failure of a system component or a simple wiring fault. Of the two possibilities, the latter is by far the most likely. In the event of failure, check the system in a logical fashion, as described below.

2 Disconnect the HT lead from the spark plug. Connect the lead to a new plug of the correct specification and lay the plug on the engine with the thread earthed **(see illustration)**. If necessary, hold the spark plug with an insulated tool.

Warning: Do not remove the spark plug from the engine to perform this check – atomised fuel being pumped out of the open spark plug hole could ignite, causing severe injury!

3 Having observed the above precautions, turn the ignition switch ON and turn the engine over on the starter motor. If the system is in good condition a regular, fat blue spark should be evident between the plug electrodes. If the spark appears thin or yellowish, or is non-existent, further investigation will be necessary. Before proceeding further, turn the ignition OFF.

Caution: Some ignition systems are designed for the combined resistance of the spark plug and spark plug cap. To avoid the risk of damaging the ICU, a spark testing tool should not be used.

4 If required, spark plug resistance can be checked with a multimeter. Remove the plug and clean the electrodes (see Chapter 1). Set the multimeter to the K-ohms scale and connect the meter probes to the terminal at the top of the plug and the central electrode **(see illustration)**. Compare the result with the reading from a new plug of the correct specification. If there is a great deal of variance between the readings, discard the old plug.

5 Ignition faults can be divided into two categories, namely those where the ignition system has failed completely, and those which are due to a partial failure. The likely faults are listed below, starting with the most probable source of failure. Work through the list systematically, referring to the subsequent sections for full details of the necessary checks and tests. **Note:** Before checking the following items ensure that the battery is fully-charged and that all fuses are in good condition.

● Loose, corroded or damaged wiring connections, broken or shorted wiring between any of the component parts of the ignition system **(see illustration 1.1)**.
● Faulty spark plug with dirty, worn or corroded plug electrodes, or incorrect gap between electrodes (see Chapter 1).
● Faulty HT coil or spark plug cap.
● Faulty ignition (main) switch (see Chapter 10).
● Faulty immobiliser (where fitted).
● Faulty source coil.
● Faulty pick-up coil.
● Faulty ICU.

6 If the above checks don't reveal the cause of the problem, have the ignition system tested by a scooter dealer.

3 HT coil and spark plug cap – check, removal and installation

Check

1 Trace the HT lead back from the spark plug cap to the HT coil and remove any body panels as required for access to the coil (see Chapter 9). Disconnect the battery negative (-ve) lead (see Chapter 10).

2 Pull the spark plug cap off the plug and inspect the cap, HT lead and coil for cracks and other damage **(see illustration)**.

3 On some scooters the ICU and HT coil are integrated in one unit **(see illustration)**. If no test specifications are available in the Data section, the only way to determine conclusively that the unit is defective is to substitute it with a known good one. If the fault is rectified, the original unit is faulty.

4 The condition of the coil primary and secondary windings can be checked with a multimeter. Note the position of the primary circuit wiring connectors, then disconnect them **(see illustration)**. **Note:** If there is only one primary circuit wire then the coil is earthed through its mounting – use the mounting as a substitute for the earth wire terminal in this check. Set the multimeter to the appropriate ohms scale and connect the meter probes to the primary circuit wiring

3.3 Combined ignition control unit (ICU) and HT coil

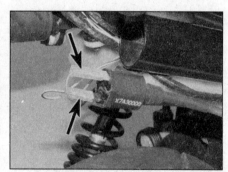

3.4a Disconnect the primary circuit connectors from the coil

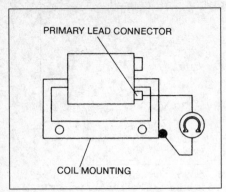

3.4b HT coil primary winding check

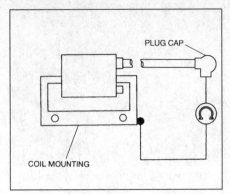

3.5 HT coil secondary winding check

terminals **(see illustration)**. This will give a resistance reading for the coil primary windings which should be consistent with the specifications in the *Data* section. If the reading is outside the specified range, it is likely the coil is defective.

5 Set the multimeter to the K-ohms scale and connect the meter probes to the earth primary circuit wiring terminal and the spark plug terminal inside the plug cap **(see illustration)**. This will give a resistance reading for the coil secondary windings. If the reading is not within the specified range, unscrew the plug cap from the HT lead and connect the probes to the earth primary circuit wiring terminal and the core of the lead. If the reading is now as specified, the plug cap is suspect. If the reading is still outside the specified range, it is likely that the coil is defective.

6 Should any of the above checks not produce the expected result, have your findings confirmed by a scooter dealer. If the coil is confirmed to be faulty, it must be renewed; the coil is a sealed unit and cannot be repaired.

7 To check the condition of the spark plug cap, set the multimeter to the appropriate ohms scale and connect the meter probes to the HT lead and plug terminals inside the cap **(see illustration)**. If the reading is outside the specified range, the cap is defective and a new one must be fitted. If the reading is as specified, the cap connection may have been faulty. Remake the connection between the cap and the HT lead and check the resistance

reading for the coil secondary windings again (see Step 5).

Removal

8 Remove any body panels as required for access (see Chapter 9). Disconnect the battery negative (-ve) lead (see Chapter 10).
9 Note the position of the primary circuit wiring connectors, then disconnect them **(see illustration 3.4a)**. Disconnect the HT lead from the spark plug.
10 Unscrew the fixings securing the coil to the frame and remove it.

Installation

11 Installation is the reverse of removal. If the coil is earthed through its mounting, ensure the mounting is clean and free from corrosion. Make sure the wiring connectors and HT lead are securely connected.

4 Immobiliser system – general information and check

General information

Caution: The use of the correct resistor type, spark plug and suppresser cap is essential to prevent interference with the immobiliser system and possible loss of key programming.

1 The system comprises a security-coded ignition key with integral transponder, the immobiliser and transponder aerial. When the

key is inserted into the ignition switch the security code is transmitted from the key to the immobiliser via the aerial which is located around the switch. The code deactivates the immobiliser and the warning LED on the instrument panel stops flashing. When the key is removed, the immobiliser is activated and the warning LED starts flashing. **Note:** *To minimise battery discharging, the warning LED goes out after a period of time although the immobiliser system remains active. Disconnecting the battery does not deactivate the immobiliser system.*

2 One master key and several ignition service keys are supplied with each machine from new. The keys and the immobiliser are encoded by the factory. The master key should be kept in a safe place and not used on a day-to-day basis.
3 If an ignition key is lost, obtain a new one from a scooter dealer and have the system recoded. The dealer will require the master key for this purpose. Once the system is recoded the lost key will not deactivate the immobiliser.
4 The ignition keys can lose their code. If the machine will not start with the ignition switched ON, and the LED continues to flash, use a spare service key or the master key and have the system, including the key that has lost its code, recoded by a scooter dealer.

Check

5 Insert the ignition key into the switch and turn the switch ON. Once the LED stops flashing, the immobiliser has been deactivated; if the machine will not start, the problem lies elsewhere. If the LED continues to flash, and using another key does not deactivate the immobiliser (see Step 4), the immobiliser is suspect.
6 Remove the body panel to access the transponder aerial (see Chapter 9) and disconnect the battery negative (-ve) terminal. Trace the transponder aerial wiring from the ignition switch to the immobiliser and disconnect the wiring **(see illustrations)**. Check the resistance in the aerial with a multimeter set to the appropriate ohms scale. Connect the meter probes to the terminals in the connector and compare the result with the specifications in the *Data* section **(see**

3.7 Measuring the resistance of the spark plug cap

4.6a Transponder aerial (arrowed) is clipped to the ignition switch

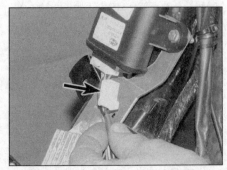

4.6b Disconnect the aerial wiring connector from the immobiliser

illustration). If the reading is not within the specification, fit a new aerial and try starting the machine again.

7 If the machine still will not start, the immobiliser should be checked by a scooter dealer. **Note:** *It is not possible to substitute an immobiliser from another machine, or a second-hand immobiliser, as this will not recognise the security code from your ignition key.*

8 When a new (uncoded) immobiliser is fitted, check that it is working before encoding it. Turn the ignition ON and start the engine; the engine should run but will not rev above 2000 rpm. If the engine runs, the immobiliser can be encoded using the master key. **Note:** *Encoding the immobiliser is irreversible – only encode a new immobiliser once you are sure the system is working correctly.*

9 If the engine does not start, the problem lies elsewhere.

10 To check the LED, remove the instrument cluster and test for continuity between the LED terminals **(see illustration)**. There should be continuity in one direction only. If there is no continuity, or continuity in both directions, renew the LED.

Malfunction codes

11 The LED should flash once when the ignition is switched ON. If the LED continues to flash and then stays on permanently to indicate an ignition fault, try using the master key to turn the ignition ON. If this works, the service key has lost its programme. If the fault persists, refer to your scooter handbook for details of malfunction codes.

---

5 Source coil and pick-up coil – check and renewal

Check

1 To check the condition of the source coil and the pick-up coil it is first necessary to identify the wiring for the individual components. Remove the body panels and alternator or engine cover as required according to model (see Chapter 9) and disconnect the battery negative (-ve) lead.

2 Trace the source coil and pick-up coil wiring from the back of the alternator housing

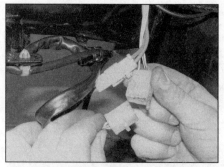
5.2 Disconnect the alternator/pick-up coil wiring connector

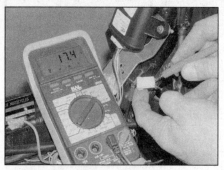
4.6c Measuring the resistance in the transponder aerial

and disconnect it at the connector **(see illustration)**. **Note:** *On some scooters, the wiring will connect directly into the ICU, on others there will be a multi-pin connector where it joins the main wiring loom.* If available, use your scooter's wiring diagram to identify the appropriate wires. Alternatively, check the colour-coding of the wires at the source coil (on the alternator stator) and the pick-up coil adjacent to the alternator rotor.

3 Using a multimeter set to the appropriate ohms scale, measure the source coil resistance by connecting the meter probes between the coil terminals on the alternator side of the connector. Now reset the multimeter and measure the pick-up coil resistance by connecting the meter probes between the pick-up terminals in the connector.

4 Compare the readings obtained with those given in the *Data* section. If the readings obtained differ greatly from those given, particularly if the meter indicates a short circuit (no measurable resistance) or an open circuit (infinite, or very high resistance), the alternator stator and pick-up coil assembly must be renewed. However, first check that the fault is not due to a damaged or broken wire from the coil to the connector; pinched or broken wires can usually be repaired.

5 Some scooters are fitted with a motorcycle-type alternator with three yellow wires from the stator. Using a multimeter set to the ohms scale, measure resistance of each coil by connecting the meter probes between the yellow wire terminals in the connector. Compare the result with the specifications in the *Data* section. Also check for continuity

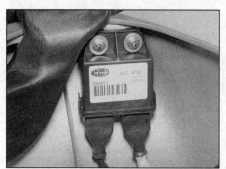
6.2a Undo the ICU fixings . . .

4.10 LED terminals (arrowed) on the instrument cluster circuit

between each terminal and earth – there should be no continuity.

6 On some scooters, there is a short wiring loom between the multi-pin connector and the ICU. To check the condition of this loom, disconnect the ICU wiring connector and test for continuity between the terminals in the ICU connector and the alternator/pick-up coil multi-pin connector.

Renewal

7 The source coil and pick-up coil are integral with the alternator stator. Refer to the relevant Section of Chapter 2 for the removal and installation procedure.

---

6 Ignition control unit (ICU) – check, removal and installation

Check

1 If the tests shown in the preceding sections have failed to isolate the cause of an ignition fault, it is possible that the ICU itself is faulty. In order to determine conclusively that the unit is defective, it should be substituted with a known good one. If the fault is rectified, the original unit is faulty. **Note:** *The ICU unit will be damaged if a non-resistor type spark plug or spark plug cap are fitted. When fitting a new ICU unit, always ensure the spark plug and cap are of the correct specification before starting the engine.*

Removal

2 Remove the body panels as required according to model (see Chapter 9) and

6.2b . . . or unclip it from its holder (arrowed)

disconnect the battery negative (-ve) lead. Disconnect the wiring connector(s) from the ICU. Unscrew the nuts and bolts securing the unit to the frame, or unclip it from its fixing, and remove the unit **(see illustrations)**.

Installation

3 Installation is the reverse of removal. Make sure the wiring connector is correctly and securely connected. **Note:** *Some scooters are fitted with a combined ICU and ignition immobiliser. When a new unit is fitted it must be encoded by a scooter dealer using your ignition master key.*

7 Ignition timing – general information and check

General information

1 Since no provision exists for adjusting the ignition timing and since no component is subject to mechanical wear, there is no need for regular checks; only if investigating a fault such as a loss of power or a misfire, should the ignition timing be checked.

2 The ignition timing is defined by the relationship between two timing marks – one on the alternator rotor and a static mark on the engine. The alignment of the two marks is checked with the engine running (dynamically) using a stroboscopic lamp. The inexpensive neon lamps should be adequate in theory, but in practice may produce a pulse of such low intensity that the timing mark on the rotor

remains indistinct. If possible, one of the more precise xenon tube lamps should be used, powered by an external source of the appropriate voltage. **Note:** *Do not use the machine's own battery as an incorrect reading may result from stray impulses within the machine's electrical system.*

3 Every engine has two marks – a static mark, either on the alternator cover or on the inside of an inspection hole, and a mark on the alternator rotor or cooling fan **(see illustrations)**. Refer to your scooter handbook for the exact location of the timing marks and the engine speed at which the marks should align.

Check

4 Warm the engine up to normal operating temperature then turn it OFF.

5 Connect the timing lamp to the spark plug HT lead as described in the manufacturer's instructions.

7.3a Static timing mark on the alternator cover

6 Start the engine and aim the light at the static timing mark. With the machine running at the specified speed, the timing mark on the rotor should align with the idle timing mark.

 The timing marks can be highlighted with white paint to make them more visible under the stroboscope light.

7 Slowly increase the engine speed whilst observing the timing mark. The timing mark should move anti-clockwise, increasing in relation to the engine speed until it reaches the full advance mark (where present).

8 If the ignition timing is incorrect, or suspected of being incorrect, one of the ignition system components is at fault, and the system must be tested as described in the preceding Sections of this Chapter.

7.3b Timing mark on the alternator rotor (arrowed)

Chapter 6
Transmission: Drive components and gearbox

Contents

Degrees of difficulty

Easy, suitable for novice with little experience	**Fairly easy,** suitable for beginner with some experience	**Fairly difficult,** suitable for competent DIY mechanic	**Difficult,** suitable for experienced DIY mechanic	**Very difficult,** suitable for expert DIY or professional

Specifications

Refer to the *Data* section at the end of this manual for servicing specifications.

1 General information

The transmission on all scooters covered by this manual is fully-automatic in operation.

Power is transmitted from the engine to the rear wheel by belt, via a variable-size drive pulley (the variator), an automatic clutch on the driven pulley, and a reduction gearbox. The variator and the automatic clutch both work on the principal of centrifugal force. **Note:** *On some scooters the internal components of the transmission may differ slightly to those described or shown. When dismantling, always note the fitted position, order and way round of each component as it is removed.*

The transmission can be worked on with the engine in the frame.

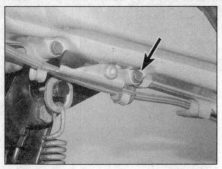

2.2 Undo the screw and remove the brake cable/hose bracket

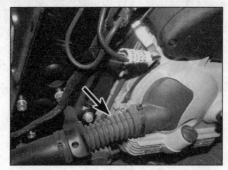

2.3a Detach the air cooling duct (arrowed)

2.3b If necessary, remove the oil filler plug

2 Drivebelt cover –
removal and installation

Removal

1 Remove any body panels as required for access to the transmission casing (see Chapter 9). If required, remove the air filter housing (se Chapter 4).

2 Undo the screw securing the rear brake cable or hydraulic hose bracket to the underside of the transmission casing and remove the bracket (see illustration).

3 Where fitted, detach the air cooling duct from the front of the cover (see illustration). On four-stroke engines, where the oil filler plug passes through the cover, remove the plug (see illustration).

4 Some scooters have a plastic trim fitted over the main belt cover. If necessary, remove the kickstart lever (see Section 3), then undo the screws securing the trim and remove it. Refit the kickstart lever – this is to prevent the kickstart shaft being accidentally knocked through the cover and dislodging the mechanism return spring.

5 On some scooters, the gearbox input shaft passes through the drivebelt cover and is supported by a bearing in the cover. To undo the nut on the outer end of the shaft, first unclip the plastic cap on the clutch bearing housing (see illustration). The clutch drum must be locked against the belt cover to prevent the shaft turning while the nut is undone. Either use a service tool to hold the clutch drum, or insert two large screwdrivers through the holes in the belt cover to engage the holes in the clutch drum. Have an assistant hold the screwdrivers while the nut is undone (see illustration). Remove the nut and washer.

6 Working in a criss-cross pattern, loosen the drivebelt cover retaining bolts and remove the bolts noting the position of any clips. **Note:** *On scooters fitted with a kickstart lever it is not necessary to remove the lever before removing the cover.*

> **HAYNES HiNT** *Make a cardboard template of the cover and punch a hole for each bolt location. This will ensure all bolts are installed correctly on reassembly – this is important as some bolts may be of different lengths.*

7 Lift off the cover and note the position of any locating dowels (see illustration). Remove the dowels for safekeeping if they are loose. **Note:** *Sealant should not be used on the cover, but if it will not lift away easily, tap it gently around the edge with a soft-faced hammer. Some scooters have a cover manufactured from composite material fitted with a gasket. If the gasket is damaged, discard it and fit a new one on reassembly.*

8 On models where the gearbox input shaft passes through the belt cover, note the spacer on the shaft (see illustration).

9 Where fitted, note the position of the kickstart quadrant and the engaging pinion (see illustration 3.2). If the starter motor engages with the variator, note how the outer end of the starter motor pinion assembly locates in the cover.

10 If fitted, undo the retaining bolt for the air cooling duct and remove the duct. Inspect the duct filter element (see Chapter 1).

11 Clean any dust or dirt from the inside of the casing with a suitable solvent, taking care to avoid contact with the belt and the drive faces of the pulleys. Any evidence of oil inside the casing suggests a worn seal either on the crankshaft or the gearbox input shaft which must be rectified. Evidence of grease inside the casing suggests worn seals either in the variator or the clutch centre which should also be rectified.

2.7 Lift off the drivebelt cover

2.5a Remove the clutch bearing cap

2.5b Lock the clutch drum with two screwdrivers and undo the nut

2.8 Note the spacer on the shaft

Installation

12 Installation is the reverse of removal, noting the following:

- *If removed, fit the dowels in the cover.*
- *If required, apply a smear of grease to the end of the starter motor pinion and to the threads of the cover bolts.*
- *On models where the gearbox input shaft passes through the belt cover, ensure the spacer is in place on the shaft.*
- *Where fitted, ensure the kickstart quadrant and engaging pinion are correctly located in the cover.*
- *Tighten the cover bolts evenly in a criss-cross pattern.*
- *Where fitted, crank the kickstart lever to ensure the mechanism engages correctly with the kickstart driven gear and that the lever returns to its proper rest position afterwards.*

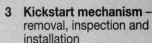

3 Kickstart mechanism – removal, inspection and installation

Removal

1 Remove the drivebelt cover (see Section 2). Where fitted, remove the mechanism cover from the inside of the drivebelt cover **(see illustration)**.
2 Pull the engaging pinion out of its recess in the cover, noting how the spring locates **(see illustration)**. Remove the washer from behind the pinion.
3 Note the rest position of the kickstart lever, then undo the lever pinch-bolt and pull the lever off the shaft **(see illustration)**.
4 Remove the circlip and washer (if fitted) from the kickstart shaft on the outside of the cover **(see illustration)**.

5 Ease the kickstart shaft out of the cover and release the tension on the kickstart return spring. Unhook the spring from the kickstart quadrant and remove the shaft **(see illustration)**.
6 Note how the return spring locates inside the cover and remove the spring **(see illustration)**. If it is a loose fit, lift out the kickstart bush **(see illustration)**.
7 Clean all the components with a suitable solvent.

Inspection

8 Check the dogs on the end of the engaging pinion and the corresponding dogs on the kickstart driven gear **(see illustration)**. Inspect the teeth on the engaging pinion and the teeth on the kickstart quadrant **(see illustration)**. Check the shafts of the engaging pinion and the kickstart quadrant, and the

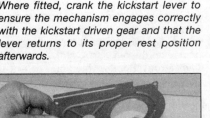

3.1 Where fitted, remove the kickstart mechanism cover

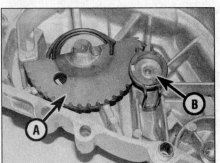

3.2 Kickstart quadrant (A) and engaging pinion (B) are located in the cover

3.3 Undo the pinch-bolt and remove the kickstart lever

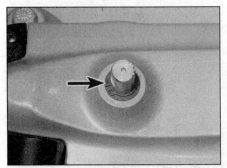

3.4 Remove the circlip (arrowed) securing the shaft

3.5 Release the tension in the spring and unhook it from the quadrant

3.6a Unhook the spring from the post (arrowed) . . .

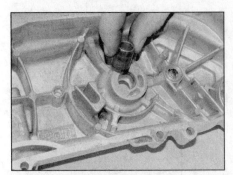

3.6b . . . and remove the kickstart bush if necessary

3.8a Check the dogs on the engaging pinion and the dogs on the driven gear

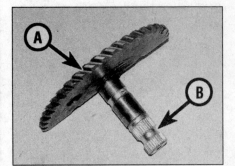

3.8b Inspect the teeth (A) and the splines (B) on the kickstart quadrant

3.11 Quadrant should butt against the stop (arrowed) on the inside of the case

3.13 Operate the kickstart lever to draw the pinion into the case

4.2a Variator pulley teeth engage in notch (arrowed)

quadrant bush, for signs of wear, and inspect the splines on the end of the quadrant shaft for damage. Renew any components that are worn or damaged.

9 Ensure the spring on the engaging pinion is a firm fit and inspect the kickstart return spring for cracks and wear at each end. When fitted, the return spring should return the kickstart lever to the rest position and hold it there; if not, it has sagged and should be renewed.

Installation

10 If removed, press the kickstart bush into the cover, then install the return spring with its long end innermost. Hook the long end around the post on the inside of the cover **(see illustration 3.6a)**.

11 Lubricate the kickstart shaft with a smear of molybdenum disulphide grease and insert it through the bush, then hook the outer end of the return spring onto the quadrant. Rotate the shaft anti-clockwise against the spring tension until the quadrant can be butted against the stop on the inside of the case **(see illustration)**. Ensure the shaft is pressed all the way into the case, then install the washer (if fitted) and circlip.

12 Fit the kickstart lever in the rest position and tighten the pinch-bolt securely. Operate the lever to check that it turns smoothly and returns to its rest position under spring pressure.

13 Lubricate the shaft of the engaging pinion with a smear of grease and install the washer,

then fit the pinion into the case. Align the spring with the detent in the case, then operate the kickstart lever to engage the pinion with the kickstart quadrant and draw the pinion into the case **(see illustration)**. Check the operation of the mechanism.

14 Where fitted, install the mechanism cover **(see illustration 3.1)**.

15 Refit the drivebelt cover (see Section 2).

---

4 Variator – removal, inspection and installation

Removal

1 Remove the drivebelt cover (see Section 2).

2 To remove the variator centre nut, the crankshaft must be locked to stop it turning. On engines with a toothed variator pulley, a service tool which bolts onto the engine case and locates between the teeth on the pulley is available to do this. Alternatively a similar tool can be made **(see illustrations)**. On engines with cooling fan blades on the variator pulley, locate a suitable holding tool in the holes provided in the pulley **(see illustration)**. A holding tool can be made from two strips of steel (see *Tool Tip*). **Note:** *The variator centre nut is tight – to avoid damage, ensure the variator pulley is held firmly before attempting to undo the nut.*

3 Undo the variator centre nut. **Note:** *Some manufacturers recommend fitting a new nut*

on reassembly – check with a scooter dealer. On some scooters, the kickstart driven gear is held in place by the nut – note how the gear locates on the outer face of the pulley **(see illustration)**. Remove the outer half of the

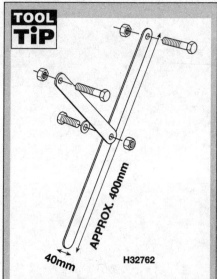

A holding tool can be made using two strips of steel bolted together in the middle, and with a nut and bolt through each end which locate into the holes in the pulley.

4.2b Lock the crankshaft with the tool (A) and undo the nut (B)

4.2c Using the holding tool to undo the variator centre nut

4.3a Note the location of the kickstart driven gear

variator pulley **(see illustration)**. Move the drivebelt aside – unless you are removing the clutch assembly, leave the belt on the clutch pulley. Mark the belt with a directional arrow if it is removed so that it can be refitted the correct way round **(see illustration)**.

4 Either hold the variator assembly and withdraw the centre sleeve, then pull the variator assembly off the crankshaft **(see illustrations)**, or pull the complete variator assembly off the shaft **(see illustration)**. **Note:** *If the variator is just being displaced, grip the assembly so that the ramp plate at the back is held into the variator body as you remove it, otherwise the rollers inside will fall out off their ramps and the variator will have to be disassembled to reposition them.*

5 Remove the washer (if fitted) from the crankshaft.

6 Where fitted, remove the screws or bolts and lift off the variator cover, then remove the

O-ring and discard it, as a new one must be fitted on reassembly **(see illustrations)**. Some restricted 50 cc machines have a restrictor plate fitted in the variator – lift out the restrictor plate **(see illustration)**.

4.3b Remove the outer half of the pulley

4.3c Mark the direction of rotation on the drivebelt

7 Lift out the ramp plate, noting how it fits, and remove the ramp guides **(see illustrations)**.

8 Lift out the rollers, noting which way round they fit **(see illustration)**.

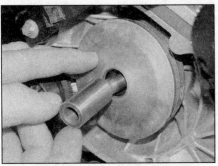

4.4a Withdraw the centre sleeve . . .

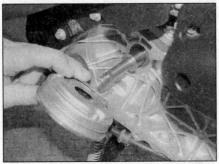

4.4b . . . then pull off the variator assembly

4.4c Hold the ramp plate (arrowed) to keep the rollers in place

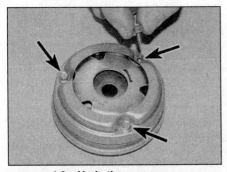

4.6a Undo the screws . . .

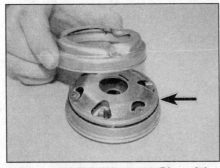

4.6b . . . and lift off the cover. Discard the O-ring (arrowed)

4.6c Where fitted, lift out the restrictor plate

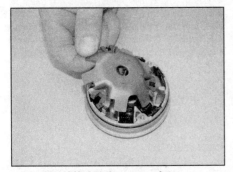

4.7a Lift out the ramp plate . . .

4.7b . . . and remove the ramp guides

4.8 Lift out the rollers

4.9 Clean the components of the variator thoroughly

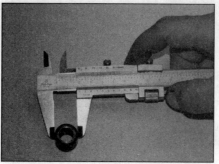

4.10 Measure the diameter of each roller

4.13 Check the splines (arrowed) for wear and the surface of the pulley for blueing

9 Clean all the components using a suitable solvent **(see illustration)**. **Note:** *Some manufacturers lubricate the rollers with high melting-point grease – refer to your scooter handbook for details.*

Inspection

10 Measure the diameter of each roller; they should all be the same size **(see illustration)**. Inspect the surface of each roller for flat spots. If any rollers are worn below the size specified in the *Data* section, or have worn flat, renew all the rollers as a set. **Note:** *Variator rollers are not interchangeable between different models. Always specify the year and model of your scooter when buying new rollers.*

11 Inspect the surface of the ramps in the variator body and the ramp plate for wear or damage. Check the slots in the ramp guides where they fit in the variator body and fit new components as necessary.

12 Inspect the surface of the variator sleeve for wear and fit a new one if necessary.

13 Check the condition of the splines in the centre of the outer half of the variator pulley and inspect the inner face of the pulley for signs of overheating or blueing, caused by the pulley running out of alignment **(see illustration)**. Renew the pulley half if it is damaged.

Installation

14 If required, lubricate the rollers and the ramps with high melting-point grease, then fit the rollers into the variator body **(see illustration 4.8)**. **Note:** *Too much grease in the variator will make it run out of balance and cause vibration.*

15 Check that the ramp guides are correctly

fitted on the ramp plate and install the plate **(see illustration 4.7b)**.

16 On restricted 50 cc machines, fit the restrictor plate.

17 Where fitted, fit a new O-ring in the groove around the variator body, then install the cover, taking care not to dislodge the O-ring, and tighten the cover screws or bolts securely.

18 Install the washer (if fitted) on the crankshaft. Grip the variator so that the ramp plate is held into the body and install the assembly and the centre sleeve (see Step 4). **Note:** *If the ramp plate moves and the rollers are dislodged, disassemble the variator and reposition the rollers correctly.*

19 Clean both inner faces of the variator pulley with a suitable solvent, then compress the clutch pulley centre spring and press the drivebelt into the clutch pulley to facilitate fitting it over the variator pulley **(see illustrations)**.

20 Install the outer half of the variator pulley, ensuring the splines align with the crankshaft. If required, install the kickstart driven gear (see Step 3). Fit the centre nut finger tight. **Note:** *A new centre nut should be fitted if recommended by the manufacturer.* Make sure the outer pulley half butts against the centre sleeve and is not skewed by the belt.

21 Install the locking tool used on removal (see Step 2) and tighten the centre nut to the specified torque setting.

22 Measure the distance between the crankcase face and the edge of the outer pulley half, then rotate the crankshaft and repeat the measuring procedure several times to ensure the outer pulley half is not skewed **(see illustration)**.

23 Ease the drivebelt out of the clutch pulley to reduce the slack in the belt **(see illustration)**, then fit the cover (see Section 2).

4.19a Clean the inner faces of the variator pulley . . .

4.19b . . . then press the belt into the clutch pulley and fit it onto the variator pulley

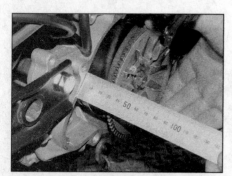

4.22 Check by measuring that the pulley is not skewed

4.23 Ease the belt into place between the two pulleys

5 Drivebelt –
inspection and renewal

Inspection

1 Most manufacturers specify service intervals for drivebelt inspection and service limits for the width of the belt, but it is good

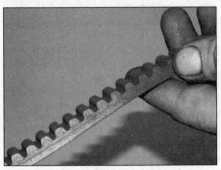

5.2a Check the belt for damage

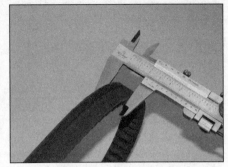

5.2b Measure the belt width

practice to check the condition of the belt whenever the cover is removed (see Section 2).

2 Check along the entire length of the belt for cracks, splits, fraying and damaged teeth and renew the belt if any such damage is found. Measure the belt width and compare the result with the specification in the *Data* section at the end of this manual **(see illustrations)**.

3 The belt will wear during the normal course of use and dust will accumulate inside the cover. However, a large amount of dust or debris inside the cover is an indication of abnormal wear and the cause, such as high spots on the pulleys or the pulleys running out of alignment, should be investigated.

Note: *Drivebelts are not interchangeable between different models. Always specify the*

year and model of your scooter when buying a new belt. If in doubt, check the part number marked on the belt.

4 Oil or grease inside the casing will contaminate the belt and prevent it gripping the pulleys (see Section 2).

Renewal

5 The drivebelt must be renewed at the specified service interval, or earlier dependant on belt condition (see Step 2). Remove the outer half of the variator pulley (see Section 4) and lift the belt off the crankshaft and the clutch pulley without disturbing the variator assembly.

6 Fit the new belt, making sure any directional arrows point in the direction of normal rotation, then install the variator outer pulley half (see Section 4).

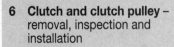

6 Clutch and clutch pulley –
  removal, inspection and
  installation

Removal

1 Remove the drivebelt (see Section 5).
2 To remove the clutch centre nut it is necessary to hold the clutch to prevent it turning. On some scooters, a holding tool that locates in the holes in the clutch drum can be used (see Section 4 *Tool Tip*); alternatively you can use a strap wrench **(see illustrations)**. *Note 1: On machines where the gearbox input shaft passes through the drivebelt cover, the clutch centre nut will already have been removed. Note any spacer on the gearbox input shaft and remove it.* **Note 2:** *Some manufacturers recommend fitting a new nut on reassembly – check with a scooter dealer.*
3 Remove the clutch drum **(see illustration)**.
4 Draw the clutch and pulley assembly off the gearbox input shaft **(see illus-tration)**.
5 To disassemble the clutch and pulley assembly, the centre spring must be compressed while the assembly nut is undone **(see illustrations)**. Most manufacturers produce a service tool to do this. Alternatively, use the set-up shown, ensuring no pressure is applied to the rim of the pulley and that there is

6.2a Prevent the clutch from turning with a home-made tool . . .

6.2b . . . or a strap wrench

6.3 Remove the clutch drum . . .

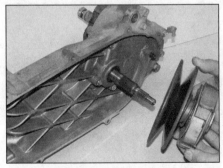

6.4 . . . then pull the clutch and pulley off the shaft

6.5a To undo the clutch assembly nut (arrowed) . . .

6.5b . . . the centre spring (arrowed) must be compressed

6.5c A home-made clamp for disassembling the clutch

6.5d Ensure the clamp does not rest on the rim (arrowed) of the pulley

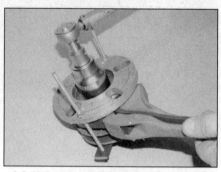

6.6 Hold the clutch with a strap wrench and undo the nut

adequate room to undo the nut **(see illustrations)**.

6 Fit a strap wrench around the clutch shoes to hold the assembly while the nut is

undone, then release the spring pressure gradually by undoing the clamp **(see illustration)**.

7 Remove the clutch shoes and backplate,

then remove the spring seat, the spring and the centre sleeve **(see illustrations)**.

8 Note the two O-rings fitted to the pulley outer half and remove them carefully **(see illustration)**. **Note:** *If the O-rings are damaged, or if grease from the clutch centre has worked its way past the O-rings, they should be renewed.*

9 Withdraw the guide pins and separate the pulley halves **(see illustrations)**.

10 Clean all the components with a suitable solvent.

Inspection

11 Check the inner surface of the clutch drum for damage and scoring and inspect the splines in the centre; renew it if necessary. Measure the internal diameter of the drum at several points to determine if it is worn or out-of-round **(see illustration)**. If it is worn or out-of-round, renew it.

12 Check the amount of friction material remaining on the clutch shoes **(see illustration)**. If the friction material has worn to the service limit specified in the *Data* section, down to the shoe, or the shoes are worn unevenly, fit a new shoe assembly.

13 Inspect the shoe springs for wear, cracks and stretching. Ensure that the shoes are not seized on their pivot pins and that the retaining circlips, where fitted, are secure on the ends of the pins **(see illustration 6.12)**. If any parts are worn or damaged, fit a new shoe assembly.

14 Check the condition of the centre spring.

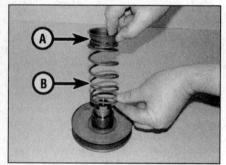

6.7a Lift off the spring seat (A) and spring (B) . . .

6.7b . . . then remove the centre sleeve

6.8 Remove the O-rings carefully

6.9a Withdraw the guide pins . . .

6.9b . . . and separate the pulley halves

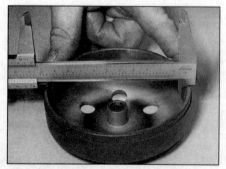

6.11 Measure the internal diameter of the drum as described

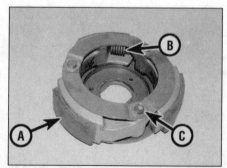

6.12 Check the clutch friction material (A), shoe springs (B) and retaining clips (C)

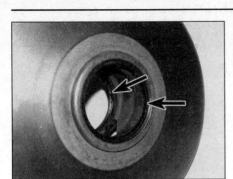

6.17 Inspect the pulley internal seals (arrowed)

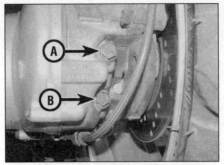

7.2 Gearbox filler plug (A) and drain plug (B)

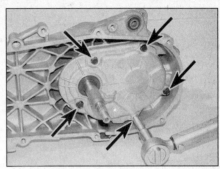

7.3 Undo the gearbox cover bolts

If it is bent or appears weak, renew it. Measure the free length of the spring and compare the result with the figure in the *Data* section. Fit a new spring if it has worn to less than the service limit.

15 Inspect the inner faces of the clutch pulley for signs of overheating or blueing, caused by the pulley running out of alignment.

16 Inspect the guide pins and the pin slots for wear.

17 Check the seals inside the pulley outer half **(see illustration)**. If the seals are worn or damaged, grease will pass onto the face of the pulley. On most scooters, two bearings are fitted in the hub of the pulley inner half; inspect the rollers of the inner bearing for flat spots and ensure the outer sealed ball-bearing turns smoothly (see *Tools and Workshop Tips* in the *Reference* section). If any of the clutch pulley internal components are worn or damaged, they must be renewed. Check with a scooter dealer as to the availability of new parts – details of bearing and seal renewal are given in *Tools and Workshop Tips*. If individual components are not available, or if a number of components are worn, fit a new clutch pulley assembly.

Installation

18 Assemble the two halves of the clutch pulley and install the guide pins and the O-rings. Lubricate the pin slots with molybdenum disulphide grease, then fit the centre sleeve, the centre spring and the spring seat.

19 Position the shoe assembly on the spring

seat and compress the spring using the same method as for disassembly (see Step 5). Ensure the flats on the shoe backplate are aligned with the pulley hub and install the assembly nut finger tight. Hold the assembly with a strap wrench around the clutch shoes and tighten the nut to the torque setting specified in the *Data* section, then release the clamp **(see illustration 6.6)**.

20 Lubricate the needle bearing in the hub of the pulley inner half with molybdenum disulphide grease and install the clutch and pulley assembly on the input shaft. Install the clutch drum, ensuring the splines align with the shaft.

21 Install the remaining components in the reverse order of removal, noting the following:

● *Where fitted, install the spacer on the gearbox shaft (see Step 2).*
● *If required, use a new clutch centre nut.*
● *Tighten the centre nut to the specified torque setting.*
● *Clean both inner faces of the clutch pulley with a suitable solvent before installing the drivebelt (see Section 5).*

7 Gearbox – removal, inspection and installation

Removal

1 Remove the clutch and clutch pulley (see Section 6). On machines fitted with a drum

rear brake, remove the rear wheel; on machines fitted with a disc rear brake, remove the rear wheel, hub and brake disc (see Chapter 8).

2 If a drain plug is fitted to the machine, drain the gearbox oil **(see illustration)**. **Note:** *Remove the filler plug to assist oil drainage.*

3 Unscrew the bolts securing the gearbox cover and remove them **(see illustration)**. **Note:** *Depending upon the design of your scooter, the gearbox cover is fitted either on the left-hand side of the transmission casing, behind the clutch, or on the right-hand side behind the rear wheel. The cover bolts are usually positioned on the same side as the cover, although on some machines with a right-hand cover, the bolts pass through the casing from the left.*

> **HAYNES HINT** *Make a cardboard template of the gearbox cover and punch a hole for each bolt location. This will ensure all bolts are installed correctly on reassembly – this is important as some bolts may be of different lengths.*

4 Carefully ease the cover away from the casing and remove it **(see illustration)**. If the cover is stuck, tap around the joint face between the cover and the casing with a soft-faced mallet to free it. Do not try to lever the cover off as this may damage the sealing surfaces. **Note:** *On gearboxes not fitted with a drain plug, position a tray beneath the casing to catch the oil when the cover is removed.*

5 If any of the gearbox shafts come out with the cover, take care not to damage any seals as the shafts are pulled through. Note the position of any dowels on the cover and remove them for safekeeping if they are loose. Discard the gasket, as a new one must be fitted on reassembly.

6 All the scooters covered by this manual have three gearbox shafts – the input shaft which carries the clutch, the output shaft which carries the rear wheel, and an intermediate shaft **(see illustration)**. Check the shafts for any thrustwashers or wave washers and remove them, noting where they fit, then lift out

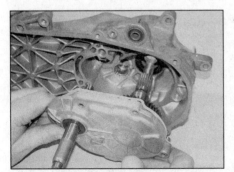

7.4 Lift away the gearbox cover

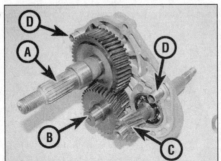

7.6a Output shaft (A), intermediate shaft (B), input shaft (C) and cover dowels (D)

7.6b Note the position of any wave washers (A) or thrustwashers (B) on the shafts

7.6c Lift out the gearbox shafts . . .

7.6d . . . noting how they fit together

the shafts **(see illustrations)**. **Note:** *The input shaft is often a press-fit in its bearing and should not be removed unless the shaft, the bearing or the oil seal is to be renewed.*

7 Check the casing and cover for any remaining washers and remove them, noting where they fit **(see illustration)**.

8 Do not remove the gear pinions from the shafts unnecessarily – they should only be removed if components are being renewed.

Inspection

9 Clean all traces of old gasket material from the case and cover mating surfaces, taking care not to scratch or gouge the soft aluminium. Wash all the components in a suitable solvent and dry them with compressed air.

10 Check the pinion teeth for cracking, chipping, pitting and other obvious wear or damage, then check for signs of scoring or blueing on the pinions and shafts caused by overheating due to inadequate lubrication **(see illustration)**.

11 Ensure that all the pinions are a tight fit on their shafts.

12 Inspect the splines and threads on the input and output shafts.

13 Renew any damaged or worn components. In some cases, the pinions are a press-fit on the shafts, or are retained by circlips allowing components to be renewed individually **(see illustration)**. Some pinions are an integral part of the shaft and on some scooters shafts are only supplied as matched items. Check with a scooter dealer as to the availability of components.

14 To remove the input shaft, first fit the clutch centre nut to protect the threads, then drive the shaft out using a soft-faced mallet on the clutch end.

15 Check the intermediate shaft thrustwashers and renew them if they are damaged or worn. Fit new ones if in any doubt.

16 Check the condition of the shaft oil seals **(see illustration)**. Some gearboxes are fitted with drain holes – if a seal fails, oil will drain out to the underside of the casing **(see illustration)**. Any loss of gearbox oil must be remedied immediately to avoid expensive damage or seizure. If the input shaft oil seal fails, oil will run out of the drain hole, if fitted, or into the drivebelt case behind the clutch. If either of the shafts has been removed, it is good practice to fit a new seal (see *Tools and Workshop Tips* in the *Reference* section).

17 Inspect the bearings (see *Tools and Workshop Tips* in the *Reference* section). **Note:** *Bearings that are fitted into blind holes require an internal bearing puller to extract them without damaging the case; consult a scooter dealer or a specialist engineer if they need removing.*

Installation

18 Installation is the reverse of removal, noting the following:

● *Ensure any washers are fitted to the shafts before assembly.*
● *Lubricate both ends of the intermediate shaft with molybdenum disulphide grease before installation.*
● *Fit any dowels into the cover.*
● *Use a new cover gasket.*
● *Smear the inside of the oil seals with grease before installing the shafts.*
● *Tighten the cover bolts evenly and in a criss-cross pattern to the torque setting specified in the Data section.*
● *If a gearbox drain plug is fitted, ensure it is tightened to the specified torque setting.*
● *Fill the gearbox with the specified amount and type of oil (see Chapter 1).*

7.7 Note the location of any inner washers

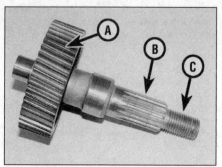

7.10 Check the pinion teeth (A), splines (B) and threads (C) for wear and damage

7.13 Pinion is retained on the shaft by the circlip (arrowed)

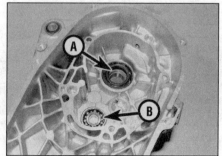

7.16a Check the condition of the oil seals (A) and bearings (B)

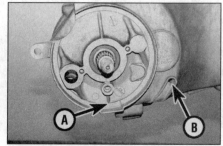

7.16b If the output shaft seal fails, oil will drain at (A); if the input shaft seal fails, oil will drain at (B)

Chapter 7
Frame and suspension

Contents

Degrees of difficulty

Easy, suitable for novice with little experience	**Fairly easy,** suitable for beginner with some experience	**Fairly difficult,** suitable for competent DIY mechanic	**Difficult,** suitable for experienced DIY mechanic	**Very difficult,** suitable for expert DIY or professional

Specifications

Refer to the *Data* section at the end of this manual for servicing specifications.

1 General information

All scooters covered by this manual are fitted with a tubular and pressed steel one-piece frame.

The engine and transmission unit is linked to the frame by a pivoting assembly at the front and by the rear shock absorber(s), making the unit an integral part of the rear suspension.

Front suspension is by a leading or trailing link arrangement with a single shock absorber, or by conventional or upside-down telescopic forks.

Ancillary items such as stands and handlebars are covered in this Chapter.

2 Frame – inspection and repair

1 The frame should not require attention unless accident damage has occurred. In most cases, frame renewal is the only satisfactory remedy for such damage. A few frame specialists have the jigs and other equipment necessary for straightening the frame to the required standard of accuracy, but even then there is no simple way of assessing to what extent the frame may have been over-stressed.

2 After a high mileage, the frame should be examined closely for signs of cracking or splitting at the welded joints. Loose engine mount and suspension bolts can cause ovaling or fracturing of the mounting points. Minor damage can often be repaired by specialist welding, depending on the extent and nature of the damage.

3 Remember that a frame which is out of alignment will cause handling problems. If misalignment is suspected as the result of an accident, it will be necessary to strip the machine completely so the frame can be thoroughly checked.

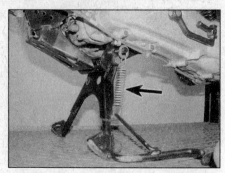

3.2a Note the location of the spring (arrowed) . . .

3.2b . . . and remove it carefully

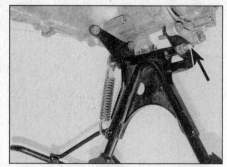

3.3 Unscrew the nut (arrowed) and withdraw the pivot bolt

3.4 Remove the stand assembly

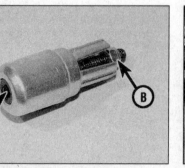

3.8 Unhook the spring and remove the pivot bolt (arrowed)

3 Stands –
removal and installation

Centre stand

1 Support the scooter securely in an upright position using an auxiliary stand. **Note:** *Do not rest the weight of the machine on the bodywork; remove the belly panels to expose the frame (see Chapter 9). Alternatively, have an assistant support the machine.*
2 Unhook the stand spring, noting how it fits, and remove the spring plate, if fitted **(see illustrations)**.
3 Unscrew the pivot bolt nut and remove the washer, then withdraw the pivot bolt and remove the stand **(see illustration)**.
4 On scooters with a stand bracket bolted to

the underside of the engine, unscrew the nuts and withdraw the bolts securing the bracket, then remove the stand and bracket as an assembly **(see illustration)**.
5 Thoroughly clean the stand and remove all road dirt and old grease. Inspect the pivot bolt and the pivot holes in the bracket for wear and renew them if necessary. Inspect the spring; if it is sagged or is cracked a new spring must be fitted. Inspect the rubber stop on the stand and renew it if it is worn or perished.
6 Installation is the reverse of removal, noting the following:
● *Apply grease to the pivot bolt and all pivot points.*
● *Tighten the nuts securely.*
● *Ensure that the spring holds the stand up securely when it is not in use – an accident is almost certain to occur if the stand*

extends while the machine is in motion. If necessary, fit a new spring.

Side stand

7 Support the scooter securely in an upright position using an auxiliary stand (see Step 1).
8 Unhook the stand spring, noting how it fits **(see illustration)**.
9 Unscrew the stand pivot bolt and remove the bolt, washer and stand **(see illustration 3.8)**. Note how the contact plate on the stand locates against the safety switch plunger when the stand is lowered.
10 Installation is the reverse of removal, noting the following:
● *Apply grease to the pivot bolt.*
● *Ensure that the stand contact plate actuates the stand switch when the stand is lowered.*
● *Check the spring tension – it must hold the stand up when it is not in use. If necessary, fit a new spring.*
● *Check the operation of the sidestand switch (see Chapter 10, Section 8).*

4 Handlebars –
removal and installation

Removal

1 Remove the handlebar covers and any body panels as necessary to access the steering stem (see Chapter 9).
2 If required, the handlebars can be displaced from the steering stem for access to the bearings without having to detach any cables, hoses or main wiring looms, or remove the switches, brake levers or master cylinders. If this is the case, ignore the Steps which do not apply.
3 Where fitted, loosen the centre screws for the bar end weights and withdraw the weights from the handlebars. Take care not to undo the screws too far and lose the nuts on the end of the screws **(see illustration)**.
4 Undo the throttle twistgrip housing screws and slide the twistgrip off the end of the handlebar (see Chapter 4).
5 Disconnect the wiring from each brake light switch **(see illustration)**.

4.3 Loosen bar end weight centre screw (A) to release nut (B)

4.5 Disconnect the brake light switch wiring connectors

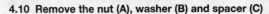
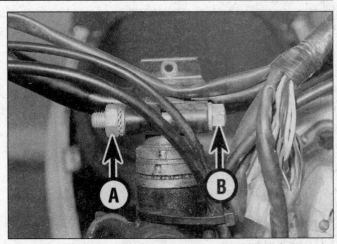

4.10 Remove the nut (A), washer (B) and spacer (C)

4.11 Undo the nut (A) and withdraw the pinch-bolt (B)

6 Undo the handlebar switch housing screws and displace the housing.

7 Check that no other electrical components are mounted on the handlebars and detach them if necessary.

8 Unscrew the brake master cylinder assembly clamp bolts and position the assembly clear of the handlebar, making sure no strain is placed on the hydraulic hose (see Chapter 8). Keep the master cylinder reservoir upright to prevent air entering the system. **Note:** *Some scooters are fitted with hydraulically-operated front and rear brakes, on others only the front brake is hydraulically-operated.*

9 Remove the left-hand grip; peel the grip off the end of the bar, or if necessary cut it off.

10 On scooters with the handlebars secured by a stem bolt, undo the nut on the stem bolt and remove the nut, washer and shaped spacer, noting how they fit **(see illustration)**. Support the handlebars and withdraw the bolt, then lift the bars off the steering stem.

11 On scooters with the handlebars secured by a clamp and pinch-bolt, undo the nut and bolt, then lift off the bars **(see illustration)**.

12 If the handlebar components have been left attached, position the bars so that no strain is placed on any of the cables, hoses or wiring, and protect the body panels to prevent scratching.

Installation

13 Installation is the reverse of removal, noting the following:

● *Tighten the handlebar stem bolt to the torque setting specified in the Data section.*
● *Use a suitable adhesive to secure the left-hand grip on the handlebar.*
● *Don't forget to reconnect the brake light switch wiring connectors.*
● *Check the operation of the brakes before riding the scooter.*

5 Steering head bearings – adjustment

1 Support the machine on the centrestand with the front wheel raised off the ground. **Note:** *Do not rest the weight of the machine on the bodywork; remove the belly panels to expose the frame (see Chapter 9).*

2 Remove the handlebar covers and any body panels as necessary to access the steering stem (see Chapter 9).

3 If required, displace the handlebars (see Section 4).

4 Some scooters are fitted with one locknut above the bearing adjuster nut, others have two locknuts. The locknut and the adjuster nut are usually held in place with a lock washer

(see illustration). Check carefully and refer to your scooter handbook for details.

5 If the lock washer has tabs which locate in notches in the locknut, first prise the tabs out of the notches. **Note:** *A tabbed lock washer should not be re-used; remove the locknut and fit a new washer after adjusting the bearings.*

6 If one locknut is fitted, loosen it using a suitable spanner, C-spanner or drift **(see illustration)**.

7 If two locknuts are fitted, unscrew the top nut then lift the tab washer off the remaining two nuts, noting how it fits **(see illustration)**. Unscrew the second locknut. A rubber washer is fitted between the second locknut and the adjuster nut. Discard it if it is crushed or damaged and fit a new one on reassembly.

8 Using either a spanner, C-spanner or drift, loosen the adjuster nut slightly to take pressure off the bearing then tighten the nut until all freeplay is removed. Check that the steering still turns freely from side-to-side. The object is to set the adjuster nut so that the bearings are under a very light loading, just enough to remove any freeplay.

Caution: Take great care not to apply excessive pressure because this will cause premature failure of the bearings.

9 With the bearings correctly adjusted, the adjuster nut must be held to prevent it from

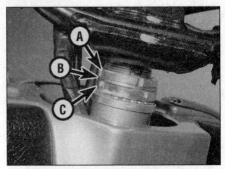

5.4 Locknut (A), washer (B), adjuster nut (C)

5.6 Remove the locknut (arrowed) and discard the lockwasher

5.7 Location of the tab washer

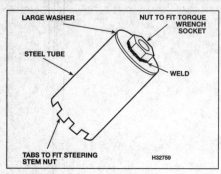

LARGE WASHER
NUT TO FIT TORQUE
WRENCH SOCKET
STEEL TUBE
WELD
TABS TO FIT STEERING
STEM NUT
H32759

5.11a Tool to adjust the steering head bearings

moving while the locknut is tightened. Where necessary, first install a new lockwasher ensuring the tabs locate correctly in the adjuster nut.

10 Where one locknut is fitted, tighten the locknut securely, then bend the remaining lockwasher tabs up to secure the locknut. **Note:** *Some manufacturers specify a torque setting for the locknut (see the Data section at the end of this manual); however to apply this a service tool or a suitable fabricated tool (see illustration 5.11a) is required and the handlebars must be displaced (see Section 4).*

11 Where two locknuts are fitted, install the rubber washer and then the second locknut, tightening it finger-tight. Hold the adjuster nut to prevent it turning, then tighten the second locknut only enough to align its notches with the notches in the adjuster nut and install the tab washer **(see illustration 5.7)**. Install the top locknut, then hold the adjuster nut to

5.11b Hold the adjuster nut and tighten the locknut with the special tool

prevent it turning and tighten the top locknut securely. If the special tool is available, tighten the locknut to the specified torque setting **(see illustrations)**.

12 Check the bearing adjustment and re-adjust if necessary, then install the remaining components in the reverse order of removal.

6 Steering stem – removal and installation

Removal

1 Remove the front wheel and, if applicable, the brake caliper (see Chapter 8). On machines where the wheel can be removed leaving the hub in place, remove the hub.

2 If the front mudguard or mudguard liner are

mounted on the front suspension, remove them (see Chapter 9).

3 Remove the handlebars (see Section 4). **Note:** *The ball-bearings in the lower steering head race may not be retained by a cage – place a clean rag on the floor beneath the steering head to catch the ball-bearings if they are loose when the steering stem is removed.*

4 Unscrew and remove the bearing adjuster locknut(s) and washer (see Section 5).

5 Support the steering stem, then unscrew the bearing adjuster nut and carefully lower the stem out of the steering head **(see illustration)**. Note which way round the adjuster nut fits.

6 The ball-bearings in the lower race will either fall out of the race or stick to the lower inner race on the steering stem. The top inner race and top bearing will remain in the top of the steering head.

7 If not already done, lift out the top inner race and the top bearing **(see illustration)**. **Note:** *On some scooters, the top inner bearing race is integral with the adjuster nut. The balls of the top bearing may be loose or they may be housed in a cage.*

8 Remove all traces of old grease from the ball-bearings and races and inspect them for wear or damage (see Section 7). **Note:** *Do not attempt to remove the outer races from the steering head or the lower bearing inner race from the steering stem unless they are to be renewed.*

Installation

9 Apply a liberal quantity of grease to the bearing inner and outer races and install the top bearing **(see illustration 6.7)**.

10 Assemble the lower race ball-bearings on the lower inner race on the steering stem; if they are a loose assembly they will be retained by the grease **(see illustration)**.

11 Carefully lift the steering stem up through the steering head, ensuring the lower race ball-bearings remain in place. Either thread the combined top inner bearing race/adjuster nut onto the stem or install the inner race and thread the adjuster nut onto the stem **(see illustrations)**. Ensure the adjuster nut is fitted the right way round.

12 Install the remaining components in the reverse order of removal.

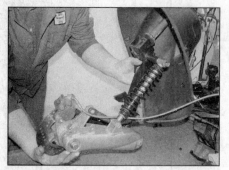

6.5 Lower the steering stem out of the steering head

6.7 Top bearing in the top of the steering head

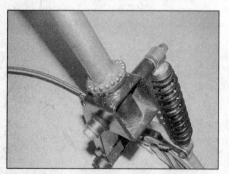

6.10 Hold the lower race ball-bearings in place with grease

6.11a Lift the steering stem into place ...

6.11b ... and install the adjuster nut

7.3a Inspect the races in the top . . .

7.3b . . . and bottom of the steering head

7.3c Lower inner race on the steering stem

7 Steering head bearings – inspection and renewal

Inspection

1 Remove the steering stem (see Section 6).
2 Remove all traces of old grease from the bearings and races and check them for wear or damage.
3 The races should be polished and free from indentations (see illustrations). The outer races are in the steering head, the top inner race is either integral with the bearing adjuster nut or it rests on top of the top bearing, and the lower inner race is on the steering stem. Inspect the ball-bearings for signs of wear, pitting or corrosion, and examine the bearing retainer cage for signs of cracks or splits, where fitted. If there are any signs of wear or damage on any of the above components both upper and lower bearing assemblies must be renewed as a set. Only remove the races from the steering head and the stem if they need to be renewed – do not re-use them once they have been removed.

Renewal

4 The outer races are an interference fit in the frame and can be tapped from position with a suitable drift (see illustration). Tap firmly and evenly around each race to ensure that it is driven out squarely. It may prove advantageous to curve the end of the drift slightly to improve access.
5 Alternatively, the races can be pulled out using a slide-hammer with internal expanding extractor.
6 The new outer races can be pressed into the frame using a drawbolt arrangement (see illustration), or by using a large diameter tubular drift which bears only on the outer edge of the race. Ensure that the drawbolt washer or drift (as applicable) bears only on the outer edge of the race and does not contact the working surface.

 HAYNES HiNT *Installation of new bearing outer races is made much easier if the races are left overnight in the freezer. This causes them to contract slightly making them a looser fit.*

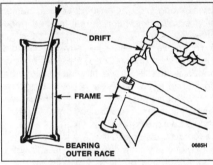

7.4 Drive the bearing outer races out with a brass drift

7 To remove the lower inner race from the steering stem, first drive a chisel between the base of the race and the bottom yoke. Work the chisel around the race to ensure it lifts squarely. Once there is clearance beneath the race, use two levers placed on opposite sides of the race to work it free, using blocks of wood to improve leverage and protect the yoke. If the race is firmly in place it will be necessary to use a bearing puller.
8 Fit the new lower inner race onto the steering stem. A length of tubing with an internal diameter slightly larger than the steering stem will be needed to tap the new bearing into position. Ensure that the drift bears only on the inner edge of the race and does not contact its working surface.
9 Install the steering stem (see Section 6).

8 Front suspension – disassembly, inspection and reassembly

Note: *Some suspension assemblies use self-locking nuts which should be discarded after use. Always use new self-locking nuts when reassembling the suspension.*

Leading link or monolever

Disassembly

1 Remove the front wheel, hub, caliper bracket and axle (see Chapter 8), and the mudguard (see Chapter 9).
2 Undo the nut and bolt securing the lower end of the shock absorber to the suspension

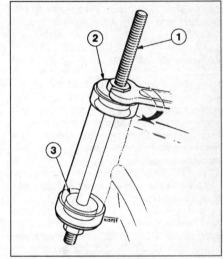

7.6 Using a drawbolt to fit the outer races in the steering head

1 Long bolt or threaded bar
2 Thick washer
3 Guide for lower race

arm. Support the arm and withdraw the bolt (see illustration).
3 Undo the nut securing the upper end of the shock absorber, then pull off the shock. If required, remove the upper mounting bolt, noting the position of any spacers.
4 Counterhold the bolt and undo the nut securing the brake caliper bracket torque arm to the suspension leg, then remove the nut,

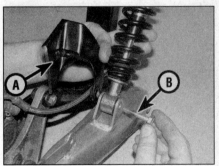

8.2 Remove the bracket (A) and withdraw the lower shock bolt (B)

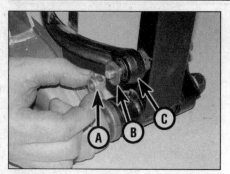

8.4 Remove the nut (A), washer (B) and torque arm (C)

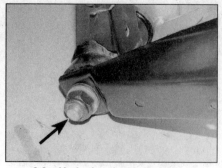

8.6a Undo the pivot bolt nut . . .

8.6b . . . and remove any washers . . .

washer and torque arm **(see illustration)**. Remove the bolt from the suspension leg if it is loose.

5 On some scooters the suspension arm pivots on rubber bushes in the bottom of the suspension leg, on others the arm turns on a pair of bearings. Before separating the arm from the suspension leg, check the condition of the bushes or bearings by moving the arm laterally against the suspension leg. If any play is felt between the arm and the leg, the bushes or bearings must be renewed. Also move the arm up-and-down. If any roughness is felt or the arm does not move smoothly and freely, the bushes, bearings or pivot bolt must be renewed. If there is no play or roughness in the suspension arm movement there is no need to disassemble the suspension further. **Note:** *Suspension rubber bushes are generally a very tight fit which requires a press for*

removal and fitting. Consult a scooter dealer or specialist engineer if the bushes need renewing.

6 To remove the suspension arm, counterhold the pivot bolt and undo the nut on the opposite end. Remove the nut, noting the position of any washers, spacers or brackets, then withdraw the pivot bolt and arm from the suspension leg **(see illustrations)**. The bolt should be a press-fit in the arm and should not be removed unnecessarily.

7 Remove any dust caps, spacers and seals from either side of the suspension leg, then remove any sleeve from inside the bearings **(see illustrations)**.

Inspection

8 Clean all components thoroughly, removing all traces of dirt, corrosion and grease. Inspect all components closely, looking for

obvious signs of wear such as heavy scoring, or for damage such as cracks or distortion.

9 Check the condition of the bearings in the suspension leg (see *Tools and Workshop Tips* in the *Reference* section). **Note:** *If ball-bearings are fitted they can be removed for cleaning and inspection, but needle roller bearings should only be removed if they are going to be renewed.* Check carefully for any retaining circlips before attempting to remove the bearings and note the position of the bearings and any sleeves or spacers.

10 Inspect the pivot bolt for wear and remove any corrosion with steel wool. Check the bolt for straightness with a straight-edge. If the bolt is worn, press it out of the suspension arm carefully to avoid damaging the locating hole and fit a new bolt. If the bolt is bent, cut off the damaged section and press the remainder out of the arm.

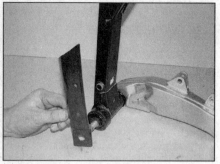

8.6c . . . or brackets . . .

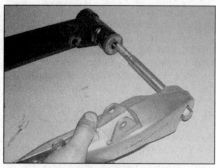

8.6d . . . then withdraw the pivot bolt and arm from the suspension leg

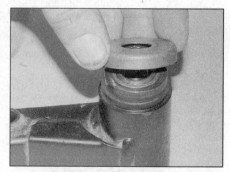

8.7a Remove the dust cap . . .

8.7b . . . and any seals . . .

8.7c . . . or spacers

8.7d Remove the bearing sleeve, where fitted

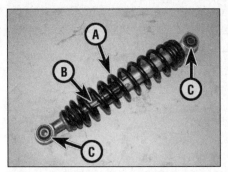

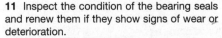

8.13 Inspect the shock spring (A), damper rod (B) and mountings (C)

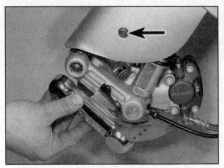

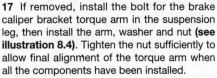

8.24 Undo the screw (arrowed) to remove the cover and pull off the trim

8.25 Remove the circlip (arrowed) and slide the bracket off

11 Inspect the condition of the bearing seals and renew them if they show signs of wear or deterioration.

12 Inspect the shock absorber for obvious physical damage and the shock spring for looseness, cracks or signs of fatigue.

13 Inspect the damper rod for signs of bending, pitting and oil leaks, and check the mountings at the top and bottom of the shock for wear or damage (see illustration). If any parts are worn or damaged, a new shock must be fitted.

Reassembly

14 If the bearings have been removed, ensure the bearing housings are thoroughly clean, then install the bearings (see Tools and Workshop Tips in the Reference section). Note: Where a bearing is retained by a circlip, drive it in only as far as is necessary to install the circlip. Ensure any bearing spacers are in place and lubricate needle roller bearings with molybdenum disulphide grease.

15 Install any seals, spacers and dust caps as necessary, then smear the pivot bolt with grease and install it through the bearings, ensuring the seals remain in position. Check that the suspension arm is fitted on the correct side of the leg, then install the washers and spacers as necessary and the pivot bolt nut.

16 If the pivot bolt nut retains the mudguard assembly, tighten the nut sufficiently to allow final positioning of the mudguard bracket when the mudguard is fitted. Otherwise, tighten the nut to the torque setting specified in the Data section at the end of this manual.

17 If removed, install the bolt for the brake caliper bracket torque arm in the suspension leg, then install the arm, washer and nut (see illustration 8.4). Tighten the nut sufficiently to allow final alignment of the torque arm when all the components have been installed.

18 Install the lower end of the shock absorber in the bracket on the monolever arm, then install the bolt. Tighten the bolt finger-tight.

19 Ensure any spacers on the upper shock mounting bolt are correctly positioned, then fit the shock onto the bolt and install the nut. Counterhold the bolt and tighten the nut to the specified torque setting.

20 Install the mudguard (see Chapter 9). If not already done, tighten the pivot bolt nut to the specified torque setting.

21 Install the axle and caliper bracket (see Chapter 8). Counterhold the bolt and tighten the nut securing the caliper bracket torque arm to the suspension leg to the specified torque setting.

22 Tighten the lower shock mounting bolt to the specified torque setting.

23 Install the hub and front wheel (see Chapter 8).

Trailing link monoshock

Disassembly

24 Remove the front wheel and, on disc brake models, the hub assembly (see Chapter 8). Where applicable, remove the suspension cover and the trailing link trim (see illustration).

25 On disc brake models, check for any play in the bearings between the trailing link arm and the brake caliper mounting bracket. Remove the circlip and slide the bracket off the arm to inspect the bearings (see illustration).

26 On some scooters, the bottom of the shock absorber is secured by two bolts, and a bracket on the top of the shock is held by two nuts (see illustrations). Alternatively, the shock is secured top and bottom by a single bolt. Undo the fixings as appropriate, noting the position of any washers or spacers, then lift the shock off (see illustration).

27 Before separating the trailing link arm from the suspension leg, check the condition of the bearings by moving the arm laterally against the leg. If any play is felt between the arm and the leg, the bearings and spacer pin must be renewed. Also move the arm up-and-down. If any roughness is felt or the arm does not move smoothly and freely, the bearings and spacer pin must be renewed. If there is no play or roughness in the suspension arm movement there is no need to disassemble the suspension further.

28 To remove the suspension arm, first remove the wheel hub assembly (see Chapter 8).

29 On some scooters, the suspension arm turns on a pivot bolt; counterhold the bolt and undo the nut on the opposite end. Remove the nut, noting the position of any washers or spacers, then withdraw the pivot bolt and arm from the suspension leg.

8.26a Undo the two bolts (arrowed) . . .

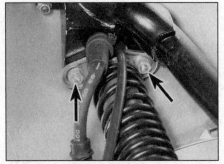

8.26b . . . and the two nuts (arrowed) . . .

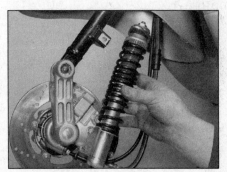

8.26c . . . and lift off the shock

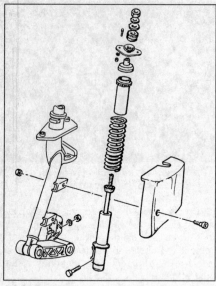

8.37 Front shock absorber components

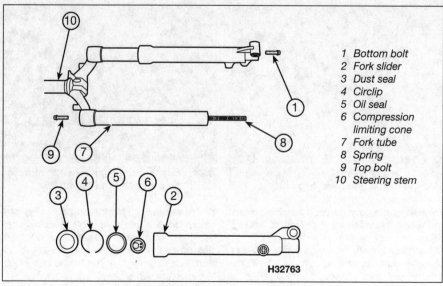

1 Bottom bolt
2 Fork slider
3 Dust seal
4 Circlip
5 Oil seal
6 Compression limiting cone
7 Fork tube
8 Spring
9 Top bolt
10 Steering stem

H32763

8.46 Typical telescopic fork components

30 Alternatively, the arm turns on a pin which is secured at each end by a push-in cap. The caps can be removed either by hitting them centrally with a suitable punch or drift, which should be wide enough to cover the raised inner section of the cap, or be levering up the outer tangs of the cap with a screwdriver. Discard the caps, as new ones must be used.

31 Drive or press out the pivot pin from the middle of the arm and separate the arm from the leg. Note the position of any O-rings and seals.

Inspection

32 Clean all components thoroughly, removing all traces of dirt, corrosion and grease. Inspect all components closely, looking for obvious signs of wear such as heavy scoring, or for damage such as cracks or distortion.

33 Check the condition of the suspension arm and brake caliper mounting bracket bearings (see *Tools and Workshop Tips* in the *Reference* section). **Note:** *If ball-bearings are fitted they can be removed for cleaning and inspection, but needle roller bearings should only be removed if they are going to be renewed.* Check carefully for any retaining circlips before attempting to remove the bearings and note the position of the bearings and any sleeves or spacers.

34 Inspect the shock absorber for obvious physical damage and the shock spring for looseness, cracks or signs of fatigue.

35 Inspect the damper rod for signs of bending, pitting and oil leaks **(see illustration 8.13)**.

36 Inspect the mountings at the top and bottom of the shock for wear or damage.

37 On some machines, the shock absorber can be disassembled and individual components renewed **(see illustration)** – check the availability of parts with a scooter dealer. Compress the spring to remove the

pressure on the spring seat at the top, then unscrew the top nut. Lift off the components of the upper mounting, noting the order in which they are fitted, then carefully release the pressure on the spring. Remove the spring, noting which way up it fits. Install the new components and reassemble the shock in the reverse order of disassembly.

Reassembly

38 If the bearings have been removed, ensure the bearing housings are thoroughly clean, then install the bearings (see *Tools and Workshop Tips* in the *Reference* section). **Note:** *Where a bearing is retained by a circlip, drive it in only as far as is necessary to install the circlip. Ensure any bearing spacers are in place and lubricate needle roller bearings with molybdenum disulphide grease*

39 Lubricate the pivot pin with molybdenum disulphide grease. Align the suspension arm with the leg, ensuring it is the right way round, then press the pin into place.

40 Fit new dust seals and O-rings as necessary.

41 Fit the new push-in caps and drive them into place using a piece of tubing that bears only on the area between the raised inner section and the raised outer tangs.

42 Install the shock absorber and tighten the nuts and bolts to the specified torque settings.

43 On disc brake models, slide the brake caliper mounting bracket onto the suspension arm and secure it with the circlip, making sure it sits properly in its groove (see Step 25). Install the hub assembly (see Step 24).

44 Install the front wheel (see Chapter 8) and the covers, where applicable.

Conventional telescopic fork

Note 1: *Two types of conventional telescopic fork are fitted to the scooters covered by this manual. On the first type, the tubes are an*

integral part of the fork yoke (Steps 45 to 62), on the second, motorcycle-type fork, the tubes are clamped in the yoke and can be removed individually for disassembly (Steps 63 to 92).

Note 2: *Always dismantle the fork legs separately to avoid interchanging parts. Check the availability of parts and the type and quantity of fork oil required with a scooter dealer before disassembling the forks. Note that on some scooters the forks are lubricated with grease.*

Disassembly

45 Remove the steering stem (see Section 6).

46 Place a suitable oil drain tray below the fork, then unscrew the bolt in the bottom of the fork slider. Discard the sealing washer, as a new one must be used on reassembly. Pull the slider off the fork tube, then pull the dust seal off the slider and, if applicable, drain the oil from the slider **(see illustration)**.

47 Remove the circlip from inside the top of the slider, then carefully prise out the oil seal, taking care not to gouge the rim of the slider when doing this. Discard the seal, as a new one must be fitted on reassembly.

48 Remove the compression limiting cone from inside the bottom of the slider, noting which way round it fits.

49 To remove the spring, unscrew the bolt in the top of the fork tube and draw the spring out of the tube. Hold the spring to prevent it from turning with the bolt. Some forks are fitted with a sealed damper unit. Unscrew the top bolt, then unscrew the damper rod from the top bolt and remove damper unit and spring together. **Note:** *Various combinations of spring and damper unit are used – some forks have only one unit fitted in one of the legs, others have a damper unit in both legs. Some forks have a damper unit fitted in one leg and a spring in the other.*

Inspection

50 Clean all parts in a suitable solvent and dry them with compressed air, if available.

51 Inspect the fork tubes for score marks, pitting or flaking of the chrome finish and excessive or abnormal wear. Check the straightness of the tubes with a straight-edge. If either of the tubes is damaged, worn or bent, fit a new fork yoke assembly.

52 Inspect the springs for cracks, sagging and other damage. No service data is available for the springs, but ensure they are both the same length. If one spring is defective renew both springs as a pair.

53 If fitted, check the operation of the damper unit. Compress the damper rod into the cartridge, then pull it out. Movement of the rod should be slow and gradual – if there is no damping action, or the movement is jerky, fit a new unit. **Note:** *If two units are fitted they should be renewed as a pair.*

54 The dust seals should be a sliding fit on the fork legs. Discard the dust seals if they are worn or perished and fit new ones (it is good practice to renew the dust seals when the forks are disassembled).

Reassembly

55 Install the compression limiting cone.

56 Lubricate the new oil seal with fork oil or grease, then press it squarely into the slider using a suitable piece of tubing or a socket until the circlip groove is visible above the seal.

> **HAYNES HINT** *Place a suitably-sized washer on top of the oil seal to protect it when pressing it into place.*

57 Once the seal is installed, fit the circlip, making sure it is correctly located in its groove. **Note:** *If the fork is lubricated with grease, apply the grease to the inside of the slider below the level of the seal.*

58 As required, check that both plugs are in the ends of the spring, then insert the spring into the slider; alternatively, install the damper unit and spring into the slider. Fit a new sealing washer to the bottom bolt, then install the bolt into the bottom of the slider and thread it into the plug in the base of the spring or into the damper unit. Press down on the spring to prevent it from turning and tighten the bolt securely.

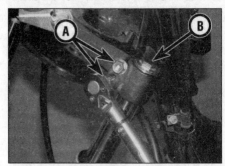

8.66 Fork leg clamp bolts (A) and fork top bolt (B)

59 If applicable, carefully pour the correct quantity of the specified fork oil into the slider (see Note 2).

60 Fit the dust seal and apply some fork oil to the lips of the seal, then insert the top of the spring into the bottom of the fork tube. Ensure the fork tube fits squarely through the oil seal and into the slider, and install the slider onto the tube until the spring contacts the top of the tube. Hold the slider in position, then install the bolt in the top of the fork tube and thread it into the plug in the top of the spring. Alternatively, extend the damper rod fully, then install the slider onto the tube and thread the damper rod into the top bolt and tighten it securely.

61 Tighten the top bolt securely.

62 Install the steering stem (see Section 6).

Motorcycle-type fork

Note 1: *Two types of conventional telescopic fork are fitted to the scooters covered by this manual. On the first type, the tubes are an integral part of the fork yoke (Steps 45 to 62), on the second, motorcycle-type fork, the tubes are clamped in the yoke and can be removed individually for disassembly (Steps 63 to 92).*

Note 2: *Always dismantle the fork legs separately to avoid interchanging parts. Check the availability of parts and the type and quantity of fork oil required with a scooter dealer before disassembling the forks. Note that on some scooters the forks are lubricated with grease.*

Removal

63 Remove the front wheel and, if applicable, the brake caliper (see Chapter 8).

64 If the front mudguard is mounted on the front suspension, remove it (see Chapter 9).

65 Remove each fork leg individually.

66 If the fork leg is going to be disassembled or the fork oil is going to be changed, loosen the fork top bolt while the leg is still clamped in the fork yoke (**see illustration**). To do this, first undo the fork leg clamp bolts and push the leg a short distance up through the yoke, then temporarily tighten the clamp bolts. Now loosen the top bolt. **Note:** *Some fork legs have a location groove for one of the clamp bolts – remove the bolt before attempting to move the leg.*

67 Undo the fork clamp bolts and remove the fork leg by twisting it and pulling it downwards (**see illustration**).

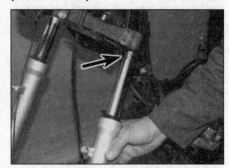

8.67 Pull the leg down – note the groove (arrowed)

> **HAYNES HINT** *If the fork legs are seized in the yokes, spray the area with penetrating oil and allow time for it to soak in before trying again.*

Installation

68 Remove all traces of corrosion from the fork tubes and the yokes. Install each fork leg individually. Slide the leg up through the yoke until the top edge of the fork tube is level with the top edge of the yoke. Where applicable, ensure the location groove for the clamp bolt is correctly aligned. **Note:** *If the fork top bolt has not been fully tightened, follow the procedure in Step 66 to tighten it before positioning the leg in the yoke.* Tighten the clamp bolts in the yoke to the torque setting specified in the *Data* section at the end of this manual.

69 Install the remaining components in the reverse order of removal. Check the operation of the front forks and brake before taking the scooter out on the road.

Disassembly

70 Remove the fork leg (see Steps 63 to 67). Always dismantle the fork legs separately to avoid interchanging parts. Store all components in separate, clearly-marked containers (**see illustration**).

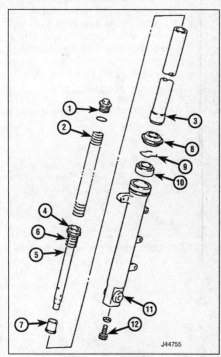

J44755

8.70 Typical motorcycle-type fork components

1 Top bolt		7 Spring seat
2 Spring		8 Dust seal
3 Fork tube		9 Circlip
4 Sealing ring		10 Oil seal
5 Damper		11 Fork slider
6 Rebound spring		12 Damper bolt

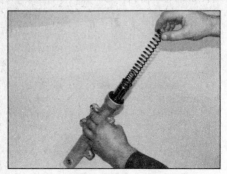

8.74 Withdraw the fork spring

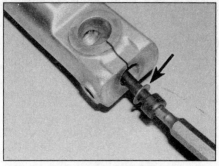

8.76 Remove the damper bolt and sealing washer (arrowed)

8.78 Withdraw the damper and rebound spring

71 The damper bolt should be loosened at this stage. Invert the fork leg and compress the fork tube in the slider so that the spring exerts maximum pressure on the damper head, then loosen the bolt in the base of the fork slider **(see illustration 8.76)**.

72 If the fork top bolt was not loosened with the fork on the scooter, carefully clamp the fork tube in a vice equipped with soft jaws, taking care not to overtighten or score the tube's surface, and loosen the top bolt.

73 Unscrew the top bolt from the top of the fork tube. If a damper rod is attached to the top bolt, loosen the locknut and unscrew the rod. Note any O-ring fitted to the top bolt; if it is damaged, fit a new one on reassembly.

 Warning: The fork spring is pressing on the fork top bolt with considerable pressure. Unscrew the bolt very carefully, keeping a downward pressure on it and release it slowly as it is likely to spring

clear. It is advisable to wear some form of eye and face protection when carrying out this operation.

74 Slide the fork tube down into the slider and withdraw the spring **(see illustration)**. Note which way up the spring is fitted.

75 Invert the fork leg over a suitable container and pump the fork vigorously to expel as much fork oil as possible.

76 Remove the previously-loosened damper bolt and its sealing washer from the bottom of the slider **(see illustration)**. Discard the sealing washer, as a new one must be used on reassembly. If the damper bolt was not loosened before dismantling the fork, temporarily install the spring and press down on it to prevent the damper from turning.

77 Pull the fork tube out of the slider.

78 Withdraw the damper and, if fitted, the rebound spring and spring seat from inside the fork tube **(see illustration)**.

79 Carefully prise out the dust seal from the

top of the slider, then remove the retaining clip and prise the oil seal out of the slider. Discard the seals, as a new ones must be used on reassembly.

Inspection

80 Follow the procedure in Steps 50 to 54 to clean and check the fork components. If either of the fork tubes appears bent, have them both checked by a scooter dealer or specialist engineer. If necessary, fit new fork tubes, do not have them straightened.

81 Where fitted, check the condition of the rebound spring as well as the main spring.

82 On some forks, no damper rod is fitted – a sealing ring is fitted around the damper which restricts the flow of oil through the fork tube. Inspect the surface of the ring and renew it if it is scored, pitted or worn **(see illustration)**. **Note:** *Do not remove the ring from the piston unless it requires renewal.*

Reassembly

83 Where fitted, slide the rebound spring onto the damper, then insert the damper into the bottom of the fork tube and install the spring seat on the bottom of the damper **(see illustration)**.

84 Lubricate the fork tube with the specified fork oil and insert the assembly into the slider. Fit a new sealing washer to the damper bolt and apply a few drops of a suitable, non-permanent thread-locking compound, then install the bolt into the bottom of the slider. Tighten the bolt to the specified torque setting. If the damper rotates inside the tube, hold it with spring pressure as on disassembly (see Step 76).

85 Push the fork tube fully into the slider, then lubricate the inside of the new oil seal with fork oil and slide it over the tube with its markings facing upwards **(see illustration)**. Press the seal into place in the slider. If necessary, use a suitable piece of tubing to tap the seal carefully into place; the tubing must be slightly larger in diameter than the fork tube and slightly smaller in diameter than the seal recess in the slider. Take care not to scratch the fork tube during this operation; if the fork tube is pushed fully into the slider any accidental scratching is confined to the area above the seal.

86 Fit the retaining clip, making sure it is correctly located in its groove **(see illustration)**.

8.82 Check the condition of the sealing ring

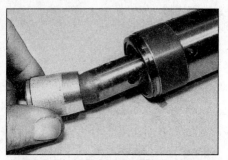

8.83 Fit the spring seat on the bottom of the damper

8.85 Install the oil seal with markings facing up

8.86 Fit the oil seal retaining clip . . .

8.87 . . . and then the dust seal

8.88 Measure the oil level with the leg fully compressed

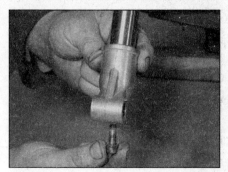

8.94a Remove the bolt and pull off the bracket

87 Lubricate the inside of the new dust seal then slide it down the fork tube and press it into position **(see illustration)**.

88 Slowly pour in the correct quantity of the specified grade of fork oil and carefully pump the fork to distribute the oil evenly; the oil level should also be measured and adjustment made by adding or subtracting oil – refer to your scooter handbook for details. Fully compress the fork tube into the slider, then measure the fork oil level from the top of the tube **(see illustration)**.

89 Pull the fork tube out of the slider to its full extension; if applicable, pull the damper rod out also. Install the spring.

90 If necessary, fit a new O-ring to the fork top bolt. If applicable, thread the bolt onto the damper rod and tighten the locknut.

91 Keep the fork leg fully extended and press down on the spring whilst threading the top bolt into the top of the fork tube. Turn the bolt carefully to ensure it is not cross-threaded. **Note:** *The top bolt can be tightened to the specified torque setting when the fork has been installed and is securely held in the bottom yoke.*

 Warning: It will be necessary to compress the spring by pressing it down with the top bolt in order to engage the threads of the top bolt with the fork tube. This is a potentially dangerous operation and should be performed with care, using an assistant if necessary. Wipe off any excess oil before starting to prevent the possibility of slipping.

92 Install the fork leg (see Steps 68 and 69).

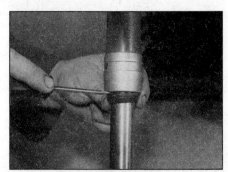

8.94b Lever off the dust seal

Upside-down fork

Seal renewal

93 Remove the front wheel and, if applicable, the brake caliper (see Chapter 8).

94 Where fitted, unscrew the bolt from the base of the fork slider which retains the axle/brake caliper bracket and draw the bracket off the slider **(see illustration)**. Where fitted, lever the dust seal off the bottom of the fork tube and remove it **(see illustration)**.

95 Where fitted, remove the circlip, then prise the oil seal out of the bottom of the fork tube, taking care not to gouge the tube or the surface of the slider.

96 Clean the bottom of the slider and the inside of the axle/brake caliper bracket and remove any traces of corrosion.

97 Smear the new oil seal with fork oil or grease, then fit it over the slider and press it into position on the bottom of the tube. If applicable, fit the circlip.

98 If applicable, smear the inside of the new

dust seal with fork oil or grease and install the seal.

99 Install the axle/brake caliper bracket and tighten the retaining bolt securely.

100 Install the remaining components in the reverse order of removal.

Disassembly

Note: *Some designs of upside-down forks are difficult to disassemble. If the fork is worn or the fork action is suspect, consult a scooter dealer – it may be more practical to renew the whole assembly. On some scooters, the forks are maintenance-free and no parts are available. Check the availability of parts and the type and quantity of fork oil required with a scooter dealer before disassembling the forks. Note that on some scooters the forks are lubricated with grease.*

101 Remove the steering stem (see Section 6). Always dismantle the fork legs separately to avoid interchanging parts. Store all components in separate, clearly marked containers **(see illustration)**.

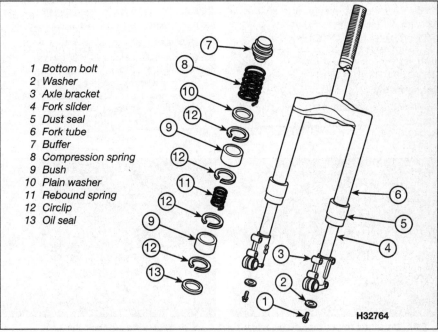

1 Bottom bolt
2 Washer
3 Axle bracket
4 Fork slider
5 Dust seal
6 Fork tube
7 Buffer
8 Compression spring
9 Bush
10 Plain washer
11 Rebound spring
12 Circlip
13 Oil seal

H32764

8.101 Typical upside-down fork components

8.103 Removing the circlip

9.3 Upper rear suspension mounting

2 The shock absorber is secured to the frame at the top and the transmission casing at the bottom. To access the upper mounting, remove the body panels as necessary according to model (see Chapter 9). If necessary, remove the air filter housing (see Chapter 4).

3 Undo and remove the nut, or the nut and bolt, securing the top of the shock absorber to the frame **(see illustration)**.

4 Undo the nut and bolt securing the bottom of the shock absorber to the transmission casing; support the shock and remove the bolt, then manoeuvre the shock away from the machine **(see illustrations)**.

Inspection

5 Inspect the shock absorber for obvious physical damage and the shock spring for looseness, cracks or signs of fatigue.

6 Inspect the damper rod for signs of bending, pitting and oil leaks and check the mountings at the top and bottom of the shock for wear or damage **(see illustration 8.13)**.

7 On some scooters, the shock absorber can be disassembled and individual components renewed **(see illustration)** – check the availability of parts with a scooter dealer. Compress the spring to remove the pressure on the spring seat at the top, then unscrew the top nut. Lift off the components of the upper mounting, noting the order in which they are fitted, then carefully release the pressure on the spring. Remove the spring, noting which way up it fits. Install the new

102 Remove the dust and oil seals (see Steps 94 and 95).

103 Remove the lower circlip from inside the bottom of the fork tube **(see illustration)**. Pull the slider out of the fork tube, together with the lower bush and rebound spring. Note the order of the fork components for reassembly. If applicable, drain the fork oil out of the slider.

104 Remove the upper bush circlip, then draw out the upper bush and remove the upper circlip. Discard the circlips, as new ones must be fitted on reassembly.

105 Withdraw the washer (where fitted), compression spring and buffer from the tube.

Inspection

106 Clean all parts in a suitable solvent and dry them with compressed air, if available.

107 Inspect the fork sliders for score marks, pitting or flaking of the chrome finish and excessive or abnormal wear. Check the straightness of the sliders with a straight-edge. If either of the sliders is damaged, worn or bent, fit a new fork yoke assembly.

108 Inspect the springs for cracks, sagging and other damage. No service data is available for the springs, but ensure both springs in each pair are the same length. If one spring is defective renew both springs as a pair.

109 Examine the working surfaces of each bush; if they are worn or scuffed, renew the bushes as a set.

Reassembly

110 Install the various components into the fork tube in the reverse order of removal. If required, pour the correct quantity of the

specified fork oil into the slider; alternatively, lubricate the inside of the fork tube and the outside of the slider with grease.

111 Install the buffer, compression spring and washer (where applicable) into the fork tube. Fit the new upper bush and circlips using a suitable piece of tubing to ensure they are squarely positioned inside the fork tube. Install the upper circlip for the lower bush inside the fork tube. Install the lower bush and spring on the slider, then fit the slider into the tube pushing it up into place. Press the lower bush into place against its upper circlip, then secure it with the lower circlip.

112 Install the remaining components in the reverse order of removal.

---

9 Rear shock absorber – removal, inspection and installation

Note: *Most scooters covered by this manual have a single rear shock absorber. On machines with twin rear shocks, the lower end of the right-hand shock is supported by a subframe which bolts to the engine case and the rear wheel axle (see Chapter 8).*

Removal

1 Support the machine on its centre stand and position a support under the rear wheel so that the engine does not drop when the shock absorber is removed, but also making sure that the weight of the machine is off the rear suspension so that the shock is not compressed.

9.4a Undo the lower rear suspension mounting . . .

9.4b . . . then lift out the shock

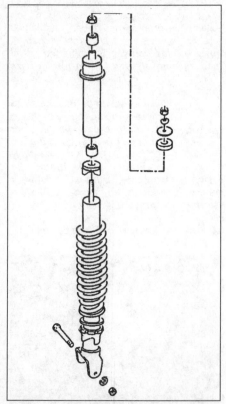

9.7 Rear shock absorber components

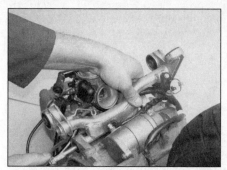

10.2a Removing a 'hanger bracket' from the engine unit

10.2b Withdraw the pivot bolt . . .

10.2c . . . and remove the bracket from the frame

components and reassemble the shock in the reverse order of disassembly.

Installation

8 Installation is the reverse of removal. Tighten the shock absorber mounting bolts to the specified torque settings.

---

10 Front engine mounting – removal, inspection and installation

Removal

Note: *On some scooters the front engine mounting is bolted to the front, lower edge of the crankcase, on others a 'hanger bracket' bolts to the top of the crankcase. In all cases, the mounting employs rubber-in-torsion 'silentbloc' bushes and damping rubbers to restrict movement.*

1 Remove the engine/transmission unit (see Chapter 2A or 2B).
2 Counterhold the engine bracket bolt(s) and undo the nut(s), then withdraw the bolt(s) and remove the engine mounting **(see illustrations)**.

Inspection

3 Thoroughly clean all components, removing all traces of dirt, corrosion and grease.
4 Inspect the silentbloc bushes closely, looking for obvious signs of deterioration such as compression and cracks, or distortion due to accident damage **(see illustration)**. The bushes are generally a very tight fit which requires a press for removal and fitting. Consult a scooter dealer or specialist engineer if the bushes need renewing.
5 Where the mounting bracket bolts to the front edge of the crankcase it should be necessary to compress the damping rubber in order to remove and install the engine bracket to frame bolt. If the bracket is not a tight fit, renew the damping rubber **(see illustration)**.

10.4 Inspect the bushes carefully . . .

6 On the hanger bracket type mounting, check for wear on the damping rubbers. If the rubbers have worn, allowing metal-to-metal contact, renew them.
7 Check the bolts for wear and check the holes in the engine bracket for wear. If the bolts are not a precise fit in the bracket the components must be renewed.

Installation

8 Installation is the reverse of removal. Smear some grease on the engine bracket bolts. Tighten all mounting bolts to the torque setting specified in the *Data* section at the end of this manual.

10.5 . . . and check the condition of the damper rubbers

Chapter 8
Brakes, wheels and tyres

Contents

Degrees of difficulty

| Easy, suitable for novice with little experience | | Fairly easy, suitable for beginner with some experience | | Fairly difficult, suitable for competent DIY mechanic | | Difficult, suitable for experienced DIY mechanic | | Very difficult, suitable for expert DIY or professional | |

Specifications

Refer to the *Data* section at the end of this manual for servicing specifications.

1 General information

The scooters covered by this manual are fitted with either hydraulic disc brakes, cable-operated drum brakes, or a combination of disc front and drum rear brakes.

Generally, the hydraulic master cylinder is integral with the brake lever, although occasionally the master cylinder is remotely-mounted and operated by a cable from the brake lever.

In view of the broad variety of wheel types and tyre sizes covered, owners are advised to refer to their scooter handbook or consult a tyre specialist for tyre choice and fitment.
Caution: Disc brake components rarely require disassembly. Do not disassemble components unless absolutely necessary. If a hydraulic brake hose is loosened, the entire system must be disassembled, drained, cleaned and then properly filled and bled upon reassembly. Do not use solvents on internal brake components. Solvents will cause the seals to swell and distort. Use only clean brake fluid, a dedicated brake cleaner or denatured alcohol for cleaning. Use care when working with brake fluid as it can injure your eyes; it will also damage painted surfaces and plastic parts.

2 Front brake pads – removal, inspection and installation

 Warning: The dust created by the brake system may contain asbestos, which is harmful to

2.1 Remove the pad cover

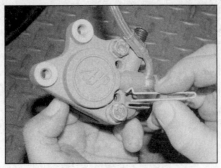

2.3a Withdraw the spring wire pins

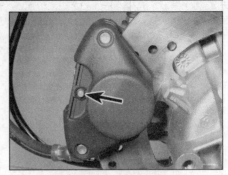

2.3b Remove the E-clip . . .

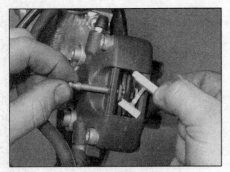

2.3c . . . and withdraw the pin – note the position of the pad spring

2.3d Drift out the pin and spring clip

disc (see Section 3). **Note:** *Do not operate the brake lever while the caliper is off the disc.*

3 The pads are retained in the caliper by pad pins. Some calipers have spring wire pins; withdraw the pins, noting how they fit **(see illustration)**. Some calipers have pressed-in steel pins – if the pin is secured with an E-clip, remove the clip and withdraw the pin, noting the position of the pad spring **(see illustrations)**. If the pin is secured with a spring clip, drift out the pin **(see illustration)**. Some calipers have screw-in pins – unscrew the pin plug, then unscrew the pin and withdraw it **(see illustrations)**.

4 If not already done, note the position of any pad springs and remove them, then lift out the pads **(see illustration)**. Note the position of any pad springs inside the caliper **(see illustration)**.

5 Inspect the surface of each pad for contamination and check that the friction material has not worn to or beyond the minimum thickness specified in the *Data* section at the end of this manual **(see illustration)**. If either pad is worn down to, or beyond, the service limit, is fouled with oil or grease, or heavily scored or damaged, both pads must be renewed. **Note:** *It is not possible to degrease the friction material; if the pads are contaminated in any way they must be renewed.*

6 If the pads are in good condition, clean them carefully using a fine wire brush which is completely free of oil and grease to remove all traces of road dirt and corrosion. Spray the caliper with a dedicated brake cleaner to

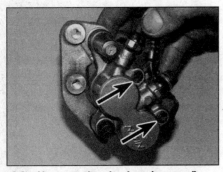

2.3e Unscrew the pin plugs (arrowed) . . .

2.3f . . . then unscrew the pad pins

your health. Never blow it out with compressed air and don't inhale any of it. An approved filtering mask should be worn when working on the brakes.

1 Where fitted, remove the pad cover from the caliper **(see illustration)**.

2 If necessary, unscrew the brake caliper mounting bolts and slide the caliper off the

2.4a Lift out the pads

2.4b Note the position of springs (arrowed) inside the caliper

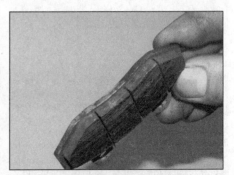

2.5 Measure the amount of friction material on each pad

remove any dust and remove any traces of corrosion which might cause sticking of the caliper/pad operation.

7 Remove all traces of corrosion from the pad pins. Inspect the pins for damage and, where applicable, loss of spring tension, and renew them if necessary. If the pins are secured by clips, ensure the clips are a tight fit on the pin, otherwise fit new clips on reassembly.

8 Remove all traces of corrosion from the pad springs; if the springs are badly worn or damaged, fit new springs.

9 Check the condition of the brake disc (see Section 4).

10 If new pads are being installed, slowly push each piston as far back into the caliper as possible using hand pressure or a piece of wood for leverage. This will displace brake fluid back into the hydraulic reservoir, so it may be necessary to remove the reservoir cap, plate and diaphragm and syphon out some fluid (depending on how much fluid was in there in the first place and how far the pistons have to be pushed in). If a piston are difficult to push back, attach a length of clear hose to the bleed valve and place the open end in a suitable container, then open the valve and try again. Take great care not to draw any air into the system and don't forget to tighten the valve once the piston has been sufficiently displaced. If in doubt, bleed the brakes afterwards (see Section 8).

Caution: Never lever the caliper against the brake disc to push a piston back into the caliper as damage to the disc will result.

11 Smear the pad pins and the backs of the pads with copper-based grease, making sure that none gets on the front or sides of the pads.

12 Installation is the reverse of removal, noting the following:
● *If applicable, ensure any pad springs are in place inside the caliper.*
● *Fit the pads into the caliper so that the friction material faces the disc.*
● *Install the pad pins and, where applicable, the pad spring.*
● *Check that the pins are correctly locked or clipped in place.*
● *Install the caliper and operate the brake lever several times to bring the pads into contact with the disc.*
● *Check the brake fluid level and top-up if necessary (see Daily (pre-ride) checks).*

13 Check the operation of the brake before riding the scooter.

3 Front brake caliper –
removal, overhaul and installation

⚠ **Warning: If a caliper indicates the need for renewal (usually due to leaking fluid or sticky operation), all old brake fluid should be flushed from the system at the same time. Also, the dust created by the**

3.1a Undo the caliper mounting bolts . . .

brake system may contain asbestos, which is harmful to your health. Never blow it out with compressed air and don't inhale any of it. An approved filtering mask should be worn when working on the brakes. Do not, under any circumstances, use petroleum-based solvents to clean brake parts. Use a dedicated brake cleaner or denatured alcohol only, as described. To prevent damage from spilled brake fluid, always cover paintwork when working on the braking system.

Note: *On some scooters, the front wheel must be removed before the caliper can be removed (see Section 14).*

Removal

1 Unscrew the brake caliper mounting bolts and slide the caliper off the disc **(see illustrations)**. **Note:** *Do not operate the brake lever while the caliper is off the disc.*

2 If the caliper is just being displaced, the brake pads can be left in place. Support the caliper with a cable tie to ensure no strain is placed on the hydraulic hose.

3 If the caliper is being cleaned and inspected, remove the brake pads (see Section 2). **Note:** *It is not necessary to disconnect the brake hose to clean and inspect the caliper.*

4 To remove the caliper from the machine, first note the alignment of the banjo fitting on the caliper, then unscrew the banjo bolt and separate the hose from the caliper **(see illustration)**. Discard the sealing washers, as new ones must be used on installation. Wrap a plastic bag tightly around the end of the

3.4 Unscrew the bolt (arrowed) to detach the hose

3.1b . . . and slide the caliper off

hose to prevent dirt entering the system and secure the hose in an upright position to minimise fluid loss. **Note:** *If you are planning to overhaul the caliper and do not have a source of compressed air to blow out the piston, just loosen the banjo bolt at this stage and retighten it lightly. The hydraulic system can then be used to force the piston out of the caliper. Disconnect the hose once the piston has been sufficiently displaced.*

Overhaul

5 Clean the exterior of the caliper with denatured alcohol or brake system cleaner. Inspect the caliper for signs of damage, especially around the mounting lugs and the bleed screw, and renew it if necessary. If hydraulic fluid is leaking from around the edge of the piston, the internal piston seal has failed **(see illustration)**. If new seals are available the caliper can be overhauled as follows, otherwise a new caliper will have to be fitted. **Note:** *The scooters covered by this manual are fitted with single piston, opposed piston or double piston calipers. If there is more than one piston in the caliper, mark each piston head and the caliper body with a suitable marker to ensure that the pistons can be matched to their original bores on reassembly.*

6 Displace the piston from its bore using either compressed air or by carefully operating the front brake lever to pump it out. If the piston is being displaced hydraulically, it may be necessary to top-up the hydraulic reservoir during the procedure. Also, have some clean rag ready to catch any spilled hydraulic fluid

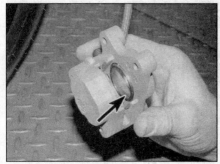

3.5 Fluid leaks indicate a failed seal

3.9 Remove the seals with a soft wooden or plastic tool – a pencil works well

when the piston reaches the end of the bore. Where two pistons are fitted, ensure that they both move freely and evenly. **Note:** *If the compressed air method is used, direct the air into the fluid inlet on the caliper. Use only low pressure to ease the piston out – if the air pressure is too high and the piston is forced out, the caliper and/or piston may be damaged.*

⚠️ **Warning: Never place your fingers in front of a piston in an attempt to catch or protect it when applying compressed air, as serious injury could result.**

7 If a piston sticks in its bore, try to displace it with compressed air (see Step 6). Where two pistons are fitted, remove the free piston first, then pack its bore with clean rag and try to displace the stuck piston. If the stuck piston cannot be displaced, a new caliper will have to be fitted.

Caution: Do not try to remove a piston by levering it out, or by using pliers or any other grips.

8 On opposed piston calipers, it may not be possible to force the pistons all the way out of their bores. Unscrew the caliper joining bolts and separate the caliper halves, noting the position of any O-rings. Discard the O-rings, as new ones must be fitted on reassembly.

9 Remove the dust seal and the piston seal from the piston bore using a soft wooden or plastic tool to avoid scratching the bore **(see illustration)**. Discard the seals, as new ones must be fitted.

10 Clean the piston and bore with clean brake fluid or brake system cleaner. If compressed air is available, blow it through

the fluid galleries in the caliper to ensure they are clear and use it to dry the parts thoroughly (make sure it is filtered and unlubricated). *Caution: Do not, under any circumstances, use a petroleum-based solvent to clean brake parts.*

11 Inspect the bore and piston for signs of corrosion, nicks and burrs and loss of plating. If surface defects are present, the caliper assembly must be renewed. If the caliper is in bad shape the master cylinder should also be checked.

12 Lubricate the new piston seal with clean brake fluid and install it in the groove in the caliper bore.

13 Lubricate the new dust seal with clean brake fluid and install it in the groove in the caliper bore.

14 Lubricate the piston with clean brake fluid and install it, closed-end first, into the caliper bore. Using your thumbs, push the piston all the way in, making sure it enters the bore squarely.

15 On opposed piston calipers, smear the new caliper body O-rings with clean brake fluid and install them in one half of the caliper. Assemble the caliper halves and tighten the joining bolts – if required, the bolts can be tightened fully once the caliper has been installed on the scooter.

Installation

16 If the brake pads have been removed, install the pads (see Section 2). If the caliper has just been displaced, install the caliper on the brake disc **(see illustration 3.1b)**.

17 Install the caliper mounting bolts, and tighten them to the torque setting specified in the *Data* section. If required, tighten the caliper joining bolts (see Step 15).

18 If the caliper was removed from the machine, or a new caliper is being fitted, connect the brake hose to the caliper, using new sealing washers on each side of the banjo fitting. Align the banjo fitting as noted on removal. Tighten the banjo bolt to the specified torque setting and top-up the hydraulic reservoir (see *Daily (pre-ride) checks*). Bleed the hydraulic system (see Section 8).

19 Check for fluid leaks and check the operation of the brake before riding the scooter.

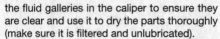

Inspection

1 Visually inspect the surface of the disc for score marks and other damage. Light scratches are normal after use and won't affect brake operation, but deep grooves and heavy score marks will reduce braking efficiency and accelerate pad wear. If a disc is badly grooved it must be machined or renewed.

2 The disc must not be machined or allowed to wear down to a thickness less than the service limit, either as listed in the *Data* section at the end of this manual, or as stamped on the disc **(see illustration)**. Check the thickness of the disc with a micrometer and renew it if necessary **(see illustration)**.

3 To check disc warpage, position the machine upright so that the wheel is raised off the ground. Attach a dial gauge to the suspension with the tip of the gauge touching the surface of the disc about 10 mm from the outer edge. Rotate the wheel and watch the gauge needle; a small amount of movement is acceptable. If excessive movement is indicated, first check the wheel bearings for play (see Section 14). If the bearings are good, the disc is warped and should be renewed.

Removal

4 Remove the front wheel (see Section 14). On some scooters it may also be necessary to remove the hub assembly.

Caution: Do not lay the wheel down and allow it to rest on the disc – the disc could become warped.

5 If you are not renewing the disc, mark the relationship of the disc to the wheel so that it can be installed in the same position. Unscrew the disc retaining bolts, loosening them a little at a time to avoid distorting the disc, then remove the disc **(see illustration)**.

Installation

6 Before installing the disc, make sure there is no dirt or corrosion where the disc seats on the hub. If the disc does not sit flat when it is

4.2a Look for thickness stamped on disc

4.2b Measuring the thickness of a disc with a micrometer

4.5 Unscrew the bolts (arrowed) to remove the disc

4.7 Brake disc directional arrow

5.2 Unscrew the clamp bolts (arrowed)

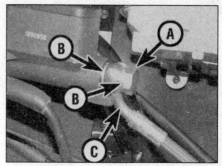

5.4 Brake hose banjo bolt (A), sealing washers (B) and banjo fitting (C)

bolted down, it will appear to be warped when checked or when the front brake is used.

7 Install the disc, making sure that the directional arrow, if applicable, points in the direction of normal wheel rotation **(see illustration)**. Align the previously applied register marks, if you are reinstalling the original disc. Install the bolts and tighten them evenly and a little at a time to the torque setting specified in the *Data* section. Clean the disc using acetone or brake system cleaner. If a new brake disc has been installed, remove any protective coating from its working surfaces.

8 If applicable, install the hub assembly, and the front wheel (see Section 14).

9 Operate the brake lever several times to bring the pads into contact with the disc. Check the operation of the brake before riding the scooter.

5 Front brake master cylinder
– removal, overhaul and installation

Handlebar-mounted

Removal

1 Remove the handlebar covers for access (see Chapter 9).

2 If the master cylinder is just being displaced, ensure the fluid reservoir cover is secure. Unscrew the master cylinder clamp bolts and remove the back of the clamp **(see illustration)** . Position the assembly clear of the handlebar, making sure no strain is placed on the brake hose and the brake light switch wiring. Keep the fluid reservoir upright to prevent air entering the hydraulic system.

3 If the master cylinder is being removed, disconnect the brake light switch wiring connector and, if required unscrew the brake light switch.

4 Unscrew the brake hose banjo bolt and detach the banjo fitting, noting its alignment with the master cylinder **(see illustration)**.

5 Once disconnected, secure the hose in an upright position to minimise fluid loss. Wrap a clean plastic bag tightly around the end to prevent dirt entering the system. Discard the sealing washers, as new ones must be fitted on reassembly.

6 Undo the master cylinder clamp bolts and remove the back of the clamp **(see illustration 5.2)**. Lift the master cylinder and reservoir away from the handlebar.

7 Undo the reservoir cover retaining screws and lift off the cover, the diaphragm plate and the diaphragm **(see illustration)**. Drain the brake fluid from the reservoir into a suitable container. Wipe any remaining fluid out of the reservoir with a clean rag.

8 If required, remove the brake lever (see Section 11).

Overhaul

Note : *If the master cylinder is leaking fluid, or if the lever does not produce a firm feel when the brake is applied, bleeding the brakes does not help (see Section 8), and the hydraulic hoses are all in good condition, then the master cylinder must be overhauled or a new one must be fitted. Check the availability of parts with a scooter dealer.*

9 Before disassembling the master cylinder, read through the entire procedure and make sure that you have obtained all the new parts required including some new DOT 4 brake fluid, some clean rags and internal circlip pliers.

Caution: Disassembly, overhaul and reassembly of the brake master cylinder must be done in a spotlessly-clean work area to avoid contamination and possible failure of the brake hydraulic system components. To prevent damage to the paint from spilled brake fluid, always cover the fuel tank and fairing when working on the master cylinder.

10 Follow Steps 3 to 8, then carefully remove the dust boot from the master cylinder to reveal the pushrod retaining circlip **(see illustration)**.

11 Depress the piston and use circlip pliers

5.7 Master cylinder cover, diaphragm plate and diaphragm

5.10 Remove the dust boot to access the pushrod circlip

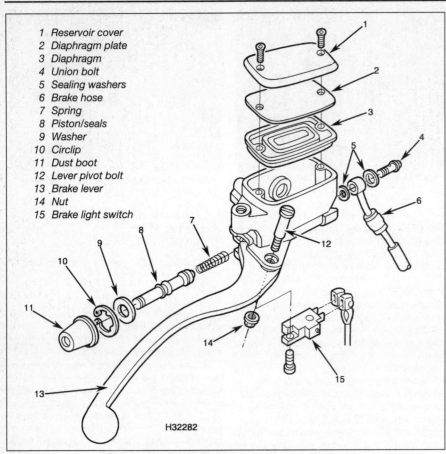

1 Reservoir cover
2 Diaphragm plate
3 Diaphragm
4 Union bolt
5 Sealing washers
6 Brake hose
7 Spring
8 Piston/seals
9 Washer
10 Circlip
11 Dust boot
12 Lever pivot bolt
13 Brake lever
14 Nut
15 Brake light switch

H32282

5.11 Typical front brake master cylinder components

to remove the circlip, then slide out the piston assembly and the spring, noting how they fit **(see illustration)**. If they are difficult to remove, apply low pressure compressed air to the fluid outlet. Lay the parts out in the proper order to prevent confusion during reassembly.
12 Clean all parts with clean brake fluid or brake system cleaner. If compressed air is available, blow it through the fluid galleries to ensure they are clear and use it to dry the parts thoroughly (make sure the air is filtered and unlubricated).
Caution: Do not, under any circumstances, use a petroleum-based solvent to clean brake parts.

13 Check the bore inside the master cylinder for corrosion, scratches, nicks and score marks. If damage or wear is evident, the master cylinder must be renewed. If the master cylinder is in poor condition, then the caliper should be checked as well.
14 The dust boot, circlip, piston assembly and spring are included in the master cylinder rebuild kit. Use all of the new parts, regardless of the apparent condition of the old ones. Fit them according to the layout of the old piston assembly.
15 Lubricate the piston assembly with clean brake fluid and install the components in the master cylinder in the reverse order of

disassembly. Depress the piston and install the new circlip, making sure it is properly located in the groove.
16 Fit the dust boot, making sure the lip is seated properly in the groove.
17 Inspect the hydraulic reservoir cap, diaphragm plate and diaphragm and renew any parts if they are damaged or deteriorated.

Installation

18 Installation is the reverse of removal, noting the following:
● *Connect the brake hose to the master cylinder, using new sealing washers on each side of the banjo union.*
● *Align the banjo union as noted on removal.*
● *Ensure the brake light wiring is connected securely.*
● *Fill the fluid reservoir with new brake fluid (see Daily (pre-ride) checks).*
● *Bleed the air from the system (see Section 8).*
● *Ensure the reservoir diaphragm is correctly seated and that the cover screws are tightened securely.*
19 Check the operation of the brake before riding the scooter.

Remotely-mounted

Removal

20 On some scooters, the master cylinder is mounted on the steering stem with a separate hydraulic reservoir. The master cylinder is activated by a cable from the brake lever. Remove the handlebar covers and the front body panels as necessary for access (see Chapter 9).
21 Remove the E-clip on the cable pivot pin, then draw out the pin and detach the cable from the master cylinder lever arm **(see illustration)**.
22 Unscrew the brake hose from the master cylinder **(see illustration)**. Secure the hose in an upright position to minimise fluid loss. Wrap a clean plastic bag tightly around the end to prevent dirt entering the system.
23 Unscrew the reservoir cap and remove the diaphragm plate and diaphragm. Drain the brake fluid from the reservoir into a suitable container.
24 Release the clip securing the reservoir hose to the union on the master cylinder, then detach the hose from the union **(see illustration)**. Wipe any remaining fluid out of the reservoir with a clean rag.

5.21 Remove the E-clip and draw out the pin

5.22 Unscrew the brake hose union (arrowed)

5.24 Release the clip (arrowed) and detach the reservoir hose

5.25 Master cylinder mounting bolts (arrowed)

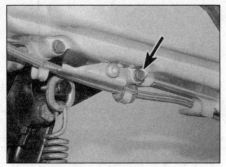

6.2 Undo the screw and remove the bracket

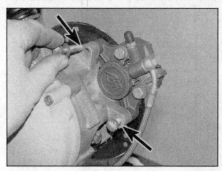

6.3 Brake caliper is secured by two bolts

25 Unscrew the master cylinder mounting bolts and remove the master cylinder **(see illustration)**.

Overhaul

26 If the necessary parts for overhauling the master cylinder are available, follow the procedure in Steps 9 to 17, otherwise fit a new master cylinder.

Installation

27 Installation is the reverse of removal, noting the following:
● Ensure the reservoir hose is secured with the clip – if the old clip has weakened, fit a new one.
● The E-clip should be a tight fit on the pivot pin – fit a new one if necessary.
● Fill the fluid reservoir with new brake fluid (see Daily (pre-ride) checks).
● Bleed the air from the system (see Section 8).
● Ensure the reservoir diaphragm is correctly seated and that the cover is tightened securely.
28 Check the operation of the brake before riding the scooter.

6 Rear disc brake – inspection, removal and installation

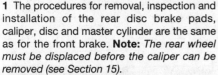

1 The procedures for removal, inspection and installation of the rear disc brake pads, caliper, disc and master cylinder are the same as for the front brake. **Note:** The rear wheel must be displaced before the caliper can be removed (see Section 15).
2 Note the routing of the rear brake hose before displacing the caliper, then undo any screws securing the hose bracket to the drivebelt cover and remove the bracket **(see illustration)**.
3 The caliper is secured to the transmission casing by two bolts **(see illustration)**.
4 If the caliper is just being displaced, secure it to the machine with a cable tie to avoid straining the hose. **Note:** Do not operate the brake lever while the caliper is off the disc.
5 After working on any component in the brake system, always check the operation of the brake before riding the scooter.

7 Brake hoses and unions – inspection and renewal

Inspection

1 Brake hose condition should be checked regularly and the hose(s) renewed at the specified interval (see Chapter 1).
2 Remove the body panels as necessary (see Chapter 9).
3 Twist and flex the hose while looking for cracks, bulges and seeping fluid. Check extra carefully where the hose connects to the banjo fittings or hose unions, as these are common areas for hose failure.
4 Inspect the banjo fittings and hose unions; if they are rusted, cracked or damaged, fit new hoses.

Renewal

5 Most brake hoses have banjo fittings on each end. Cover the surrounding area with plenty of rags and unscrew the banjo bolt, noting the alignment of the fitting with the master cylinder or brake caliper **(see illustration)**. Free the hose from any clips or guides and remove it, noting its routing. Discard the sealing washers. On some hoses, one end is secured by a union nut; hold the hose to prevent it twisting while the nut is being undone **(see illustration 5.22). Note:** Do not operate the brake lever while a brake hose is disconnected.
6 Position the new hose, making sure it is not twisted or otherwise strained, and ensure that it is correctly routed through any clips or guides and is clear of all moving components.
7 Check that the fittings align correctly, then install the banjo bolts, using new sealing washers on both sides of the fittings **(see illustration 5.4)**. Tighten the banjo bolts securely. If the hose is secured by a union nut at one end, install that end first to avoid twisting the hose while the nut is being tightened. Take care not to overtighten the union nut.
8 Flush the old brake fluid from the system, refill with new brake fluid and bleed the air from the system (see Section 8).
9 Check the operation of the brakes before riding the scooter.

8 Brake system – bleeding and fluid change

Caution: Support the scooter in a upright position and ensure that the hydraulic reservoir is level while carrying-out these procedures.

Bleeding

1 Bleeding the brakes is simply the process of removing air from the brake fluid reservoir, master cylinder, the hose and the brake caliper. Bleeding is necessary whenever a brake system connection is loosened, or when a component is renewed. Leaks in the system may also allow air to enter, but leaking brake fluid will reveal their presence and warn you of the need for repair.
2 To bleed the brake, you will need some new DOT 4 brake fluid, a small container partially-filled with new brake fluid, a length of clear vinyl or plastic hose, some rags and a spanner to fit the brake caliper bleed valve.
3 Remove the handlebar covers or body panels for access to the fluid reservoir (see Chapter 9) and cover any painted components to prevent damage in the event that brake fluid is spilled.
4 Remove the reservoir cover, diaphragm plate and diaphragm, and slowly pump the brake lever a few times until no air bubbles can be seen floating up from the holes in the bottom of the reservoir. This bleeds air from the master cylinder end of the system. Temporarily refit the reservoir cover.

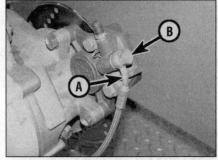

7.5 Note the alignment of the fitting (A) before undoing the bolt (B)

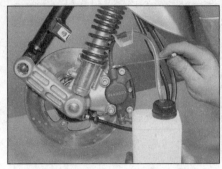

8.5a Pull off the dust cap

8.5b Set-up for bleeding the brakes

8.6 Check the fluid level regularly

5 Pull the dust cap off the caliper bleed valve (see illustration). Attach one end of the clear hose to the bleed valve and submerge the other end in the brake fluid in the container (see illustration). Note: *To avoid damaging the bleed valve during the procedure, loosen it and then tighten it temporarily with a ring spanner before attaching the hose. With the hose attached, the valve can then be opened and closed with an open-ended spanner.*
6 Check the fluid level in the reservoir. Do not allow the fluid level to drop below the half-way mark during the procedure (see illustration).
7 Carefully pump the brake lever three or four times and hold it in while opening the caliper bleed valve. When the valve is opened, brake fluid will flow out of the caliper into the clear hose and the lever will move toward the handlebar.
8 Tighten the bleed valve, then release the brake lever gradually. Repeat the process until no air bubbles are visible in the brake fluid leaving the caliper and the lever is firm when applied. On completion, disconnect the hose, ensure the bleed valve is tightened securely and fit the dust cap.
9 Top-up the reservoir, install the diaphragm, diaphragm plate and cover, and wipe up any spilled brake fluid. Check the entire system for fluid leaks.

HAYNES HiNT *If it's not possible to produce a firm feel to the lever the fluid may be aerated. Let the brake fluid in the system stabilise for a few hours and then repeat the procedure when the tiny bubbles in the system have settled out. To speed this process up, tie the front brake lever to the handlebar so that the system is pressurised.*

Fluid change

Note: *Some manufacturers recommend back-filling the hydraulic system with a syringe to avoid troublesome air locks (see Steps 16 to 22).*
10 Changing the brake fluid is a similar process to bleeding the brakes and requires the same materials plus a suitable tool for

syphoning the fluid out of the hydraulic reservoir. Also ensure that the container is large enough to take all the old fluid when it is flushed out of the system.
11 Follow the procedure in Step 5, then remove the reservoir cap, diaphragm plate and diaphragm and syphon the old fluid out of the reservoir. Fill the reservoir with new brake fluid, then follow the procedure in Step 7.
12 Retighten the bleed valve, then release the brake lever gradually. Keep the reservoir topped-up with new fluid at all times or air may enter the system and greatly increase the length of the task. Repeat the process until new fluid can be seen emerging from the bleed valve.

HAYNES HiNT *Old brake fluid is invariably much darker in colour than new fluid, making it easy to see when all old fluid has been expelled from the system.*

13 Disconnect the hose, ensure the bleed valve is tightened securely and install the dust cap.
14 Top-up the reservoir, install the diaphragm, diaphragm plate and cover, and wipe up any spilled brake fluid. Check the entire system for fluid leaks.
15 Check the operation of the brakes before riding the scooter.
16 If, after changing the brake fluid, it proves impossible to obtain a firm feel at the brake lever, it may be necessary to back-fill the system. To back-fill the hydraulic system, remove the reservoir cover, diaphragm plate and diaphragm and syphon the old fluid out of the reservoir. Temporarily refit the reservoir cover but do not tighten the fixing screws.
17 Remove the brake caliper and slowly push the pistons as far back into the caliper as possible using hand pressure or a piece of wood for leverage, then syphon any residual fluid from the reservoir. Leave the cover off the reservoir. Refit the brake caliper.
18 Fill a suitable syringe with approximately 40 ml of new brake fluid and connect a short length of hose to the syringe. Bleed any air from the syringe and hose, then connect the hose to the caliper bleed valve. **Note:** *To avoid damaging the bleed valve during the procedure, loosen it and then tighten it temporarily with a*

ring spanner before attaching the hose. With the hose attached, the valve can then be opened and closed with an open-ended spanner.
19 Open the bleed valve and carefully inject fluid into the system until the level in the reservoir is up to the half-way mark. Tighten the bleed valve, disconnect the hose and refit the dust cap.
20 Operate the brake lever carefully several times to bring the pads into contact with the disc, then check the fluid level in the reservoir and top-up if necessary (see *Daily (pre-ride) checks*).
21 Install the diaphragm, diaphragm plate and cover, and wipe up any spilled brake fluid. Check the system for fluid leaks.
22 Check the operation of the brakes before riding the scooter.

9 Drum brakes – inspection, shoe removal and installation

⚠ **Warning: The dust created by the brake system may contain asbestos, which is harmful to your health. Never blow it out with compressed air and don't inhale any of it. An approved filtering mask should be worn when working on the brakes.**

Inspection

1 Some scooters are fitted with a brake wear indicator; if the wear indicator aligns with the index mark when the brake is applied, the shoes should be renewed (see illustration).

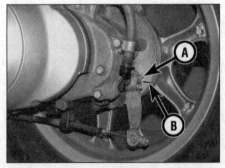

9.1 Brake wear indicator (A) and alignment mark (B)

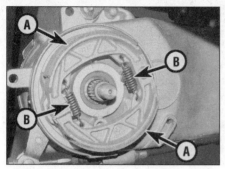

9.2 Check the friction material (A) and springs (B)

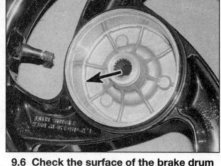

9.6 Check the surface of the brake drum (arrowed)

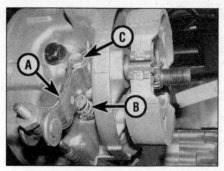

9.8 Brake arm (A), spring (B) and pinch-bolt (C)

2 Alternatively, remove the wheel (see Section 14 or 15). On some front suspension types, the brake backplate will remain on the suspension arm, on others it will be necessary to remove the backplate from the wheel. Check the amount of friction material on the brake shoes and compare the result with the specification in the *Data* section at the end of this manual **(see illustration)**. If the friction material has worn down to the minimum thickness, fit new brake shoes.

3 Inspect the friction material for contamination. If it is fouled with oil or grease, or heavily scored or damaged, both shoes must be renewed as a set. Note that it is not possible to degrease the friction material; if the shoes are contaminated in any way they must be renewed.

4 If the shoes are in good condition, clean them carefully using a fine wire brush which is completely free of oil and grease to remove all traces of dust and corrosion.

5 Check the condition of the brake shoe springs; they should hold the shoes tightly in place against the operating cam and pivot post **(see illustration 9.2)**. Remove the shoes (see Steps 11 to 12) and renew the springs if they appear weak or are obviously deformed or damaged.

6 Clean the surface of the brake drum using brake system cleaner. Examine the surface for scoring and excessive wear **(see illustration)**. While light scratches are to be expected, any heavy scoring will impair braking and there is no satisfactory way of removing them; in this

event the wheel should be renewed, although you could consult a specialist engineer who might be able to skim the surface.

7 Measure the internal diameter of the brake drum with a vernier caliper; take several measurements to ensure the drum has not worn out-of-round. If the drum is out-of-round, fit a new wheel.

8 To check and lubricate the brake cam, first remove the brake shoes (see Steps 11 to 12). Note the position of the brake arm and spring, then loosen the brake arm pinch-bolt and pull the cam out of the backplate or casing **(see illustration)**. Clean all traces of old grease off the cam and shaft. If the bearing surfaces of the cam or shaft are worn the cam should be renewed.

9 Lubricate the shaft with a smear of copper grease; position the brake arm and spring and install the cam in the backplate or casing, then tighten the pinch-bolt securely. Lubricate the cam and the pivot post with a smear of copper grease and install the brake shoes.

Shoe removal and installation

10 Remove the wheel (see Section 14 or 15).

11 If the shoes are not going to be renewed they must be installed in their original positions; mark them to aid reassembly. Note how the springs are fitted.

12 Grasp the outer edge of each shoe and fold them inwards towards each other to release the spring tension and remove the shoes **(see illustration)**. Remove the springs from the shoes.

13 To install the shoes, first lubricate the cam and the pivot post with a smear of copper grease and hook the springs into the shoes **(see illustration)**. Position the shoes in a V on the cam and pivot post, then fold them down into position. Operate the brake arm to check that the cam and shoes work correctly.

14 Install the wheel and test the operation of the brake before riding the scooter.

10 Brake cable – renewal

1 Remove the body panels as necessary (see Chapter 9).

2 Fully unscrew the adjuster on the lower end of the cable, then release the cable from the stop on the backplate. Disconnect the cable from the brake arm **(see illustration)**.

3 Free the cable from any clips or guides.

4 Pull the outer cable out of the handlebar lever bracket and free the inner cable end from its socket in the underside of the lever **(see illustrations)**.

5 Withdraw the cable from the scooter, noting its routing.

6 Installation is the reverse of removal. Make sure the cable is correctly routed and clipped into place. Lubricate the cable nipple at the handlebar end with grease before fitting it into the lever and adjust the cable freeplay (see Chapter 1).

9.12 Fold the shoes as shown to release the spring tension

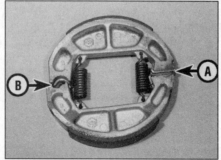

9.13 Assemble the shoes and springs as shown – flat ends (A) and rounded ends (B)

10.2 Release the cable from the brake arm

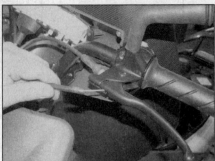

10.4a Pull the cable out of the handlebar bracket . . .

10.4b . . . and release the inner cable end from the lever

11.1 Brake lever pivot bolt locknut

> **HAYNES HiNT**
>
> *When fitting a new cable, tape the lower end of the new cable to the upper end of the old cable before removing it from the machine. Slowly pull the lower end of the old cable out, guiding the new cable down into position. Using this method will ensure the cable is routed correctly.*

7 Check the operation of the brake before riding the scooter.

11 Brake levers –
removal and installation

Removal

1 Unscrew the lever pivot bolt locknut, then withdraw the pivot bolt and remove the lever **(see illustration)**. Where applicable, slacken the brake cable and detach it from the underside of the lever as you remove it.

Installation

2 Installation is the reverse of removal. Apply grease to the pivot bolt shank and the contact areas between the lever and its bracket, and to the brake cable nipple (where applicable).

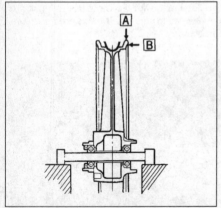

12.2 Check the wheel for radial (out-of-round) runout (A) and axial (side-to-side) runout (B)

12 Wheels –
inspection and repair

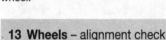

1 In order to carry out a proper inspection of the wheels, it is necessary to support the scooter upright so that the wheel being inspected is raised off the ground. Clean the wheels thoroughly to remove mud and dirt that may interfere with the inspection procedure or mask defects. Make a general check of the wheels (see Chapter 1) and tyres (see *Daily (pre-ride) checks*).
2 If available, attach a dial gauge to the suspension (front) or the transmission casing (rear) with the tip of the gauge touching the side of the rim. Spin the wheel slowly and check the axial (side-to-side) runout of the rim **(see illustration)**.
3 In order to accurately check radial (out-of-round) runout with the dial gauge, the wheel should be removed from the machine, and the tyre removed from the wheel. With the axle clamped in a vice or jig and the dial gauge positioned on the top of the rim, the wheel can be rotated to check the runout.
4 An easier, though slightly less accurate, method is to attach a stiff wire pointer to the front suspension or transmission casing with the end of the pointer a fraction of an inch from the edge of the wheel rim where the wheel and tyre join. If the wheel is true, the distance from the pointer to the rim will be constant as the wheel is rotated. **Note:** *If wheel runout is excessive, check the wheel bearings very carefully before renewing the wheel (see Section 16).*
5 The wheels should also be visually inspected for cracks, flat spots on the rim and other damage. Look very closely for dents in

the area where the tyre bead contacts the rim. Dents in this area may prevent complete sealing of the tyre against the rim, which leads to deflation of the tyre over a period of time. If damage is evident, or if runout is excessive, the wheel will have to be renewed. Never attempt to repair a damaged cast alloy wheel.

13 Wheels – alignment check

1 Misalignment of the wheels can cause strange and potentially serious handling problems and will most likely be due to bent frame or suspension components as the result of an accident. If the frame or suspension are at fault, repair by a frame specialist or using new parts are the only options.
2 To check wheel alignment you will need an assistant, a length of string or a perfectly straight piece of wood and a ruler. A plumb bob or spirit level for checking that the wheels are vertical will also be required. Support the scooter in an upright position on its centre stand.
3 If a string is used, have your assistant hold one end of it about halfway between the floor and the centre of the rear wheel, with the string touching the back edge of the rear tyre sidewall.
4 Run the other end of the string forward and pull it tight so that it is roughly parallel to the floor. Slowly bring the string into contact with the front sidewall of the rear tyre, then turn the front wheel until it is parallel with the string. Measure the distance (offset) from the front tyre sidewall to the string **(see illustration)**.

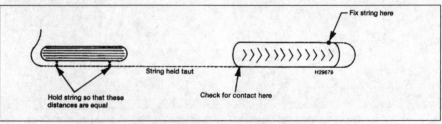

Fix string here

String held taut

Hold string so that these distances are equal

Check for contact here

H29679

13.4 Wheel alignment check using string

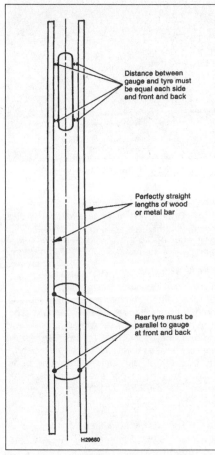

13.6 Wheel alignment check using a straight-edge

Note: *Where the same size tyre is fitted front and rear, there should be no offset.*

5 Repeat the procedure on the other side of the machine. The distance from the front tyre sidewall to the string should be equal on both sides.

6 As previously mentioned, a perfectly straight length of wood or metal bar may be substituted for the string **(see illustration)**.

7 If the distance between the string and tyre is greater on one side, or if the rear wheel appears to be out of alignment, have your machine checked by a scooter dealer.

8 If the front-to-back alignment is correct, the

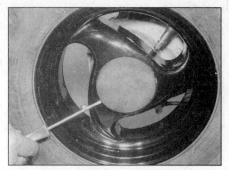

14.2a Lever off the centre cover

wheels still may be out of alignment vertically.
9 Using a plumb bob or spirit level, check the rear wheel to make sure it is vertical. To do this, hold the string of the plumb bob against the tyre upper sidewall and allow the weight to settle just off the floor. If the string touches both the upper and lower tyre sidewalls and is perfectly straight, the wheel is vertical. If it is not, adjust the centre stand by using spacers under its feet until it is.
10 Once the rear wheel is vertical, check the front wheel in the same manner. If both wheels are not perfectly vertical, the frame and/or major suspension components are bent.

---

14 Front wheel and hub assembly – removal and installation

Leading and trailing link suspension

Drum brake wheel

1 Support the machine in an upright position with the front wheel off the ground. If required, disconnect the front brake cable from the brake arm and backplate (see Section 10).
2 On some scooters, the wheel is secured on a fixed axle; lever off the hub centre cover using a small flat-bladed screwdriver **(see illustration)**. Where fitted, remove the split pin from the end of the axle then remove the cage nut **(see illustration)**. Discard the split pin, as a new one must be used. Undo the hub centre

14.2b Remove the split pin

nut, then remove the washer and draw the wheel of the axle **(see illustrations)**.
3 On some scooters, the wheel is secured on a knock-out axle; counterhold the axle and undo the axle nut, then support the wheel and withdraw the axle. Note how the brake backplate locates against the suspension arm and how the speedometer drive gearbox locates in the hub.
4 Check the condition of the wheel bearings (see Section 16).
5 If applicable, clean the axle and remove any corrosion using steel wool. Check the axle for straightness by rolling it on a flat surface such a piece of plate glass. If the axle is bent, renew it.
6 Installation is the reverse of removal – ensure all the components align, then tighten the hub or axle nut to the torque specified in the *Data* section at the end of this manual. Where applicable, fit a new split pin to secure the cage nut. Adjust the front brake cable (see Chapter 1).

Drum brake hub assembly

Note: *On scooters with a separate hub assembly, the assembly incorporates the brake backplate.*

7 Remove the wheel (see above).
8 Remove the suspension shock absorber (see Chapter 7).
9 If necessary, disconnect the speedometer cable from the hub.
10 The hub assembly is secured by a circlip; remove the circlip and washer, they draw the assembly off the axle.
11 Check the condition of the bearings in the

14.2c Undo the centre nut . . .

14.2d . . . and remove the washer

14.2e Lift off the wheel

14.14 Front wheel is retained by bolts (arrowed)

14.22a Remove the split pin (arrowed) . . .

14.22b . . . and the cage nut

hub (see Section 16). Examine the hub seals for wear and damage – if grease is passing the seals they should be renewed (see *Tools and Workshop Tips* in the *Reference* section). Clean the axle and remove any corrosion using steel wool.

12 Installation is the reverse of removal, noting the following:

● *Lubricate the axle, bearings and speedometer drive with grease.*
● *Ensure the circlip is properly seated in its groove.*

Disc brake wheel

Caution: Don't lay the wheel down and allow it to rest on the disc – the disc could become warped. Set the wheel on wood blocks so the disc doesn't support the weight of the wheel.

13 Support the machine in an upright position with the front wheel off the ground.
14 On some scooters, the wheel is secured

to the hub assembly; undo the bolts securing the wheel to the hub and lift the wheel off **(see illustration)**. Installation is the reverse of removal – tighten the wheel bolts to the torque specified in the *Data* section.

15 On some scooters, the wheel is secured on a knock-out axle; counterhold the axle and undo the axle nut, then support the wheel and withdraw the axle. Lower the wheel and lift off the speedometer drive gearbox, noting how it fits. Disengage the brake disc from the caliper and remove the wheel. **Note:** *Do not operate the brake lever while the caliper is off the disc.*

16 Note the position of any axle spacers and remove them from the wheel for safekeeping.
17 Check the condition of the wheel bearings (see Section 16).
18 Clean the axle and remove any corrosion using steel wool. Check the axle for straightness (see Step 5).
19 Installation is the reverse of removal – ensure the speedometer drive gearbox is

correctly located and the axle spacers are in place. Tighten the axle nut to the torque specified in the *Data* section.

20 Check the operation of the front brake before riding the scooter.

Disc brake hub assembly

21 Remove the wheel (see above).
22 Where fitted, remove the split pin from the end of the axle then remove the cage nut **(see illustrations)**. Discard the split pin, as a new one must be used. Have an assistant apply the front brake, then loosen the hub centre nut. Undo the brake caliper mounting bolts and displace the caliper (see Section 3). **Note:** *Do not operate the brake lever while the caliper is off the disc.*

23 Unscrew the hub centre nut and remove the nut and washer **(see illustration)**.
24 Draw the hub assembly off the axle **(see illustration)**.
25 If applicable, note how the speedometer drive tabs on the back of the hub locate in the speedometer gearbox in the brake caliper bracket **(see illustrations)**.
26 Check the condition of the hub bearings and seals, and the axle (see Step 11).
27 If applicable, disconnect the speedometer cable from the speedometer gearbox in the brake caliper bracket. **Note:** *On some scooters, the speedometer is electronically activated and the electrical wire and drive housing are a one-piece unit. Do not attempt disconnected them.* Undo the bolt securing the brake torque arm to the caliper bracket, then slide the bracket off the axle **(see illustration)**.

14.23 Remove the centre nut and washer

14.24 Pull the hub assembly off the axle

14.25a Note how the speedometer drive tabs (arrowed) . . .

14.25b . . . locate in the speedometer gearbox (arrowed)

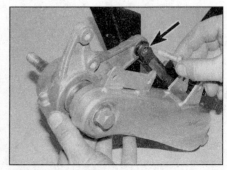

14.27 Undo the torque arm bolt (arrowed)

28 Installation is the reverse of removal, noting the following:
● *Lubricate the axle, bearings and speedometer drive with grease.*
● *Ensure the speedometer drive tabs are correctly located.*
● *Tighten the hub nut and brake caliper bolts to the torque specified in the Data section.*
● *Where applicable, fit a new split pin to secure the cage nut.*

Telescopic fork

Wheel removal

Caution: Don't lay the wheel down and allow it to rest on the disc – the disc could become warped. Set the wheel on wood blocks so the disc doesn't support the weight of the wheel.

29 Support the machine in an upright position with the front wheel off the ground.
30 On drum brake models, disconnect the brake cable (see Section 10).
31 Unscrew the brake caliper mounting bolts and displace the caliper (see Section 3). **Note:** *Do not operate the brake lever while the caliper is off the disc.*
32 If required, disconnect the speedometer cable from the speedometer gearbox **(see illustration)**. **Note:** *On some scooters, the speedometer is electronically-activated and the electrical wire and drive housing are a one-piece unit. Do not attempt disconnected them.*
33 Counterhold the axle and undo the axle nut, then support the wheel and withdraw the axle from the wheel and front suspension **(see illustrations)**. Lower the wheel out of the forks and lift off the speedometer gearbox **(see illustration)**.
34 Note the position of any axle spacers and remove them from the wheel for safekeeping.
35 Clean the axle and remove any corrosion using steel wool. Check the axle for straightness by rolling it on a flat surface such as a piece of plate glass. If the axle is bent, renew it.
36 Check the condition of the wheel bearings (see Section 16).

Wheel installation

37 Manoeuvre the wheel into position, making sure the directional arrow on the tyre is pointing in the normal direction of rotation.

14.32 Disconnect the speedometer cable

14.33b ... then support the wheel and withdraw the axle

On models with a cable-activated speedometer, apply some grease to the inside of the speedometer gearbox. Install the speedometer gearbox, ensuring it locates correctly on the wheel hub **(see illustrations)**.
38 Lubricate the axle with a smear of grease. Lift the wheel into place between the forks and install any axle spacers. Check that the speedometer gearbox is located correctly against the inside of the fork **(see illustration)**. On drum brake models, ensure the brake backplate is located correctly against the inside of the fork.
39 Slide the axle in carefully ensuring all the components remain in alignment.
40 Install the axle nut and tighten it to the torque setting specified in the *Data* section.
41 As necessary, install the brake caliper, making sure the pads sit squarely on each side of the disc (see Section 3). Connect the speedometer cable. On drum brake models,

14.33a Undo the axle nut ...

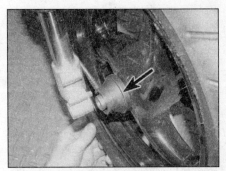
14.33c Lift off the speedometer gearbox

connect the brake cable (see Section 10) and adjust it (see Chapter 1).
42 Move the scooter off its stand, apply the front brake and pump the front forks a few times to settle all components in position.
43 Check the operation of the front brake before riding the scooter.

15 Rear wheel and hub assembly – removal and installation

Note: *It may not be possible to remove the rear wheel with the exhaust system in place. If necessary, remove the complete system – do not remove the exhaust system mounting bolts and attempt to lever the wheel behind the silencer with the exhaust manifold still connected; damage to the manifold studs and cylinder will result.*

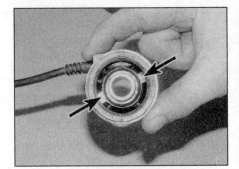
14.37a Tabs in the speedometer gearbox (arrowed) ...

14.37b ... locate against tabs on the wheel hub (arrowed)

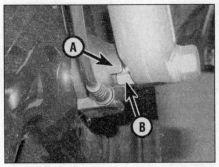
14.38 Note how the speedometer gearbox (A) locates against the fork slider (B)

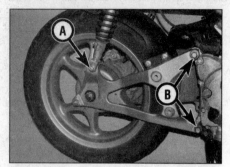

15.3 Bolt (A) secures shock to subframe; bolts (B) secure subframe to engine

15.5 Remove the hub centre nut and washer

15.6 Lift off the rear subframe

Drum brake models

Wheel

1 Position the scooter on its centre stand and support it so that the rear wheel is off the ground.
2 If necessary, remove the exhaust system (see Chapter 4).
3 On scooters with twin rear shock absorbers, undo the bolt securing the lower end of the right-hand shock to the subframe and displace the shock, then undo the bolts securing the subframe to the engine casing **(see illustration)**.
4 Lever the centre cover off with a small flat-bladed screwdriver. Where fitted, remove the split pin from the end of the axle then remove the cage nut **(see illustrations 14.22a and 14.22b)**. Discard the split pin, as a new one must be used.
5 Have an assistant apply the rear brake, then unscrew the hub centre nut and remove the nut and washer **(see illustration)**.

6 If applicable, lift off the rear subframe and slide any spacers off the axle **(see illustration)**. Check the condition of the bearing and seals in the subframe (see *Tools and Workshop Tips* in the *Reference* section). If there is any doubt about the condition of the bearing, renew it.
7 Slide the wheel off the axle and manoeuvre it out of the back of the machine **(see illustrations)**.
8 Inspect the splines on the axle and on the inside of the hub for wear and damage **(see illustration)**. If the splines are worn, both components should be renewed. To renew the axle the gearbox must first be disassembled (see Chapter 6).
9 Installation is the reverse of removal – slide the wheel onto the axle carefully to avoid disturbing the alignment of the brake shoes. Tighten the hub centre nut to the torque setting specified in the *Data* section at the end of this manual. Where applicable, fit a new split pin to secure the cage nut.

10 Check the operation of the rear brake before riding the scooter.

Disc brake models

Wheel

11 Position the scooter on its centre stand and support it so that the rear wheel is off the ground.
12 If necessary, remove the exhaust system (see Chapter 4).
13 Have an assistant apply the rear brake, then undo the bolts securing the wheel to the hub assembly and remove the wheel **(see illustration)**. **Note:** *On scooters with twin rear shocks, follow the procedure in Steps 3 and 6 to remove the subframe.*
14 Installation is the reverse of removal – tighten the wheel bolts to the torque setting specified in the *Data* section.

Hub assembly

15 If required, remove the wheel.
16 Lever the centre cover off with a small flat-bladed screwdriver. Where fitted, remove the split pin from the end of the axle then remove the cage nut **(see illustrations 14.22a and 14.22b)**. Discard the split pin, as a new one must be used.
17 Have an assistant apply the rear brake, then loosen the hub centre nut.
18 Undo the brake caliper mounting bolts and displace the caliper (see Section 3). **Note:** *Do not operate the brake lever while the caliper is off the disc.*
19 Undo the hub centre nut and remove the nut, then draw the hub assembly off the axle **(see illustration)**.

15.7a Slide the wheel off the axle . . .

15.7b . . . and withdraw it from the machine

15.8 Inspect the splines for wear and damage

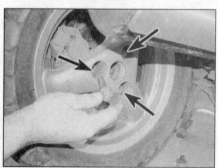

15.13 Undo the bolts (arrowed) and lift off the wheel

15.19 remove the nut (A), washer (B) and hub assembly (C)

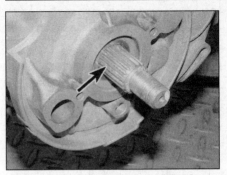

15.20a Inspect the splines on the axle . . .

15.20b . . . and inside the hub (arrowed)

16.2a Remove any spacers . . .

20 Inspect the splines on the axle and on the inside of the hub for wear and damage (**see illustrations**). If the splines are worn, both components should be renewed. To renew the axle the gearbox must first be disassembled (see Chapter 6).

21 Installation is the reverse of removal – tighten the hub centre nut to the torque setting specified in the *Data* section. Where applicable, fit a new split pin to secure the cage nut.

22 Check the operation of the rear brake before riding the scooter.

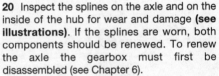

16 Wheel bearings – check and renewal

Note: *The front wheel bearings are located inside the wheel hub and, where applicable, inside the separate hub assembly. There are no rear wheel bearings as such, the rear axle/gearbox output shaft bearings are located inside the gearbox (see Chapter 6). On scooters with twin rear shock absorbers, also check the condition of the bearing in the rear subframe (see Section 15).*

Check

1 Remove the wheel and, if applicable, the hub assembly (see Section 14).
Caution: Don't lay the wheel down and allow it to rest on the brake disc – it could become warped. Set the wheel on wood blocks so the wheel rim supports the weight of the wheel.
2 Remove any spacers and dust caps from the wheel hub (**see illustrations**).
3 Inspect the bearings (see *Tools and Workshop Tips* in the *Reference* section). If necessary, lever out the bearing seals with a flat-bladed screwdriver to gain access to the bearings and fit new seals on reassembly. Wash needle roller bearings with a suitable solvent so that they can be inspected properly. **Note:** *Caged ball-bearings can be removed for checking and re-used if they are good, but needle roller bearings must be renewed once they have been removed.*
4 If there is any doubt about the condition of a bearing, renew it. **Note:** *Always renew the wheel bearings in sets, never individually.*

Renewal

5 If not already done, lever out the bearing seal. Check for any retaining circlips and remove them (**see illustration**).
6 To remove the bearings from the hub assembly, stand the assembly on a suitable spacer to allow the bearings to be driven out. Note the position of the bearings before removing them.
Caution: Don't support the hub on the brake disc when driving out the bearings.
7 To remove a caged ball-bearing, use a metal rod (preferably a brass drift punch) inserted through the centre of the bearing on one side of the wheel hub or hub assembly, to tap evenly around the outer race of the bearing on the other side (**see illustrations**). The bearing spacer will come out with the bearing. Use a drawbolt to remove a needle roller bearing (see *Tools and Workshop Tips* in the *Reference* section).
8 Turn the hub over and remove the

remaining bearing using the same procedure.
9 Thoroughly clean the bearing housings with a suitable solvent and inspect them for scoring and wear. If a housing is damaged, indicating that the bearing has seized and spun in use, it may be possible to secure the new bearing in place with a suitable bearing locking solution.
10 Install a new bearing into its seat in one side of the hub, with the marked or sealed side facing outwards (see *Tools and Workshop Tips* in the *Reference* section), then turn the hub over, install the bearing spacer and install the other new bearing. **Note:** *Needle roller bearings should be installed using a drawbolt.*
11 If applicable, secure the bearing with the circlip and ensure the circlip is properly located in its groove.
12 Install new bearing seals.
13 Install the hub assembly and/or the wheel as applicable (see Section 14).

16.2b . . . and dust caps

16.5 Remove the circlip (arrowed)

16.7a Driving a bearing out of the hub

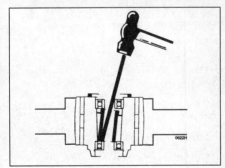

16.7b Locate the rod as shown when driving out a bearing

17 Tyres – general information and fitting

General information

1 Tyre sizes and tyre pressures are given in the *Data* section at the end of this manual.

2 Refer to *Daily (pre-ride) checks* at the beginning of this manual for tyre maintenance.

Fitting new tyres

3 When selecting new tyres, refer to the tyre information given in the owners handbook. Ensure that front and rear tyre types are compatible, the correct size and correct speed rating. If necessary seek advice from a tyre fitting specialist.

4 It is recommended that tyres are fitted by a tyre specialist rather than attempted in the home workshop. This is particularly relevant in the case of tubeless tyres because the force required to break the seal between the wheel rim and tyre bead is substantial, and is usually beyond the capabilities of an individual working with normal tyre levers. Additionally, the specialist will be able to balance the wheels after tyre fitting.

5 Note that although punctured tubeless tyres can in some cases be repaired, some manufacturers do not recommend the use of repaired tyres.

Chapter 9
Bodywork

Contents

Degrees of difficulty

Easy, suitable for novice with little experience		Fairly easy, suitable for beginner with some experience		Fairly difficult, suitable for competent DIY mechanic		Difficult, suitable for experienced DIY mechanic		Very difficult, suitable for expert DIY or professional	

1 General information

Almost all the functional components of the scooters covered by this manual are enclosed by body panels, making removal of relevant panels a necessary part of most servicing and maintenance procedures. Panel removal is straightforward, and as well as facilitating access to mechanical components, it avoids the risk of accidental damage to the panels.

Most panels are retained by screws and inter-locking tabs, although in some cases trim clips are used (see Section 5). Always check the details in your scooter handbook and follow the advice given at the beginning of Section 8 before removing the panels.

2 Rear view mirrors – removal and installation

Removal

Note: *If the mirror stem is covered by a rubber boot, pull back the lower end of the boot to expose the top of the fixing.*

1 Where the mirror threads into a housing, slacken the locknut then unscrew the mirror **(see illustrations)**.

2 Where the mirror passes through a bore and is secured by a nut, unscrew the nut from the underside and remove the mirror **(see illustration)**.

Installation

3 Installation is the reverse of removal. Position the mirror as required, then hold it in place and tighten the nut.

2.1a Slacken the nut . . .

2.1b . . . then unscrew the mirror

2.2 Undo the nut from the bottom of the stem and remove the mirror

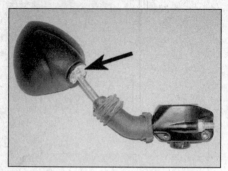

2.4 Rear view mirror adjuster screws

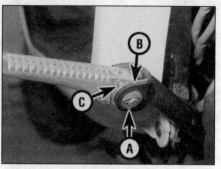

3.1 Remove the split pin (A) to release the pivot pin. Note the detent plate (B) and ball (C)

3.2 Undo the nut to remove the footrest

4 Some mirrors have screw fixings on the back of the mirror head. To adjust the angle of the mirror, pull back the upper end of the boot on the stem to expose the adjuster screws **(see illustration)**. Loosen the screws and set the mirror to the required position, then tighten the screws and refit the boot.

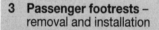

3 Passenger footrests – removal and installation

Note: *Some scooters are fitted with folding passenger footrests. Different methods of securing the footrests are employed – study the design before attempting to remove the footrest.*

Removal

1 If applicable, remove the split pin and washer or spring clip from the bottom of the footrest pivot pin, then withdraw the pivot pin and remove the footrest **(see illustration)**. Some footrests are held in position with a detent plate, ball and spring; note how they are fitted and take care that they do not spring out when removing the footrest.
2 On some scooters the footrest is secured by a pivot bolt. Counterhold the bolt and undo the nut on the underside of the footrest **(see illustration)**. **Note:** *It may be necessary to remove a cover or lift a floor mat to access the bolt.* Withdraw the bolt and slide the footrest out of the bracket.

Installation

3 Installation is the reverse of removal.

Apply a smear of grease to the pivot pin or bolt and ensure any washers or spacers are fitted on the bolt before it is installed. If applicable, tighten the nut enough to allow the footrest to pivot without binding in the bracket. Alternatively, install the spring clip, ensuring it is a firm fit, or fit a new split pin.

4 Seat and storage compartment – removal and installation

Seat

1 Release the seat catch and swing the seat upright.
2 The seat is retained by the hinge at the front of the seat base **(see illustration)**. Support the seat and undo the hinge bolts, then lift the seat away.
3 The seat latch mechanism is actuated either by a rod or cable from the seat lock **(see illustrations)**. To remove the seat lock, first remove the storage compartment (see Steps 7 to 10). Unclip the rod from the lock or unclip the cable from the back of the side panel and the lock **(see illustrations)**, then remove the side panel (see Section 8).
4 The lock is retained in a recess in the panel by a spring clip. Pull off the spring clip, note how the lock locates in the

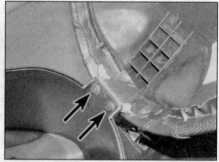

4.2 Undo the hinge bolts to remove the seat

4.3a Latch mechanism is actuated either by rod . . .

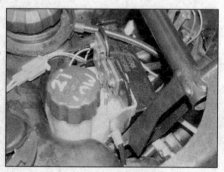

4.3b . . . or by cable

4.3c Unclip the cable from the stop on the panel . . .

4.3d . . . then from the back of the lock

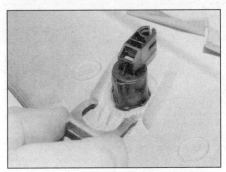

4.4 Pull off the clip to remove the lock

4.8 Remove the collars from the fuel and oil tank filler necks

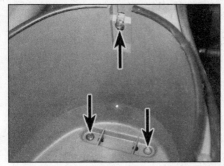

4.9a Storage compartment is retained by screws . . .

panel recess, then remove the lock (see illustration).

5 Check the operation of the latch mechanism and lubricate it with a smear of grease.

6 Installation is the reverse of removal.

 Warning: Ensure the actuating rod or cable is properly connected to the lock before closing the seat, otherwise you will have no way of releasing the latch.

Storage compartment

7 Unlock the seat and swing it upright. Generally, an engine access panel is fitted in the bottom of the compartment, although this offers limited access to the engine; for better access remove the storage compartment as follows. **Note:** *On most scooters, the storage compartment can be removed with the seat attached.*

8 Where fitted, remove any sealing collars from around the fuel and oil tank filler necks – it will be necessary to unscrew the tank caps to remove the collars (see illustration). Refit the tank caps.

9 Undo the screws or flange nuts securing the storage compartment to the frame edge (see illustrations). Note that on some scooters, the screws also secure some body panels.

10 Check that no electrical components such as relays or fuseboxes are clipped to the compartment, then lift it out (see illustration).

11 Installation is the reverse of removal.

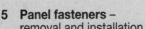
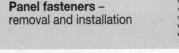

5   Panel fasteners –
removal and installation

1 Before removing any body panel, study it closely, noting the position of the fasteners and associated fittings.

2 Once the evident fasteners have been removed, try to remove the panel but DO NOT FORCE IT – if it will not release, check that all fasteners have been removed.

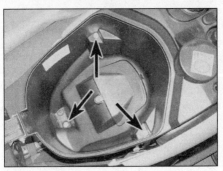

4.9b . . . or by flange nuts

On some panels, fasteners are located inside glove compartments or fuel filler flaps, or behind blanking plugs (see illustrations). **Note:** *Adjacent panels are often joined together by tabs and slots (see Step 16).*

3 Note all the fasteners and associated fittings removed with the panel to be sure of returning everything to its correct place on installation.

> **HAYNES HiNT** *Make a cardboard template of the panel and punch a hole for each fastener location. This will ensure all fasteners are installed correctly on reassembly – this is important as some fasteners may be of different sizes or lengths.*

5.2a Check for fasteners inside compartments . . .

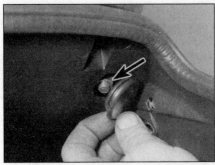

4.10 Detach any electrical components from the compartment

4 Before installing a panel, check that all fasteners and fittings are in good condition and renew any that are damaged.

5 Tighten the fasteners securely, but be careful not to overtighten any of them or the panel may break (not always immediately) due to uneven stress. Take particular care when tightening self-tapping screws into plastic lugs on the backs of panels – if the lugs break the panel will have to be renewed.

Trim clips

6 Two types of trim clips are used. If the centre pin is flush with the head of the trip clip, push the centre into the body, then draw the clip out of the panel (see

5.2b . . . or behind blanking plugs

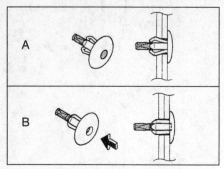

5.6a Trim clip removal

A Clip installed
B Clip with centre pin pushed in ready for removal

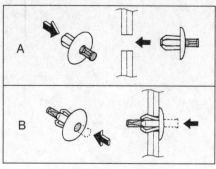

5.6b Trim clip installation

A Clip ready for installation
B Clip being secured in panel

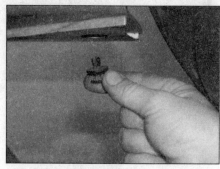

5.7 Pull out the centre pin to remove the clip

illustration). Before installing the this type of trim clip, first push the centre back out so that it protrudes from the top of the clip **(see illustration)**. Fit the clip into its hole, then push the centre in so that it is flush with the top of the clip.

7 Alternatively, if the centre pin has a raised head, pull the pin out, then draw the clip out of the panel **(see illustration)**. To install the clip, fit the clip into its hole, then push the centre in until it clicks into place.

Quick-release screws

8 To undo a quick-release screw, turn it anti-clockwise until resistance is felt – the screw will normally turn between 90° and 180°. As the panel is removed, note the alignment between the screw and its retaining mechanism.

9 To install a quick-release screw, first ensure it is correctly aligned, then turn it clockwise

until resistance is felt – the screw should now be locked.

Self-tapping screws

10 When the panel is removed, note the location of the screws. If they engage in plastic lugs on the back of an adjacent panel, check the condition of each lug and ensure it is not split or the thread stripped. If necessary, repair a damaged lug with a proprietary repair kit (see Section 6).

11 If the screws engage in U-clips, check that the clips are a firm fit on the mounting lug and that they are not sprained **(see illustration)**. If necessary, fit new U-clips.

Shouldered screws

12 Shouldered screws are designed to retain a panel in conjunction with a spacer or rubber bush **(see illustration)**. Ensure the correct

components are in place on the screw before installing it, otherwise the panel will not be held firmly. Do not pack a shouldered screw with washers – this will place undue pressure on the panel and cause cracking.

Wellnuts

13 Wellnuts have a metal thread retained inside a rubber bush; the bush is a firm press-fit in a body panel or windscreen **(see illustration)**. Avoid overtightening the screw, otherwise the bush will twist in the panel and damage the locating hole.

Peg and grommet

14 Ease the panel back and exert firm, even pressure to pull the peg out of the rubber grommet **(see illustration)**. If the peg is a tight fit, use a lubricating spray to release it. Do not rock the panel as the peg may snap.

15 If the grommet has split or hardened with age, renew it.

> **HAYNES HiNT** *Note that a small amount of lubricant (liquid soap or similar) applied to rubber mounting grommets will assist the lugs to engage without the need for undue pressure.*

Tab and slot

16 The edges of adjacent panels are often joined by tabs and slots – once all the fixing screws have been removed, slide these panels apart rather than pull them **(see illustration)**.

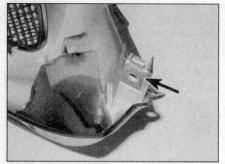

5.11 U-clip (arrowed) should be a firm fit

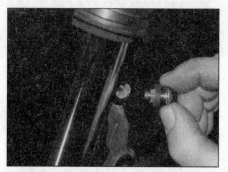

5.12 Shouldered screw and rubber bush

5.13 Wellnut threads are retained inside rubber bush

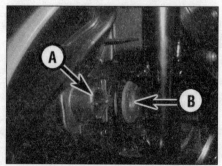

5.14 Peg (A) is secured in rubber grommet (B)

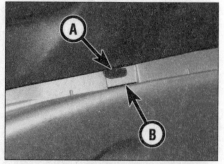

5.16 Hooked tab (A) locates in slot (B)

6 Panel repair

1 In the case of damage to the body panels, it is usually necessary to remove the broken panel and use a new (or second-hand) one. There are however some shops that specialise in 'plastic welding', so it may be worthwhile seeking the advice of one of these specialists before scrapping an expensive component.
2 Proprietary repair kits can be obtained for repair of small components **(see illustration)**.

7 Fuel and oil tanks –
removal and installation

6.2 A typical repair kit

⚠️ *Warning: Refer to the precautions given in Chapter 4, Section, 1 before proceeding.*

Fuel tank

1 Generally, the fuel tank is located underneath the seat, although on some scooters the tank is underneath the floor panel. The location of the fuel filler is a good guide to the location of the tank.
2 Remove the body panels as necessary on your scooter to access the tank (see Section 8).
3 Disconnect the battery negative (-ve) lead and disconnect the fuel gauge sender wiring connector (see Chapter 10).
4 If the tank is located underneath the seat, fuel flow to the carburettor will be controlled by a tap on the underside of the tank. Disconnect the fuel and vacuum hoses from the unions on the tap (see Chapter 4). Drain any residual fuel in the fuel hose into a suitable container.
5 If the tank is located underneath the floor panel, fuel flow to the carburettor will be controlled by a pump mounted on the frame alongside the fuel tank. Disconnect the fuel hose between the tank and the pump at the pump, and drain any residue fuel in the hose

into a suitable container. The fuel hose should be clamped to prevent fuel leakage using any of the methods shown in *Tools and Workshop Tips* in the *Reference* section.
6 Undo the fixings securing the tank to the frame, noting the location of any washers, then lift out the tank. Note the routing of any tank vent hoses.

⚠️ *Warning: If the fuel tank is removed from the scooter, it should not be placed in an area where sparks or open flames could ignite the fumes coming out of the tank. Be especially careful inside garages where a natural gas-type appliance is located, because the pilot light could cause an explosion.*

7 Installation is the reverse of removal, noting the following:
● *Ensure no wiring is trapped between the tank and the frame.*
● *Tighten the fixings securely.*
● *Ensure the fuel and vacuum hoses are a tight fit on their unions.*
● *Ensure any vent hoses are correctly routed.*

Oil tank

8 Generally, the oil tank is located underneath the seat, either alongside or below the fuel tank. If necessary, remove the fuel tank (see above).
9 Disconnect the oil level warning light sensor wiring connector.
10 Release the clip securing the oil hose from

the tank to the oil filter and detach the hose from the filter. Clamp the hose to prevent oil loss (see Step 5). Wrap a clean plastic bag around the oil filter to prevent dirt entering the system and secure the filter in an upright position to minimise oil loss.
11 Undo the tank fixings, noting the location of any washers, then lift out the tank.
12 Installation is the reverse of removal, noting the following:
● *Ensure no wiring is trapped between the tank and the frame.*
● *Tighten the fixings securely.*
● *Ensure the oil hose is pushed fully onto the union on the filter and secure it with the clip.*
● *Bleed any air trapped in the filter (see Chapter 1).*

8 Body panels –
removal and installation

1 In most cases, adjacent body panels are linked together with some form of fixing and it is usually necessary to remove panels in a specific order – refer to your scooter handbook for details. Removing service panels, rear carriers and the under seat storage compartment often allows access to concealed panel fixings.
2 In some cases the aid of an assistant will be required when removing panels, to avoid the risk of straining tabs or damaging paintwork. Where assistance was required to remove a panel, make sure your assistant is on hand to install it.
3 Check that all mounting brackets are straight and repair or renew them if necessary before attempting to install the a panel.
4 The following information is intended as a general guide to panel removal.

Handlebar covers

5 Remove the handlebar covers to gain access to the instrument cluster, brake master cylinder(s) and, where applicable, the headlight unit.
6 The covers are usually screwed and clipped together – remove the fixings and ease them apart carefully **(see illustrations)**.

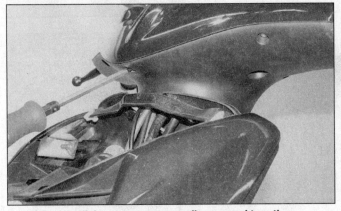

8.6a Handlebar covers are usually screwed together . . .

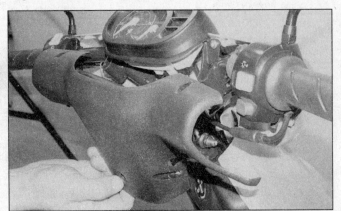

8.6b . . . and secured to the handlebars

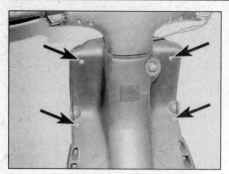

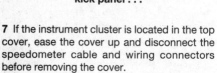

8.11a Front panel fixings in the kick panel . . .

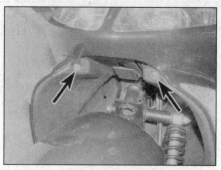

8.11b . . . and on the front underside (arrowed)

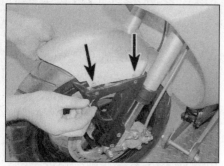

8.14 Front mudguard secured by screws (arrowed) to separate bracket

7 If the instrument cluster is located in the top cover, ease the cover up and disconnect the speedometer cable and wiring connectors before removing the cover.

8 Note any cut-out in the covers for the throttle cable.

9 On some scooters, the handlebar switches are located in the covers – take care not to strain the switch wiring when removing the covers.

10 On some scooters, the handlebars must be removed in order to remove the lower cover (see Chapter 7).

Front panel

11 Generally, the front panel is secured by fixings through the kick panel and, where fitted, the glove compartment. Also check for fixings underneath the front of the panel

above the front wheel **(see illustrations)**.

12 If the headlight unit is located in the front panel, ease the panel forward and disconnect the light wiring connectors before removing the panel.

13 On some liquid-cooled scooters, the radiator is located behind the front panel. The grille in the front panel should be kept free from obstructions.

Front mudguard

14 On some scooters, the mudguard is mounted on the front suspension, on others it is secured to the front body panels **(see illustration)**.

15 It may be necessary to remove the front wheel before removing the mudguard.

16 Note the location of any guides for the speedometer cable and front brake

hose/cable on the mudguard. Ensure the cables are correctly routed on installation.

Kick panel

17 Generally, the kick panel is secured to the main frame tube and is clipped to the floor panel along its lower edge **(see illustration)**.

18 Remove the kick panel to gain access to the main headlight/ignition wiring loom and the throttle cable. On some two-stroke scooters with a cable-operated oil pump, the cable splitter is located behind the kick panel.

Belly panel

19 The belly panel may be either a one or two-piece assembly; check along the centre of the panel underneath the scooter for joining screws.

20 On some scooters, the top edge of the belly panel is secured to the floor panel with tabs and slots; check carefully before removing the panel to avoid breaking the tabs **(see illustrations)**.

Side panels

21 Remove the side panels to gain access to the engine, fuel tank and carburettor, and upper rear suspension mounting(s).

22 On some scooters, the side panels can be removed as an assembly once the seat and storage compartment have been removed; on others, a separate rear cowling is fitted **(see illustrations)**.

23 Note the location of the tail light unit. On

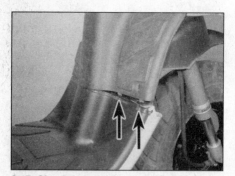

8.17 Check for tabs (arrowed) between the floor and kick panels

8.20a Remove the belly panel carefully . . .

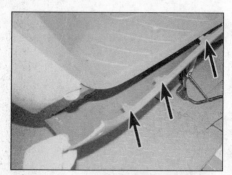

8.20b . . . to avoid breaking the tabs (arrowed)

8.22a Side panels may be removed as an assembly . . .

8.22b . . . or individually, depending on design

8.22c Some scooters have a separate rear cowling

8.26a Check for floor panel fixings behind blanking plugs . . .

8.26b . . . underneath floor mats . . .

8.26c . . . and on the underside of the panel

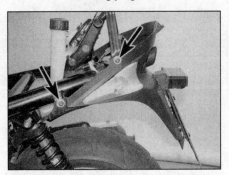

8.29 Mudguard fixings (arrowed). Note the turn signals and number plate light are part of the assembly

some scooters the tail light is located in a body panel assembly; disconnect the light wiring connectors before removing the assembly. On some scooters, it is necessary to remove the light lens to access panel fixing screws.

24 If applicable, note the position of the seat lock and disconnect the latch mechanism before removing the appropriate panel (see Section 4).

Floor panel

25 The floor panel is secured to the main frame tube and support brackets. On most scooters, it is necessary to remove some of the adjacent panels before the floor panel will lift off. Check for tab and slot fixings to the kick panel, belly panel and the side panels.

26 Panel fixings are often located underneath rubber mats, metal trim panels or behind blanking plugs; also check on the underside of the floor panel (see illustrations).

27 It may be necessary to remove the passenger footrests before the floor panel will lift off (see Section 3).

28 On installation, ensure no cables, hoses or wiring are trapped between the panel and the frame.

Rear mudguard

29 On most scooters the mudguard is secured to the rear of the frame underneath the side panels or rear cowling (see illustration).

30 Check the location of the rear turn signals and, where fitted, the number plate light, and disconnect the wiring if applicable before removing the mudguard.

Chapter 10
Electrical systems

Contents

Degrees of difficulty

Easy, suitable for novice with little experience	Fairly easy, suitable for beginner with some experience	Fairly difficult, suitable for competent DIY mechanic	Difficult, suitable for experienced DIY mechanic	Very difficult, suitable for expert DIY or professional 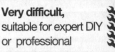

Specifications

Refer to the *Data* section at the end of this manual for servicing specifications.

1 General information

All the scooters covered by this manual have 12 volt electrical systems charged by a three-phase alternator with a separate regulator/rectifier. The regulator maintains the charging system output within a specified range to prevent overcharging, and the rectifier converts the AC (alternating current) output of the alternator to DC (direct current) to power the lights and other components, and to charge the battery.

The four electrical systems covered in this Chapter – lighting, signalling, starting and charging – are each illustrated by a general wiring diagram which shows how the system components are linked together. Follow the diagrams when tracing faults and compare them with the wiring diagram in your scooter handbook, noting any additional features specific to your scooter.

The location of electrical components such as relays, resistors and diodes varies enormously; refer to the wiring diagram in your handbook and trace the wiring to the component, removing any body panels as necessary to gain access (see Chapter 9). **Note:** *Keep in mind that electrical parts, once purchased, cannot be returned. To avoid unnecessary expense, make very sure the faulty component has been positively identified before buying a new part.*

2 Electrical systems – fault finding

 Warning: To prevent the risk of short circuits, the ignition (main) switch must always be OFF and the battery negative (-ve) terminal should be disconnected before any of the scooter's other electrical components are disturbed. Don't forget to reconnect the terminal securely once work is finished or if battery power is needed for circuit testing.

Tracing faults

1 A typical electrical circuit consists of an electrical component, the switches, relays, etc, related to that component, and the wiring and connectors that link the component to both the battery and the frame. To aid in locating any electrical problem, refer to the relevant system wiring diagram in this manual and then to the diagram in your scooter handbook.
2 Study the wiring diagram thoroughly to get a complete picture of what makes up each individual circuit. Trouble spots, for instance, can often be narrowed down by noting if other components related to that circuit are operating properly or not. If several components or circuits fail at one time, chances are the fault lies in the system fuse or earth connection.
3 Electrical problems often stem from simple causes, such as loose or corroded connections or a blown fuse. Prior to any electrical fault finding, always check the condition of the fuse, wires and connections in the problem circuit.

Intermittent failures can be especially frustrating, since you can't always duplicate the failure when it's convenient to test. In such situations, a good practice is to clean all connections in the affected circuit, whether or not they appear to be good. All of the connections and wires should also be wiggled to check for looseness which can cause intermittent failure.
4 If testing instruments are going to be used, use the wiring diagram to plan where you will make the necessary connections in order to accurately pinpoint the trouble spot.

Using test equipment

5 The basic tools needed for electrical fault finding include a battery and bulb test circuit, a continuity tester, a test light, and a jumper wire. A multimeter capable of reading volts, ohms and amps is also very useful as an alternative to the above, and is necessary for performing more extensive tests and checks **(see illustration)**.

2.5 A multimeter is capable of reading ohms, amps and volts

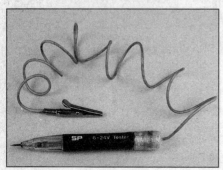

2.6a A test light . . .

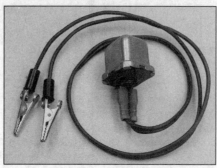

2.6b . . . or buzzer can be used for simple voltage checks

with your skin, or painted or plastic surfaces of the scooter. Rinse off any spills immediately with plenty of water. Check with the local authorities about disposing of an old battery. Many communities will have collection centres which will see that batteries are disposed of safely.

Removal and installation

1 Refer to your scooter handbook and remove the battery access panel.
2 Undo the negative (-ve) terminal screw first and disconnect the lead from the battery, then unscrew the positive (+ve) terminal screw and disconnect the lead **(see illustration)**.
3 Undo the battery strap or displace the strap and lift the battery from its holder.
4 Before installation, clean the battery terminals, terminal screws, nuts and lead ends with a wire brush, knife or steel wool to ensure a good electrical connection.
5 Install the battery, then reconnect the leads, connecting the positive (+ve) lead first, and secure the battery strap.

> **HAYNES HINT** *Battery corrosion can be kept to a minimum by applying a layer of petroleum jelly to the terminals after the cables have been connected.*

6 Voltage checks should be performed if a circuit is not functioning properly. Connect one lead of a test light or voltmeter to either the negative battery terminal or a known good earth **(see illustrations)**. Connect the other lead to a connector in the circuit being tested, preferably nearest to the battery or fuse. If the bulb lights, voltage is reaching that point, which means the part of the circuit between that connector and the battery is problem-free. Continue checking the remainder of the circuit in the same manner. When you reach a point where no voltage is present, the problem lies between there and the last good test point. Most of the time the problem is due to a loose connection. Keep in mind that some circuits only receive voltage when the ignition is ON.
7 One method of finding short circuits is to remove the fuse and connect a test light or voltmeter to the fuse terminals. There should be no load in the circuit (it should be switched off). Move the wiring harness from side-to-side while watching the test light. If the bulb lights, there is a short to earth somewhere in that area, probably where insulation has rubbed off a wire. The same test can be performed on other components in the circuit, including the switch.
8 An earth check should be done to see if a component is earthed properly. Disconnect the battery and connect one lead of a self-powered test light (continuity tester) to a known good earth **(see illustrations)**. Connect the other lead to the wire or earth connection being tested. If the bulb lights, the earth is good. If the bulb does not light, the earth is not good.

9 A continuity check is performed to see if a circuit, section of circuit or individual component is capable of passing electricity through it. Disconnect the battery and connect one lead of a self-powered test light (continuity tester) to one end of the circuit being tested and the other lead to the other end of the circuit. If the bulb lights, there is continuity, which means the circuit is passing electricity through it properly. Switches can be checked in the same way.

> **HAYNES HINT** *Remember that all electrical circuits are designed to conduct electricity from the battery, through the wires, switches, relays, etc, to the electrical component (light bulb, motor, etc). From there it is directed to the frame (earth) where it is passed back to the battery. Electrical problems are basically an interruption in the flow of electricity from the battery or back to it.*

3 Battery – removal, installation and checks

> ⚠️ **Warning: Be extremely careful when handling or working around the battery. Do not allow electrolyte to come in contact**

6 Fit the battery access panel.

Inspection and maintenance
Conventional battery

7 The battery fitted to most scooters covered by this manual is of the conventional lead-acid type, requiring regular checks of the electrolyte level (see Chapter 1) in addition to those detailed below.
8 Check the battery terminals and leads for tightness and corrosion. If corrosion is evident, undo the terminal screws and disconnect the leads from the battery, disconnecting the negative (-ve) terminal first. Wash the terminals and lead ends in a solution of baking soda and hot water and dry them thoroughly. If necessary, further clean the terminals and lead ends with a wire brush, knife or steel wool. Reconnect the leads, connecting the negative (-ve) terminal last,

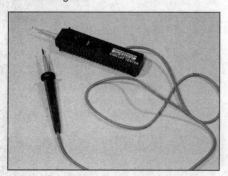

2.8a Continuity can be checked with a battery powered tester . . .

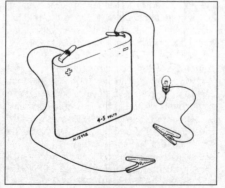

2.8b . . . or a battery and bulb circuit

3.2 Disconnect the negative (-ve) lead first, then the positive (+ve) lead

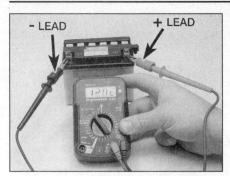

3.12 Measuring battery open-circuit voltage

and apply a thin coat of petroleum jelly to the connections to slow further corrosion.

9 The battery case should be kept clean to prevent current leakage, which can discharge the battery over a period of time (especially when it sits unused). Wash the outside of the case with a solution of baking soda and water. Rinse the battery thoroughly, then dry it.

10 Look for cracks in the case and renew the battery if any are found. If acid has been spilled on the battery holder or surrounding bodywork, neutralise it with a baking soda and water solution, dry it thoroughly, then touch up any damaged paint.

11 If the machine is not used for long periods of time, disconnect the leads from the battery terminals, negative (-ve) terminal first. Refer to Section 4 and charge the battery once every month to six weeks.

12 The condition of the battery can be assessed by measuring the voltage present at the battery terminals with a multimeter. Connect the meter positive (+ve) probe to the battery positive (+ve) terminal, and the negative (-ve) probe to the battery negative (-ve) terminal **(see illustration)**. Compare the reading with the specifications given in the *Data* section at the end of this manual. If the voltage falls below 12 volts the battery must be removed, disconnecting the negative (-ve) terminal first, and recharged as described below in Section 4. **Note:** *Before taking the*

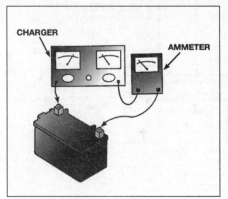

4.3 If the charger has no built-in ammeter, connect one in series as shown. DO NOT connect the ammeter between the battery terminals or it will be ruined

measurement, wait at least 30 minutes after any charging has taken place (including running the engine).

13 If battery condition is suspect, connect the multimeter to the battery terminals as before (see Step 12), turn the ignition ON and press the starter button. If the meter reading drops below 8 volts a new battery is required.

Maintenance-free (MF) battery

14 If your scooter is fitted with an MF battery, inspect the terminals and case as for a conventional battery (see Steps 8 to 10). If the machine is not used for long periods of time, disconnect the leads from the battery terminals and charge the battery periodically (see Step 11).

15 Battery condition can be assessed as for a conventional battery (see Steps 12 and 13).

4 Battery – charging

Caution: Be extremely careful when handling or working around the battery. The electrolyte is very caustic and an explosive gas (hydrogen) is given off when the battery is charging.

1 Ensure the charger is suitable for charging a 12V battery.

2 Remove the battery (see Section 3). Connect the charger to the battery **BEFORE** switching the charger on. Make sure that the positive (+ve) lead on the charger is connected to the positive (+ve) terminal on the battery, and the negative (-ve) lead is connected to the negative (-ve) terminal.

3 Refer to your scooter handbook for the recommend battery charging rate – manufacturers generally recommend a rate of no more than 0.5 amps. Exceeding this figure can cause the battery to overheat, buckling the plates and rendering it useless. Few owners will have access to an expensive current controlled charger, so if a normal domestic charger is used check that after a possible initial peak, the charge rate falls to a safe level **(see illustration)**. If the battery

5.2a Remove the fuse to check it

becomes hot during charging **STOP**. Further charging will cause damage.

4 When charging a maintenance-free battery, make sure that you use a regulated battery charger.

5 If the recharged battery discharges rapidly if left disconnected it is likely that an internal short caused by physical damage or sulphation has occurred. A new battery will be required. A sound item will tend to lose its charge at about 1% per day.

6 Install the battery (see Section 3).

5 Fuses – check and renewal

1 The electrical systems are protected by fuses; on some scooters, only one (main) fuse is fitted, on others the individual electrical systems are protected by their own (secondary) fuses. Refer to the *Data* section and to your scooter handbook for details and for the location of the fuse holders.

2 A blown fuse is easily identified by a break in the element – pull the fuse out of its holder to check it visually **(see illustrations)**. The fuse is clearly marked with its rating and must only be renewed with a fuse of the correct rating. It is advisable to carry spare fuses on the scooter at all times.

⚠ *Warning: Never put in a fuse of a higher rating or bridge the terminals with any other substitute, however temporary it may be. Serious damage may be done to the circuit, or a fire may start.*

3 If the fuse blows, be sure to check the wiring circuit very carefully for evidence of a short-circuit. Look for bare wires and chafed, melted or burned insulation. If the fuse is renewed before the cause is located, the new fuse will blow immediately.

4 Occasionally the fuse will blow or cause an open-circuit for no obvious reason. Corrosion of the fuse ends and fuse holder terminals may occur and cause poor fuse contact. If this happens, remove the corrosion with a wire brush or steel wool, then spray the fuse ends and fuse holder terminals with electrical contact cleaner.

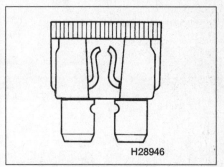

5.2b A blown fuse can be identified by a break in the element

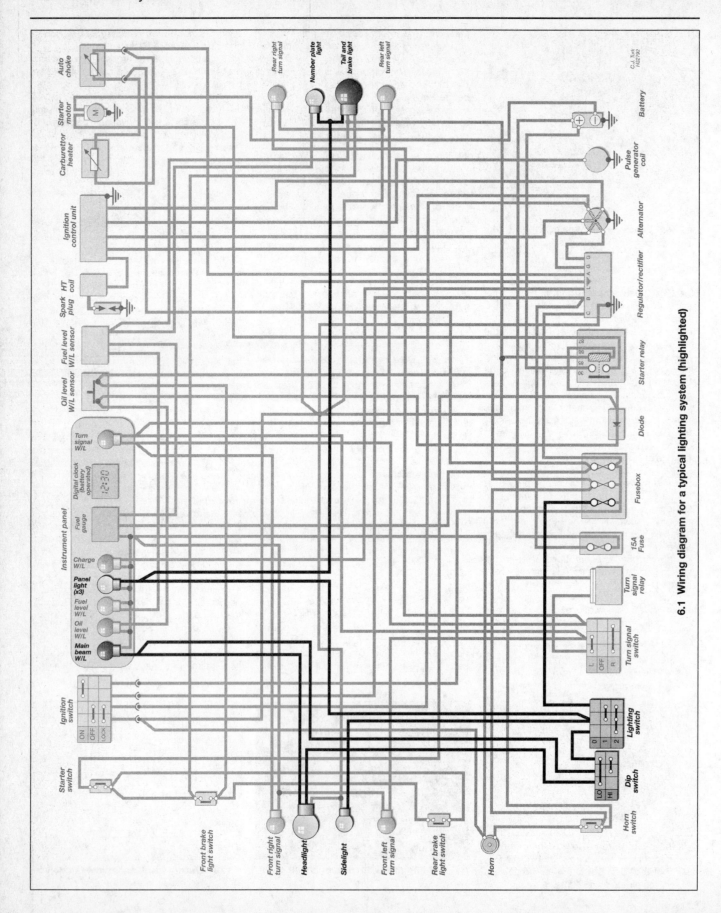

6.1 Wiring diagram for a typical lighting system (highlighted)

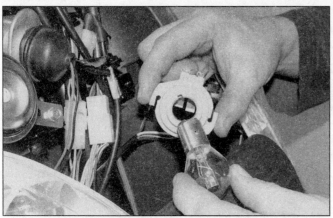

6.3a Checking the headlight bulb terminals . . .

6.3b . . . and the tail light terminals (arrowed)

6 Lighting system – check

1 The lighting system consists of the headlight, sidelight, tail light, brake light, instrument panel lights, handlebar switches and fuse (see illustration opposite).

2 On most of the scooters covered by this manual, the engine must be running for any of the lights to work. If none of the lights work, always check the fuse (where fitted) and alternator lighting coil before proceeding (see Section 9). If applicable, check the condition of the lighting resistor (see Step 11).

Lights

Note: *To remove the bulbs, refer to your scooter handbook for details.*

3 If a light fails to work, first check the bulb and the terminals in the bulbholder or the bulb wiring connector (see illustrations). Note: *If the headlight bulb is of the quartz-halogen type, do not touch the bulb glass as skin acids will shorten the bulb's service life. If the bulb is accidentally touched, it should be wiped carefully when cold with a rag soaked in methylated spirit and dried before fitting.*

⚠️ **Warning: Allow the bulb time to cool before removing it if the headlight has just been on.**

4 Next check for voltage on the supply side of the bulbholder or wiring connector with a test light or multimeter with the light switch ON. Don't forget that the engine may have to be running to do this check (see Step 2). When checking the headlight, select either high or low beam at the handlebar switch. When checking the brake light, pull the brake lever in.

5 If no voltage is indicated, check the wiring between the bulbholder and the light switch, then check the switch (see Steps 12 to 16).

6 If voltage is indicated, check for continuity between the earth wire terminal and an earth point on the scooter frame. If there is no continuity, check the earth circuit for a broken or poor connection.

Instrument panel lights

Note: *On some scooters, the panel is illuminated with LEDs. If an LED fails, it may be necessary to renew the complete panel circuit – check the availability of parts with a scooter dealer.*

7 If one light fails to work, check the bulb and the bulb terminals (see illustration). If none of the lights work, refer to the wiring diagram in your scooter handbook, then check for voltage on the supply side of the instrument cluster wiring connector, if necessary with the engine running and light switch ON (see illustration).

8 If no voltage is indicated, check the wiring

between the connector, the light switch and the ignition switch, then check the switches themselves.

9 If voltage is indicated, disconnect the connector and check for continuity between the power supply wire terminal on the instrument cluster and the corresponding terminals in the bulbholders; no continuity indicates a break in the circuit.

10 If continuity is present, check for continuity between the earth wire terminal in the wiring connector and an earth point on the scooter frame. If there is no continuity, check the earth circuit for a broken or poor connection.

Lighting system resistor

11 On some scooters, the lighting system is protected by a resistor (see illustration). To test the resistor, substitute it with a known good one or have the resistance checked by a scooter dealer.

Handlebar switches

12 Generally speaking, the switches are reliable and trouble-free. Most problems, when they do occur, are caused by dirty or corroded contacts, but wear and breakage of internal parts is a possibility that should not be overlooked when tracing a fault. If breakage does occur, the entire switch and related wiring harness will have to be renewed as individual parts are not available.

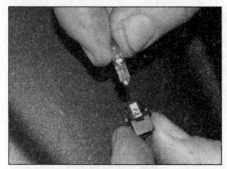

6.7a Pull the instrument panel bulb out of its holder

6.7b Instrument cluster wiring connectors

6.11 A typical lighting system resistor

6.14a Trace the wiring to the connectors . . .

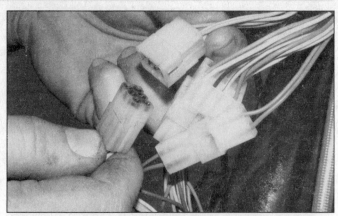

6.14b . . . and disconnect them to test the handlebar switches

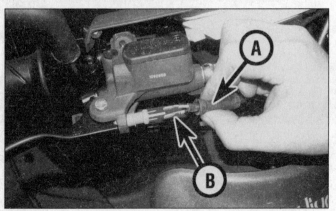

6.17a Pull back the boot (A) and disconnect the wires (B)

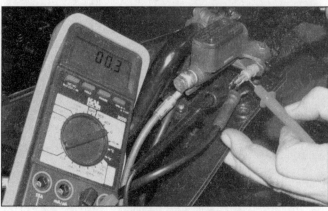

6.17b Testing the continuity of the brake light switch

13 The switches can be checked for continuity using a multimeter or test light and battery. Always disconnect the battery negative (-ve) lead, which will prevent the possibility of a short circuit, before making the checks.

14 Remove the body panels as necessary to trace the wiring from the switch in question back to its connector (see Chapter 9). Disconnect the relevant wiring connector **(see illustrations)**. Refer to the wiring diagram in your scooter handbook and check for continuity between the terminals of the switch wiring with the switch in the various positions (ie, switch OFF – no continuity; switch ON – continuity).

15 If the checks indicate a problem exists, remove the switch housing and spray the switch contacts with electrical contact cleaner. If they are accessible, the contacts can be scraped clean carefully with a knife or polished with crocus cloth. If switch components are damaged or broken, it will be obvious when the switch is disassembled.

16 Clean the inside of the switch body thoroughly and smear the contacts with suitable grease before reassembly.

Brake light switches

17 Remove the handlebar cover (see Chapter 9), then disconnect the switch wiring connectors **(see illustration)**. Using a

continuity tester, connect a probe to each terminal on the switch. With the brake lever at rest, there should be no continuity. Pull the brake lever in – there should now be continuity **(see illustration)**. If not, fit a new switch.

18 If the switch is good, refer the wiring diagram in your scooter handbook to check the brake light circuit using a multimeter or test light (see Section 2).

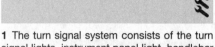

7 Turn signal system – check

1 The turn signal system consists of the turn signal lights, instrument panel light, handlebar switch, relay and fuse **(see illustration opposite)**.

2 On most of the scooters covered by this manual, the engine must be running for the turn signal lights to work. If none of the lights work, always check the fuse (where fitted) and alternator lighting coil before proceeding (see Section 9).

Turn signal lights

3 Most turn signal problems are the result of a failed bulb or corroded socket. This is especially true when the turn signals function properly in one direction, but not in the other.

Follow the procedures described in Section 6 to check the bulbs and the sockets, the operation of the turn signal switch and the turn signal warning light in the instrument cluster.

Turn signal relay

4 If the bulbs and sockets are good, test the power supply to the turn signal relay **(see illustration)**. Disconnect the relay wiring connector and check for voltage at the input wire terminal in the connector with the engine running, using a multimeter or test light connected to a good earth. Turn the engine OFF. If there is no voltage, use the wiring diagram in your scooter handbook to check the supply circuit.

7.4 A typical turn signal relay

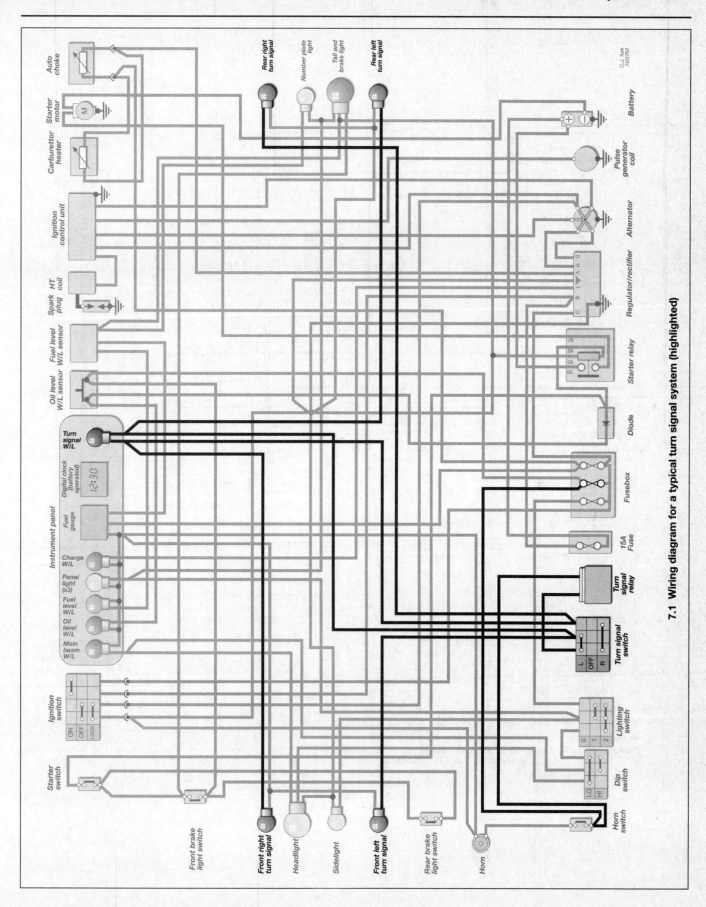

7.1 Wiring diagram for a typical turn signal system (highlighted)

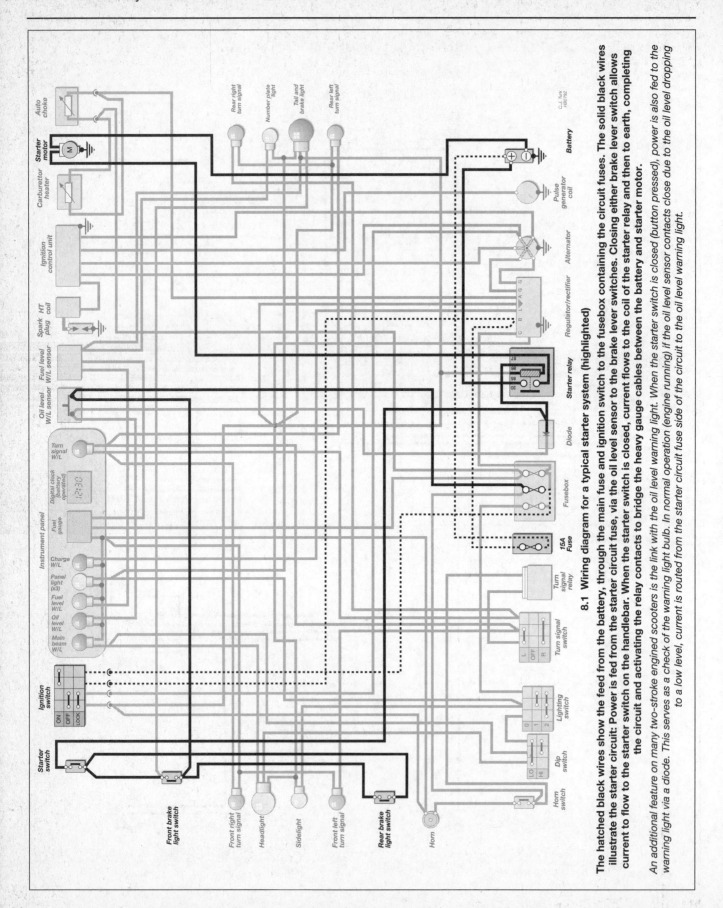

8.1 Wiring diagram for a typical starter system (highlighted)

The hatched black wires show the feed from the battery, through the main fuse and ignition switch to the fusebox containing the circuit fuses. The solid black wires illustrate the starter circuit: Power is fed from the starter circuit fuse, via the oil level sensor to the brake lever switches. Closing either brake lever switch allows current to flow to the starter switch on the handlebar. When the starter switch is closed, current flows to the coil of the starter relay and then to earth, completing the circuit and activating the relay contacts to bridge the heavy gauge cables between the battery and starter motor.

An additional feature on many two-stroke engined scooters is the link with the oil level warning light. When the starter switch is closed (button pressed), power is also fed to the warning light via a diode. In normal operation (engine running) if the oil level sensor contacts close due to the oil level dropping to a low level, current is routed from the starter circuit fuse side of the circuit to the oil level warning light. This serves as a check of the warning light bulb.

5 If there is voltage, reconnect the wiring connector to the relay and use a test light to check for voltage on the output side of the relay wiring connector with the engine running. The light should flash; if it does not, fit a new relay.

8 Starter system – check

1 The starter system consists of the starter switch, starter motor, battery, relay and fuse **(see illustration opposite)**. On some scooters, one or both of the brake light switches and, where fitted, the side stand switch, are part of a safety circuit which prevents the engine starting unless the brake is held on and the side stand is up.

2 On most two-stroke engined scooters, a diode links the starter circuit with the oil level warning light; this serves to check that the warning light bulb is sound. A similar system may also be fitted to check that the fuel level warning light bulb is sound.

3 If the starter circuit is faulty, first check the fuse (see Section 5). Also check that the battery is fully-charged (see Section 3).

Starter relay

4 To locate the starter relay, either trace the lead from the positive terminal of the battery to the relay, or trace the lead back from the starter motor to the relay **(see illustration)**.

5 Disconnect the starter motor lead from the relay. With the ignition switch ON, press the starter switch. The relay should be heard to click. Switch the ignition OFF.

6 If the relay wasn't heard to click in the test above, remove it from the scooter for further testing. Ensure that the ignition is OFF and

8.4 Starter motor relay

disconnect the battery negative (-ve) lead beforehand. Take note of the wire connections to the starter relay, then disconnect the heavy gauge battery and starter motor cables from the relay terminals, followed by the wire connector. Move the relay to the bench for testing. Connect a multi-meter set to the ohms (resistance) range across the battery and starter motor terminals of the relay (these are the terminals for the heavy gauge cables). Using a fully charged battery (the scooter's battery will do) and short jumper wires, connect the other terminals of the relay to the battery **(see illustration)**. If the relay if working correctly, continuity should be indicated on the meter when battery power is applied. Note that the wire terminal numbers shown on the illustration may be stamped on the relay, particularly on European models.

7 If the relay is good, refer to the wiring diagram in your scooter handbook and check the other components in the starter circuit as described below. If all components are good, check the wiring between the various components.

Oil level warning light and diode

8 The oil level warning light in the instrument

cluster should come on temporarily when the starter button is pressed as a check of the warning bulb. If the light fails to come on, first check the bulb (see Section 6), then check the wiring between the instrument cluster and the diode.

9 The diode will only allow current to pass in one direction. This is usually represented by an arrowhead on the diode housing and may also be shown on the wiring diagram.

10 Unplug the diode from the wiring harness, taking note of the wire locations. Use a multimeter set to the ohms or diode test function, connect its probes across the two terminals of the diode. Continuity (zero resistance) should be indicated when connecting the probes one way, then no continuity (infinite resistance) should be shown when reversing the probes.

11 If the tests indicate the same condition in both directions, the diode is faulty.

Side stand switch

12 The side stand switch is mounted on the stand bracket **(see illustration)**. To test the switch, trace the wiring back to the connector and disconnect it.

13 Connect a multimeter or continuity tester to the terminals on the switch side of the connector. With the sidestand up there should be continuity (zero resistance) between the terminals, with the stand down there should be no continuity (infinite resistance).

14 If the switch does not work as expected, check that the fault is not caused by a sticking switch plunger due to the ingress of road dirt; spray the switch with a water dispersant aerosol. If the switch still does not work it is defective and must be renewed.

Starter motor

15 To remove the starter motor, first

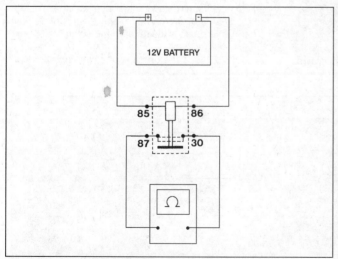

8.6 Starter relay test

8.12 Location of the side stand switch

8.15 Disconnect the wire from the starter motor terminal

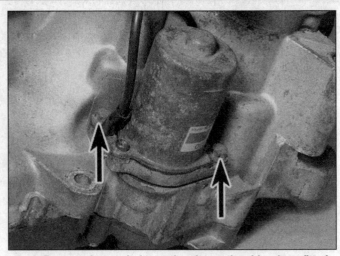

8.16 Remove the two bolts, noting the earth cable where fitted

disconnect the battery negative (-ve) lead. If accessible, disconnect the wire from the starter motor terminal (see illustration). Alternatively, trace the wire from the starter motor terminal and disconnect it at the connector.

16 Unscrew the two bolts securing the starter motor to the crankcase; note any earth wire secured by the bolts (see illustration).

17 Withdraw the starter motor. If not already done, disconnect the wire from the motor terminal. Remove the O-ring from the end of

the motor body and discard it, as a new one must be fitted on reassembly (see illustration).

18 Installation is the reverse of removal. Where fitted, apply a smear of engine oil to the new body O-ring and secure the earth wire with one of the mounting bolts.

19 The parts of the starter motor that are most likely to wear are the brushes, the commutator and the bearings. If the motor is suspect, it can be inspected as follows. Note: A number of different starter motors are fitted across the range of scooters covered by this

manual. Before disassembling the motor, check the availability of new parts with a scooter dealer. If parts are not available it may be worthwhile consulting an auto-electrician before buying a new motor, as sometimes, depending on the nature of the fault, they can be repaired. When disassembling the motor, carefully note the correct fitted position of each component before removing it, as the procedure given below is general and does not cover the specific components of each type of motor.

20 Remove the starter motor (see Steps 15 to 17), then undo the screws or bolts securing the housing to the end cover and draw the housing off, leaving the armature in place in the cover (see illustrations). Note the position of any housing seals and remove them carefully. Note: If there is oil inside the starter motor the internal cover seal has failed – check the availability of a new seal or cover assembly with a scooter dealer.

21 Withdraw the armature from the cover, noting any shims or washers on either or both ends of the armature shaft, and noting how the brushes locate onto the commutator (see illustration).

22 Slide the brushes out from their holders;

8.17 O-ring fitted to the starter motor body

8.20a Undo the screws . . .

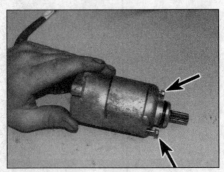

8.20b . . . or the bolts . . .

8.20c . . . and remove the housing

8.21 Withdraw the armature, noting how it fits

8.22a Displace the brushes . . .

8.22b . . . and remove the brush springs

note the position of the brush springs and remove them for safekeeping if they are loose **(see illustrations)**.

23 Check that the brushes are firmly attached to their terminals. If the brushes are excessively worn, cracked or chipped, they should be renewed, otherwise a new starter motor must be fitted. Note that some starter motors are fitted with separate brush plates **(see illustration)**.

24 Inspect the commutator bars on the armature for scoring, scratches and discoloration **(see illustration)**. The commutator can be cleaned and polished with crocus cloth, but do not use sandpaper or emery paper. After cleaning, wipe away any residue with a cloth soaked in electrical system cleaner or denatured alcohol.

25 Using an multimeter or test light and battery, check for continuity between the commutator bars **(see illustration)**. Continuity (zero resistance) should exist between each bar and all of the others.

26 Also, check for continuity between the commutator bars and the armature shaft **(see illustration)**. There should be no continuity (infinite resistance) between the commutator and the shaft. If the checks indicate otherwise, the armature is defective.

27 Check the front end of the armature shaft for worn or chipped teeth. Check the condition of the bearing which may be either on the armature or in the motor cover **(see illustration)**.

28 Reassemble the starter motor in the reverse order of disassembly, noting the following:
● *Press the brushes into their holders against the pressure of their springs, then fit the armature into the end cover carefully to avoid damaging the seal.*
● *Ensure each brush is pressed against the*

commutator by its spring and is free to move easily in its holder.
● *Lubricate the bush in the end of the housing with a smear of grease.*

9 Charging system – check

1 If the performance of the charging system is suspect, the system as a whole should be checked first, followed by testing of the

8.23 Brushes mounted on separate brush plate

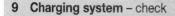

8.24 Inspect the commutator bars (arrowed)

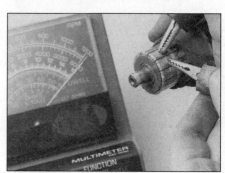

8.25 Continuity should exist between the commutator bars

8.26 There should be no continuity between the commutator bars and the armature shaft

8.27 Bearing (arrowed) located in starter motor cover

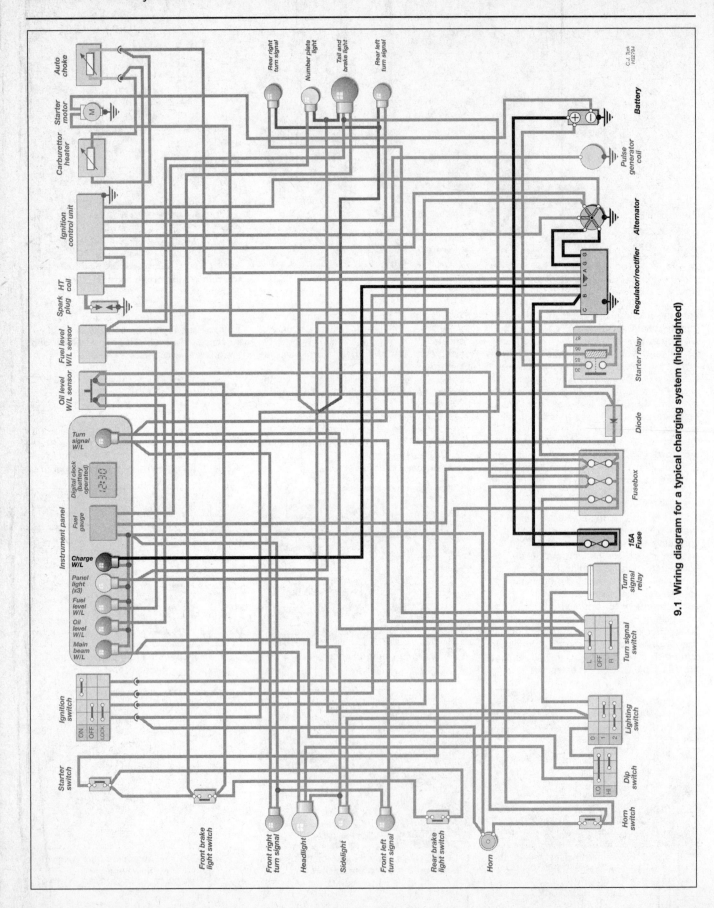

9.1 Wiring diagram for a typical charging system (highlighted)

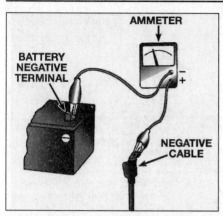

9.5 Checking the charging system leakage rate – connect the meter as shown

individual components and circuits **(see illustration opposite)**. **Note:** *Before beginning the checks, make sure the battery is fully-charged and that all circuit connections are clean and tight.*

2 Checking the output of the charging system and the performance of the various components within the charging system requires the use of a multimeter – if a multimeter is not available, have the system tested a scooter dealer or auto-electrician.

3 When making the checks, follow the procedures carefully to prevent incorrect connections or short circuits, as irreparable damage to electrical system components may result if short circuits occur.

Leakage test

4 Disconnect the battery negative (-ve) terminal.

5 Set the multimeter to the amps function and connect its negative (-ve) probe to the battery negative (-ve) terminal, and positive (+ve) probe to the disconnected negative (-ve) lead **(see illustration)**. Always set the meter to a high amps range initially and then bring it down to the mA (milliAmps) range; if there is a high current flow in the circuit it may blow the meter's fuse.

Caution: Always connect an ammeter in series, never in parallel with the battery, otherwise it will be damaged. Do not turn the ignition ON or operate the starter motor when the meter is connected – a

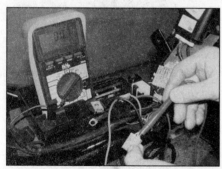

9.15 Checking the resistance in the alternator coils

sudden surge in current will blow the meter's fuse.

6 While manufacturers figures may vary, if the current leakage indicated exceeds 1 mA, there is probably a short circuit in the wiring. Disconnect the meter and reconnect the negative (-ve) lead to the battery, tightening it securely,

7 If current leakage is indicated, refer to the wiring diagram in your scooter handbook and systematically disconnect individual electrical components and repeat the test until the source is identified.

Alternator

Regulated output test

8 Start the engine and warm it up to normal operating temperature, then stop the engine and turn the ignition OFF.

9 Support the scooter on its centre stand with the rear wheel clear of the ground.

10 To check the regulated voltage output, set the multimeter to the 0 to 50 volts DC scale (voltmeter). Connect the meter positive (+ve) probe to the battery positive (+ve) terminal, and the negative (-ve) probe to the battery negative (-ve) terminal.

11 Start the engine and slowly increase the engine speed to a fast idle; the regulated voltage should be as specified in the *Data* section at the end of this manual. Now turn the headlight ON and note the reading – there should be no significant change in the output voltage. **Note:** *As a general rule, if a regulated voltage is not specified, the meter reading should be between 13 to 16 volts.*

12 If the voltage is not within these limits, there is a fault either in the regulator/rectifier or the alternator itself. If available, substitute the regulator/rectifier with a known good one and test again; if the voltage is still outside the specified limits, check the alternator coil resistance (see Steps 14 to 17).

13 Some manufacturers only specify an unregulated alternator output. This check requires a wring diagram and test details

> **HAYNES HINT** *Clues to a faulty regulator are constantly blowing bulbs, with brightness varying considerably with engine speed, and battery overheating.*

specific to your scooter, and is best undertaken by a scooter dealer or auto-electrician.

Coils resistance test

14 Disconnect the battery negative (-ve) terminal. Trace the wiring from the alternator cover and disconnect it at the connector.

15 Refer to the wiring diagram in your scooter handbook and identify the wire terminals for the charging coil and lighting coil in the alternator side of the connector. **Note:** *For alternators with three charging coil wires of the same colour code, see Step 16.* Set the multimeter to the ohms x 1 scale and connect the meter probes to the charging coil wire terminal and to earth, and then to the lighting coil terminal and earth. This will give resistance readings for the coils which should be consistent with the specifications in the *Data* section **(see illustration)**.

16 Alternatively, set the multimeter to the ohms x 1 scale and check the resistance between one pair of wire terminals at a time and note the three readings obtained. Also check for continuity between each terminal and earth. The readings should be consistent with the specifications in the *Data* section and there should be no continuity (infinite resistance) between any of the terminals and earth.

17 If the readings obtained differ greatly from those given in the *Data* section, particularly if the meter indicates a short circuit (no measurable resistance) or an open circuit (infinite, or very high resistance), the alternator stator assembly must be renewed. However, first check that the fault is not due to a damaged or broken wire from the alternator to the connector; pinched or broken wires can usually be repaired.

18 Refer to the procedure in Chapter 2A or 2B, as applicable, for details of alternator removal and installation.

10 Ignition (main) switch – check, removal and installation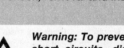

 Warning: To prevent the risk of short circuits, disconnect the battery negative (-ve) lead before making any ignition (main) switch checks.

Check

1 Remove any body panels as required for access (see Chapter 9). Ensure the battery negative (-ve) lead is disconnected, then pull back the boot on the wiring connector and disconnect the connector **(see illustration)**.

2 Refer to the wiring diagram in your scooter handbook, then using a multimeter or continuity tester, check the continuity of the connector terminal pairs. Continuity should exist between the connected terminals when the switch is in the indicated position.

3 If the switch fails any of the tests, renew it.

Removal

4 Disconnect the battery negative (-ve) lead and the switch wiring connector (see Step 1).

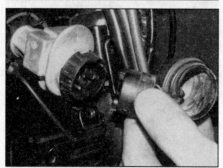

10.1 Disconnect the ignition switch wiring connector

10.4 Where fitted, unclip the immobiliser ring

10.5 Ignition switch is secured by a shear bolt (arrowed)

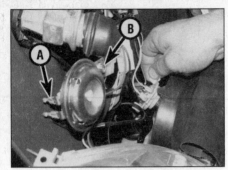

11.2 Horn wiring connectors (A) and mounting bolt (B)

If applicable, unclip the immobiliser transponder aerial from the front of the switch **(see illustration)**.

5 The switch is secured to the frame by a shear bolt **(see illustration)**. To remove the bolt, drill off the bolt head, then remove the switch. The threaded section of the bolt can then be unscrewed with pliers.

Installation

6 Installation is the reverse of removal. Operate the key to ensure the steering lock mechanism is correctly aligned with the frame and steering stem before tightening the shear bolt, then tighten the bolt until the head snaps off.

7 Reconnect the battery negative (-ve) lead once all electrical connections have been made to the switch.

11 Horn – check and renewal

Check

1 Remove any body panels as required for access to the horn (see Chapter 9).

2 Disconnect the wiring connectors from the horn and ensure that the contacts are clean and free from corrosion **(see illustration)**.

3 To test the horn, use jumper wires to connect one of the horn terminals to the

battery positive (+ve) terminal and the other horn terminal to the battery negative (-ve) terminal. If the horn sounds, check the handlebar switch (see Section 6) and the wiring between the switch and the horn.

4 If the horn doesn't sound, renew it.

Renewal

5 Disconnect the wiring connectors from the horn, then unscrew the bolt securing the horn and remove it.

6 Install the horn and tighten the mounting bolt securely. Connect the wiring connectors and test the horn.

12 Fuel gauge and level sender – check and renewal

> ⚠ **Warning: Petrol (gasoline) is extremely flammable, so take extra precautions when you work on any part of the fuel system. Don't smoke or allow open flames or bare light bulbs near the work area, and don't work in a garage where a natural gas-type appliance is present. If you spill any fuel on your skin, rinse it off immediately with soap and water. When you perform any kind of work on the fuel system, wear safety glasses and have a fire extinguisher suitable for a class B type fire (flammable liquids) on hand.**

12.1 Fuel level sender wiring connector

12.3 Fuel level sender unit

Fuel gauge

Check

1 Disconnect the wiring connector from the top of the fuel level sender **(see illustration)**.

2 Connect a jumper wire between the terminals on the wiring loom side of the connector. With the ignition switched ON, the fuel gauge should read FULL. If it doesn't, check the wiring between the connector and the gauge. If the wiring is good, then the gauge is confirmed faulty. **Note:** *On most scooters, the fuel gauge is integral with the instrument cluster, for which no individual parts are available. If the fuel gauge is faulty, the entire cluster must be renewed.*

Fuel level sender

Check

3 Disconnect the wiring connector from the fuel level sender (see Step 1), then unscrew the sender from the tank and remove the sender unit **(see illustration)**. **Note:** *On some scooters the sender is retained by a locking ring.*

> ⚠ **Warning: Block the opening in the tank to prevent the escape of petrol fumes and accidental fuel spillage.**

4 Check the operation of the sender; the arm should move freely without binding. Also check that the float is held securely on the arm and that it is not damaged. This will usually be apparent by the presence of fuel inside the float. If any of the component parts are faulty or damaged, fit a new sender.

5 If the sender is good, check the wiring between the sender and the gauge.

6 If a fault persists with the fuel gauge and both the gauge and sender appear good, have the sender resistance checked by a scooter dealer.

Renewal

7 Check the condition of the sender O-ring and fit a new one if it is deformed or perished. Insert the sender carefully into the tank, then lock it in position.

Data section

Contents

Note: *The specifications available at the time of writing are given on the Data Sheets; consult a scooter dealer for any other settings.*

Aprilia Leonardo 125

Engine .... 124 cc single-cylinder four-stroke
Cooling system .... Liquid-cooled
Fuel system .... Mikuni BS26 CV carburettor
Ignition system .... CDI
Transmission .... Variable speed automatic, belt-driven
Suspension .... Upside-down telescopic front, swingarm with twin
                              adjustable shock rear
Brakes .... 220 mm disc front, 190 mm disc rear
Tyres .... 130/70 x 12 front, 140/70 x 12 rear
Wheelbase .... 1320 mm
Weight .... 136 kg
Fuel tank capacity .... 9.5 litres

Engine

Spark plug type .... NGK CR8E
Electrode gap .... 0.6 mm
Idle speed (rpm) .... 1600 rpm
Engine oil .... SAE 5W 40 four-stroke
                              motorcycle oil
Oil capacity .... 1.1 litres
Bore x stroke .... 56.4 x 50 mm
Coolant .... 50% distilled water,
                              50% corrosion
                              inhibiting ethylene
                              glycol anti-freeze
Coolant capacity .... 1.2 litres

Fuel system

Throttle twistgrip freeplay ... 2 to 3 mm
Main jet 107.5
Pilot jet 42.5
Starter jet 25
Needle type/clip position ..... 4DX8-3 (3rd groove
                              from top)
Pilot screw setting .... 1¼ turns out
Float height .... 21.4 mm

Ignition system

HT coil primary resistance ...... 0.5 to 2.0 ohm
HT coil secondary resistance
  (without plug cap) .... 4.8 to 7.2 K-ohms
Pick-up coil resistance .... 192 to 288 ohms

Transmission

Gearbox oil .... SAE 75W/90 API GL4 oil
Gearbox oil capacity .... 90 ml

Brakes

Fluid type .... DOT 4
Pad minimum thickness .... 1.0 mm
Disc thickness (service limit) ... 3.6 mm

Tyre pressures

Front .... 28 psi (1.9 bar)
Rear .... 29 psi (2.0 bar)

Electrical system

Battery
  Capacity .... 12 V, 12 Ah
Alternator
  Output (regulated) .... 13 to 15 V (DC)
  Charging coil resistance ..... 0.1 to 1.0 ohms
Fuse (main) .... 20 Amps
Fuse (secondary) .... 15 and 7.5 Amps
Bulbs
  Headlight (main/dipped) ...... 35/35 W
  Sidelight .... 3 W
  Brake/tail light .... 21/5 W
  Turn signal lights .... 10 W
  Instrument and warning lights ... 2 and 1.2 W

Torque wrench settings

Engine mounting bolt .... 50 Nm
Exhaust manifold nuts .... 30 Nm
Exhaust system mounting bolt .... 27 Nm
Engine oil drain plug .... 15 Nm
Oil filter cover bolt .... 12 Nm
Gearbox oil drain plug .... 15 Nm
Rear shock absorber mountings
  Lower bolt .... 20 Nm
  Upper bolt .... 20 Nm
Rear subframe bolts .... 27 Nm
Steering head bearing locknut ... 110 Nm
Handlebar stem bolt .... 35 Nm
Front fork leg clamp bolts ..... 25 Nm
Front axle nut .... 50 Nm
Front axle pinch-bolt .... 12 Nm
Rear hub nut .... 110 Nm
Disc brake caliper mounting bolts ... 27 Nm
Disc mounting bolts .... 27 Nm
Brake hose banjo bolts .... 18.5 Nm

Aprilia Rally 50

Engine

Engine	49 cc single-cylinder two-stroke
Cooling system	Air or liquid-cooled
Fuel system	Dell'Orto PHBN 12 slide carburettor
Ignition system	CDI
Transmission	Variable speed automatic, belt-driven
Suspension	Upside down telescopic front, swingarm with single shock rear
Brakes	190 mm disc front, 190 mm disc or 110 mm drum rear
Tyres	120/80 x 12 front, 130/80 x 12 rear
Wheelbase	1250 mm
Weight	94 kg
Fuel tank capacity	6.0 litres

Engine

Spark plug type	
Air-cooled engine	NGK BR7 HS
Liquid-cooled engine	NGK BR8 HS
Electrode gap	0.5 to 0.6 mm
Idle speed (rpm)	1700 to 1900 rpm
Oil tank capacity	1.3 litres
Bore x stroke	40.0 x 39.2 mm
Coolant	50% distilled water, 50% corrosion inhibiting ethylene glycol anti-freeze
Coolant capacity	0.8 litres

Fuel system

Throttle twistgrip freeplay	2 to 3 mm
Main jet	90
Pilot jet	50
Starter jet	46
Needle type/ - clip position	3SI12 - 3/5
Pilot screw setting	1½ turns out
Float height	12 to 17 mm

Tyre pressures

Front	17 psi (1.2 bar)
Rear	22 psi (1.5 bar)

Electrical system

Battery	
Capacity	12 V, 4 Ah
Alternator	
Output (regulated)	13 to 15 Volts (DC)
Fuse (main)	7.5 Amps
Bulbs	
Headlight (main/dipped)	35/35 W
Sidelight	3 W
Brake/tail light	10/5 W
Turn signal lights	10 W
Instrument and warning lights	1.2 W

Ignition system

HT coil primary resistance	0.56 to 0.84 ohms
HT coil secondary resistance (without plug cap)	4.5 to 7.5 K-ohms
Source coil resistance	640 to 960 ohms
Pick-up coil resistance	400 to 600 ohms

Transmission

Variator roller diameter (service limit)	14.5 mm
Belt width (service limit)	15.5 mm
Gearbox oil	SAE 75W/90 API GL4 oil
Gearbox oil capacity	110 ml

Brakes

Disc brake	
Fluid type	DOT 4
Pad minimum thickness	1.0 mm
Disc thickness (service limit)	3.2 mm
Drum brake	
Brake shoe lining thickness	
Service limit	1.0 mm
Brake lever freeplay	10 mm

Torque wrench settings

Engine mounting bolt	50 Nm
Exhaust manifold nuts	12 Nm
Exhaust system mounting bolt	25 Nm
Cylinder head nuts	10 Nm
Spark plug	20 Nm
Alternator rotor nut	38 Nm
Starter motor bolts	13 Nm
Clutch assembly nut	50 Nm
Variator centre nut	33 Nm
Crankcase bolt	9 Nm
Gearbox oil drain plug	18 Nm
Gearbox cover bolts	12 Nm
Rear shock absorber mountings	
Lower bolt	25 Nm
Upper bolt	50 Nm
Handlebar stem bolt	50 Nm
Front axle nut	50 Nm
Front axle pinch-bolt	12 Nm
Rear hub nut	110 Nm
Rear wheel bolts (disc brake)	50 Nm
Disc brake caliper mounting bolts	
Front	25 Nm
Rear	27 Nm
Disc mounting bolts	27 Nm

Engine

Engine	49 cc single-cylinder two-stroke
Cooling system	Air or liquid-cooled
Fuel system	Dell'Orto PHBN 12 slide carburettor
Ignition system	CDI
Transmission	Variable speed automatic, belt-driven
Suspension	Telescopic front, swingarm with single shock rear
Brakes	155 mm disc front, 110 mm drum rear
Tyres	100/90 x 10 front, 100/90 x 10 rear
Wheelbase	1180 mm
Weight	87 kg
Fuel tank capacity	8.0 litres

Engine

Spark plug type	
Air-cooled engine	NGK BR8 HS
Liquid-cooled engine	NGK BR8 HS
Electrode gap	0.5 to 0.6 mm
Idle speed (rpm)	1700 to 1900 rpm
Oil tank capacity	1.6 litres
Bore x stroke	40.0 x 39.2 mm
Coolant	50% distilled water, 50% corrosion inhibiting ethylene glycol anti-freeze
Coolant capacity	1.0 litres

Fuel system

Throttle twistgrip freeplay	2 to 3 mm
Main jet	90
Pilot jet	50
Starter jet	46
Needle type/ - clip position	3SI12 - 3/5
Pilot screw setting	1½ turns out
Float height	12 to 17 mm

Tyre pressures

Front	25 psi (1.7 bar)
Rear	28 psi (1.9 bar)

Electrical system

Battery	
Capacity	12 V, 4 Ah
Alternator	
Output (regulated)	13 to 15 Volts (DC)
Fuse (main)	7.5 Amps
Bulbs	
Headlight (main/dipped)	35/35 W
Sidelight	3 W
Brake/tail light	10/5 W
Turn signal lights	10 W
Instrument and warning lights	1.2 W

Ignition system

HT coil primary resistance	0.56 to 0.84 ohms
HT coil secondary resistance (without plug cap)	4.5 to 7.5 K-ohms
Source coil resistance	640 to 960 ohms
Pick-up coil resistance	400 to 600 ohms

Transmission

Variator roller diameter (service limit)	14.5 mm
Belt width (service limit)	15.5 mm
Gearbox oil	SAE 75W/90 API GL4 oil
Gearbox oil capacity	110 ml

Brakes

Disc brake	
Fluid type	DOT 4
Pad minimum thickness	1.0 mm
Disc thickness (service limit)	3.2 mm
Drum brake	
Brake shoe lining thickness	
Service limit	1.0 mm
Brake lever freeplay	10 mm

Torque wrench settings

Engine mounting bolt	60 Nm
Exhaust manifold nuts	10 Nm
Exhaust system mounting bolt	25 Nm
Cylinder head nuts	10 Nm
Spark plug	20 Nm
Alternator rotor nut	38 Nm
Starter motor bolts	13 Nm
Clutch assembly nut	50 Nm
Variator centre nut	33 Nm
Crankcase bolt	9 Nm
Gearbox oil drain plug	18 Nm
Gearbox cover bolts	12 Nm
Rear shock absorber mountings	
Lower bolt	18 Nm
Upper bolt	32 Nm
Handlebar stem bolt	50 Nm
Front axle nut	50 Nm
Rear hub nut	110 Nm
Disc brake caliper mounting bolts	27 Nm
Disc mounting bolts	27 Nm

Aprilia SR50 (1994 to 1999)

(General)

Engine	49 cc single-cylinder two-stroke Minarelli engine with horizontal cylinder
Cooling system	Air or liquid-cooled
Fuel system	Dell'Orto PHBN 12 slide carburettor
Ignition system	CDI
Transmission	Variable speed automatic, belt-driven
Suspension	Telescopic front, swingarm with single shock rear
Brakes	190 mm disc front, 190 mm disc or 110 mm drum rear
Tyres	130/60 x 13 front, 130/60 x 13 rear
Wheelbase	1250 mm
Weight	99 kg
Fuel tank capacity	8.0 litres

Engine

Spark plug type		
Air-cooled engine		NGK BR7 HS
Liquid-cooled engine		NGK BR8 HS
Electrode gap		0.5 to 0.6 mm
Idle speed (rpm)		1700 to 1900 rpm
Oil tank capacity		1.6 litres
Bore x stroke		40.0 x 39.2 mm
Coolant		50% distilled water, 50% corrosion inhibiting ethylene glycol anti-freeze
Coolant capacity		1.2 litres

Fuel system

Throttle twistgrip freeplay	2 to 3 mm
Main jet	90
Pilot jet	50
Starter jet	46
Needle type/ - clip position	3SI12 - 3/5
Pilot screw setting	1½ turns out
Float height	12 to 17 mm

Tyre pressures

Front	25 psi (1.7 bar)
Rear	28 psi (1.9 bar)

Electrical system

Battery	
Capacity	12 V, 4 Ah
Alternator	
Output (regulated)	13 to 15 Volts (DC)
Fuse (main)	7.5 Amps
Bulbs	
Headlight (main/dipped)	35/35 W
Sidelight	3 W
Brake/tail light	10/5 W
Turn signal lights	10 W
Instrument and warning lights	1.2 W

Ignition system

HT coil primary resistance	0.56 to 0.84 ohms
HT coil secondary resistance (without plug cap)	4.5 to 7.5 K-ohms
Source coil resistance	640 to 960 ohms
Pick-up coil resistance	400 to 600 ohms

Transmission

Variator roller diameter (service limit)	14.5 mm
Belt width (service limit)	15.5 mm
Gearbox oil	SAE 75W/90 API GL4 oil
Gearbox oil capacity	110 ml

Brakes

Disc brake	
Fluid type	DOT 4
Pad minimum thickness	1.0 mm
Disc thickness (service limit)	3.2 mm
Drum brake	
Brake shoe lining thickness	
Service limit	1.0 mm
Brake lever freeplay	10 mm

Torque wrench settings

Engine mounting bolt	50 Nm
Exhaust manifold nuts	12 Nm
Exhaust system mounting bolt	25 Nm
Cylinder head nuts	10 Nm
Spark plug	20 Nm
Alternator rotor nut	38 Nm
Starter motor bolts	13 Nm
Clutch assembly nut	50 Nm
Variator centre nut	33 Nm
Crankcase bolt	9 Nm
Gearbox oil drain plug	18 Nm
Gearbox cover bolts	12 Nm
Rear shock absorber mountings	
Lower bolt	25 Nm
Upper bolt	50 Nm
Handlebar stem bolt	50 Nm
Front axle nut	50 Nm
Front axle pinch-bolt	12 Nm
Rear hub nut	110 Nm
Rear wheel bolts (disc brake)	50 Nm
Disc brake caliper mounting bolts	
Front	25 Nm
Rear	27 Nm
Disc mounting bolts	27 Nm

Engine no. prefix

Engine no. prefix	C301M
Frame no. prefix	ZAPC3
Engine	49 cc single cylinder two-stroke
Cooling system	Air-cooled
Fuel system	Weber 18 OM / Dell'Orto PHVA 17.5 RD carburettor
Ignition system	CDI
Transmission	Variable speed automatic, belt driven
Suspension	Telescopic front, swingarm with single adjustable shock rear
Brakes	200 mm disc front, 110 mm drum rear
Tyres	120/90 x 10 front and rear
Wheelbase	1220 mm
Weight	92 kg
Fuel tank capacity	6.5 litres

Engine

Spark plug type	Champion RN2C
Electrode gap	0.6 to 0.7 mm
Idle speed (rpm)	1700 to 1900 rpm
Engine oil	Two-stroke injector oil
Oil tank capacity	1.6 litres
Bore x stroke	40.0 x 39.3 mm
Piston oversizes available	+ 0.20 and + 0.40 mm
Piston to bore clearance (standard)	0.055 to 0.069 mm
Piston ring installed end gap	
Standard	0.10 to 0.25 mm

Fuel system

Throttle twistgrip freeplay	2 to 6 mm
Main jet	
Weber	60
Dell'Orto	56
Pilot jet	
Weber	30
Dell'Orto	32
Starter jet	50
Needle type / position	
Weber	AK (3rd notch from top)
Dell'Orto	A22 (1st notch from top)
Pilot screw setting	
Weber	2½ turns out
Dell'Orto	1½ turns out
Fuel level	3.5 mm
Automatic choke resistance	35 ohms

Ignition system

Source coil resistance	800 to 1100 ohms
Pick-up coil resistance	90 to 140 ohms

Transmission

Belt width (service limit)	17.5 mm
Variator rollers diameter	
Service limit	18.5 mm
Recommended lubricant	lithium soap grease
Clutch lining thickness (service limit)	1.0 mm
Clutch spring free length (service limit)	110 mm
Gearbox oil	SAE 80W/90 API GL4
Gearbox oil capacity	75 ml

Tyre pressures

Front	19 psi (1.3 bar)
Rear	26 psi (1.8 bar)

Electrical system

Battery	
Capacity	12 V, 3.6 Ah
Alternator	
Output (unregulated)	25 to 30 V (AC)
Fuse	7.5 Amps
Bulbs	
Headlight (main/dipped)	35/35 W
Sidelight	3 W
Brake/tail light	21/5 W
Turn signal lights	10 W
Instrument and warning lights	LEDs

Brakes

Disc brake	
Fluid type	DOT 4
Pad minimum thickness	1.5 mm
Disc thickness (service limit)	3.5 mm
Drum brake	
Brake shoe lining thickness	
Service limit	1.5 mm

Torque wrench settings

Cylinder head nuts	11 Nm
Crankcase bolts	13 Nm
Engine mounting bolt	41 Nm
Exhaust system mounting bolt	24 Nm
Alternator rotor nut	44 Nm
Variator centre nut	44 Nm
Clutch centre nut	44 Nm
Clutch assembly nut	60 Nm
Rear shock absorber mountings	
Lower bolt	41 Nm
Upper bolt	25 Nm
Steering head bearing locknut	40 Nm
Handlebar stem bolt	50 Nm
Front fork leg clamp bolts	25 Nm
Front fork leg top nuts (where fitted)	25 nm
Front fork leg bottom bolts	20 Nm
Front axle nut	50 Nm
Rear hub nut	126 Nm
Disc brake caliper mounting bolts	25 Nm
Disc mounting bolts	6.5 Nm
Brake hose banjo bolts	20 Nm

Gilera Runner 50 (1997 to 2005)

Engine no. prefix	C141M, C142M, C362M and C364M
Frame no. prefix	ZAPC
Engine	49 cc single-cylinder two-stroke
Cooling system	Liquid-cooled
Fuel system	Weber 12 OM slide carburettor
Ignition system	CDI
Transmission	Variable speed automatic, belt-driven
Suspension	Upside-down telescopic front, swingarm with single adjustable shock rear
Brakes	220 mm disc front, 110 mm drum or 220 mm disc rear
Tyres	120/70 x 12 front, 130/70 x 12 rear
Wheelbase	1290 mm
Weight	98 kg
Fuel tank capacity	8.5 litres

Tyre pressures

Front	17 psi (1.2 bar)
Rear	23 psi (1.6 bar)

Electrical system

Battery	
Capacity	12 V, 4 Ah
Alternator	
Output (unregulated)	25 to 30 V (AC)
Fuse	7.5 Amps
Bulbs	
Headlight (main/dipped)	35/35 W
Sidelight	5 W
Brake/tail light	21/5 W
Turn signal lights	10 W
Instrument and warning lights	1.2 W

Torque wrench settings

Cylinder head nuts	10 Nm
Crankcase bolts	12 Nm
Engine mounting bolt	41 Nm
Exhaust manifold nuts	10 Nm
Exhaust system mounting bolt	24 Nm
Thermostat housing bolt	4 Nm
Alternator rotor nut	44 Nm
Variator centre nut	44 Nm
Clutch centre nut	44 Nm
Clutch assembly nut	60 Nm
Gearbox oil drain plug	5 Nm
Rear shock absorber mountings	
Lower bolt	41 Nm
Upper bolt	25 Nm
Steering head bearing locknut	40 Nm
Handlebar stem bolt	70 Nm
Front fork leg top nuts	25 Nm
Front fork leg bottom bolts	50 Nm
Front axle nut	25 Nm
Rear wheel bolts	25 Nm
Rear hub nut	125 Nm
Disc brake caliper mounting bolts	25 Nm
Disc mounting bolts	15 Nm
Brake hose banjo bolts	18 Nm

Engine

Spark plug type	Champion N84
Electrode gap	0.5 mm
Idle speed (rpm)	1800 rpm
Engine oil	Two-stroke injector oil
Oil tank capacity	1.8 litres
Bore x stroke	40.0 x 39.3 mm
Piston oversizes available	+ 0.20 and + 0.40 mm
Piston to bore clearance (standard)	0.04 to 0.05 mm
Piston ring installed end gap	
Standard	0.10 to 0.25 mm
Coolant	50% distilled water, 50% corrosion inhibiting ethylene glycol anti-freeze
Coolant capacity	0.9 litres

Ignition system

Source coil resistance	800 to 1100 ohms
Pick-up coil resistance	90 to 140 ohms

Transmission

Belt width (service limit)	17.5 mm
Variator rollers	
Recommended lubricant	lithium soap grease
Gearbox oil	SAE 80W/90 API GL4
Gearbox oil capacity	75 ml

Fuel system

Throttle twistgrip freeplay	2 to 6 mm
Main jet	100
Pilot jet	34 L
Needle type / position	U (2nd notch from top)
Pilot screw setting	2¼ turns out
Fuel level	3.5 mm
Automatic choke resistance	35 ohms

Brakes

Disc brake	
Fluid type	DOT 4
Pad minimum thickness	1.5 mm
Drum brake	
Brake shoe lining thickness	
Service limit	1.5 mm

Engine no. prefix	C461M
Frame no. prefix	ZAPC
Engine	49 cc single cylinder two-stroke
Cooling system	Liquid-cooled
Fuel system	Dell'Orto PHVA 17.5 slide carburettor
Ignition system	CDI
Transmission	Variable speed automatic, belt driven
Suspension	Upside-down telescopic front, swingarm with single adjustable shock rear
Brakes	220 mm disc front, 175 mm disc rear
Tyres	120/70 x 14 front, 140/60 x 13 rear
Wheelbase	1270 mm
Fuel tank capacity	7 litres

Tyre pressures

Front	24 psi (1.7 bar)
Rear	30 psi (2.1 bar)

Electrical system

Battery	
Capacity	12 V, 4 Ah
Voltage (fully charged)	V
Alternator output (unregulated)	25 to 30 V (AC) @ 3000 rpm
Fuse	7.5 Amps
Bulbs	
Headlight (main/dipped)	35/35 W
Sidelight	5 W
Brake/tail light	21/5 W
Turn signal lights	10 W

Engine

Spark plug type	Champion RN1C
Electrode gap	0.45 to 0.55 mm
Idle speed (rpm)	1800 rpm
Engine oil	JASO FC grade two-stroke engine oil
Oil tank capacity	1.6 litres
Bore x stroke	40.0 x 39.3 mm
Piston oversizes available	+ 0.20 and + 0.40 mm
Piston to bore clearance (standard)	0.04 to 0.06 mm
Piston ring installed end gap	
Standard	0.10 to 0.25 mm
Coolant	50% distilled water, 50% corrosion inhibiting ethylene glycol anti-freeze
Coolant capacity	0.9 litres

Ignition system

Source coil resistance	1.0 ohm
Pick-up coil resistance	170 ohms

Transmission

Belt width (service limit)	17.5 mm
Clutch lining thickness (service limit)	1 mm
Clutch spring free length	118 mm
Gearbox oil	SAE 80W/90 API GL4
Gearbox oil capacity	75 ml

Fuel system

Main jet	53
Pilot jet	32
Needle type / position	A22 (1st notch from top)
Pilot screw setting	1½ turns out

Brakes

Disc brake	
Fluid type	DOT 4
Pad minimum thickness	1.5 mm

Torque wrench settings

Spark plug	25 to 30 Nm
Cylinder head nuts	10 to 11 Nm
Crankcase bolts	12 to 13 Nm
Engine mounting bolt	33 to 41 Nm
Exhaust manifold nuts	9 to 10 Nm
Exhaust system mounting bolt	22 to 24 Nm
Thermostat housing bolt	3 to 4 Nm
Alternator rotor nut	40 to 44 Nm
Variator centre nut	40 to 44 Nm
Clutch centre nut	40 to 44 Nm
Clutch assembly nut	55 to 60 Nm
Gearbox oil drain plug	3 to 5 Nm
Rear shock absorber mountings	
Lower bolt	33 to 41 Nm
Upper bolt	20 to 25 Nm
Steering head bearing locknut	30 to 40 Nm
Handlebar stem bolt	65 to 70 Nm
Front fork leg top nuts	20 to 25 Nm
Front fork leg bottom bolts	20 to 25 Nm
Front axle nut	45 to 50 Nm
Rear wheel bolts	20 to 25 Nm
Rear hub nut	100 to 125 Nm
Disc brake caliper mounting bolts	20 to 25 Nm
Front disc mounting bolts	12 to 15 Nm
Rear disc mounting bolts	6.0 to 6.5 Nm
Brake hose banjo bolts	13 to 18 Nm

Gilera Runner FX125 and FXR180

Engine no. prefix

FX125	M071M
FXR180	M081M

Frame no. prefix

FX125	ZAPM 070
FXR180	ZAPM 080

Engine

	123 cc single cylinder two-stroke
Cooling system	Liquid-cooled
Fuel system	Mikuni VM20 slide carburettor
Ignition system	CDI

Transmission

Variable speed automatic, belt driven

Suspension

Upside-down telescopic front, swingarm with single adjustable shock rear

Brakes

220 mm disc front, 140 mm drum rear or 240 mm disc rear

Tyres

120/70 x 12 front, 130/70 x 12 rear or 130/60 x 13 rear (1999-on)

Wheelbase	1303 mm
Weight	115 kg
Fuel tank capacity	9 litres or 12 litres (1999-on)

Engine

Spark plug type	Champion RN2C
Electrode gap	0.6 to 0.7 mm
Idle speed (rpm)	1400 to 1600 rpm
Engine oil	Two-stroke injector oil
Oil tank capacity	1.8 litres

Bore x stroke

FX125	55.0 x 52 mm
FXR180	65.6 x 52 mm

Piston oversizes available

FX125 only	+ 0.20, + 0.40 and + 0.60 mm

Piston to bore clearance (standard)

FX125	0.05 to 0.06 mm
FXR180	0.04 to 0.05 mm

Piston ring installed end gap

Standard	0.20 to 0.35 mm
Coolant	50% distilled water, 50% corrosion inhibiting ethylene glycol anti-freeze
Coolant capacity	1.74 litres

Ignition system

HT coil primary resistance	0.5 ohm
HT coil secondary resistance	4.55 to 5.05 K-ohms
Source coil resistance	122 to 132 ohms
Pick-up coil resistance	102 to 112 ohms

Fuel system

Main jet

FX125	85
FXR180	97.5

Pilot jet

FX125	35
FXR180	27.5

Starter jet	gs 40

Needle type / position

FX125	3CK01 (3rd notch from top)
FXR180	3DJ8 (3rd notch from top)

Pilot screw setting	1¼ turns out
Fuel level	6.5 mm
Automatic choke resistance	35 ohms

Transmission

Belt width (service limit)	20.5 mm
Variator rollers diameter	
Recommended lubricant	lithium soap grease
Gearbox oil	SAE 80W/90 API GL4
Gearbox oil capacity	80 ml

Tyre pressures

Front	20 psi (1.4 bar)
Rear	23 psi (1.6 bar)

Brakes

Disc brake

Fluid type	DOT 4
Pad minimum thickness	1.5 mm

Drum brake

Brake shoe lining thickness

Service limit	1.5 mm

Electrical system

Battery capacity

FX125	12 V, 9 Ah
FXR180	12 V, 12 Ah

Alternator

Output (unregulated)	27 to 31 V (AC)
Fuse (main)	25 Amps
Fuseholder	10 and 7.5 Amps

Bulbs

Headlight (main/dipped)	55/55 W
Sidelight	5 W
Brake/tail light	21/5 W
Turn signal lights	10 W
Instrument and warning lights	1.2 W

Torque wrench settings

Cylinder head cover bolts	10 Nm
Cylinder head nuts	10 Nm
Crankcase bolts	12 Nm
Engine mounting bolt	41 Nm
Exhaust manifold nuts	10 Nm
Exhaust system mounting bolt	24 Nm
Thermostat housing bolt	4 Nm
Alternator rotor nut	56 Nm
Variator centre nut	80 Nm
Clutch centre nut	56 Nm
Clutch assembly nut	60 Nm
Gearbox oil drain plug	5 Nm
Rear shock absorber mountings	
Lower bolt	41 Nm
Upper bolt	25 Nm
Steering head bearing locknut	40 Nm
Handlebar stem bolt	70 Nm
Front fork leg top nuts	25 Nm
Front fork leg bottom bolts	25 Nm
Front axle nut	50 Nm
Rear wheel bolts	25 Nm
Rear hub nut	130 Nm
Disc brake caliper mounting bolts	25 Nm
Disc mounting bolts	15 Nm
Brake hose banjo bolts	25 Nm

Gilera Runner VX125 and VXR180/200

Engine no. prefix	M241M (VX125), M242M (VXR180), M242M 1001 (VXR200)
Frame no. prefix	ZAPM 24
Engine	Single cylinder, four valve, four-stroke LEADER
Cooling system	Liquid-cooled
Fuel system	Walbro WVF-7C carburettor
Carburettor type	WVF-7C (VX125), WVF-7D (VXR180), WVF-7H (VXR200)
Ignition system	Inductive discharge with electronic variable advance
Transmission	Variable ratio automatic, belt driven
Suspension	Telescopic front, swingarm with twin adjustable shocks rear
Brakes	220 mm disc front, 200 mm disc rear
Tyres	120/70 x 12 front, 130/70 x 12 rear
Wheelbase	1350 mm
Weight	132 kg
Fuel tank capacity	12 litres

Engine

Spark plug type	NGK CR 8EB
Electrode gap	0.7 to 0.8 mm
Idle speed (rpm)	1600 to 1700 rpm
Engine oil	SAE 5W/40 synthetic four-stroke oil
Oil capacity	1.0 litre
Bore x stroke	
VX125	57.0 x 48.6 mm
VXR180	69.0 x 48.6 mm
VXR200	72.0 x 48.6 mm
Piston oversizes (VX125 only)	+ 0.20, + 0.40 and + 0.60 mm
Piston to bore clearance (standard)	
VX125	0.045 to 0.059 mm
VXR180/200	0.030 to 0.044 mm
Piston ring installed end gap (standard)	
Top ring	0.20 to 0.40 mm
Second ring	0.10 to 0.30 mm
Oil control ring	0.15 to 0.35 mm
Valve clearance	
Intake	0.10 mm
Exhaust	0.15 mm
Camshaft height (standard)	
Intake	30.285 mm
Exhaust	29.209 mm
Coolant	50% distilled water, 50% corrosion inhibiting ethylene glycol anti-freeze
Coolant capacity	0.9 litre

Brakes

Disc brake	
Fluid type	DOT 4
Pad minimum thickness	1.5 mm

Ignition system

Spark plug cap resistance	5 K-ohms
Pick-up coil resistance	105 to 124 ohms
HT coil primary resistance	0.4 to 0.5 ohm
HT coil secondary resistance	2.7 to 3.3 K-ohms

Fuel system

	VX125	VXR180/200
Main jet	108	118
Pilot jet	36	34
Starter jet	50	50
Needle type / position		
VX125	51C (2nd notch from top)	
VXR180	465 (3rd notch from top)	
VXR200	465 (2nd notch from top)	
Float level	Parallel to gasket face	
Automatic choke resistance	approx. 30 ohms (cold)	

Transmission

Belt width (service limit)	
VX125	21.5 mm
VXR180/200	19.5 mm
Variator rollers	
Standard diameter	18.9 to 19.1 mm
Service limit	18.5 mm
Recommended lubricant	Do not lubricate
Clutch lining thickness (service limit)	1 mm
Clutch spring free length (standard)	106 mm
Gearbox oil	SAE 80W/90 API GL4
Gearbox oil capacity	150 ml

Tyre pressures

Front	20 psi (1.4 bar)
Rear	23 psi (1.6 bar) solo, 26 psi (1.8 bar) with pillion

Electrical system

Battery	
Capacity	12 V, 10 Ah
Alternator	
Output (regulated)	15.2 V (DC)
Charging coil resistance	0.7 to 0.9 ohms
Fuse	15A x 2 and 5A x 4
Bulbs	
Headlight (separate lights)	55 W main, 55 W dip
Sidelight	5 W
Brake/tail light	21/5 W
Turn signal lights	10 W
Instrument and warning lights	1.2 W

Torque wrench settings

Spark plug	12 to 14 Nm
Valve cover bolts	11 to 13 Nm
Cylinder head nuts	27 to 29 Nm
Cylinder head bolts	11 to 13 Nm
Cam chain tensioner spring cap bolt	5 to 6 Nm
Camshaft sprocket bolt	11 to 15 Nm
Engine oil drain plug	24 to 30 Nm
Engine mounting bolt	33 to 41 Nm
Exhaust manifold nuts	16 to 18 Nm
Exhaust system mounting bolt at crankcase	20 to 25 Nm
Exhaust system mounting bolts at swingarm	24 to 27 Nm
Alternator rotor nut	54 to 60 Nm
Variator centre nut	75 to 83 Nm
Clutch centre nut	54 to 60 Nm
Clutch assembly nut	55 to 60 Nm
Drive cover screws	11 to 13 Nm
Crankcase bolts	11 to 13 Nm
Gearbox oil drain plug	15 to 17 Nm
Gearbox cover bolts	24 to 27 Nm
Rear shock absorber mountings	
Lower bolt	33 to 41 Nm
Upper bolt	20 to 25 Nm
Steering head bearing locknut	30 to 40 Nm
Handlebar stem bolt	45 to 50 Nm
Front fork leg top nuts	20 to 25 Nm
Front fork leg bottom bolts	20 to 25 Nm
Front axle nut	45 to 50 Nm
Rear wheel bolts	20 to 25 Nm
Rear hub nut	104 to 126 Nm
Disc brake calliper mounting bolts	20 to 25 Nm
Disc mounting bolts	
Front	11 to 13 Nm
Rear	14 to 17 Nm
Brake hose banjo bolts	20 to 25 Nm

Gilera SKP50 (Stalker)

Engine no. prefix ...

Engine no. prefix	C131M
Frame no. prefix	ZAPC13
Engine	49 cc single-cylinder two-stroke
Cooling system	Air-cooled
Fuel system	Weber 12 OM slide carburettor
Ignition system	CDI
Transmission	Variable speed automatic, belt-driven
Suspension	Upside-down telescopic front, swingarm with single adjustable shock rear
Brakes	190 mm disc front, 110 mm drum or 175 mm disc rear
Tyres	120/90 x 10 front, 130/90 x 10 rear
Wheelbase	1230 mm
Weight	87 kg
Fuel tank capacity	6.0 litres

Engine

Spark plug type	Champion N2C
Electrode gap	0.5 to 0.6 mm
Idle speed (rpm)	1800 to 2000 rpm
Engine oil	Two-stroke injector oil
Oil tank capacity	1.2 litres
Bore x stroke	40.0 x 39.3 mm
Piston oversizes available	+ 0.20 and + 0.40 mm
Piston to bore clearance (standard)	0.045 to 0.055 mm
Piston ring installed end gap	
Standard	0.10 to 0.25 mm

Fuel system

Throttle twistgrip freeplay	2 to 6 mm
Main jet	72
Pilot jet	34
Starter jet	50
Needle type / position	V (3rd notch from top)
Pilot screw setting	2¾ turns out
Fuel level	3.5 mm
Automatic choke resistance	35 ohms

Tyre pressures

Front	18 psi (1.2 bar)
Rear	23 psi (1.6 bar)

Electrical system

Battery	
Capacity	12 V, 4 Ah
Alternator	
Output (unregulated)	25 to 30 V (AC)
Fuse	7.5 Amps
Bulbs	
Headlight (main/dipped)	35/35 W
Sidelight	5 W
Brake/tail light	21/5 W
Turn signal lights	10 W
Instrument and warning lights	1.2 and 2 W

Ignition system

Source coil resistance	800 to 1100 ohms
Pick-up coil resistance	90 to 140 ohms

Transmission

Belt width (service limit)	17.5 mm
Variator rollers	
Recommended lubricant	lithium soap grease
Gearbox oil	SAE 80W/90 API GL4
Gearbox oil capacity	75 ml

Brakes

Disc brake	
Fluid type	DOT 4
Pad minimum thickness	1.5 mm
Drum brake	
Brake shoe lining thickness	
Service limit	1.5 mm

Torque wrench settings

Cylinder head nuts	11 Nm
Crankcase bolts	12 Nm
Engine mounting bolt	41 Nm
Exhaust manifold nuts	10 Nm
Exhaust system mounting bolt	24 Nm
Alternator rotor nut	44 Nm
Variator centre nut	44 Nm
Clutch centre nut	44 Nm
Clutch assembly nut	60 Nm
Gearbox oil drain plug	4 Nm
Rear shock absorber mountings	
Lower bolt	41 Nm
Upper bolt	25 Nm
Steering head bearing locknut	40 Nm
Handlebar stem bolt	21.5 Nm
Front fork leg top nuts	25 Nm
Front fork leg bottom bolts	25 Nm
Front axle nut	50 Nm
Rear wheel bolts	25 Nm
Rear hub nut	110 Nm
Disc brake caliper mounting bolts	25 Nm
Disc mounting bolts	
Front	15 Nm
Rear	6.5 Nm
Brake hose banjo bolts	12 Nm

Engine

Engine	124 cc single-cylinder two-stroke
Cooling system	liquid-cooled
Fuel system	PB20 slide carburettor
Ignition system	CDI
Transmission	Variable speed automatic, belt-driven
Suspension	Telescopic front, swingarm with single adjustable shock rear
Brakes	Disc front, drum rear
Tyres	110/90 x 12 front, 130/70 x 12 rear
Wheelbase	1450 mm
Weight (dry)	149 kg
Fuel tank capacity	12 litres

Engine

Spark plug type	NGK BR8ES
Electrode gap	0.7 to 0.8 mm
Idle speed (rpm)	1500 rpm
Engine oil	Two-stroke injector oil
Oil tank capacity	1.2 litres
Bore x stroke	54.0 x 54.5 mm
Piston diameter (standard)	53.93 to 53.95 mm
Piston to bore clearance (standard)	0.06 to 0.07 mm
Piston ring installed end gap (service limit)	0.65 mm
Coolant	50% distilled water, 50% corrosion inhibiting ethylene glycol anti-freeze
Coolant capacity	1.2 litres

Fuel system

Throttle twistgrip freeplay	2 to 6 mm
Main jet	108
Pilot jet	40
Pilot screw setting	1¾ turns out
Float height	8.8 mm
Automatic choke resistance	1.5 to 5.6 ohms

Transmission

Belt width (service limit)	21.5 mm
Variator rollers diameter	
Standard	23.08 mm
Service limit	22.50 mm
Clutch lining thickness (service limit)	2.0 mm
Clutch spring free length (service limit)	99.6 mm
Gearbox oil	SAE 10W-30 oil
Gearbox oil capacity	180 ml

Brakes

Fluid type	DOT 4
Disc brake	
Disc thickness (service limit)	3.5 mm
Drum brake	
Drum internal diameter (service limit)	161 mm
Brake lever freeplay	10 to 20 mm

Tyre pressures

Front	25 psi (1.75 bar)
Rear	29 psi (2.0 bar)

Electrical system

Battery	
Capacity	12 V, 8 Ah
Voltage (fully charged)	13 to 13.2 V
Alternator	
Output (regulated)	14.5 to 15.3 V (DC)
Charging coil resistance	0.1 to 0.5 ohms
Fuse (main)	30 Amps
Fuse (secondary)	2 x 15 and 3 x 10 Amps
Bulbs	
Headlight (main/dipped)	55/55 W
Sidelight	5 W
Brake/tail light	21/5 W
Turn signal lights	21 W
Instrument and warning lights	1.7 and 2 W

Torque wrench settings

Cylinder head nuts	22 Nm
Cylinder base nuts	22 Nm
Crankcase bolts	10 Nm
Engine mounting bolt	62 Nm
Exhaust manifold nuts	29 Nm
Exhaust system mounting bolts	
8 mm	34 Nm
10 mm	49 Nm
Water pump impeller nut	10 Nm
Alternator rotor nut	64 Nm
Alternator stator bolts	12 Nm
Variator centre nut	93 Nm
Clutch centre nut	74 Nm
Clutch assembly nut	78 Nm
Gearbox oil filler plug	13 Nm
Gearbox oil drain plug	13 Nm
Gearbox cover bolts	22 Nm
Rear shock absorber mounting bolts	39 Nm
Steering head bearing locknut	74 Nm
Handlebar stem bolt	59 Nm
Front fork leg clamp bolts	40 Nm
Front fork leg bottom bolts	20 Nm
Front axle nut	69 Nm
Rear hub nut	118 Nm
Disc brake caliper mounting bolts	31 Nm
Disc mounting bolts	42 Nm
Brake hose banjo bolts	34 Nm

Honda FES250 Foresight

Engine

Engine	249 cc single-cylinder four-stroke
Cooling system	liquid-cooled
Fuel system	VE3BB CV carburettor
Ignition system	CDI
Transmission	Variable speed automatic, belt-driven
Suspension	Telescopic front, swingarm with single adjustable shock rear
Brakes	Disc front, drum rear
Tyres	110/90 x 12 front, 130/70 x 12 rear
Wheelbase	1450 mm
Weight (dry)	150 kg
Fuel tank capacity	12 litres

Tyre pressures

Front	25 psi (1.75 bar)
Rear	29 psi (2.0 bar)

Electrical system

Battery	
Capacity	12 V, 10 Ah
Voltage (fully charged)	13 to 13.2 V
Alternator	
Output (regulated)	14.5 to 15.3 V (DC)
Charging coil resistance	0.1 to 0.5 ohms
Fuse (main)	30 Amps
Fuse (secondary)	2 x 15 and 3 x 10 Amps
Bulbs	
Headlight (main/dipped)	55/55 W
Sidelight	5 W
Brake/tail light	21/5 W
Turn signal lights	21 W
Instrument and warning lights	1.7 and 3 W

Torque wrench settings

Cylinder head cap nuts	24 Nm
Cam chain tensioner cap bolt	22 Nm
Engine mounting bolt	59 Nm
Engine bracket to frame bolt	78 Nm
Engine bracket pivot bolt	62 Nm
Engine tension rod nut	20 Nm
Exhaust manifold nuts	29 Nm
Exhaust system mounting bolts	34 Nm
Water pump impeller nut	12 Nm
Alternator rotor nut	116 Nm
Alternator stator bolts	12 Nm
Variator centre nut	93 Nm
Clutch centre nut	74 Nm
Clutch assembly nut	78 Nm
Gearbox oil filler plug	13 Nm
Gearbox oil drain plug	13 Nm
Gearbox cover bolts	25 Nm
Rear shock absorber mounting bolts	39 Nm
Steering head bearing locknut	74 Nm
Handlebar stem bolt	88 Nm
Front fork leg bottom bolts	20 Nm
Front axle nut	69 Nm
Rear hub nut	118 Nm
Disc brake caliper mounting bolts	31 Nm
Disc mounting bolts	42 Nm
Brake hose banjo bolts	34 Nm

Engine

Spark plug type	NGK DPR7EA-9
Electrode gap	0.8 to 0.9 mm
Idle speed (rpm)	1500 rpm
Engine oil	SAE 10W/40 four-stroke motorcycle oil
Oil capacity	1.3 litres
Bore x stroke	72.7 x 60.0 mm
Piston diameter (service limit)	72.65 mm
Cylinder diameter (service limit)	73.01 mm
Piston to bore clearance (service limit)	0.10 mm
Piston ring installed end gap (service limit)	
Top ring	0.50 mm
Second ring	0.65 mm
Oil control ring	0.90 mm
Valve clearance	Refer to handbook
Valve spring free length (service limit)	29.5 mm
Inner spring (intake and exhaust)	29.5 mm
Outer spring (intake and exhaust)	38.4 mm
Camshaft lobe height (service limit)	
Intake	34.181 mm
Exhaust	34.062 mm
Coolant	50% distilled water, 50% corrosion inhibiting ethylene glycol anti-freeze
Coolant capacity	1.2 litres

Fuel system

Throttle twistgrip freeplay	2 to 6 mm
Main jet	105
Pilot jet	40
Pilot screw setting	2½ turns out
Float height	18.5 mm
Automatic choke resistance	10 K-ohms

Transmission

Belt width (service limit)	22.3 mm
Variator rollers diameter	
Standard	23.08 mm
Service limit	22.50 mm
Clutch lining thickness (service limit)	0.5 mm
Clutch spring free length (service limit)	127.8 mm
Gearbox oil	SAE 10W-30 oil
Gearbox oil capacity	200 ml

Brakes

Fluid type	DOT 4
Disc brake	
Pad minimum thickness	To wear limit indicator
Disc thickness (service limit)	3.5 mm
Drum brake	
Drum internal diameter (service limit)	161 mm
Brake shoe lining thickness	
Service limit	To wear limit indicator
Brake lever freeplay	20 to 30 mm

Honda NES125 @125

Engine

Engine	124.6 cc single cylinder four-stroke
Cooling system	Liquid-cooled
Fuel system	VK4AA CV carburettor
Ignition system	CDI

Transmission

	Variable speed automatic, belt driven

Suspension

	Telescopic front, swingarm with twin adjustable shock rear

Brakes	disc front, drum rear
Tyres	110/90 x 13 front, 130/70 x 13 rear
Wheelbase	1328 mm
Weight (dry)	131 kg
Fuel tank capacity	9 litres

Engine

Spark plug type	NGK CR8EH-9
Electrode gap	0.8 to 0.9 mm
Idle speed (rpm)	1500 rpm
Engine oil	SAE 10W/40 four-stroke motorcycle oil
Oil capacity	1.0 litre
Bore x stroke	52.4 x 57.8 mm
Piston diameter service limit	52.30 mm
Cylinder bore service limit	52.44 mm
Piston to bore clearance (service limit)	0.10 mm
Piston ring installed end gap (standard/service limit)	
Top ring	0.15 to 0.30 mm/ 0.50 mm
Second ring	0.30 to 0.45 mm/ 0.65 mm
Oil control ring	0.20 to 0.70 mm/ 0.90 mm
Valve clearance	
Intake	0.16 mm
Exhaust	0.25 mm
Valve spring free length	
Standard	36.2 mm
Service limit	34.4 mm
Camshaft height service limit	
Intake	29.637 mm
Exhaust	29.395 mm
Coolant	50% distilled water, 50% corrosion inhibiting ethylene glycol anti-freeze
Coolant capacity	0.95 litre

Ignition system

Honda's specified testing procedure for the ignition system components requires specialist equipment not available to the DIY mechanic.

Electrical system

Battery	
Capacity	12 V, 6 Ah
Voltage (fully charged)	13 to 13.2 V
Alternator	
Output (regulated)	15.5 V (DC)
Charging coil resistance	0.1 to 0.5 ohms
Fuse (main)	30 Amps
Fuse (secondary)	1 x 15 and 4 x 10 Amps
Bulbs	
Headlight (main/dipped)	55 W
Sidelight	5 W
Brake/tail light	21/5 W
Turn signal lights	21 W
Instrument and warning lights	1.7 W

Fuel system

Throttle twistgrip freeplay	2 to 6 mm
Main jet	112
Pilot jet	35
Needle type / position	not available
Pilot screw setting	1⅞ turns out
Float height	18.2 mm
Automatic choke resistance	not available

Transmission

Belt width (service limit)	21.5 mm
Variator rollers	
Standard diameter	20.0 mm
Service limit	19.5 mm
Clutch lining thickness (service limit)	2 mm
Clutch spring free length (standard)	143.3 mm
Gearbox oil	SAE 90 hypoid gear oil
Gearbox oil capacity	220 ml

Brakes

Disc brake	
Fluid type	DOT 4
Pad minimum thickness	To wear limit indicator
Disc thickness (service limit)	3.5 mm
Drum brake	
Drum internal diameter (service limit)	131 mm
Shoe lining minimum thickness	To wear limit indicator
Brake lever freeplay	15 to 25 mm

Torque wrench settings

Valve cover bolts	12 Nm
Cylinder head nuts	27 Nm
Cylinder head bolts	12 Nm
Cam chain tensioner bolts	12 Nm
Camshaft sprocket bolts	9 Nm
Engine oil drain plug	20 Nm
Engine mounting bolts	49 Nm
Exhaust manifold nuts	29 Nm
Exhaust system mounting bolts	49 Nm
Water pump cover bolts	12 Nm
Water pump impeller nut	12 Nm
Thermostat cover bolts	10 Nm
Alternator rotor nut	116 Nm
Variator centre nut	59 Nm
Clutch centre nut	49 Nm
Clutch assembly nut	54 Nm
Crankcase bolts	12 Nm
Gearbox oil filler plug	13 Nm
Gearbox oil drain plug	27 Nm
Gearbox cover bolts	27 Nm
Rear shock absorber mountings	
Lower bolt	25 Nm
Upper bolt	39 Nm
Rear sub frame bolts	40 Nm
Steering head bearing locknut	68 Nm
Handlebar stem bolt	39 Nm
Front fork leg clamp bolts	40 Nm
Front axle nut	68 Nm
Rear hub nut	118 Nm
Disc brake caliper mounting bolts	30 Nm
Disc mounting bolts	42 Nm
Brake hose banjo bolts	34 Nm

Tyre pressures

Front	24.5 psi (1.7 bar)
Rear	29 psi (2.0 bar)

Honda SCV100 Lead

Engine

Engine	102cc single cylinder 4-stroke
Cooling system	Air cooled
Fuel system	VK0AC CV carburettor
Ignition system	CDI
Transmission	Variable speed automatic belt driven
Suspension	Trailing link front, single non adjustable shock rear
Brakes	Drum front and rear
Tyres	90/100 x 10 front, 90/100 x 10 rear
Wheelbase	1235 mm
Weight (dry)	102 kg (224lbs)
Fuel tank capacity	6.0 litres

Engine

Spark plug type	NGK CR6HSA
Electrode gap	0.6 to 0.7 mm
Idle speed (rpm)	1800 ± 100 min
Engine oil	viscosity SAE 10W-30
Oil capacity	800 ml
Bore x stroke	50.0 x 52.0 mm
Piston diameter service limit	49.90 mm
Piston to bore clearance (service limit)	0.10 mm
Piston ring installed end gap (service limit)	0.45 mm
Valve clearance	
Intake and exhaust	0.12 to 0.16 mm
Valve spring free length (service limit)	
Inner spring	29.1 mm
Outer spring	31.5 mm
Camshaft lobe height (service limit)	
Intake	29.283 mm
Exhaust	28.997 mm

Fuel system

Main jet	85
Pilot jet	35
Pilot screw setting	1¾ turns out
Float height	13 mm
Throttle twistgrip freeplay	2 to 6 mm

Electrical system

Battery	
Capacity	12V , 4Ah
Voltage (fully charged)	12.8V
Alternator regulated output	14 to 15V @ 5000 rpm
Charging coil	12 to 13.6V @ 5000 rpm
Lighting coil	
Charging coil resistance	0.4 to 1.0 ohms
Lighting coil resistance	0.2 to 0.8 ohms
Fuse (main)	10 A
Bulbs	
Headlight (main/dipped)	35/35 W
Sidelight	5 W
Brake/tail light	5/21 W
Turn signal lights	21 W
Instrument and turn signal warning light	3 W

Ignition system

Honda's specified testing procedure for the ignition system components requires specialist equipment not available to the DIY mechanic.

Transmission

Belt width (service limit)	17.5 mm
Variator rollers (service limit)	15.40 mm
Clutch lining thickness (service limit)	2.0 mm
Clutch spring free length (service limit)	105 mm
Gearbox oil	SAE 90 hypoid gear oil
Gearbox oil capacity	120 ml

Brakes

Drum internal diameter (service limit)	131 mm
Shoe lining minimum thickness	to wear limit indicator
Brake lever freeplay	10 to 20 mm

Torque wrench settings

Alternator rotor nut	39 Nm
Camshaft sprocket bolts	9 Nm
Camchain tensioner blade pivot bolt	10 Nm
Camchain tensioner plug	4 Nm
Clutch assembly nut	54 Nm
Clutch centre nut	39 Nm
Crankcase bolts	13 Nm
Cylinder head/rocker nuts	16 Nm
Engine mounting bracket nut	69 Nm
Engine mounting nut	49 Nm
Engine oil drain plug	24 Nm
Engine oil strainer cap	20 Nm
Fan cover bolt	10 Nm
Front axle nut	59 Nm
Front suspension bottom link-to-fork bracket nuts	28 Nm
Front fork suspension unit retaining bolt	32 Nm
Gearbox oil filler plug	13 Nm
Gearbox oil drain plug	13 Nm
Handlebar stem bolt	34 Nm
Oil pump mounting bolts	10 Nm
Rear axle nut	118 Nm
Rear shock absorber mountings	
lower bolt	22 Nm
upper bolt	39 Nm
Rear wheel – to – hub nuts	30 Nm
Steering head nut	68 Nm
Valve cover bolts	12 Nm
Variator centre nut	59 Nm

Tyre pressures

Front	22 psi (1.5 bar)
Rear	29 psi (2.0 bar)

Honda SES 125 Dylan

Engine

Engine	124.6 cc single cylinder four-stroke
Cooling system	Liquid-cooled
Fuel system	VK4AA CV carburettor
Ignition system	CDI
Transmission	Variable speed automatic, belt driven
Suspension	Telescopic front, swingarm with twin adjustable shock rear
Brakes	disc front, drum rear
Tyres	110/90 x 13 front, 130/70 x 13 rear
Wheelbase	1328 mm
Weight (dry)	122 kg
Fuel tank capacity	9.0 litres

Engine

Spark plug type	NGK CR8EH-9
Electrode gap	0.8 to 0.9 mm
Idle speed (rpm)	1600 rpm
Engine oil	SAE 10W/40 four-stroke motorcycle oil
Oil capacity	1.0 litre
Bore x stroke	52.4 x 57.8 mm
Piston diameter service limit	52.30 mm
Cylinder bore service limit	52.44 mm
Piston to bore clearance (service limit)	0.10 mm
Piston ring installed end gap (standard/service limit)	
Top ring	0.15 to 0.30 mm/ 0.50 mm
Second ring	0.30 to 0.45 mm/ 0.65 mm
Oil control ring	0.20 to 0.70 mm/ 0.90 mm
Valve clearance	
Intake	0.16 mm
Exhaust	0.25 mm
Valve spring free length	
Standard	36.2 mm
Service limit	34.4 mm
Camshaft height service limit	
Intake	29.637 mm
Exhaust	29.395 mm
Coolant	50% distilled water, 50% corrosion inhibiting ethylene glycol anti-freeze
Coolant capacity	0.95 litre

Fuel system

Throttle twistgrip freeplay	2 to 6 mm
Main jet	112
Pilot jet	35
Needle type / position	not available
Pilot screw setting	1⅞ turns out
Float height	18.2 mm
Automatic choke resistance	not available

Transmission

Belt width (service limit)	21.5 mm
Variator rollers	
Standard diameter	20.0 mm
Service limit	19.5 mm
Clutch lining thickness (service limit)	2 mm
Clutch spring free length (standard)	143.3 mm
Gearbox oil	SAE 90 hypoid gear oil
Gearbox oil capacity	220 ml

Brakes

Disc brake	
Fluid type	DOT 4
Pad minimum thickness	To wear limit indicator
Disc thickness (service limit)	3.5 mm
Drum brake	
Drum internal diameter (service limit)	131 mm
Shoe lining minimum thickness	To wear limit indicator
Brake lever freeplay	15 to 25 mm

Ignition system

Honda's specified testing procedure for the ignition system components requires specialist equipment not available to the DIY mechanic.

Tyre pressures

Front	24.5 psi (1.7 bar)
Rear	29 psi (2.0 bar)

Electrical system

Battery	
Capacity	12 V, 6 Ah
Voltage (fully charged)	13 to 13.2 V
Alternator	
Output (regulated)	15.5 V (DC)
Charging coil resistance	0.1 to 0.5 ohms
Lighting coil resistance	0.1 to 0.5 ohms
Fuse (main)	30 Amps
Fuse (secondary)	1 x 15 and 4 x 10 Amps
Bulbs	
Headlight (main/dipped)	60/55 W
Sidelight	5 W
Brake/tail light	21/5 W
Turn signal lights	21 W
Instrument and warning lights	1.2 W

Torque wrench settings

Valve cover bolts	12 Nm
Cylinder head nuts	27 Nm
Cylinder head bolts	12 Nm
Cam chain tensioner bolts	12 Nm
Camshaft sprocket bolts	9 Nm
Engine oil drain plug	20 Nm
Engine mounting bolts	49 Nm
Exhaust manifold nuts	29 Nm
Exhaust system mounting bolts	49 Nm
Water pump cover bolts	12 Nm
Water pump impeller nut	12 Nm
Thermostat cover bolts	10 Nm
Alternator rotor nut	116 Nm
Variator centre nut	59 Nm
Clutch centre nut	49 Nm
Clutch assembly nut	54 Nm
Crankcase bolts	12 Nm
Gearbox oil filler plug	13 Nm
Gearbox oil drain plug	27 Nm
Gearbox cover bolts	27 Nm
Rear shock absorber mountings	
Lower bolt	25 Nm
Upper bolt	39 Nm
Rear sub frame bolts	40 Nm
Steering head nut	68 Nm
Handlebar stem bolt	44 Nm
Front fork leg clamp bolts	40 Nm
Front axle nut	78 Nm
Rear hub nut	128 Nm
Disc brake caliper mounting bolts	30 Nm
Disc mounting bolts	42 Nm
Brake hose banjo bolts	34 Nm

Honda SFX50 Data 17

Engine

Engine	49 cc single-cylinder two-stroke
Cooling system	Air-cooled
Fuel system	PB2BN slide carburettor
Ignition system	CDI
Transmission	Variable speed automatic, belt-driven
Suspension	Telescopic front, swingarm with single shock rear
Brakes	Disc front, drum rear
Tyres	90/90 x 10 front, 90/90 x 10 rear
Wheelbase	1215 mm
Weight (dry)	71 kg
Fuel tank capacity	6 litres

Engine

Spark plug type	NGK BR6HSA
Electrode gap	0.6 to 0.7 mm
Idle speed (rpm)	1800 rpm
Engine oil	Two-stroke injector oil
Oil tank capacity	1.2 litres
Bore x stroke	39.0 x 41.4 mm
Piston diameter (service limit)	38.90 mm
Cylinder diameter (service limit)	39.05 mm
Piston to bore clearance (service limit)	0.10 mm
Piston ring installed end gap	
Standard	0.10 to 0.25 mm
Service limit	0.40 mm

Fuel system

Throttle twistgrip freeplay	2 to 6 mm
Main jet	80
Pilot jet	35
Needle type / position	J63S (3rd notch)
Pilot screw setting	1½ turns out
Float height	8.6 mm
Automatic choke resistance	3.2 to 5.6 ohms

Tyre pressures

Front	18 psi (1.3 bar)
Rear	29 psi (2.0 bar)

Electrical system

Battery	
Capacity	12 V, 2.3 Ah
Voltage (fully charged)	13 to 13.2 V
Alternator	
Output (regulated)	14 to 15 V (DC)
Charging coil resistance	0.2 to 1.0 ohms
Lighting coil resistance	0.1 to 0.8 ohms
Fuse	15 + 10 Amps
Bulbs	
Headlight (main/dipped)	25/25 W
Sidelight	5 W
Brake/tail light	21/5 W
Turn signal lights	10 W
Instrument and warning lights	2 W

Ignition system

HT coil primary resistance	0.1 to 0.3 ohm
HT coil secondary resistance	6.5 to 9.7 K-ohms
Spark plug cap resistance	3.8 to 6.2 K-ohms
Pick-up coil resistance	50 to 200 ohms

Transmission

Belt width (service limit)	17.5 mm
Variator rollers diameter	
Standard	15.92 to 16.08 mm
Service limit	15.40 mm
Clutch lining thickness (service limit)	2 mm
Clutch spring free length (service limit)	92.8 mm
Gearbox oil	SAE 10W-40 oil
Gearbox oil capacity	100 ml

Brakes

Disc brake	
Fluid type	DOT 4
Disc thickness (service limit)	3.5 mm
Drum brake	
Drum internal diameter (service limit)	111 mm
Brake lever freeplay	10 to 20 mm

Torque wrench settings

Cylinder head bolts	10 Nm
Crankcase bolts	10 Nm
Engine mounting bolt	50 Nm
Exhaust manifold nuts	16 Nm
Exhaust system mounting bolts	27 Nm
Alternator rotor nut	40 Nm
Variator centre nut	42 Nm
Clutch centre nut	40 Nm
Clutch assembly nut	55 Nm
Gearbox oil filler plug	12 Nm
Gearbox oil drain plug	12 Nm
Rear shock absorber mountings	
Lower bolt	25 Nm
Upper bolt	40 Nm
Steering head bearing locknut	70 Nm
Handlebar stem bolt	40 Nm
Front fork leg clamp bolts	27 Nm
Front axle nut	45 Nm
Rear hub nut	120 Nm
Disc brake caliper mounting bolts	32 Nm
Disc mounting bolts	43 Nm
Brake hose banjo bolts	30 Nm

Honda SGX50 Sky

Engine

Engine	49 cc single-cylinder two-stroke
Cooling system	Air-cooled
Fuel system	PB2BN slide carburettor
Ignition system	CDI
Transmission	Variable speed automatic, belt-driven
Suspension	Telescopic front, swingarm with single shock rear
Brakes	Disc front, drum rear
Tyres	2.50 x 16 front, 2.75 x 16 rear
Wheelbase	1230 mm
Weight (dry)	72.2 kg
Fuel tank capacity	4.5 litres

Engine

Spark plug type	NGK BR6HSA
Electrode gap	0.6 to 0.7 mm
Idle speed (rpm)	1800 rpm
Engine oil	Two-stroke injector oil
Oil tank capacity	1.2 litres
Bore x stroke	39.0 x 41.4 mm
Piston diameter (service limit)	38.90 mm
Cylinder diameter (service limit)	39.05 mm
Piston to bore clearance (service limit)	0.10 mm
Piston ring installed end gap	
Standard	0.10 to 0.25 mm
Service limit	0.40 mm

Fuel system

Throttle twistgrip freeplay	2 to 6 mm
Main jet	72
Pilot jet	35
Needle type / position	J63U (3rd notch from top)
Pilot screw setting	3 turns out
Float height	14.3 mm
Automatic choke resistance	3.2 to 5.6 ohms

Ignition system

HT coil secondary resistance	550 to 650 ohms
Spark plug cap resistance	4.95 to 5.05 K-ohms
Pick-up coil resistance	150 to 200 ohms

Transmission

Belt width (service limit)	17.0 mm
Variator rollers diameter	
Standard	15.92 to 16.08 mm
Service limit	15.40 mm
Clutch lining thickness (service limit)	2 mm
Clutch spring free length (service limit)	92.8 mm
Gearbox oil	SAE 10W-40 oil
Gearbox oil capacity	100 ml

Brakes

Disc brake	
Fluid type	DOT 4
Disc thickness (service limit)	3.0 mm
Drum brake	
Drum internal diameter (service limit)	111 mm
Brake shoe lining thickness	
Service limit	1.5 mm
Brake lever freeplay	10 to 20 mm

Tyre pressures

Front	25 psi (1.75 bar)
Rear	33 psi (2.25 bar)

Electrical system

Battery	
Capacity	12 V, 3 Ah
Voltage (fully charged)	13 to 13.2 V
Alternator	
Output (regulated)	14 to 15 V (DC)
Charging coil resistance	0.7 to 1.1 ohms
Fuse (main)	15 Amps
Fuse (secondary)	10 Amps
Bulbs	
Headlight (main/dipped)	35/35 W
Sidelight	5 W
Brake/tail light	21/5 W
Turn signal lights	10 W
Instrument and warning lights	2 W

Torque wrench settings

Cylinder head bolts	10 Nm
Crankcase bolts	10 Nm
Engine mounting bolt	50 Nm
Exhaust manifold nuts	16 Nm
Exhaust system mounting bolts	27 Nm
Alternator rotor nut	40 Nm
Variator centre nut	42 Nm
Clutch centre nut	40 Nm
Clutch assembly nut	55 Nm
Gearbox oil filler plug	12 Nm
Gearbox oil drain plug	12 Nm
Rear shock absorber mountings	
Lower bolt	25 Nm
Upper bolt	40 Nm
Steering head bearing locknut	70 Nm
Handlebar stem bolt	40 Nm
Front fork leg clamp bolts	27 Nm
Front axle nut	45 Nm
Rear hub nut	120 Nm
Disc brake caliper mounting bolts	32 Nm
Disc mounting bolts	43 Nm
Brake hose banjo bolts	30 Nm

Honda SH50

Engine

Engine	49 cc single-cylinder two-stroke
Cooling system	Air-cooled
Fuel system	PB2BR slide carburettor
Ignition system	CDI
Transmission	Variable speed automatic, belt-driven
Suspension	Telescopic front, swingarm with twin shock rear
Brakes	Disc front, drum rear
Tyres	2.50 x 16 front, 2.75 x 16 rear
Wheelbase	1267 mm
Weight (dry)	83.8 kg
Fuel tank capacity	6.3 litres

Engine

Spark plug type	NGK BR6HSA
Electrode gap	0.6 to 0.7 mm
Idle speed (rpm)	1800 rpm
Engine oil	Two-stroke injector oil
Oil tank capacity	1.2 litres
Bore x stroke	39.0 x 41.4 mm
Piston diameter (service limit)	38.90 mm
Cylinder diameter (service limit)	39.05 mm
Piston to bore clearance (service limit)	0.10 mm
Piston ring installed end gap	
Standard	0.10 to 0.25 mm
Service limit	0.40 mm

Fuel system

Throttle twistgrip freeplay	2 to 6 mm
Main jet	82
Needle type / position	J63U (3rd notch from top)
Pilot screw setting	1⅜ turns out
Float height	8.6 mm
Automatic choke resistance	3.2 to 5.6 ohms

Ignition system

HT coil primary resistance	0.1 to 0.3 ohm
HT coil secondary resistance	2.7 to 3.5 K-ohms
Spark plug cap resistance	3.8 to 6.2 K-ohms
Pick-up coil resistance	50 to 200 ohms

Transmission

Belt width (service limit)	17.0 mm
Variator rollers diameter	
Standard	15.92 to 16.08 mm
Service limit	15.40 mm
Clutch lining thickness (service limit)	2 mm
Clutch spring free length (service limit)	92.8 mm
Gearbox oil	SAE 10W-40 oil
Gearbox oil capacity	100 ml

Brakes

Disc brake	
Fluid type	DOT 4
Disc thickness (service limit)	3.0 mm
Drum brake	
Drum internal diameter (service limit)	111 mm
Brake shoe lining thickness	
Service limit	1.5 mm
Brake lever freeplay	10 to 20 mm

Tyre pressures

Front	25 psi (1.75 bar)
Rear	33 psi (2.25 bar)

Electrical system

Battery	
Capacity	12 V, 2.3 Ah
Voltage (fully charged)	13 to 13.2 V
Alternator	
Output (regulated)	14 to 15 V (DC)
Charging coil resistance	0.2 to 1.0 ohms
Lighting coil resistance	0.1 to 0.8 ohms
Fuse (main)	15 Amps
Fuse (secondary)	10 Amps
Bulbs	
Headlight (main/dipped)	35/35 W
Sidelight	5 W
Brake/tail light	21/5 W
Turn signal lights	10 W
Instrument and warning lights	2 W

Torque wrench settings

Cylinder head bolts	18 Nm
Crankcase bolts	10 Nm
Engine mounting bolts	50 Nm
Exhaust manifold nuts	12 Nm
Exhaust system mounting bolts	27 Nm
Alternator rotor nut	40 Nm
Alternator stator bolts	10 Nm
Variator centre nut	42 Nm
Clutch centre nut	40 Nm
Clutch assembly nut	55 Nm
Gearbox oil filler plug	12 Nm
Gearbox cover bolts	10 Nm
Rear shock absorber mountings	
Lower bolt	24 Nm
Upper bolt	39 Nm
Steering head bearing locknut	68 Nm
Handlebar stem bolt	44 Nm
Front fork leg clamp bolts	
Upper	26 Nm
Lower	18 Nm
Front fork leg bottom bolts	20 Nm
Front axle nut	58 Nm
Rear hub nut	118 Nm
Disc brake caliper mounting bolts	32 Nm
Disc mounting bolts	42 Nm
Brake hose banjo bolts	30 Nm

Honda SH125

Engine

Engine	124 cc single-cylinder four-stroke
Cooling system	Liquid-cooled
Fuel system	VK4AA CV carburettor
Ignition system	CDI
Transmission	Variable speed automatic, belt-driven
Suspension	Telescopic front, swingarm with twin adjustable shock rear
Brakes	Disc front, drum rear
Tyres	100/80 x 16 front, 120/80 x 16 rear
Wheelbase	1335 mm
Weight	131 kg

Engine

Spark plug type	NGK CR8EH-9
Electrode gap	0.8 to 0.9 mm
Idle speed (rpm)	1500 rpm
Engine oil	SAE 10W/40 four-stroke motorcycle oil
Oil capacity	1.0 litre
Bore x stroke	52.4 x 57.8 mm
Piston diameter service limit	52.30 mm
Cylinder bore service limit	52.44 mm
Piston to bore clearance	0.10 mm
(service limit)	
Piston ring installed end gap (standard/service limit)	
Top ring	0.15 to 0.30 mm/0.50 mm
Second ring	0.30 to 0.45 mm/0.65 mm
Oil control ring	0.20 to 0.70 mm/0.90 mm
Valve clearance	
Intake	0.16 mm
Exhaust	0.25 mm
Valve spring free length	
Standard	36.2 mm
Service limit	34.4 mm
Camshaft lobe height service limit	
Intake	29.637 mm
Exhaust	29.395 mm
Coolant	50% distilled water, 50% corrosion inhibiting ethylene glycol anti-freeze
Coolant capacity	0.95 litre

Fuel system

Throttle twistgrip freeplay	2 to 6 mm
Main jet	112
Pilot jet	35
Pilot screw setting	1⅞ turns out
Float height	18.2 mm

Ignition system

Honda's specified testing procedure for the ignition system components requires specialist equipment not available to the DIY mechanic.

Transmission

Belt width service limit	21.5 mm
Variator rollers	
Standard diameter	20.0 mm
Service limit	19.5 mm
Clutch lining thickness service limit	2 mm
Clutch spring free length	
(standard)	143.3 mm
Gearbox oil	SAE 90 hypoid gear oil
Gearbox oil capacity	220 ml

Brakes

Disc brake	
Fluid type	DOT 4
Pad minimum thickness	To wear limit indicator
Disc thickness (service limit)	3.5 mm
Drum brake	
Drum internal diameter	131 mm
(service limit)	
Shoe lining minimum thickness	To wear limit indicator
Brake lever freeplay	15 to 25 mm

Tyre pressures

Front	25 psi (1.75 bar)
Rear	25 psi (1.75 bar)

Electrical system

Battery	
Capacity	12 V, 6 Ah
Voltage (fully charged)	14.5 to 15.3 V
Alternator	
Output (regulated)	15.5 V (DC)
Charging coil resistance	0.1 to 0.5 ohms
Lighting coil resistance	0.1 to 0.5 ohms
Fuse (main)	30 Amps
Fuse (secondary)	2 x 15 and 5 x 10 Amps
Bulbs	
Headlight (main/dipped)	55/55 W
Sidelight	5 W
Brake/tail light	21/5 W
Turn signal lights	21 W
Instrument and warning lights	1.7 W

Torque wrench settings

Valve cover bolts	12 Nm
Cylinder head nuts	27 Nm
Cylinder head bolts	12 Nm
Cam chain tensioner bolts	12 Nm
Camshaft sprocket bolts	9 Nm
Engine oil drain plug	20 Nm
Engine mounting bolts	49 Nm
Exhaust manifold nuts	9 Nm
Exhaust system mounting bolts	49 Nm
Water pump cover bolts	12 Nm
Water pump impeller nut	12 Nm
Oil pump mounting bolts	12 Nm
Thermostat cover bolts	10 Nm
Alternator rotor nut	116 Nm
Variator centre nut	59 Nm
Clutch centre nut	49 Nm
Clutch assembly nut	54 Nm
Crankcase bolts	12 Nm
Gearbox oil filler plug	13 Nm
Gearbox oil drain plug	27 Nm
Gearbox cover bolts	27 Nm
Rear shock absorber mountings	
Lower bolt	25 Nm
Upper bolt	39 Nm
Rear sub frame bolts	40 Nm
Steering head bearing locknut	68 Nm
Handlebar stem bolt	39 Nm
Front fork leg clamp bolts	40 Nm
Front axle nut	68 Nm
Rear hub nut	118 Nm
Disc brake caliper mounting bolts	30 Nm
Disc mounting bolts	42 Nm
Brake hose banjo bolts	34 Nm

Electrical system

Battery	
Capacity	12 V, 2.3 Ah
Voltage (fully charged)	13 to 13.2 V
Alternator	
Output (regulated)	14 to 15 V (DC)
Charging coil resistance	0.7 to 1.1 ohms
Fuse (main)	15 Amps
Fuse (secondary)	10 Amps
Bulbs	
Headlight (main/dipped)	25/25 W
Sidelight	5 W
Brake/tail light	21/5 W
Turn signal lights	10 W
Instrument and warning lights	2 W

Torque wrench settings

Cylinder head bolts	10 Nm
Crankcase bolts	10 Nm
Engine mounting bolt	50 Nm
Exhaust manifold nuts	16 Nm
Exhaust system mounting bolts	32 Nm
Alternator rotor nut	40 Nm
Variator centre nut	42 Nm
Clutch centre nut	40 Nm
Clutch assembly nut	55 Nm
Gearbox oil filler plug	12 Nm
Gearbox oil drain plug	12 Nm
Rear shock absorber mountings	
Lower bolt	26 Nm
Upper bolt	18 Nm
Steering head bearing locknut	78 Nm
Handlebar stem bolt	44 Nm
Front fork leg clamp bolts	39 Nm
Front axle nut	59 Nm
Rear wheel nuts	64 Nm
Rear hub nut	118 Nm
Disc brake caliper mounting bolts	31 Nm
Disc mounting bolts	42 Nm
Brake hose banjo bolts	30 Nm

Engine

Engine	49 cc single-cylinder two-stroke
Cooling system	Air-cooled
Fuel system	PHVA 12FS slide carburettor
Ignition system	CDI
Transmission	Variable speed automatic, belt-driven
Suspension	Telescopic front, swingarm with single shock rear
Brakes	Single disc front, single disc rear
Tyres	
Model S	120/70 x 13 front, 140/60 x 13 rear
Model X	120/80 x 12 front, 120/80 x 12 rear
Wheelbase	1265 mm
Weight (dry)	97 kg
Fuel tank capacity	6 litres

Transmission

Belt width (service limit)	17 mm
Variator rollers diameter	
Standard	15.92 to 16.08 mm
Service limit	15.40 mm
Clutch lining thickness	
(service limit)	2 mm
Clutch spring free length	
(service limit)	92.8 mm
Gearbox oil	SAE 10W-40 oil
Gearbox oil capacity	100 ml

Brakes

Disc brake	
Fluid type	DOT 4
Disc thickness (service limit)	
Front	3.0 mm
Rear	2.5 mm

Tyre pressures

Front	
Model S	25 psi (1.75 bar)
Model X	18 psi (1.25 bar)
Rear	
Model S	29 psi (2.00 bar)
Model X	25 psi (1.75 bar)

Engine

Spark plug type	NGK BR6HSA
Electrode gap	0.6 to 0.7 mm
Idle speed (rpm)	1800 rpm
Bore x stroke	39.0 x 41.4 mm
Piston diameter (service limit)	38.90 mm
Cylinder diameter (service limit)	39.05 mm
Piston to bore clearance	
(service limit)	0.10 mm
Piston ring installed end gap	
Standard	0.10 to 0.25 mm
Service limit	0.40 mm

Fuel system

Throttle twistgrip freeplay	2 to 6 mm
Main jet	72
Pilot jet	35
Needle type / position	A30 (2nd notch)
Pilot screw setting	3 turns out
Float height	14.3 mm
Automatic choke resistance	3.2 to 5.6 ohms

Ignition system

HT coil primary resistance	0.1 to 0.3 ohm
HT coil secondary resistance	6.5 to 9.7 K-ohms
Spark plug cap resistance	3.8 to 6.2 K-ohms
Pick-up coil resistance	50 to 200 ohms

Malaguti F12 50 Phantom air-cooled

Engine

Engine	49 cc single-cylinder two-stroke
Cooling system	Air-cooled
Fuel system	Dell'Orto PHVA 12 slide carburettor
Ignition system	CDI
Transmission	Variable speed automatic, belt-driven
Suspension	Telescopic forks front, swingarm with single adjustable shock rear
Brakes	190 mm disc front, 110 mm drum or 190 mm disc rear
Tyres	120/70 x 12 front, 130/70 x 12 rear
Wheelbase	1240 mm
Weight (dry)	88 kg
Fuel tank capacity	8.5 litres

Engine

Spark plug type	NGK BR8HS or Champion RL 78/C
Electrode gap	0.5 to 0.6 mm
Idle speed (rpm)	1600 to 1800 rpm
Engine oil	Q8 City Bike Ultra
Oil tank capacity	1.4 litres
Bore x stroke	40.0 x 39.2 mm
Piston diameter (standard)	39.97 mm
Piston oversizes available	None
Piston to bore clearance	
Standard	0.034 mm
Service limit	0.047 mm
Piston ring installed end gap	0.15 to 0.35 mm

Fuel system

Throttle twistgrip freeplay	1 to 3 mm
Main jet	78
Pilot jet	38
Starter jet	48
Needle type	F12

Ignition system

HT coil primary resistance	0.30 to 0.50 ohm
HT coil secondary resistance	4.2 to 5.2 K-ohms
Spark plug cap resistance	5.3 K-ohms
Pick-up coil resistance	116 to 118 ohms

Electrical system

Battery	
Capacity	12 V, 4 Ah
Alternator	
Output (unregulated)	55 V (AC)
Charging coil resistance	0.80 ohms
Lighting coil resistance	0.60 ohms
Fuse (main)	10 Amps
Bulbs	
Headlight (main/dipped)	35/35 W
Sidelight	5 W
Brake/tail light	21/5 W
Turn signal lights	10 W
Instrument lights	1.2 W
Warning lights	LED panel

Transmission

Belt width	
Standard	16.8 mm
Service limit	15.5 mm
Variator rollers	
Standard diameter	15.0 mm
Service limit	14.5 mm
Clutch lining thickness	
Standard	4.0 mm
Service limit	2.5 mm
Clutch spring free length	
Standard	121.7 mm
Service limit	106.7 mm
Gearbox oil capacity	120 ml

Brakes

Disc brake	
Fluid type	DOT 4
Pad minimum thickness	2.0 mm
Disc minimum thickness	2.0 mm
Drum brake	
Brake lining minimum thickness	2 mm
Brake lever freeplay	10 mm

Tyre pressures

Front	26 psi (1.8 bar)
Rear	28 psi (1.9 bar)

Torque wrench settings

Cylinder head nuts	15 Nm
Crankcase bolts	12 Nm
Engine mounting bolts	62 Nm
Intake manifold bolts	8 Nm
Exhaust manifold nuts	8 Nm
Exhaust system mounting bolts	
8 mm	25 Nm
6 mm	8 Nm
Oil pump mounting bolts	4 Nm
Alternator rotor nut	38 Nm
Alternator stator bolts	9 Nm
Variator centre nut	33 Nm
Clutch centre nut	40 Nm
Clutch assembly nut	50 Nm
Gearbox oil filler plug	12 Nm
Gearbox oil drain plug	12 Nm
Gearbox cover bolts	12 Nm
Rear shock absorber	
Upper mounting bolt	40 Nm
Lower mounting bolt	24 Nm
Steering head bearing adjuster locknut	140 Nm
Handlebar stem bolt	50 Nm
Front axle	45 Nm
Front axle pinch-bolt	24 Nm
Rear hub nut	100 Nm
Disc brake caliper mounting bolts	30 Nm
Brake hose banjo bolts	28 Nm

Malaguti F12 50 Phantom liquid-cooled

Engine

Engine	49 cc single-cylinder two-stroke
Cooling system	Liquid-cooled
Fuel system	Dell'Orto PHVA 12 slide carburettor
Ignition system	CDI
Transmission	Variable speed automatic, belt-driven
Suspension	Telescopic forks front, swingarm with single adjustable shock rear
Brakes	190 mm disc front, 110 mm drum or 190 mm disc rear
Tyres	120/70 x 12 front, 130/70 x 12 rear
Wheelbase	1240 mm
Weight (dry)	92 kg
Fuel tank capacity	8.5 litres

Engine

Spark plug type	NGK BR8HS or Champion RL 78/C
Electrode gap	0.5 to 0.6 mm
Idle speed (rpm)	1600 to 1800 rpm
Engine oil	Q8 City Bike Ultra
Oil tank capacity	1.4 litres
Bore x stroke	40.0 x 39.2 mm
Piston diameter (standard)	39.97 mm
Piston oversizes available	None
Piston to bore clearance	
Standard	0.029 mm
Service limit	0.042 mm
Piston ring installed end gap	0.15 to 0.35 mm
Coolant	50% distilled water, 50% corrosion inhibiting ethylene glycol anti-freeze
Coolant capacity	1.1 litres

Fuel system

Throttle twistgrip freeplay	1 to 3 mm
Main jet	78
Pilot jet	38
Starter jet	48
Needle type	F12

Tyre pressures

Front	26 psi (1.8 bar)
Rear	28 psi (1.9 bar)

Electrical system

Battery	
Capacity	12 V, 4 Ah
Alternator	
Output (unregulated)	55 V (AC)
Charging coil resistance	0.80 ohms
Lighting coil resistance	0.60 ohms
Fuse (main)	10 Amps
Bulbs	
Headlight (main/dipped)	35/35 W
Sidelight	5 W
Brake/tail light	21/5 W
Turn signal lights	10 W
Instrument lights	1.2 W
Warning lights	LED panel

Ignition system

HT coil primary resistance	0.30 to 0.50 ohm
HT coil secondary resistance	4.2 to 5.2 K-ohms
Spark plug cap resistance	5.3 K-ohms
Pick-up coil resistance	116 to 118 ohms

Transmission

Belt width	
Standard	16.8 mm
Service limit	15.5 mm
Variator rollers	
Standard diameter	15.0 mm
Service limit	14.5 mm
Clutch lining thickness	
Standard	4.0 mm
Service limit	2.5 mm
Clutch spring free length	
Standard	121.7 mm
Service limit	106.7 mm
Gearbox oil capacity	120 ml

Brakes

Disc brake	
Fluid type	DOT 4
Pad minimum thickness	2.0 mm
Disc minimum thickness	2.0 mm
Drum brake	
Brake lining minimum thickness	2 mm
Brake lever freeplay	10 mm

Torque wrench settings

Cylinder head nuts	15 Nm
Crankcase bolts	12 Nm
Engine mounting bolts	62 Nm
Intake manifold bolts	8 Nm
Exhaust manifold nuts	8 Nm
Exhaust system mounting bolts	
8 mm	25 Nm
6 mm	8 Nm
Oil pump mounting bolts	4 Nm
Alternator rotor nut	38 Nm
Alternator stator bolts	9 Nm
Variator centre nut	33 Nm
Clutch centre nut	40 Nm
Clutch assembly nut	50 Nm
Gearbox oil filler plug	12 Nm
Gearbox oil drain plug	12 Nm
Gearbox cover bolts	12 Nm
Rear shock absorber mounting	
Upper bolt	40 Nm
Lower bolt	24 Nm
Steering head bearing adjuster locknut	140 Nm
Handlebar stem bolt	50 Nm
Front axle	45 Nm
Front axle pinch-bolt	24 Nm
Rear hub nut	100 Nm
Disc brake caliper mounting bolts	30 Nm
Brake hose banjo bolts	28 Nm

Engine

Engine	49 cc single-cylinder two-stroke
Cooling system	Liquid-cooled
Fuel system	Dell'Orto PHVA 12 slide carburettor
Ignition system	CDI
Transmission	Variable speed automatic, belt-driven
Suspension	Telescopic forks front, swingarm with single adjustable shock rear
Brakes	200 mm disc front, 190 mm disc rear
Tyres	120/70 x 12 front, 130/70 x 12 rear
Wheelbase	1240 mm
Weight	86 kg
Fuel tank capacity	8.5 litres

Tyre pressures

Front	26 psi (1.8 bar)
Rear	28 psi (1.9 bar)

Electrical system

Battery	
Capacity	12 V, 4 Ah
Alternator	
Output (unregulated)	55 V (AC)
Charging coil resistance	0.80 ohms
Lighting coil resistance	0.60 ohms
Fuse (main)	10 Amps
Bulbs	
Headlight (main/dipped)	35/35 W
Sidelight	5 W
Brake/tail light	21/5 W
Turn signal lights	10 W
Instrument lights	1.2 W
Warning lights	LED panel

Engine

Spark plug type	NGK BR8HS or Champion RL 78/C
Electrode gap	0.5 to 0.6 mm
Idle speed (rpm)	1600 to 1800 rpm
Engine oil	Q8 City Bike Ultra
Oil tank capacity	1.6 litres
Bore x stroke	40.0 x 39.2 mm
Piston diameter (standard)	39.97 mm
Piston oversizes available	None
Piston to bore clearance	
Standard	0.029 mm
Service limit	0.042 mm
Piston ring installed end gap	0.15 to 0.35 mm
Coolant	50% distilled water, 50% corrosion inhibiting ethylene glycol anti-freeze
Coolant capacity	1.1 litres

Ignition system

HT coil primary resistance	0.30 to 0.50 ohm
HT coil secondary resistance	4.2 to 5.2 K-ohms
Spark plug cap resistance	5.3 K-ohms
Pick-up coil resistance	116 to 118 ohms

Transmission

Belt width	
Standard	16.8 mm
Service limit	15.5 mm
Variator rollers	
Standard diameter	15.0 mm
Service limit	14.5 mm
Clutch lining thickness	
Standard	4.0 mm
Service limit	2.5 mm
Clutch spring free length	
Standard	121.7 mm
Service limit	106.7 mm
Gearbox oil capacity	110 ml

Torque wrench settings

Cylinder head nuts	15 Nm
Crankcase bolts	12 Nm
Engine mounting bolt	62 Nm
Intake manifold bolts	8 Nm
Exhaust manifold nuts	8 Nm
Exhaust system mounting bolts	
8 mm	25 Nm
6 mm	8 Nm
Oil pump mounting bolts	4 Nm
Alternator rotor nut	38 Nm
Alternator stator bolts	9 Nm
Variator centre nut	33 Nm
Clutch centre nut	40 Nm
Clutch assembly nut	50 Nm
Gearbox oil filler plug	12 Nm
Gearbox oil drain plug	12 Nm
Gearbox cover bolts	12 Nm
Rear shock absorber	
Upper mounting bolt	40 Nm
Lower mounting bolt	24 Nm
Steering head bearing adjuster locknut	140 Nm
Handlebar stem bolt	50 Nm
Front axle	45 Nm
Front axle pinch-bolt	24 Nm
Rear hub nut	100 Nm
Disc brake caliper mounting bolts	30 Nm
Brake hose banjo bolts	28 Nm

Fuel system

Throttle twistgrip freeplay	1 to 3 mm
Main jet	78
Pilot jet	38
Starter jet	48
Needle type	F12

Brakes

Disc brake	
Fluid type	DOT 4
Pad minimum thickness	2.0 mm
Disc minimum thickness	2.0 mm

Malaguti F15 50 Firefox

Engine

Engine	49 cc single-cylinder two-stroke
Cooling system	Liquid-cooled
Fuel system	Dell'Orto PHVA 12 slide carburettor
Ignition system	CDI

Transmission

Transmission	Variable speed automatic, belt-driven

Suspension

Suspension	Telescopic forks front, swingarm with single adjustable shock rear

Brakes	190 mm disc front, 110 mm drum or 190 mm disc rear
Tyres	120/70 x 12 front, 130/70 x 12 rear
Wheelbase	1268 mm
Weight (dry)	96 kg
Fuel tank capacity	7.0 litres

Engine

Spark plug type	NGK BR8HS or Champion RL 78/C
Electrode gap	0.5 to 0.6 mm
Idle speed (rpm)	1600 to 1800 rpm
Engine oil	Q8 City Bike Ultra
Oil tank capacity	1.6 litres
Bore x stroke	40.0 x 39.2 mm
Piston diameter (standard)	39.97 mm
Piston oversizes available	None
Piston to bore clearance	
Standard	0.029 mm
Service limit	0.042 mm
Piston ring installed end gap	0.15 to 0.35 mm
Coolant	50% distilled water, 50% corrosion inhibiting ethylene glycol anti-freeze
Coolant capacity	1.1 litres

Fuel system

Throttle twistgrip freeplay	1 to 3 mm
Main jet	78
Pilot jet	38
Starter jet	48
Needle type	F12

Tyre pressures

Front	26 psi (1.8 bar)
Rear	28 psi (1.9 bar)

Electrical system

Battery	
Capacity	12 V, 4 Ah
Alternator	
Output (unregulated)	55 V (AC)
Charging coil resistance	0.80 ohms
Lighting coil resistance	0.60 ohms
Fuse (main)	10 Amps
Bulbs	
Headlight (main/dipped)	35/35 W
Sidelight	5 W
Brake/tail light	21/5 W
Turn signal lights	10 W
Instrument lights	1.2 W
Warning lights	LED panel

Ignition system

HT coil primary resistance	0.30 to 0.50 ohm
HT coil secondary resistance	4.2 to 5.2 K-ohms
Spark plug cap resistance	5.3 K-ohms
Pick-up coil resistance	116 to 118 ohms

Transmission

Belt width	
Standard	16.8 mm
Service limit	15.5 mm
Variator rollers	
Standard diameter	15.0 mm
Service limit	14.5 mm
Clutch lining thickness	
Standard	4.0 mm
Service limit	2.5 mm
Clutch spring free length	
Standard	121.7 mm
Service limit	106.7 mm
Gearbox oil capacity	110 ml

Torque wrench settings

Cylinder head nuts	15 Nm
Crankcase bolts	12 Nm
Engine mounting bolt	62 Nm
Intake manifold bolts	8 Nm
Exhaust manifold nuts	8 Nm
Exhaust system mounting bolts	
8 mm	25 Nm
6 mm	8 Nm
Oil pump mounting bolts	4 Nm
Alternator rotor nut	38 Nm
Alternator stator bolts	9 Nm
Variator centre nut	33 Nm
Clutch centre nut	40 Nm
Clutch assembly nut	50 Nm
Gearbox oil filler plug	12 Nm
Gearbox oil drain plug	12 Nm
Gearbox cover bolts	12 Nm
Rear shock absorber	
Upper mounting bolt	40 Nm
Lower mounting bolt	24 Nm
Steering head bearing adjuster locknut	140 Nm
Handlebar stem bolt	50 Nm
Front axle	45 Nm
Front axle pinch-bolt	24 Nm
Rear hub nut	100 Nm
Disc brake caliper mounting bolts	30 Nm
Brake hose banjo bolts	28 Nm

Brakes

Disc brake	
Fluid type	DOT 4
Pad minimum thickness	2.0 mm
Disc minimum thickness	2.0 mm
Drum brake	
Brake lining minimum thickness	2 mm
Brake lever freeplay	10 mm

Malaguti Madison 125 and 150

Engine
Engine	Single-cylinder four-stroke
Cooling system	Liquid-cooled
Fuel system	Teikei 224V - YD CV carburettor
Ignition system	CDI

Transmission
	Variable speed automatic, belt-driven

Suspension
	Telescopic forks front, swingarm with twin adjustable shock rear

Brakes
Brakes	240 mm disc front, 220 mm disc rear
Tyres	120/70 x 13 front, 130/60 x 13 rear
Wheelbase	1445 mm
Weight (dry)	150 kg
Fuel tank capacity	12 litres

Tyre pressures
Front	29 psi (2.0 bar)
Rear	29 psi (2.0 bar) Solo, 32 psi (2.2 bar) with pillion

Electrical system
Battery	
Capacity	12 V, 9 Ah
Alternator	
Output (unregulated)	85 to 90 V (AC)
Output (regulated)	13.5 V (DC)
Lighting coil resistance	0.8 to 0.9 ohms
Fuse (main)	15 Amps
Fuse (secondary)	5 Amps
Bulbs	
Headlight (main/dipped)	35/35 W
Sidelight	3 W
Brake/tail light	21/5 W
Turn signal lights	10 W
Instrument light	2 W
Warning lights	1.2 W

Torque wrench settings
Cylinder head nuts	22 Nm
Cylinder head bolts	12 Nm
Cam chain tensioner cap bolt	8 Nm
Cam chain tensioner bolts	10 Nm
Camshaft sprocket bolt	25 Nm
Engine mounting bolt	32 Nm
Intake manifold bolts	10 Nm
Exhaust manifold nuts	8 Nm
Exhaust system mounting bolts	42 Nm
Alternator rotor nut	70 Nm
Variator centre nut	55 Nm
Clutch centre nut	60 Nm
Clutch assembly nut	90 Nm
Crankcase bolts	10 Nm
Gearbox oil drain plug	22 Nm
Gearbox cover bolts	16 Nm
Rear shock absorber	
Upper mounting bolt	45 Nm
Lower mounting bolt	24 Nm
Rear sub frame bolts	23 Nm
Steering head bearing locknut	140 Nm
Handlebar stem bolt	50 Nm
Handlebar clamp bolts	30 Nm
Front fork leg clamp bolts	32 Nm
Front fork leg bottom bolts	24 Nm
Front axle	45 Nm
Rear hub nut	100 Nm
Disc brake caliper mounting bolts	30 Nm
Brake hose banjo bolts	28 Nm

Engine
Spark plug type	NGK CR8E
Electrode gap	0.6 to 0.7 mm
Idle speed (rpm)	1600 to 1800 rpm
Engine oil	10W 40 four-stroke motorcycle oil
Oil capacity	1.4 litres
Bore x stroke	
125 cc	53.7 x 54.8 mm
150 cc	59.5 x 54.8 mm
Cylinder bore service limit	+ 0.05 mm
Piston to bore clearance	
Standard	0.025 to 0.035 mm
Service limit	0.15 mm
Piston ring installed end gap (standard/service limit)	
125 cc	
Top ring	0.15 to 0.25 mm/ 0.40 to 0.45 mm
Second ring	0.15 to 0.30 mm/ 0.45 to 0.60 mm
150 cc	
Top ring	0.15 to 0.30 mm/ 0.40 to 0.45 mm
Second ring	0.30 to 0.45 mm/ 0.45 to 0.60 mm
Oil control ring	0.20 to 0.70 mm
Valve clearance	
Intake	0.10 to 0.14 mm
Exhaust	0.16 to 0.20 mm
Valve spring free length service limit	39.84 mm
Camshaft lobe height service limit	30.711 mm
Coolant	50% distilled water, 50% corrosion inhibiting ethylene glycol anti-freeze
Coolant capacity	1 litre

Fuel system
Throttle twistgrip freeplay	1 to 5 mm	
	125 cc	**150 cc**
Carburettor type	5DS	5KD
Main jet 1	116	114
Pilot jet	39	36
Starter jet	50	47
Needle type	4E31	4E32
Pilot screw setting (turns out)	2½	3
Float height	27 mm	27 mm
Fuel level	5 to 6 mm below joint	

Ignition system
HT coil primary resistance	0.40 to 0.60 ohm
HT coil secondary resistance	7.5 to 8.5 K-ohms
Pick-up coil resistance	110 to 115 ohms

Transmission
Belt width	
Standard (service limit)	22.0 mm (19.8 mm)
Variator rollers	
Standard dia. (service limit)	20.0 mm (19.5 mm)
Recommended lubricant	Shell BT No 3
Clutch lining thickness (service limit)	1.0 mm
Gearbox oil	T35 80W
Gearbox oil capacity	140 ml

Brakes
Disc brake	
Fluid type	DOT 4
Pad minimum thickness	2.0 mm
Disc thickness (service limit)	2.0 mm
Drum brake	
Shoe lining minimum thickness	2 mm
Brake lever freeplay	10 mm

Engine

Engine	49 cc single-cylinder two-stroke
Cooling system	Air-cooled
Fuel system	Gurtner PA390 slide carburettor
Ignition system	CDI
Transmission	Variable speed automatic, belt-driven
Suspension	Upside down telescopic front, swingarm with single shock rear
Brakes	190 mm disc front, 110 mm drum rear
Tyres	120/70 x 12 front, 130/70 x 12 rear
Wheelbase	1360 mm
Weight	99 kg
Fuel tank capacity	8.3 litres

Engine

Spark plug type	NGK BR7HS
Electrode gap	0.6 to 0.7 mm
Idle speed (rpm)	1600 rpm
Engine oil	JASO FC, API TC semi-synthetic
Oil tank capacity	1.3 litres
Bore x stroke	40.0 x 39.1 mm
Piston diameter (standard)	39.85 mm
Piston to bore clearance	
Standard	0.15 mm
Piston rings	
Installed end gap	0.20 to 0.35 mm

Fuel system

Throttle twistgrip freeplay	2 to 5 mm
Main jet	74
Pilot jet	42
Starter jet	45
Needle type / position	L3035H (top notch)
Pilot screw setting	1⅛ turns out
Float height	Not adjustable
Automatic choke resistance	approx. 5.0 ohms @ 20°C

Ignition system

HT coil primary resistance	0.20 to 0.31 ohm
HT coil secondary resistance	2.4 to 3.6 K-ohms
Spark plug cap resistance	4.5 to 5.5 K-ohms
Source coil resistance	
AEC 400 system	0.44 to 0.66 K-ohms
ACI 100 system	0.64 to 0.96 ohms
Pick-up coil resistance	108 to 132 ohms
Immobiliser transponder aerial resistance	13.6 to 20.4 ohms

Transmission

Variator rollers	
Standard diameter	16 mm
Recommended lubricant	Esso SKF LGHT 3/0.4
Clutch spring free length	103.5 mm
Gearbox oil	80W-90 scooter gear oil
Gearbox oil capacity	120 ml

Brakes

Disc brake	
Fluid type	DOT 4
Pad minimum thickness	1.5 mm
Disc thickness	
Standard	3.5 mm
Service limit	3.0 mm
Drum brake	
Drum internal diameter	110 mm
Brake shoe lining thickness	
Standard	4 mm
Brake lever freeplay	10 to 20 mm

Tyre pressures

Front	19 psi (1.3 bar)
Rear	23 psi (1.6 bar)

Electrical system

Battery	
Capacity	12 V, 4 Ah
Voltage (fully charged)	14 to 15 V
Alternator	
Output (unregulated)	18 to 22 V (AC)
Output (regulated)	14 to 15 V (DC)
Charging coil resistance	0.53 to 0.88 ohms
Lighting coil resistance	0.45 to 0.75 ohms
Fuse (main)	5 Amps
Bulbs	
Headlight (main/dipped)	35/35 W
Brake/tail light	21/5 W
Turn signal lights	10 W
Instrument and warning lights	1.2 W

Torque wrench settings

Cylinder head bolts	15 Nm
Crankcase bolts	12 Nm
Engine mounting bolt	60 Nm
Intake manifold bolts	10 Nm
Exhaust manifold nuts	16 Nm
Exhaust system mounting bolts	25 Nm
Oil pump mounting bolts	8 Nm
Alternator rotor nut	40 Nm
Alternator stator bolts	10 Nm
Variator centre nut	40 Nm
Clutch centre nut	45 Nm
Clutch assembly nut	50 Nm
Gearbox oil filler plug	12 Nm
Gearbox oil drain plug	12 Nm
Gearbox cover bolts	10 Nm
Shock absorber mountings (front and rear)	
Lower bolt	25 Nm
Upper bolt	50 Nm
Steering head bearing adjuster nut	
Initial setting	40 Nm
Final setting	23 Nm
Steering head bearing locknut	80 Nm
Handlebar stem bolt	40 Nm
Front axle nut	70 Nm
Rear hub nut	120 Nm
Disc brake caliper mounting bolts	35 Nm
Brake disc mounting bolts	32 Nm

Peugeot Elyseo 100

Engine

Engine	99 cc single-cylinder two-stroke
Cooling system	Air-cooled
Fuel system	Dell'Orto 17.5 ES slide carburettor
Ignition system	CDI
Transmission	Variable speed automatic, belt-driven
Suspension	Telescopic front, swingarm with single shock rear
Brakes	226 mm disc front, 110 mm drum rear
Tyres	120/70 x 12 front, 130/70 x 12 rear
Wheelbase	1368 mm
Weight	113 kg
Fuel tank capacity	8.3 litres

Engine

Spark plug type	NGK BR8ES
Electrode gap	0.6 to 0.7 mm
Idle speed (rpm)	1600 rpm
Engine oil	JASO FC, API TC semi-synthetic
Oil tank capacity	1.4 litres
Bore x stroke	50.6 x 49.7 mm
Piston diameter (standard)	50.45 mm
Piston to bore clearance	
Standard	0.15 mm
Piston rings	
Installed end gap	0.30 to 0.45 mm

Fuel system

Throttle twistgrip freeplay	2 to 5 mm
Main jet	81
Pilot jet	30
Starter jet	65
Needle type / position	A11 (2nd notch from top)
Pilot screw setting	2 turns out
Float height	Not adjustable
Automatic choke resistance	approx. 5.0 ohms @ 20°C

Ignition system

HT coil primary resistance	0.20 to 0.31 ohm
HT coil secondary resistance	2.4 to 3.6 K-ohms
Spark plug cap resistance	4.5 to 5.5 K-ohms
Source coil resistance	
AEC 400 system	0.44 to 0.66 K-ohms
ACI 100 system	0.64 to 0.96 ohms
Pick-up coil resistance	108 to 132 ohms
Immobiliser transponder aerial resistance	13.6 to 20.4 ohms

Transmission

Variator rollers	
Standard diameter (models up to 1999)	19 mm
Standard diameter (2000-on models)	18 mm
Recommended lubricant	Esso SKF LGHT 3/0.4
Clutch spring free length	105.5 mm
Gearbox oil	80W-90 scooter gear oil
Gearbox oil capacity	120 ml

Brakes

Disc brake	
Fluid type	DOT 4
Pad minimum thickness	1.5 mm
Disc thickness	
Standard	4.0 mm
Service limit	3.5 mm
Drum brake	
Drum internal diameter	110 mm
Brake shoe lining thickness	
Standard	4 mm
Brake lever freeplay	10 to 20 mm

Tyre pressures

Front	19 psi (1.3 bar)
Rear	23 psi (1.6 bar)

Electrical system

Battery	
Capacity	12 V, 8 Ah
Voltage (fully charged)	14 to 15 V
Alternator	
Output (unregulated)	18 to 22 V (AC)
Output (regulated)	14 to 15 V (DC)
Charging coil resistance	0.58 to 0.88 ohms
Lighting coil resistance	0.45 to 0.75 ohms
Fuse (main)	5 Amps
Bulbs	
Headlight (main/dipped)	35/35 W
Sidelight	5 W
Brake/tail light	21/5 W
Licence plate light	5 W
Turn signal lights	10 W
Instrument and warning lights	1.2 W

Torque wrench settings

Cylinder head bolts	15 Nm
Crankcase bolts	12 Nm
Engine mounting bolt	60 Nm
Intake manifold bolts	10 Nm
Exhaust manifold nuts	16 Nm
Exhaust system mounting bolts	25 Nm
Oil pump mounting bolts	8 Nm
Alternator rotor nut	40 Nm
Alternator stator bolts	10 Nm
Variator centre nut	40 Nm
Clutch centre nut	45 Nm
Clutch assembly nut	50 Nm
Gearbox oil filler plug	12 Nm
Gearbox oil drain plug	12 Nm
Gearbox cover bolts	10 Nm
Shock absorber mountings (front and rear)	
Lower bolt	25 Nm
Upper bolt	50 Nm
Steering head bearing adjuster nut	
Initial setting	40 Nm
Final setting	23 Nm
Steering head bearing locknut	80 Nm
Handlebar stem bolt	40 Nm
Front axle nut	70 Nm
Rear hub nut	120 Nm
Disc brake caliper mounting bolts	35 Nm
Brake disc mounting bolts	32 Nm

Engine no. prefix / Frame no. prefix / Engine

Engine no. prefix	FD1
Frame no. prefix	VGAG2AB
Engine	124 cc single-cylinder four-stroke
Cooling system	Liquid-cooled
Fuel system	Mikuni BS26 CV carburettor
Ignition system	CDI
Transmission	Variable speed automatic, belt-driven
Suspension	Telescopic front, swingarm with twin adjustable shock rear
Brakes	226 mm disc front, 210 mm disc or 130 mm drum rear
Tyres	120/70 x 12 front, 130/70 x 12 rear
Wheelbase	1368 mm
Weight	140 kg
Fuel tank capacity	8.5 litres

Engine

Spark plug type	NGK CR7E
Electrode gap	0.6 to 0.7 mm
Idle speed (rpm)	1600 rpm
Engine oil	SAE 10W 40 four-stroke motorcycle oil
Oil capacity	1.25 litres
Bore x stroke	57.0 x 48.9 mm
Piston ring installed end gap	0.15 to 0.35 mm
Valve clearance	
Intake	0.10 to 0.15 mm
Exhaust	0.25 to 0.30 mm
Coolant	Procor 3000 or equivalent
Coolant capacity	1.5 litres

Fuel system

Throttle twistgrip freeplay	2 to 5 mm
Main jet	125
Pilot jet	35
Starter jet	25
Needle type / position	4CZ3 (2nd notch from top)
Pilot screw setting	2 turns out
Float height	Not adjustable

Ignition system

HT coil primary resistance	0.20 to 0.31 ohm
HT coil secondary resistance	2.4 to 3.6 K-ohms
Spark plug cap resistance	4.5 to 5.5 K-ohms
Source coil resistance	
AEC 400 system	0.44 to 0.66 K-ohms
ACI 100 system	0.64 to 0.96 ohms
Pick-up coil resistance	108 to 132 ohms
Immobiliser transponder aerial resistance	13.6 to 20.4 ohms

Electrical system

Battery	
Capacity	12 V, 12 Ah
Voltage (fully charged)	14 to 15 V
Alternator	
Output (unregulated)	18 to 22 V (AC)
Output (regulated)	14 to 15 V (DC)
Stator coil resistance	0.3 to 5.0 ohms
Fuse (main)	20 A and 5 Amps
Bulbs	
Headlight (main/dipped)	60/55 W
Sidelight	5 W
Brake/tail light	21/5 W
Licence plate light	5 W
Turn signal lights	10 W
Instrument and warning lights	1.2 W

Torque wrench settings

Valve cover bolts	10 Nm
Cylinder head bolts	10 Nm
Cylinder head nuts	23 Nm
Cylinder bolt	12 Nm
Cam chain tensioner bolts	10 Nm
Camshaft sprocket bolt	23 Nm
Engine oil drain plug	40 Nm
Engine mounting bolt	60 Nm
Intake manifold bolts	10 Nm
Exhaust manifold nuts	18 Nm
Exhaust system mounting bolts	25 Nm
Oil pump mounting bolts	10 Nm
Alternator rotor nut	70 Nm
Alternator stator bolts	10 Nm
Variator centre nut	70 Nm
Clutch centre nut	70 Nm
Clutch assembly nut	50 Nm
Crankcase bolts	10 Nm
Gearbox oil filler plug	12 Nm
Gearbox oil drain plug	12 Nm
Gearbox cover bolts	10 Nm
Rear shock absorber mountings	
Lower bolt	25 Nm
Upper bolt	50 Nm
Steering head bearing adjuster nut	
Initial setting	40 Nm
Final setting	23 Nm
Steering head bearing locknut	80 Nm
Handlebar stem bolt	40 Nm
Front axle nut	53 Nm
Rear hub nut	120 Nm
Disc brake caliper mounting bolts	35 Nm
Brake disc mounting bolts	32 Nm

Transmission

Variator rollers (standard diameter)	20 mm
Gearbox oil	80W-90 scooter gear oil
Gearbox oil capacity	120 ml

Brakes

Disc brake	
Fluid type	DOT 4
Pad minimum thickness	1.5 mm
Disc thickness (front)	
Standard	4.0 mm (4.5 mm M model)
Service limit	3.5 mm (4.0 mm M model)
Disc thickness (rear)	
Standard	4.0 mm
Service limit	3.5 mm
Drum brake	
Drum internal diameter	130 mm
Brake shoe lining thickness	
Standard	4 mm
Brake lever freeplay	10 to 20 mm

Tyre pressures

Front	22 psi (1.5 bar)
Rear	26 psi (1.8 bar)

Peugeot Elystar 125 and 150 Advantage

Data 30

Model code		G2AB (125), G2AC (150)
Engine		125/151 cc single cylinder four-stroke
Cooling system		Liquid-cooled
Fuel system		Dell'Orto PHCF24 slide carburettor
Ignition system		CDI
Transmission		Variable speed automatic, belt driven
Suspension		Telescopic front, swingarm with twin adjustable shock rear
Brakes		226 mm disc front, 210 mm disc rear
Tyres		120/70 x 12 front, 130/70 x 12 rear
Wheelbase		1368 mm
Weight		149 kg
Fuel tank capacity		8.5 litres

Engine

Spark plug type	NGK CR7E
Electrode gap	0.6 to 0.7 mm
Idle speed (rpm)	1600 rpm
Engine oil	SAE 10W/40 four-stroke motorcycle oil
Oil capacity	1.25 litres
Bore x stroke	
125	57.0 x 48.9 mm
150	57.0 x 58.9 mm
Piston rings installed end gap	0.15 to 0.35 mm
Valve clearance	
Intake	0.10 to 0.15 mm
Exhaust	0.25 to 0.30 mm
Coolant	Procor 3000 or equivalent
Coolant capacity	1.6 litres

Fuel system

Main jet	93 (125), 97 (150)
Pilot jet	40 (125), 46 (150)
Starter jet	38
Needle type / position	SH 89 (3rd notch from top)
Pilot screw setting	
125	2½ turns out
150	3 turns out

Ignition system

HT coil primary resistance	0.20 to 0.31 ohm
HT coil secondary resistance	2.4 to 3.6 K-ohms
Spark plug cap resistance	4.5 to 5.5 K-ohms
Pick-up coil resistance	108 to 132 ohms

Transmission

Gearbox oil	80W/90 scooter gear oil
Gearbox oil capacity	120 ml

Brakes

Disc brake	
Fluid type	DOT 4
Pad minimum thickness	1.5 mm
Front disc thickness:	
Standard	4.5 mm
Service limit	4.0 mm
Rear disc thickness:	
Standard	4.0 mm
Service limit	3.5 mm

Tyre pressures

Front	22 psi (1.5 bar)
Rear	26 psi (1.8 bar)

Electrical system

Battery	
Capacity	12 V, 12 Ah
Voltage (fully charged)	14 to 15 V
Alternator	
Output (regulated)	14 to 15 V (DC)
Stator coil resistance	0.5 ohms
Fuses	20 A and 5 A
Bulbs	
Headlight (main/dipped)	60/55 W
Sidelight	5 W
Brake/tail light	21/5 W
Licence plate light	5 W
Turn signal lights	10 W
Instrument and warning lights	1.2 W

Torque wrench settings

Cylinder head nuts	23 Nm
Crankcase bolts	8 to 10 Nm
Spark plug	10 Nm
Exhaust manifold nuts	15 to 18 Nm
Rear shock absorber mountings	
Lower bolt	20 to 25 Nm
Upper bolt	43 to 50 Nm
Steering column upper nut	60 to 80 Nm
Front axle nut	47 to 53 Nm
Rear hub nut	100 to 120 Nm
Brake caliper mounting bolts	25 to 35 Nm
Brake disc mounting bolts	27 to 32 Nm

Engine

Engine	49 cc single-cylinder two-stroke
Cooling system	Air-cooled
Fuel system	Gurtner PA358 slide carburettor
Ignition system	CDI
Transmission	Variable speed automatic, belt-driven
Suspension	Telescopic front, swingarm with single shock rear
Brakes	226 mm disc front, 110 mm drum rear
Tyres	80/80 x 16 front, 100/70 x 16 rear
Wheelbase	1311 mm
Weight	100 kg
Fuel tank capacity	8.0 litres

Engine

Spark plug type	NGK BR7HS
Electrode gap	0.6 mm
Idle speed (rpm)	1600 rpm
Engine oil	JASO FC, API TC semi-synthetic
Oil tank capacity	1.2 litres
Bore x stroke	40.0 x 39.1 mm
Piston diameter (standard)	39.85 mm
Piston to bore clearance	0.15 mm
Piston rings	
Installed end gap	0.20 to 0.35 mm

Fuel system

Throttle twistgrip freeplay	2 to 5 mm
Main jet	52
Pilot jet	36
Starter jet	50
Needle type	L3035F
Pilot screw setting	1½ turns out
Float height	Not adjustable
Automatic choke resistance	approx. 5.0 ohms @ 20°C

Ignition system

HT coil primary resistance	0.15 to 0.25 ohm
HT coil secondary resistance	3.6 to 4.5 K-ohms
Spark plug cap resistance	4.5 to 5.5 K-ohms
Source coil resistance	
AEC 400 system	0.44 to 0.66 K-ohms
ACI 100 system	0.64 to 0.96 ohms
Pick-up coil resistance	102 to 138 ohms
Immobiliser transponder aerial resistance	13.6 to 20.4 ohms

Transmission

Variator rollers	
Standard diameter	16 mm
Recommended lubricant	Esso SKF LGHT 3/0.4
Clutch spring free length	103.5 mm
Gearbox oil	80W-90 scooter gear oil
Gearbox oil capacity	120 ml

Brakes

Disc brake	
Fluid type	DOT 4
Pad minimum thickness	1.5 mm
Disc thickness	
Standard	4.0 mm
Service limit	3.0 mm
Drum brake	
Drum internal diameter	110 mm
Brake shoe lining thickness	
Standard	3 to 3.8 mm
Brake lever freeplay	10 to 20 mm

Tyre pressures

Front	26 psi (1.8 bar)
Rear	29 psi (2.0 bar)

Electrical system

Battery	
Capacity	12 V, 4 Ah
Voltage (fully charged)	14 to 15 V
Alternator	
Output (unregulated)	18 to 22 V (AC)
Output (regulated)	14 to 15 V (DC)
Charging coil resistance	0.64 to 0.96 ohms
Lighting coil resistance	0.48 to 0.72 ohms
Fuse (main)	5 Amps
Bulbs	
Headlight (main/dipped)	35/35 W
Sidelight	5 W
Brake/tail light	21/5 W
Turn signal lights	10 W
Instrument and warning lights	1.2 W

Torque wrench settings

Cylinder head bolts	15 Nm
Crankcase bolts	12 Nm
Engine mounting bolt	70 Nm
Intake manifold bolts	10 Nm
Exhaust system mounting bolts	16 Nm
Oil pump mounting bolts	25 Nm
Alternator rotor nut	8 Nm
Alternator stator bolts	40 Nm
Variator centre nut	10 Nm
Clutch centre nut	40 Nm
Clutch assembly nut	45 Nm
Gearbox oil filler plug	50 Nm
Gearbox oil drain plug	12 Nm
Gearbox cover bolts	12 Nm
Shock absorber mountings (front and rear)	10 Nm
Lower bolt	25 Nm
Upper bolt	50 Nm
Steering head bearing adjuster nut	
Initial setting	40 Nm
Final setting	23 Nm
Steering head bearing locknut	80 Nm
Handlebar stem bolt	40 Nm
Front axle nut	70 Nm
Rear hub nut	120 Nm
Disc brake caliper mounting bolts	35 Nm
Brake disc mounting bolts	32 Nm

Peugeot Looxor 100

Engine

Engine	99 cc single-cylinder two-stroke
Cooling system	Air-cooled
Fuel system	Gurtner PY slide carburettor
Ignition system	CDI
Transmission	Variable speed automatic, belt-driven
Suspension	Telescopic front, swingarm with single shock rear
Brakes	226 mm disc front, 190 mm disc rear
Tyres	80/80 x 16 front, 100/70 x 16 rear
Wheelbase	1311 mm
Weight	107 kg
Fuel tank capacity	8.0 litres

Engine

Spark plug type	NGK BR7HS
Electrode gap	0.6 mm
Idle speed (rpm)	1600 rpm
Engine oil	JASO FC, API TC semi-synthetic
Oil tank capacity	1.2 litres
Bore x stroke	50.6 x 49.7 mm
Piston diameter (standard)	50.45 mm
Piston to bore clearance	
Standard	0.15 mm
Piston rings	
Installed end gap	0.30 to 0.45 mm

Tyre pressures

Front	26 psi (1.8 bar)
Rear	29 psi (2.0 bar)

Electrical system

Battery	
Capacity	12 V, 4 Ah
Voltage (fully charged)	14 to 15 V
Alternator	
Output (unregulated)	18 to 22 V (AC)
Output (regulated)	14 to 15 V (DC)
Charging coil resistance	0.64 to 0.96 ohms
Lighting coil resistance	0.48 to 0.72 ohms
Fuse (main)	5 Amps
Bulbs	
Headlight (main/dipped)	35/35 W
Sidelight	5 W
Brake/tail light	21/5 W
Turn signal lights	10 W
Instrument and warning lights	1.2 W

Ignition system

HT coil primary resistance	0.15 to 0.25 ohm
HT coil secondary resistance	3.6 to 4.5 K-ohms
Spark plug cap resistance	4.5 to 5.5 K-ohms
Source coil resistance	
AEC 400 system	0.44 to 0.66 K-ohms
ACI 100 system	0.64 to 0.96 ohms
Pick-up coil resistance	102 to 138 ohms
Immobiliser transponder aerial resistance	13.6 to 20.4 ohms

Torque wrench settings

Cylinder head bolts	15 Nm
Crankcase bolts	12 Nm
Engine mounting bolt	70 Nm
Intake manifold bolts	10 Nm
Exhaust manifold nuts	16 Nm
Exhaust system mounting bolts	25 Nm
Oil pump mounting bolts	8 Nm
Alternator rotor nut	40 Nm
Alternator stator bolts	10 Nm
Variator centre nut	40 Nm
Clutch centre nut	45 Nm
Clutch assembly nut	50 Nm
Gearbox oil filler plug	12 Nm
Gearbox oil drain plug	12 Nm
Gearbox cover bolts	10 Nm
Shock absorber mountings (front and rear)	
Lower bolt	25 Nm
Upper bolt	50 Nm
Steering head bearing adjuster nut	
Initial setting	40 Nm
Final setting	23 Nm
Steering head bearing locknut	80 Nm
Handlebar stem bolt	40 Nm
Front axle nut	70 Nm
Rear hub nut	120 Nm
Disc brake caliper mounting bolts	35 Nm
Brake disc mounting bolts	32 Nm

Transmission

Variator rollers	
Standard diameter	18 mm
Recommended lubricant	Esso SKF LGHT 3/0.4
Clutch spring free length	105.5 mm
Gearbox oil	80W-90 scooter gear oil
Gearbox oil capacity	120 ml

Fuel system

Throttle twistgrip freeplay	2 to 5 mm
Main jet	88
Pilot jet	45
Starter jet	62
Needle type	L3035F
Pilot screw setting	1¾ turns out
Float height	Not adjustable
Automatic choke resistance	approx. 5.0 ohms @ 20°C

Brakes

Disc brake	
Fluid type	DOT 4
Pad minimum thickness	1.5 mm
Disc thickness	
Standard	4.0 mm
Service limit	3.0 mm

Peugeot Looxor 125 and 150

Engine

Engine	Single-cylinder four-stroke
Cooling system	Air-cooled
Fuel system	Walbro CV carburettor
Ignition system	CDI
Transmission	Variable speed automatic, belt-driven
Suspension	Telescopic front, swingarm with single shock rear
Brakes	226 mm disc front, 200 mm disc rear
Tyres	80/80 x 16 front, 110/80 x 14 rear
Wheelbase	1311 mm
Weight	115 kg
Fuel tank capacity	8.5 litres

Engine

Spark plug type	NGK CR7E
Electrode gap	0.6 mm
Idle speed (rpm)	1600 rpm
Engine oil	SAE 15W 40 four-stroke motorcycle oil
Bore x stroke	
125 cc	57.0 x 48.6 mm
150 cc	62.6 x 48.6 mm
Piston rings installed end gap	
Top ring	0.15 to 0.40 mm
Second ring	0.20 to 0.50 mm
Oil control ring	0.20 to 0.50 mm
Valve clearance	
Intake	0.10 mm
Exhaust	0.15 mm

Fuel system

Throttle twistgrip freeplay	2 to 5 mm
Main jet	
125 cc	84
150 cc	82
Pilot jet	
125 cc	33
150 cc	34
Starter jet	48
Needle type / position	
125 cc	DCK (2nd notch from top)
150 cc	52K (2nd notch from top)
Pilot screw setting	2¼ turns out

Electrical system

Battery	
Capacity	12 V, 4 Ah
Voltage (fully charged)	14 to 15 V
Alternator	
Output (unregulated)	18 to 22 V (AC)
Output (regulated)	14 to 15 V (DC)
Charging coil resistance	0.64 to 0.96 ohms
Lighting coil resistance	0.48 to 0.72 ohms
Fuse (main)	5 Amps
Bulbs	
Headlight (main/dipped)	35/35 W
Sidelight	5 W
Brake/tail light	21/5 W
Turn signal lights	10 W
Instrument and warning lights	1.2 W

Ignition system

HT coil primary resistance	0.15 to 0.25 ohm
HT coil secondary resistance	3.6 to 4.5 K-ohms
Spark plug cap resistance	4.5 to 5.5 K-ohms
Source coil resistance	
AEC 400 system	0.44 to 0.66 K-ohms
ACI 100 system	0.64 to 0.96 ohms
Pick-up coil resistance	102 to 138 ohms
Immobiliser transponder aerial resistance	13.6 to 20.4 ohms

Transmission

Gearbox oil	80W-90 scooter gear oil
Gearbox oil capacity	120 ml

Brakes

Disc brake	
Fluid type	DOT 4
Pad minimum thickness	1.5 mm
Disc thickness	
Standard	4.0 mm
Service limit	3.5 mm

Tyre pressures

Front	26 psi (1.8 bar)
Rear	33 psi (2.3 bar)

Torque wrench settings

Valve cover bolts	10 Nm
Cylinder head bolts	10 Nm
Cylinder head nuts	28 Nm
Cylinder bolt	12 Nm
Cam chain tensioner bolts	10 Nm
Camshaft sprocket bolt	23 Nm
Engine oil drain plug	40 Nm
Engine mounting bolt	62 Nm
Intake manifold bolts	10 Nm
Exhaust manifold nuts	16 Nm
Exhaust system mounting bolts	25 Nm
Oil pump mounting bolts	10 Nm
Alternator rotor nut	70 Nm
Alternator stator bolts	10 Nm
Variator centre nut	70 Nm
Clutch centre nut	70 Nm
Clutch assembly nut	50 Nm
Crankcase bolts	10 Nm
Gearbox oil filler plug	12 Nm
Gearbox oil drain plug	12 Nm
Gearbox cover bolts	10 Nm
Rear shock absorber mountings	
Lower bolt	25 Nm
Upper bolt	50 Nm
Steering head bearing adjuster nut	
Initial setting	40 Nm
Final setting	23 Nm
Steering head bearing locknut	80 Nm
Handlebar stem bolt	40 Nm
Front axle nut	53 Nm
Rear hub nut	120 Nm
Disc brake caliper mounting bolts	35 Nm
Brake disc mounting bolts	32 Nm

Peugeot Ludix 50

Tyre pressures

Front	19 psi (1.3 bar)
Rear	23 psi (1.6 bar)

Electrical system

Battery

Capacity	12 V, 4 Ah
Voltage (fully charged)	14 to 15 V

Alternator

Output (unregulated)	18 to 22 V (AC)
Output (regulated)	14 to 15 V (DC)
Charging coil resistance	0.53 to 0.88 ohm
Lighting coil resistance	0.45 to 0.75 ohm
Fuse (main)	7.5 A

Bulbs

Headlight	15 W
Brake/tail light	5 W x 3 or 10/5 W x 1
Turn signal lights	10 W
Instrument and warning lights	1.2 W and 2.0 W

Torque wrench settings

Cylinder head bolts	12 to 15 Nm
Crankcase bolts	8 to 12 Nm
Exhaust manifold nuts	15 to 18 Nm
Spark plug	20 Nm
Front wheel	60 to 70 Nm
Rear wheel	100 to 120 Nm
Steering column upper nut	70 to 80 Nm
Shock absorber mountings (front and rear):	
Lower bolt	20 to 25 Nm
Upper bolt	43 to 50 Nm
Disc brake caliper mounting bolts	25 to 35 Nm
Brake disc mounting bolts	27 to 32 Nm

Model code

Model code	L1AACA (Snake), L1AAM (One), L1AABA (Elegance), L1AABM (Classic), L1AAAA (Trend), L1ACCA (Blaster)

Engine

Cooling system	49 cc single cylinder two-stroke
Fuel system	Liquid-cooled (Blaster), Air-cooled (all other models)
	Gurtner PYA (Blaster), Gurtner PY12 (all other models) slide carburettor
Ignition system	CDI
Transmission	Variable speed automatic, belt driven
Suspension	USD telescopic front, swingarm with single shock rear
Brakes	disc or drum front, drum rear

Tyres

Snake and Blaster	120/90 x 10 front, 130/90 x 10 rear
One	90/90 x 10 front and rear
Elegance and Classic	80/80 x 14 front and rear
Trend	100/80 x 10 front and rear

Wheelbase

Snake, One, Trend and Blaster	1210 mm
Elegance and Classic	1235 mm
Weight	81.5 kg (Blaster), 66 to 76 kg (all other models)
Fuel tank capacity	5.5 litres

Ignition system

HT coil primary resistance	0.20 to 0.31 ohm
HT coil secondary resistance	2.4 to 3.6 K-ohms
Spark plug cap resistance	4.5 to 5.5 K-ohms
Pick-up coil resistance	108 to 132 ohms

Transmission

Gearbox oil	80W/90 scooter gear oil
Gearbox oil capacity	120 ml

Engine

Spark plug type	
One, Elegance, Classic and Trend	NGK BR7HS
Snake and Blaster	NGK CR7EB
Electrode gap	0.6 to 0.7 mm
Idle speed (rpm)	1600 rpm
Engine oil	JASO FC, API TC semi-synthetic two-stroke oil
Oil tank capacity	1.2 litres
Bore x stroke	39.9 x 39.8 mm
Piston rings	
Installed end gap	0.015 to 0.035 mm

Brakes

Disc brake

Fluid type	DOT 4
Pad minimum thickness	1.5 mm
Disc thickness:	
Standard	3.0 mm
Service limit	2.5 mm

Drum brake

Drum internal diameter	110 mm
Brake shoe lining thickness	
Standard	3.8 mm

Fuel system – Snake, One, Elegance, Classic and Trend

Main jet	56
Pilot jet	36
Starter jet	45
Needle type	L5035E
Pilot screw setting	1¼ to 1½ turns out

Fuel system – Blaster

Main jet	55
Pilot jet	42
Starter jet	45
Needle type	L3035F
Pilot screw setting	0 to ¾ turn out

Engine

Engine no. prefix	FL1
Frame no. prefix	VGAS1B
Engine	49 cc single-cylinder two-stroke
Cooling system	Liquid-cooled
Fuel system	Gurtner PA370 slide carburettor
Ignition system	CDI
Transmission	Variable speed automatic, belt-driven
Suspension	Monolever front, swingarm with single shock rear
Brakes	180 mm disc front, 110 mm drum
Tyres	120/70 x 12 front, 140/70 x 12 rear
Wheelbase	1225 mm
Weight (dry)	90 kg
Fuel tank capacity	7.2 litres

Tyre pressures

Front	19 psi (1.3 bar)
Rear	23 psi (1.6 bar)

Electrical system

Battery	
Capacity	12 V, 4 Ah
Voltage (fully charged)	14 to 15 V
Alternator	
Output (unregulated)	18 to 22 V (AC)
Output (regulated)	14 to 15 V (DC)
Charging coil resistance	0.64 to 0.96 ohms
Lighting coil resistance	0.48 to 0.72 ohms
Fuse (main)	5 Amps
Bulbs	
Headlight (main/dipped)	35/35 W
Sidelight	5 W
Brake/tail light	21/5 W
Turn signal lights	10 W
Instrument and warning lights	1.2 W

Torque wrench settings

Cylinder head bolts	15 Nm
Crankcase bolts	12 Nm
Engine mounting bolt	60 Nm
Intake manifold bolts	10 Nm
Exhaust manifold nuts	16 Nm
Exhaust system mounting bolts	25 Nm
Oil pump mounting bolts	8 Nm
Water pump mounting bolts	10 Nm
Alternator rotor nut	40 Nm
Alternator stator bolts	10 Nm
Variator centre nut	40 Nm
Clutch centre nut	45 Nm
Clutch assembly nut	50 Nm
Gearbox oil filler plug	12 Nm
Gearbox oil drain plug	12 Nm
Gearbox cover bolts	10 Nm
Shock absorber mountings (front and rear)	
Lower bolt	25 Nm
Upper bolt	50 Nm
Front monolever arm pivot bolt	90 Nm
Steering head bearing adjuster nut	
Initial setting	40 Nm
Final setting	23 Nm
Steering head bearing locknut	80 Nm
Handlebar stem bolt	40 Nm
Front and rear wheel bolts	40 Nm
Front hub nut	70 Nm
Rear hub nut	120 Nm
Disc brake caliper mounting bolts	35 Nm
Brake disc mounting bolts	32 Nm

Engine

Spark plug type	NGK BR7HS
Electrode gap	0.6 mm
Idle speed (rpm)	1500 rpm
Engine oil	JASO FC, API TC semi-synthetic
Oil tank capacity	1.3 litres
Bore x stroke	40.0 x 39.1 mm
Piston diameter (standard)	39.85 mm
Piston to bore clearance	
Standard	0.15 mm
Piston rings	
Installed end gap	0.24 mm
Service limit	0.26 mm
Coolant	50% distilled water, 50% corrosion inhibiting ethylene glycol anti-freeze
Temperature sender resistance	
@ 20°C	1.19 to 2.58 K-ohms
@ 90°C	92 to 124 ohms

Ignition system

HT coil primary resistance	0.15 to 0.25 ohm
HT coil secondary resistance	3.6 to 4.5 K-ohms
Spark plug cap resistance	4.5 to 5.5 K-ohms
Source coil resistance	
AEC 400 system	0.44 to 0.66 K-ohms
ACI 100 system	0.64 to 0.96 ohms
Pick-up coil resistance	102 to 138 ohms
Immobiliser transponder aerial resistance	13.6 to 20.4 ohms

Transmission

Variator rollers	
Standard diameter	16 mm
Recommended lubricant	Esso SKF LGHT 3/0.4
Clutch spring free length	103.5 mm
Gearbox oil	80W-90 scooter gear oil
Gearbox oil capacity	120 ml

Brakes

Disc brake	
Fluid type	DOT 4
Pad minimum thickness	1.5 mm
Disc thickness	
Standard	3.5 mm
Service limit	3.0 mm
Drum brake	
Drum internal diameter	110 mm
Brake shoe lining thickness	
Standard	4 mm
Brake lever freeplay	10 to 20 mm

Fuel system

Throttle twistgrip freeplay	2 to 5 mm
Main jet	72
Pilot jet	36
Starter jet	50
Needle type / position	L3035H (top notch)
Pilot screw setting	1⅛ turns out
Float height	Not adjustable
Automatic choke resistance	approx. 5.0 ohms @ 20°C

Peugeot Speedfight 2 50 liquid-cooled

Engine no. prefix / Frame no. prefix

Engine no. prefix	FL1
Frame no. prefix	VGAS1B
Engine	49 cc single-cylinder two-stroke
Cooling system	Liquid-cooled
Fuel system	Gurtner PA370 slide carburettor
Ignition system	CDI
Transmission	Variable speed automatic, belt-driven
Suspension	Monolever front, swingarm with single shock rear
Brakes	180 mm disc front, 180 mm disc or 110 mm drum rear
Tyres	
Front	120/70 x 12
Rear	140/70 x 12 ('00 to '02), 130/70 x 12 ('03-on)
Wheelbase	1225 mm
Weight	101 kg
Fuel tank capacity	7.0 litres

Engine

Spark plug type	NGK BR7HS
Electrode gap	0.6 to 0.7 mm
Idle speed (rpm)	1500 rpm
Engine oil	JASO FC, API TC semi-synthetic
Oil tank capacity	1.3 litres
Bore x stroke	40.0 x 39.1 mm
Piston diameter (standard)	39.85 mm
Piston to bore clearance	
Standard	0.15 mm
Piston rings	
Installed end gap	0.20 mm
Service limit	0.35 mm
Coolant	50% distilled water, 50% corrosion inhibiting ethylene glycol anti-freeze
Temperature sender resistance	
@ 20°C	1.19 to 2.58 K-ohms
@ 90°C	92 to 124 ohms

Fuel system

Throttle twistgrip freeplay	2 to 5 mm
Main jet	72
Pilot jet	36
Starter jet	50
Needle type / position	L3035H (top notch)
Pilot screw setting	1½ turns out
Float height	Not adjustable
Automatic choke resistance	approx. 5.0 ohms @ 20°C

Ignition system

HT coil primary resistance	0.20 to 0.31 ohm
HT coil secondary resistance	2.4 to 3.6 K-ohms
Spark plug cap resistance	4.5 to 5.5 K-ohms
Source coil resistance	
AEC 400 system	0.44 to 0.66 K-ohms
ACI 100 system	0.64 to 0.96 K-ohms
Pick-up coil resistance	108 to 132 ohms
Immobiliser transponder aerial resistance	13.6 to 20.4 ohms

Transmission

Variator rollers	
Standard diameter	16 mm
Recommended lubricant	Esso SKF LGHT 3/0.4
Clutch spring free length	103.5 mm
Gearbox oil	80W-90 scooter gear oil
Gearbox oil capacity	120 ml

Brakes

Disc brake	
Fluid type	DOT 4
Pad minimum thickness	1.5 mm
Disc thickness	
Standard	3.5 mm
Service limit	3.0 mm
Drum brake	
Brake shoe lining thickness	4 mm
Drum internal diameter	110 mm

Tyre pressures

Front	19 psi (1.3 bar)
Rear	23 psi (1.6 bar)

Electrical system

Battery	
Capacity	12 V, 4 Ah
Voltage (fully charged)	14 to 15 V
Alternator	
Output (unregulated)	18 to 22 V (AC)
Output (regulated)	14 to 15 V (DC)
Charging coil resistance	0.53 to 0.88 ohms
Lighting coil resistance	0.45 to 0.75 ohms
Fuse (main)	5 Amps
Bulbs	
Headlight (main/dipped)	35/35 W
Brake/tail light	21/5 W
Turn signal lights	10 W
Instrument and warning lights	1.2 W

Torque wrench settings

Cylinder head bolts	15 Nm
Crankcase bolts	12 Nm
Engine mounting bolt	60 Nm
Intake manifold bolts	18 Nm
Exhaust system mounting bolts	25 Nm
Oil pump mounting bolts	8 Nm
Water pump mounting bolts	10 Nm
Alternator rotor nut	40 Nm
Alternator stator bolts	10 Nm
Variator centre nut	40 Nm
Clutch centre nut	45 Nm
Clutch assembly nut	50 Nm
Gearbox oil filler plug	12 Nm
Gearbox oil drain plug	12 Nm
Gearbox cover bolts	10 Nm
Shock absorber mountings (front and rear)	
Lower bolt	25 Nm
Upper bolt	50 Nm
Front monolever arm pivot bolt	90 Nm
Steering head bearing adjuster nut	
Initial setting	40 Nm
Final setting	23 Nm
Steering head bearing locknut	80 Nm
Handlebar stem bolt	40 Nm
Front and rear wheel bolts	40 Nm
Front hub nut	70 Nm
Rear hub nut	120 Nm
Disc brake caliper and disc mounting bolts	
Front	35 Nm
Rear	32 Nm

Peugeot Speedfight and Speedfight 2 100

Engine no. prefix	FB6
Frame no. prefix	VGAS2A
Engine	
Cooling system	99 cc single-cylinder two-stroke
Fuel system	Air-cooled
	Dell'Orto PHVA slide carburettor
Ignition system	CDI
Transmission	Variable speed automatic, belt-driven
Suspension	Monolever front, swingarm with single shock rear
Brakes	180 mm disc front, 180 mm disc rear
Tyres	
Front	120/70 x 12
Rear	130/70 x 12 ('97 to '02), 140/70 x 12 ('03-on)
Wheelbase	1225 mm
Weight	101 kg
Fuel tank capacity	7.0 litres

Engine

Spark plug type	NGK BR8ES
Electrode gap	0.6 to 0.7 mm
Idle speed (rpm)	1600 rpm
Engine oil	JASO FC, API TC semi-synthetic
Oil tank capacity	1.3 litres
Bore x stroke	50.6 x 49.7 mm
Piston diameter (standard)	50.45 mm
Piston to bore clearance	
Standard	0.15 mm
Piston rings	
Installed end gap	0.30 mm
Service limit	0.45 mm

Fuel system

Throttle twistgrip freeplay	2 to 5 mm
Main jet	83
Pilot jet	30
Starter jet	65
Needle type / position	A11 (2nd notch from top)
Pilot screw setting	1¾ turns out
Float height	Not adjustable
Automatic choke resistance	approx. 5.0 ohms @ 20°C

Ignition system

HT coil primary resistance	0.20 to 0.31 ohm
HT coil secondary resistance	2.4 to 3.6 K-ohms
Spark plug cap resistance	4.5 to 5.5 K-ohms
Source coil resistance	
AEC 400 system	0.44 to 0.66 K-ohms
ACI 100 system	0.64 to 0.96 ohms
Pick-up coil resistance	108 to 132 ohms
Immobiliser transponder aerial resistance	13.6 to 20.4 ohms

Transmission

Variator rollers	
Speedfight standard diameter	19 mm
Speedfight 2 standard diameter	18 mm
Recommended lubricant	Esso SKF LGHT 3/0.4
Clutch spring free length	105.5 mm
Gearbox oil	80W-90 scooter gear oil
Gearbox oil capacity	120 ml

Brakes

Disc brake	
Fluid type	DOT 4
Pad minimum thickness	1.5 mm
Disc thickness	
Standard	3.5 mm
Service limit	3.0 mm

Tyre pressures

Front	19 psi (1.3 bar)
Rear	23 psi (1.6 bar)

Electrical system

Battery	
Capacity	12 V, 4 Ah
Voltage (fully charged)	14 to 15 V
Alternator	
Output (unregulated)	18 to 22 V (AC)
Output (regulated)	14 to 15 V (DC)
Charging coil resistance	0.53 to 0.88 ohms
Lighting coil resistance	0.45 to 0.75 ohms
Fuse (main)	5 Amps
Bulbs	
Headlight (main/dipped)	35/35 W
Sidelight	5 W
Brake/tail light	21/5 W
Licence plate light	5 W
Turn signal lights	10 W
Instrument and warning lights	1.2 W

Torque wrench settings

Cylinder head bolts	15 Nm
Crankcase bolts	12 Nm
Engine mounting bolt	60 Nm
Intake manifold bolts	10 Nm
Exhaust manifold nuts	18 Nm
Exhaust system mounting bolts	25 Nm
Oil pump mounting bolts	8 Nm
Alternator rotor nut	40 Nm
Alternator stator bolts	10 Nm
Variator centre nut	40 Nm
Clutch centre nut	45 Nm
Clutch assembly nut	50 Nm
Gearbox oil filler plug	12 Nm
Gearbox oil drain plug	12 Nm
Gearbox cover bolts	10 Nm
Shock absorber mountings (front and rear)	
Lower bolt	25 Nm
Upper bolt	50 Nm
Front monolever arm pivot bolt	90 Nm
Steering head bearing adjuster nut	
Initial setting	40 Nm
Final setting	23 Nm
Steering head bearing locknut	80 Nm
Handlebar stem bolt	40 Nm
Front and rear wheel bolts	40 Nm
Front hub nut	70 Nm
Rear hub nut	120 Nm
Disc brake caliper and disc mounting bolts	
Front	35 Nm
Rear	32 Nm

Tyre pressures

Front	19 psi (1.3 bar)
Rear	23 psi (1.6 bar)

Electrical system

Battery

Capacity	12 V, 4 Ah
Voltage (fully charged)	14 to 15 V

Alternator

Output (unregulated)	18 to 22 V (AC)
Output (regulated)	14 to 15 V (DC)
Charging coil resistance	0.53 to 0.88 ohms
Lighting coil resistance	0.45 to 0.75 ohms
Fuse (main)	5 Amps

Bulbs

Headlight (main/dipped)	35/35 W
Sidelight	5 W
Brake/tail light	21/5 W
Turn signal lights	10 W
Instrument and warning lights	1.2 W (LED – Metal-X)

Torque wrench settings

Cylinder head bolts	15 Nm
Crankcase bolts	12 Nm
Engine mounting bolt	60 Nm
Intake manifold bolts	10 Nm
Exhaust manifold nuts	16 Nm
Exhaust system mounting bolts	25 Nm
Oil pump mounting bolts	8 Nm
Alternator rotor nut	40 Nm
Alternator stator bolts	10 Nm
Variator centre nut	40 Nm
Clutch centre nut	45 Nm
Clutch assembly nut	50 Nm
Gearbox oil filler plug	12 Nm
Gearbox oil drain plug	12 Nm
Gearbox cover bolts	10 Nm
Shock absorber mountings (front and rear)	
Lower bolt	25 Nm
Upper bolt	50 Nm
Steering head bearing adjuster nut	
Initial setting	40 Nm
Final setting	23 Nm
Steering head bearing locknut	80 Nm
Handlebar stem bolt	40 Nm
Front axle nut	70 Nm
Rear hub nut	120 Nm
Disc brake caliper mounting bolts	35 Nm
Brake disc mounting bolts	32 Nm

Engine

Engine	49 cc single-cylinder two-stroke
Cooling system	Air-cooled
Fuel system	Gurtner PA360 or 370 slide carburettor
Ignition system	CDI
Transmission	Variable speed automatic, belt-driven
Suspension	Telescopic front, swingarm with single shock rear
Brakes	190 mm disc front, 110 mm drum rear

Tyres

Road	120/70 x 12 front, 130/70 x 12 rear
Off road and Metal-X	120/90 x 10 front, 130/90 x 10 rear
Wheelbase	1250 mm
Weight (dry)	83 to 88 kg
Fuel tank capacity	6 litres

Ignition system

HT coil primary resistance	0.20 to 0.31 ohm
HT coil secondary resistance	2.4 to 3.6 K-ohms
Spark plug cap resistance	4.5 to 5.5 K-ohms
Source coil resistance	
AEC 400 system	0.44 to 0.66 K-ohms
ACI 100 system	0.64 to 0.96 ohms
Pick-up coil resistance	108 to 132 ohms
Immobiliser transponder aerial resistance	13.6 to 20.4 ohms

Transmission

Variator rollers	
Standard diameter	16 mm
Recommended lubricant	Esso SKF LGHT 3/0.4
Clutch spring free length	103.5 mm
Gearbox oil	80W-90 scooter gear oil
Gearbox oil capacity	120 ml

Brakes

Disc brake

Fluid type	DOT 4
Pad minimum thickness	1.5 mm
Disc thickness	
Standard	3.5 mm
Service limit	3.0 mm

Drum brake

Drum internal diameter	110 mm
Brake shoe lining thickness	
Standard	4 mm
Brake lever freeplay	10 to 20 mm

Engine

Spark plug type	NGK BR7HS
Electrode gap	0.6 to 0.7 mm
Idle speed (rpm)	1600 rpm
Engine oil	JASO FC, API TC semi-synthetic
Oil tank capacity	1.3 litres
Bore x stroke	40.0 x 39.1 mm
Piston diameter (standard)	39.85 mm
Piston to bore clearance	
Standard	0.15 mm
Piston rings	
Installed end gap	0.15 to 0.35 mm

Fuel system

Throttle twistgrip freeplay	2 to 5 mm
Main jet	72
Pilot jet	42
Starter jet	45
Needle type / position	L3035H (top notch)
Pilot screw setting	1⅛ to 1¼ turns out
Float height	Not adjustable
Automatic choke resistance	approx. 5.0 ohms @ 20°C

Peugeot Trekker 100

Engine no. prefix	FB6
Frame no. prefix	VGAS2A
Engine	99 cc single-cylinder two-stroke
Cooling system	Air-cooled
Fuel system	Dell'Orto PHVA slide carburettor
Ignition system	CDI
Transmission	Variable speed automatic, belt-driven
Suspension	Telescopic front, swingarm with single shock rear
Brakes	190 mm disc front, 110 mm drum rear
Tyres	120/70 x 12 front, 130/70 x 12 rear
Wheelbase	1250 mm
Weight	94 kg
Fuel tank capacity	6 litres

Engine

Spark plug type	NGK BR8ES
Electrode gap	0.6 to 0.7 mm
Idle speed (rpm)	1600 rpm
Engine oil	JASO FC, API TC semi-synthetic
Oil tank capacity	1.3 litres
Bore x stroke	50.6 x 49.7 mm
Piston diameter (standard)	50.45 mm
Piston to bore clearance	
Standard	0.15 mm
Piston rings	
Installed end gap	0.30 mm
Service limit	0.45 mm

Fuel system

Throttle twistgrip freeplay	2 to 5 mm
Main jet	83
Pilot jet	30
Starter jet	65
Needle type / position	A11 (2nd notch from top)
Pilot screw setting	1¾ turns out
Float height	Not adjustable
Automatic choke resistance	approx. 5.0 ohms @ 20°C

Tyre pressures

Front	19 psi (1.3 bar)
Rear	23 psi (1.6 bar)

Electrical system

Battery	
Capacity	12 V, 4 Ah
Voltage (fully charged)	14 to 15 V
Alternator	
Output (unregulated)	18 to 22 V (AC)
Output (regulated)	14 to 15 V (DC)
Charging coil resistance	0.53 to 0.88 ohms
Lighting coil resistance	0.45 to 0.75 ohms
Fuse (main)	5 Amps
Bulbs	
Headlight (main/dipped)	35/35 W
Sidelight and licence plate light	5 W
Brake/tail light	21/5 W
Turn signal lights	10 W
Instrument and warning lights	1.2 W

Ignition system

HT coil primary resistance	0.20 to 0.31 ohm
HT coil secondary resistance	2.4 to 3.6 K-ohms
Spark plug cap resistance	4.5 to 5.5 K-ohms
Source coil resistance	
AEC 400 system	0.44 to 0.66 K-ohms
ACI 100 system	0.64 to 0.96 ohms
Pick-up coil resistance	108 to 132 ohms
Immobiliser transponder aerial resistance	13.6 to 20.4 ohms

Transmission

Variator rollers	
Standard diameter	19 mm
Recommended lubricant	Esso SKF LGHT 3/0.4
Clutch spring free length	105.5 mm
Gearbox oil	80W-90 scooter gear oil
Gearbox oil capacity	120 ml

Brakes

Disc brake	
Fluid type	DOT 4
Pad minimum thickness	1.5 mm
Disc thickness	
Standard	3.5 mm
Service limit	3.0 mm
Drum brake	
Drum internal diameter	110 mm
Brake shoe lining thickness	
Standard	4 mm
Brake lever freeplay	10 to 20 mm

Torque wrench settings

Cylinder head bolts	15 Nm
Crankcase bolts	12 Nm
Engine mounting bolt	60 Nm
Intake manifold bolts	10 Nm
Exhaust manifold nuts	16 Nm
Exhaust system mounting bolts	25 Nm
Oil pump mounting bolts	8 Nm
Alternator rotor nut	40 Nm
Alternator stator bolts	10 Nm
Variator centre nut	40 Nm
Clutch centre nut	45 Nm
Clutch assembly nut	50 Nm
Gearbox oil filler plug	12 Nm
Gearbox oil drain plug	12 Nm
Gearbox cover bolts	10 Nm
Shock absorber mountings (front and rear)	
Lower bolt	25 Nm
Upper bolt	50 Nm
Steering head bearing adjuster nut	
Initial setting	40 Nm
Final setting	23 Nm
Steering head bearing locknut	80 Nm
Handlebar stem bolt	40 Nm
Front axle nut	70 Nm
Rear hub nut	120 Nm
Disc brake caliper mounting bolts	35 Nm
Brake disc mounting bolts	32 Nm

Peugeot Vivacity 50

Engine no. prefix ...
Engine no. prefix	FB2
Frame no. prefix	VGAS1A
Engine	49 cc single-cylinder two-stroke
Cooling system	Air-cooled
Fuel system	Gurtner PA370 slide carburettor
Ignition system	CDI
Transmission	Variable speed automatic, belt-driven
Suspension	Upside down telescopic front, swingarm with single shock rear
Brakes	190 mm disc front, 110 mm drum rear
Tyres	120/70 x 12 front, 130/70 x 12 rear
Wheelbase	1249 mm
Weight (dry)	81 kg
Fuel tank capacity	6 litres

Engine
Spark plug type	NGK BR7HS
Electrode gap	0.6 to 0.7 mm
Idle speed (rpm)	1600 rpm
Engine oil	JASO FC, API TC semi-synthetic
Oil tank capacity	1.3 litres
Bore x stroke	40.0 x 39.1 mm
Piston diameter (standard)	39.85 mm
Piston to bore clearance	
Standard	0.15 mm
Piston rings	
Installed end gap	0.2 mm
Service limit	0.35 mm

Fuel system
Throttle twistgrip freeplay	2 to 5 mm
Main jet	72
Pilot jet	42
Starter jet	45
Needle type / position	L3035H (top notch)
Pilot screw setting	1½ turns out
Float height	Not adjustable
Automatic choke resistance	approx. 5.0 ohms @ 20°C

Ignition system
HT coil primary resistance	0.23 to 0.28 ohm
HT coil secondary resistance	2.7 to 3.3 K-ohms
Spark plug cap resistance	4.5 to 5.5 K-ohms
Source coil resistance	
AEC 400 system	0.44 to 0.66 K-ohms
ACI 100 system	0.64 to 0.96 ohms
Pick-up coil resistance	108 to 132 ohms
Immobiliser transponder aerial resistance	13.6 to 20.4 ohms

Transmission
Variator rollers	
Standard diameter	16 mm
Recommended lubricant	Esso SKF LGHT 3/0.4
Clutch spring free length	103.5 mm
Gearbox oil	80W-90 scooter gear oil
Gearbox oil capacity	120 ml

Brakes
Disc brake	
Fluid type	DOT 4
Pad minimum thickness	1.5 mm
Disc thickness	
Standard	3.5 mm
Service limit	3.0 mm
Drum brake	
Drum internal diameter	110 mm
Brake shoe lining thickness	
Standard	4 mm
Brake lever freeplay	10 to 20 mm

Tyre pressures
Front	19 psi (1.3 bar)
Rear	23 psi (1.6 bar)

Electrical system
Battery	
Capacity	12 V, 4 Ah
Voltage (fully charged)	14 to 15 V
Alternator	
Output (unregulated)	18 to 22 V (AC)
Output (regulated)	14 to 15 V (DC)
Charging coil resistance	0.53 to 0.88 ohms
Lighting coil resistance	0.48 to 0.75 ohms
Fuse (main)	5 Amps
Bulbs	
Headlight (main/dipped)	35/35 W
Brake/tail light	21/5 W
Turn signal lights	10 W
Instrument and warning lights	1.2 W

Torque wrench settings
Cylinder head bolts	15 Nm
Crankcase bolts	12 Nm
Engine mounting bolt	60 Nm
Intake manifold bolts	10 Nm
Exhaust manifold nuts	16 Nm
Exhaust system mounting bolts	25 Nm
Oil pump mounting bolts	8 Nm
Alternator rotor nut	40 Nm
Alternator stator bolts	10 Nm
Variator centre nut	40 Nm
Clutch centre nut	45 Nm
Clutch assembly nut	50 Nm
Gearbox oil filler plug	12 Nm
Gearbox oil drain plug	12 Nm
Gearbox cover bolts	10 Nm
Shock absorber mountings (front and rear)	
Lower bolt	25 Nm
Upper bolt	50 Nm
Steering head bearing adjuster nut	
Initial setting	40 Nm
Final setting	23 Nm
Steering head bearing locknut	80 Nm
Handlebar stem bolt	40 Nm
Front axle nut	70 Nm
Rear hub nut	120 Nm
Disc brake caliper mounting bolts	35 Nm
Brake disc mounting bolts	32 Nm

Peugeot Vivacity 100

Data 41

Engine no. prefix — FB6
Frame no. prefix — VGAS2A
Engine — 99 cc single-cylinder two-stroke
  Cooling system — Air-cooled
  Fuel system — Dell'Orto PHVA slide carburettor
  Ignition system — CDI
Transmission — Variable speed automatic, belt-driven
Suspension — Upside down telescopic front, swingarm with single shock rear
Brakes — 190 mm disc front, 110 mm drum rear
Tyres — 120/70 x 12 front, 130/70 x 12 rear
Wheelbase — 1250 mm
Weight (dry) — 90 kg
Fuel tank capacity — 6 litres

Engine

Spark plug type	NGK BR8ES
Electrode gap	0.6 to 0.7 mm
Idle speed (rpm)	1600 rpm
Engine oil	JASO FC, API TC semi-synthetic
Oil tank capacity	1.3 litres
Bore x stroke	50.6 x 49.7 mm
Piston diameter (standard)	50.45 mm
Piston to bore clearance	
Standard	0.15 mm
Piston rings	
Installed end gap	0.30 mm
Service limit	0.45 mm

Fuel system

Throttle twistgrip freeplay	2 to 5 mm
Main jet	83
Pilot jet	30
Starter jet	65
Needle type / position	A11 (2nd notch from top)
Pilot screw setting	1¾ turns out
Float height	Not adjustable
Automatic choke resistance	approx. 5.0 ohms @ 20°C

Tyre pressures

Front	19 psi (1.3 bar)
Rear	23 psi (1.6 bar)

Electrical system

Battery	
Capacity	12 V, 4 Ah
Voltage (fully charged)	14 to 15 V
Alternator	
Output (unregulated)	18 to 22 V (AC)
Output (regulated)	14 to 15 V (DC)
Charging coil resistance	0.53 to 0.88 ohms
Lighting coil resistance	0.45 to 0.75 ohms
Fuse (main)	5 Amps
Bulbs	
Headlight (main/dipped)	35/35 W
Sidelight	5 W
Brake/tail light	21/5 W
Turn signal lights	10 W
Instrument and warning lights	1.2 W

Ignition system

HT coil primary resistance	0.23 to 0.28 ohm
HT coil secondary resistance	2.7 to 3.3 K-ohms
Spark plug cap resistance	4.5 to 5.5 K-ohms
Source coil resistance	
AEC 400 system	0.44 to 0.66 K-ohms
ACI 100 system	0.64 to 0.96 ohms
Pick-up coil resistance	108 to 132 ohms
Immobiliser transponder aerial resistance	13.6 to 20.4 ohms

Transmission

Variator rollers	
Standard diameter	19 mm
Recommended lubricant	Esso SKF LGHT 3/0.4
Clutch spring free length	105.5 mm
Gearbox oil	80W-90 scooter gear oil
Gearbox oil capacity	120 ml

Brakes

Disc brake	
Fluid type	DOT 4
Pad minimum thickness	1.5 mm
Disc thickness	
Standard	3.5 mm
Service limit	3.0 mm
Drum brake	
Drum internal diameter	110 mm
Brake shoe lining thickness	
Standard	4 mm
Brake lever freeplay	10 to 20 mm

Torque wrench settings

Cylinder head bolts	15 Nm
Crankcase bolts	12 Nm
Engine mounting bolt	60 Nm
Intake manifold bolts	10 Nm
Exhaust manifold nuts	16 Nm
Exhaust system mounting bolts	25 Nm
Oil pump mounting bolts	8 Nm
Alternator rotor nut	40 Nm
Alternator stator bolts	10 Nm
Variator centre nut	40 Nm
Clutch centre nut	45 Nm
Clutch assembly nut	50 Nm
Gearbox oil filler plug	12 Nm
Gearbox oil drain plug	12 Nm
Gearbox cover bolts	10 Nm
Shock absorber mountings (front and rear)	
Lower bolt	25 Nm
Upper bolt	50 Nm
Steering head bearing adjuster nut	
Initial setting	40 Nm
Final setting	23 Nm
Steering head bearing locknut	80 Nm
Handlebar stem bolt	40 Nm
Front axle nut	70 Nm
Rear hub nut	120 Nm
Disc brake caliper mounting bolts	35 Nm
Brake disc mounting bolts	32 Nm

Peugeot Zenith

Engine no. prefix	FB0
Frame no. prefix	VGAFE05
Engine	49 cc single-cylinder two-stroke
Cooling system	Air-cooled
Fuel system	Gurtner PA341 slide carburettor
Ignition system	CDI
Transmission	Variable speed automatic, belt-driven
Suspension	Telescopic hydraulic fork with single shock rear
Brakes	95 mm drum front, 110 mm drum rear
Tyres	90/90 x 10 front, 90/90 x 10 rear
Wheelbase	1200 mm
Weight (dry)	68 kg
Fuel tank capacity	5.4 litres

Engine

Spark plug type	NGK BR7HS
Electrode gap	0.6 mm
Idle speed (rpm)	1500 rpm
Engine oil	JASO FC, SAE 20 semi-synthetic
Oil tank capacity	1.3 litres
Bore x stroke	40.0 x 39.1 mm
Piston diameter (standard)	39.85 mm
Piston oversizes available	None
Piston to bore clearance (standard)	0.15 mm
Piston ring installed end gap	0.24 mm

Fuel system

Throttle twistgrip freeplay	5 mm
Main jet	72
Pilot jet	36
Starter jet	50
Needle type / position	L3035H (top notch)
Pilot screw setting	1⅛ turns out
Float level	not adjustable
Automatic choke resistance	approx. 5.0 ohms @ 20°C

Ignition system

HT coil primary resistance	0.15 to 0.25 ohm
HT coil secondary resistance	3.6 to 4.5 K-ohms
Spark plug cap resistance	4.5 to 5.5 K-ohms
Source coil resistance	540 to 740 ohms
Pick-up coil resistance	100 to 123 ohms

Transmission

Variator rollers	greased
Recommended lubricant	Esso SKF LGHT 3/0.4
Gearbox oil	80W-90 scooter gear oil
Gearbox oil capacity	120 ml

Brakes

Brake lever freeplay	10 to 20 mm
Drum internal diameter	110 mm
Brake shoe lining thickness (standard)	4 mm

Tyre pressures

Front	26 psi (1.8 bar)
Rear	32 psi (2.2 bar)

Electrical system

Battery	
Capacity	12 V, 4 Ah
Voltage (fully charged)	14 to 15 V
Alternator	
Output (unregulated)	18 to 22 V (AC)
Output (regulated)	14 to 15 V (DC)
Charging coil resistance	0.7 ohms ± 25%
Lighting coil resistance	0.6 ohms ± 25%
Fuse (main)	5 Amps
Bulbs	
Headlight (main/dipped)	15/15 W
Brake/tail light	21/5 W
Turn signal lights	10 W
Instrument and warning lights	1.2 W

Torque wrench settings

Cylinder head bolts	15 Nm
Alternator rotor nut	40 Nm
Alternator stator bolts	10 Nm
Crankcase bolts	12 Nm
Engine mounting bolts	60 Nm
Inlet manifold bolts	10 Nm
Exhaust manifold nuts	16 Nm
Exhaust system mounting bolts	25 Nm
Oil pump mounting bolts	8 Nm
Variator centre nut	40 Nm
Clutch centre nut	45 Nm
Gearbox oil filler plug	12 Nm
Gearbox oil drain plug	12 Nm
Gearbox cover bolts	10 Nm
Rear shock absorber mountings	
Lower bolt	25 Nm
Upper bolt	50 Nm
Steering head bearing adjuster nut	
Initial setting	40 Nm
Final setting	23 Nm
Steering head bearing locknut	80 Nm
Handlebar stem bolt	40 Nm
Front axle nut	70 Nm
Rear wheel bolts	40 Nm

Piaggio B125 (Beverly)

Engine no. prefix, etc.

Engine no. prefix	M284M
Frame no. prefix	ZAPM 284
Engine	124cc single cylinder, four valve, four-stroke LEADER
Cooling system	Liquid-cooled
Fuel system	Walbro WVF 7C or 7G carburettor, or Keihin CVEK30
Ignition system	CDI
Transmission	Variable speed automatic, belt driven
Suspension	Telescopic front, swingarm with twin adjustable shock rear
Brakes	Disc front, disc rear
Tyres	110/70 x 16 front, 140/70 x 16 rear
Wheelbase	1475 mm
Weight (dry)	149 kg
Fuel tank capacity	10.0 litres

Engine

Spark plug type	NGK CR8EB
Electrode gap	0.7 to 0.8 mm
Idle speed (rpm)	1600 to 1700 rpm
Engine oil	5W 40 API SJ synthetic engine oil
Oil capacity	1.1 litre
Bore x stroke	57.0 x 48.6 mm
Piston diameter (standard)	56.94 to 56.97 mm
Piston to bore clearance (standard)	0.045 to 0.059 mm
Piston ring installed end gap (standard)	
Top ring	0.15 to 0.30 mm
Second ring	0.10 to 0.30 mm
Oil control ring	0.15 to 0.35 mm
Piston ring installed end gap (service limit)	1 mm
Valve clearance	
Intake	0.10 mm
Exhaust	0.15 mm
Valve spring free length	Not available
Camshaft height (standard)	
Intake	30.285 mm
Exhaust	29.209 mm
Coolant	50% distilled water, 50% corrosion inhibiting ethylene glycol anti-freeze
Coolant capacity	1.2 litres

Ignition system

HT coil primary resistance	0.4 to 0.5 ohms
HT coil secondary resistance	1.7 to 2.3 K-ohms
Pick-up coil resistance	105 to 124 ohms

Fuel system – Walbro carburettor

Throttle twistgrip freeplay	1 to 3 mm
Main jet	108
Pilot jet	36
Starter jet	50
Needle type / position	51C (2nd notch from top)
Pilot screw setting	2⅝ ± ½
Float height	Bottom edge parallel to gasket face
Automatic choke resistance	approx. 40 ohms

Fuel system – Keihin carburettor

Throttle twistgrip freeplay	1 to 3 mm
Main jet	105
Pilot jet	35
Starter jet	42
Needle type / position	2.450
Pilot screw setting	2 ± ¼
Float height	Bottom edge parallel to gasket face
Automatic choke resistance	approx. 20 ohms

Transmission

Belt width service limit	21.5 mm
Variator rollers minimum diameter	18.5 mm
Clutch lining thickness	1.0 mm
Clutch spring free length	106 mm
Gearbox oil	SAE 80W/90 API GL4
Gearbox oil capacity	250 ml

Brakes

Fluid type	DOT 4
Pad minimum thickness	1.5 mm

Tyre pressures

Front	29 psi (2.0 bar)
Rear	32 psi (2.2 bar) solo, 36 psi (2.5 bar) pillion

Electrical system

Battery	
Capacity	12 V, 12 Ah
Alternator	
Output (regulated)	15.2 V (DC)
Fuses	15A x 2, 10A x 1, 7.5A x 2, 4A x 3
Bulbs	
Headlight	55 W x 2
Sidelight	5 W x 2
Tail light	3 W x 2
Brake light	10 W
Turn signal lights	10 W
Instrument lights	2 W x 5
Licence plate light and helmet compartment light	5 W

Torque wrench settings

Valve cover bolts	6 to 7 Nm
Cylinder head nuts	9 to 11 Nm, +180°
Cylinder head bolts	11 to 12 Nm
Cam chain tensioner bolts	11 to 13 Nm
Camshaft sprocket bolt	11 to 15 Nm
Engine mounting bolt	33 to 41 Nm
Exhaust manifold nuts	16 to 18 Nm
Exhaust system mounting bolts	27 to 30 Nm
Water pump cover screws	3 to 4 Nm
Engine oil drain plug	24 to 30 Nm
Oil pump sprocket bolt	10 to 14 Nm
Oil pump mounting bolts	4 to 6 Nm
Alternator rotor nut	52 to 58 Nm
Alternator stator bolts	3 to 4 Nm
Variator centre nut	75 to 83 Nm
Clutch centre nut	45 to 50 Nm
Clutch assembly nut	54 to 60 Nm
Crankcase bolts	11 to 13 Nm
Gearbox oil drain plug	15 to 17 Nm
Gearbox cover bolts	24 to 27 Nm
Rear shock absorber mountings	33 to 41 Nm
Steering head bearing adjuster nut	10 to 13 Nm
Steering head bearing locknut	30 to 36 Nm
Handlebar stem bolt	45 to 50 Nm
Front axle nut	45 to 50 Nm
Rear hub nut	104 to 126 Nm
Disc brake caliper mounting bolts	20 to 25 Nm
Brake hose banjo bolt	12 to 16 Nm

Piaggio Fly 50 2T

Engine no. prefix	C441M
Frame no. prefix	ZAPM 44100
Engine	50cc Single cylinder two-stroke
Cooling system	Air-cooled
Fuel system	Dell 'orto PHVA 17.5 RD
Ignition system	CDI
Transmission	Variable speed (CVT) with automatic clutch
Suspension	Telescopic front with single shock rear
Brakes	Single disc front, Drum rear
Tyres	Tubeless 120/70-12 front and rear
Wheelbase	1340 mm
Weight (dry)	97 kg
Fuel tank capacity	7.2 litres

Engine

Spark plug type	Champion RGN2C
Electrode gap	0.6 to 0.7 mm
Idle speed (rpm)	1800 to 2000 rpm
Engine oil	Selenia HT 2T two-stroke injector oil
Oil tank capacity	1.2 litres
Bore x stroke	40 x 39.3 mm
Piston diameter (standard)	39.943 to 39.971 mm
Piston to bore clearance (standard)	0.055 to 0.069 mm
Piston ring installed end gap (standard)	0.10 to 0.25 mm

Fuel system

Main jet	53
Pilot jet	32
Starter jet	50
Needle type / position	A22/1st notch from top
Pilot screw setting	1½ turns out
Fuel level	5 mm (non adjustable)
Automatic choke resistance	30 to 40 ohm

Tyre pressures

Front	26 psi (1.8 Bar)
Rear	29 psi (2.0 Bar)

Electrical system

Battery	
Capacity	12 V 4 Ah
Alternator	
Output (unregulated)	25 to 30 V (ac) at 3000 rpm
Fuse (main)	10 A
Bulbs	
Headlight (main/dipped)	60 / 55 W
Sidelight	5 W
Brake/tail light	21 / 5 W
Turn signal lights	10 W
Instrument and warning lights	1.2 and / or 2.0 W

Ignition system

Source coil resistance	800 to 1100 ohms
Pick-up coil resistance	90 to 140 ohms

Transmission

Belt width service limit	17.5 mm
Variator rollers minimum diameter	18.5 mm
Clutch lining thickness	1 mm
Clutch spring free length	110 mm
Gearbox oil	SAE 80W/90 API GL4
Gearbox oil capacity	Approx 85 ml

Brakes

Disc brake	
Fluid type	DOT 4
Pad minimum thickness	1.5 mm
Drum brake	
Shoe lining minimum thickness	1.5 mm
Brake lever freeplay	10 to 15 mm

Torque wrench settings

Cylinder head nuts	10 to 11Nm
Crankcase bolts	12 to 13 Nm
Engine mounting bolt	33 to 41 Nm
Exhaust system mounting bolts to crankcase	22 to 24 Nm
Alternator rotor nut	40 to 44 Nm
Variator centre nut	40 to 44 Nm
Clutch centre nut	40 to 44 Nm
Clutch assembly nut	55 to 60 Nm
Gearbox oil drain plug	3 to 5 Nm
Drive belt cover bolts	12 to 13 Nm
Rear shock absorber mountings	
Lower bolt	33 to 41 Nm
Upper bolt	20 to 25 Nm
Steering head bearing adjuster nut	8 to 10 Nm
Steering head bearing locknut	35 to 40 Nm
Handlebar stem bolt	50 to 55 Nm
Front axle nut	45 to 50 Nm
Rear hub nut	104 to 126 Nm
Disc brake caliper mounting bolts	20 to 25 Nm
Brake hose banjo bolt at caliper	19 to 24 Nm
Brake hose banjo bolt at master cylinder	16 to 20 Nm

Piaggio Fly 50 4T

Engine no. prefix ... C442M
Frame no. prefix ... ZAPM44200
Engine ... 49.9 cc single cylinder 2-valve four-stroke
  Cooling system ... Air-cooled
  Fuel system ... Keihin CVK 18 CV carburettor
  Ignition system ... CDI
Transmission ... Variable speed automatic, belt driven
Suspension ... Telescopic front, swingarm with single shock rear
Brakes ... Disc front, drum rear
Tyres ... 120/70 x 12 front and rear
Wheelbase ... 1340 mm
Weight (dry) ... 102 kg
Fuel tank capacity ... 7.2 litres

Engine

Spark plug type	NGK CR8EB
Electrode gap	0.7 to 0.8 mm
Idle speed (rpm)	1900 to 2000 rpm
Engine oil	5W/40 API SL synthetic oil
Oil capacity	850 ml
Bore x stroke	39.0 x 41.8 mm
Piston diameter (standard)	38.954 to 38.982 mm
Piston to bore clearance (standard)	0.032 to 0.051 mm
Piston ring installed end gap	
Top ring	0.08 to 0.20 mm
Second ring	0.05 to 0.20 mm
Oil control ring	0.02 to 0.70 mm
Valve clearance	
Intake	0.10 mm
Exhaust	0.15 mm
Camshaft height (standard)	25.935 mm

Fuel system

Main jet	75
Pilot jet	35
Starter jet	40
Needle type	NGBA
Pilot screw setting	1¾ turns out
Float level	parallel to gasket face
Automatic choke resistance	6 ohms ± 5%

Electrical system

Battery capacity	12 V, 9 Ah
Alternator	
Output (unregulated)	25 to 35 V (AC) at 2000 rpm
Fuse (main)	10 A
Bulbs	
Headlight (main/dipped)	35/35 W
Sidelight	5 W
Brake/tail light	21/5 W
Licence plate light	1.2 W x 2
Turn signal lights	10 W
Instrument and warning lights	1.2 W and 2.0 W

Ignition system

Source coil resistance	1 ohm
Pick-up coil resistance	170 ohms

Transmission

Belt width service limit	17.5 mm
Clutch lining minimum thickness	1.0 mm
Clutch spring free length	118 mm
Gearbox oil	SAE 80W/90 API GL4
Gearbox oil capacity	85 ml

Brakes

Disc brake	
Fluid type	DOT 4
Pad minimum thickness	1.5 mm
Drum brake	
Shoe lining minimum thickness	1.5 mm
Brake lever freeplay	10 to 15 mm
Front fork oil	30 ml of SAE 20W fork oil

Torque wrench settings

Spark plug	10 to 15 Nm
Valve cover bolts	8 to 10 Nm
Cylinder head nuts	
Initial setting	6 to 7 Nm
Final setting	+90° +90°
Cylinder head bolts	8 to 10 Nm
Cam chain tensioner bolts	8 to 10 Nm
Camshaft sprocket bolt	12 to 14 Nm
Engine mounting bolt	33 to 41 Nm
Engine oil drain plug	25 to 28 Nm
Oil pump mounting bolts	5 to 6 Nm
Alternator rotor nut	52 to 58 Nm
Variator centre nut	18 to 20 Nm
	+90°
Clutch centre nut	40 to 44 Nm
Clutch assembly nut	55 to 60 Nm
Crankcase bolts	8 to 10 Nm
Drive belt cover screws	11 to 13 Nm
Front shock absorber mountings	20 to 25 Nm
Rear shock absorber mountings	
Lower bolt	33 to 41 Nm
Upper bolt	20 to 25 Nm
Steering head bearing adjuster nut	8 to 10 Nm
Steering head bearing locknut	35 to 40 Nm
Handlebar stem nut	50 to 55 Nm
Front hub nut	45 to 50 Nm
Rear hub nut	104 to 126 Nm
Disc brake caliper mounting bolts	24 to 27 Nm
Brake hose banjo bolt at caliper	19 to 24 Nm
Brake hose banjo bolt at master cylinder	16 to 20 Nm

Tyre pressures

Front	26 psi (1.8 bar)
Rear	29 psi (2.0 bar) solo, 33 psi (2.3 bar) pillion

Engine no. prefix, Frame no. prefix

Engine no. prefix	M421M
Frame no. prefix	ZAPM42100
Engine	125cc single cylinder 4-stroke LEADER
Cooling system	Air-cooled
Fuel system	Keihin CVEK 26
Ignition system	CDI
Transmission	Variable speed automatic, belt driven
Suspension	Telescopic front, single shock absorber rear
Brakes	Single disc (front), drum (rear)
Tyres	120/70 x 12 front and rear
Wheelbase	1330 mm
Weight (dry)	112kg
Fuel tank capacity	7.2 litres

Engine

Spark plug type	NGKCR7EB
Electrode gap	0.7 to 0.8 mm
Idle speed (rpm)	1600 to 1800 rpm
Engine oil	5W / 40 API SL synthetic oil
Oil tank capacity	approx 1 litre
Bore x stroke	57 x 48.6 mm
Piston diameter (standard)	56.933 mm to 57.561 mm
Piston to bore clearance (standard)	0.040 to 0.054 mm
Piston ring installed end gap (standard)	0.15 mm to 0.30 mm

Fuel system

Main jet	82
Pilot jet	35
Starter jet	42
Needle type / position	NELA
Pilot screw setting	1¾ turns out
Float height	Not available
Automatic choke resistance	20 ohms

Electrical system

Battery	
Capacity	12A, 4Ah
Alternator	
Output (regulated)	15.2 V (DC)
Charging coil resistance	0.7 to 0.9 ohms
Fuse (main)	15 A
Bulbs	
Headlight (main/dipped)	60/55 W
Sidelight	5 W
Brake/tail light	21/5 W
Turn signal lights	10 W
Instrument and warning lights	1.2 W and/or 2.0 W

Ignition system

Source coil resistance	0.7 to 0.9 ohms
Pick-up coil resistance	1.5 to 124 ohms

Transmission

Belt width service limit	21.5 mm
Variator rollers minimum diameter	18.5 mm
Clutch lining thickness	1 mm
Clutch spring free length	106 mm
Gearbox oil	SAE 80W/90 API GL4
Gearbox oil capacity	approx 200 cc

Brakes

Disc brake	
Fluid type	DOT 4
Pad minimum thickness	1.5 mm
Drum brake	
Shoe lining minimum thickness	1.5 mm
Brake lever freeplay	10 to 15 mm

Torque wrench settings

Cylinder head nuts	28 to 30 Nm
Crankcase bolts	11 to 13 Nm
Engine mounting bolt	33 to 41 Nm
Exhaust manifold nuts	16 to 18 Nm
Exhaust system mounting bolts to crankcase	24 to 27 Nm
Oil pump mounting bolts	5 to 6 Nm
Alternator rotor nut	52 to 58 Nm
Alternator screws	3 to 4 Nm
Variator centre nut	75 to 83 Nm
Clutch centre nut	50 to 56 Nm
Clutch assembly nut	55 to 60 Nm
Gearbox oil drain plug	15 to 17 Nm
Drive belt cover bolt	11 to 13 Nm
Rear shock absorber mountings	
Lower bolt	33 to 41 Nm
Upper bolt	20 to 25 Nm
Steering head bearing adjuster nut	8 to 10 Nm
Steering head bearing locknut	35 to 40 Nm
Handlebar stem bolt	50 to 55 Nm
Front axle nut	45 to 50 Nm
Rear hub nut	104 to 126 Nm
Disc brake caliper mounting bolts	24 to 27 Nm
Brake hose banjo bolt	19 to 24 Nm
Brake hose banjo bolt at caliper	19 to 24 Nm
Engine oil filter	27 to 33 Nm
Engine oil drain plug	24 to 30 Nm

Tyre pressures

Front	26 psi (1.8 Bar)
Rear	29 psi (2.0 Bar)

Piaggio Hexagon 125

Engine

Engine no. prefix	EXS 1M
Frame no. prefix	EXS 1T
Engine	Single-cylinder two-stroke
Cooling system	Liquid-cooled
Fuel system	Mikuni VM slide carburettor
Ignition system	CDI
Transmission	Variable speed automatic, belt-driven
Suspension	Trailing link front, swingarm with single shock rear
Brakes	Disc front, drum rear
Tyres	100/80 x 10 front, 130/70 x 10 rear
Wheelbase	1400 mm
Weight (dry)	138 kg
Fuel tank capacity	10.0 litres

Tyre pressures

Front	26 psi (1.8 bar)
Rear	33 psi (2.3 bar)

Electrical system

Battery	
Capacity	12 V, 9 Ah
Alternator	
Output (unregulated)	27 to 31 V (AC)
Fuse (main)	25 Amps
Fuses (secondary)	10, 7.5 and 4 Amps
Bulbs	
Headlight (main/dipped)	60/55 W
Sidelight	5 W
Brake/tail light	21/5 W
Turn signal lights	10 W
Instrument and warning lights	1.2 W

Engine

Spark plug type	Champion N2C or NGK B9ES
Electrode gap	0.5 to 0.6 mm
Idle speed (rpm)	1600 to 1800 rpm
Engine oil	Two-stroke injector oil
Oil tank capacity	1.5 litres
Bore x stroke	55.0 x 52.0 mm
Piston diameter (standard)	54.94 to 54.97 mm
Piston to bore clearance (standard)	0.052 to 0.062 mm
Piston ring installed end gap (standard)	0.20 to 035 mm
Coolant	50% distilled water, 50% corrosion inhibiting ethylene glycol anti-freeze
Coolant capacity	1 litre

Ignition system

HT coil primary resistance	0.48 to 0.52 ohms
HT coil secondary resistance	4.6 to 5.2 K-ohms
Source coil resistance	122 to 132 ohms
Pick-up coil resistance	102 to 112 ohms

Transmission

Belt width service limit	21.0 mm
Variator rollers minimum diameter	18.5 mm
Clutch lining thickness (service limit)	1.0 mm
Clutch spring free length	136 mm
Gearbox oil	SAE 80W/90 API GL4
Gearbox oil capacity	85 ml

Fuel system

Throttle twistgrip freeplay	1 to 3 mm
Main jet	82.5
Pilot jet	35
Starter jet	40
Needle type / position	3CK01 (3rd notch from top)
Pilot screw setting	1½ turns out
Fuel level	3.5 mm
Automatic choke resistance	approx. 30.0 to 40.0 ohms @ 20°C

Brakes

Disc brake	
Fluid type	DOT 4
Pad minimum thickness	1.5 mm
Drum brake	
Shoe lining minimum thickness	1.5 mm
Brake lever freeplay	10 to 15 mm

Torque wrench settings

Cylinder head nuts	22 Nm
Crankcase bolts	13 Nm
Engine mounting bolt	41 Nm
Exhaust manifold nuts	11 Nm
Exhaust system mounting bolts	24 Nm
Oil pump mounting bolts	4 Nm
Alternator rotor nut	56 Nm
Alternator stator bolts	4 Nm
Variator centre nut	80 Nm
Clutch centre nut	56 Nm
Clutch assembly nut	60 Nm
Gearbox oil filler plug	5 Nm
Gearbox cover bolts	15 Nm
Front shock absorber mountings	10 Nm
Rear shock absorber mountings	
Lower bolt	41 Nm
Upper bolt	25 Nm
Steering head bearing adjuster nut	10 Nm
Steering head bearing locknut	40 Nm
Handlebar stem bolt	50 Nm
Front wheel bolts	25 Nm
Front hub nut	90 Nm
Rear hub nut	110 Nm
Disc brake caliper mounting bolts	25 Nm
Brake hose banjo bolt	25 Nm

Piaggio Super Hexagon 125

Engine

Engine no. prefix	M201M
Frame no. prefix	ZAPM
Engine	Single-cylinder four-stroke
Cooling system	Liquid-cooled
Fuel system	Walbro WVF 7A CV carburettor
Ignition system	CDI
Transmission	Variable speed automatic, belt-driven
Suspension	Trailing link front, swingarm with twin adjustable shock rear
Brakes	Disc front, disc rear
Tyres	120/70 x 11 front, 130/70 x 11 rear
Wheelbase	1450 mm
Weight (dry)	139 kg
Fuel tank capacity	11.4 litres

Engine

Spark plug type	Champion RG 4HC or NGK CR9EB
Electrode gap	0.5 to 0.6 mm
Idle speed (rpm)	1600 to 1700 rpm
Engine oil	5W 40 API SJ synthetic engine oil
Oil capacity	1.0 litre
Bore x stroke	57.0 x 48.6 mm
Piston diameter (standard)	56.94 to 56.97 mm
Piston to bore clearance (standard)	0.045 to 0.059 mm
Piston ring installed end gap (standard)	
Top ring	0.20 to 0.40 mm
Second ring	0.10 to 0.30 mm
Oil control ring	0.15 to 0.35 mm
Piston ring installed end gap (service limit)	1 mm
Valve clearance	
Intake	0.10 mm
Exhaust	0.15 mm
Camshaft lobe height (standard)	
Intake	30.285 mm
Exhaust	29.209 mm
Coolant	50% distilled water, 50% corrosion inhibiting ethylene glycol anti-freeze
Coolant capacity	1.2 litres

Fuel system

Throttle twistgrip freeplay	1 to 3 mm
Main jet	108
Pilot jet	34
Starter jet	50
Needle type / position	51C (2nd notch from top)
Pilot screw setting	3 turns out
Float height	Bottom edge parallel to gasket face
Automatic choke resistance	approx. 30 ohms @ 20°C

Ignition system

HT coil primary resistance	0.4 to 0.5 ohms
HT coil secondary resistance	2.7 to 3.3 K-ohms
Pick-up coil resistance	105 to 124 ohms

Transmission

Belt width service limit	21.5 mm
Variator rollers minimum diameter	18.5 mm
Clutch lining thickness (service limit)	1.0 mm
Clutch spring free length	106 mm
Gearbox oil	SAE 80W/90 API GL4
Gearbox oil capacity	150 ml

Brakes

Fluid type	DOT 4
Pad minimum thickness	1.5 mm

Tyre pressures

Front	26 psi (1.8 bar)
Rear	32 psi (2.2 bar)

Electrical system

Battery	
Capacity	12 V, 12 Ah
Alternator	
Output (unregulated)	27 to 31 V (AC)
Fuse (main)	15 Amps
Fuses (secondary)	10, 7.5 and 5 Amps
Bulbs	
Headlight (main/dipped)	55/55 W
Sidelight	5 W
Brake/tail light	21/5 W
Turn signal lights	10 W
Instrument and warning lights	1.2 W

Torque wrench settings

Valve cover bolts	13 Nm
Cylinder head nuts	30 Nm
Cylinder head bolts	13 Nm
Cam chain tensioner bolts	13 Nm
Camshaft sprocket bolt	15 Nm
Engine mounting bolt	41 Nm
Exhaust manifold nuts	33 Nm
Exhaust system mounting bolts	27 Nm
Water pump impeller	12 Nm
Engine oil drain plug	30 Nm
Oil pump sprocket bolt	13 Nm
Oil pump mounting bolts	6 Nm
Alternator rotor nut	60 Nm
Alternator stator bolts	12 Nm
Variator centre nut	83 Nm
Clutch centre nut	60 Nm
Clutch assembly nut	60 Nm
Crankcase bolts	13 Nm
Gearbox oil filler plug	13 Nm
Gearbox oil drain plug	13 Nm
Gearbox cover bolts	25 Nm
Front shock absorber mountings	
Lower bolt	27 Nm
Upper bolt	30 Nm
Rear shock absorber mountings	
Lower bolt	41 Nm
Upper bolt	25 Nm
Rear sub frame bolts	25 Nm
Steering head bearing adjuster nut	10 Nm
Steering head bearing locknut	40 Nm
Handlebar stem bolt	38 Nm
Front wheel bolts	25 Nm
Front hub nut	85 Nm
Rear hub nut	126 Nm
Disc brake caliper mounting bolts	25 Nm
Brake hose banjo bolt	25 Nm

Piaggio Super Hexagon 180

Engine no. prefix	M202M
Frame no. prefix	ZAPM
Engine	Single-cylinder four-stroke
Cooling system	Liquid-cooled
Fuel system	Walbro WVF 7B CV carburettor
Ignition system	CDI
Transmission	Variable speed automatic, belt-driven
Suspension	Trailing link front, swingarm with twin adjustable shock rear
Brakes	Disc front, disc rear
Tyres	120/70 x 11 front, 130/70 x 11 rear
Wheelbase	1450 mm
Weight (dry)	139 kg
Fuel tank capacity	11.4 litres

Engine

Spark plug type	Champion RG 4HC or NGK CR9EB
Electrode gap	0.5 to 0.6 mm
Idle speed (rpm)	1600 to 1700 rpm
Engine oil	5W 40 API SJ synthetic engine oil
Oil capacity	1.0 litre
Bore x stroke	69.0 x 48.6 mm
Piston diameter (standard)	68.941 to 68.955 mm
Piston to bore clearance (standard)	0.045 to 0.059 mm
Piston ring installed end gap (standard)	
Top ring	0.20 to 0.40 mm
Second ring	0.10 to 0.30 mm
Oil control ring	0.15 to 0.35 mm
Piston ring installed end gap (service limit)	1 mm
Valve clearance	
Intake	0.10 mm
Exhaust	0.15 mm
Camshaft lobe height (standard)	
Intake	30.285 mm
Exhaust	29.209 mm
Coolant	50% distilled water, 50% corrosion inhibiting ethylene glycol anti-freeze
Coolant capacity	1.2 litres

Electrical system

Battery	
Capacity	12 V, 12 Ah
Alternator	
Output (unregulated)	27 to 31 V (AC)
Fuse (main)	15 Amps
Fuses (secondary)	10, 7.5 and 5 Amps
Bulbs	
Headlight (main/dipped)	55/55 W
Sidelight	5 W
Brake/tail light	21/5 W
Turn signal lights	10 W
Instrument and warning lights	1.2 W

Fuel system

Throttle twistgrip freeplay	1 to 3 mm
Main jet	118
Pilot jet	34
Starter jet	50
Needle type / position	465 (2nd notch from top)
Pilot screw setting	3 turns out
Float height	Bottom edge parallel to gasket face
Automatic choke resistance	approx. 30 ohms @ 20°C

Ignition system

HT coil primary resistance	0.4 to 0.5 ohms
HT coil secondary resistance	2.7 to 3.3 K-ohms
Pick-up coil resistance	105 to 124 ohms

Transmission

Belt width service limit	21.5 mm
Variator rollers minimum diameter	18.5 mm
Clutch lining thickness (service limit)	1.0 mm
Clutch spring free length	106 mm
Gearbox oil	SAE 80W/90 API GL4
Gearbox oil capacity	150 ml

Brakes

Fluid type	DOT 4
Pad minimum thickness	1.5 mm

Tyre pressures

Front	26 psi (1.8 bar)
Rear	32 psi (2.2 bar)

Torque wrench settings

Valve cover bolts	13 Nm
Cylinder head nuts	30 Nm
Cylinder head bolts	13 Nm
Cam chain tensioner bolts	13 Nm
Camshaft sprocket bolt	15 Nm
Engine mounting bolt	41 Nm
Exhaust manifold nuts	33 Nm
Exhaust system mounting bolts	27 Nm
Water pump impeller	12 Nm
Engine oil drain plug	30 Nm
Oil pump sprocket bolt	13 Nm
Oil pump mounting bolts	6 Nm
Alternator rotor nut	60 Nm
Alternator stator bolts	12 Nm
Variator centre nut	83 Nm
Clutch centre nut	60 Nm
Clutch assembly nut	60 Nm
Crankcase bolts	13 Nm
Gearbox oil filler plug	13 Nm
Gearbox oil drain plug	13 Nm
Gearbox cover bolts	25 Nm
Front shock absorber mountings	
Lower bolt	27 Nm
Upper bolt	30 Nm
Rear shock absorber mountings	
Lower bolt	41 Nm
Upper bolt	25 Nm
Rear sub frame bolts	25 Nm
Steering head bearing adjuster nut	10 Nm
Steering head bearing locknut	40 Nm
Handlebar stem bolt	38 Nm
Front wheel bolts	25 Nm
Front hub nut	85 Nm
Rear hub nut	126 Nm
Disc brake caliper mounting bolts	25 Nm
Brake hose banjo bolt	25 Nm

Engine no. prefix C151M
Frame no. prefix ZAPC15
Engine
Cooling system .... 50 cc single cylinder two-stroke
Fuel system .... Air cooled
Ignition system .... Weber 120M
Transmission .... CDI
Suspension .... Variable speed automatic, belt driven
Brakes .... Telescopic forks / swingarm monoshock
Tyres .... Single disc (front), Drum (rear)
Wheelbase .... 70/90-16 front, 90/80-16 rear
Weight (dry) .... 1285 mm
Fuel tank capacity .... 88 kg
5.5 litres

Engine
Spark plug type .... Champion N2C
Electrode gap .... 0.5 to 0.6 mm
Idle speed (rpm) .... 1700 to 1900 rpm
Engine oil .... Good quality two-stroke injecto oil

Oil tank capacity .... 1.7 litres
Bore x stroke .... 40.0 mm x 39.9 mm
Piston diameter (standard) ..... 39.943 mm to
39.971 mm
Piston to bore clearance (standard) .. 0.055 to 0.069 mm
Piston ring installed end gap .... 0.10 to 0.25 mm

Fuel system
Main jet 63
Pilot jet 38L
Starter jet 50
Needle type / position .... V (2nd notch from top)
Fuel level height .... 5 mm (not adjustable)
Automatic choke resistance ..... 30 to 40 ohms

Tyre pressures
Front tyre pressure .... 26 psi (1.8 bar)
Rear tyre pressure .... 29 psi (2.0 bar)

Electrical system
Battery
Capacity .... 12 V, 4 Ah
Alternator:
Output (unregulated) .... 25 to 30 V (ac)
at 3000 rpm
Fuse (main) .... 7.5 A
Bulbs:
Headlight (main/dipped) ...... 35 / 35 W
Sidelight .... 4 W
Brake/tail light .... 21 / 5 W
Turn signal lights .... 10 W
Instrument and warning lights .. 1.2 and / or 2.0 W

Ignition system
Source coil resistance .... 930 to 1030 ohms
Pick-up coil resistance .... 83 to 93 ohms

Transmission
Belt width .... 17.5 mm
Variator rollers .... 18.5 mm
Clutch lining thickness .... 1 mm
Gearbox oil .... SAE 80W/90 API GL4
Gearbox oil capacity .... approx 100 ml

Brakes
Disc brake:
Fluid type .... DOT 4
Pad minimum thickness .... 1.5 mm
Drum brake:
Brake shoe lining thickness
(standard) .... 1.5 mm
Brake lever freeplay .... 10 to 15 mm

Torque wrench settings
Cylinder head bolts .... 10 to 11 Nm
Alternator rotor nut .... 40 to 44 Nm
Alternator stator bolts .... 3 to 4 Nm
Crankcase bolts .... 11 to 13 Nm
Engine mounting bolts .... 33 to 41 Nm
Variator centre nut .... 18 to 20 Nm
+90°
Clutch centre nut .... 40 to 44 Nm
Clutch assembly nut .... 55 to 60 Nm
Gearbox cover bolts .... 12 to 13 Nm
Rear shock absorber mountings
Lower bolt .... 33 to 41 Nm
Upper bolt .... 20 to 25 Nm
Handlebar stem bolt .... 40 to 50 Nm
Front axle nut .... 40 to 50 Nm
Rear hub nut .... 90 to 110 Nm
Disc brake caliper mounting bolts .. 20 to 25 Nm
Brake hose banjo bolts .... 15 to 25 Nm

Piaggio Liberty 50 4T

Data 51

Engine no. prefix	C422M
Frame no. prefix	ZAPC 422
Engine	49.93 cc single cylinder 2-valve 4-stroke
Cooling system	Air-cooled
Fuel system	Keihin CVK 18
Ignition system	CDI
Transmission	Variable speeed automatic, belt driven
Suspension	Telescopic forks, swingarm monoshock
Brakes	Single disc (front), drum (rear)
Tyres	90/80 x 16 (front), 110/80-14 (rear)
Wheelbase	1330 mm
Weight (dry)	88 kg
Fuel tank capacity	6.0 litres

Tyre pressures

Front tyre pressure	29 psi (2.0 bar)
Rear tyre pressure	32 psi (2.2 bar)

Electrical system

Battery capacity	12 V, 9 Ah
Alternator output (unregulated)	25 to 35 V (ac)
	@ 2000 rpm
Fuse (main)	10 A
Bulbs:	
Headlight (main/dipped)	35/35 W
Sidelight	5 W
Brake/tail light	21/5 W
Turn signal lights	10 W
Instrument and warning lights	1.2 W and 2.0 W

Engine

Spark plug type	NGK CR9EB or Champion RG 4HC
Electrode gap	0.7 to 0.8 mm
Idle speed (rpm)	1900 to 2000 rpm
Engine oil	SAE 5W/40, API SL synthetic four-stroke oil
Oil tank capacity	850 ml
Bore x stroke	39.0 x 41.8 mm
Piston to bore clearance	0.032 to 0.051 mm
Piston ring installed end gap (standard)	
Top ring	0.08 to 0.20 mm
Second ring	0.05 to 0.20 mm
Oil ring	0.20 to 0.70 mm
Valve clearance	
Intake	0.10 mm
Exhaust	0.15 mm

Ignition system

Source coil resistance	1 ohm
Pick-up coil resistance	170 ohms

Transmission

Belt width service limit	17.5 mm
Clutch lining thickness service limit	1 mm
Clutch spring free length (standard)	118 mm
Gearbox oil	SAE 80W/90 API GL4
Gearbox oil capacity	85 ml

Fuel system

Main jet	75
Pilot jet	35
Starter jet	48
Needle type / position	NACA
Pilot screw setting	2⅞ turns out
Float level	Parallel to gasket face
Automatic choke resistance	6 ± 5 ohms

Brakes

Disc brake:	
Fluid type	DOT 4
Pad minimum thickness	1.5 mm

Torque wrench settings

Spark plug	10 to 15 Nm
Valve cover bolts	8 to 10 Nm
Cylinder head bolts	6 to 7 Nm, +90° +90°
Camshaft sprocket bolt	12 to 14 Nm
Camchain tensioner bolts	8 to 10 Nm
Camchain tensioner spring cap bolt	5 to 6 Nm
Alternator rotor nut	52 to 58 Nm
Alternator stator bolts	3 to 4 Nm
Crankcase bolts	8 to 10 Nm
Engine mounting bolts	33 to 41 Nm
Oil pump mounting bolts	5 to 6 Nm
Variator centre nut	18 to 20 Nm, +90°
Clutch centre nut	40 to 44 Nm
Clutch assembly nut	55 to 60 Nm
Drive belt cover screws	12 to 13 Nm
Disc brake caliper mounting bolts	20 to 25 Nm
Disc mounting bolts	8 to 12 Nm

Piaggio Liberty 125 (2001 to 2003)

Engine no. prefix	M222M
Frame no. prefix	ZAP M222
Engine	Single-cylinder four-stroke 2-valve LEADER
Cooling system	Air-cooled
Fuel system	Walbro WVF 6B CV carburettor
Ignition system	CDI
Transmission	Variable speed automatic, belt-driven
Suspension	Telescopic front, swingarm with single adjustable shock rear
Brakes	Disc front, drum rear
Tyres	80/80 x 16 front, 110/80 x 14 rear
Wheelbase	1285 mm
Weight	97 kg
Fuel tank capacity	7.0 litres

Electrical system

Battery	
Capacity	12 V, 9 Ah
Alternator	
Output (unregulated)	27 to 31 V (AC)
Fuse (main)	15 Amps
Fuses (secondary)	10, 7.5 and 5 Amps
Bulbs	
Headlight (main/dipped)	35/35 W
Sidelight	5 W
Brake/tail light	21/5 W
Turn signal lights	10 W
Instrument and warning lights	1.2 W

Torque wrench settings

Valve cover bolts	12 Nm
Cylinder head nuts	
Initial setting	7 Nm
Final setting	+90° +90°
Cylinder head bolts	13 Nm
Cam chain tensioner bolts	10 Nm
Camshaft sprocket bolt	15 Nm
Engine mounting bolt	41 Nm
Exhaust manifold nuts	11 Nm
Exhaust system mounting bolts	27 Nm
Engine oil drain plug	28 Nm
Oil pump sprocket bolt	13 Nm
Oil pump mounting bolts	6 Nm
Alternator rotor nut	58 Nm
Alternator stator bolts	4 Nm
Variator centre nut	83 Nm
Clutch centre nut	60 Nm
Clutch assembly nut	60 Nm
Crankcase bolts	13 Nm
Gearbox oil filler plug	5 Nm
Gearbox oil drain plug	17 Nm
Gearbox cover bolts	13 Nm
Rear shock absorber mountings	
Lower bolt	41 Nm
Upper bolt	25 Nm
Steering head bearing adjuster nut	10 Nm
Steering head bearing locknut	40 Nm
Handlebar stem bolt	55 Nm
Front axle nut	50 Nm
Front axle pinch-bolts	7 Nm
Rear hub nut	126 Nm
Disc brake caliper mounting bolts	25 Nm
Brake hose banjo bolt	25 Nm

Ignition system

Source coil resistance	300 to 400 ohms
Pick-up coil resistance	90 to 140 ohms

Transmission

Belt width service limit	21.5 mm
Variator rollers minimum diameter	18.5 mm
Clutch lining thickness	1.0 mm
Clutch spring free length	106 mm
Gearbox oil	SAE 80W/90 API GL4
Gearbox oil capacity	100 ml

Brakes

Disc brake	
Fluid type	DOT 4
Pad minimum thickness	1.5 mm
Drum brake	
Shoe lining minimum thickness	1.5 mm
Brake lever freeplay	10 to 15 mm

Tyre pressures

Front	26 psi (1.8 bar)
Rear	29 psi (2.0 bar)

Engine

Spark plug type	Champion RG 4HC or NGK CR8EB
Electrode gap	0.7 to 0.8 mm
Idle speed (rpm)	1600 to 1700 rpm
Engine oil	5W 40 API SJ synthetic engine oil
Oil capacity	1.0 litre
Bore x stroke	57.0 x 48.6 mm
Piston diameter (standard)	56.93 to 56.96 mm
Piston to bore clearance (standard)	0.040 to 0.054 mm
Piston ring installed end gap (service limit)	
Top ring	0.40 mm
Second ring	0.50 mm
Oil control ring	0.50 mm
Valve clearance	
Intake	0.10 mm
Exhaust	0.15 mm
Camshaft lobe height (standard)	27.8 mm

Fuel system

Throttle twistgrip freeplay	1 to 3 mm
Main jet	84
Pilot jet	33
Starter jet	48
Needle type / position	DCK (2nd notch from top)
Float height	Bottom edge parallel to gasket face
Automatic choke resistance	approx. 30 ohms @ 20°C

Piaggio Liberty 125 (2004-on)

Engine no. prefix	M381M
Frame no. prefix	ZAP M381
Engine	Single cylinder four-stroke 2-valve LEADER
Cooling system	Air-cooled
Fuel system	Keihin CVEK26 carburettor
Ignition system	CDI
Transmission	Variable speed automatic, belt driven
Suspension	Telescopic front, swingarm with single adjustable shock rear
Brakes	Disc front, drum rear
Tyres	90/80 x 16 front, 110/80 x 14 rear
Wheelbase	1335 mm
Weight	99 kg
Fuel tank capacity	6.0 litres

Engine

Spark plug type	Champion RG 6YC or NGK CR7EB
Electrode gap	0.8 mm
Idle speed (rpm)	1600 to 1800 rpm
Engine oil	5W 40 API SJ synthetic engine oil
Oil capacity	1.0 litre
Bore x stroke	57.0 x 48.6 mm
Piston to bore clearance (standard)	
With cast iron cylinder	0.046 to 0.060 mm
With aluminium cylinder	0.040 to 0.054 mm
Piston oversizes	+ 0.20, + 0.40 and + 0.60 mm
Piston ring installed end gap (service limit)	
Top and second rings	0.15 to 0.30 mm
Oil control ring	0.15 to 0.35 mm
Valve clearance	
Intake	0.10 mm
Exhaust	0.15 mm
Valve spring free length	33.9 to 34.4 mm
Camshaft lobe height (standard)	
Intake	27.512 mm
Exhaust	27.212 mm

Fuel system

Main jet	82
Pilot jet	35
Starter jet	42
Needle type	NELA
Pilot screw setting	1¾ turns out
Float height	Bottom edge parallel to gasket face
Automatic choke resistance	approx. 20 ohms @ 24°C

Tyre pressures

Front	29 psi (2.0 bar)
Rear	32 psi (2.2 bar) solo, 36 psi (2.5 bar) pillion

Electrical system

Battery	
Capacity	12 V, 9 Ah
Alternator	
Output (regulated)	15.2 V (DC)
Charging coil resistance	0.7 to 0.9 ohms
Fuse	15A x 1 and 7.5A x 4
Bulbs	
Headlight (main/dipped)	60/55 W
Sidelight	5 W
Brake/tail light	21/5 W
Licence plate light	5 W
Turn signal lights	10 W
Instrument and warning lights	1.2 W and 2.0 W

Ignition system

HT coil primary resistance	0.4 to 0.5 ohm
HT coil secondary resistance	2.7 to 3.3 K-ohms
Spark plug cap resistance	5 K-ohms
Pick-up coil resistance	104 to 124 ohms

Transmission

Belt width service limit	21.5 mm
Variator rollers minimum diameter	18.5 mm
Clutch lining thickness	1.0 mm
Clutch spring free length	106 mm
Gearbox oil	SAE 80W/90 API GL4
Gearbox oil capacity	200 ml

Brakes

Disc brake	
Fluid type	DOT 4
Pad minimum thickness	1.5 mm
Drum brake	
Shoe lining minimum thickness	1.5 mm
Brake lever freeplay	10 to 15 mm

Torque wrench settings

Spark plug	12 to 14 Nm
Valve cover bolts	3 to 4 Nm
Cylinder head nuts	28 to 30 Nm
Cylinder head bolts	11 to 13 Nm
Cam chain tensioner bolts	11 to 13 Nm
Cam chain tensioner spring cap bolt	5 to 6 Nm
Camshaft sprocket bolt	12 to 14 Nm
Engine mounting bolt	33 to 41 Nm
Oil pump sprocket bolt	10 to 14 Nm
Oil pump mounting bolts	5 to 6 Nm
Alternator rotor nut	52 to 58 Nm
Alternator stator bolts	3 to 4 Nm
Variator centre nut	75 to 83 Nm
Clutch centre nut	54 to 60 Nm
Clutch assembly nut	55 to 60 Nm
Drive belt cover screws	11 to 13 Nm
Crankcase bolts	11 to 13 Nm
Gearbox cover bolts	24 to 27 Nm
Rear shock absorber mountings	
Lower bolt	33 to 41 Nm
Upper bolt	20 to 25 Nm
Rear hub nut	104 to 126 Nm

Piaggio NRG 50 MC²

Engine no. prefix	CO 41M
Frame no. prefix	ZAP CO
Engine	49 cc single-cylinder two-stroke
Cooling system	Liquid-cooled
Fuel system	Dell'Orto PHVA slide carburettor
Ignition system	CDI
Transmission	Variable speed automatic, belt-driven
Suspension	Upside down telescopic front, swingarm with single shock rear
Brakes	Disc front, drum or disc rear
Tyres	130/60 x 13 front, 130/60 x 13 rear
Wheelbase	1260 mm
Weight (dry)	94 kg
Fuel tank capacity	5.5 litres

Engine

Spark plug type	Champion N84 or Bosch W2CC
Electrode gap	0.5 to 0.6 mm
Idle speed (rpm)	1800 to 2000 rpm
Engine oil	Two-stroke injector oil
Oil tank capacity	1.3 litres
Bore x stroke	40.0 x 39.3 mm
Piston diameter (standard)	39.94 to 39.96 mm
Piston to bore clearance (standard)	0.045 to 0.055 mm
Piston ring installed end gap (standard)	0.10 to 0.25 mm
Coolant	50% distilled water, 50% corrosion inhibiting ethylene glycol anti-freeze
Coolant capacity	1 litre

Fuel system

Throttle twistgrip freeplay	1 to 3 mm
Main jet	66
Pilot jet	38
Starter jet	60
Needle type / position	A15 (2nd notch from top)
Float height	5 mm (not adjustable)
Automatic choke resistance	approx. 30.0 to 40.0 ohms @ 20°C

Ignition system

Source coil resistance	930 to 1030 ohms
Pick-up coil resistance	83 to 93 ohms

Transmission

Belt width service limit	17.5 mm
Variator rollers minimum diameter	18.5 mm
Clutch spring free length	110 mm
Gearbox oil	SAE 80W/90 API GL4
Gearbox oil capacity	80 ml

Brakes

Disc brake	
Fluid type	DOT 4
Pad minimum thickness	1.5 mm
Drum brake	
Shoe lining minimum thickness	1.5 mm
Brake lever freeplay	10 to 15 mm

Tyre pressures

Front	19 psi (1.3 bar)
Rear	25 psi (1.7 bar)

Electrical system

Battery	
Capacity	12 V, 4 Ah
Alternator	
Output (unregulated)	25 to 30 V (AC)
Fuse (main)	7.5 Amps
Bulbs	
Headlight (main/dipped)	35/35 W
Sidelight	5 W
Brake/tail light	21/5 W
Turn signal lights	10 W
Instrument and warning lights	1.2 W

Torque wrench settings

Cylinder head nuts	11 Nm
Crankcase bolts	13 Nm
Engine mounting bolt	41 Nm
Exhaust manifold nuts	11 Nm
Exhaust system mounting bolts	24 Nm
Oil pump mounting bolts	4 Nm
Alternator rotor nut	44 Nm
Alternator stator bolts	4 Nm
Variator centre nut	44 Nm
Clutch centre nut	44 Nm
Clutch assembly nut	60 Nm
Gearbox oil filler plug	5 Nm
Gearbox cover bolts	13 Nm
Rear shock absorber mountings	
Lower bolt	41 Nm
Upper bolt	25 Nm
Steering head bearing adjuster nut	10 Nm
Steering head bearing locknut	40 Nm
Handlebar stem bolt	50 Nm
Front axle nut	52 Nm
Rear hub nut	126 Nm
Disc brake caliper mounting bolts	25 Nm
Brake hose banjo bolt	25 Nm

Piaggio NRG 50 MC³ DD and DT

Engine no. prefix	CO 41M (DD), C215M (DT)
Frame no. prefix	ZAP C18 (DD), ZAP C21 (DT)
Engine	
Cooling system	49 cc single cylinder two-stroke
Fuel system	Liquid-cooled (DD), Air-cooled (DT)
Ignition system	Dell'Orto PHVA 17.5 carburettor
	CDI
Transmission	Variable speed automatic, belt driven
Suspension	Upside down telescopic front, swingarm with single shock rear
Brakes	Disc front, drum or disc rear
Tyres	130/60 x 13 front and rear
Wheelbase	1280 mm
Weight (dry)	94 to 96 kg
Fuel tank capacity	7.5 litres

Engine

Spark plug type	Champion RN2C or NGK BR9ES
Electrode gap	0.5 to 0.6 mm
Idle speed (rpm)	1700 to 1900 rpm
Engine oil	Two-stroke injector oil
Oil tank capacity	1.3 litres
Bore x stroke	40.0 x 39.3 mm
Piston diameter (standard)	39.94 to 39.96 mm
Piston to bore clearance (standard)	
DD model	0.045 to 0.055 mm
DT model	0.050 to 0.060 mm
Piston ring installed end gap (standard)	0.10 to 0.25 mm
Coolant (DD)	50% distilled water, 50% corrosion inhibiting ethylene glycol anti-freeze
Coolant capacity (DD)	1 litre

Fuel system

Main jet	53
Pilot jet	32
Starter jet	50
Needle type / position	A22 (1st notch from top)
Pilot screw setting	1½
Float height	5 mm (not adjustable)
Automatic choke resistance	approx. 30.0 to 40.0 ohms @ 20°C

Electrical system

Battery	
Capacity	12 V, 4 Ah
Alternator	
Output (unregulated)	25 to 30 V (AC) at 3000 rpm
Fuse (main)	7.5 Amps
Bulbs	
Headlight (main/dipped)	35/35 W
Sidelight	4 W
Brake/tail light	21/5 W
Turn signal lights	10 W
Instrument and warning lights	1.2 W

Ignition system

Source coil resistance	930 to 1030 ohms
Pick-up coil resistance	83 to 93 ohms

Transmission

Belt width service limit	17.5 mm
Variator rollers minimum diameter	18.5 mm
Clutch lining thickness	1 mm
Clutch spring free length	110 mm
Gearbox oil	SAE 80W/90 API GL4
Gearbox oil capacity	80 to 85 ml

Brakes

Disc brake	
Fluid type	DOT 4
Pad minimum thickness	1.5 mm
Drum brake	
Shoe lining minimum thickness	1.5 mm
Brake lever freeplay	10 to 15 mm

Torque wrench settings

Cylinder head nuts	10 to 11 Nm
Crankcase bolts	12 to 13 Nm
Engine mounting bolt	33 to 41 Nm
Alternator rotor nut	40 to 44 Nm
Variator centre nut	40 to 44 Nm
Clutch centre nut	40 to 44 Nm
Clutch assembly nut	40 to 44 Nm
Gearbox cover bolts and drive belt cover screws	12 to 13 Nm
Rear shock absorber mountings	
Lower bolt	33 to 41 Nm
Upper bolt	20 to 25 Nm
Steering head bearing adjuster nut	8 to 10 Nm
Steering head bearing locknut	35 to 40 Nm
Handlebar stem bolt	45 to 50 Nm
Front axle nut	40 to 50 Nm
Rear hub nut	90 to 110 Nm
Disc brake caliper mounting bolts	20 to 25 Nm
Brake hose banjo bolt	15 to 25 Nm

Tyre pressures

Front	19 psi (1.3 bar)
Rear	26 to 29 psi (1.8 to 2.0 bar)

Piaggio NRG Power DT

Engine no. prefix	C453M
Frame no. prefix	ZAPC45300
Engine	49 cc single cylinder two-stroke
Cooling system	Air-cooled
Fuel system	Dell'Orto PHVA 17.5RD slide carburettor
Ignition system	CDI
Transmission	Variable speed automatic belt driven
Suspension	Telescopic front with single shock rear
Brakes	Single disc (front), drum (rear)
Tyres	120/70 x 13 front, 140/60 x 13 rear
Wheelbase	1270 mm
Weight (dry)	95 kg
Fuel tank capacity	6.5 litres

Engine

Spark plug type	Champion RN2C
Electrode gap	0.6 to 0.7 mm
Idle speed (rpm)	1800 to 2000 rpm
Engine oil	Good quality synthetic 2-stroke injector oil
Oil tank capacity	1.2 litres
Bore x stroke	40.0 x 39.3 mm
Piston diameter (standard)	39.940 to 39.960 mm
Piston to bore clearance (standard)	0.050 to 0.060 mm
Piston ring installed end gap (standard)	0.10 to 0.25 mm

Fuel system

Main jet	53
Pilot jet	32
Starter jet	50
Needle type / position	A22 (1st notch from top)
Pilot screw setting	1½ turns out
Fuel level	5 mm (not adjustable)
Automatic choke resistance	30 to 40 ohms

Ignition system

Source coil resistance	1.0 ohm
Pick-up coil resistance	170 ohms

Transmission

Belt width service limit	17.5 mm
Variator rollers minimum diameter	18.5 mm
Clutch lining thickness service limit	1 mm
Clutch spring free length	110 mm
Gearbox oil	SAE 80W/90 API GL4
Gearbox oil capacity	Approx 85 ml

Brakes

Disc brake	
Fluid type	DOT 4
Pad minimum thickness	1.5 mm
Drum brake	
Shoe lining minimum thickness	1.5 mm
Brake lever freeplay	10 to 15 mm

Tyre pressures

Front	17.5 psi (1.2 bar)
Rear	27 psi (1.8 bar)

Electrical system

Battery	
Capacity	12 V 4 Ah
Alternator	
Output (unregulated)	25 to 30 V (ac) at 3000 rpm
Fuse (main)	7.5 A
Bulbs	
Headlight (main/dipped)	35 / 35 W
Sidelight	3 W
Brake/tail light	LED
Turn signal lights	10 W
Instrument and warning lights	1.2 and / or 2.0 W

Torque wrench settings

Cylinder head nuts	10 to 11 Nm
Crankcase bolts	12 to 13 Nm
Engine mounting bolt	33 to 41 Nm
Exhaust system mounting bolts to crankcase	22 to 24 Nm
Alternator rotor nut	40 to 44 Nm
Variator centre nut	40 to 44 Nm
Clutch centre nut	40 to 44 Nm
Clutch assembly nut	55 to 60 Nm
Gearbox oil drain plug	3 to 5 Nm
Drive belt cover bolts	12 to 13 Nm
Rear shock absorber mountings	
Lower bolt	33 to 41 Nm
Upper bolt	20 to 25 Nm
Steering head bearing adjuster nut	8 to 10 Nm
Steering head bearing locknut	35 to 40 Nm
Handlebar stem bolt	45 to 50 Nm
Front axle nut	45 to 50 Nm
Rear hub nut	104 to 126 Nm
Disc brake caliper mounting bolts	20 to 25 Nm
Brake hose banjo bolt at caliper	20 to 25 Nm
Brake hose banjo bolt at master cylinder	13 to 18 Nm

Piaggio NRG Power DD

Engine no. prefix	C451M
Frame no. prefix	ZAPC45100
Engine	50cc Single cylinder Hi-Per 2 PRO
Cooling system	Liquid-cooled
Fuel system	Dell 'Orto PHVA 17.5 ID slide carburettor
Ignition system	CDI
Transmission	Variable speed automatic, belt driven
Suspension	Upside down telescopic forks / swingarm monoshock
Brakes	Single disc (front and rear)
Tyres	130/60-13
Wheelbase	1280 mm
Weight (dry)	99 kg
Fuel tank capacity	6.5 litres

Engine

Spark plug type	Champion RN1C
Electrode gap	0.6 to 0.7 mm
Idle speed (rpm)	1800 to 2000 rpm
Engine oil	API TC synthetic two-stroke injector oil
Oil tank capacity	1.2 litres
Bore x stroke	40 x 39.3 mm
Piston diameter (standard)	39.943 to 39.971 mm
Piston to bore clearance (standard)	0.047 to 0.061 mm
Piston ring installed end gap (standard)	0.10 to 0.25 mm
Coolant	50% distilled water, 50% corrosion inhibiting ethylene glycol anti-freeze
Coolant capacity	1 litre

Fuel system

Main jet	53
Pilot jet	32
Starter jet	50
Needle type / position	A22 (1st notch from top)
Pilot screw setting	1½ turns out
Fuel level height	5 mm (not adjustable)
Automatic choke resistance	30 to 40 ohms

Tyre pressures

Front	17.5 psi (1.2 bar)
Rear	24.5 psi (1.7 bar)

Electrical system

Battery	
Capacity	12 V, 4 Ah
Alternator	
Output (unregulated)	25 to 30 V (ac) at 3000 rpm
Fuse (main)	7.5 A
Bulbs	
Headlight (main/dipped)	35 / 35 W
Sidelight	3 W
Brake/tail light	LED
Turn signal lights	10 W
Instrument and warning lights	1.2 and / or 2.0 W

Ignition system

Source coil resistance	1.0 ohm
Pick-up coil resistance	170 ohm

Transmission

Belt width service limit	17.5 mm
Variator rollers minimum diameter	18.5 mm
Clutch lining thickness	1 mm
Clutch spring free length	106 mm
Gearbox oil	SAE 80W/90 API GL4
Gearbox oil capacity	approx 85 ml

Brakes

Disc brake	
Fluid type	DOT 4
Pad minimum thickness	1.5 mm
Drum brake	
Shoe lining minimum thickness	1.5 mm
Brake lever freeplay	10 to 15 mm

Torque wrench settings

Cylinder head nuts	10 to 11 Nm
Crankcase bolts	12 to 13 Nm
Engine mounting bolt	33 to 41 Nm
Exhaust system mounting bolts to crankcase	22 to 24 Nm
Alternator rotor nut	40 to 44 Nm
Variator centre nut	18 to 20 Nm
	+90°
Clutch centre nut	40 to 44 Nm
Clutch assembly nut	55 to 60 Nm
Gearbox oil drain plug	3 to 5 Nm
Drive belt cover bolts	12 to 13 Nm
Rear shock absorber mountings	
Lower bolt	33 to 41 Nm
Upper bolt	20 to 25 Nm
Steering head bearing adjuster nut	8 to 10 Nm
Steering head bearing locknut	35 to 40 Nm
Handlebar stem bolt	45 to 50 Nm
Front wheel axle nut	45 to 50 Nm
Front wheel axle pinch bolts	6 to 7 Nm
Rear hub nut	104 to 126 Nm
Disc brake caliper mounting bolts	20 to 25 Nm
Brake hose banjo bolt at caliper	20 to 25 Nm
Brake hose banjo bolt at master cylinder	13 to 18 Nm

Piaggio Skipper 125

Engine no. prefix	CSM 1M
Frame no. prefix	CSM 1T
Engine	
Cooling system	Single-cylinder two-stroke
Fuel system	Air-cooled
Ignition system	Mikuni VM slide carburettor
	CDI
Transmission	Variable speed automatic, belt-driven
Suspension	Trailing link front, swingarm with single shock rear
Brakes	Disc front, drum rear
Tyres	100/80 x 10 front, 110/80 x 10 rear
Wheelbase	1250 mm
Weight (dry)	95 kg
Fuel tank capacity	8.0 litres

Electrical system

Battery	
Capacity	12 V, 9 Ah
Alternator	
Output (unregulated)	27 to 31 V (AC)
Fuse (main)	15 Amps
Fuses (secondary)	10, 7.5 and 4 Amps
Bulbs	
Headlight (main/dipped)	35/35 W
Sidelight	5 W
Brake/tail light	21/5 W
Turn signal lights	10 W
Instrument and warning lights	1.2 W

Torque wrench settings

Cylinder head nuts	23 Nm
Crankcase bolts	13 Nm
Engine mounting bolt	41 Nm
Exhaust manifold nuts	11 Nm
Exhaust system mounting bolts	24 Nm
Oil pump mounting bolts	4 Nm
Alternator rotor nut	56 Nm
Alternator stator bolts	4 Nm
Variator centre nut	80 Nm
Clutch centre nut	56 Nm
Clutch assembly nut	60 Nm
Gearbox oil filler plug	5 Nm
Gearbox cover bolts	15 Nm
Front shock absorber mountings	10 Nm
Rear shock absorber mountings	
Lower bolt	41 Nm
Upper bolt	25 Nm
Steering head bearing adjuster nut	10 Nm
Steering head bearing locknut	40 Nm
Handlebar stem bolt	50 Nm
Front wheel bolts	25 Nm
Front hub nut	90 Nm
Rear hub nut	110 Nm
Disc brake caliper mounting bolts	25 Nm
Brake hose banjo bolt	25 Nm

Engine

Spark plug type	Champion N2C or NGK B9ES
Electrode gap	0.5 to 0.6 mm
Idle speed (rpm)	1600 to 1800 rpm
Engine oil	Two-stroke injector oil
Oil tank capacity	1.5 litres
Bore x stroke	55.0 x 52.0 mm
Piston diameter (standard)	54.95 to 54.98 mm
Piston to bore clearance (standard)	0.04 to 0.05 mm
Piston ring installed end gap (standard)	0.20 to 035 mm

Ignition system

Source coil resistance	930 to 1030 ohms
Pick-up coil resistance	83 to 93 ohms

Transmission

Belt width service limit	21.0 mm
Variator rollers minimum diameter	18.5 mm
Clutch spring free length	136 mm
Gearbox oil	SAE 80W/90 API GL4
Gearbox oil capacity	85 ml

Fuel system

Throttle twistgrip freeplay	1 to 3 mm
Main jet	82.5
Pilot jet	35
Starter jet	40
Needle type / position	3CK01 (3rd notch from top)
Pilot screw setting	1¾ turns out
Fuel level	3.5 mm
Automatic choke resistance	approx. 30.0 to 40.0 ohms @ 20°C

Brakes

Disc brake	
Fluid type	DOT 4
Pad minimum thickness	1.5 mm
Drum brake	
Shoe lining minimum thickness	1.5 mm

Tyre pressures

Front	19 psi (1.3 bar)
Rear	26 psi (1.8 bar)

Piaggio Skipper ST125

Engine

Frame no. prefix	ZAP M
Engine	Single-cylinder four-stroke
Cooling system	Air-cooled
Fuel system	Walbro WVF 6A CV carburettor
Ignition system	CDI
Transmission	Variable speed automatic, belt-driven
Suspension	Upside down telescopic front, swingarm with single shock rear
Brakes	Disc front, drum rear
Tyres	120/70 x 12 front, 130/70 x 12 rear
Wheelbase	1320 mm
Weight	108 kg
Fuel tank capacity	9.5 litres

Electrical system

Battery	
Capacity	12 V, 9 Ah
Alternator	
Output (unregulated)	27 to 31 V (AC)
Fuse (main)	15 Amps
Fuses (secondary)	10, 7.5 and 5 Amps
Bulbs	
Headlight (main/dipped)	35/35 W
Sidelight	5 W
Brake/tail light	21/5 W
Turn signal lights	10 W
Instrument and warning lights	1.2 W

Torque wrench settings

Valve cover bolts	12 Nm
Cylinder head nuts	
Initial setting	7 Nm
Final setting	+90° +90°
Cylinder head bolts	13 Nm
Cam chain tensioner bolts	10 Nm
Camshaft sprocket bolt	15 Nm
Engine mounting bolt	41 Nm
Exhaust manifold nuts	11 Nm
Exhaust system mounting bolts	27 Nm
Engine oil drain plug	28 Nm
Oil pump sprocket bolt	13 Nm
Oil pump mounting bolts	6 Nm
Alternator rotor nut	58 Nm
Alternator stator bolts	4 Nm
Variator centre nut	83 Nm
Clutch centre nut	60 Nm
Clutch assembly nut	60 Nm
Crankcase bolts	13 Nm
Gearbox oil filler plug	5 Nm
Gearbox oil drain plug	17 Nm
Gearbox cover bolts	13 Nm
Rear shock absorber mountings	
Lower bolt	41 Nm
Upper bolt	25 Nm
Steering head bearing adjuster nut	10 Nm
Steering head bearing locknut	40 Nm
Handlebar stem bolt	70 Nm
Front axle nut	50 Nm
Rear hub nut	126 Nm
Disc brake caliper mounting bolts	25 Nm
Brake hose banjo bolt	25 Nm

Engine

Spark plug type	Champion RG 4HC or NGK CR8E
Electrode gap	0.7 to 0.8 mm
Idle speed (rpm)	1600 to 1700 rpm
Engine oil	5W 40 API SJ synthetic engine oil
Oil capacity	1.0 litre
Bore x stroke	57.0 x 48.6 mm
Piston diameter (standard)	56.93 to 56.96 mm
Piston to bore clearance (standard)	0.040 to 0.054 mm
Piston ring installed end gap (service limit)	
Top ring	0.40 mm
Second ring	0.50 mm
Oil control ring	0.50 mm
Valve clearance	
Intake	0.10 mm
Exhaust	0.15 mm
Camshaft lobe height (standard)	27.8 mm

Ignition system

Source coil resistance	300 to 400 ohms
Pick-up coil resistance	90 to 140 ohms

Transmission

Belt width service limit	21.5 mm
Variator rollers minimum diameter	18.5 mm
Clutch lining thickness	1.0 mm
Clutch spring free length	106 mm
Gearbox oil	SAE 80W/90 API GL4
Gearbox oil capacity	100 ml

Fuel system

Throttle twistgrip freeplay	1 to 3 mm
Main jet	82
Pilot jet	34
Starter jet	48
Needle type / position	52K (2nd/3rd notch from top)
Float height	Bottom edge parallel to gasket face
Automatic choke resistance	approx. 30 ohms @ 20°C

Brakes

Disc brake	
Fluid type	DOT 4
Pad minimum thickness	1.5 mm
Drum brake	
Shoe lining minimum thickness	1.5 mm
Brake lever freeplay	10 to 15 mm

Tyre pressures

Front	19 psi (1.3 bar)
Rear	26 psi (1.8 bar)

Piaggio Typhoon 50 and 80 (1993 to 2000)

Engine no. prefix	TEC 1M, TEC 2M and TEC 3M (50cc), TE8 1M (80cc)
Frame no. prefix	TEC 1T and ZAPC19 (50cc), TE8 1T (80cc)
Engine	
Cooling system	Single-cylinder two-stroke
Fuel system	Air-cooled
Ignition system	Dell'Orto PHVA slide carburettor
	CDI
Transmission	Variable speed automatic, belt-driven
Suspension	Upside down telescopic front, swingarm with single shock rear
Brakes	Disc front, drum rear
Tyres	120/90 x 10 front, 120/90 x 10 rear
Wheelbase	1280 mm
Weight (dry)	83 kg and 94 kg
Fuel tank capacity	5.5 litres (50cc), 7.0 litres (80cc)

Engine

Spark plug type	Champion N2C or NGK B9ES
Electrode gap	0.5 to 0.6 mm
Idle speed (rpm)	1800 to 2000 rpm
Engine oil	Two-stroke injector oil
Oil tank capacity	1.5 litres
Bore x stroke	
50 cc	40.0 x 39.3 mm
80 cc	46.5 x 44.0 mm
Piston diameter (standard)	
50 cc	39.94 to 39.96 mm
80 cc	46.46 to 46.49 mm
Piston to bore clearance (standard)	
50 cc	0.045 to 0.055 mm
80 cc	0.025 to 0.035 mm
Piston ring installed end gap (standard)	0.10 to 0.25 mm

Fuel system

Throttle twistgrip freeplay	1 to 3 mm
Main jet	
50 cc	70
80 cc	62
Pilot jet	
50 cc	36
80 cc	34
Starter jet	60
Needle type / position	
50 cc	A12 (2nd notch from top)
80 cc	A7 (4th notch from top)
Pilot screw setting	
50 cc	Not available
80 cc	4½ turns out
Float height	5 mm (not adjustable)
Automatic choke resistance	approx. 30.0 to 40.0 ohms @ 20°C

Ignition system

Source coil resistance	930 to 1030 ohms
Pick-up coil resistance	83 to 93 ohms

Transmission

Belt width service limit	17.5 mm
Variator rollers minimum diameter	18.5 mm
Clutch spring free length	110 mm
Gearbox oil	SAE 80W/90 API GL4
Gearbox oil capacity	85 ml

Brakes

Disc brake	
Fluid type	DOT 4
Pad minimum thickness	1.5 mm
Drum brake	
Shoe lining minimum thickness	1.5 mm
Brake lever freeplay	10 to 15 mm

Tyre pressures

Front	19 psi (1.3 bar)
Rear	26 psi (1.8 bar)

Electrical system

Battery	
Capacity	12 V, 4 Ah
Alternator	
Output (unregulated)	25 to 30 V (AC)
Fuse (main)	7.5 Amps
Bulbs	
Headlight (main/dipped)	35/35 W
Sidelight	5 W
Brake/tail light	21/5 W
Turn signal lights	10 W
Instrument and warning lights	1.2 W

Torque wrench settings

Cylinder head nuts	11 Nm
Crankcase bolts	13 Nm
Engine mounting bolt	41 Nm
Exhaust manifold nuts	11 Nm
Exhaust system mounting bolts	24 Nm
Oil pump mounting bolts	4 Nm
Alternator rotor nut	44 Nm
Alternator stator bolts	4 Nm
Variator centre nut	44 Nm
Clutch centre nut	44 Nm
Clutch assembly nut	60 Nm
Gearbox oil filler plug	5 Nm
Gearbox cover bolts	13 Nm
Rear shock absorber mountings	
Lower bolt	41 Nm
Upper bolt	25 Nm
Steering head bearing adjuster nut	10 Nm
Steering head bearing locknut	40 Nm
Handlebar stem bolt	50 Nm
Front axle nut	50 Nm
Rear hub nut	110 Nm

Piaggio Typhoon 50 (2001-on)

Engine no. prefix	C215M and C216M
Frame no. prefix	ZAP C29
Engine	Single cylinder two-stroke
Cooling system	Air-cooled
Fuel system	Dell'Orto PHVA 17.5 slide carburettor
Ignition system	CDI
Transmission	Variable speed automatic, belt driven
Suspension	Upside down telescopic front, swingarm with single shock rear
Brakes	Disc front, drum rear
Tyres	120/90 x 10 front, 120/90 x 10 rear
Wheelbase	1260 mm
Weight (dry)	84 kg
Fuel tank capacity	5.5 litres

Engine

Spark plug type	Champion RN2C
Electrode gap	0.6 to 0.7 mm
Idle speed (rpm)	1800 to 2000 rpm
Engine oil	JASO FC Two-stroke engine oil
Oil tank capacity	1.5 litres
Bore x stroke	40.0 x 39.3 mm
Piston diameter (standard)	39.94 to 39.96 mm
Piston to bore clearance (standard)	0.055 to 0.069 mm
Piston ring installed end gap (standard)	0.10 to 0.25 mm

Fuel system

Main jet	53
Pilot jet	32
Starter jet	50
Needle type / position	A22 (1st notch from top)
Pilot screw setting	1½ turns out

Ignition system

Source coil resistance	1 ohm
Pick-up coil resistance	170 ohms

Transmission

Belt width service limit	17.5 mm
Variator rollers minimum diameter	18.5 mm
Clutch lining minimum thickness	1 mm
Clutch spring free length	118 mm
Clutch spring free length service limit	113 mm
Gearbox oil	SAE 80W/90 API GL4
Gearbox oil capacity	80 ml

Brakes

Disc brake	
Fluid type	DOT 4
Pad minimum thickness	1.5 mm
Drum brake	
Shoe lining minimum thickness	1.5 mm
Brake lever freeplay	10 to 15 mm

Tyre pressures

Front	19 psi (1.3 bar)
Rear	26 psi (1.8 bar)

Electrical system

Battery	
Capacity	12 V, 4 Ah
Alternator	
Output (unregulated)	25 to 30 V (AC) @ 3000 rpm
Fuse (main)	7.5 Amps
Bulbs	
Headlight (main/dipped)	35/35 W
Sidelight	5 W
Brake/tail light	21/5 W
Turn signal lights	10 W
Instrument and warning lights	1.2 W

Torque wrench settings

Spark plug	25 to 30 Nm
Cylinder head nuts	10 to 11 Nm
Crankcase bolts	12 to 13 Nm
Engine mounting bolt	33 to 41 Nm
Exhaust system-to-crankcase bolt	22 to 24 Nm
Oil pump mounting bolts	3 to 4 Nm
Alternator rotor nut	40 to 44 Nm
Alternator stator bolts	3 to 4 Nm
Variator centre nut	40 to 44 Nm
Clutch centre nut	40 to 44 Nm
Clutch assembly nut	55 to 60 Nm
Gearbox oil drain plug	3 to 5 Nm
Gearbox cover bolts	12 to 13 Nm
Drivebelt cover screws	12 to 13 Nm
Rear shock absorber mountings	
Lower bolt	33 to 41 Nm
Upper bolt	20 to 25 Nm
Steering head bearing adjuster nut	8 to 10 Nm
Steering head bearing locknut	35 to 40 Nm
Handlebar stem bolt	45 to 50 Nm
Front axle nut	45 to 50 Nm
Rear hub nut	104 to 126 Nm

Piaggio Typhoon 125

Engine no. prefix	CO 21M
Frame no. prefix	ZAP CO
Engine	
Cooling system	Single-cylinder two-stroke
Cooling system	Air-cooled
Fuel system	Mikuni VM slide carburettor
Ignition system	CDI
Transmission	Variable speed automatic, belt-driven
Suspension	Upside down front, swingarm with single shock rear
Brakes	Disc front, drum rear
Tyres	120/90 x 10 front, 120/90 x 10 rear
Wheelbase	1280 mm
Weight (dry)	106 kg
Fuel tank capacity	8.0 litres

Engine

Spark plug type	Champion N2C or NGK B9ES
Electrode gap	0.5 to 0.6 mm
Idle speed (rpm)	1600 to 1800 rpm
Engine oil	Two-stroke injector oil
Oil tank capacity	1.5 litres
Bore x stroke	55.0 x 52.0 mm
Piston diameter (standard)	54.95 to 54.98 mm
Piston to bore clearance (standard)	0.04 to 0.05 mm
Piston ring installed end gap (standard)	0.20 to 035 mm

Fuel system

Throttle twistgrip freeplay	1 to 3 mm
Main jet	82.5
Pilot jet	35
Starter jet	40
Needle type / position	3CK01 (3rd notch from top)
Pilot screw setting	1¾ turns out
Fuel level	3.5 mm
Automatic choke resistance	approx. 30.0 to 40.0 ohms @ 20°C

Ignition system

Source coil resistance	930 to 1030 ohms
Pick-up coil resistance	83 to 93 ohms

Transmission

Belt width service limit	21.0 mm
Variator rollers minimum diameter	18.5 mm
Clutch spring free length	136 mm
Gearbox oil	SAE 80W/90 API GL4
Gearbox oil capacity	85 ml

Brakes

Disc brake	
Fluid type	DOT 4
Pad minimum thickness	1.5 mm
Drum brake	
Shoe lining minimum thickness	1.5 mm
Brake lever freeplay	10 to 15 mm

Tyre pressures

Front	19 psi (1.3 bar)
Rear	26 psi (1.8 bar)

Electrical system

Battery	
Capacity	12 V, 9 Ah
Alternator	
Output (unregulated)	27 to 31 V (AC)
Fuse (main)	15 Amps
Fuses (secondary)	10, 7.5 and 4 Amps
Bulbs	
Headlight (main/dipped)	35/35 W
Sidelight	5 W
Brake/tail light	21/5 W
Turn signal lights	10 W
Instrument and warning lights	1.2 W

Torque wrench settings

Cylinder head nuts	23 Nm
Crankcase bolts	13 Nm
Engine mounting bolt	41 Nm
Exhaust manifold nuts	11 Nm
Exhaust system mounting bolts	24 Nm
Oil pump mounting bolts	4 Nm
Alternator rotor nut	56 Nm
Alternator stator bolts	4 Nm
Variator centre nut	80 Nm
Clutch centre nut	56 Nm
Clutch assembly nut	60 Nm
Gearbox oil filler plug	5 Nm
Gearbox cover bolts	15 Nm
Rear shock absorber mountings	
Lower bolt	41 Nm
Upper bolt	25 Nm
Steering head bearing adjuster nut	10 Nm
Steering head bearing locknut	40 Nm
Handlebar stem bolt	50 Nm
Front axle nut	50 Nm
Rear hub nut	110 Nm

Piaggio X8 125

Data 63

Electrical system

Battery	
Capacity	12 V, 12 Ah
Alternator output (regulated)	14 to 15.2 V (DC)
Fuse (main)	15 A
Bulbs:	
Headlight (main/dipped)	55 W x 2
Sidelight	4 W x 2
Tail light	5 W x 2
Brake light	2.3 W x 5
Turn signal lights	10 W
Trunk light	5 W
Licence plate light	5 W
Instrument and warning lights	2.0 W x 5

Torque wrench settings

Cylinder head nuts	28 to 30 Nm
Alternator rotor nut	54 to 60 Nm
Alternator stator bolts	3 to 4 Nm
Crankcase bolts	11 to 13 Nm
Engine mounting bolts	33 to 41 Nm
Exhaust manifold nuts	16 to 18 Nm
Exhaust system mounting bolts	15 to 20 Nm
Exhaust system-to-swingarm bolt	27 to 30 Nm
Oil pump mounting bolts	5 to 6 Nm
Variator centre nut	75 to 83 Nm
Clutch centre nut	54 to 60 Nm
Clutch assembly nut	55 to 60 Nm
Gearbox oil drain plug	15 to 17 Nm
Gearbox cover bolts	24 to 27 Nm
Rear shock absorber mountings	
Lower bolt	33 to 41 Nm
Upper bolt	20 to 25 Nm
Steering head bearing adjuster nut	10 to 13 Nm then loosen by 90°
Steering head bearing locknut	30 to 33 Nm
Handlebar stem bolt	43 to 47 Nm
Front wheel axle nut	45 to 50 Nm
Front wheel axle pinch bolts	6 to 7 Nm
Front disc caliper-to-brake bolts	42 to 52 Nm
Brake hose banjo bolts	20 to 25 Nm
Rear brake caliper bolts	20 to 25 Nm

Engine

Engine no. prefix	M363M
Frame no. prefix	ZAPM36300
Engine	124 cc single cylinder four-stroke LEADER
Cooling system	Liquid-cooled
Fuel system	Walbro WVF/7R or Keihin CVEK-30
Ignition system	CDI
Transmission	Variable speed sutomatic, belt driven
Suspension	Telescopic forks, swingarm and twin shock
Brakes	Single disc (front and rear)
Tyres	120/70 x 14 front, 130/70 x 12 rear
Wheelbase	1490 mm
Weight (dry)	157 kg
Fuel tank capacity	9.5 litres

Engine

Spark plug type	Champion RG4HC
Electrode gap	0.7 to 0.8 mm
Idle speed (rpm)	1600 to 1700 rpm
Engine oil	SAE 5 W/40 API SG Synthetic oil
Engne oil capacity	Approx 1litre
Bore x stroke	57.0 mm x 48.6 mm
Pis on diameter (standard)	56.945 mm
Piston to bore clearance service limit	0.045 mm to 0.059 mm
Piston ring installed end gap	
Top ring	0.15 to 0.30 mm
Second ring	0.10 to 0.30 mm
Oil control ring	0.15 to 0.35 mm
Coolant	50% distilled water and 50% ethylene glycol antifreeze ethylene glycol anti-freeze
Coolant capacity	Approx 2 litres

Ignition system

Source coil resistance	0.7 to 0.9 ohm
Pick-up coil resistance	105 to 124 ohms

Transmission

Belt width	21.5 mm
Variator rollers	18.5 mm
Clutch lining thickness	1 mm
Gearbox oil	SAE 80W/90 API GL4
Gearbox oil capacity	Approx 150 ml

Fuel system – Walbro carburettor

Main jet	103
Pilot jet	38
Starter jet	48
Needle type / position	653 (2nd notch from top)
Pilot screw setting	2⅞ turns out
Float level	Bottom edge parallel to gasket face
Automatic choke resistance	40 ohms

Brakes

Disc brake:	
Fluid type	DOT 4
Pad minimum thickness	1.5 mm

Tyre pressures

Front tyre pressure	29 psi (2.0 bar)
Rear tyre pressure	32 psi (2.2 bar)

Piaggio X9 125 (inc. Evolution)

Engine no. prefix	M223M (X9), M23XM (X9 Evo)
Frame no. prefix	ZAP M23
Engine	124cc single cylinder, four valve, four-stroke LEADER
Cooling system	Liquid-cooled
Fuel system	Walbro WVF 7C or 7G CV carburettor, or Keihin CVK30 carburettor
Ignition system	CDI
Transmission	Variable speed automatic, belt driven
Suspension	Telescopic front, swingarm with twin adjustable shock rear
Brakes	Disc front, disc rear
Tyres	120/70 x 14 front, 140/60 x 14 rear
Wheelbase	1495 mm (X9), 1500 mm (X9 Evo)
Weight (dry)	159 kg (X9), 165 kg (X9 Evo)
Fuel tank capacity	14.5 litres

Engine

Spark plug type	NGK CR8EB
Electrode gap	0.7 to 0.8 mm
Idle speed (rpm)	1600 to 1700 rpm
Engine oil	5W 40 API SJ synthetic engine oil
Oil capacity	1.0 litre
Bore x stroke	57.0 x 48.6 mm
Piston diameter (standard)	56.94 to 56.97 mm
Piston to bore clearance (standard)	0.045 to 0.059 mm
Piston ring installed end gap (standard)	
Top ring	0.20 to 0.40 mm
Second ring	0.10 to 0.30 mm
Oil control ring	0.15 to 0.35 mm
Piston ring installed end gap (service limit)	1 mm
Valve clearance	
Intake	0.10 mm
Exhaust	0.15 mm
Valve spring free length	Not available
Camshaft lobe height (standard)	
Intake	30.285 mm
Exhaust	29.209 mm
Coolant	50% distilled water, 50% corrosion inhibiting ethylene glycol anti-freeze
Coolant capacity	1.2 litres

Ignition system

HT coil primary resistance	0.4 to 0.5 ohms
HT coil secondary resistance	2.7 to 3.3 K-ohms
Pick-up coil resistance	105 to 124 ohms

Fuel system – Walbro carburettor

Throttle twistgrip freeplay	1 to 3 mm
Main jet	108
Pilot jet	36
Starter jet	50
Needle type (position)	51C (2nd notch from top)
Pilot screw setting	2⅝ ± ½ turns out
Float height	Bottom edge parallel to gasket face
Automatic choke resistance	30 to 40 ohms

Fuel system – Keihin carburettor

Throttle twistgrip freeplay	1 to 3 mm
Main jet	105
Pilot jet	35
Starter jet	42
Needle type (position)	NDYA (fixed)
Pilot screw setting	2 ± ¼ turns out
Float height	Bottom edge parallel to gasket face
Automatic choke resistance	approx. 20.0 ohms

Transmission

Belt width service limit	21.5 mm
Variator rollers minimum diameter	18.5 mm
Clutch lining thickness	1.0 mm
Clutch spring free length	106 mm
Gearbox oil	SAE 80W/90 API GL4
Gearbox oil capacity	150 ml

Brakes

Fluid type	DOT 4
Pad minimum thickness	1.5 mm

Tyre pressures

Front	29 psi (2.0 bar)
Rear	32 psi (2.2 bar) solo, 36 psi (2.5 bar) pillion

Electrical system

Battery	
Capacity	12 V, 12 Ah
Alternator	
Output (regulated)	14 to 15 V (DC)
Charging coil resistance	0.7 to 0.9 ohms
Fuses (X9)	15A x 2, 10A x 4, 7.5A x 1, 5A x 1
Fuses (X9 Evolution)	15A x 2, 10A x 3, 7.5A x 3
Bulbs	
Headlights	55W x 2
Sidelight	5W x 2
Tail light	5W x 2
Brake light	2.3W x 5
Licence plate light and trunk light	5W
Turn signal lights	10 W

Torque wrench settings

Valve cover bolts	13 Nm (X9), 6 to 7 Nm (X9 Evo)
Cylinder head nuts	27 to 29 Nm
Cylinder head bolts	11 to 13 Nm
Cam chain tensioner bolts	11 to 13 Nm
Camshaft sprocket bolt	11 to 15 Nm
Engine mounting bolt	33 to 41 Nm
Exhaust manifold nuts	16 to 18 Nm
Exhaust system mounting bolts	15 to 20 Nm
Water pump cover screws	3 to 4 Nm
Engine oil drain plug	24 to 30 Nm
Oil pump sprocket bolt	10 to 14 Nm
Oil pump mounting bolts	5 to 6 Nm
Alternator rotor nut	54 to 60 Nm
Alternator stator bolts	3 to 4 Nm
Variator centre nut	75 to 83 Nm
Clutch centre nut	55 to 60 Nm
Clutch assembly nut	54 to 60 Nm
Crankcase bolts	11 to 13 Nm
Gearbox oil drain plug	15 to 17 Nm
Gearbox cover bolts	24 to 27 Nm
Rear shock absorber mountings	33 to 41 Nm
Steering head bearing adjuster nut	8 to 10 Nm
Steering head bearing locknut	27 to 33 Nm
Handlebar stem bolt	43 to 47 Nm
Front axle nut	45 to 50 Nm
Rear hub nut	104 to 126 Nm
Disc brake caliper mounting bolts	20 to 25 Nm
Brake hose banjo bolt	17 to 20 Nm

Piaggio Zip 50

Data 65

Engine

Engine no. prefix	NSL 1M
Frame no. prefix	ZAP CO
Engine	49 cc single-cylinder two-stroke
Cooling system	Air-cooled
Fuel system	Dell'Orto PHVA slide carburettor
Ignition system	CDI
Transmission	Variable speed automatic, belt-driven
Suspension	Telescopic front, swingarm with single shock rear
Brakes	Drum front, drum rear
Tyres	90/90 x 10 front, 90/90 x 10 rear
Wheelbase	1160 mm
Weight (dry)	71 kg
Fuel tank capacity	4 litres

Engine

Spark plug type	Champion N2C or NGK B9ES
Electrode gap	0.5 to 0.6 mm
Idle speed (rpm)	1800 to 2000 rpm
Engine oil	Two-stroke injector oil
Oil tank capacity	1.5 litres
Bore x stroke	40.0 x 39.3 mm
Piston diameter (standard)	39.94 to 39.96 mm
Piston to bore clearance (standard)	0.045 to 0.055 mm
Piston ring installed end gap (standard)	0.10 to 0.25 mm

Fuel system

Throttle twistgrip freeplay	1 to 3 mm
Main jet	70
Pilot jet	38
Starter jet	60
Needle type / position	A15 (2nd notch from top)
Float height	5 mm (not adjustable)
Automatic choke resistance	approx. 30.0 to 40.0 ohms @ 20°C

Ignition system

Source coil resistance	930 to 1030 ohms
Pick-up coil resistance	83 to 93 ohms

Transmission

Belt width service limit	17.5 mm
Variator rollers minimum diameter	18.5 mm
Clutch spring free length	110 mm
Gearbox oil	SAE 80W/90 API GL4
Gearbox oil capacity	85 ml

Brakes

Shoe lining minimum thickness	1.5 mm
Brake lever freeplay	10 to 15 mm

Tyre pressures

Front	17 psi (1.2 bar)
Rear	25 psi (1.7 bar)

Electrical system

Battery	
Capacity	12 V, 4 Ah
Alternator	
Output (unregulated)	25 to 30 V (AC)
Fuse (main)	7.5 Amps
Bulbs	
Headlight (main/dipped)	35/35 W
Sidelight	5 W
Brake/tail light	21/5 W
Turn signal lights	10 W
Instrument and warning lights	1.2 W

Torque wrench settings

Cylinder head nuts	11 Nm
Crankcase bolts	13 Nm
Engine mounting bolt	41 Nm
Exhaust manifold nuts	11 Nm
Exhaust system mounting bolts	24 Nm
Oil pump mounting bolts	4 Nm
Alternator rotor nut	44 Nm
Alternator stator bolts	4 Nm
Variator centre nut	44 Nm
Clutch centre nut	44 Nm
Clutch assembly nut	60 Nm
Gearbox oil filler plug	5 Nm
Gearbox cover bolts	13 Nm
Rear shock absorber mountings	
Lower bolt	41 Nm
Upper bolt	25 Nm
Steering head bearing adjuster nut	10 Nm
Steering head bearing locknut	40 Nm
Handlebar stem bolt	50 Nm
Front axle nut	50 Nm
Rear hub nut	110 Nm

Piaggio Zip 50 Cat

Engine

Engine no. prefix	C251M
Frame no. prefix	ZAP C25
Engine	49 cc single cylinder two-stroke
Cooling system	Air-cooled
Fuel system	Dell'Orto PHVA carburettor
Ignition system	CDI
Transmission	Variable speed automatic, belt driven
Suspension	Telescopic front, swingarm with single shock rear
Brakes	175 mm disc front, 110 mm drum rear
Tyres	110/80 x 10 front, 120/70 x 10 rear
Wheelbase	1180 mm
Weight (dry)	84 kg
Fuel tank capacity	7.5 litres

Engine

Spark plug type	Champion RN2C
Electrode gap	0.6 to 0.7 mm
Idle speed (rpm)	1700 to 1900 rpm
Engine oil	Two-stroke injector oil
Oil tank capacity	1.4 litres
Bore x stroke	40.0 x 39.3 mm
Piston to bore clearance (standard)	0.055 to 0.069 mm
Piston ring installed end gap (standard)	0.10 to 0.25 mm

Fuel system

Main jet	56
Pilot jet	32
Starter jet	50
Needle type / position	A22 (1st notch from top)
Pilot screw setting	1½ turns out

Ignition system

Source coil resistance	930 to 1030 ohms
Pick-up coil resistance	83 to 93 ohms

Electrical system

Battery capacity	12 V, 3.6 Ah
Alternator output (unregulated)	26 to 30 V (AC) @ 3000 rpm
Fuse (main)	7.5 Amps
Bulbs	
Headlight (main/dipped)	35/35 W
Sidelight	5 W
Tail light	5 W
Brake light	10 W
Turn signal lights	10 W (front), 5 W (rear)
Instrument and warning lights	1.2 W

Transmission

Belt width service limit	17.5 mm
Variator rollers minimum diameter	18.5 mm
Clutch lining thickness	1 mm
Clutch spring free length	110 mm
Gearbox oil	SAE 80W/90 API GL4
Gearbox oil capacity	75 ml

Brakes

Brake fluid type	DOT 4
Pad minimum thickness	1.5 mm

Torque wrench settings

Spark plug	25 to 30 Nm
Cylinder head nuts	10 to 11 Nm
Crankcase bolts	12 to 13 Nm
Engine mounting bolt	33 to 41 Nm
Oil pump mounting bolts	3 to 4 Nm
Alternator rotor nut	40 to 44 Nm
Alternator stater screws	3 to 4 Nm
Variator centre nut	40 to 44 Nm
Clutch centre nut	40 to 44 Nm
Clutch assembly nut	55 to 60 Nm
Gearbox cover bolts	12 to 13 Nm
Drivebelt cover screws	12 to 13 Nm
Rear shock absorber mountings	
Lower bolt	33 to 41 Nm
Upper bolt	20 to 25 Nm
Steering head bearing adjuster nut	8 to 10 Nm
Steering head bearing locknut	30 to 40 Nm
Handlebar stem bolt	20 to 22 Nm
Front axle nut	43 to 52 Nm
Rear hub nut	104 to 126 Nm
Front brake caliper bolts	20 to 25 Nm
Front disc bolts	5.0 to 6.5 Nm
Front brake hose banjo bolt	20 to 25 Nm

Tyre pressures

Front	19 psi (1.3 bar)
Rear	26 to 29 psi (1.8 to 2.0 bar)

Engine no. prefix C11 1M
Frame no. prefix .... ZAP C11
Engine ....
Cooling system .... 49 cc single-cylinder two-stroke
Fuel system .... Liquid-cooled
Ignition system .... Dell'Orto PHVA slide carburettor
.... CDI
Transmission .... Variable speed automatic, belt-driven
Suspension .... Trailing link front, swingarm with single shock rear
Brakes .... Disc front, drum rear
Tyres .... 100/80 x 10 front, 100/80 x 10 rear
Wheelbase .... 1160 mm
Weight (dry) .... 77 kg
Fuel tank capacity .... 4 litres

Engine

Spark plug type .... Champion N2C or
.... NGK B9ES
Electrode gap .... 0.5 to 0.6 mm
Idle speed (rpm) .... 1800 to 2000 rpm
Engine oil .... Two-stroke injector oil
Oil tank capacity .... 1.5 litres
Bore x stroke .... 40.0 x 39.3 mm
Piston diameter (standard) .... 39.94 to 39.96 mm
Piston to bore clearance
 (standard) .... 0.045 to 0.055 mm
Piston ring installed end gap
 (standard) .... 0.10 to 0.25 mm
Coolant .... 50% distilled water,
.... 50% corrosion
.... inhibiting ethylene
.... glycol anti-freeze
Coolant capacity .... 1 litre

Fuel system

Throttle twistgrip freeplay .... 1 to 3 mm
Main jet 75
Pilot jet 34
Starter jet 50
Needle type / position .... SA2 (3rd notch from top)
Float height .... 5 mm (not adjustable)
Automatic choke resistance .... approx. 30.0 to
.... 40.0 ohms @ 20°C

Ignition system

Source coil resistance .... 930 to 1030 ohms
Pick-up coil resistance .... 83 to 93 ohms

Transmission

Belt width service limit .... 17.5 mm
Variator rollers minimum diameter .... 18.5 mm
Clutch spring free length .... 110 mm
Gearbox oil .... SAE 80W/90 API GL4
Gearbox oil capacity .... 80 ml

Tyre pressures

Front .... 20 psi (1.4 bar)
Rear .... 26 psi (1.8 bar)

Electrical system

Battery
 Capacity .... 12 V, 4 Ah
Alternator
 Output (unregulated) .... 25 to 30 V (AC)
 Fuse (main) .... 7.5 Amps
Bulbs
 Headlight (main/dipped) .... 35/35 W
 Sidelight .... 5 W
 Brake/tail light .... 21/5 W
 Turn signal lights .... 10 W
 Instrument and warning lights .... 1.2 W

Brakes

Disc brake
 Fluid type .... DOT 4
 Pad minimum thickness .... 1.5 mm
Drum brake
 Shoe lining minimum thickness .... 1.5 mm
 Brake lever freeplay .... 10 to 15 mm

Torque wrench settings

Cylinder head nuts .... 11 Nm
Crankcase bolts .... 13 Nm
Engine mounting bolt .... 41 Nm
Exhaust manifold nuts .... 11 Nm
Exhaust system mounting bolts .... 24 Nm
Oil pump mounting bolts .... 4 Nm
Alternator rotor nut .... 44 Nm
Alternator stator bolts .... 4 Nm
Variator centre nut .... 44 Nm
Clutch centre nut .... 44 Nm
Clutch assembly nut .... 60 Nm
Gearbox oil filler plug .... 5 Nm
Gearbox cover bolts .... 13 Nm
Front shock absorber mountings .... 10 Nm
Rear shock absorber mountings
 Lower bolt .... 41 Nm
 Upper bolt .... 25 Nm
Steering head bearing adjuster nut .... 10 Nm
Steering head bearing locknut .... 40 Nm
Handlebar stem bolt .... 50 Nm
Front wheel bolts .... 25 Nm
Front hub nut .... 90 Nm
Rear hub nut .... 110 Nm
Disc brake caliper mounting bolts .... 25 Nm
Brake hose banjo bolt .... 25 Nm

Engine no. prefix	C252M (50 cc), M252M (100 cc)
Frame no. prefix	ZAPC25 (50 cc), LEMM252 (100 cc)
Engine	49.9 cc and 96.2 cc single cylinder 2-valve four-stroke
Cooling system	Air-cooled
Fuel system	Keihin CVK 18 (50 cc), CVK 20 (100 cc) CV carburettor
Ignition system	CDI
Transmission	Variable speed automatic, belt driven
Suspension	Telescopic front, swingarm with single shock rear
Brakes	Disc front, drum rear
Tyres	100/80 x 10 front, 120/70 x 10 rear
Wheelbase	1250 mm (50 cc), 1200 mm (100 cc)
Weight (dry)	84 kg (50 cc), 89 cc (100 cc)
Fuel tank capacity	7.5 litres (50 cc), 7 litres (100 cc)

Engine

Spark plug type	Champion RG4HC/RG4PHP or NGK CR9EB
Electrode gap	0.7 to 0.8 mm
Idle speed (rpm)	
50 cc	1900 to 2000 rpm
100 cc	1350 to 1650 rpm
Engine oil	5W40 API SL synthetic oil
Oil capacity	850 ml
Bore x stroke	
50 cc	39.0 x 41.8 mm
100 cc	50.0 x 49.0 mm
Piston diameter (standard)	
50 cc	38.95 to 38.98 mm
100 cc	49.962 to 49.976 mm
Piston to bore clearance (standard)	
50 cc	0.025 to 0.039 mm
100 cc	0.038 to 0.052 mm
Piston ring installed end gap - 50 cc	
Top ring	0.08 to 0.20 mm
Second ring	0.05 to 0.20 mm
Oil control ring	0.20 to 0.70 mm
Piston ring installed end gap - 100 cc	
Top and second rings	0.10 to 0.25 mm
Oil control ring	0.20 to 0.70 mm
Valve clearance	
Intake	0.10 mm
Exhaust	0.15 mm
Camshaft height (standard)	25.935 mm

Ignition system

Source coil resistance	1 ohm
Pick-up coil resistance	170 ohms

Fuel system

Main jet	75
Pilot jet	35
Starter jet	42 (50 cc), 45 (100 cc)
Needle type	NACA (50 cc), ADA (100 cc)
Float level	parallel to gasket face
Automatic choke resistance	6 ohms ± 5%

Transmission

Belt width service limit	17.5 mm
Variator rollers minimum diameter (50 cc models)	18.5 mm
Clutch lining minimum thickness	1.0 mm
Clutch spring free length	110 mm (50 cc), 118 mm (100 cc)
Gearbox oil	SAE 80W/90 API GL4
Gearbox oil capacity	80 ml

Brakes and suspension

Disc brake	
Fluid type	DOT 4
Pad minimum thickness	1.5 mm
Drum brake	
Shoe lining minimum thickness	1.5 mm
Brake lever freeplay	10 to 15 mm
Front fork oil	
50 cc	25 ml of SAE 20W fork oil
100 cc	30 ml of SAE 20W fork oil

Tyre pressures

Front	19 psi (1.3 bar)
Rear	23 to 26 psi (1.6 to 1.8 bar)

Electrical system

Battery	
Capacity	12 V, 7 Ah (9 Ah early models)
Alternator	
Output (unregulated)	25 to 35 V (AC) at 2000 rpm
Fuse (main)	10 A
Bulbs	
Headlight (main/dipped)	35/35 W
Sidelight (100 models)	5 W x 2
Tail light	5 W x 2
Brake light	10 W
Turn signal lights	10 W front, 5 W rear
Instrument and warning lights	1.2 W

Torque wrench settings

Spark plug	10 to 15 Nm
Valve cover bolts	8 to 10 Nm
Cylinder head nuts	
Initial setting	6 to 7 Nm
Final setting	+90° +90°
Cylinder head bolts	8 to 10 Nm
Cam chain tensioner bolts	8 to 10 Nm
Camshaft sprocket bolt	12 to 14 Nm
Engine mounting bolt	33 to 41 Nm
Engine oil drain plug	25 to 28 Nm
Oil pump mounting bolts	5 to 6 Nm
Alternator rotor nut	40 to 44 Nm
Alternator stator bolts	3 to 4 Nm
Variator centre nut	18 to 20 Nm +90°
Clutch centre nut	40 to 44 Nm
Clutch assembly nut	55 to 60 Nm
Crankcase bolts	8 to 10 Nm
Gearbox cover bolts and drive belt cover screws	11 to 13 Nm
Front shock absorber mountings	
50 cc	8 to 10 Nm
100 cc	20 to 25 Nm
Rear shock absorber mountings	
Lower bolt	33 to 41 Nm
Upper bolt	20 to 25 Nm
Steering head bearing adjuster nut	8 to 10 Nm
Steering head bearing locknut	30 to 40 Nm
Handlebar stem bolt	20 to 22 Nm
Front hub nut	43 to 52 Nm
Rear hub nut	
50 cc	115 to 125 Nm
100 cc	104 to 126 Nm
Disc brake caliper mounting bolts	20 to 25 Nm
Brake hose banjo bolt	20 to 25 Nm

Engine

Cooling system	Single-cylinder four-stroke
Fuel system	Air-cooled
Ignition system	Walbro WVF 6A CV carburettor
Transmission	CDI
Suspension	Variable speed automatic, belt-driven
Brakes	Trailing link front, swingarm with single adjustable shock rear
Tyres	Disc front, drum rear
Wheelbase	100/80 x 10 front, 120/70 x 10 rear
Weight	1220 mm
Fuel tank capacity	95 kg
	7.5 litres

Electrical system

Battery		
Capacity		12 V, 9 Ah
Alternator		
Output (unregulated)		27 to 31 V (AC)
Fuse (main)		15 Amps
Fuses (secondary)		10, 7.5 and 5 Amps
Bulbs		
Headlight (main/dipped)		35/35 W
Sidelight		5 W
Brake/tail light		21/5 W
Turn signal lights		10 W
Instrument and warning lights		1.2 W

Torque wrench settings

Valve cover bolts	12 Nm
Cylinder head nuts	
Initial setting	7 Nm
Final setting	+90° +90°
Cylinder head bolts	13 Nm
Cam chain tensioner bolts	10 Nm
Camshaft sprocket bolt	15 Nm
Engine mounting bolt	41 Nm
Exhaust manifold nuts	11 Nm
Exhaust system mounting bolts	27 Nm
Engine oil drain plug	28 Nm
Oil pump sprocket bolt	13 Nm
Oil pump mounting bolts	6 Nm
Alternator rotor nut	58 Nm
Alternator stator bolts	4 Nm
Variator centre nut	83 Nm
Clutch centre nut	60 Nm
Clutch assembly nut	60 Nm
Crankcase bolts	13 Nm
Gearbox oil filler plug	5 Nm
Gearbox oil drain plug	17 Nm
Gearbox cover bolts	13 Nm
Front shock absorber mountings	25 Nm
Rear shock absorber mountings	
Lower bolt	41 Nm
Upper bolt	25 Nm
Steering head bearing adjuster nut	10 Nm
Steering head bearing locknut	40 Nm
Handlebar stem bolt	70 Nm
Front wheel bolts	25 Nm
Front hub nut	90 Nm
Rear hub nut	125 Nm
Disc brake caliper mounting bolts	25 Nm
Brake hose banjo bolt	25 Nm

Engine

Spark plug type	Champion RG 6YC or NGK CR7EB
Electrode gap	0.7 to 0.8 mm
Idle speed (rpm)	1600 to 1700 rpm
Engine oil	5W 40 API SJ synthetic engine oil
Oil capacity	1.0 litre
Bore x stroke	57.0 x 48.6 mm
Piston diameter (standard)	56.93 to 56.96 mm
Piston to bore clearance (standard)	0.040 to 0.054 mm
Piston ring installed end gap (service limit)	
Top ring	0.40 mm
Second ring	0.50 mm
Oil control ring	0.50 mm
Valve clearance	
Intake	0.10 mm
Exhaust	0.15 mm
Camshaft lobe height (standard)	27.8 mm

Ignition system

Source coil resistance	300 to 400 ohms
Pick-up coil resistance	90 to 140 ohms

Transmission

Belt width service limit	21.5 mm
Variator rollers minimum diameter	18.5 mm
Clutch lining thickness	1.0 mm
Clutch spring free length	106 mm
Gearbox oil	SAE 80W/90 API GL4
Gearbox oil capacity	100 ml

Fuel system

Throttle twistgrip freeplay	1 to 3 mm
Main jet	82
Pilot jet	34
Starter jet	48
Needle type / position	52K (2nd/3rd notch from top)
Float height	Bottom edge parallel to gasket face
Automatic choke resistance	approx. 30 ohms @ 20°C

Brakes

Disc brake	
Fluid type	DOT 4
Pad minimum thickness	1.5 mm
Drum brake	
Shoe lining minimum thickness	1.5 mm
Brake lever freeplay	10 to 15 mm

Tyre pressures

Front	19 psi (1.3 bar)
Rear	26 psi (1.8 bar)

Suzuki AN125

Engine

Engine	125 cc single-cylinder four-stroke
Cooling system	Air-cooled
Fuel system	Mikuni BS26SS CV carburettor
Ignition system	CDI
Transmission	Variable speed automatic, belt-driven
Suspension	Telescopic front, swingarm with single shock rear
Brakes	Disc front, drum rear
Tyres	3.50 x 10 front, 3.50 x 10 rear
Wheelbase	1300 mm
Weight (dry)	99 kg
Fuel tank capacity	7.3 litres

Engine

Spark plug type	NGK CR8E
Electrode gap	0.7 to 0.8 mm
Idle speed (rpm)	1500 to 1700 rpm
Engine oil	SAE 10W 40 four-stroke motorcycle oil
Oil capacity	0.9 litres
Bore x stroke	52.0 x 58.6 mm
Piston diameter service limit	51.88 mm
Cylinder bore service limit	52.10 mm
Piston to bore clearance (service limit)	0.120 mm
Piston ring installed end gap (service limit)	0.50 mm
Valve clearance	0.08 to 0.13 mm
Valve spring free length (service limit)	
Inner	29.7 mm
Outer	29.6 mm
Camshaft lobe height (service limit)	
Intake	32.67 mm
Exhaust	32.55 mm

Fuel system

Throttle twistgrip freeplay	3 to 6 mm
Main jet	97.15
Pilot jet	40
Needle type	4CX2 (4th notch from top)
Pilot screw setting	2½
Float height	21.4 mm

Electrical system

Battery	
Capacity	12 V, 10 Ah
Voltage (fully charged)	14 to 15 V
Alternator	
Output (regulated)	13.0 to 16.0 V (DC)
Charging coil resistance	No resistance
Fuse (main)	15 Amps
Bulbs	
Headlight (main/dipped)	30/30 W
Sidelight	5 W
Brake/tail light	21/5 W
Turn signal lights	10 W
Instrument and warning lights	1.7 W
Turn signal warning light	3.4 W
Storage compartment light	2 W

Ignition system

HT coil primary resistance	0.09 to 0.13 ohms
HT coil secondary resistance	11 to 18 K-ohms
Pick-up coil resistance	157 to 235 ohms
Source coil resistance	130 to 195 ohms

Transmission

Belt width (service limit)	18.0 mm
Variator rollers diameter (service limit)	16.4 mm
Clutch lining thickness (service limit)	2.0 mm
Clutch spring free length (service limit)	71.6 mm
Gearbox oil	SAE 10W-40 oil
Gearbox oil capacity	90 ml

Brakes

Disc brake	
Fluid type	DOT 4
Pad minimum thickness	To wear limit indicator
Disc thickness (service limit)	3.5 mm
Drum brake	
Drum internal diameter (service limit)	120.7 mm
Shoe lining minimum thickness	To wear limit indicator
Brake lever freeplay	15 to 25 mm

Tyre pressures

Front	18.0 psi (1.25 bar)
Rear	29.0 psi (2.00 bar)

Torque wrench settings

Valve cover bolts	14 Nm
Camshaft journal holder bolts	10 Nm
Camshaft sprocket bolts	10 Nm
Cylinder head nuts (internal)	23 Nm
Cylinder head nuts (external)	10 Nm
Cylinder base nuts	10 Nm
Cam chain tensioner bolts	10 Nm
Engine mounting bolt	85 Nm
Engine mounting bracket bolt	102 Nm
Exhaust manifold nuts	23 Nm
Exhaust system mounting bolts	23 Nm
Engine oil drain plug	18 Nm
Oil pump drive gear nut	80 Nm
Alternator rotor nut	80 Nm
Variator centre nut	60 Nm
Clutch centre nut	60 Nm
Clutch assembly nut	60 Nm
Gearbox oil filler plug	12 Nm
Gearbox oil drain plug	5.5 Nm
Gearbox cover bolts	10 Nm
Rear shock absorber mountings	
Lower bolt	29 Nm
Upper bolt	29 Nm
Steering head bearing locknut	30 Nm
Handlebar clamp bolt	49 Nm
Handlebar stem bolt	25 Nm
Front axle nut	53 Nm
Front fork leg bottom bolt	23 Nm
Front fork leg clamp bolts	23 Nm
Rear hub nut	75 Nm
Disc brake caliper mounting bolts	26 Nm
Disc mounting bolts	23 Nm
Brake hose banjo bolts	23 Nm

Suzuki AP50

Engine

Engine	49 cc single-cylinder two-stroke
Cooling system	Air-cooled
Fuel system	Mikuni VM 14SH slide carburettor
Ignition system	CDI
Transmission	Variable speed automatic, belt-driven
Suspension	Telescopic front, swingarm with single shock rear
Brakes	Disc front, drum rear
Tyres	90/90 x 10 front, 90/90 x 10 rear
Wheelbase	1195 mm
Weight (dry)	76 kg
Fuel tank capacity	5.0 litres

Engine

Spark plug type	NGK BPR6HS
Electrode gap	0.6 to 0.7 mm
Idle speed (rpm)	1500 to 1900 rpm
Engine oil	JASO FC, SAE 20 semi-synthetic
Oil tank capacity	0.8 litres
Bore x stroke	41.0 x 37.4 mm
Piston diameter service limit	40.885 mm
Piston oversizes available	+ 0.5 and + 1.0 mm
Cylinder bore service limit	41.075 mm
Piston to bore clearance (service limit)	0.120 mm
Piston ring installed end gap (service limit)	0.80 mm

Fuel system

Throttle twistgrip freeplay	3 to 6 mm
Main jet	55
Pilot jet	17.5
Starter jet	25
Needle type / position	3L30 (4th notch from top)
Float height	16 to 18 mm

Tyre pressures

Front	18 psi (1.2 bar)
Rear	25 psi (1.7 bar)

Electrical system

Battery	
Capacity	12 V, 4 Ah
Voltage (fully charged)	14 to 15 V
Alternator	
Output (regulated)	13.0 to 15.0 V (DC)
Charging coil resistance	0.5 to 1.2 ohms
Lighting coil resistance	0.3 to 1.0 ohms
Fuse (main)	10 Amps
Bulbs	
Headlight (main/dipped)	25/25 W
Sidelight	5 W
Brake/tail light	21/5 W
Turn signal lights	10 W
Instrument and warning lights	1.2 W

Ignition system

HT coil secondary resistance	14 to 30 K-ohms
Pick-up coil resistance	170 to 270 ohms

Transmission

Belt width (service limit)	16 mm
Clutch lining thickness (service limit)	2 mm
Clutch spring free length (service limit)	104.5 mm
Gearbox oil	SAE 10W-40 oil
Gearbox oil capacity	90 ml

Brakes

Disc brake	
Fluid type	DOT 4
Pad minimum thickness	To wear limit indicator
Disc thickness	
Standard	4.0 mm
Service limit	3.5 mm
Drum brake	
Drum internal diameter service limit	120.7 mm
Brake shoe lining thickness	
Standard	4 mm
Service limit	1.5 mm
Brake lever freeplay	15 to 25 mm

Torque wrench settings

Cylinder head bolts	10 Nm
Engine mounting bolt	60 Nm
Exhaust manifold nuts	10 Nm
Exhaust system mounting bolts	23 Nm
Oil pump mounting bolts	4 Nm
Alternator rotor nut	40 Nm
Variator centre nut	50 Nm
Clutch centre nut	50 Nm
Clutch assembly nut	50 Nm
Gearbox oil filler plug	12 Nm
Gearbox oil drain plug	5.5 Nm
Rear shock absorber mountings	
Lower bolt	32 Nm
Upper bolt	29 Nm
Steering head bearing locknut	80 Nm
Handlebar stem bolt	25 Nm
Handlebar clamp bolt	49 Nm
Front fork leg clamp bolts	23 Nm
Front axle nut	42 Nm
Rear hub nut	75 Nm
Disc brake caliper mounting bolts	26 Nm
Disc mounting bolts	23 Nm
Brake hose banjo bolts	23 Nm

Suzuki AY50 Katana

Engine

Engine	49 cc single cylinder two-stroke
Cooling system	Air-cooled
Fuel system	Keihin PWS 14 carburettor
Ignition system	CDI
Transmission	Variable speed automatic, belt driven
Suspension	Upside down telescopic front, swingarm with single shock rear
Brakes	disc front, drum rear
Tyres	120/70 x 12 front, 130/70 x 12 rear
Wheelbase	1260 mm
Weight (dry)	77 kg
Fuel tank capacity	6.8 litres

Engine

Spark plug type		
V to Y models		NGK BPR6HS
K1-on models		NGK BPR7HS
Electrode gap		0.6 to 0.7 mm
Idle speed (rpm)		1500 to 1900 rpm
Engine oil		JASO FC, SAE 20 semi-synthetic
Oil tank capacity		1.2 litres
Bore x stroke		41.0 x 37.4 mm
Piston diameter (service limit)		40.885 mm
Piston oversizes available		+ 0.5 and + 1.0 mm
Cylinder diameter (service limit)		41.075 mm
Piston to bore clearance (service limit)		0.120 mm
Piston ring installed end gap (service limit)		0.80 mm

Fuel system

Throttle twistgrip freeplay		
V to W models		3 to 6 mm
X models on		2 to 4 mm
Main jet		
V to K3 models		60
K4-on models		65
Pilot jet		
V to K1 models		45
K2-on models		40
Needle type / position		
V to K2 models		N4VJ (4th notch)
K3-on models		N5GJ (3rd notch)
Pilot screw setting		1¾ turns out
Float level		4.6 to 5.6 mm

Ignition system

HT coil secondary resistance	4 to 10 K-ohms
Pick-up coil resistance	100 to 270 ohms

Transmission

Belt width (service limit)	16 mm
Clutch lining thickness (service limit)	2 mm
Clutch spring free length (service limit)	104.5 mm
Gearbox oil	SAE 10W-40 oil
Gearbox oil capacity	130 ml

Brakes

Disc brake	
Fluid type	DOT 4
Disc thickness:	
Standard	4.0 mm
Service limit	3.5 mm
Drum brake	
drum internal diameter (service limit)	120.7 mm
Brake shoe lining thickness	
Standard	4 mm
Service limit	1.5 mm
Brake lever freeplay	15 to 20 mm

Tyre pressures

Front tyre pressure	18 psi (1.2 bar)
Rear tyre pressure	25 psi (1.7 bar)

Electrical system

Battery	
Capacity	
V to Y models	12 V, 4 Ah
K1 models on	12 V, 3 Ah
Alternator	
Output (regulated)	13.5 to 15.5 V (DC)
Charging coil resistance	
V to Y models	0.1 to 1.2 ohms
K1 models on	0.2 to 1.5 ohms
Fuse (main)	10 Amps
Bulbs	
Headlight (main/dipped)	35/35 W
Sidelight	5 W
Brake/tail light	21/5 W
Turn signal lights	10 W
Instrument and warning lights	1.2 W
Warning lights	2W (highbeam light 1.7W)

Torque wrench settings

Cylinder head bolts	10 Nm
Alternator rotor nut	40 Nm
Engine mounting bolt	60 Nm
Exhaust manifold nuts	10 Nm
Oil pump mounting bolts	4 Nm
Variator centre nut	50 Nm
Clutch centre nut	50 Nm
Clutch assembly nut	50 Nm
Gearbox oil filler plug	12 Nm
Gearbox oil drain plug	5.5 Nm
Rear shock absorber mountings	
Lower bolt	35 Nm
Upper bolt	29 Nm
Steering head bearing locknut	30 Nm
Handlebar stem bolt	50 Nm
Front axle nut	42 Nm
Rear hub nut	75 Nm
Disc brake caliper mounting bolts	26 Nm
Disc mounting bolts	23 Nm
Brake hose banjo bolts	23 Nm

Engine

Engine	49 cc single cylinder two-stroke
Cooling system	Liquid cooled
Fuel system	Keihin PWS 12 carburettor
Ignition system	CDI

Transmission

Transmission	Variable ration automatic (CVT)

Suspension

Suspension	Inverted telescopic, coil spring front, swingarm coil spring oil damped rear

Brakes

Brakes	disc front (all models), drum rear (WW models), disc rear (WX–on models)

Tyres	120/70 x 12 front, 130/70 x 12 rear
Wheelbase	1260 mm
Weight (dry)	83 kg
Fuel tank capacity	6.8 litres

Engine

Spark plug type	NGK BPR6HS
Electrode gap	0.6 to 0.7 mm
Idle speed (rpm)	
WW to WK2 models	1500 to 1900 rpm
WK3 onward	1700 to 2100 rpm
Engine oil	Suzuki CCI super oil or equivalent
Oil tank capacity	1.2 litres
Bore x stroke	41.0 x 37.4 mm
Piston diameter (service limit)	40.890 mm
Piston to bore clearance (service limit)	0.120 mm
Cylinder diameter (service limit)	41.105 mm
Piston ring installed end gap (service limit)	0.80 mm
Coolant	50:50 distilled water and ethylene glycol anti-freeze

Fuel system

Throttle twistgrip freeplay	
WW models	3 to 6 mm
WX–on models	2 to 4 mm
Main jet	
WW to WK2 modles	60
WK3–on models	62
Pilot jet	45
Needle type / position	
WW to WK2 models	N4WA (3rd notch from top)
WK3–on models	N5GJ (2nd notch from top)
Pilot screw setting	
WW to WK2 models	1¾ turns out
WK3–on models	1½ turns out
Float level	4.6 to 5.6 mm

Tyre pressures

Front tyre pressure	18 psi (1.2 bar)
Rear tyre pressure	25 psi (1.7 bar)

Electrical system

Battery	
Capacity	12 V, 3 Ah
Alternator	
Output (regulated)	13.5 to 15.5 V (DC)
Charging coil resistance	0.2 to 1.5 ohms
Fuse (main)	10 Amps
Bulbs	
Headlight (main/dipped)	15 W
Sidelight	3 W
Brake/tail light	21/5 W
Turn signal lights	10 W
Instrument and warning lights	1.2 W
Warning lights	2 W (high beam light 1.7 W)

Ignition system

HT coil secondary resistance	4 to 10 K-ohms
Pick-up coil resistance	100 to 270 ohms

Transmission

Belt width (service limit)	
WW models	16 mm
WX onwards	17.4 mm
Clutch lining thickness (service limit)	2 mm
Clutch spring free length (service limit)	104.5 mm
Gearbox oil	SAE 10W–40 oil
Gearbox oil capacity	130 ml

Brakes

Disc brake	
Fluid type	DOT 4
Disc thickness:	
Standard	4.0 mm
Service limit	3.5 mm
Drum brake	
drum internal diameter (service limit)	120.7 mm
Brake shoe lining thickness	
Standard	4 mm
Service limit	1.5 mm
Brake lever freeplay	15 to 20 mm

Torque wrench settings

Cylinder head bolts	10 Nm
Alternator rotor nut	40 Nm
Engine mounting bolt	60 Nm
Exhaust manifold nuts	10 Nm
Oil pump mounting bolts	4 Nm
Variator centre nut	50 Nm
Clutch centre nut	50 Nm
Clutch assembly nut	50 Nm
Gearbox oil filler plug	12 Nm
Gearbox oil drain plug	5.5 Nm
Rear shock absorber mountings	
Lower bolt	35 Nm
Upper bolt	29 Nm
Steering head bearing locknut	30 Nm
Handlebar stem bolt	50 Nm
Front axle nut	42 Nm
Rear hub nut	75 Nm
Disc brake caliper mounting bolts	26 Nm
Disc mounting bolts	23 Nm
Brake hose banjo bolts	23 Nm

Suzuki UH125 Burgman

Electrical system

Battery	
Capacity	12 V, 10 Ah
Voltage (fully charged)	14 to 15 V
Alternator	
Output (regulated)	13.5 to 15.0 V (DC)
Charging coil resistance	0.50 to 0.62 ohms
Fuse (main)	20 Amps
Bulbs	
Headlight (main/dipped)	35/35 W
Sidelight	5 W
Brake/tail light	21/5 W
Turn signal lights	21 W
Instrument and warning lights	1.2 W
Storage compartment light	5 W

Torque wrench settings

Valve cover bolts	14 Nm
Camshaft journal holder bolt	10 Nm
Camshaft sprocket bolt	15 Nm
Cylinder head nuts	10 Nm
Cylinder head bolts	42 Nm
Cylinder base nuts	10 Nm
Crankcase bolts	
M8	Initial 13 Nm, final 22 Nm
M6	11 Nm
Engine mounting bolt	102 Nm
Engine mounting bracket bolt	85 Nm
Exhaust manifold nuts	23 Nm
Exhaust system mounting bolts	23 Nm
Engine oil drain plug	23 Nm
Water pump mounting bolts	10 Nm
Oil pump mounting bolts	10 Nm
Alternator rotor nut	80 Nm
Variator centre nut	90 Nm
Clutch centre nut	60 Nm
Clutch assembly nut	60 Nm
Gearbox oil filler plug	12 Nm
Gearbox oil drain plug	12 Nm
Gearbox cover bolts	22 Nm
Rear shock absorber mountings	
Lower and upper bolt	29 Nm
Steering head bearing locknut	30 Nm
Handlebar clamp bolt	50 Nm
Handlebar stem bolt	25 Nm
Front axle nut	44 Nm
Front fork leg bottom bolt	18 Nm
Front fork leg clamp bolts	23 Nm
Rear hub nut	75 Nm
Disc brake caliper mounting bolts	25 Nm
Disc mounting bolts	23 Nm
Brake hose banjo bolts	23 Nm

Engine

Engine	125 cc single-cylinder four-stroke
Cooling system	Liquid-cooled
Fuel system	Keihin CVK 24 CV carburettor
Ignition system	CDI
Transmission	Variable speed automatic, belt-driven
Suspension	Telescopic front, swingarm with twin adjustable shock rear
Brakes	Disc front, disc rear and drum parking brake
Tyres	110/90 x 12 front, 130/70 x 12 rear
Wheelbase	1450 mm
Weight (dry)	139 kg
Fuel tank capacity	10.0 litres

Ignition system

HT coil primary resistance	0.09 to 0.13 ohms
HT coil secondary resistance	15.4 to 18.1 K-ohms
Pick-up coil resistance	148 to 222 ohms

Engine

Spark plug type	NGK CR8E
Electrode gap	0.7 to 0.8 mm
Idle speed (rpm)	1500 to 1700 rpm
Engine oil	SAE 10W 40 four-stroke motorcycle oil
Oil capacity	1.5 litres
Bore x stroke	57.0 x 48.8 mm
Piston diameter service limit	56.88 mm
Cylinder bore service limit	57.09 mm
Piston to bore clearance (service limit)	0.120 mm
Piston ring installed end gap (service limit)	0.70 mm
Valve clearance	
Intake	0.05 to 0.10 mm
Exhaust	0.10 to 0.15 mm
Valve spring free length (service limit)	
Inner	35.0 mm
Outer	37.8 mm
Camshaft lobe height (service limit)	
Intake	32.16 mm
Exhaust	31.62 mm
Coolant	50% distilled water, 50% corrosion inhibiting ethylene glycol anti-freeze
Coolant capacity	1.25 litres

Transmission

Belt width (service limit)	21.1 mm
Clutch lining thickness (service limit)	2 mm
Clutch spring free length (service limit)	142.5 mm
Gearbox oil	SAE 10W-40 oil
Gearbox oil capacity	130 ml

Brakes

Disc brake	
Fluid type	DOT 4
Pad minimum thickness	1.0 mm
Disc thickness	
Standard	3.8 to 4.2 mm
Service limit	3.5 mm
Parking drum brake	
Drum internal diameter service limit	130.7 mm
Brake shoe lining thickness	
Standard	4 mm
Service limit	1.5 mm
Brake lever freeplay	15 to 25 mm

Fuel system

Throttle twistgrip freeplay	2 to 4 mm
Main jet	115
Pilot jet	35
Needle type	NCHA
Pilot screw setting	fixed
Float height	15 to 17 mm
Fuel level	6 to 8 mm

Tyre pressures

Front	29 psi (2.00 bar)
Rear	33 psi (2.25 bar)

Sym DD50 City Trek

Engine

Engine	49 cc single-cylinder two-stroke
Cooling system	Air-cooled
Fuel system	PB2BE slide carburettor
Ignition system	CDI
Transmission	Variable speed automatic, belt-driven
Suspension	Telescopic front, swingarm with single shock rear
Brakes	110 drum/160 mm disc front, 95 mm drum rear
Tyres	100/90 x 10 front, 100/90 x 10 rear
Wheelbase	1155 mm
Weight (dry)	80 kg
Fuel tank capacity	7.5 litres

Engine

Spark plug type	NGK BR8HSA
Electrode gap	0.6 to 0.7 mm
Idle speed (rpm)	2000 rpm
Engine oil	JASO FC, SAE 20 semi-synthetic
Oil tank capacity	1.2 litres
Bore x stroke	39.0 x 41.4 mm
Piston diameter (service limit)	38.935 mm
Cylinder diameter (service limit)	39.050 mm
Piston to bore clearance	
Standard	0.04 to 0.05 mm
Service limit	0.10 mm
Piston ring installed end gap	
Standard	0.10 to 0.25 mm
Service limit	0.40 mm

Fuel system

Throttle twistgrip freeplay	2 to 6 mm
Main jet	82
Pilot screw setting	1¾ turns out
Float height	8.6 mm
Automatic choke resistance	approx. 10 ohms @ 20°C

Ignition system

HT coil primary resistance	0.19 to 0.23 K-ohms
HT coil secondary resistance	5.0 to 6.2 K-ohms
Spark plug cap resistance	3.1 to 3.2 K-ohms
Pick-up coil resistance	50 to 200 ohms

Transmission

Belt width	
Standard	18.0 mm
Service limit	16.5 mm
Variator rollers	
Standard diameter	15.92 to 16.08 mm
Service limit	15.40 mm
Clutch lining thickness (service limit)	2.0 mm
Clutch spring free length (service limit)	92.7 mm
Gearbox oil	SAE 140 hypoid gear oil
Gearbox oil capacity	100 ml

Brakes

Disc brake	
Fluid type	DOT 4
Pad minimum thickness	2.0 mm
Disc thickness	
Standard	3.5 mm
Service limit	2.0 mm
Drum brake	
Brake shoe lining thickness	
Standard	4.0 mm
Service limit	2.0 mm
Brake lever freeplay	10 to 20 mm

Tyre pressures

Front	22 psi (1.50 bar)
Rear	33 psi (2.25 bar)

Electrical system

Battery	
Capacity	12 V, 3 Ah
Voltage (fully charged)	13 to 13.2 V
Alternator	
Output (regulated)	14 to 15 V (DC)
Charging coil resistance	0.2 to 1.0 ohms
Lighting coil resistance	0.2 to 0.8 ohms
Fuse (main)	7 Amps
Bulbs	
Headlight (main/dipped)	35/35 W
Sidelight	3 W
Brake/tail light	18/5 W
Turn signal lights	10 W
Instrument and warning lights	3 W

Torque wrench settings

Cylinder head bolts	10 Nm
Crankcase bolts	10 Nm
Engine mounting bolts	60 Nm
Inlet manifold bolts	10 Nm
Exhaust manifold nuts	12 Nm
Exhaust system mounting bolts	32 Nm
Alternator rotor nut	38 Nm
Alternator stator bolts	10 Nm
Variator centre nut	38 Nm
Clutch centre nut	38 Nm
Clutch assembly nut	55 Nm
Gearbox oil drain plug	13 Nm
Rear shock absorber mounting	
Lower bolt	27 Nm
Upper bolt	40 Nm
Steering head bearing locknut	70 Nm
Handlebar stem bolt	50 Nm
Front fork leg clamp bolts	25 Nm
Front axle nut	60 Nm
Rear hub nut	110 Nm
Front and rear wheel bolts	25 Nm
Disc brake caliper mounting bolts	30 Nm
Disc mounting bolts	44 Nm
Brake hose banjo bolts	34 Nm

Sym Jet 50 and 100

Data 76

Engine
Engine	49 cc and 101 cc single-cylinder two-stroke
Cooling system	Air-cooled
Fuel system	PB2BE slide carburettor
Ignition system	CDI
Transmission	Variable speed automatic, belt-driven
Suspension	Telescopic front, swingarm with single shock rear
Brakes	273 mm disc front, 130 mm drum rear
Tyres	100/90 x 12 front, 130/70 x 12 rear
Wheelbase	1273 mm
Weight	94 and 97 kg
Fuel tank capacity	6.3 litres

Engine
Spark plug type	
50 cc	NGK BR8HSA
100 cc	NGKBR6HSA
Electrode gap	0.6 to 0.7 mm
Idle speed	2000 rpm
Engine oil	JASO FC, SAE 20 semi-synthetic
Oil tank capacity	1.2 litres
Bore x stroke	
50 cc	39 x 41.4 mm
100 cc	51 x 49.6 mm
Piston diameter service limit	
50 cc	38.935 mm
100 cc	50.935 mm
Cylinder bore service limit	
50 cc	39.050 mm
100 cc	51.050 mm
Piston to bore clearance (service limit)	0.10 mm
Piston ring installed end gap	
Standard	0.10 to 0.25 mm
Service limit	0.40 mm

Fuel system
Throttle twistgrip freeplay	2 to 6 mm
Pilot screw setting	1⅜ turns out
Float height	8.8 mm
Automatic choke resistance	approx. 10 ohms @ 20°C

Tyre pressures
Front	25 psi (1.75 bar)
Rear	29 psi (2.00 bar)

Electrical system
Battery	
Capacity	12 V, 5 Ah
Voltage (fully charged)	13 to 13.2 V
Alternator	
Output (regulated)	14 to 15 V (DC)
Charging coil resistance	0.2 to 1.0 ohms
Lighting coil resistance	0.1 to 0.8 ohms
Fuse (main)	7 Amps
Bulbs	
Headlight (main/dipped)	35/35 W
Sidelight	5 W
Brake/tail light	21/5 W
Turn signal lights	10 W
Instrument and warning lights	3 W

Ignition system
HT coil primary resistance	0.19 to 0.23 K-ohms
HT coil secondary resistance	3.6 to 3.9 K-ohms
Spark plug cap resistance	4.3 to 5.7 K-ohms
Pick-up coil resistance	50 to 200 ohms

Transmission
Belt width	
Standard	18.0 mm
Service limit	16.5 mm
Variator rollers	
Standard diameter	15.92 to 16.08 mm
Service limit	15.40 mm
Clutch lining thickness (service limit)	2.0 mm
Clutch spring free length (service limit)	82.5 mm
Gearbox oil	SAE 140 hypoid gear oil
Gearbox oil capacity	120 ml

Brakes
Disc brake	
Fluid type	DOT 4
Pad minimum thickness	2.0 mm
Disc thickness	
Standard	4.0 mm
Service limit	3.5 mm
Drum brake	
Brake shoe lining thickness	
Standard	4.0 mm
Service limit	2.0 mm
Brake lever freeplay	10 to 20 mm

Torque wrench settings
Cylinder head bolts	20 Nm
Crankcase bolts	15 Nm
Engine mounting bolt	55 Nm
Inlet manifold bolts	12 Nm
Exhaust manifold nuts	14 Nm
Exhaust system mounting bolts	32 Nm
Alternator rotor nut	45 Nm
Alternator stator bolts	10 Nm
Variator centre nut	60 Nm
Starter clutch centre nut	45 Nm
Clutch centre nut	45 Nm
Clutch assembly nut	60 Nm
Gearbox oil drain plug	13 Nm
Rear shock absorber mounting	
Lower bolt	30 Nm
Upper bolt	45 Nm
Steering head bearing locknut	50 Nm
Handlebar stem bolt	50 Nm
Front axle nut	70 Nm
Rear hub nut	130 Nm
Wheel rim nuts	25 Nm
Disc brake caliper mounting bolts	35 Nm
Disc mounting bolts	22 Nm
Brake hose banjo bolts	40 Nm

Sym Shark 50

Engine

Engine	49 cc single-cylinder two-stroke
Cooling system	Air-cooled
Fuel system	PB2BE slide carburettor
Ignition system	CDI
Transmission	Variable speed automatic, belt-driven
Suspension	Telescopic front, swingarm with single shock rear
Brakes	273 mm disc front, 130 mm drum rear
Tyres	100/90 x 12 front, 130/70 x 12 rear
Wheelbase	1335 mm
Weight	112 kg
Fuel tank capacity	7.5 litres

Engine

Spark plug type	NGK BR8HSA
Electrode gap	0.6 to 0.7 mm
Idle speed (rpm)	2000 rpm
Engine oil	JASO FC, SAE 20 semi-synthetic
Oil tank capacity	1.2 litres
Bore x stroke	39.0 x 41.4 mm
Piston diameter (service limit)	38.935 mm
Cylinder diameter (service limit)	39.050 mm
Piston to bore clearance	
Standard	0.04 to 0.05 mm
Service limit	0.10 mm
Piston ring installed end gap	
Standard	0.10 to 0.25 mm
Service limit	0.40 mm

Fuel system

Throttle twistgrip freeplay	2 to 6 mm
Pilot screw setting	1⅜ turns out
Float height	8.8 mm
Automatic choke resistance	approx. 10 ohms @ 20°C

Tyre pressures

Front	22 psi (1.50 bar)
Rear	25 psi (1.75 bar)

Electrical system

Battery	
Capacity	12 V, 4 Ah
Voltage (fully charged)	13 to 13.2 V
Alternator	
Output (regulated)	14 to 15 V (DC)
Charging coil resistance	0.2 to 1.0 ohms
Lighting coil resistance	0.1 to 0.8 ohms
Fuse (main)	7 Amps
Bulbs	
Headlight (main/dipped)	35/35 W
Sidelight	5 W
Brake/tail light	21/5 W
Turn signal lights	10 W
Instrument and warning lights	3 W and LEDs

Ignition system

HT coil primary resistance	0.19 to 0.23 K-ohms
HT coil secondary resistance	3.6 to 3.9 K-ohms
Spark plug cap resistance	4.3 to 5.7 K-ohms
Pick-up coil resistance	50 to 200 ohms

Transmission

Belt width	
Standard	18.0 mm
Service limit	16.5 mm
Variator rollers	
Standard diameter	15.92 to 16.08 mm
Service limit	15.40 mm
Clutch lining thickness	
(service limit)	2.0 mm
Clutch spring free length	
(service limit)	82.5 mm
Gearbox oil	SAE 140 hypoid gear oil
Gearbox oil capacity	120 ml

Brakes

Disc brake	
Fluid type	DOT 4
Pad minimum thickness	2.0 mm
Disc thickness	
Standard	3.5 mm
Service limit	2.0 mm
Drum brake	
Brake shoe lining thickness	
Standard	4.0 mm
Service limit	2.0 mm
Brake lever freeplay	10 to 20 mm

Torque wrench settings

Cylinder head bolts	20 Nm
Crankcase bolts	15 Nm
Engine mounting bolt	55 Nm
Inlet manifold bolts	12 Nm
Exhaust manifold nuts	14 Nm
Exhaust system mounting bolts	32 Nm
Alternator rotor nut	45 Nm
Alternator stator bolts	10 Nm
Variator centre nut	60 Nm
Starter clutch centre nut	45 Nm
Clutch centre nut	45 Nm
Clutch assembly nut	60 Nm
Gearbox oil drain plug	13 Nm
Rear shock absorber mounting	
Lower bolt	30 Nm
Upper bolt	45 Nm
Steering head bearing locknut	50 Nm
Handlebar stem bolt	50 Nm
Front axle nut	70 Nm
Rear hub nut	130 Nm
Wheel rim nuts	25 Nm
Disc brake caliper mounting bolts	35 Nm
Disc mounting bolts	22 Nm
Brake hose banjo bolts	40 Nm

Sym Super Fancy and City Hopper

Engine	
Engine	49 cc single-cylinder two-stroke
Cooling system	Air-cooled
Fuel system	PB2BE slide carburettor
Ignition system	CDI
Transmission	Variable speed automatic, belt-driven
Suspension	Trailing link front, swingarm with single shock rear
Brakes	110 drum/160 mm disc front, 110 mm drum rear
Tyres	100/90 x 10 front, 100/90 x 10 rear
Wheelbase	1210 mm
Weight (dry)	79 kg
Fuel tank capacity	6.5 litres

Engine	
Spark plug type	NGK BR8HSA
Electrode gap	0.6 to 0.7 mm
Idle speed (rpm)	2000 rpm
Engine oil	JASO FC, SAE 20 semi-synthetic
Oil tank capacity	1.2 litres
Bore x stroke	39.0 x 41.4 mm
Piston diameter (service limit)	38.935 mm
Cylinder diameter (service limit)	39.050 mm
Piston to bore clearance	
Standard	0.04 to 0.05 mm
Service limit	0.10 mm
Piston ring installed end gap	
Standard	0.10 to 0.25 mm
Service limit	0.40 mm

Fuel system	
Throttle twistgrip freeplay	2 to 6 mm
Pilot screw setting	1⅜ turns out
Float height	8.8 mm
Automatic choke resistance	approx. 10 ohms @ 20°C

Tyre pressures	
Front	22 psi (1.50 bar)
Rear	25 psi (1.75 bar)

Electrical system	
Battery	
Capacity	12 V, 4 Ah
Voltage (fully charged)	13 to 13.2 V
Alternator	
Output (regulated)	14 to 15 V (DC)
Charging coil resistance	0.2 to 1.0 ohms
Lighting coil resistance	0.1 to 0.8 ohms
Fuse (main)	7 Amps
Bulbs	
Headlight (main/dipped)	35/35 W
Sidelight	3 W
Brake/tail light	18/5 W
Turn signal lights	10 W
Instrument and warning lights	3 W and LEDs

Ignition system	
HT coil primary resistance	0.19 to 0.23 K-ohms
HT coil secondary resistance	3.6 to 3.9 K-ohms
Spark plug cap resistance	4.3 to 5.7 K-ohms
Pick-up coil resistance	50 to 200 ohms

Transmission	
Belt width	
Standard	18.0 mm
Service limit	16.5 mm
Variator rollers	
Standard diameter	15.92 to 16.08 mm
Service limit	15.40 mm
Clutch lining thickness	
(service limit)	2.0 mm
Clutch spring free length	
(service limit)	82.5 mm
Gearbox oil	SAE 140 hypoid gear oil
Gearbox oil capacity	120 ml

Brakes	
Disc brake	
Fluid type	DOT 4
Pad minimum thickness	2.0 mm
Disc thickness	
Standard	3.5 mm
Service limit	2.0 mm
Drum brake	
Brake shoe lining thickness	
Standard	4.0 mm
Service limit	2.0 mm
Brake lever freeplay	10 to 20 mm

Torque wrench settings	
Cylinder head bolts	20 Nm
Crankcase bolts	15 Nm
Engine mounting bolt	55 Nm
Inlet manifold bolts	12 Nm
Exhaust manifold nuts	14 Nm
Exhaust system mounting bolts	32 Nm
Alternator rotor nut	45 Nm
Alternator stator bolts	10 Nm
Variator centre nut	60 Nm
Starter clutch centre nut	45 Nm
Clutch centre nut	45 Nm
Clutch assembly nut	60 Nm
Gearbox oil drain plug	13 Nm
Rear shock absorber mounting	
Lower bolt	30 Nm
Upper bolt	45 Nm
Steering head bearing locknut	50 Nm
Handlebar stem bolt	50 Nm
Front suspension bolts	30 Nm
Front axle nut	70 Nm
Rear hub nut	130 Nm
Wheel rim nuts	25 Nm
Disc brake caliper mounting bolts	35 Nm
Disc mounting bolts	22 Nm
Brake hose banjo bolts	40 Nm

Vespa ET2 50

Engine no. prefix	C161M
Frame no. prefix	ZAPC16
Engine	49 cc single-cylinder two-stroke
Cooling system	Air-cooled
Fuel system	Weber 12 OM slide carburettor
Ignition system	CDI
Transmission	Variable speed automatic, belt-driven
Suspension	Trailing link front, swingarm with single shock rear
Brakes	Disc front, drum rear
Tyres	100/80 x 10 front, 120/70 x 10 rear
Wheelbase	1260 mm
Weight (dry)	71 kg
Fuel tank capacity	8.6 litres

Engine

Spark plug type	Champion N2C or NGK B9ES
Electrode gap	0.5 to 0.6 mm
Idle speed (rpm)	1600 to 1800 rpm
Engine oil	Two-stroke injector oil
Oil tank capacity	1.35 litres
Bore x stroke	40.0 x 39.3 mm
Piston diameter (standard)	39.94 to 39.96 mm
Piston to bore clearance (standard)	0.045 to 0.055 mm
Piston ring installed end gap (standard)	0.10 to 0.25 mm

Fuel system

Throttle twistgrip freeplay	1 to 3 mm
Main jet	76
Pilot jet	34
Starter jet	50
Needle type / position	V (2nd notch from top)
Pilot screw setting	2½ to 3½
Float height	3.5 mm (not adjustable)
Automatic choke resistance	approx. 30.0 to 40.0 ohms @ 20°C

Ignition system

Source coil resistance	850 to 1050 ohms
Pick-up coil resistance	100 to 130 ohms

Transmission

Belt width service limit	17.5 mm
Variator rollers minimum diameter	18.5 mm
Clutch spring free length	110 mm
Gearbox oil	SAE 80W/90 API GL4
Gearbox oil capacity	75 ml

Brakes

Disc brake	
Fluid type	DOT 4
Pad minimum thickness	1.5 mm
Drum brake	
Shoe lining minimum thickness	1.5 mm
Brake lever freeplay	10 to 15 mm

Tyre pressures

Front	19 psi (1.3 bar)
Rear	26 psi (1.8 bar)

Electrical system

Battery	
Capacity	12 V, 4 Ah
Alternator	
Output (unregulated)	25 to 30 V (AC)
Fuse (main)	7.5 Amps
Bulbs	
Headlight (main/dipped)	35/35 W
Sidelight	5 W
Brake/tail light	21/5 W
Turn signal lights	10 W
Instrument and warning lights	1.2 W

Torque wrench settings

Cylinder head nuts	11 Nm
Crankcase bolts	13 Nm
Engine mounting bolt	41 Nm
Exhaust manifold nuts	11 Nm
Exhaust system mounting bolts	24 Nm
Oil pump mounting bolts	4 Nm
Alternator rotor nut	44 Nm
Alternator stator bolts	4 Nm
Variator centre nut	44 Nm
Clutch centre nut	44 Nm
Clutch assembly nut	60 Nm
Gearbox oil filler plug	5 Nm
Gearbox cover bolts	13 Nm
Front shock absorber mountings	10 Nm
Rear shock absorber mountings	
Lower bolt	41 Nm
Upper bolt	25 Nm
Steering head bearing adjuster nut	10 Nm
Steering head bearing locknut	40 Nm
Handlebar stem bolt	50 Nm
Front wheel bolts	25 Nm
Front hub nut	90 Nm
Rear hub nut	110 Nm
Disc brake caliper mounting bolts	25 Nm
Brake hose banjo bolt	25 Nm

Vespa ET4 50

Engine no. prefix
Engine no. prefix	C261M
Frame no. prefix	ZAPC26

Engine
Cooling system	Air-cooled
Fuel system	Keihin CVK 18 carburettor
Ignition system	CDI

Transmission
	Variable speed automatic, belt driven

Suspension
	Trailing link front, swingarm with single shock rear

Brakes	Disc front, drum rear
Tyres	100/80 x 10 front, 120/70 x 10 rear
Wheelbase	1275 mm
Weight (dry)	105 kg
Fuel tank capacity	9.0 litres

Engine
Spark plug type	Champion RG4 PHP
Electrode gap	0.7 to 0.8 mm
Idle speed (rpm)	1900 to 2000 rpm
Engine oil	5W40 API SJ synthetic oil
Oil capacity	850 ml
Bore x stroke	39.0 x 41.8 mm
Piston diameter (standard)	38.95 to 38.98 mm
Piston to bore clearance (standard)	0.025 to 0.039 mm
Piston ring installed end gap	
Top ring	0.08 to 0.20 mm
Second ring	0.05 to 0.20 mm
Oil control ring	0.02 to 0.70 mm
Valve clearance	
Intake	0.10 mm
Exhaust	0.15 mm
Valve spring free length	Not available
Camshaft height (standard)	25.935 mm

Fuel system
Throttle twistgrip freeplay	1 to 3 mm
Main jet	75
Pilot jet	35
Starter jet	42
Needle type / position	NACA
Automatic choke resistance	6 ohms ± 5%

Electrical system
Battery		
Capacity		12 V, 9 Ah
Alternator		
Output (unregulated)		25 to 30 V (AC)
Fuse (main)		10 Amps
Bulbs		
Headlight (main/dipped)		35/35 W
Sidelight		5 W
Brake/tail light		21/5 W
Turn signal lights		10 W
Instrument and warning lights		1.2 W

Ignition system
Source coil resistance	850 to 1050 ohms
Pick-up coil resistance	100 to 130 ohms

Transmission
Belt width service limit	17.5 mm
Variator rollers minimum diameter	18.5 mm
Clutch lining minimum thickness	1.0 mm
Clutch spring free length	118 mm
Gearbox oil	SAE 80W/90 API GL4
Gearbox oil capacity	80 ml

Brakes
Disc brake	
Fluid type	DOT 4
Pad minimum thickness	1.5 mm
Drum brake	
Shoe lining minimum thickness	1.5 mm
Brake lever freeplay	10 to 15 mm

Tyre pressures
Front	19 psi (1.3 bar)
Rear	26 psi (1.8 bar)

Torque wrench settings
Valve cover bolts	8 to 10 Nm
Cylinder head nuts	
Initial setting	6 to 7 Nm
Final setting	+90° +90°
Cylinder head bolts	8 to 10 Nm
Cam chain tensioner bolts	8 to 10 Nm
Camshaft sprocket bolt	12 to 14 Nm
Engine mounting bolt	33 to 41 Nm
Exhaust manifold nuts	11 Nm
Exhaust system mounting bolts	24 Nm
Engine oil drain plug	25 to 28 Nm
Oil pump sprocket bolt	14 Nm
Oil pump mounting bolts	5 to 6 Nm
Alternator rotor nut	40 to 44 Nm
Alternator stator bolts	3 to 4 Nm
Variator centre nut	18 to 20 Nm
	+90°
Clutch centre nut	40 to 44 Nm
Clutch assembly nut	55 to 60 Nm
Crankcase bolts	8 to 10 Nm
Gearbox oil drain plug	3 to 5 Nm
Gearbox cover bolts	11 to 13 Nm
Front shock absorber mountings	20 to 27 Nm
Rear shock absorber mountings	
Lower bolt	33 to 41 Nm
Upper bolt	20 to 25 Nm
Steering head bearing adjuster nut	8 to 10 Nm
Steering head bearing locknut	30 to 40 Nm
Handlebar stem bolt	45 to 50 Nm
Front wheel bolts	20 to 25 Nm
Front hub nut	75 to 90 Nm
Rear hub nut	115 to 125 Nm
Disc brake caliper mounting bolts	20 to 25 Nm
Brake hose banjo bolt	20 to 25 Nm

Vespa ET4 125 1996 to 1998

Engine no. prefix	MO41M
Frame no. prefix	ZAP MO4
Engine	125 cc single-cylinder four-stroke
Cooling system	Air-cooled
Fuel system	Mikuni BS24 CV carburettor
Ignition system	CDI
Transmission	Variable speed automatic, belt-driven
Suspension	Trailing link front, swingarm with single shock rear
Brakes	Disc front, drum rear
Tyres	100/80 x 10 front, 120/70 x 10 rear
Wheelbase	1275 mm
Weight	109 kg
Fuel tank capacity	9.0 litres

Engine

Spark plug type	Champion RG4 HC or NGK CR8E
Electrode gap	0.7 to 0.8 mm
Idle speed (rpm)	1570 to 1630 rpm
Engine oil	20W synthetic engine oil
Oil capacity	0.85 litres
Bore x stroke	57.0 x 48.6 mm
Piston diameter (standard)	56.93 to 56.95 mm
Piston to bore clearance (standard)	0.050 to 0.060 mm
Piston ring installed end gap (service limit)	
Top ring	0.50 mm
Second ring	0.40 mm
Oil control ring	0.50 mm
Valve clearance	0.15 mm
Valve spring free length (service limit)	29.5 mm

Fuel system

Throttle twistgrip freeplay	1 to 3 mm
Main jet	87.5
Pilot jet	20
Starter jet	35
Needle type / position	4CZ6 (2nd notch from top)
Float height	12.2 mm
Automatic choke resistance	approx. 30.0 to 40.0 ohms @ 20°C

Electrical system

Battery	
Capacity	12 V, 9 Ah
Alternator	
Output (unregulated)	25 to 30 V (AC)
Fuse (main)	7.5 Amps
Bulbs	
Headlight (main/dipped)	35/35 W
Sidelight	5 W
Brake/tail light	21/5 W
Turn signal lights	10 W
Instrument and warning lights	1.2 W

Ignition system

Source coil resistance	300 to 400 ohms
Pick-up coil resistance	90 to 140 ohms

Transmission

Belt width service limit	17.2 mm
Variator rollers minimum diameter	21.9 mm
Clutch lining minimum thickness	1.0 mm
Clutch spring free length	127 mm
Gearbox oil	SAE 80W/90 API GL4
Gearbox oil capacity	90 ml

Brakes

Disc brake	
Fluid type	DOT 4
Pad minimum thickness	1.5 mm
Drum brake	
Shoe lining minimum thickness	1.5 mm
Brake lever freeplay	10 to 15 mm

Tyre pressures

Front	19 psi (1.3 bar)
Rear	26 psi (1.8 bar)

Torque wrench settings

Valve cover bolts	12 Nm
Cylinder head nuts	29 Nm
Cylinder head bolt	13 Nm
Cam chain tensioner bolts	10 Nm
Camshaft sprocket bolt	13 Nm
Engine mounting bolt	41 Nm
Exhaust manifold nuts	11 Nm
Exhaust system mounting bolts	27 Nm
Engine oil drain plug	30 Nm
Oil pump sprocket bolt	13 Nm
Oil pump mounting bolts	6 Nm
Alternator rotor nut	58 Nm
Alternator stator bolts	4 Nm
Variator centre nut	83 Nm
Clutch centre nut	50 Nm
Clutch assembly nut	60 Nm
Crankcase bolts	13 Nm
Gearbox oil filler plug	5 Nm
Gearbox oil drain plug	17 Nm
Gearbox cover bolts	13 Nm
Front shock absorber mountings	25 Nm
Rear shock absorber mountings	
Lower bolt	41 Nm
Upper bolt	25 Nm
Steering head bearing adjuster nut	10 Nm
Steering head bearing locknut	40 Nm
Handlebar stem bolt	50 Nm
Front wheel bolts	25 Nm
Front hub nut	90 Nm
Rear hub nut	125 Nm
Disc brake caliper mounting bolts	25 Nm
Brake hose banjo bolt	25 Nm

Vespa ET4 125 with LEADER engine (1999-on)

Engine no. prefix	MO41M
Frame no. prefix	ZAP M19
Engine	
	125 cc single-cylinder four-stroke
Cooling system	Air-cooled
Fuel system	Walbro WVF 6B CV carburettor
Ignition system	CDI
Transmission	Variable speed automatic, belt-driven
Suspension	Trailing link front, swingarm with single adjustable shock rear
Brakes	Disc front, drum rear
Tyres	100/80 x 10 front, 120/70 x 10 rear
Wheelbase	1275 mm
Weight	109 kg
Fuel tank capacity	9.0 litres

Engine

Spark plug type	Champion RG4 HC or NGK CR8E
Electrode gap	0.7 to 0.8 mm
Idle speed (rpm)	1600 to 1700 rpm
Engine oil	5W 40 API SJ synthetic engine oil
Oil capacity	1.0 litre
Bore x stroke	57.0 x 48.6 mm
Piston diameter (standard)	56.93 to 56.96 mm
Piston to bore clearance (standard)	0.040 to 0.054 mm
Piston ring installed end gap (service limit)	
Top ring	0.40 mm
Second ring	0.50 mm
Oil control ring	0.50 mm
Valve clearance	
Intake	0.10 mm
Exhaust	0.15 mm
Camshaft lobe height (standard)	27.8 mm

Fuel system

Throttle twistgrip freeplay	1 to 3 mm
Main jet	84
Pilot jet	33
Starter jet	48
Needle type / position	DCK (2nd notch from top)
Float height	Bottom edge parallel to gasket face
Automatic choke resistance	approx. 30 ohms @ 20°C

Ignition system

Source coil resistance	300 to 400 ohms
Pick-up coil resistance	90 to 140 ohms

Transmission

Belt width service limit	21.5 mm
Variator rollers minimum diameter	18.5 mm
Clutch lining minimum thickness	1.0 mm
Clutch spring free length	106 mm
Gearbox oil	SAE 80W/90 API GL4
Gearbox oil capacity	100 ml

Brakes

Disc brake	
Fluid type	DOT 4
Pad minimum thickness	1.5 mm
Drum brake	
Shoe lining minimum thickness	1.5 mm
Brake lever freeplay	10 to 15 mm

Tyre pressures

Front	19 psi (1.3 bar)
Rear	26 psi (1.8 bar)

Electrical system

Battery	
Capacity	12 V, 9 Ah
Alternator	
Output (unregulated)	25 to 30 V (AC)
Fuse (main)	7.5 Amps
Bulbs	
Headlight (main/dipped)	35/35 W
Sidelight	5 W
Brake/tail light	21/5 W
Turn signal lights	10 W
Instrument and warning lights	1.2 W

Torque wrench settings

Valve cover bolts	12 Nm
Cylinder head nuts	
Initial setting	7 Nm
Final setting	+90° +90°
Cylinder head bolts	13 Nm
Cam chain tensioner bolts	10 Nm
Camshaft sprocket bolt	15 Nm
Engine mounting bolt	41 Nm
Exhaust manifold nuts	11 Nm
Exhaust system mounting bolts	27 Nm
Engine oil drain plug	28 Nm
Oil pump sprocket bolt	13 Nm
Oil pump mounting bolts	6 Nm
Alternator rotor nut	58 Nm
Alternator stator bolts	4 Nm
Variator centre nut	83 Nm
Clutch centre nut	60 Nm
Clutch assembly nut	60 Nm
Crankcase bolts	13 Nm
Gearbox oil filler plug	5 Nm
Gearbox oil drain plug	17 Nm
Gearbox cover bolts	13 Nm
Front shock absorber mountings	25 Nm
Rear shock absorber mountings	
Lower bolt	41 Nm
Upper bolt	25 Nm
Steering head bearing adjuster nut	10 Nm
Steering head bearing locknut	40 Nm
Handlebar stem bolt	50 Nm
Front wheel bolts	25 Nm
Front hub nut	90 Nm
Rear hub nut	125 Nm
Disc brake caliper mounting bolts	25 Nm
Brake hose banjo bolt	25 Nm

Engine

Engine no. prefix	M311M
Frame no. prefix	ZAPM 311
Engine	124 cc single cylinder, four valve, four-stroke LEADER
Cooling system	Liquid-cooled
Fuel system	Walbro WVF-7 OR Keihin CVK 30 carburettor
Ignition system	Inductive discharge with electronic variable advance
Transmission	Variable ratio automatic, belt driven
Suspension	Trailing link front, swingarm with twin adjustable shocks rear
Brakes	220 mm disc front, 220 mm disc rear
Tyres	120/70 x 12 front, 130/70 x 12 rear
Wheelbase	1395 mm
Weight (dry)	140 kg
Fuel tank capacity	9.5 litres

Engine

Spark plug type	Champion RG4HC
Electrode gap	0.7 to 0.8 mm
Idle speed (rpm)	1600 to 1700 rpm
Engine oil	SAE 5W/40 synthetic four-stroke oil
Oil capacity	1.0 litre
Bore x stroke	57.0 x 48.6 mm
Piston over sizes available	+ 0.20, + 0.40 and + 0.60 mm
Piston to bore clearance (standard)	0.045 to 0.059 mm
Piston ring installed end gap (standard)	
Top ring	0.15 to 0.30 mm
Second ring	0.10 to 0.30 mm
Oil control ring	0.15 to 0.35 mm
Valve clearance	
Intake	0.10 mm
Exhaust	0.15 mm
Camshaft height (standard)	
Intake	30.285 mm
Exhaust	29.209 mm
Coolant	50% distilled water, 50% corrosion inhibiting ethylene glycol anti-freeze
Coolant capacity	2.1 to 2.15 litre

Fuel system – Walbro carburettor

Main jet	103
Pilot jet	38
Starter jet	60
Needle type / position	653 (2nd notch from top)
Pilot screw setting	2⅞ ± ½ turns out
Float level	parallel to gasket face
Automatic choke resistance	approx. 40 ohms (cold)

Fuel system – Keihin carburettor

Main jet	98
Pilot jet	38
Starter jet	42
Needle type (position)	NDVA (fixed)
Pilot screw setting	2 ± ¼ turns out
Float level	parallel to gasket face
Automatic choke resistance	approx. 20 ohms (cold)

Ignition system

HT coil primary resistance	0.4 to 0.5 ohm
HT coil secondary resistance	2.7 to 3.3 K-ohms
Spark plug cap resistance	5 K-ohms
Pick-up coil resistance	105 to 124 ohms

Transmission

Belt width (service limit)	21.5 mm
Variator rollers	
Standard diameter	18.9 to 19.1 mm
Service limit	18.5 mm
Recommended lubricant	Do not lubricate
Clutch lining thickness (service limit)	1 mm
Clutch spring free length (standard)	106 mm
Gearbox oil	SAE 80W/90 API GL4
Gearbox oil capacity	150 ml

Brakes

Disc brake	
Fluid type	DOT 4
Pad minimum thickness	1.5 mm

Tyre pressures

Front	26 psi (1.8 bar)
Rear	29 psi (2.0 bar) solo, 32 psi (2.2 bar) pillion

Electrical system

Battery capacity	12 V, 12 Ah
Alternator	
Output (regulated)	15.2 V (DC)
Charging coil resistance	0.7 to 0.9 ohms
Fuse	1 x 15A, 1 x 10A, 3 x 7.5A and 2 x 5A
Bulbs	
Headlight	60/55 W
Sidelight	5 W
Brake/tail light	8 x 2.3 W
Turn signal lights	10 W
Instrument and warning lights	1.2 W and 2 W

Torque wrench settings

Spark plug	12 to 14 Nm
Valve cover bolts	6 to 7 Nm
Cylinder head nuts	6 to 8 Nm + 180°
Cylinder head bolts	11 to 13 Nm
Cam chain tensioner spring cap bolt	5 to 6 Nm
Camshaft sprocket bolt	11 to 15 Nm
Engine oil drain plug	24 to 30 Nm
Engine oil filter	8 to 10 Nm
Engine sump cover bolts	10 to 14 Nm
Engine mounting bolt	33 to 41 Nm
Exhaust manifold nuts	13 to 15 Nm
Exhaust system mounting bolt	20 to 25 Nm
Water pump mounting screws	3 to 4 Nm
Thermostat cover bolts	3 to 4 Nm
Alternator rotor nut	54 to 60 Nm
Variator centre nut	75 to 83 Nm
Clutch centre nut	55 to 60 Nm
Clutch assembly nut	54 to 60 Nm
Drive belt cover screws	11 to 13 Nm
Crankcase bolts	11 to 13 Nm
Gearbox oil drain plug	15 to 17 Nm
Gearbox cover bolts	24 to 27 Nm
Rear shock absorber mountings	
Lower bolt	33 to 41 Nm
Upper bolt	20 to 25 Nm
Steering head bearing locknut	30 to 40 Nm
Handlebar stem bolt	45 to 50 Nm
Front fork leg top nuts	20 to 30 Nm
Front fork leg bottom bolts	20 to 27 Nm
Front axle nut	75 to 90 Nm
Wheel bolts	20 to 25 Nm
Rear hub nut	104 to 126 Nm
Disc brake calliper mounting bolts	20 to 25 Nm
Disc mounting bolts	
Front	6 Nm
Rear	11 to 13 Nm
Brake hose banjo bolts	20 to 25 Nm

Engine no. prefix	M312M
Frame no. prefix	ZAPM 312
Engine	197.75 cc single cylinder, four valve, four-stroke LEADER
Cooling system	Liquid-cooled
Fuel system	Walbro WVF-7 or Keihin CVK 30 carburettor
Ignition system	Inductive discharge with electronic variable advance
Transmission	Variable ratio automatic, belt driven
Suspension	Trailing link front, swingarm with twin adjustable shocks rear
Brakes	220 mm disc front, 220 mm disc rear
Tyres	120/70 x 12 front, 130/70 x 12 rear
Wheelbase	1395 mm
Weight (dry)	140 kg
Fuel tank capacity	9.5 litres

Engine

Spark plug type	Champion RG 6 YC
Electrode gap	0.7 to 0.8 mm
Idle speed (rpm)	1600 to 1700 rpm
Engine oil	SAE 5W/40 synthetic four-stroke oil
Oil capacity	1.0 litre
Bore x stroke	72.0 x 48.6 mm
Piston to bore clearance (standard)	0.030 to 0.044 mm
Piston ring installed end gap (standard)	
Top ring	0.15 to 0.30 mm
Second ring and oil control ring	0.20 to 0.40 mm
Valve clearance	
Intake	0.10 mm
Exhaust	0.15 mm
Camshaft lobe height (standard)	
Intake	30.285 mm
Exhaust	29.209 mm
Coolant	50% distilled water, 50% corrosion inhibiting ethylene glycol anti-freeze
Coolant capacity	2.1 to 2.15 litre

Fuel system – Walbro carburettor

Main jet	95
Pilot jet	33
Starter jet	120
Needle type / position	495 (2nd notch from top)
Pilot screw setting	2 ± ½ turns out
Float level	parallel to gasket face
Automatic choke resistance	approx. 40 ohms (cold)

Fuel system – Keihin carburettor

Main jet	92
Pilot jet	38
Starter jet	142
Needle type (position)	NDAA (fixed)
Pilot screw setting	2 ¼ ± ¼ turns out
Float level	parallel to gasket face
Automatic choke resistance	approx. 20 ohms (cold)

Ignition system

HT coil primary resistance	0.4 to 0.5 ohm
HT coil secondary resistance	2.7 to 3.3 K-ohms
Spark plug cap resistance	5 K-ohms
Pick-up coil resistance	105 to 124 ohms

Transmission

Belt width (service limit)	19.5 mm
Variator rollers	
Standard diameter	20.5 to 20.7 mm
Service limit	20.0 mm
Recommended lubricant	Do not lubricate
Clutch lining thickness (service limit)	1 mm
Clutch spring free length (standard)	123 mm
Gearbox oil	SAE 80W/90 API GL4
Gearbox oil capacity	150 ml

Brakes

Disc brake	
Fluid type	DOT 4
Pad minimum thickness	1.5 mm

Tyre pressures

Front	26 psi (1.8 bar)
Rear	29 psi (2.0 bar) solo, 32 psi (2.2 bar) pillion

Electrical system

Battery capacity	12 V, 12 Ah
Alternator	
Output (regulated)	15.2 V (DC)
Charging coil resistance	0.7 to 0.9 ohms
Fuse	1 x 15A, 1 x 10A, 3 x 7.5A and 2 x 5A
Bulbs	
Headlight	60/55W
Sidelight	5W
Brake/tail light	8 x 2.3W
Turn signal lights	10W
Instrument and warning lights	1.2W and 2W

Torque wrench settings

Spark plug	12 to 14 Nm
Valve cover bolts	6 to 7 Nm
Cylinder head nuts	6 to 8 Nm + 180°
Cylinder head bolts	11 to 13 Nm
Cam chain tensioner spring cap bolt	5 to 6 Nm
Camshaft sprocket bolt	11 to 15 Nm
Engine oil drain plug	24 to 30 Nm
Engine oil filter	8 to 10 Nm
Engine sump cover bolts	10 to 14 Nm
Engine mounting bolt	33 to 41 Nm
Exhaust manifold nuts	13 to 15 Nm
Exhaust system mounting bolt	20 to 25 Nm
Water pump mounting screws	3 to 4 Nm
Thermostat cover bolts	3 to 4 Nm
Alternator rotor nut	54 to 60 Nm
Variator centre nut	75 to 83 Nm
Clutch centre nut	55 to 60 Nm
Clutch assembly nut	54 to 60 Nm
Drive belt cover screws	11 to 13 Nm
Crankcase bolts	11 to 13 Nm
Gearbox oil drain plug	15 to 17 Nm
Gearbox cover bolts	24 to 27 Nm
Rear shock absorber mountings	
Lower bolt	33 to 41 Nm
Upper bolt	20 to 25 Nm
Steering head bearing locknut	30 to 40 Nm
Handlebar stem bolt	45 to 50 Nm
Front fork leg top nuts	20 to 30 Nm
Front fork leg bottom bolts	20 to 27 Nm
Front axle nut	75 to 90 Nm
Wheel bolts	20 to 25 Nm
Rear hub nut	104 to 126 Nm
Disc brake calliper mounting bolts	20 to 25 Nm
Disc mounting bolts	
Front	6 Nm
Rear	11 to 13 Nm
Brake hose banjo bolts	20 to 25 Nm

Vespa LX2 50

Engine no. prefix C381M
Frame no. prefix .... ZAPC 38101
Engine .... 50 cc single cylinder two-stroke
Cooling system .... Air cooled
Fuel system .... Dell 'Orto PHVA 17.5RD
Ignition system .... CDI
Transmission .... Variable speed automatic, belt driven
Suspension .... (Front) trailing link and monoshock, (Rear) swingarm
Brakes .... Single disc (front), drum (rear)
Tyres .... 110/70-11 (front), 120/70-10 (rear)
Wheelbase .... 1280 mm
Weight (dry) .... 96 kg
Fuel tank capacity .... 8.5 litres

Engine

Spark plug type	Champion RGN2C
Electrode gap	0.6 to 0.7 mm
Idle speed (rpm)	1800 to 2000 rpm
Engine oil	Selenia HI 2T two-stroke injector oil
Oil tank capacity	1.2 litres
Bore x stroke	40.0 mm x 39.3 mm
Piston diameter (standard)	39.943 to 39.971 mm
Piston to bore clearance (standard)	0.055 to 0.069 mm
Piston ring installed end gap (clearance)	0.10 to 0.25 mm

Fuel system

Main jet	53
Pilot jet	32
Starter jet	50
Needle type / position	A22 (1st notch from top)
Pilot screw setting	1½ turns out
Fuel level	5 mm (not adjustable)
Automatic choke resistance	30 to 40 ohms

Tyre pressures

Front tyre pressure	23 psi (1.6 bar)
Rear tyre pressure	29 psi (2.0 bar)

Electrical system

Battery	
Capacity	12 V, 4 Ah
Alternator:	
Output (unregulated)	25 to 30 C (ac) at 3000 rpm
Fuse (main)	7.5 A
Bulbs:	
Headlight (main/dipped)	35/35 W
Sidelight	3 W
Brake/tail light	21/5 W
Turn signal lights	10 W
Instrument and warning lights .	1.2 and/or 2.0 W

Ignition system

Source coil resistance	800 to 1100 ohms
Pick-up coil resistance	90 to 140 ohms

Transmission

Belt width	17.5 mm
Variator rollers	18.5 mm
Clutch lining thickness	1 mm
Gearbox oil	SAE 80W/90 API GL4
Gearbox oil capacity	Approx 85 ml

Brakes

Disc brake:	
Fluid type	DOT 4
Pad minimum thickness	1.5 mm
Drum brake:	
Shoe lining thickness	1.5 mm
Brake lever freeplay	10 to 15 mm

Torque wrench settings

Cylinder head bolts	22 to 23 Nm
Alternator rotor nut	52 to 56 Nm
Crankcase bolts	13 Nm
Engine mounting bolts	33 to 41 Nm
Exhaust system mounting bolts to crankcase .	22 to 24 Nm
Variator centre nut	40 to 44 Nm
Clutch assembly nut	55 to 60 Nm
Clutch centre nut	40 to 44 Nm
Gearbox oil drain plug	3 to 5 Nm
Drive belt cover bolts	12 to 13 Nm
Rear shock absorber mountings	
Lower bolt	33 to 41 Nm
Upper bolt	20 to 25 Nm
Steering head bearing adjuster nut .	8 to 10 Nm
Steering head bearing locknut .	35 to 40 Nm
Handlebar stem bolt	45 to 50 Nm
Front wheel bolts	20 to 25 Nm
Front wheel axle nut	75 to 90 Nm
Disc brake caliper mounting bolts	20 to 25 Nm
Brake hose banjo bolts	20 to 22 Nm

Tyre pressures

Front tyre pressure	23 psi (1.6 bar)
Rear tyre pressure	29 psi (2.0 bar)

Electrical system

Battery capacity	12 V, 9 Ah
Alternator:	
Output (unregulated)	25 to 35 V (ac)
	at 3000 rpm
Fuse (main)	10 A
Bulbs:	
Headlight (main/dipped)	60/55 W
Sidelight	5 W
Brake/tail light	21/5 W
Turn signal lights	10 W
Instrument and warning lights	1.2 W and 2.0 W

Torque wrench settings

Spark plug	10 to 15 Nm
Cylinder head nuts	6 to 7 Nm, +90° +90°
Alternator rotor nut	40 to 44 Nm
Crankcase bolts	8 to 10 Nm
Engine mounting bolts	33 to 41 Nm
Engine oil drain bolt	25 to 28 Nm
Exhaust system mounting bolts to crankcase	22 to 24 Nm
Oil pump mounting bolts	5 to 6 Nm
Variator centre nut	18 to 20 Nm +90°
Clutch centre nut	40 to 44 Nm
Clutch assembly nut	55 to 60 Nm
Gearbox oil drain plug	3 to 5 Nm
Drive belt cover bolts	11 to 13 Nm
Rear shock absorber mountings	
Lower bolt	33 to 41 Nm
Upper bolt	20 to 25 Nm
Steering head bearing adjuster nut	8 to 10 Nm
Steering head bearing locknut	35 to 40 Nm
Handlebar stem bolt	45 to 50 Nm
Front wheel bolts	20 to 25 Nm
Front wheel axle nut	75 to 90 Nm
Disc brake caliper mounting bolts	20 to 25 Nm
Brake hose banjo bolt at caliper	20 to 22 Nm
Brake hose banjo bolt at master cylinder	8 to 12 Nm

Engine no. prefix	C383M
Frame no. prefix	ZAPC38300
Engine	49 cc single cylinder four-stroke
Cooling system	Air-cooled
Fuel system	Keihin CVK 18 carburettor
Ignition system	CDI
Transmission	Variable speed automatic, belt driven
Suspension	Trailing link front, swingarm with single shock rear
Brakes	Disc (front), Drum (rear)
Tyres	110/70 x 11 front, 120/70 x 10 rear
Wheelbase	1290 mm
Weight (dry)	102 kg
Fuel tank capacity	8.5 litres

Ignition system

Source coil resistance	1.0 ohm
Pick-up coil resistance	170 ohms

Transmission

Belt width	17.5 mm
Variator rollers	18.5 mm
Clutch lining thickness	1 mm
Clutch spring free length	110 mm
Gearbox oil	SAE 80W/90 API GL4
Gearbox oil capacity	Approx 85 ml

Brakes

Disc brake:	
Fluid type	DOT 4
Pad minimum thickness	1.5 mm
Drum brake:	
Shoe lining thickness	1.5 mm
Brake lever freeplay	10 to 15 mm

Engine

Spark plug type	NGK CR8EB
Electrode gap	0.7 to 0.8 mm
Idle speed (rpm)	1900 to 2000 rpm
Engine oil	5W/40 API SG synthetic oil
Oil tank capacity	850 ml
Bore x stroke	39.0 x 41.8 mm
Piston diameter (standard)	38.954 to 38.975 mm
Piston to bore clearance (standard)	0.032 to 0.046 mm
Piston ring installed end gap	
Top ring	0.08 to 0.20 mm
Second ring	0.05 to 0.20 mm
Oil control ring	0.20 to 0.70 mm

Fuel system

Main jet	75
Pilot jet	35
Starter jet	40
Needle type	NGBA
Pilot screw setting	1½ turns out
Float level	parallel to gasket face
Automatic choke resistance	30 to 40 ohms

Vespa LX4 125

Frame no. prefix
Frame no. prefix ZAPM44100

Engine
Engine	124 cc Single cylinder four-stroke LEADER
Cooling system	Air-cooled
Fuel system	Keihin CVEK 26 carburettor
Ignition system	CDI
Transmission	Variable speed automatic, belt driven
Suspension	Swingarm and monoshock
Brakes	Single disc (front), drum (rear)
Tyres	110/70 x 11 front, 120/70 x 10 rear
Wheelbase	1280 mm
Weight (dry)	110 kg
Fuel tank capacity ...	8.5 litres

Electrical system
Battery capacity	12 V, 9 Ah
Alternator:	
Output (regulated) ...	15.2 V (DC)
Charging coil resistance	0.7 to 0.9 ohms
Fuse (main)	15 A
Bulbs:	
Headlight (main/dipped)	35/35 W
Sidelight	4 W
Brake/tail light	21/5 W
Turn signal lights	10 W
Instrument and warning lights	1.2 W and 2.0 W

Engine
Spark plug type	Champion RG6YC
Electrode gap	0.7 to 0.8 mm
Idle speed (rpm)	1600 to 1800 rpm
Engine oil	5W / 40 API SG synthetic oil
Oil tank capacity	approx 1 litre
Bore x stroke	57.0 x 48.6 mm
Piston diameter (standard)	56.933 to 57.561 mm
Piston oversizes available	+0.20mm, +0.40mm and +0.60 mm
Piston to bore clearance (standard)	0.040 to 0.054 mm
Piston ring installed end gap (clearance)	
Top ring	0.15 to 0.30 mm
Second ring	0.10 to 0.30 mm
Oil ring	0.15 to 0.30 mm

Ignition system
Source coil resistance	0.7 to 0.9 ohm
Pick-up coil resistance	105 to 124 ohms

Transmission
Belt width	21.5 mm
Variator rollers	18.5 mm
Clutch lining thickness	1 mm
Gearbox oil	SAE 80W/90 API GL4
Gearbox oil capacity .	Approx 100 ml

Brakes
Disc brake:	
Fluid type	DOT 4
Pad minimum thickness	1.5 mm
Drum brake:	
Shoe lining thickness	1.5 mm
Brake lever freeplay .	10 to 15 mm

Fuel system
Main jet	82
Pilot jet	35
Starter jet	42
Needle type	NELA
Pilot screw setting ...	1½ turns out
Float level	12.2 mm
Automatic choke resistance	20 ohms

Tyre pressures
Front tyre pressure ...	23 psi (1.6 bar)
Rear tyre pressure	29 psi (2.0 bar) solo, 33 psi (2.3 bar) pillion

Torque wrench settings
Spark plug	12 to 14 Nm
Cylinder head bolts	7 Nm, +90° +90°
Alternator rotor nut	52 to 58 Nm
Crankcase bolts	11 to 13 Nm
Engine mounting bolts	33 to 41 Nm
Engine oil drain bolt	24 to 30 Nm
Exhaust manifold nuts	16 to 18 Nm
Exhaust system mounting bolts to crankcase	24 to 27 Nm
Oil pump mounting bolts ..	5 to 6 Nm
Variator centre nut	75 to 83 Nm
Clutch assembly nut	45 to 50 Nm
Clutch centre nut	54 to 60 Nm
Gearbox oil drain plug	15 to 17 Nm
Drive belt cover bolts	24 to 27 Nm
Rear shock absorber mountings	
Lower bolt	33 to 41 Nm
Upper bolt	20 to 25 Nm
Steering head bearing adjuster nut	8 to 10 Nm
Steering head bearing locknut	30 to 40 Nm
Handlebar stem bolt	45 to 50 Nm
Front wheel axle nut	75 to 90 Nm
Front wheel bolts	20 to 25 Nm
Rear hub nut	104 to 126 Nm
Disc brake caliper mounting bolts	20 to 25 Nm
Brake hose banjo bolt at caliper	20 to 25 Nm
Brake hose banjo bolt at master cylinder	8 to 12 Nm

Data 88

Yamaha CS50 JogR and MBK Mach G 50

Engine

Engine	49 cc single-cylinder two-stroke
Cooling system	Air-cooled
Fuel system	Dell'Orto PHBN or Gurtner PY12 slide carburettor
Ignition system	CDI
Transmission	Variable speed automatic, belt-driven
Suspension	Telescopic front, swingarm with single shock rear
Brakes	190 mm disc front, 110 mm drum rear
Tyres	110/70 x 12 front, 120/70 x 12 rear
Wheelbase	1210 mm
Weight	81kg
Fuel tank capacity	5.5 litres

Engine

Spark plug type	NGK BR8HS
Electrode gap	0.6 to 0.7 mm
Idle speed (rpm)	1650 to 1950 rpm
Engine oil	JASO FC grade two-stroke engine oil
Oil tank capacity	1.4 litres
Bore x stroke	40.0 x 39.2 mm
Piston diameter (standard)	39.952 to 39.972 mm
Cylinder bore	
Standard	39.993 to 40.012 mm
Service limit	40.1 mm
Piston to bore clearance (standard)	0.034 to 0.047 mm
Piston ring installed end gap	
Standard	0.15 to 35 mm
Service limit	0.6 mm

Fuel system

Throttle twistgrip freeplay	2 to 5 mm
Dell'Orto PHBNVA	
Main jet	65
Pilot jet	36
Starter jet	50
Needle type / position	A20 (3rd notch from top)
Pilot screw setting	2 turns out
Float height	15 to 17 mm
Gurtner PY12	
Main jet	62
Pilot jet	38
Starter jet	42
Needle type / position	B10A (2nd notch from top)
Pilot screw setting	1¾ turns out
Float height	15 to 17 mm

Ignition system

HT coil primary resistance	0.56 to 0.84 ohms
HT coil secondary resistance	5.68 to 8.52 K-ohms
Spark plug cap resistance	10 K-ohms
Pick-up coil resistance	400 to 600 ohms

Transmission

Belt width (service limit)	15.7 mm
Variator rollers diameter (service limit)	14.5 mm
Clutch lining thickness (service limit)	1.0 mm
Clutch spring free length (service limit)	106.7 mm
Gearbox oil	SAE 10W 30 oil
Gearbox oil capacity	110 ml

Brakes

Disc brake	
Fluid type	DOT 4
Pad thickness (service limit)	0.5 mm
Disc thickness (service limit)	3.2 mm
Drum brake	
Drum internal diameter (service limit)	110.5 mm
Brake shoe lining thickness	
Standard	4.0 mm
Service limit	2.0 mm
Brake lever freeplay	10 to 20 mm

Tyre pressures

Front	22 psi (1.5 bar)
Rear	22 psi (1.5 bar)

Electrical system

Battery	
Capacity	12 V, 4 Ah
Alternator	
Output (regulated)	12 to 15 V (DC)
Charging coil resistance	0.288 to 0.432 ohms
Lighting coil resistance	0.116 to 0.264 ohms
Fuse (main)	7.5 Amps
Bulbs	
Headlight (main/dipped)	35/35 W
Sidelight	5 W
Brake/tail light	21/5 W
Turn signal lights	10 W
Instrument and warning lights	1.2 and 2W

Torque wrench settings

Cylinder head nuts	14 Nm
Crankcase bolts	10 Nm
Engine mounting bolt	84 Nm
Exhaust manifold nuts	9 Nm
Exhaust system mounting bolts	26 Nm
Oil pump mounting bolts	4 Nm
Alternator rotor nut	35 Nm
Alternator stator bolts	8.5 Nm
Variator centre nut	33 Nm
Clutch centre nut	40 Nm
Clutch assembly nut	50 Nm
Gearbox oil drain plug	18 Nm
Gearbox cover bolts	10 Nm
Rear shock absorber mountings	
Lower bolt	18 Nm
Upper bolt	31.5 Nm
Steering head bearing locknut	75 Nm
Handlebar stem bolt	42.5 Nm
Front fork leg bottom bolt	23 Nm
Front fork leg clamp bolt	30 Nm
Front axle nut	47.5 Nm
Rear hub nut	125 Nm
Disc brake caliper mounting bolts	23 Nm
Disc mounting bolts	23 Nm
Brake hose banjo bolts	23 Nm

Yamaha CS50Z Jog RR

Data 89

Engine

Engine	49cc, single cylinder two-stroke
Cooling system	Liquid-cooled
Fuel system	Dell'Orto PHVA 12ZS/l
Ignition system	CDI
Transmission	Variable speed automatic, belt driven
Suspension	Telescopic front fork, swingarm with single shock rear
Brakes	Front disc, rear drum
Tyres	110/70-12/47 L front, 120/70-12/51L or 130/70-12/56L rear
Wheelbase	1210 mm
Weight (wet)	83.7 kg
Fuel tank capacity	5.5 litre

Engine

Spark plug type	NGK BR 8HS
Electrode gap	0.6 to 0.7 mm
Idle speed (rpm)	1650 to 1950 mm
Engine oil	JASO FC grade two-stroke engine oil
Oil tank capacity	1.4 litre
Bore x stroke	40.0 x 39.2 mm
Piston diameter (standard)	39.957 to 39.997 mm
Cylinder bore diameter	
Standard	39.993 to 40.012 mm
Service limit	40.1 mm
Piston to bore clearance (standard)	0.029 to 0.042 mm
Piston ring installed end gap	0.15 to 0.35 mm
Coolant	50% distilled water, 50% corrosion inhibiting ethylene glycol anti-freeze
Coolant capacity	0.91 litre

Fuel system

Main jet	65
Pilot jet	36
Starter jet	50
Needle type / position	A35 (4th or 5th groove from top)
Pilot screw setting	1¾ ± ⅛ turns out
Float level	15 to 17 mm

Ignition system

HT coil primary resistance	0.56 to 0.84 ohm
HT coil secondary resistance	5.68 to 8.52 K-ohms
Spark plug cap resistance	10 K-ohms
Pick-up coil resistance	460 to 600 ohms

Transmission

Belt width	15.7 mm
Variator rollers	14.5 mm
Clutch lining thickness service limit	1 mm
Clutch spring free length service limit	106.7 mm
Gearbox oil	10W/30 type SE or higher engine oil or GL gear oil
Gearbox oil capacity	110 ml

Brakes and suspension

Disc brake:	
Fluid type	DOT 4
Pad minimum thickness	0.5 mm
Drum brake:	
Shoe lining minimum thickness	2 mm
Brake lever freeplay	5 to 10 mm at lever end
Fork oil capacity	45 ml
Fork oil type	10 W

Tyre pressures

Front tyre pressure	25 psi (1.75 bar)
Rear tyre pressure	33 psi (2.27 bar)

Electrical system

Battery capacity	12 V, 4 Ah
Alternator output	
Charging coil resistance	0.288 to 0.432 ohms
Regulated output	12 V (DC) @ 3000 rpm, 15 V (DC) or less @ 8000 rpm or more
Fuse (main)	7.5 A
Bulbs:	
Headlight (main/dipped)	35/35 W
Sidelight	5 W
Brake/tail light	21/5 W
Licence plate light	5 W
Turn signal lights	10 W (rear), 16 W (front)
Instrument and warning lights	1.2 W

Torque wrench settings

Cylinder head bolts	14 Nm
Crankcase bolts	10 Nm
Engine mounting bolts	84 Nm
Exhaust manifold nuts	9 Nm
Exhaust system mounting bolts	26 Nm
Oil pump mounting bolts	4 Nm
Alternator rotor nut	43 Nm
Alternator stator plate bolts	9 Nm
Variator centre nut	33 Nm
Clutch centre nut	40 Nm
Clutch assembly nut	50 Nm
Gearbox oil drain plug	18 Nm
Drive belt cover bolts	9 Nm
Rear shock absorber mountings	
Lower bolt	18 Nm
Upper bolt	32 Nm
Steering head bearing adjuster	38 Nm, slacken ½ turn, then 6.5 Nm
Steering head bearing locknut	43 Nm
Steering stem nut	75 Nm
Handlebar stem bolt	43 Nm
Front axle nut	47.5 Nm
Rear hub nut	125 Nm
Front fork damper rod bolt	23 Nm
Front fork pinch bolts in lower yoke	30 Nm
Disc caliper mounting bolts	23 Nm
Brake hose banjo bolts	23 Nm

Yamaha CW / BW and MBK Rocket

Engine

Engine	49 cc single-cylinder two-stroke
Cooling system	Air-cooled
Fuel system	Dell'Orto PHBN slide carburettor
Ignition system	CDI
Transmission	Variable speed automatic, belt-driven
Suspension	Telescopic front, swingarm with single shock rear
Brakes	Disc front, drum rear
Tyres	120/90 x 10 front, 130/90 x 10 rear
Wheelbase	1206 mm
Weight	83 kg
Fuel tank capacity	6.5 litres

Engine

Spark plug type	NGK BR8HS
Electrode gap	0.5 to 0.7 mm
Idle speed (rpm)	1800 to 2200 rpm
Engine oil	Semi-synthetic two-stroke engine oil
Bore x stroke	40.0 x 39.2 mm
Piston diameter (standard)	39.952 to 39.972 mm
Cylinder bore service limit	40.10 mm
Piston to bore clearance (service limit)	0.1 mm
Piston ring installed end gap (service limit)	0.70 mm

Fuel system

Throttle twistgrip freeplay	1.5 to 3.5 mm
Main jet	90
Pilot jet	36
Starter jet	40
Needle type / position	211GA (3rd notch from top)
Pilot screw setting	1½ turns out

Ignition system

HT coil primary resistance	0.32 to 0.48 ohms
HT coil secondary resistance	5.68 to 8.52 K-ohms
Spark plug cap resistance	5 K-ohms
Pick-up coil resistance	400 to 600 ohms
Source coil resistance	640 to 960 ohms

Transmission

Belt width (service limit)	15.7 mm
Variator rollers diameter (service limit)	14.5 mm
Clutch lining thickness (service limit)	1 mm
Clutch spring free length (service limit)	106.7 mm
Gearbox oil	SAE 10W 30 oil
Gearbox oil capacity	130 ml

Brakes

Disc brake	
Fluid type	DOT 4
Pad thickness (service limit)	0.5 mm
Disc thickness (service limit)	3.2 mm
Drum brake	
Drum internal diameter (service limit)	110.5 mm
Brake shoe lining thickness	
Standard	4.0 mm
Service limit	2.0 mm
Brake lever freeplay	10 to 20 mm

Tyre pressures

Front	22 psi (1.5 bar)
Rear	22 psi (1.5 bar)

Electrical system

Battery	
Capacity	12 V, 4 Ah
Alternator	
Output (regulated)	13 to 14 V (DC)
Charging coil resistance	0.48 to 0.72 ohms
Lighting coil resistance	0.32 to 0.48 ohms
Fuse (main)	7 Amps
Bulbs	
Headlight (main/dipped)	35/35 W
Sidelight	5 W
Brake/tail light	21/5 W
Turn signal lights	10 W
Instrument and warning lights	1.2 W

Torque wrench settings

Cylinder head nuts	10 Nm
Crankcase bolts	13 Nm
Engine mounting bolt	84 Nm
Exhaust manifold nuts	9 Nm
Exhaust system mounting bolts	26 Nm
Oil pump mounting bolts	4 Nm
Alternator rotor nut	37.5 Nm
Alternator stator bolts	8 Nm
Variator centre nut	30 Nm
Clutch centre nut	40 Nm
Clutch assembly nut	50 Nm
Gearbox oil drain plug	18 Nm
Gearbox cover bolts	9 Nm
Rear shock absorber mountings	
Lower bolt	16 Nm
Upper bolt	31.5 Nm
Steering head bearing locknut	27.5 Nm
Handlebar stem bolt	60 Nm
Front fork leg bottom bolt	23 Nm
Front fork leg clamp bolt	30 Nm
Front axle nut	35 Nm
Rear hub nut	105 Nm
Disc brake caliper mounting bolts	23 Nm
Disc mounting bolts	23 Nm
Brake hose banjo bolts	23 Nm

Engine

Engine	49 cc single-cylinder two-stroke
Cooling system	Air-cooled
Fuel system	Dell'Orto PHBN or Teikei 5FX / 5LH slide carburettor
Ignition system	CDI
Transmission	Variable speed automatic, belt-driven
Suspension	Telescopic front, swingarm with single shock rear
Brakes	190 mm disc front, 110 mm drum rear
Tyres	120/80 x 12 front, 130/90 x 10 rear
Wheelbase	1202 mm
Weight	81kg
Fuel tank capacity	6.5 litres

Tyre pressures

Front	22 psi (1.5 bar)
Rear	22 psi (1.5 bar)

Electrical system

Battery	
Capacity	12 V, 4 Ah
Alternator	
Output (regulated)	13 to 14 V (DC)
Charging coil resistance	0.48 to 0.72 ohms
Lighting coil resistance	0.39 to 0.50 ohms
Fuse (main)	7 Amps
Bulbs	
Headlight (main/dipped)	35/35 W
Sidelight	5 W
Brake/tail light	21/5 W
Turn signal lights	10 W
Instrument and warning lights	1.2 W

Engine

Spark plug type	NGK BR8HS
Electrode gap	0.5 to 0.7 mm
Idle speed (rpm)	1600 to 2000 rpm
Engine oil	JASO FC grade two-stroke engine oil
Oil tank capacity	1.4 litres
Bore x stroke	40.0 x 39.2 mm
Piston diameter (standard)	39.952 to 39.972 mm
Cylinder bore (standard)	39.993 to 40.012 mm
Piston to bore clearance (service limit)	0.1 mm
Piston ring installed end gap (standard)	0.15 to 35 mm

Ignition system

HT coil primary resistance	0.32 to 0.48 ohms
HT coil secondary resistance	5.68 to 8.52 K-ohms
Spark plug cap resistance	5 K-ohms
Pick-up coil resistance	400 to 600 ohms
Source coil resistance	640 to 960 ohms

Transmission

Belt width (service limit)	14.9 mm
Variator rollers diameter (service limit)	14.5 mm
Clutch lining thickness (service limit)	1.0 mm
Clutch spring free length (service limit)	106.7 mm
Gearbox oil	SAE 10W 30 oil
Gearbox oil capacity	130 ml

Fuel system

Throttle twistgrip freeplay	1.5 to 3.5 mm
Dell'Orto PHBN	
Main jet	90
Pilot jet	36
Starter jet	40
Needle type / position	A21 (3rd notch from top)
Pilot screw setting	1% turns out
Teikei 5FX / 5LH	
Main jet	88/80
Pilot jet	50/42
Starter jet	46
Needle type / position	3S12/3S14 (3rd/2nd notch from top)
Pilot screw setting	1½ turns out

Brakes

Disc brake	
Fluid type	DOT 4
Pad thickness (service limit)	0.5 mm
Disc thickness (service limit)	3.2 mm
Drum brake	
Drum internal diameter (service limit)	110.5 mm
Brake shoe lining thickness	
Standard	4.0 mm
Service limit	2.0 mm
Brake lever freeplay	10 to 20 mm

Torque wrench settings

Cylinder head nuts	10 Nm
Crankcase bolts	13 Nm
Engine mounting bolt	50 Nm
Exhaust manifold nuts	8.5 Nm
Exhaust system mounting bolts	29 Nm
Oil pump mounting bolts	3 Nm
Alternator rotor nut	35 Nm
Alternator stator bolts	8.5 Nm
Variator centre nut	65 Nm
Clutch centre nut	40 Nm
Clutch assembly nut	30 Nm
Gearbox oil drain plug	17.5 Nm
Gearbox cover bolts	10 Nm
Rear shock absorber mountings	
Lower bolt	17.5 Nm
Upper bolt	31.5 Nm
Steering head bearing locknut	75 Nm
Handlebar stem bolt	60 Nm
Front fork leg bottom bolt	32.5 Nm
Front axle nut	35 Nm
Rear hub nut	103.5 Nm
Disc brake caliper mounting bolts	23 Nm
Disc mounting bolts	23 Nm
Brake hose banjo bolts	23 Nm

Engine

Engine	124 cc, single cylinder four-stroke
Cooling system	Air-cooled
Fuel system	Keihin CVK24
Ignition system	CDI
Transmission	Variable speed automatic, belt-driven
Suspension	Telescopic front fork, rear swingarm with single shock
Brakes	Single front disc, rear drum
Tyres	110/70 x 12 47 L front, 120/70 x 12 58 L rear
Wheelbase	1295 mm
Weight (dry)	114 kg
Fuel tank capacity	7.1 litre

Engine

Spark plug type	CR7E (NGK)
Electrode gap	0.6 to 0.7 mm
Idle speed (rpm)	1700 to 1800 rpm
Engine oil	SAE 20W/40 SE, SAE 10W/30 SE or SAE 10W/40 SE
Oil capacity	0.9 to 1.0 litre
Bore x stroke	52.4 x 57.9 mm
Piston diameter (standard)	52.375 to 52.390 mm
Piston to bore clearance (standard)	0.02 mm
Piston ring installed end gap	0.10 to 0.25 mm

Fuel system

Throttle twistgrip freeplay	3 to 5 mm
Main jet	105
Pilot jet	35
Starter jet	55
Needle type / position	106 – CO17 E4000
Pilot screw setting	2 turns out
Float height	20.5 mm
Carburettor heater coil resistance	25 to 34 ohms @ 24°C

Electrical system

Battery capacity	12 V, 6 Ah
Alternator:	
regulated output	14 V (DC) @5000 rpm
Charging coil resistance	0.56 to 0.84 ohm
Fuse (main)	30 A
Circuit fuses	2 x 15 A, 2 x 7.5 A
Bulbs:	
Headlight (main/dipped)	60 / 55 W
Sidelight	5 W
Brake/tail light	21/5 W
Turn signal lights	10 W front, 16 W rear
Instrument and warning lights	1.7 W

Ignition system

HT coil primary resistance	0.168 to 0.252 ohm
HT coil secondary resistance	2.4 to 3.6 K-ohms
Spark plug cap resistance	8 to 12 K-ohms
Pick-up coil resistance	248 to 372 ohms

Transmission

Belt width service limit	19.8 mm
Variator roller service limit	19.5 mm
Clutch lining thickness service limit	2 mm
Clutch spring free length service limit	110.6 mm
Gearbox oil	SAE 10W/30SE Hypoid gear oil
Gearbox oil capacity	130 ml

Brakes and suspension

Disc brake:	
Fluid type	DOT 4
Pad minimum thickness	1.5 mm
Drum brake:	
Shoe lining minimum thickness	1 mm
Brake lever freeplay	10 to 20 mm
Fork oil capacity	116 ± 2.5 ml
Fork oil type	10W

Tyre pressures

Front tyre pressure	25 psi (1.75 bar)
Rear tyre pressure	29 psi (2.0 bar)

Torque wrench settings

Cylinder head nuts	22 Nm
Cylinder head bolts	10 Nm
Alternator rotor bolts	70 Nm
Alternator stator bolts	7 Nm
Crankcase bolts	13 Nm
Engine mounting bolts	32 Nm
Exhaust system mountings:	
M8 bolts	31 Nm
M10 bolts	53 Nm
Exhaust manifold nuts	13 Nm
Oil pump bolts	4 Nm
Engine oil drain bolt and oil strainer cover bolt	20 Nm
Variator centre nut	45 Nm
Clutch centre nut	60 Nm
Gearbox oil drain plug	23 Nm
Drive belt cover bolts	10 Nm
Front fork damper rod bolt	30 Nm
Front fork top bolt	45 Nm
Front fork pinch bolts	23 Nm
Rear shock absorber mountings	
Lower bolt	18 Nm
Upper bolt	32 Nm
Steering head bearing adjuster nut	38 Nm, then slacken ½ turn
Steering head bearing locknut	13 Nm
Steering stem nut	66 Nm
Handlebar stem bolt	60 Nm
Front wheel axle nut	70 Nm
Rear hub nut	105 Nm
Disc brake caliper mounting bolts	49 Nm
Brake hose banjo bolts	30 Nm

Yamaha XN125 Teo's and MBK Doodo 125

Engine
Engine	124 cc single-cylinder four-stroke
Cooling system	Liquid-cooled
Fuel system	Teikei 5DS/1 CV carburettor
Ignition system	CDI
Transmission	Variable speed automatic, belt-driven
Suspension	Telescopic front, swingarm with twin adjustable shock rear
Brakes	220 mm disc front, 130 mm drum rear
Tyres	120/70 x 12 front, 120/70 x 12 rear
Wheelbase	1315 mm
Weight	123 kg
Fuel tank capacity	10 litres

Tyre pressures
Front	26 psi (1.8 bar)
Rear	29 psi (2.0 bar)

Electrical system
Battery	
Capacity	12 V, 8 Ah
Alternator	
Output (regulated)	14 V (DC)
Charging coil resistance	0.6 to 0.9 ohms
Fuse (main)	20 Amps
Fuse (cooling fan)	7.5 Amps
Bulbs	
Headlight (main/dipped)	35/35 W
Sidelight	5 W
Brake/tail light	21/5 W
Turn signal lights	10 W
Instrument and warning lights	1.2 W

Torque wrench settings
Cylinder head nuts	22 Nm
Cylinder head bolts	12 Nm
Cam chain tensioner bolts	10 Nm
Camshaft sprocket bolt	30 Nm
Engine oil drain plug	32 Nm
Engine mounting bolt	43 Nm
Exhaust manifold nuts	11 Nm
Exhaust system mounting bolts	27 Nm
Water pump cover bolts	7 Nm
Thermostat cover bolts	9 Nm
Oil pump mounting bolts	6.5 Nm
Alternator rotor nut	70 Nm
Alternator stator bolts	7 Nm
Variator centre nut	60 Nm
Clutch centre nut	55 Nm
Clutch assembly nut	90 Nm
Crankcase bolts	9 Nm
Gearbox oil drain plug	22 Nm
Gearbox cover bolts	6.5 Nm
Rear shock absorber mountings	
Lower bolt	17.5 Nm
Upper bolt	32 Nm
Steering head bearing locknut	75 Nm
Handlebar stem bolt	60 Nm
Front fork leg bottom bolt	23 Nm
Front fork leg clamp bolt	33 Nm
Front axle nut	70 Nm
Rear hub nut	103.5 Nm
Disc brake caliper mounting bolts	22 Nm
Disc mounting bolts	23 Nm
Brake hose banjo bolts	26 Nm

Engine
Spark plug type	NGK CR8E
Electrode gap	0.5 to 0.7 mm
Idle speed (rpm)	1600 to 1800 rpm
Engine oil	SAE 10W 40 four-stroke motorcycle oil
Oil capacity	1.4 litres
Bore x stroke	53.7 x 54.8 mm
Piston diameter (standard)	53.760 to 54.8 mm
Cylinder bore	
Standard	52.002 to 53.675 mm
Piston to bore clearance (service limit)	0.15 mm
Piston ring installed end gap (standard/service limit)	
Top ring	0.15 to 25 mm/0.40 mm
Second ring	0.15 to 30 mm/0.45 mm
Oil control ring	0.2 to 0.7 mm
Valve clearance	
Intake	0.10 to 0.14 mm
Exhaust	0.16 to 0.20 mm
Valve spring free length	
Standard	41.94 mm
Service limit	39.84 mm
Camshaft lobe height	
Standard	30.811 to 30.911 mm
Service limit	30.711 mm
Coolant	50% distilled water, 50% corrosion inhibiting ethylene glycol anti-freeze
Coolant capacity	1.1 litres

Fuel system
Throttle twistgrip freeplay	1.5 to 3 mm
Main jet	116
Pilot jet	38
Needle type / position	4E31 (3rd notch from top)
Pilot screw setting	2½ turns out
Fuel level	7.5 mm

Ignition system
HT coil primary resistance	0.19 to 0.27 ohms
HT coil secondary resistance	6.3 to 9.5 K-ohms
Spark plug cap resistance	10 K-ohms
Pick-up coil resistance	248 to 372 ohms
Source coil resistance	720 to 1080 ohms

Transmission
Belt width service limit	18.9 mm
Variator rollers diameter (service limit)	19.5 mm
Clutch lining thickness (service limit)	1.0 mm
Gearbox oil	SAE 10W 30 oil
Gearbox oil capacity	150 ml

Brakes
Disc brake	
Fluid type	DOT 4
Pad thickness service limit	2 mm
Disc thickness (standard)	4.5 mm
Drum brake	
Shoe lining minimum thickness	2 mm
Brake lever freeplay	10 to 20 mm

Yamaha XQ125 Maxster and MBK Thunder 125

Tyre pressures

Front	22 psi (1.5 bar)
Rear	22 psi (1.5 bar)

Electrical system

Battery	
Capacity	12 V, 8 Ah
Alternator	14 V (DC)
Output (regulated)	0.6 to 0.9 ohms
Charging coil resistance	20 Amps
Fuse (main)	7.5 Amps
Cooling fan fuse	
Bulbs	
Headlight (main/dipped)	35/35 W
Sidelight	5 W
Brake/tail light	21/5 W
Turn signal lights	10 W
Instrument and warning lights	1.2 W

Torque wrench settings

Cylinder head nuts	22 Nm
Cylinder head bolts	12 Nm
Cylinder base bolt	12 Nm
Camshaft sprocket bolt	30 Nm
Cam chain tensioner bolt	10 Nm
Engine oil drain plug	22 Nm
Engine mounting bolt	55 Nm
Exhaust manifold bolts	11 Nm
Exhaust system mounting bolts	27 Nm
Oil pump mounting bolts	6.5 Nm
Alternator rotor nut	70 Nm
Alternator stator bolts	7 Nm
Variator centre nut	60 Nm
Clutch centre nut	55 Nm
Clutch assembly nut	90 Nm
Crankcase bolts	9 Nm
Gearbox oil drain plug	22 Nm
Gearbox cover bolts	6.5 Nm
Rear shock absorber mountings	
Lower bolt	18 Nm
Upper bolt	32 Nm
Rear sub frame bolts	42 Nm
Steering head bearing locknut	75 Nm
Handlebar stem bolt	60 Nm
Front fork leg bottom bolt	23 Nm
Front fork leg clamp bolt	33 Nm
Front axle nut	70 Nm
Rear wheel bolts	47 Nm
Rear hub nut	104 Nm
Disc brake caliper mounting bolts	23 Nm
Disc mounting bolts	23 Nm
Brake hose banjo bolts	23 Nm

Engine

Engine	124 cc single-cylinder four-stroke
Cooling system	Liquid-cooled
Fuel system	Teikei TK5DS CV carburettor
Ignition system	CDI
Transmission	Variable speed automatic, belt-driven
Suspension	Telescopic front, swingarm with twin shock rear
Brakes	245 mm disc front, 220 mm disc rear
Tyres	130/60 x 13 front, 140/60 x 13 rear
Wheelbase	1400 mm
Weight	130 kg
Fuel tank capacity	7.5 litres

Ignition system

HT coil primary resistance	0.32 to 0.48 ohms
HT coil secondary resistance	5.7 to 8.5 K-ohms
Spark plug cap resistance	10 K-ohms
Pick-up coil resistance	248 to 372 ohms
Source coil resistance	720 to 1080 ohms

Transmission

Belt width (service limit)	16.0 mm
Variator rollers diameter	
(service limit)	14.5 mm
Clutch lining thickness	
(service limit)	2.5 mm
Clutch spring free length	
(service limit)	73 mm
Gearbox oil	SAE 85W 140 oil
Gearbox oil capacity	150 ml

Brakes

Disc brake	
Fluid type	DOT 4
Pad thickness (service limit)	2.0 mm
Disc thickness (service limit)	3.2 mm
Brake lever freeplay	10 to 20 mm
Drum brake	
Drum internal diameter	
(service limit)	110.5 mm
Brake shoe lining thickness	
Standard	4.0 mm
Service limit	2.0 mm
Brake lever freeplay	10 to 20 mm

Engine

Spark plug type	NGK CR8E
Electrode gap	0.5 to 0.7 mm
Idle speed (rpm)	1600 to 1800 rpm
Engine oil	10W 30 four-stroke motorcycle engine oil
Oil capacity	1.4 litres
Bore x stroke	52.0 x 47.6 mm
Piston diameter (standard)	53.670 to 53.687 mm
Cylinder bore (standard)	53.700 to 53.705 mm
Piston to bore clearance (service limit)	0.15 mm
Piston ring installed end gap	
Top ring (service limit)	0.50 mm
Second ring (service limit)	0.65 mm
Oil control ring (standard)	0.2 to 0.7 mm
Valve clearance	
Intake	0.10 to 0.14 mm
Exhaust	0.16 to 0.20 mm
Valve spring free length	
Standard	41.94 mm
Service limit	39.84 mm
Camshaft lobe height (service limit)	30.711 mm
Coolant	50% distilled water, 50% corrosion inhibiting ethylene glycol anti-freeze
Coolant capacity	1.25 litres

Fuel system

Throttle twistgrip freeplay	1.5 to 3 mm
Main jet	116
Pilot jet	38
Starter jet	45
Needle type / position	4E31 (3rd notch from top)
Pilot screw setting	2¼ turns out
Fuel level	5 to 6 mm

Yamaha YN50 Neo's and MBK Ovetto 50

Engine

Engine	49 cc single-cylinder two-stroke
Cooling system	Air-cooled
Fuel system	Dell'Orto PHVA 12 slide carburettor
Ignition system	CDI
Transmission	Variable speed automatic, belt-driven
Suspension	Telescopic front, swingarm with single shock rear
Brakes	disc front, drum rear
Tyres	120/70 x 12 front, 130/70 x 12 rear
Wheelbase	1280 mm
Weight	87 kg
Fuel tank capacity	6.5 litres

Engine

Spark plug type	NGK BR8HS
Electrode gap	0.6 to 0.7 mm
Idle speed (rpm)	1800 rpm
Engine oil	JASO FC two-stroke engine oil
Oil tank capacity	1.2 litres
Bore x stroke	40.0 x 39.2 mm
Piston diameter (standard)	39.952 to 39.972 mm
Cylinder bore service limit	40.1 mm
Piston to bore clearance (standard)	0.034 to 0.047 mm
Piston ring installed end gap (service limit)	0.60 mm

Fuel system

Throttle twistgrip freeplay	1.5 to 3.5 mm
Main jet	78
Pilot jet	36
Starter jet	45
Needle type / position	A12 (3rd notch from top)
Pilot screw setting	1½ turns out
Float height	15 to 17 mm

Tyre pressures

Front	25 psi (1.75 bar)
Rear	29 psi (2.00 bar)

Electrical system

Battery	
Capacity	12 V, 4 Ah
Alternator	
Output (regulated)	14 to 15 V (DC)
Charging coil resistance	0.5 to 0.7 ohms
Lighting coil resistance	0.4 to 0.6 ohms
Fuse (main)	7 Amps
Bulbs	
Headlight (main/dipped)	25/25 W
Sidelight	5 W
Brake/tail light	21/5 W
Turn signal lights	10 W
Instrument and warning lights	1.2 and 2 W

Ignition system

HT coil primary resistance	0.56 to 0.84 ohms
HT coil secondary resistance	5.68 to 8.52 K-ohms
Pick-up coil resistance	400 to 600 ohms

Transmission

Belt width (service limit)	15.7 mm
Variator rollers diameter (service limit)	14.5 mm
Clutch lining thickness (service limit)	1 mm
Clutch spring free length (service limit)	90.4 mm
Gearbox oil	SAE 10W 30 oil
Gearbox oil capacity	110 ml

Brakes

Disc brake	
Fluid type	DOT 4
Pad thickness (service limit)	0.8 mm
Disc thickness (service limit)	3.0 mm
Drum brake	
Drum internal diameter (service limit)	110.5 mm
Brake shoe lining thickness	
Standard	4.0 mm
Service limit	2.0 mm
Brake lever freeplay	5 to 10 mm

Torque wrench settings

Cylinder head nuts	14 Nm
Crankcase bolts	10 Nm
Engine mounting bolt	84 Nm
Exhaust manifold nuts	9 Nm
Exhaust system mounting bolts	26 Nm
Oil pump mounting bolts	4 Nm
Alternator rotor nut	43 Nm
Alternator stator bolts	8 Nm
Variator centre nut	33 Nm
Clutch centre nut	40 Nm
Clutch assembly nut	50 Nm
Gearbox oil filler plug	12 Nm
Gearbox oil drain plug	5.5 Nm
Gearbox cover bolts	9 Nm
Rear shock absorber mountings	
Lower bolt	18 Nm
Upper bolt	Not available
Steering head bearing locknut	48 Nm
Handlebar stem bolt	43 Nm
Front fork leg bottom bolt	23 Nm
Front fork leg clamp bolt	30 Nm
Front axle nut	48 Nm
Rear hub nut	125 Nm
Disc brake caliper mounting bolts	23 Nm
Disc mounting bolts	20 Nm
Brake hose banjo bolts	23 Nm

Yamaha YN100 Neo's and MBK Ovetto 100

Engine
Cooling system	101 cc single-cylinder two-stroke
	Air-cooled
Fuel system	Teikei Y16P slide carburettor
Ignition system	CDI

Transmission — Variable speed automatic, belt-driven

Suspension — Telescopic front, swingarm with single shock rear

Brakes — 190 mm disc front, 110 mm drum rear

Tyres — 120/70 x 12 front, 130/70 x 12 rear

Fuel tank capacity — 5.5 litres

Engine
Spark plug type	NGK BR8HS
Electrode gap	0.6 to 0.7 mm
Idle speed (rpm)	1700 to 1900 rpm
Engine oil	JASO FC grade two-stroke engine oil
Oil tank capacity	1.2 litres
Bore x stroke	52.0 x 47.6 mm
Piston diameter (standard)	51.995 to 51.970 mm
Cylinder bore	
Standard	52.002 to 52.012 mm
Service limit	52.1 mm
Piston to bore clearance (standard)	0.042 to 0.047 mm
Piston ring installed end gap (standard)	0.15 to 35 mm

Fuel system
Throttle twistgrip freeplay	2 to 5 mm
Main jet	76
Pilot jet	44
Starter jet	42
Needle type / position	3S0E (3rd notch from top)
Pilot screw setting	1¼ turns out
Float height	15 to 17 mm

Tyre pressures
Front	25 psi (1.75 bar)
Rear	29 psi (2.00 bar)

Electrical system
Battery	
Capacity	12 V, 4 Ah
Alternator	
Output (regulated)	12 to 15 V (DC)
Charging coil resistance	0.5 to 0.7 ohms
Lighting coil resistance	0.4 to 0.6 ohms
Fuse (main)	7 Amps
Bulbs	
Headlight (main/dipped)	35/35 W
Sidelight	5 W
Brake/tail light	21/5 W
Turn signal lights	10 W
Instrument and warning lights	1.2 and 2W

Ignition system
HT coil primary resistance	0.32 to 0.48 ohms
HT coil secondary resistance	5.68 to 8.52 K-ohms
Spark plug cap resistance	5 K-ohms
Pick-up coil resistance	400 to 600 ohms
Source coil resistance	640 to 960 ohms

Transmission
Belt width (service limit)	16.0 mm
Variator rollers diameter (service limit)	14.5 mm
Clutch lining thickness (service limit)	2.5 mm
Clutch spring free length (service limit)	81.0 mm
Gearbox oil	SAE 10W 30 oil
Gearbox oil capacity	130 ml

Brakes
Disc brake	
Fluid type	DOT 4
Pad thickness (service limit)	0.8 mm
Disc thickness (service limit)	3.0 mm
Drum brake	
Drum internal diameter (service limit)	110.5 mm
Brake shoe lining thickness (service limit)	2.0 mm
Brake lever freeplay	5 to 10 mm

Torque wrench settings
Cylinder head nuts	14 Nm
Crankcase bolts	12 Nm
Engine mounting bolt	84 Nm
Exhaust manifold nuts	9 Nm
Exhaust system mounting bolts	26 Nm
Oil pump mounting bolts	4 Nm
Alternator rotor nut	43 Nm
Alternator stator bolts	8 Nm
Variator centre nut	45 Nm
Clutch centre nut	50 Nm
Clutch assembly nut	50 Nm
Gearbox oil drain plug	18 Nm
Gearbox cover bolts	12 Nm
Rear shock absorber mountings	
Lower bolt	20 Nm
Upper bolt	39 Nm
Steering head bearing locknut	48 Nm
Handlebar stem bolt	43 Nm
Front fork leg bottom bolt	23 Nm
Front fork leg clamp bolt	30 Nm
Front axle nut	48 Nm
Rear hub nut	120 Nm
Disc brake caliper mounting bolts	23 Nm
Disc mounting bolts	20 Nm
Brake hose banjo bolts	23 Nm

Yamaha YP125 Majesty and MBK Skyliner 125

Engine

Engine	124 cc single-cylinder four-stroke
Cooling system	Liquid-cooled
Fuel system	Teikei Z24V-1D CV carburettor
Ignition system	CDI
Transmission	Variable speed automatic, belt-driven
Suspension	Telescopic front, swingarm with twin adjustable shock rear
Brakes	220 mm disc front, 190 mm disc rear
Tyres	120/70 x 12 front, 130/70 x 12 rear
Wheelbase	1480 mm
Weight	141 kg
Fuel tank capacity	10.5 litres

Electrical system

Battery		
Capacity		12 V, 6 Ah
Alternator		14 V (DC)
Output (regulated)		0.6 to 0.9 ohms
Charging coil resistance		20 Amps
Fuse (main)		4 Amps
Fuse (cooling fan)		
Bulbs		
Headlight (main/dipped)		35/35 W
Sidelight		5 W
Brake/tail light		21/5 W
Turn signal lights		10 W
Instrument and warning lights		1.2 W

Ignition system

HT coil primary resistance	0.19 to 0.27 ohms
HT coil secondary resistance	6.3 to 9.5 K-ohms
Spark plug cap resistance	10 K-ohms
Pick-up coil resistance	248 to 372 ohms
Source coil resistance	720 to 1080 ohms

Transmission

Belt width (standard)	21.0 mm
Clutch lining thickness	
(service limit)	1.5 mm
Gearbox oil	SAE 10W 30 oil
Gearbox oil capacity	150 ml

Torque wrench settings

Cylinder head nuts	22 Nm
Cylinder head bolts	12 Nm
Cam chain tensioner bolts	6.5 Nm
Camshaft sprocket bolt	30 Nm
Engine oil drain plug	32 Nm
Engine mounting bolt	55 Nm
Exhaust manifold nuts	10 Nm
Exhaust system mounting bolts	31 Nm
Water pump cover bolts	10 Nm
Thermostat cover bolts	10 Nm
Oil pump mounting bolts	6.5 Nm
Alternator rotor nut	70 Nm
Alternator stator bolts	7 Nm
Variator centre nut	55 Nm
Clutch centre nut	60 Nm
Clutch assembly nut	60 Nm
Crankcase bolts	9 Nm
Gearbox oil drain plug	22 Nm
Gearbox cover bolts	10 Nm
Rear shock absorber mountings	
Lower bolt	35 Nm
Upper bolt	32 Nm
Steering head bearing locknut	75 Nm
Handlebar stem bolt	42 Nm
Front fork leg bottom bolt	23 Nm
Front fork leg clamp bolt	23 Nm
Front axle nut	70 Nm
Rear hub nut	105 Nm
Disc brake caliper mounting bolts	
Front	23 Nm
Rear	28 Nm
Disc mounting bolts	23 Nm
Brake hose banjo bolts	30 Nm

Engine

Spark plug type	NGK CR8E
Electrode gap	0.7 to 0.8 mm
Idle speed (rpm)	1600 to 1800 rpm
Engine oil	SAE 10W 40 four-stroke motorcycle oil
Oil capacity	1.4 litres
Bore x stroke	53.7 x 54.8 mm
Piston diameter (standard)	53.700 to 53.687 mm
Cylinder bore (standard)	52.002 to 53.705 mm
Piston to bore clearance (service limit)	0.15 mm
Piston ring installed end gap (standard/service limit)	
Top ring	0.15 to 25 mm/0.50 mm
Second ring	0.15 to 30 mm/0.65 mm
Oil control ring	0.2 to 0.7 mm
Valve clearance	
Intake	0.10 to 0.14 mm
Exhaust	0.16 to 0.20 mm
Valve spring free length	
Standard	41.94 mm
Service limit	39.84 mm
Camshaft height	
Standard	30.811 to 30.911 mm
Service limit	30.711 mm
Coolant	50% distilled water, 50% corrosion inhibiting ethylene glycol anti-freeze
Coolant capacity	1.1 litres

Brakes

Fluid type	DOT 4
Pad thickness	
Standard	4.5 mm
Service limit	
Front	0.8 mm
Rear	0.5 mm
Disc thickness	
Front	
Standard	4.5 mm
Service limit	4.0 mm
Rear	
Standard	5.0 mm
Brake lever freeplay	2 to 5 mm

Fuel system

Throttle twistgrip freeplay	3 to 5 mm
Main jet	116
Pilot jet	38
Starter jet	45
Needle type / position	4E31 (3rd notch from top)
Pilot screw setting	2½ turns out

Tyre pressures

Front	28 psi (1.9 bar)
Rear	32 psi (2.2 bar)

Engine

Engine	249 cc single-cylinder four-stroke
Cooling system	Liquid-cooled
Fuel system	Teikei Y28V-1A CV carburettor
Ignition system	CDI
Transmission	Variable speed automatic, belt-driven
Suspension	Telescopic front, swingarm with twin adjustable shock rear
Brakes	245 mm disc front, 160 mm drum rear
Tyres	110/90 x 12 front, 130/70 x 12 rear
Wheelbase	1480 mm
Weight	158 kg
Fuel tank capacity	11.0 litres

Engine

Spark plug type	NGK DR8EA
Electrode gap	0.6 to 0.7 mm
Idle speed (rpm)	1450 to 1550 rpm
Engine oil	SAE 10W 40 four-stroke motorcycle oil
Oil capacity	1.4 litres
Bore x stroke	69.0 x 66.8 mm
Piston diameter (standard)	68.965 to 68.980 mm
Cylinder bore service limit	69.1 mm
Piston to bore clearance (service limit)	0.15 mm
Piston ring installed end gap (standard/service limit)	
Top ring	0.15 to 30 mm/0.45 mm
Second ring	0.30 to 45 mm/0.70 mm
Oil control ring	0.2 to 0.7 mm
Valve clearance	
Intake	0.08 to 0.12 mm
Exhaust	0.16 to 0.20 mm
Valve spring free length (standard/service limit)	
Inner spring	38.10 mm/36.1 mm
Outer spring	36.93 mm/35.0 mm
Camshaft height service limit	36.45 mm
Coolant	50% distilled water, 50% corrosion inhibiting ethylene glycol anti-freeze
Coolant capacity	1.4 litres

Fuel system

Throttle twistgrip freeplay	3 to 5 mm
Main jet	130
Pilot jet	44
Needle type / position	5D32 (3rd notch from top)
Pilot screw setting	1⅞ turns out
Float height	27 mm

Ignition system

HT coil primary resistance	3.6 to 4.8 ohms
HT coil secondary resistance	10.7 to 14.5 K-ohms
Spark plug cap resistance	5 K-ohms
Pick-up coil resistance	168 to 252 ohms

Transmission

Belt width service limit	21.0 mm
Variator rollers diameter service limit	19.5 mm
Clutch lining thickness service limit	2.0 mm
Gearbox oil	SAE 10W 40 oil
Gearbox oil capacity	250 ml

Brakes

Disc brake	
Fluid type	DOT 4
Pad thickness service limit	0.8 mm
Disc thickness (standard)	4.0 mm
Drum brake	
Shoe lining minimum thickness	2.0 mm
Brake lever freeplay	2 to 5 mm

Tyre pressures

Front	25 psi (1.75 bar)
Rear	29 psi (2.00 bar)

Electrical system

Battery	
Capacity	12 V, 6 Ah
Alternator	
Output (regulated)	14 V (DC)
Charging coil resistance	0.8 to 1.0 ohms
Fuse (main)	20 Amps
Fuse (cooling fan)	3 Amps
Bulbs	
Headlight (main/dipped)	60/55 W
Sidelight	4 W
Brake/tail light	21/5 W
Turn signal lights	21 W
Instrument and warning lights	3.4 and 1.7 W

Torque wrench settings

Valve cover bolts	10 Nm
Cylinder head nuts	22 Nm
Cylinder head bolts	10 Nm
Cam chain tensioner bolts	10 Nm
Camshaft sprocket bolt	60 Nm
Engine oil drain plug	22 Nm
Engine mounting bolt	32 Nm
Exhaust manifold nuts	20 Nm
Exhaust system mounting bolts	53 Nm
Water pump cover bolts	10 Nm
Thermostat cover bolts	10 Nm
Oil pump mounting bolts	7 Nm
Alternator rotor nut	80 Nm
Alternator stator bolts	7 Nm
Variator centre nut	60 Nm
Clutch centre nut	60 Nm
Clutch assembly nut	90 Nm
Crankcase bolts	10 Nm
Gearbox oil drain plug	22 Nm
Gearbox cover bolts	18 Nm
Rear shock absorber mountings	
Lower bolt	19 Nm
Upper bolt	40 Nm
Steering head bearing locknut	75 Nm
Handlebar stem nut	139 Nm
Handlebar clamp bolts	23 Nm
Front fork leg bottom bolts	23 Nm
Front fork leg clamp bolts	23 Nm
Front axle nut	70 Nm
Rear hub nut	135 Nm
Disc brake caliper mounting bolt	23 Nm
Disc caliper bracket bolts	49 Nm
Disc mounting bolts	23 Nm
Brake hose banjo bolts	26 Nm

Yamaha YQ50 Aerox and MBK Nitro 50

Engine

Engine	49 cc single-cylinder two-stroke
Cooling system	Liquid-cooled
Fuel system	Dell'Orto PHBN 12HS slide carburettor
Ignition system	CDI
Transmission	Variable speed automatic, belt-driven
Suspension	Telescopic front, swingarm with single shock rear
Brakes	190 mm disc front, 190 mm disc rear
Tyres	130/60 x 13 front, 140/60 x 13 rear
Wheelbase	1256 mm
Weight	97 kg
Fuel tank capacity	7.0 litres

Engine

Spark plug type	NGK BR8HS
Electrode gap	0.5 to 0.7 mm
Idle speed (rpm)	1600 to 2000 rpm
Engine oil	JASO FC two-stroke engine oil
Bore x stroke	40.0 x 39.2 mm
Piston diameter (standard)	39.957 to 39.977 mm
Cylinder bore service limit	40.1 mm
Piston to bore clearance (service limit)	0.1 mm
Piston ring installed end gap (standard)	0.15 to 0.35 mm
Coolant	50% distilled water, 50% corrosion inhibiting ethylene glycol anti-freeze
Coolant capacity	1.2 litres

Fuel system

Throttle twistgrip freeplay	1 to 3 mm
Main jet	86
Pilot jet	36
Starter jet	45
Needle type / position	A12 (2nd notch from top)
Pilot screw setting	1⅛ turns out
Float height	15 to 17 mm

Tyre pressures

Front	22 psi (1.5 bar)
Rear	22 psi (1.5 bar)

Electrical system

Battery	
Capacity	12 V, 4 Ah
Alternator	
Output (regulated)	13 to 14 V (DC)
Charging coil resistance	0.48 to 0.72 ohms
Lighting coil resistance	0.32 to 0.48 ohms
Fuse (main)	7.5 Amps
Bulbs	
Headlight (main/dipped)	35/35 W
Sidelight	5 W
Brake/tail light	21/5 W
Turn signal lights	10 W
Instrument and warning lights	1.2 W

Ignition system

HT coil primary resistance	0.56 to 0.84 ohms
HT coil secondary resistance	5.68 to 8.52 K-ohms
Spark plug cap resistance	5 K-ohms
Pick-up coil resistance	400 to 600 ohms
Source coil resistance	640 to 960 ohms

Transmission

Belt width (service limit)	15.7 mm
Variator rollers diameter (service limit)	14.5 mm
Clutch lining thickness (service limit)	1 mm
Clutch spring free length (service limit)	106.7 mm
Gearbox oil	SAE 10W 30 oil
Gearbox oil capacity	130 ml

Brakes

Fluid type	DOT 4
Pad thickness (service limit)	2.0 mm
Disc thickness (service limit)	3.2 mm
Brake lever freeplay	10 to 20 mm

Torque wrench settings

Cylinder head nuts	14 Nm
Crankcase bolts	13 Nm
Engine mounting bolt	50 Nm
Exhaust manifold bolts	7 Nm
Exhaust system mounting bolts	29 Nm
Oil pump mounting bolts	4 Nm
Alternator rotor nut	37.5 Nm
Alternator stator bolts	8.5 Nm
Variator centre nut	33 Nm
Clutch centre nut	30 Nm
Clutch assembly nut	50 Nm
Gearbox oil drain plug	17.5 Nm
Gearbox cover bolts	10 Nm
Rear shock absorber mountings	
Lower bolt	16 Nm
Upper bolt	Not available
Steering head bearing locknut	22.5 Nm
Handlebar stem bolt	60 Nm
Front fork leg bottom bolt	23 Nm
Front fork leg clamp bolt	30 Nm
Front axle nut	35 Nm
Rear wheel bolts	47 Nm
Rear hub nut	120 Nm
Disc brake caliper mounting bolts	23 Nm
Disc mounting bolts	23 Nm
Brake hose banjo bolts	23 Nm

Yamaha YQ100 Aerox and MBK Nitro 100

Engine .... 101 cc single-cylinder two-stroke
Cooling system .... Air-cooled
Fuel system .... Teikei TK16 slide carburettor
Ignition system .... CDI
Transmission .... Variable speed automatic, belt-driven
Suspension .... Telescopic front, swingarm with single shock rear
Brakes .... 190 mm disc front, 130 mm drum rear
Tyres .... 130/60 x 13 front, 140/60 x 13 rear
Wheelbase .... 1272 mm
Weight .... 57 kg
Fuel tank capacity .... 7.0 litres

Tyre pressures

Front .... 22 psi (1.5 bar)
Rear .... 22 psi (1.5 bar)

Electrical system

Battery
  Capacity .... 12 V, 3 Ah
Alternator
  Output (regulated) .... 13 to 14 V (DC)
  Charging coil resistance .... 0.48 to 0.72 ohms
  Lighting coil resistance .... 0.40 to 0.60 ohms
Fuse (main) .... 7.5 Amps
Bulbs
  Headlight (main/dipped) .... 35/35 W
  Sidelight .... 5 W
  Brake/tail light .... 21/5 W
  Turn signal lights .... 10 W
  Instrument and warning lights .... 1.2 W

Engine

Spark plug type .... NGK BR8HS
Electrode gap .... 0.5 to 0.7 mm
Idle speed (rpm) .... 1800 to 2200 rpm
Engine oil .... JASO FC two-stroke engine oil
Oil tank capacity .... 1.3 litres
Bore x stroke .... 52.0 x 47.6 mm
Piston diameter (standard) .... 51.958 to 51.967 mm
Cylinder bore (standard) .... 52.002 to 52.012 mm
Piston to bore clearance (service limit) .. 0.1 mm
Piston ring installed end gap (standard) .. 0.15 to 0.35 mm

Ignition system

HT coil primary resistance .... 0.32 to 0.48 ohms
HT coil secondary resistance .... 5.68 to 8.52 K-ohms
Spark plug cap resistance .... 5 K-ohms
Pick-up coil resistance .... 400 to 600 ohms
Source coil resistance .... 640 to 960 ohms

Transmission

Belt width (service limit) .... 16.0 mm
Variator rollers diameter (service limit) .. 14.5 mm
Clutch lining thickness (service limit) .. 2.5 mm
Clutch spring free length (service limit) .. 73 mm
Gearbox oil .... SAE 85W 140 oil
Gearbox oil capacity .... 130 ml

Torque wrench settings

Cylinder head nuts .... 14 Nm
Crankcase bolts .... 12 Nm
Engine mounting bolt .... 50 Nm
Exhaust manifold bolts .... 8.5 Nm
Exhaust system mounting bolts .... 29 Nm
Oil pump mounting bolts .... 4 Nm
Alternator rotor nut .... 43 Nm
Alternator stator bolts .... 8 Nm
Variator centre nut .... 45 Nm
Clutch centre nut .... 40 Nm
Clutch assembly nut .... 50 Nm
Gearbox oil drain plug .... 18 Nm
Gearbox cover bolts .... 12 Nm
Rear shock absorber mountings
  Lower bolt .... 17.5 Nm
  Upper bolt .... 31.5 Nm
Steering head bearing locknut .... 75 Nm
Handlebar stem bolt .... 60 Nm
Front fork leg bottom bolt .... 23 Nm
Front fork leg clamp bolt .... 30 Nm
Front axle nut .... 35 Nm
Rear wheel bolts .... 47 Nm
Rear hub nut .... 125 Nm
Disc brake caliper mounting bolts ..... 31 Nm
Disc mounting bolts .... 23 Nm
Brake hose banjo bolts .... 23 Nm

Brakes

Disc brake
  Fluid type .... DOT 4
  Pad thickness (service limit) .... 2.0 mm
  Disc thickness (service limit) ...... 3.2 mm
  Brake lever freeplay .... 10 to 20 mm
Drum brake
  Drum internal diameter (service limit) .. 110.5 mm
  Brake shoe lining thickness
    Standard .... 4.0 mm
    Service limit .... 2.0 mm
  Brake lever freeplay .... 10 to 20 mm

Fuel system

Throttle twistgrip freeplay .... 1.5 to 3 mm
Main jet 76
Pilot jet 44
Starter jet 43
Needle type / position .... 3SOF (3rd notch from top)
Pilot screw setting .... 1% turns out

Reference

Tools and Workshop Tips

Buying tools

A toolkit is a fundamental requirement for servicing and repairing a scooter. Although there will be an initial expense in building up enough tools for servicing, this will soon be offset by the savings made by doing the job yourself. As experience and confidence grow, additional tools can be added to enable the repair and overhaul of the scooter. Many of the specialist tools are expensive and not often used so it may be preferable to hire them, or for a group of friends or scooter club to join in the purchase.

As a rule, it is better to buy more expensive, good quality tools. Cheaper tools are likely to wear out faster and need to be renewed more often, nullifying the original saving.

 Warning: To avoid the risk of a poor quality tool breaking in use, causing injury or damage to the component being worked on, always aim to purchase tools which meet the relevant national safety standards.

The following lists of tools do not represent the manufacturer's service tools, but serve as a guide to help the owner decide which tools are needed for this level of work. In addition, items such as an electric drill, hacksaw, files, soldering iron and a workbench equipped with a vice, may be needed. Although not classed as tools, a selection of bolts, screws, nuts, washers and pieces of tubing always come in useful.

For more information about tools, refer to the Haynes *Motorcycle Workshop Practice Techbook* (Bk. No. 3470).

Manufacturer's service tools

Inevitably certain tasks require the use of a service tool. Where possible an alter native tool or method of approach is recommended, but sometimes there is no option if personal injury or damage to the component is to be avoided. Where required, service tools are referred to in the relevant procedure.

Service tools can usually only be purchased from a scooter dealer and are identified by a part number. Some of the commonly-used tools, such as rotor pullers, are available in aftermarket form from mail-order motorcycle tool and accessory suppliers.

Maintenance and minor repair tools

- [ ] *Set of flat-bladed screwdrivers*
- [ ] *Set of Phillips head screwdrivers*
- [ ] *Combination open-end and ring spanners*
- [ ] *Socket set (3/8 inch or 1/2 inch drive)*
- [ ] *Set of Allen keys or bits*
- [ ] *Set of Torx keys or bits*
- [ ] *Pliers, cutters and self-locking grips (Mole grips)*
- [ ] *Adjustable spanners*
- [ ] *C-spanners*
- [ ] *Tread depth gauge and tyre pressure gauge*
- [ ] *Cable oiler clamp*
- [ ] *Feeler gauges*
- [ ] *Spark plug gap measuring tool*
- [ ] *Spark plug spanner or deep plug sockets*
- [ ] *Wire brush and emery paper*
- [ ] *Calibrated syringe, measuring vessel and funnel*
- [ ] *Oil filter adapters (4-stroke engines)*
- [ ] *Oil drainer can or tray*
- [ ] *Pump type oil can*
- [ ] *Grease gun*
- [ ] *Straight-edge and steel rule*
- [ ] *Continuity tester*
- [ ] *Battery charger*
- [ ] *Hydrometer (for battery specific gravity check)*
- [ ] *Anti-freeze tester (for liquid-cooled engines)*

Repair and overhaul tools

- [ ] *Torque wrench (small and mid-ranges)*
- [ ] *Conventional, plastic or soft-faced hammers*
- [ ] *Impact driver set*
- [ ] *Vernier gauge*
- [ ] *Circlip pliers (internal and external, or combination)*
- [ ] *Set of cold chisels and punches*
- [ ] *Selection of pullers*
- [ ] *Breaker bars*
- [ ] *One-man brake bleeder kit*
- [ ] *Wire stripper and crimper tool*
- [ ] *Multimeter (measures amps, volts and ohms)*
- [ ] *Stroboscope (for dynamic timing checks)*
- [ ] *Hose clamp*
- [ ] *Clutch holding tool*

Specialist tools

- [ ] *Micrometers (external type)*
- [ ] *Telescoping gauges*
- [ ] *Dial gauge*
- [ ] *Stud extractor*
- [ ] *Screw extractor set*
- [ ] *Bearing driver set*
- [ ] *Valve spring compressor (4-stroke engines)*
- [ ] *Piston pin drawbolt tool*
- [ ] *Piston ring clamp*

1.1 Hydraulic motorcycle ramp

1.2 Use an approved can only for storing petrol (gasoline)

1.3 A fire extinguisher, goggles, mask and protective gloves should be at hand in the workshop

1 Workshop equipment and facilities

The workbench

● Work is made much easier by raising the scooter up on a ramp – components are much more accessible if raised to waist level. The hydraulic or pneumatic types seen in the dealer's workshop are a sound investment if you undertake a lot of repairs or overhauls (see illustration 1.1).
● If raised off ground level, the scooter must be supported on the ramp to avoid it falling. Most ramps incorporate a front wheel locating clamp which can be adjusted to suit different diameter wheels. When tightening the clamp, take care not to mark the wheel rim or damage the tyre – use wood blocks on each side to prevent this.

Fumes and fire

● Refer to the Safety first! page at the beginning of the manual for full details. Make sure your workshop is equipped with a fire extinguisher suitable for fuel-related fires (Class B fire – flammable liquids) – it is not sufficient to have a water-filled extinguisher.
● Always ensure adequate ventilation is available. Unless an exhaust gas extraction system is available for use, ensure that the engine is run outside of the workshop.
● If working on the fuel system, make sure

the workshop is ventilated to avoid a build-up of fumes. This applies equally to fume build-up when charging a battery. Do not smoke or allow anyone else to smoke in the workshop.

Fluids

● If you need to drain fuel from the tank, store it in an approved container marked as suitable for the storage of petrol (gasoline) (see illustration 1.2). Do not store fuel in glass jars or bottles.
● Use proprietary engine degreasers or solvents which have a high flash-point, such as paraffin (kerosene), for cleaning off oil, grease and dirt – never use petrol (gasoline) for cleaning. Wear rubber gloves when handling solvent and engine degreaser. The fumes from certain solvents can be dangerous – always work in a well-ventilated area.

Dust, eye and hand protection

● Protect your lungs from inhalation of dust particles by wearing a filtering mask over the nose and mouth. Many frictional materials still contain asbestos which is dangerous to your health. Protect your eyes from spouts of liquid and sprung components by wearing a pair of protective goggles (see illustration 1.3).
● Protect your hands from contact with solvents, fuel and oils by wearing rubber gloves. Alternatively apply a barrier cream to your hands before starting work. If handling hot components or fluids, wear suitable gloves to protect your hands from scalding and burns.

What to do with old fluids

● Old cleaning solvent, fuel, coolant and oils should not be poured down domestic drains or onto the ground. Package the fluid up in old oil containers, label it accordingly, and take it to a garage or disposal facility. Contact your local authority for location of such sites.

2 Fasteners – screws, bolts and nuts

Fastener types and applications

Bolts and screws

● Fastener head types are either of hexagonal, Torx or splined design, with internal and external versions of each type (see illustrations 2.1 and 2.2); splined head fasteners are not in common use on scooters. The conventional slotted or Phillips head design is used for certain screws. Bolt or screw length is always measured from the underside of the head to the end of the item (see illustration 2.11).
● Certain fasteners on the scooter have a tensile marking on their heads, the higher the marking the stronger the fastener. High tensile fasteners generally carry a 10 or higher marking. Never replace a high tensile fastener with one of a lower tensile strength.

Washers (see illustration 2.3)

● Plain washers are used between a fastener

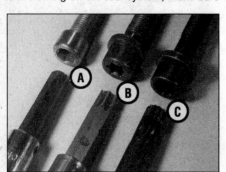

2.1 Internal hexagon/Allen (A), Torx (B) and splined (C) fasteners, with corresponding bits

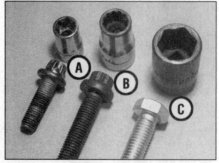

2.2 External Torx (A), splined (B) and hexagon (C) fasteners, with corresponding sockets

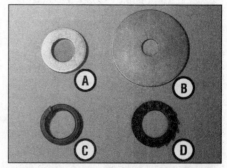

2.3 Plain washer (A), penny washer (B), spring washer (C) and serrated washer (D)

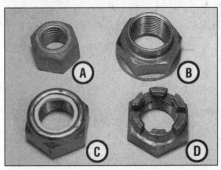

2.4 Plain nut (A), shouldered locknut (B), nylon insert nut (C) and castellated nut (D)

2.5 Bend split pin (cotter pin) arms as shown (arrows) to secure a castellated nut

2.6 Bend split pin (cotter pin) arms as shown to secure a plain nut

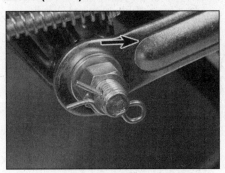

2.7 Correct fitting of R-pin. Arrow indicates forward direction

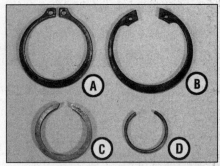

2.8 External stamped circlip (A), internal stamped circlip (B), machined circlip (C) and wire circlip (D)

head and a component to prevent damage to the component or to spread the load when torque is applied. Plain washers can also be used as spacers or shims in certain assemblies. Copper or aluminium plain washers are often used as sealing washers on drain plugs.

● The split-ring spring washer works by applying axial tension between the fastener head and component. If flattened, it is fatigued and must be renewed. If a plain (flat) washer is used on the fastener, position the spring washer between the fastener and the plain washer.

● Serrated star type washers dig into the fastener and component faces, preventing loosening. They are often used on electrical earth (ground) connections to the frame.

● Cone type washers (sometimes called Belleville) are conical and when tightened apply axial tension between the fastener head and component. They must be installed with the dished side against the component and often carry an OUTSIDE marking on their outer face. If flattened, they are fatigued and must be renewed.

● Tab washers are used to lock plain nuts or bolts on a shaft. A portion of the tab washer is bent up hard against one flat of the nut or bolt to prevent it loosening. Due to the tab washer being deformed in use, a new tab washer should be used every time it is disturbed.

● Wave washers are used to take up endfloat on a shaft. They provide light springing and prevent excessive side-to-side play of a component. Can be found on rocker arm shafts.

Nuts and split pins

● Conventional plain nuts are usually six-sided (see illustration 2.4). They are sized by thread diameter and pitch. High tensile nuts carry a number on one end to denote their tensile strength.

● Self-locking nuts either have a nylon insert, or two spring metal tabs, or a shoulder which is staked into a groove in the shaft – their advantage over conventional plain nuts is a resistance to loosening due to vibration. The nylon insert type can be used a number of times, but must be renewed when the friction of the nylon insert is reduced, ie when the nut spins freely on the shaft. The spring tab type

can be reused unless the tabs are damaged. The shouldered type must be renewed every time it is disturbed.

● Split pins (cotter pins) are used to lock a castellated nut to a shaft or to prevent slackening of a plain nut. Common applications are wheel axles and brake torque arms. Because the split pin arms are deformed to lock around the nut a new split pin must always be used on installation – always fit the correct size split pin which will fit snugly in the shaft hole. Make sure the split pin arms are correctly located around the nut (see illustrations 2.5 and 2.6).

● R-pins (shaped like the letter R), or slip pins as they are sometimes called, are sprung and can be reused if they are otherwise in good condition. Always install R-pins with their closed end facing forwards (see illustration 2.7).

Caution: If the castellated nut slots do not align with the shaft hole after tightening to the torque setting, tighten the nut until the

next slot aligns with the hole – never slacken the nut to align its slot.

Circlips (see illustration 2.8)

● Circlips (sometimes called snap-rings) are used to retain components on a shaft or in a housing and have corresponding external or internal ears to permit removal. Parallel-sided (machined) circlips can be installed either way round in their groove, whereas stamped circlips (which have a chamfered edge on one face) must be installed with the chamfer facing away from the direction of thrust load (see illustration 2.9).

● Always use circlip pliers to remove and install circlips; expand or compress them just enough to remove them. After installation, rotate the circlip in its groove to ensure it is securely seated. If installing a circlip on a splined shaft, always align its opening with a shaft channel to ensure the circlip ends are well supported and unlikely to catch (see illustration 2.10).

● Circlips can wear due to the thrust of components and become loose in their

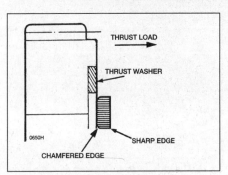

2.9 Correct fitting of a stamped circlip

2.10 Align circlip opening with shaft channel

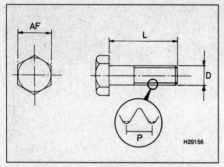

2.11 Fastener length (L), thread diameter (D), thread pitch (P) and head size (AF)

2.12 Using a thread gauge to measure pitch

2.13 A sharp tap on the head of a fastener will often break free a corroded thread

grooves, with the subsequent danger of becoming dislodged in operation. For this reason, renewal is advised every time a circlip is disturbed.

● Wire circlips are commonly used as piston pin retaining clips. If a removal tang is provided, long-nosed pliers can be used to dislodge them, otherwise careful use of a small flat-bladed screwdriver is necessary. Wire circlips should be renewed every time they are disturbed.

Thread diameter and pitch

● Diameter of a male thread (screw, bolt or stud) is the outside diameter of the threaded portion (see illustration 2.11). Most scooter manufacturers use the ISO (International Standards Organisation) metric system expressed in millimetres, eg M6 refers to a 6 mm diameter thread. Sizing is the same for nuts, except that the thread diameter is measured across the valleys of the nut.

● Pitch is the distance between the peaks of the thread (see illustration 2.11). It is expressed in millimetres, thus a common bolt size may be expressed as 6.0 x 1.0 mm (6 mm thread diameter and 1 mm pitch). Generally pitch increases in proportion to thread diameter, although there are always exceptions.

● Thread diameter and pitch are related for conventional fastener applications and the accompanying table can be used as a guide. Additionally, the AF (Across Flats), spanner or socket size dimension of the bolt or nut (see illustration 2.11) is linked to thread and pitch specification. Thread pitch can be measured with a thread gauge (see illustration 2.12).

● The threads of most fasteners are of the right-hand type, ie they are turned clockwise to tighten and anti-clockwise to loosen. The reverse situation applies to left-hand thread fasteners, which are turned anti-clockwise to tighten and clockwise to loosen. Left-hand threads are used where rotation of a component might loosen a conventional right-hand thread fastener.

AF size	Thread diameter x pitch (mm)
8 mm	M5 x 0.8
8 mm	M6 x 1.0
10 mm	M6 x 1.0
12 mm	M8 x 1.25
14 mm	M10 x 1.25
17 mm	M12 x 1.25

Seized fasteners

● Corrosion of external fasteners due to water or reaction between two dissimilar metals can occur over a period of time. It will build up sooner in wet conditions or in countries where salt is used on the roads during the winter. If a fastener is severely corroded it is likely that normal methods of removal will fail and result in its head being ruined. When you attempt removal, the fastener thread should be heard to crack free and unscrew easily – if it doesn't, stop there before damaging something.

● A smart tap on the head of the fastener will often succeed in breaking free corrosion which has occurred in the threads (see illustration 2.13).

● An aerosol penetrating fluid (such as WD-40) applied the night beforehand may work its way down into the thread and ease removal.

Depending on the location, you may be able to make up a Plasticine well around the fastener head and fill it with penetrating fluid.

● If you are working on an engine internal component, corrosion will most likely not be a problem due to the well lubricated environment. However, components can be very tight and an impact driver is a useful tool in freeing them (see illustration 2.14).

● Where corrosion has occurred between dissimilar metals (eg steel and aluminium alloy), the application of heat to the fastener head will create a disproportionate expansion rate between the two metals and break the seizure caused by the corrosion. Whether heat can be applied depends on the location of the fastener – any surrounding components likely to be damaged must first be removed (see illustration 2.15). Heat can be applied using a paint stripper heat gun or clothes iron, or by immersing the component in boiling water – wear protective gloves to prevent scalding or burns to the hands.

● As a last resort, it is possible to use a hammer and cold chisel to work the fastener head unscrewed (see illustration 2.16). This will damage the fastener, but more importantly extreme care must be taken not to damage the surrounding component.

Caution: Remember that the component being secured is generally of more value than the bolt, nut or screw – when the fastener is freed, do not unscrew it with force, instead work the fastener back and forth when resistance is felt to prevent thread damage.

2.14 Using an impact driver to free a fastener

2.15 Using heat to free a seized fastener

2.16 Using a hammer and chisel to free a seized fastener

2.17 Using a stud extractor tool to remove a broken crankcase stud

2.18 Two nuts can be locked together to unscrew a stud from a component

2.19 When using a screw extractor, first drill a hole in the fastener . . .

Broken fasteners and damaged heads

● If the shank of a broken bolt or screw is accessible you can grip it with self-locking grips. The knurled wheel type stud extractor tool or self-gripping stud puller tool is particularly useful for removing the long studs which screw into the cylinder mouth surface of the crankcase or bolts and screws from which the head has broken off (see illustration 2.17). Studs can also be removed by locking two nuts together on the threaded end of the stud and using a spanner on the lower nut (see illustration 2.18).

● A bolt or screw which has broken off below or level with the casing must be extracted using a screw extractor set. Centre punch the fastener to centralise the drill bit, then drill a hole in the fastener (see illustration 2.19). Select a drill bit which is approximately half to three-quarters the diameter of the fastener and drill to a depth which will accommodate the extractor. Use the largest size extractor

possible, but avoid leaving too small a wall thickness otherwise the extractor will merely force the fastener walls outwards wedging it in the casing thread.

● If a spiral type extractor is used, thread it anti-clockwise into the fastener. As it is screwed in, it will grip the fastener and unscrew it from the casing (see illustration 2.20).

 Warning: Stud extractors are very hard and may break off in the fastener if care is not taken – ask an engineer about spark erosion if this happens.

● If a taper type extractor is used, tap it into the fastener so that it is firmly wedged in place. Unscrew the extractor (anti-clockwise) to draw the fastener out.

● Alternatively, the broken bolt/screw can be drilled out and the hole retapped for an oversize bolt/screw or a diamond-section thread insert. It is essential that the drilling is carried out squarely and to the correct depth, otherwise the casing may be ruined – if in

doubt, entrust the work to an engineer.

● Bolts and nuts with rounded corners cause the correct size spanner or socket to slip when force is applied. Of the types of spanner/socket available always use a six-point type rather than an eight or twelve-point type – better grip is obtained. Surface drive spanners grip the middle of the hex flats, rather than the corners, and are thus good in cases of damaged heads (see illustration 2.21).

● Slotted-head or Phillips-head screws are often damaged by the use of the wrong size screwdriver. Allen-head and Torx-head screws are much less likely to sustain damage. If enough of the screw head is exposed you can use a hacksaw to cut a slot in its head and then use a conventional flat-bladed screwdriver to remove it. Alternatively use a hammer and cold chisel to tap the head of the fastener around to slacken it. Always replace damaged fasteners with new ones, preferably Torx or Allen-head type.

2.20 . . . then thread the extractor anti-clockwise into the fastener

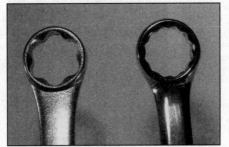

2.21 Comparison of surface drive ring spanner (left) with 12-point type (right)

A dab of valve grinding compound between the screw head and screw-driver tip will often give a good grip.

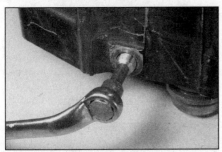

2.22 A thread repair tool being used to correct an internal thread

2.23 A thread repair tool being used to correct an external thread

Thread repair

● Threads (particularly those in aluminium alloy components) can be damaged by overtightening, being assembled with dirt in the threads, or from a component working loose and vibrating. Eventually the thread will fail completely, and it will be impossible to tighten the fastener.

● If a thread is damaged or clogged with old locking compound it can be renovated with a thread repair tool (thread chaser) (see illustrations 2.22 and 2.23); special thread

2.24 Using a thread restorer file

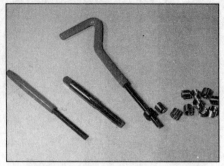

2.25 Obtain a thread insert kit to suit the thread diameter and pitch required

2.26 To install a thread insert, first drill out the original thread . . .

chasers are available for spark plug hole threads. The tool will not cut a new thread, but clean and true the original thread. Make sure that you use the correct diameter and pitch tool. Similarly, external threads can be cleaned up with a die or a thread restorer file **(see illustration 2.24)**.

● It is possible to drill out the old thread and retap the component to the next thread size. This will work where there is enough surrounding material and a new bolt or screw can be obtained. Sometimes, however, this is not possible – such as where the bolt/screw passes through another component which must also be suitably modified, also in cases where a spark plug or oil drain plug cannot be obtained in a larger diameter thread size.

● The diamond-section thread insert (often known by its popular trade name of Heli-Coil)

is a simple and effective method of renewing the thread and retaining the original size. A kit can be purchased which contains the tap, insert and installing tool **(see illustration 2.25)**. Drill out the damaged thread with the size drill specified **(see illustration 2.26)**. Carefully retap the thread **(see illustration 2.27)**. Install the insert on the installing tool and thread it slowly into place using a light downward pressure **(see illustrations 2.28 and 2.29)**. When positioned between a 1/4 and 1/2 turn below the surface withdraw the installing tool and use the break-off tool to press down on the tang, breaking it off **(see illustration 2.30)**.

● There are epoxy thread repair kits on the market which can rebuild stripped internal threads, although this repair should not be used on high load-bearing components.

Thread locking and sealing compounds

● Locking compounds are used in locations where the fastener is prone to loosening due to vibration or on important safety-related items which might cause loss of control of the scooter if they fail. It is also used where important fasteners cannot be secured by other means such as lockwashers or split pins.

● Before applying locking compound, make sure that the threads (internal and external) are clean and dry with all old compound removed. Select a compound to suit the component being secured – a non-permanent general locking and sealing type is suitable for most applications, but a high strength type is needed for permanent fixing of studs in castings. Apply a drop or two of the compound to the first few threads of the fastener, then thread it into place and tighten to the specified torque. Do not apply excessive thread locking compound otherwise the thread may be damaged on subsequent removal.

● Certain fasteners are impregnated with a dry film type coating of locking compound on their threads. Always renew this type of fastener if disturbed.

● Anti-seize compounds, such as copper-based greases, can be applied to protect threads from seizure due to extreme heat and corrosion. A common instance is spark plug threads and exhaust system fasteners.

2.27 . . . tap a new thread . . .

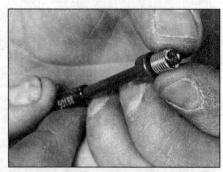

2.28 . . . fit insert on the installing tool . . .

2.29 . . . and thread into the component . . .

2.30 . . . break off the tang when complete

3 Measuring tools and gauges

Feeler gauges

● Feeler gauges (or blades) are used for measuring small gaps and clearances **(see illustration 3.1)**. They can also be used to measure endfloat (sideplay) of a component on a shaft where access is not possible with a dial gauge.

● Feeler gauge sets should be treated with care and not bent or damaged. They are etched with their size on one face. Keep them

3.1 Feeler gauges are used for measuring small gaps and clearances – thickness is marked on one face of gauge

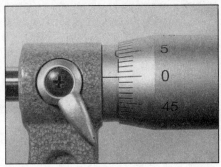

3.2 Check micrometer calibration before use

● To use, first make sure that the item being measured is clean. Place the anvil of the micrometer (1) against the item and use the thimble (2) to bring the spindle (3) lightly into contact with the other side of the item **(see illustration 3.3)**. Don't tighten the thimble down because this will damage the micrometer – instead use the ratchet (4) on the end of the micrometer. The ratchet mechanism applies a measured force preventing damage to the instrument.

● The micrometer is read by referring to the linear scale on the sleeve and the annular scale on the thimble. Read off the sleeve first to obtain the base measurement, then add the fine measurement from the thimble to obtain the overall reading. The linear scale on the sleeve represents the measuring range of the micrometer (eg 0 to 25 mm). The annular scale on the thimble will be in graduations of 0.01 mm (or as marked on the frame) – one full revolution of the thimble will move 0.5 mm on the linear scale. Take the reading where the datum line on the sleeve intersects the thimble's scale. Always position the eye directly above the scale otherwise an inaccurate reading will result.

In the example shown the item measures 2.95 mm **(see illustration 3.4)**:

Linear scale	2.00 mm
Linear scale	0.50 mm
Annular scale	0.45 mm
Total figure	**2.95 mm**

Most micrometers have a locking lever (6) on the frame to hold the setting in place, allowing the item to be removed from the micrometer.

● Some micrometers have a vernier scale on their sleeve, providing an even finer measurement to be taken, in 0.001 increments of a millimetre. Take the sleeve and thimble measurement as described above, then check which graduation on the vernier scale aligns with that of the annular scale on the thimble **Note:** *The eye must be perpendicular to the scale when taking the vernier reading – if necessary rotate the body of the micrometer to ensure this.* Multiply the vernier scale figure by 0.001 and add it to the base and fine measurement figures.

clean and very lightly oiled to prevent corrosion build-up.

● When measuring a clearance, select a gauge which is a light sliding fit between the two components. You may need to use two gauges together to measure the clearance accurately.

Micrometers

● A micrometer is a precision tool capable of measuring to 0.01 or 0.001 of a millimetre. It should always be stored in its case and not in the general toolbox. It must be kept clean and never dropped, otherwise its frame or measuring anvils could be distorted resulting in inaccurate readings.

● External micrometers are used for measuring outside diameters of components and have many more applications than internal micrometers. Micrometers are available in different size ranges, eg 0 to 25 mm, 25 to 50 mm, and upwards in 25 mm steps; some large micrometers have interchangeable anvils to allow a range of measurements to be taken. Generally the largest precision measurement you are likely to take on a scooter is the piston diameter.

● Internal micrometers (or bore micrometers) are used for measuring inside diameters, such as valve guides and cylinder bores. Telescoping gauges and small hole gauges are used in conjunction with an external micrometer, whereas the more expensive internal micrometers have their own measuring device.

External micrometer

Note: *The conventional analogue type instrument is described. Although much easier to read, digital micrometers are considerably more expensive.*

● Always check the calibration of the micrometer before use. With the anvils closed (0 to 25 mm type) or set over a test gauge (for the larger types) the scale should read zero **(see illustration 3.2)**; make sure that the anvils (and test piece) are clean first. Any discrepancy can be adjusted by referring to the instructions supplied with the tool. Remember that the micrometer is a precision measuring tool – don't force the anvils closed, use the ratchet (4) on the end of the micrometer to close it. In this way, a measured force is always applied.

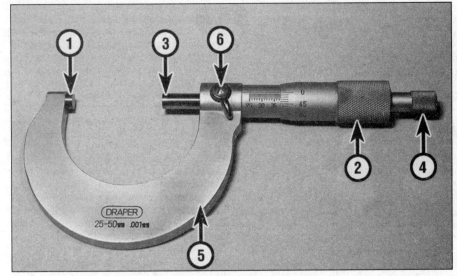

3.3 Micrometer component parts

1	Anvil	3	Spindle	5	Frame
2	Thimble	4	Ratchet	6	Locking lever

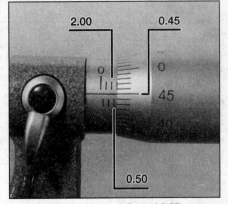

3.4 Micrometer reading of 2.95 mm

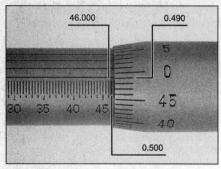

3.5 Micrometer reading of 46.99 mm on linear and annular scales . . .

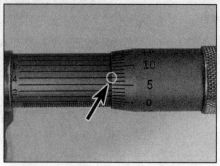

3.6 . . . and 0.004 mm on vernier scale

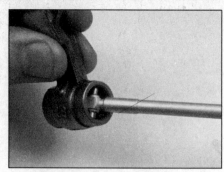

3.7 Expand the telescoping gauge in the bore, lock its position . . .

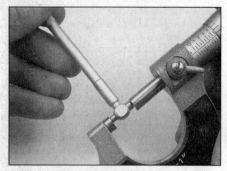

3.8 . . . then measure the gauge with a micrometer

3.9 Expand the small hole gauge in the bore, lock its position . . .

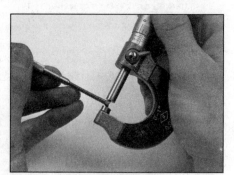

3.10 . . . then measure the gauge with a micrometer

In the example shown the item measures 46.994 mm **(see illustrations 3.5 and 3.6)**:

Linear scale (base)	46.000 mm
Linear scale (base)	00.500 mm
Annular scale (fine)	00.490 mm
Vernier scale	00.004 mm
Total figure	**46.994 mm**

Internal micrometer

● Internal micrometers are available for measuring bore diameters, but are expensive and unlikely to be available for home use. It is suggested that a set of telescoping gauges and small hole gauges, both of which must be used with an external micrometer, will suffice for taking internal measurements on a scooter.
● Telescoping gauges can be used to measure internal diameters of components. Select a gauge with the correct size range, make sure its ends are clean and insert it into the bore. Expand the gauge, then lock its position and withdraw it from the bore (see illustration 3.7). Measure across the gauge ends with a micrometer **(see illustration 3.8)**.
● Very small diameter bores (such as valve guides) are measured with a small hole gauge. Once adjusted to a slip-fit inside the component, its position is locked and the gauge withdrawn for measurement with a micrometer **(see illustrations 3.9 and 3.10)**.

Vernier caliper

Note: *The conventional linear and dial gauge type instruments are described. Digital types are easier to read, but are far more expensive.*
● The vernier caliper does not provide the precision of a micrometer, but is versatile in being able to measure internal and external diameters. Some types also incorporate a depth gauge. It is ideal for measuring clutch plate friction material and spring free lengths.
● To use the conventional linear scale vernier, slacken off the vernier clamp screws (1) and set its jaws over (2), or inside (3), the item to be measured **(see illustration 3.11)**. Slide the jaw into contact, using the thumb-wheel (4) for fine movement of the sliding scale (5) then tighten the clamp screws (1). Read off the main scale (6) where the zero on the sliding scale (5) intersects it, taking the whole number to the left of the zero; this provides the base measurement. View along the sliding scale and select the division which lines up exactly with any of the divisions on the main scale, noting that the divisions usually represents 0.02 of a millimetre. Add this fine measurement to the base measurement to obtain the total reading.

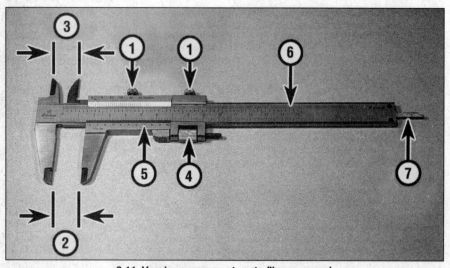

3.11 Vernier component parts (linear gauge)

1	Clamp screws	3	Internal jaws	5	Sliding scale	7	Depth gauge
2	External jaws	4	Thumbwheel	6	Main scale		

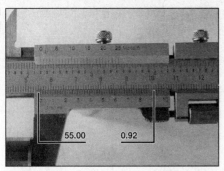

3.12 Vernier gauge reading of 55.92 mm

In the example shown the item measures 55.92 mm **(see illustration 3.12)**:

Base measurement	55.00 mm
Fine measurement	00.92 mm
Total figure	**55.92 mm**

● Some vernier calipers are equipped with a dial gauge for fine measurement. Before use, check that the jaws are clean, then close them fully and check that the dial gauge reads zero. If necessary adjust the gauge ring accordingly. Slacken the vernier clamp screw (1) and set its jaws over (2), or inside (3), the item to be measured **(see illustration 3.13)**. Slide the jaws into contact, using the thumbwheel (4) for fine movement. Read off the main scale (5) where the edge of the sliding scale (6) intersects it, taking the whole number to the left of the zero; this provides the base measurement. Read off the needle position on the dial gauge (7) scale to provide the fine measurement; each division represents 0.05 of a millimetre. Add this fine measurement to the base measurement to obtain the total reading.

In the example shown the item measures 55.95 mm **(see illustration 3.14)**:

Base measurement	55.00 mm
Fine measurement	00.95 mm
Total figure	**55.95 mm**

Dial gauge or DTI (Dial Test Indicator)

● A dial gauge can be used to accurately measure small amounts of movement. Typical uses are measuring shaft runout or shaft endfloat (sideplay) and setting piston position for ignition timing on two-strokes. A dial gauge

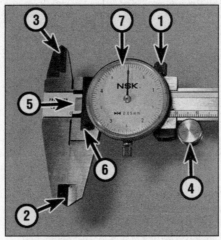

3.13 Vernier component parts (dial gauge)

1	Clamp screw	5	Main scale
2	External jaws	6	Sliding scale
3	Internal jaws	7	Dial gauge
4	Thumbwheel		

set usually comes with a range of different probes and adapters and mounting equipment.
● The gauge needle must point to zero when at rest. Rotate the ring around its periphery to zero the gauge.
● Check that the gauge is capable of reading the extent of movement in the work. Most gauges have a small dial set in the face which records whole millimetres of movement as well as the fine scale around the face periphery which is calibrated in 0.01 mm divisions. Read off the small dial first to obtain the base measurement, then add the measurement from the fine scale to obtain the total reading.

In the example shown the gauge reads 1.48 mm **(see illustration 3.15)**:

Base measurement	1.00 mm
Fine measurement	0.48 mm
Total figure	**1.48 mm**

● If measuring shaft runout, the shaft must be supported in vee-blocks and the gauge mounted on a stand perpendicular to the shaft. Rest the tip of the gauge against the centre of the shaft and rotate the shaft slowly whilst watching the gauge reading **(see illustration 3.16)**. Take several measurements along the length of the shaft and record the maximum

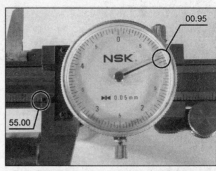

3.14 Vernier gauge reading of 55.95 mm

gauge reading as the amount of runout in the shaft. **Note:** *The reading obtained will be total runout at that point – some manufacturers specify that the runout figure is halved to compare with their specified runout limit.*
● Endfloat (sideplay) measurement requires that the gauge is mounted securely to the surrounding component with its probe touching the end of the shaft. Using hand pressure, push and pull on the shaft noting the maximum endfloat recorded on the gauge **(see illustration 3.17)**.
● A dial gauge with suitable adapters can be used to determine piston position BTDC on two-stroke engines for the purposes of ignition timing. The gauge, adapter and suitable length probe are installed in the place of the spark plug and the gauge zeroed at TDC. If the piston position is specified as 1.14 mm BTDC, rotate the engine back to 2.00 mm BTDC, then slowly forwards to 1.14 mm BTDC.

4 Torque and leverage

What is torque?

● Torque describes the twisting force about a shaft. The amount of torque applied is determined by the distance from the centre of the shaft to the end of the lever and the amount of force being applied to the end of the lever; distance multiplied by force equals torque.
● The manufacturer applies a measured

3.15 Dial gauge reading of 1.48 mm

3.16 Using a dial gauge to measure shaft runout

3.17 Using a dial gauge to measure shaft endfloat

4.1 Set the torque wrench index mark to the setting required, in this case 12 Nm

4.2 Angle tightening can be accomplished with a torque-angle gauge . . .

4.3 . . . or by marking the angle on the surrounding component

torque to a bolt or nut to ensure that it will not slacken in use and to hold two components securely together without movement in the joint. The actual torque setting depends on the thread size, bolt or nut material and the composition of the components being held.
● Too little torque may cause the fastener to loosen due to vibration, whereas too much torque will distort the joint faces of the component or cause the fastener to shear off. Always stick to the specified torque setting.

Using a torque wrench

● Check the calibration of the torque wrench and make sure it has a suitable range for the job. Torque wrenches are available in Nm (Newton-metres), kgf m (kilograms-force metre), lbf ft (pounds-feet), lbf in (inch-pounds). Do not confuse lbf ft with lbf in.
● Adjust the tool to the desired torque on the scale (see illustration 4.1). If your torque wrench is not calibrated in the units specified, carefully convert the figure (see *Conversion Factors*). A manufacturer sometimes gives a torque setting as a range (8 to 10 Nm) rather than a single figure – in this case set the tool midway between the two settings. The same torque may be expressed as 9 Nm ± 1 Nm. Some torque wrenches have a method of locking the setting so that it isn't inadvertently altered during use.
● Install the bolts/nuts in their correct location and secure them lightly. Their threads must be clean and free of any old locking compound. Unless specified the threads and flange should be dry – oiled threads are necessary in certain

circumstances and the manufacturer will take this into account in the specified torque figure. Similarly, the manufacturer may also specify the application of thread-locking compound.
● Tighten the fasteners in the specified sequence until the torque wrench clicks, indicating that the torque setting has been reached. Apply the torque again to double-check the setting. Where different thread diameter fasteners secure the component, as a rule tighten the larger diameter ones first.
● When the torque wrench has been finished with, release the lock (where applicable) and fully back off its setting to zero – do not leave the torque wrench tensioned. Also, do not use a torque wrench for slackening a fastener.

Angle-tightening

● Manufacturers often specify a figure in degrees for final tightening of a fastener. This usually follows tightening to a specific torque setting.
● A degree disc can be set and attached to the socket (see illustration 4.2) or a protractor can be used to mark the angle of movement on the bolt/nut head and the surrounding casting (see illustration 4.3).

Loosening sequences

● Where more than one bolt/nut secures a component, loosen each fastener evenly a little at a time. In this way, not all the stress of the joint is held by one fastener and the components are not likely to distort.
● If a tightening sequence is provided, work

in the REVERSE of this, but if not, work from the outside in, in a criss-cross sequence (see illustration 4.4).

Tightening sequences

● If a component is held by more than one fastener it is important that the retaining bolts/nuts are tightened evenly to prevent uneven stress build-up and distortion of sealing faces. This is especially important on high-compression joints such as the cylinder head.
● A sequence is usually provided by the manufacturer, either in a diagram or actually marked in the casting. If not, always start in the centre and work outwards in a criss-cross pattern (see illustration 4.5). Start off by securing all bolts/nuts finger-tight, then set the torque wrench and tighten each fastener by a small amount in sequence until the final torque is reached. By following this practice, the joint will be held evenly and will not be distorted. Important joints, such as the cylinder head and big-end fasteners often have two- or three-stage torque settings.

Applying leverage

● Use tools at the correct angle. Position a socket wrench or spanner on the bolt/nut so that you pull it towards you when loosening. If this can't be done, push the spanner without curling your fingers around it (see illustration 4.6) – the spanner may slip or the fastener loosen suddenly, resulting in your fingers being crushed against a component.
● Additional leverage is gained by extending the length of the lever. The best way to do this is to use a breaker bar instead of the regular length tool, or to slip a length of tubing over the end of the spanner or socket wrench.
● If additional leverage will not work, the fastener head is either damaged or firmly corroded in place (see *Fasteners*).

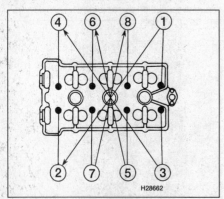

4.4 When slackening, work from the outside inwards

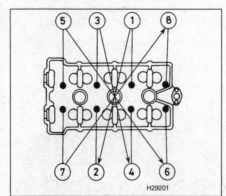

4.5 When tightening, work from the inside outwards

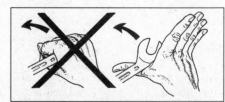

4.6 If you can't pull on the spanner to loosen a fastener, push with your hand open

5.1 Using a bearing driver against the bearing's outer race

5.2 Using a large socket against the bearing's outer race

5.3 This bearing puller clamps behind the bearing and pressure is applied to the shaft end to draw the bearing off

5 Bearings

Bearing removal and installation

Drivers and sockets

● Before removing a bearing, always inspect the casing to see which way it must be driven out – some casings will have retaining plates or a cast step. Also check for any identifying markings on the bearing and if installed to a certain depth, measure this at this stage. Some roller bearings are sealed on one side – take note of the original fitted position.

● Bearings can be driven out of a casing using a bearing driver tool (with the correct size head) or a socket of the correct diameter. Select the driver head or socket so that it contacts the outer race of the bearing, not the balls/rollers or inner race. Always support the casing around the bearing housing with wood blocks, otherwise there is a risk of fracture. The bearing is driven out with a few blows on the driver or socket from a heavy mallet. Unless access is severely restricted (as with wheel bearings), a pin-punch is not recommended unless it is moved around the bearing to keep it square in its housing.

● The same equipment can be used to install bearings. Make sure the bearing housing is supported on wood blocks and line up the bearing in its housing. Fit the bearing as noted on removal – generally they are installed with their marked side facing outwards. Tap the bearing squarely into its housing using a driver or socket which bears only on the bearing's outer race – contact with the bearing balls/rollers or inner race will destroy it **(see illustrations 5.1 and 5.2)**.

● Check that the bearing inner race and balls/rollers rotate freely.

Pullers and slide-hammers

● Where a bearing is pressed on a shaft a puller will be required to extract it **(see illustration 5.3)**. Make sure that the puller clamp or legs fit securely behind the bearing and are unlikely to slip out. If pulling a bearing off a gear shaft for example, you may have to locate the puller behind a gear pinion if there is no access to the race and draw the gear pinion off the shaft as well **(see illustration 5.4)**.

Caution: Ensure that the puller's centre bolt locates securely against the end of the shaft and will not slip when pressure is applied. Also ensure that puller does not damage the shaft end.

● Operate the puller so that its centre bolt exerts pressure on the shaft end and draws the bearing off the shaft.

● When installing the bearing on the shaft, tap only on the bearing's inner race – contact with the balls/rollers or outer race with destroy the bearing. Use a socket or length of tubing as a drift which fits over the shaft end **(see illustration 5.5)**.

5.4 Where no access is available to the rear of the bearing, it is sometimes possible to draw off the adjacent component

5.5 When installing a bearing on a shaft use a piece of tubing which bears only on the bearing's inner race

● Where a bearing locates in a blind hole in a casing, it cannot be driven or pulled out as described above. A slide-hammer with knife-edged bearing puller attachment will be required. The puller attachment passes through the bearing and when tightened expands to fit firmly behind the bearing **(see illustration 5.6)**. By operating the slide-hammer part of the tool the bearing is jarred out of its housing **(see illustration 5.7)**.

● It is possible, if the bearing is of reasonable weight, for it to drop out of its housing if the casing is heated as described opposite. If this method is attempted, first prepare a work surface which will enable the casing to be tapped face down to help dislodge the bearing – a wood surface is ideal since it will not damage the casing's gasket surface.

5.6 Expand the bearing puller so that it locks behind the bearing . . .

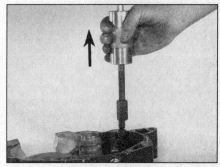

5.7 . . . attach the slide hammer to the bearing puller

5.8 Tapping a casing face down on wood blocks can often dislodge a bearing

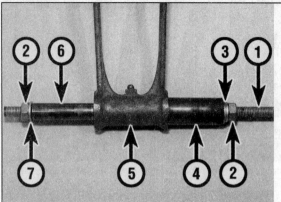

1 Bolt or length of threaded bar
2 Nuts
3 Washer (external diameter greater than tubing internal diameter)
4 Tubing (internal diameter sufficient to accommodate bearing)
5 Suspension arm with bearing
6 Tubing (external diameter slightly smaller than bearing)
7 Washer (external diameter slightly smaller than bearing)

5.9 Drawbolt component parts assembled on a suspension arm

Wearing protective gloves, tap the heated casing several times against the work surface to dislodge the bearing under its own weight (see illustration 5.8).

● Bearings can be installed in blind holes using the driver or socket method described above.

Drawbolts

● Where a bearing or bush is set in the eye of a component, such as a suspension linkage arm or connecting rod small-end, removal by drift may damage the component. Furthermore, a rubber bushing in a shock absorber eye cannot successfully be driven out of position. If access is available to a engineering press, the task is straightforward. If not, a drawbolt can be fabricated to extract the bearing or bush.

● To extract the bearing/bush you will need a long bolt with nut (or piece of threaded bar with two nuts), a piece of tubing which has an

internal diameter larger than the bearing/bush, another piece of tubing which has an external diameter slightly smaller than the bearing/bush, and a selection of washers (see illustrations 5.9 and 5.10). Note that the pieces of tubing must be of the same length, or longer, than the bearing/bush.

● The same kit (without the pieces of tubing) can be used to draw the new bearing/bush back into place (see illustration 5.11).

Temperature change

● If the bearing's outer race is a tight fit in the casing, the aluminium casing can be heated to release its grip on the bearing. Aluminium will expand at a greater rate than the steel bearing outer race. There are several ways to do this, but avoid any localised extreme heat

(such as a blow torch) – aluminium alloy has a low melting point.

● Approved methods of heating a casing are using a domestic oven (heated to 100°C) or immersing the casing in boiling water (see illustration 5.12). Low temperature range localised heat sources such as a paint stripper heat gun or clothes iron can also be used (see illustration 5.13). Alternatively, soak a rag in boiling water, wring it out and wrap it around the bearing housing.

⚠ Warning: All of these methods require care in use to prevent scalding and burns to the hands. Wear protective gloves when handling hot components.

● If heating the whole casing note that plastic components, such as the oil pressure switch, may suffer – remove them beforehand.

● After heating, remove the bearing as described above. You may find that the expansion is sufficient for the bearing to fall out of the casing under its own weight or with a light tap on the driver or socket.

● If necessary, the casing can be heated to aid bearing installation, and this is sometimes the recommended procedure if the scooter manufacturer has designed the housing and bearing fit with this intention.

● Installation of bearings can be eased by placing them in a freezer the night before installation. The steel bearing will contract slightly, allowing easy insertion in its housing. This is often useful when installing steering head outer races in the frame.

Bearing types and markings

● Plain bearings, ball bearings, needle roller bearings and tapered roller bearings will all be found on scooters (see illustrations 5.14 and 5.15). The ball and roller types are usually caged between an inner and outer race, but uncaged variations may be found.

● Plain bearings are sometimes found at the crankshaft main and connecting rod big-end where they are good at coping with high loads. They are made of a phosphor-bronze material and are impregnated with self-lubricating properties.

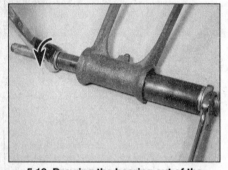

5.10 Drawing the bearing out of the suspension arm

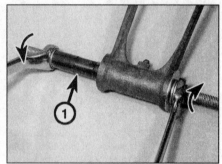

5.11 Installing a new bearing (1) in the suspension arm

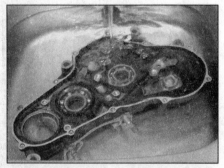

5.12 A casing can be immersed in a sink of boiling water to aid bearing removal

5.13 Using a localised heat source to aid bearing removal

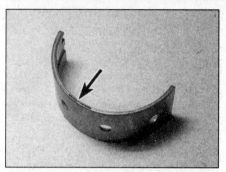

5.14 Bearings are either plain or grooved. They are usually identified by colour code (arrow)

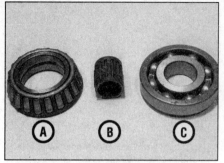

5.15 Tapered roller bearing (A), needle roller bearing (B) and ball journal bearing (C)

5.16 Typical bearing marking

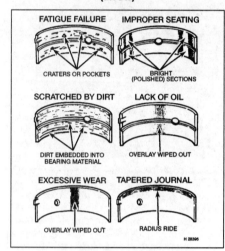

5.17 Typical bearing failures

5.18 Example of ball journal bearing with damaged balls and cages

5.19 Hold outer race and listen to inner race when spun

● Ball bearings and needle roller bearings consist of a steel inner and outer race with the balls or rollers between the races. They require constant lubrication by oil or grease and are good at coping with axial loads. Tapered roller bearings consist of rollers set in a tapered cage set on the inner race; the outer race is separate. They are good at coping with axial loads and prevent movement along the shaft – a typical application is in the steering head.

● Bearing manufacturers produce bearings to ISO size standards and stamp one face of the bearing to indicate its internal and external diameter, load capacity and type **(see illustration 5.16)**.

● Metal bushes are usually of phosphor-bronze material. Rubber bushes are used in suspension mounting eyes. Fibre bushes have also been used in suspension pivots.

Bearing fault finding

● If a bearing outer race has spun in its housing, the housing material will be damaged. You can use a bearing locking compound to bond the outer race in place if damage is not too severe.

● Plain bearings will fail due to damage of their working surface, as a result of lack of lubrication, corrosion or abrasive particles in the oil **(see illustration 5.17)**. Small particles

of dirt in the oil may embed in the bearing material whereas larger particles will score the bearing and shaft journal. If a number of short journeys are made, insufficient heat will be generated to drive off condensation which has built up on the bearings.

● Ball and roller bearings will fail due to lack of lubrication or damage to the balls or rollers. Tapered roller bearings can be damaged by overloading them. Unless the bearing is sealed on both sides, wash it in paraffin (kerosene) to remove all old grease then allow it to dry. Make a visual inspection looking to dented balls or rollers, damaged cages and worn or pitted races **(see illustration 5.18)**.

● A ball bearing can be checked for wear by listening to it when spun. Apply a film of light oil to the bearing and hold it close to the ear – hold the outer race with one hand and spin the inner race with the other hand **(see illustration 5.19)**. The bearing should be almost silent when spun; if it grates or rattles it is worn.

6 Oil seals

Oil seal removal and installation

● Oil seals should be renewed every time a component is dismantled. This is because the seal lips will become set to the sealing surface and will not necessarily reseal.

● Oil seals can be prised out of position using a large flat-bladed screwdriver **(see**

illustration 6.1). In the case of crankcase seals, check first that the seal is not lipped on the inside, preventing its removal with the crankcases joined.

● New seals are usually installed with their marked face (containing the seal reference code) outwards and the spring side towards the fluid being retained. In certain cases, such as a two-stroke engine crankshaft seal, a double lipped seal may be used due to there being fluid or gas on each side of the joint.

● Use a bearing driver or socket which bears only on the outer hard edge of the seal to install it in the casing – tapping on the inner edge will damage the sealing lip.

Oil seal types and markings

● Oil seals are usually of the single-lipped type. Double-lipped seals are found where a liquid or gas is on both sides of the joint.

6.1 Prise out oil seals with a large flat-bladed screwdriver

6.2 These oil seal markings indicate inside diameter, outside diameter and seal thickness

● Oil seals can harden and lose their sealing ability if the scooter has been in storage for a long period – renewal is the only solution.
● Oil seal manufacturers also conform to the ISO markings for seal size – these are moulded into the outer face of the seal **(see illustration 6.2)**.

7 Gaskets and sealants

Types of gasket and sealant

● Gaskets are used to seal the mating surfaces between components and keep lubricants, fluids, vacuum or pressure contained within the assembly. Aluminium gaskets are sometimes found at the cylinder joints, but most gaskets are paper-based. If the mating surfaces of the components being joined are undamaged the gasket can be installed dry, although a dab of sealant or grease will be useful to hold it in place during assembly.
● RTV (Room Temperature Vulcanising) silicone rubber sealants cure when exposed to moisture in the atmosphere. These sealants are good at filling pits or irregular gasket faces, but will tend to be forced out of the joint under very high torque. They can be used to replace a paper gasket, but first make sure that the width of the paper gasket is not essential to the shimming of internal components. RTV sealants should not be used on components containing petrol (gasoline).
● Non-hardening, semi-hardening and hard

7.1 If a pry point is provided, apply gently pressure with a flat-bladed screwdriver

setting liquid gasket compounds can be used with a gasket or between a metal-to-metal joint. Select the sealant to suit the application: universal non-hardening sealant can be used on virtually all joints; semi-hardening on joint faces which are rough or damaged; hard setting sealant on joints which require a permanent bond and are subjected to high temperature and pressure. **Note:** *Check first if the paper gasket has a bead of sealant impregnated in its surface before applying additional sealant.*
● When choosing a sealant, make sure it is suitable for the application, particularly if being applied in a high-temperature area or in the vicinity of fuel. Certain manufacturers produce sealants in either clear, silver or black colours to match the finish of the engine.
● Do not over-apply sealant. That which is squeezed out on the outside of the joint can be wiped off, whereas an excess of sealant on the inside can break off and clog oilways.

Breaking a sealed joint

● Age, heat, pressure and the use of hard setting sealant can cause two components to stick together so tightly that they are difficult to separate using finger pressure alone. Do not resort to using levers unless there is a pry point provided for this purpose **(see illustration 7.1)** or else the gasket surfaces will be damaged.
● Use a soft-faced hammer **(see illustration 7.2)** or a wood block and conventional hammer to strike the component near the mating surface. Avoid hammering against cast extremities since they may break off. If this method fails, try using a wood wedge between the two components.

7.2 Tap around the joint with a soft-faced mallet if necessary – don't strike cooling fins

Most components have one or two hollow locating dowels between the two gasket faces. If a dowel cannot be removed, do not resort to gripping it with pliers – it will almost certainly be distorted. Install a close-fitting socket or Phillips screwdriver into the dowel and then grip the outer edge of the dowel to free it.

Caution: If the joint will not separate, double-check that you have removed all the fasteners.

Removal of old gasket and sealant

● Paper gaskets will most likely come away complete, leaving only a few traces stuck on the sealing faces of the components. It is imperative that all traces are removed to ensure correct sealing of the new gasket.
● Very carefully scrape all traces of gasket away making sure that the sealing surfaces are not gouged or scored by the scraper **(see illustrations 7.3, 7.4 and 7.5)**. Stubborn

7.3 Paper gaskets can be scraped off with a gasket scraper tool . . .

7.4 . . . a knife blade . . .

7.5 . . . or a household scraper

7.6 Fine abrasive paper is wrapped around a flat file to clean up the gasket face

deposits can be removed by spraying with an aerosol gasket remover. Final preparation of the gasket surface can be made with very fine abrasive paper or a plastic kitchen scourer **(see illustrations 7.6 and 7.7)**.

● Old sealant can be scraped or peeled off components, depending on the type originally used. Note that gasket removal compounds are available to avoid scraping the components clean; make sure the gasket remover suits the type of sealant used.

8 Hoses

Clamping to prevent flow

● Small-bore flexible hoses can be clamped to prevent fluid flow whilst a component is worked on. Whichever method is used, ensure that the hose material is not

7.7 A kitchen scourer can be used on stubborn deposits

permanently distorted or damaged by the clamp.

a) A brake hose clamp available from auto accessory shops **(see illustration 8.1)**.

b) A wingnut type hose clamp **(see illustration 8.2)**.

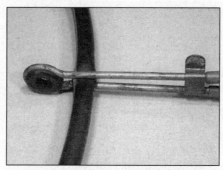

8.1 Hoses can be clamped with an automotive brake hose clamp . . .

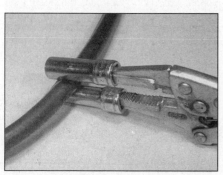

8.3 . . . two sockets and a pair of self-locking grips . . .

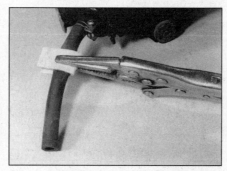

8.4 . . . or thick card and self-locking grips

c) Two sockets placed each side of the hose and held with straight-jawed self-locking grips **(see illustration 8.3)**.

d) Thick card each side of the hose held between straight-jawed self-locking grips **(see illustration 8.4)**.

Freeing and fitting hoses

● Always make sure the hose clamp is moved well clear of the hose end. Grip the hose with your hand and rotate it whilst pulling it off the union. If the hose has hardened due to age and will not move, slit it with a sharp knife and peel its ends off the union **(see illustration 8.5)**.

● Resist the temptation to use grease or soap on the unions to aid installation; although it helps the hose slip over the union it will equally aid the escape of fluid from the joint. It is preferable to soften the hose ends in hot water and wet the inside surface of the hose with water or a fluid which will evaporate.

8.2 . . . a wingnut type hose clamp . . .

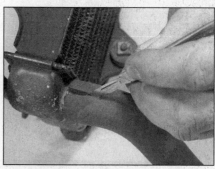

8.5 Cutting a coolant hose free with a sharp knife

About the MOT Test

In the UK, all vehicles more than three years old are subject to an annual test to ensure that they meet minimum safety requirements. A current test certificate must be issued before a machine can be used on public roads, and is required before a road fund licence can be issued. Riding without a current test certificate will also invalidate your insurance.

For most owners, the MOT test is an annual cause for anxiety, and this is largely due to owners not being sure what needs to be checked prior to submitting the scooter for testing. The simple answer is that a fully roadworthy scooter will have no difficulty in passing the test.

This is a guide to getting your scooter through the MOT test. Obviously it will not be possible to examine the scooter to the same standard as the professional MOT tester, particularly in view of the equipment required for some of the checks. However, working through the following procedures will enable you to identify any problem areas before submitting the scooter for the test.

It has only been possible to summarise the test requirements here, based on the regulations in force at the time of printing. Test standards are becoming increasingly stringent, although there are some exemptions for older vehicles. More information about the MOT test can be obtained from the TSO publications, *How Safe is your Motorcycle* and *The MOT Inspection Manual for Motorcycle Testing*.

Many of the checks require that one of the wheels is raised off the ground. Additionally, the help of an assistant may prove useful.

Check that the frame number is clearly visible.

Electrical System

Lights, turn signals, horn and reflector

✔ With the ignition on, check the operation of the following electrical components. **Note:** *The electrical components on certain small-capacity machines are powered by the generator, requiring that the engine is run for this check.*

a) *Headlight and tail light. Check that both illuminate in the low and high beam switch positions.*
b) *Position lights. Check that the front position (or sidelight) and tail light illuminate in this switch position.*
c) *Turn signals. Check that all flash at the correct rate, and that the warning light(s) function correctly. Check that the turn signal switch works correctly.*
d) *Hazard warning system (where fitted). Check that all four turn signals flash in this switch position.*

e) *Brake stop light. Check that the light comes on when the front and rear brakes are independently applied. Models first used on or after 1st April 1986 must have a brake light switch on each brake.*
f) *Horn. Check that the sound is continuous and of reasonable volume.*

✔ Check that there is a red reflector on the rear of the machine, either mounted separately or as part of the tail light lens.
✔ Check the condition of the headlight, tail light and turn signal lenses.

Headlight beam height

✔ The MOT tester will perform a headlight beam height check using specialised beam setting equipment **(see illustration 1)**. This equipment will not be available to the home mechanic, but if you suspect that the headlight is incorrectly set or may have been maladjusted in the past, you can perform a rough test as follows.

✔ Position the scooter in a straight line facing a brick wall. The scooter must be off its stand, upright and with a rider seated. Measure the height from the ground to the centre of the headlight and mark a horizontal line on the wall at this height. Position the scooter 3.8 metres from the wall and draw a vertical line up the wall central to the centreline of the scooter. Switch to dipped beam and check that the beam pattern falls slightly lower than the horizontal line and to the left of the vertical line **(see illustration 2)**.

Headlight beam height checking equipment

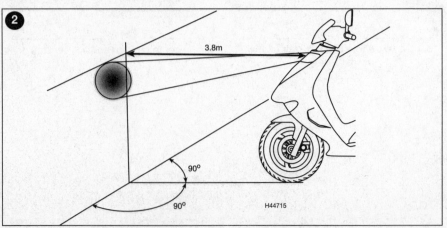

3.8m

90°

90°

H44715

Home workshop beam alignment check

Exhaust System

Exhaust

✔ Check that the exhaust mountings are secure and that the system does not foul any of the rear suspension components.

✔ Start the scooter. When the revs are increased, check that the exhaust is neither holed nor leaking from any of its joints. On a linked system, check that the collector box is not leaking due to corrosion.

✔ Note that the exhaust decibel level ("loudness" of the exhaust) is assessed at the discretion of the tester. If the scooter was first used on or after 1st January 1985 the silencer must carry the BSAU 193 stamp, or a marking relating to its make and model, or be of OE (original equipment) manufacture. If the silencer is marked NOT FOR ROAD USE, RACING USE ONLY or similar, it will fail the MOT.

Steering and Suspension

Steering

✔ With the front wheel raised off the ground, rotate the steering from lock to lock. The handlebar or switches must not contact anything. Problems can be caused by damaged lock stops on the lower yoke and frame, or by the fitting of non-standard handlebars.

✔ When performing the lock to lock check, also ensure that the steering moves freely without drag or notchiness. Steering movement can be impaired by poorly routed cables, or by overtight head bearings or worn bearings. The tester will perform a check of the steering head bearing lower race by mounting the front wheel on a surface plate, then performing a lock to lock check with the weight of the machine on the lower bearing (see illustration 3).

✔ Grasp the fork sliders (lower legs) and attempt to push and pull on the forks (see illustration 4). Any play in the steering head bearings will be felt. Note that in extreme cases, wear of the front fork bushes can be misinterpreted for head bearing play.

✔ Check that the handlebars are securely mounted.

✔ Check that the handlebar grip rubbers are secure. They should by bonded to the bar left end and to the throttle twistgrip on the right end.

Front suspension

✔ With the scooter off the stand, hold the front brake on and pump the front suspension up and down (see illustration 5). Check that the movement is adequately damped.

✔ Inspect the area above and around the front fork oil seals (see illustration 6). There should be no sign of oil on the fork tube (stanchion) nor leaking down the slider (lower leg).

✔ On models with leading or trailing link front suspension, check that there is no freeplay in the linkage when moved from side to side.

Front wheel mounted on a surface plate for steering head bearing lower race check

Checking the steering head bearings for freeplay

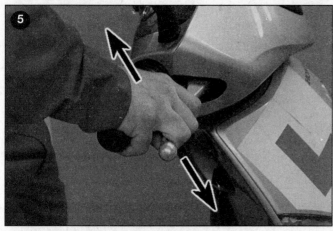

Hold the front brake on and pump the front suspension up and down to check operation

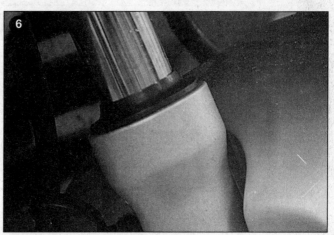

Inspect the area around the fork dust seal for oil leakage

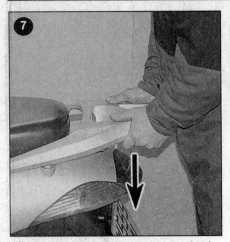

Bounce the rear of the scooter to check rear suspension operation

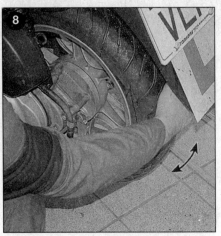

Grasp the rear wheel to check for play in the engine-to-frame mountings

Rear suspension

✔ With the scooter off the stand and an assistant supporting the scooter by its handlebars, bounce the rear suspension (see illustration 7). Check that the suspension components do not foul the bodywork and check that the shock absorber(s) provide adequate damping.

✔ Visually inspect the shock absorber(s) and check that there is no sign of oil leakage from its damper.

✔ With the rear wheel raised off the ground, grasp the wheel as shown and attempt to move it from side to side (see illustration 8). Any play in the engine-to-frame mountings will be felt as movement.

Brakes, Wheels and Tyres

Brakes

✔ With the wheel raised off the ground, apply the brake then free it off, and check that the wheel is about to revolve freely without brake drag.

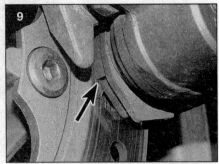

Brake pad wear can usually be viewed without removing the caliper. Some pads have wear indicator grooves (arrow)

✔ On disc brakes, examine the disc itself. Check that it is securely mounted and not cracked.

✔ On disc brakes, view the pad material through the caliper mouth and check that the pads are not worn down beyond the limit (see illustration 9).

✔ On drum brakes, check that when the brake is applied the angle between the operating

On drum brakes, check the angle of the operating lever with the brake fully applied. Most drum brakes have a wear indicator pointer and scale

lever and cable or rod is not too great (see illustration 10). Check also that the operating lever doesn't foul any other components.

✔ On disc brakes, examine the flexible hoses from top to bottom. Have an assistant hold the brake on so that the fluid in the hose is under pressure, and check that there is no sign of fluid leakage, bulges or cracking. If there are any metal brake pipes or unions, check that these are free from corrosion and damage.

✔ The MOT tester will perform a test of the scooter's braking efficiency based on a calculation of rider and scooter weight. Although this cannot be carried out at home, you can at least ensure that the braking systems are properly maintained. For hydraulic disc brakes, check the fluid level, lever/pedal feel (bleed of air if its spongy) and pad material. For drum brakes, check adjustment, cable or rod operation and shoe lining thickness.

Wheels and tyres

✔ Check the wheel condition. Cast wheels should be free from cracks and if of the built-up design, all fasteners should be secure.

✔ With the wheel raised off the ground, spin the wheel and visually check that the tyre and wheel run true. Check that the tyre does not foul the suspension or mudguards.

✔ With the wheel raised off the ground, grasp the wheel and attempt to move it about the axle (see illustration 11). Any play felt here indicates wheel bearing failure.

✔ Check the tyre tread depth, tread condition and sidewall condition (see illustration 12).

✔ Check the tyre type. Front and rear tyre types must be compatible and be suitable for

Check for wheel bearing play by trying to move the wheel about the axle (spindle)

Checking the tyre tread depth

Tyre direction of rotation arrow can be found on tyre sidewall

Two straight-edges are used to check wheel alignment

road use. Tyres marked NOT FOR ROAD USE, COMPETITION USE ONLY or similar, will fail the MOT.

✔ If the tyre sidewall carries a direction of rotation arrow, this must be pointing in the direction of normal wheel rotation **(see illustration 13)**.

✔ Check that the wheel axle nuts (where applicable) are properly secured. A self-locking nut or castellated nut with a split-pin or R-pin can be used.

✔ Wheel alignment is checked with the scooter off the stand and a rider seated. With the front wheel pointing straight ahead, two perfectly straight lengths of metal or wood and placed against the sidewalls of both tyres **(see illustration 14)**. The gap each side of the front tyre must be equidistant on both sides. Incorrect wheel alignment may be due to a cocked rear wheel or in extreme cases, a bent frame.

General checks and condition

✔ Check the security of all major fasteners, bodypanels, seat and mudguards.

✔ Check that the pillion footrests, handlebar levers and stand are securely mounted.

✔ Check for corrosion on the frame or any load-bearing components. If severe, this may affect the structure, particularly under stress.

Conversion Factors

Length (distance)

Inches (in)	x 25.4	= Millimetres (mm)	x 0.0394	= Inches (in)
Feet (ft)	x 0.305	= Metres (m)	x 3.281	= Feet (ft)
Miles	x 1.609	= Kilometres (km)	x 0.621	= Miles

Volume (capacity)

Cubic inches (cu in; in³)	x 16.387	= Cubic centimetres (cc; cm³)	x 0.061	= Cubic inches (cu in; in³)
Imperial pints (Imp pt)	x 0.568	= Litres (l)	x 1.76	= Imperial pints (Imp pt)
Imperial quarts (Imp qt)	x 1.137	= Litres (l)	x 0.88	= Imperial quarts (Imp qt)
Imperial quarts (Imp qt)	x 1.201	= US quarts (US qt)	x 0.833	= Imperial quarts (Imp qt)
US quarts (US qt)	x 0.946	= Litres (l)	x 1.057	= US quarts (US qt)
Imperial gallons (Imp gal)	x 4.546	= Litres (l)	x 0.22	= Imperial gallons (Imp gal)
Imperial gallons (Imp gal)	x 1.201	= US gallons (US gal)	x 0.833	= Imperial gallons (Imp gal)
US gallons (US gal)	x 3.785	= Litres (l)	x 0.264	= US gallons (US gal)

Mass (weight)

Ounces (oz)	x 28.35	= Grams (g)	x 0.035	= Ounces (oz)
Pounds (lb)	x 0.454	= Kilograms (kg)	x 2.205	= Pounds (lb)

Force

Ounces-force (ozf; oz)	x 0.278	= Newtons (N)	x 3.6	= Ounces-force (ozf; oz)
Pounds-force (lbf; lb)	x 4.448	= Newtons (N)	x 0.225	= Pounds-force (lbf; lb)
Newtons (N)	x 0.1	= Kilograms-force (kgf; kg)	x 9.81	= Newtons (N)

Pressure

Pounds-force per square inch (psi; lbf/in²; lb/in²)	x 0.070	= Kilograms-force per square centimetre (kgf/cm²; kg/cm²)	x 14.223	= Pounds-force per square inch (psi; lbf/in²; lb/in²)
Pounds-force per square inch (psi; lbf/in²; lb/in²)	x 0.068	= Atmospheres (atm)	x 14.696	= Pounds-force per square inch (psi; lbf/in²; lb/in²)
Pounds-force per square inch (psi; lbf/in²; lb/in²)	x 0.069	= Bars	x 14.5	= Pounds-force per square inch (psi; lbf/in²; lb/in²)
Pounds-force per square inch (psi; lbf/in²; lb/in²)	x 6.895	= Kilopascals (kPa)	x 0.145	= Pounds-force per square inch (psi; lbf/in²; lb/in²)
Kilopascals (kPa)	x 0.01	= Kilograms-force per square centimetre (kgf/cm²; kg/cm²)	x 98.1	= Kilopascals (kPa)
Millibar (mbar)	x 100	= Pascals (Pa)	x 0.01	= Millibar (mbar)
Millibar (mbar)	x 0.0145	= Pounds-force per square inch (psi; lbf/in²; lb/in²)	x 68.947	= Millibar (mbar)
Millibar (mbar)	x 0.75	= Millimetres of mercury (mmHg)	x 1.333	= Millibar (mbar)
Millibar (mbar)	x 0.401	= Inches of water (inH₂O)	x 2.491	= Millibar (mbar)
Millimetres of mercury (mmHg)	x 0.535	= Inches of water (inH₂O)	x 1.868	= Millimetres of mercury (mmHg)
Inches of water (inH₂O)	x 0.036	= Pounds-force per square inch (psi; lbf/in²; lb/in²)	x 27.68	= Inches of water (inH₂O)

Torque (moment of force)

Pounds-force inches (lbf in; lb in)	x 1.152	= Kilograms-force centimetre (kgf cm; kg cm)	x 0.868	= Pounds-force inches (lbf in; lb in)
Pounds-force inches (lbf in; lb in)	x 0.113	= Newton metres (Nm)	x 8.85	= Pounds-force inches (lbf in; lb in)
Pounds-force inches (lbf in; lb in)	x 0.083	= Pounds-force feet (lbf ft; lb ft)	x 12	= Pounds-force inches (lbf in; lb in)
Pounds-force feet (lbf ft; lb ft)	x 0.138	= Kilograms-force metres (kgf m; kg m)	x 7.233	= Pounds-force feet (lbf ft; lb ft)
Pounds-force feet (lbf ft; lb ft)	x 1.356	= Newton metres (Nm)	x 0.738	= Pounds-force feet (lbf ft; lb ft)
Newton metres (Nm)	x 0.102	= Kilograms-force metres (kgf m; kg m)	x 9.804	= Newton metres (Nm)

Power

Horsepower (hp)	x 745.7	= Watts (W)	x 0.0013	= Horsepower (hp)

Velocity (speed)

Miles per hour (miles/hr; mph)	x 1.609	= Kilometres per hour (km/hr; kph)	x 0.621	= Miles per hour (miles/hr; mph)

Fuel consumption*

Miles per gallon (mpg)	x 0.354	= Kilometres per litre (km/l)	x 2.825	= Miles per gallon (mpg)

Temperature

Degrees Fahrenheit = (°C x 1.8) + 32   Degrees Celsius (Degrees Centigrade; °C) = (°F - 32) x 0.56

It is common practice to convert from miles per gallon (mpg) to litres/100 kilometres (l/100km), where mpg x l/100 km = 282

This Section provides an easy reference-guide to the more common faults that are likely to afflict your machine. Obviously, the opportunities are almost limitless for faults to occur as a result of obscure failures, and to try and cover all eventualities would require a book. Indeed, a number have been written on the subject.

Successful troubleshooting is not a mysterious 'black art' but the application of a bit of knowledge combined with a systematic and logical approach to the problem. Approach any troubleshooting by first accurately identifying the symptom and then checking through the list of possible causes, starting with the simplest or most obvious and progressing in stages to the most complex.

Take nothing for granted, but above all apply liberal quantities of common sense.

The main symptom of a fault is given in the text as a major heading below which are listed the various systems or areas which may contain the fault. Details of each possible cause for a fault and the remedial action to be taken are given, in brief, in the paragraphs below each heading. Further information should be sought in the relevant Chapter.

1 Engine doesn't start or is difficult to start

- ☐ Starter motor doesn't rotate
- ☐ Starter motor rotates but engine does not turn over
- ☐ Starter works but engine won't turn over (seized)
- ☐ No fuel flow
- ☐ Engine flooded
- ☐ No spark or weak spark
- ☐ Compression low
- ☐ Stalls after starting
- ☐ Rough idle

2 Poor running at low speed

- ☐ Spark weak
- ☐ Fuel/air mixture incorrect
- ☐ Compression low
- ☐ Poor acceleration

3 Poor running or no power at high speed

- ☐ Firing incorrect
- ☐ Fuel/air mixture incorrect
- ☐ Compression low
- ☐ Knocking or pinking
- ☐ Miscellaneous causes

4 Overheating

- ☐ Engine overheats
- ☐ Firing incorrect
- ☐ Fuel/air mixture incorrect
- ☐ Compression too high
- ☐ Engine load excessive
- ☐ Lubrication inadequate
- ☐ Miscellaneous causes

5 Transmission problems

- ☐ No drive to rear wheel
- ☐ Vibration
- ☐ Poor performance
- ☐ Clutch not disengaging completely

6 Abnormal engine noise

- ☐ Knocking or pinking
- ☐ Piston slap or rattling
- ☐ Valve noise
- ☐ Other noise

7 Abnormal frame and suspension noise

- ☐ Front end noise
- ☐ Shock absorber noise
- ☐ Brake noise

8 Excessive exhaust smoke

- ☐ White smoke (four-stroke engines)
- ☐ White/blue smoke (two-stroke engines)
- ☐ Black smoke
- ☐ Brown smoke

9 Poor handling or stability

- ☐ Handlebar hard to turn
- ☐ Handlebar shakes or vibrates excessively
- ☐ Handlebar pulls to one side
- ☐ Poor shock absorbing qualities

10 Braking problems – disc brakes

- ☐ Brakes are ineffective
- ☐ Brake lever pulsates
- ☐ Brakes drag

11 Braking problems – drum brakes

- ☐ Brakes are ineffective
- ☐ Brake lever pulsates
- ☐ Brakes drag

12 Electrical problems

- ☐ Battery dead or weak
- ☐ Battery overcharged

1 Engine doesn't start or is difficult to start

Starter motor doesn't rotate

☐ Fuse blown. Check fuse and starter circuit (Chapter 10).
☐ Battery voltage low. Check and recharge battery (Chapter 10).
☐ Starter motor defective. Make sure the wiring to the starter is secure. Make sure the starter relay clicks when the start button is pushed. If the relay clicks, then the fault is in the wiring or motor.
☐ Starter relay faulty. Check it (Chapter 10).
☐ Starter switch on handlebar not contacting. The contacts could be wet, corroded or dirty. Disassemble and clean the switch (Chapter 10).
☐ Wiring open or shorted. Check all wiring connections and harnesses to make sure that they are dry, tight and not corroded. Also check for broken or frayed wires that can cause a short to earth.
☐ Ignition (main) switch defective. Check the switch according to the procedure in Chapter 10. Renew the switch if it is defective.

Starter motor rotates but engine does not turn over

☐ Starter pinion assembly or starter clutch defective. Inspect and repair or renew (Chapter 2A or 2B).
☐ Damaged pinion assembly or starter gears. Inspect and renew the damaged parts (Chapter 2A or 2B).

Starter works but engine won't turn over (seized)

☐ Seized engine caused by one or more internally damaged components. Failure due to wear, abuse or lack of lubrication. On all engines damage can include piston, cylinder, connecting rod, crankshaft, bearings and additionally on four-strokes, valves, camshaft, camchain. Refer to Chapter 2A or 2B for engine disassembly.

No fuel flow

☐ No fuel in tank.
☐ Fuel hose or tank vent hose trapped. Check the hoses.
☐ Fuel filter clogged. Remove the tap and clean the filter, or check the in-line fuel filter.
☐ Fuel tap vacuum hose split or detached. Check the hose.
☐ Fuel tap diaphragm split. Renew the tap (Chapter 4).
☐ Fuel hose clogged. Remove the fuel hose and carefully blow through it.
☐ Float needle valve or carburettor jets clogged. The carburettor should be removed and overhauled if draining the float chamber doesn't solve the problem.

Engine flooded

☐ Float height or fuel level too high. Check as described in Chapter 4.
☐ Float needle valve worn or stuck open. A piece of dirt, rust or other debris can cause the valve to seat improperly, causing excess fuel to be admitted to the float chamber. In this case, the float chamber should be cleaned and the needle valve and seat inspected. If the needle and seat are worn, then the leaking will persist and the parts should be renewed (Chapter 4).

No spark or weak spark

☐ Ignition switch OFF.
☐ Battery voltage low. Check and recharge the battery as necessary (Chapter 10).
☐ Spark plug dirty, defective or worn out. Locate reason for fouled plug using spark plug condition chart at the end of this manual and follow the plug maintenance procedures (Chapter 1).

Condition is especially applicable to two-stroke engines due to the oily nature of their lubrication system.

☐ Spark plug cap or secondary (HT) wiring faulty. Check condition. Replace either or both components if cracks or deterioration are evident (Chapter 5).
☐ Spark plug cap not making good contact. Make sure that the plug cap fits snugly over the plug end.
☐ Ignition control unit (ICU) defective. Check the unit, referring to Chapter 5 for details.
☐ Pick-up coil or source coil defective. Check the unit, referring to Chapter 5 for details.
☐ Ignition HT coil defective. Check the coil, referring to Chapter 5.
☐ Ignition switch shorted. This is usually caused by water, corrosion, damage or excessive wear. The switch can be disassembled and cleaned with electrical contact cleaner. If cleaning does not help, renew the switch (Chapter 10).
☐ Wiring shorted or broken. Make sure that all wiring connections are clean, dry and tight. Look for chafed and broken wires (Chapters 5 and 10).

Compression low

☐ Spark plug loose. Remove the plug and inspect its threads (Chapter 1).
☐ Cylinder head not sufficiently tightened down. If the cylinder head is suspected of being loose, then there's a chance that the gasket or head is damaged if the problem has persisted for any length of time. The head nuts should be tightened to the proper torque in the correct sequence (Chapter 2A or 2B).
☐ Low crankcase compression on two-stroke engines due to worn crankshaft oil seals. Condition will upset the fuel/air mixture. Renew the seals (Chapter 2A).
☐ Improper valve clearance (four-strokes). This means that the valve is not closing completely and compression pressure is leaking past the valve. Check and adjust the valve clearances (Chapter 1).
☐ Cylinder and/or piston worn. Excessive wear will cause compression pressure to leak past the rings. This is usually accompanied by worn rings as well. A top-end overhaul is necessary (Chapter 2A or 2B).
☐ Piston rings worn, weak, broken, or sticking. Broken or sticking piston rings usually indicate a lubrication or carburation problem that causes excess carbon deposits or seizures to form on the pistons and rings. Top-end overhaul is necessary (Chapter 2A or 2B).
☐ Cylinder head gasket damaged. If a head is allowed to become loose, or if excessive carbon build-up on the piston crown and combustion chamber causes extremely high compression, the head gasket may leak. Retorquing the head is not always sufficient to restore the seal, so gasket renewal is necessary (Chapter 2A or 2B).
☐ Cylinder head warped. This is caused by overheating or improperly tightened head nuts. Machine shop resurfacing or head renewal is necessary (Chapter 2A or 2B).
☐ Valve spring broken or weak (four-stroke engines). Caused by component failure or wear; the springs must be renewed (Chapter 2B).
☐ Valve not seating properly (four-stroke engines). This is caused by a bent valve (from over-revving or improper valve adjustment), burned valve or seat (improper carburation) or an accumulation of carbon deposits on the seat (from carburation or lubrication problems). The valves must be cleaned and/or renewed and the seats serviced if possible (Chapter 2B).

Stalls after starting

- [ ] Faulty automatic choke. Check connections and movement (Chapter 4).
- [ ] Ignition malfunction (Chapter 5).
- [ ] Carburettor malfunction (Chapter 4).
- [ ] Fuel contaminated. The fuel can be contaminated with either dirt or water, or can change chemically if the machine is allowed to sit for several months or more. Drain the tank and carburettor (Chapter 4).
- [ ] Inlet air leak. Check for loose carburettor-to-inlet manifold connection, loose carburettor top (Chapter 4).
- [ ] Engine idle speed incorrect. Turn idle adjusting screw until the engine idles at the specified rpm (Chapter 1).

Rough idle

- [ ] Ignition malfunction (Chapter 5).
- [ ] Idle speed incorrect (Chapter 1).
- [ ] Carburettor malfunction (Chapter 4).
- [ ] Fuel contaminated. The fuel can be contaminated with either dirt or water, or can change chemically if the machine is allowed to sit for several months or more. Drain the tank and carburettor (Chapter 4).
- [ ] Inlet air leak. Check for loose carburettor-to-inlet manifold connection, loose carburettor top (Chapter 4).
- [ ] Air filter clogged. Clean or renew the air filter element (Chapter 1).

2 Poor running at low speeds

Spark weak

- [ ] Battery voltage low. Check and recharge battery (Chapter 10).
- [ ] Spark plug fouled, defective or worn out. Refer to Chapter 1 for spark plug maintenance.
- [ ] Spark plug cap or HT wiring defective. Refer to Chapter 5 for details on the ignition system.
- [ ] Spark plug cap not making contact.
- [ ] Incorrect spark plug. Wrong type, heat range or cap configuration. Check and install correct plug listed in Chapter 1.
- [ ] Ignition control unit (ICU) defective. See Chapter 5.
- [ ] Pick-up coil defective. See Chapter 5.
- [ ] Ignition HT coil defective. See Chapter 5.

Fuel/air mixture incorrect

- [ ] Pilot screw out of adjustment (Chapter 4).
- [ ] Pilot jet or air passage clogged. Remove and clean the carburettor (Chapter 4).
- [ ] Air bleed hole clogged. Remove carburettor and blow out all passages (Chapter 4).
- [ ] Air filter clogged, poorly sealed or missing (Chapter 1).
- [ ] Air filter housing poorly sealed. Look for cracks, holes or loose screws and renew or repair defective parts.
- [ ] Fuel level too high or too low. Check the float height and fuel level (Chapter 4).
- [ ] Carburettor inlet manifold loose. Check for cracks, breaks, tears or loose fixings.

Compression low

- [ ] Spark plug loose. Remove the plug and inspect its threads (Chapter 1).
- [ ] Cylinder head not sufficiently tightened down. If the cylinder head is suspected of being loose, then there's a chance that the gasket or head is damaged if the problem has persisted for any length of time. The head nuts should be tightened to the proper torque in the correct sequence (Chapter 2A or 2B).
- [ ] Improper valve clearance (four-stroke engines). This means that the valve is not closing completely and compression pressure is leaking past the valve. Check and adjust the valve clearances (Chapter 1).
- [ ] Low crankcase compression on two-stroke engines due to worn crankshaft oil seals. Condition will upset the fuel/air mixture. Renew the seals (Chapter 2A).
- [ ] Cylinder and/or piston worn. Excessive wear will cause compression pressure to leak past the rings. This is usually accompanied by worn rings as well. A top-end overhaul is necessary (Chapter 2A or 2B).
- [ ] Piston rings worn, weak, broken, or sticking. Broken or sticking piston rings usually indicate a lubrication or carburation problem that causes excess carbon deposits or seizures to form on the pistons and rings. Top-end overhaul is necessary (Chapter 2A or 2B).
- [ ] Cylinder head gasket damaged. If a head is allowed to become loose, or if excessive carbon build-up on the piston crown and combustion chamber causes extremely high compression, the head gasket may leak. Retorquing the head is not always sufficient to restore the seal, so gasket renewal is necessary (Chapter 2A or 2B).
- [ ] Cylinder head warped. This is caused by overheating or improperly tightened head nuts. Machine shop resurfacing or head replacement is necessary (Chapter 2A or 2B).
- [ ] Valve spring broken or weak (four-stroke engines). Caused by component failure or wear; the springs must be replaced (Chapter 2B).
- [ ] Valve not seating properly (four-stroke engines). This is caused by a bent valve (from over-revving or improper valve adjustment), burned valve or seat (improper carburation) or an accumulation of carbon deposits on the seat (from carburation or lubrication problems). The valves must be cleaned and/or renewed and the seats serviced if possible (Chapter 2B).

Poor acceleration

- [ ] Carburettor leaking or dirty. Overhaul the carburettor (Chapter 4).
- [ ] Faulty automatic choke (Chapter 4).
- [ ] Timing not advancing. The pick-up coil or the ignition control unit (ICU) may be defective (Chapter 5). If so, they must be renewed, as they can't be repaired.
- [ ] Engine oil viscosity too high (four-stroke engines). Using a heavier oil than that recommended in Chapter 1 can damage the oil pump or lubrication system and cause drag on the engine.
- [ ] Brakes dragging. On disc brakes, usually caused by debris which has entered the brake piston seals, or from a warped disc or bent axle, or cable out of adjustment where appropriate. On drum brakes, cable out of adjustment, shoe return spring broken. Repair as necessary (Chapter 8).
- [ ] Clutch slipping, drive belt worn, or variator faulty (Chapter 6).

3 Poor running or no power at high speed

Firing incorrect

☐ Air filter clogged. Clean or renew filter (Chapter 1).
☐ Spark plug fouled, defective or worn out. See Chapter 1 for spark plug maintenance.
☐ Spark plug cap or HT wiring defective. See Chapter 5 for details of the ignition system.
☐ Spark plug cap not in good contact (Chapter 5).
☐ Incorrect spark plug. Wrong type, heat range or cap configuration. Check and install correct plug listed in Chapter 1.
☐ Ignition control unit or HT coil defective (Chapter 5).

Fuel/air mixture incorrect

☐ Main jet clogged. Dirt, water or other contaminants can clog the main jet. Clean the fuel tap filter, the in-line filter, the float chamber and the jets and carburettor orifices (Chapter 4).
☐ Main jet wrong size. The standard jetting is for sea level atmospheric pressure and oxygen content.
☐ Air bleed holes clogged. Remove and overhaul carburettor (Chapter 4).
☐ Air filter clogged, poorly sealed, or missing (Chapter 1).
☐ Air filter housing or duct poorly sealed. Look for cracks, holes or loose clamps or screws, and renew or repair defective parts.
☐ Fuel level too high or too low. Check the float height or fuel level (Chapter 4).
☐ Carburettor inlet manifold loose. Check for cracks, breaks, tears or loose fixings.

Compression low

☐ Spark plug loose. Remove the plug and inspect its threads. Reinstall and tighten to the specified torque (Chapter 1).
☐ Cylinder head not sufficiently tightened down. If the cylinder head is suspected of being loose, then there's a chance that the gasket or head is damaged if the problem has persisted for any length of time. The head nuts should be tightened to the proper torque in the correct sequence (Chapter 2A or 2B).
☐ Improper valve clearance (four-stroke engines). This means that the valve is not closing completely and compression pressure is leaking past the valve. Check and adjust the valve clearances (Chapter 1).
☐ Low crankcase compression on two-stroke engines due to worn crankshaft oil seals. Condition will upset the fuel/air mixture. Renew the seals (Chapter 2A).
☐ Cylinder and/or piston worn. Excessive wear will cause compression pressure to leak past the rings. This is usually accompanied by worn rings as well. A top-end overhaul is necessary (Chapter 2A or 2B).
☐ Piston rings worn, weak, broken, or sticking. Broken or sticking piston rings usually indicate a lubrication or carburation problem that causes excess carbon deposits or seizures to form on the pistons and rings. Top-end overhaul is necessary (Chapter 2A or 2B).
☐ Cylinder head gasket damaged. If a head is allowed to become loose, or if excessive carbon build-up on the piston crown and combustion chamber causes extremely high compression, the head gasket may leak. Retorquing the head is not always sufficient to restore the seal, so gasket replacement is necessary (Chapter 2A or 2B).
☐ Cylinder head warped. This is caused by overheating or improperly tightened head nuts. Cylinder head skimming or head replacement is necessary (Chapter 2A or 2B).
☐ Valve spring broken or weak (four-stroke engines). Caused by component failure or wear; the springs must be renewed (Chapter 2B).
☐ Valve not seating properly (four-stroke engines). This is caused by a bent valve (from over-revving or improper valve adjustment), burned valve or seat (improper carburation) or an accumulation of carbon deposits on the seat (from carburation or lubrication problems). The valves must be cleaned and/or renewed and the seats serviced if possible (Chapter 2B).

Knocking or pinking

☐ Carbon build-up in combustion chamber. Use of a fuel additive that will dissolve the adhesive bonding the carbon particles to the crown and chamber is the easiest way to remove the build-up. Otherwise, the cylinder head will have to be removed and decarbonised (Chapter 2A or 2B). On two-stroke engines, the regular service interval for cylinder head decarbonisation should be adhered to.
☐ Incorrect or poor quality fuel. Old or improper grades of fuel can cause detonation. This causes the piston to rattle, thus the knocking or pinking sound. Drain old fuel and always use the recommended fuel grade.
☐ Spark plug heat range incorrect. Uncontrolled detonation indicates the plug heat range is too hot. The plug in effect becomes a glow plug, raising cylinder temperatures. Install the proper heat range plug (Chapter 1).
☐ Improper air/fuel mixture. This will cause the cylinders to run hot, which leads to detonation. Clogged jets or an air leak can cause this imbalance. See Chapter 4.

Miscellaneous causes

☐ Throttle valve doesn't open fully. Adjust the throttle twistgrip freeplay (Chapter 1).
☐ Clutch slipping, drive belt worn, or speed governor faulty (Chapter 6).
☐ Timing not advancing (Chapter 5).
☐ Engine oil viscosity too high (four-stroke engines). Using a heavier oil than the one recommended in Chapter 1 can damage the oil pump or lubrication system and cause drag on the engine.
☐ Brakes dragging. On disc brakes, usually caused by debris which has entered the brake piston seals, or from a warped disc or bent axle, or cable out of adjustment where appropriate. On drum brakes, cable out of adjustment, shoe return spring broken. Repair as necessary (Chapter 8).

4 Overheating

Engine overheats – liquid-cooled engines

☐ Coolant level low. Check and add coolant (Chapter 1).
☐ Leak in cooling system. Check cooling system hoses and radiator for leaks and other damage. Repair or renew parts as necessary (Chapter 3).
☐ Thermostat sticking open or closed. Check and renew as described in Chapter 3.
☐ Coolant passages clogged. Drain and flush the entire system, then refill with fresh coolant.
☐ Water pump defective. Remove the pump and check the components (Chapter 3).
☐ Clogged radiator fins. Clean them by blowing compressed air through the fins from the back of the radiator.
☐ Cooling fan or fan switch fault (Chapter 3).

Engine overheats – air-cooled engines

☐ Air cooling ducts or engine cowling blocked or incorrectly fitted.
☐ Problem with cooling fan.

Firing incorrect

☐ Spark plug fouled, defective or worn out. See Chapter 1 for spark plug maintenance.
☐ Incorrect spark plug.
☐ Ignition control unit defective (Chapter 5).
☐ Faulty ignition HT coil (Chapter 5).

Fuel/air mixture incorrect

☐ Main jet clogged. Dirt, water or other contaminants can clog the main jet. Clean the fuel tap filter, the in-line filter, the float chamber and the jets and carburettor orifices (Chapter 4).
☐ Main jet wrong size. The standard jetting is for sea level atmospheric pressure and oxygen content.
☐ Air bleed holes clogged. Remove and overhaul carburettor (Chapter 4).
☐ Air filter clogged, poorly sealed, or missing (Chapter 1).
☐ Air filter housing or duct poorly sealed. Look for cracks, holes or loose clamps or screws, and renew or repair defective parts.
☐ Fuel level too high or too low. Check the float height or fuel level (Chapter 4).
☐ Carburettor inlet manifold loose. Check for cracks, breaks, tears or loose fixings.

Compression too high

☐ Carbon build-up in combustion chamber. Use of a fuel additive that will dissolve the adhesive bonding the carbon particles to the piston crown and chamber is the easiest way to remove the build-up. Otherwise, the cylinder head will have to be removed and decarbonised (Chapter 2A or 2B). On two-stroke engines, the regular service interval for cylinder head decarbonisation should be adhered to.
☐ Improperly machined head surface or installation of incorrect size cylinder base gasket during engine assembly.

Engine load excessive

☐ Clutch slipping, drive belt worn, or variator faulty (Chapter 6).
☐ Engine oil level too high (four-stroke engines). The addition of too much oil will cause pressurisation of the crankcase and inefficient engine operation. Check Specifications and drain to proper level (Chapter 1).
☐ Engine oil viscosity too high (four-stroke engines). Using a heavier oil than the one recommended in Chapter 1 can damage the oil pump or lubrication system as well as cause drag on the engine.
☐ Brakes dragging. On disc brakes, usually caused by debris which has entered the brake piston seals, or from a warped disc or bent axle, or cable out of adjustment where appropriate. On drum brakes, cable out of adjustment, shoe return spring broken. Repair as necessary (Chapter 8).

Lubrication inadequate

☐ Engine oil level too low (four-stroke engines). Friction caused by intermittent lack of lubrication or from oil that is overworked can cause overheating. The oil provides a definite cooling function in the engine. Check the oil level (Chapter 1).
☐ Oil pump out of adjustment (two-stroke engines) . Adjust pump cable (Chapter 1).
☐ Poor quality oil or incorrect viscosity or type. Oil is rated not only according to viscosity but also according to type. Some oils are not rated high enough for use in this engine. Check the Specifications section and change to the correct oil (Chapter 1). On two-stroke engines, make sure that you use a two-stroke oil which is suitable for oil injection engines.

Miscellaneous causes

☐ Modification to exhaust system. Most aftermarket exhaust systems cause the engine to run leaner, which make them run hotter. When installing an accessory exhaust system, always obtain advice on rejetting the carburettor.

5 Transmission problems

No drive to rear wheel

☐ Drive belt broken (Chapter 6).
☐ Clutch not engaging (Chapter 6).
☐ Clutch or drum excessively worn (Chapter 6).

Transmission noise or vibration

☐ Bearings worn. Also includes the possibility that the shafts are worn. Overhaul the transmission (Chapter 6).
☐ Gears worn or chipped (Chapter 6).
☐ Clutch drum worn unevenly (Chapter 6).
☐ Worn bearings or bent shaft (Chapter 6).
☐ Loose clutch nut or drum nut (Chapter 6).

Poor performance

☐ Variator worn or insufficiently greased (Chapter 6).
☐ Weak or broken driven pulley spring (Chapter 6).
☐ Clutch or drum excessively worn (Chapter 6).
☐ Grease on clutch friction material (Chapter 6).
☐ Drive belt excessively worn (Chapter 6).

Clutch not disengaging completely

☐ Weak or broken clutch springs (Chapter 6).
☐ Engine idle speed too high (Chapter 1).

6 Abnormal engine noise

Knocking or pinking

☐ Carbon build-up in combustion chamber. Use of a fuel additive that will dissolve the adhesive bonding the carbon particles to the piston crown and chamber is the easiest way to remove the build-up. Otherwise, the cylinder head will have to be removed and decarbonised (Chapter 2A or 2B). On two-stroke engines, always decarbonise the cylinder head and piston crown at the recommended service interval (Chapter 1).

☐ Incorrect or poor quality fuel. Old or improper fuel can cause detonation. This causes the pistons to rattle, thus the knocking or pinking sound. Drain the old fuel and always use the recommended grade fuel (Chapter 4).

☐ Spark plug heat range incorrect. Uncontrolled detonation indicates that the plug heat range is too hot. The plug in effect becomes a glow plug, raising cylinder temperatures. Install the proper heat range plug (Chapter 1).

☐ Improper air/fuel mixture. This will cause the cylinder to run hot and lead to detonation. Clogged jets or an air leak can cause this imbalance. See Chapter 4.

Piston slap or rattling

☐ Cylinder-to-piston clearance excessive. Caused by improper assembly. Inspect and overhaul top-end parts (Chapter 2A or 2B).

☐ Connecting rod bent. Caused by over-revving, trying to start a badly flooded engine or from ingesting a foreign object into the combustion chamber. Renew the damaged parts (Chapter 2A or 2B).

☐ Piston pin or piston pin bore worn or seized from wear or lack of lubrication. Renew damaged parts (Chapter 2A or 2B).

☐ Piston ring(s) worn, broken or sticking. Overhaul the top-end (Chapter 2A or 2B).

☐ Piston seizure damage. Usually from lack of lubrication or overheating. Renew the piston and where possible, rebore the cylinder, as necessary (Chapter 2A or 2B). On two-stroke engines, check that the oil pump is correctly adjusted.

☐ Connecting rod upper or lower end clearance excessive. Caused by excessive wear or lack of lubrication. Renew worn parts.

Valve noise – four-stroke engines

☐ Incorrect valve clearances. Adjust the clearances by referring to Chapter 1.

☐ Valve spring broken or weak. Check and renew weak valve springs (Chapter 2B).

☐ Camshaft bearings worn or damaged. Lack of lubrication at high rpm is usually the cause of damage. Insufficient oil or failure to change the oil at the recommended intervals are the chief causes. (Chapter 2B).

Other noise

☐ Exhaust pipe leaking at cylinder head connection. Caused by improper fit of pipe or loose exhaust flange. All exhaust fasteners should be tightened evenly and carefully. Failure to do this will lead to a leak.

☐ Crankshaft runout excessive. Caused by a bent crankshaft (from over-revving) or damage from an upper cylinder component failure.

☐ Engine mounting bolts loose. Tighten all engine mount bolts (Chapter 2A or 2B).

☐ Crankshaft bearings worn (Chapter 2A or 2B).

☐ Camshaft drive gear assembly defective (four-stroke engines). Replace according to the procedure in Chapter 2B.

7 Abnormal frame and suspension noise

Front end noise

☐ Steering head bearings loose or damaged. Clicks when braking. Check and adjust or replace as necessary (Chapters 1 and 7).

☐ Bolts loose. Make sure all bolts are tightened to the specified torque (Chapter 7).

☐ Fork tube bent. Good possibility if machine has been in a collision. Renew the tube or the fork assembly (Chapter 7).

☐ Front axle nut loose. Tighten to the specified torque (Chapter 8).

☐ Loose or worn wheel or hub bearings. Check and renew as needed (Chapter 8).

Shock absorber noise

☐ Fluid level incorrect. Indicates a leak caused by defective seal. Shock will be covered with oil. Renew the shock (Chapter 7).

☐ Defective shock absorber with internal damage. This is in the body of the shock and can't be remedied. The shock must be renewed (Chapter 7).

☐ Bent or damaged shock body. Renew the shock (Chapter 7).

☐ Loose or worn suspension linkage components. Check and renew as necessary (Chapter 7).

Brake noise

☐ Squeal caused by dust on brake pads or shoes. Usually found in combination with glazed pads or shoes. Clean using brake cleaning solvent (Chapter 8).

☐ Contamination of brake pads or shoes. Oil or brake fluid causing brake to chatter or squeal. Renew pads or shoes (Chapter 8).

☐ Pads or shoes glazed. Caused by excessive heat from prolonged use or from contamination. Do not use sandpaper, emery cloth, carborundum cloth or any other abrasive to roughen the pad surfaces as abrasives will stay in the pad material and damage the disc or drum. A very fine flat file can be used, but pad or shoe renewal is advised (Chapter 8).

☐ Disc or drum warped. Can cause a chattering, clicking or intermittent squeal. Usually accompanied by a pulsating lever and uneven braking. Check the disc runout and the drum ovality (Chapter 8).

☐ Loose or worn wheel (front) or transmission (rear) bearings. Check and renew as needed (Chapters 8 or 6).

8 Excessive exhaust smoke

White smoke – four-stroke engines (oil burning)

- ☐ Piston oil ring worn. The ring may be broken or damaged, causing oil from the crankcase to be pulled past the piston into the combustion chamber. Renew the rings (Chapter 2B).
- ☐ Cylinder worn, or scored. Caused by overheating or oil starvation. The cylinder will have to be rebored and an oversize piston installed (Chapter 2B).
- ☐ Valve stem oil seal damaged or worn. Renew oil seals (Chapter 2B).
- ☐ Valve guide worn. Inspect the valve guides and if worn seek the advice of a scooter dealer (Chapter 2B).
- ☐ Engine oil level too high, which causes the oil to be forced past the rings. Drain oil to the proper level (*Daily (pre-ride) checks*).
- ☐ Head gasket broken between oil return and cylinder. Causes oil to be pulled into the combustion chamber. Renew the head gasket and check the head for warpage (Chapter 2B).
- ☐ Abnormal crankcase pressurisation, which forces oil past the rings.

White/blue smoke – two-stroke engines (oil burning)

- ☐ Oil pump cable adjustment incorrect. Check throttle cable/oil pump cable adjustment (Chapter 1).
- ☐ Accumulated oil deposits in the exhaust system. If the scooter is used for short journeys only, the oil residue from the exhaust gases will condense in the cool silencer. Take the scooter for a long run to burn off the accumulated oil residue.

Black smoke (over-rich mixture)

- ☐ Air filter clogged. Clean or renew the element (Chapter 1).
- ☐ Main jet too large or loose. Compare the jet size to the Specifications (Chapter 4).
- ☐ Automatic choke faulty (Chapter 4).
- ☐ Fuel level too high. Check and adjust the float height or fuel level as necessary (Chapter 4).
- ☐ Float needle valve held off needle seat. Clean the float chamber and fuel line and renew the needle and seat if necessary (Chapter 4).

Brown smoke (lean mixture)

- ☐ Main jet too small or clogged. Lean condition caused by wrong size main jet or by a restricted orifice. Clean float chamber and jets and compare jet size to specifications (Chapter 4).
- ☐ Fuel flow Insufficient. Float needle valve stuck closed due to chemical reaction with old fuel. Float height or fuel level Incorrect. Restricted fuel hose. Clean hose and float chamber and adjust float if necessary.
- ☐ Carburettor inlet manifold clamp loose (Chapter 4).
- ☐ Air filter poorly sealed or not installed (Chapter 1).
- ☐ Ignition timing incorrect (Chapter 5).

9 Poor handling or stability

Handlebar hard to turn

- ☐ Steering head bearing adjuster nut too tight. Check adjustment as described in Chapter 1.
- ☐ Bearings damaged. Roughness can be felt as the bars are turned from side-to-side. Replace bearings and races (Chapter 7).
- ☐ Races dented or worn. Denting results from wear in only one position (eg, straight ahead), from a collision or hitting a pothole or from dropping the machine. Renew races and bearings (Chapter 7).
- ☐ Steering stem lubrication inadequate. Causes are grease getting hard from age or being washed out by high pressure car washes. Disassemble steering head and repack bearings (Chapter 7).
- ☐ Steering stem bent. Caused by a collision, hitting a pothole or by dropping the machine. Renew damaged part. Don't try to straighten the steering stem (Chapter 7).
- ☐ Front tyre air pressure too low (*Daily (pre-ride) checks*).

Handlebar shakes or vibrates excessively

- ☐ Tyres worn (Chapter 8).
- ☐ Suspension pivots worn. Renew worn components (Chapter 7).
- ☐ Wheel rim(s) warped or damaged. Inspect wheels for runout (Chapter 8).
- ☐ Wheel bearings worn. Worn wheel bearings (front) or transmission bearings (rear) can cause poor tracking. Worn front bearings will cause wobble (Chapter 8).
- ☐ Handlebar mountings loose (Chapter 7).
- ☐ Front suspension bolts loose. Tighten them to the specified torque (Chapter 7).

- ☐ Engine mounting bolts loose. Will cause excessive vibration with increased engine rpm (Chapter 2A or 2B).

Handlebar pulls to one side

- ☐ Frame bent. Definitely suspect this if the machine has been in a collision. May or may not be accompanied by cracking near the bend. Renew the frame (Chapter 7).
- ☐ Wheels out of alignment. Caused by improper location of axle spacers or from bent steering stem or frame (Chapter 7 or 8).
- ☐ Steering stem bent. Caused by impact damage or by dropping the machine. Renew the steering stem (Chapter 7).
- ☐ Fork tube bent (telescopic fork models). Disassemble the forks and renew the damaged parts (Chapter 7).

Poor shock absorbing qualities

Too hard:
- a) Fork grease or oil quantity excessive (Chapter 7).
- b) Fork grease or oil viscosity too high. Refer to your scooter handbook or check with a scooter dealer.
- c) Suspension bent. Causes a harsh, sticking feeling (Chapter 7).
- d) Fork or front shock internal damage (Chapter 7).
- e) Rear shock internal damage (Chapter 7).
- f) Tyre pressure too high (Chapter 1).

Too soft:
- a) Fork grease or oil viscosity too light. Refer to your scooter handbook or check with a scooter dealer.
- b) Fork or shock spring(s) weak or broken (Chapter 7).
- c) Shock internal damage or leakage (Chapter 7).

10 Braking problems – disc brakes

Brakes are ineffective

- ☐ Air in brake hose. Caused by inattention to master cylinder fluid level or by leakage. Locate problem and bleed brake (Chapter 8).
- ☐ Pads or disc worn (Chapter 8).
- ☐ Brake fluid leak. Locate problem and rectify (Chapter 8).
- ☐ Contaminated pads. Caused by contamination with oil, grease, brake fluid, etc. Renew pads. Clean disc thoroughly with brake cleaner (Chapter 8).
- ☐ Brake fluid deteriorated. Fluid is old or contaminated. Drain system, replenish with new fluid and bleed the system (Chapter 8).
- ☐ Master cylinder internal parts worn or damaged causing fluid to bypass (Chapter 8).
- ☐ Master cylinder bore scratched by foreign material or broken spring. Repair or renew master cylinder (Chapter 8).
- ☐ Disc warped. Renew disc (Chapter 8).
- ☐ On some scooters the master cylinder is operated by a short cable from the handlebar lever. Check that the cable is correctly adjusted and moves freely (Chapter 8).

Brake lever pulsates

- ☐ Disc warped. Renew disc (Chapter 8).
- ☐ Axle bent. Renew axle (Chapter 8).
- ☐ Brake caliper bolts loose (Chapter 8).
- ☐ Wheel warped or otherwise damaged (Chapter 8).
- ☐ Wheel or hub bearings damaged or worn (Chapter 8).

Brakes drag

- ☐ Master cylinder piston seized. Caused by wear or damage to piston or cylinder bore (Chapter 8).
- ☐ Lever balky or stuck. Check pivot and lubricate (Chapter 8).
- ☐ Brake caliper piston seized in bore. Caused by wear or ingestion of dirt past deteriorated seal (Chapter 8).
- ☐ Brake pads damaged. Pad material separated from backing plate. Usually caused by faulty manufacturing process or from contact with chemicals. Renew pads (Chapter 8).
- ☐ Pads improperly installed (Chapter 8).

11 Braking problems – drum brakes

Brakes are ineffective

- ☐ Cable incorrectly adjusted. Check cable (Chapter 1).
- ☐ Shoes or drum worn (Chapter 8).
- ☐ Contaminated shoes. Caused by contamination with oil, grease, brake fluid, etc. Renew shoes. Clean drum thoroughly with brake cleaner (Chapter 8).
- ☐ Brake lever arm incorrectly positioned, or cam excessively worn (Chapter 8).

Brake lever pulsates

- ☐ Drum warped. Renew drum (Chapter 8).
- ☐ Axle bent. Renew axle (Chapter 8).
- ☐ Wheel warped or otherwise damaged (Chapter 8).
- ☐ Wheel/hub bearings (front) or transmission bearings (rear) damaged or worn (Chapter 8).

Brakes drag

- ☐ Cable incorrectly adjusted or requires lubrication. Check cable (Chapter 1).
- ☐ Shoe return springs broken (Chapter 8).
- ☐ Lever balky or stuck. Check pivot and lubricate (Chapter 8).
- ☐ Lever arm or cam binds. Caused by inadequate lubrication or damage (Chapter 8).
- ☐ Brake shoe damaged. Friction material separated from shoe. Usually caused by faulty manufacturing process or from contact with chemicals. Renew shoes (Chapter 8).
- ☐ Shoes improperly installed (Chapter 8).

12 Electrical problems

Battery dead or weak

- ☐ Battery faulty. Caused by sulphated plates which are shorted through sedimentation. Also, broken battery terminal making only occasional contact (Chapter 10).
- ☐ Battery cables making poor electrical contact (Chapter 10).
- ☐ Load excessive. Caused by addition of high wattage lights or other electrical accessories.
- ☐ Ignition (main) switch defective. Switch either earths internally or fails to shut off system. Renew the switch (Chapter 10).
- ☐ Regulator/rectifier defective (Chapter 10).
- ☐ Alternator stator coil open or shorted (Chapter 10).
- ☐ Wiring faulty. Wiring either shorted to earth or connections loose in ignition, charging or lighting circuits (Chapter 10).

Battery overcharged

- ☐ Regulator/rectifier defective. Overcharging is noticed when battery gets excessively warm (Chapter 10).
- ☐ Battery defective. Renew battery (Chapter 10).
- ☐ Battery amperage too low, wrong type or size. Install manufacturer's specified amp-hour battery to handle charging load (Chapter 10).

Note: *References throughout this index are in the form "Chapter Number" • "Page Number"*

Haynes Motorcycle Manuals – The Complete List

Title	Book No
APRILIA RS50 (99 - 06) & RS125 (93 - 06)	4298
Aprilia RSV1000 Mille (98 - 03) ♦	4255
BMW 2-valve Twins (70 - 96) ♦	0249
BMW K100 & 75 2-valve Models (83 - 96) ♦	1373
BMW R850, 1100 & 1150 4-valve Twins (93 - 04) ♦	3466
BMW R1200 (04 - 06) ♦	4598
BSA Bantam (48 - 71)	0117
BSA Unit Singles (58 - 72)	0127
BSA Pre-unit Singles (54 - 61)	0326
BSA A7 & A10 Twins (47 - 62)	0121
BSA A50 & A65 Twins (62 - 73)	0155
DUCATI 600, 620, 750 and 900 2-valve V-Twins (91 - 05) ♦	3290
Ducati MK III & Desmo Singles (69 - 76) ◊	0445
Ducati 748, 916 & 996 4-valve V-Twins (94 - 01) ♦	3756
GILERA Runner, DNA, Ice & SKP/Stalker (97 - 07)	4163
HARLEY-DAVIDSON Sportsters (70 - 03) ♦	2534
Harley-Davidson Shovelhead and Evolution Big Twins (70 - 99) ♦	2536
Harley-Davidson Twin Cam 88 (99 - 03) ♦	2478
HONDA NB, ND, NP & NS50 Melody (81 - 85) ◊	0622
Honda NE/NB50 Vision & SA50 Vision Met-in (85 - 95) ◊	1278
Honda MB, MBX, MT & MTX50 (80 - 93)	0731
Honda C50, C70 & C90 (67 - 03)	0324
Honda XR80/100R & CRF80/100F (85 - 04)	2218
Honda XL/XR 80, 100, 125, 185 & 200 2-valve Models (78 - 87)	0566
Honda H100 & H100S Singles (80 - 92) ◊	0734
Honda CB/CD125T & CM125C Twins (77 - 88) ◊	0571
Honda CG125 (76 - 07) ◊	0433
Honda NS125 (86 - 93)	3056
Honda CBR125R (04 - 07)	4620
Honda MBX/MTX125 & MTX200 (83 - 93) ◊	1132
Honda CD/CM185 200T & CM250C 2-valve Twins (77 - 85)	0572
Honda XL/XR 250 & 500 (78 - 84)	0567
Honda XR250L, XR250R & XR400R (86 - 03)	2219
Honda CB250 & CB400N Super Dreams (78 - 84) ◊	0540
Honda CR Motocross Bikes (86 - 01)	2222
Honda CRF250 & CRF450 (02 - 06)	2630
Honda CBR400RR Fours (88 - 99) ◊ ♦	3552
Honda VFR400 (NC30) & RVF400 (NC35) V-Fours (89 - 98) ◊ ♦	3496
Honda CB500 (93 - 01) ◊	3753
Honda CB400 & CB550 Fours (73 - 77)	0262
Honda CX/GL500 & 650 V-Twins (78 - 86)	0442
Honda CBX550 Four (82 - 86) ◊	0940
Honda XL600R & XR600R (83 - 00)	2183
Honda XL600/650V Transalp & XRV750 Africa Twin (87 to 07) ♦	3919
Honda CBR600F1 & 1000F Fours (87 - 96) ♦	1730
Honda CBR600F2 & F3 Fours (91 - 98) ♦	2070
Honda CBR600F4 (99 - 06) ♦	3911
Honda CB600F Hornet & CBF600 (98 - 06) ◊ ♦	3915
Honda CBR600RR (03 - 06) ♦	4590
Honda CB650 sohc Fours (78 - 84)	0665
Honda NTV600 Revere, NTV650 and NT650V Deauville (88 - 05) ◊ ♦	3243
Honda Shadow VT600 & 750 (USA) (88 - 03)	2312
Honda CB750 sohc Four (69 - 79)	0131
Honda V45/65 Sabre & Magna (82 - 88)	0820
Honda VFR750 & 700 V-Fours (86 - 97) ♦	2101
Honda VFR800 V-Fours (97 - 01) ♦	3703
Honda VFR800 V-Tec V-Fours (02 - 05) ♦	4196
Honda CB750 & CB900 dohc Fours (78 - 84)	0535
Honda VTR1000 (FireStorm, Super Hawk) & XL1000V (Varadero) (97 - 00) ♦	3744
Honda CBR900RR FireBlade (92 - 99) ♦	2161
Honda CBR900RR FireBlade (00 - 03) ♦	4060
Honda CBR1000RR Fireblade (04 - 07) ♦	4604
Honda CBR1100XX Super Blackbird (97 - 07) ♦	3901
Honda ST1100 Pan European V-Fours (90 - 02) ♦	3384
Honda Shadow VT1100 (USA) (85 - 98)	2313
Honda GL1000 Gold Wing (75 - 79)	0309
Honda GL1100 Gold Wing (79 - 81)	0669

Title	Book No
Honda Gold Wing 1200 (USA) (84 - 87)	2199
Honda Gold Wing 1500 (USA) (88 - 00)	2225
KAWASAKI AE/AR 50 & 80 (81 - 95)	1007
Kawasaki KC, KE & KH100 (75 - 99)	1371
Kawasaki KMX125 & 200 (86 - 02) ◊	3046
Kawasaki 250, 350 & 400 Triples (72 - 79)	0134
Kawasaki 400 & 440 Twins (74 - 81)	0281
Kawasaki 400, 500 & 550 Fours (79 - 91)	0910
Kawasaki EN450 & 500 Twins (Ltd/Vulcan) (85 - 04)	2053
Kawasaki EX500 (GPZ500S) & ER500 (ER-5) (87 - 05) ♦	2052
Kawasaki ZX600 (ZZ-R600 & Ninja ZX-6) (90 - 06) ♦	2146
Kawasaki ZX-6R Ninja Fours (95 - 02) ♦	3541
Kawasaki ZX-6R (03 - 06) ♦	4742
Kawasaki ZX600 (GPZ600R, GPX600R, Ninja 600R & RX) & ZX750 (GPX750R, Ninja 750R) ♦	1780
Kawasaki 650 Four (76 - 78)	0373
Kawasaki Vulcan 700/750 & 800 (85 - 04) ♦	2457
Kawasaki 750 Air-cooled Fours (80 - 91)	0574
Kawasaki ZR550 & 750 Zephyr Fours (90 - 97) ♦	3382
Kawasaki Z750 & Z1000 (03 - 08) ♦	4762
Kawasaki ZX750 (Ninja ZX-7 & ZXR750) Fours (89 - 96) ♦	2054
Kawasaki Ninja ZX-7R & ZX-9R (94 - 04) ♦	3721
Kawasaki 900 & 1000 Fours (73 - 77)	0222
Kawasaki ZX900, 1000 & 1100 Liquid-cooled Fours (83 - 97) ♦	1681
KTM EXC Enduro & SX Motocross (00 - 07) ♦	4629
MOTO GUZZI 750, 850 & 1000 V-Twins (74 - 78)	0339
MZ ETZ Models (81 - 95) ◊	1680
NORTON 500, 600, 650 & 750 Twins (57 - 70)	0187
Norton Commando (68 - 77)	0125
PEUGEOT Speedfight, Trekker & Vivacity Scooters (96 - 05) ◊	3920
PIAGGIO (Vespa) Scooters (91 - 06) ◊	3492
SUZUKI GT, ZR & TS50 (77 - 90) ◊	0799
Suzuki TS50X (84 - 00) ◊	1599
Suzuki 100, 125, 185 & 250 Air-cooled Trail bikes (79 - 89)	0797
Suzuki GP100 & 125 Singles (78 - 93) ◊	0576
Suzuki GS, GN, GZ & DR125 Singles (82 - 05) ◊	0888
Suzuki 250 & 350 Twins (68 - 78)	0120
Suzuki GT250X7, GT200X5 & SB200 Twins (78 - 83) ◊	0469
Suzuki GS/GSX250, 400 & 450 Twins (79 - 85)	0736
Suzuki GS500 Twin (89 - 06) ♦	3238
Suzuki GS550 (77 - 82) & GS750 Fours (76 - 79)	0363
Suzuki GS/GSX550 4-valve Fours (83 - 88)	1133
Suzuki SV650 & SV650S (99 - 05) ♦	3912
Suzuki GSX-R600 & 750 (96 - 00) ♦	3553
Suzuki GSX-R600 (01 - 03), GSX-R750 (00 - 03) & GSX-R1000 (01 - 02) ♦	3986
Suzuki GSX-R600/750 (04 - 05) & GSX-R1000 (03 - 06) ♦	4382
Suzuki GSF600, 650 & 1200 Bandit Fours (95 - 06) ♦	3367
Suzuki Intruder, Marauder, Volusia & Boulevard (85 - 06) ♦	2618
Suzuki GS850 Fours (78 - 88)	0536
Suzuki GS1000 Four (77 - 79)	0484
Suzuki GSX-R750, GSX-R1100 (85 - 92), GSX600F, GSX750F, GSX1100F (Katana) Fours ♦	2055
Suzuki GSX600/750F & GSX750 (98 - 02) ♦	3987
Suzuki GS/GSX1000, 1100 & 1150 4-valve Fours (79 - 88)	0737
Suzuki TL1000S/R & DL1000 V-Strom (97 - 04) ♦	4083
Suzuki GSX1300R Hayabusa (99 - 04) ♦	4184
Suzuki GSX1400 (02 - 07) ♦	4758
TRIUMPH Tiger Cub & Terrier (52 - 68)	0414
Triumph 350 & 500 Unit Twins (58 - 73)	0137
Triumph Pre-Unit Twins (47 - 62)	0251
Triumph 650 & 750 2-valve Unit Twins (63 - 83)	0122
Triumph Trident & BSA Rocket 3 (69 - 75)	0136
Triumph Bonneville (01 - 07) ♦	4364
Triumph Daytona, Speed Triple, Sprint & Tiger (97 - 05) ♦	3755
Triumph Triples and Fours (carburettor engines) (91 - 04) ♦	2162
VESPA P/PX125, 150 & 200 Scooters (78 - 06)	0707
Vespa Scooters (59 - 78)	0126
YAMAHA DT50 & 80 Trail Bikes (78 - 95) ◊	0800
Yamaha T50 & 80 Townmate (83 - 95) ◊	1247
Yamaha YB100 Singles (73 - 91) ◊	0474

Title	Book No
Yamaha RS/RXS100 & 125 Singles (74 - 95)	0331
Yamaha RD & DT125LC (82 - 87) ◊	0887
Yamaha TZR125 (87 - 93) & DT125R (88 - 02) ◊	1655
Yamaha TY50, 80, 125 & 175 (74 - 84) ◊	0464
Yamaha XT & SR125 (82 - 03) ◊	1021
Yamaha Trail Bikes (81 - 00)	2350
Yamaha 2-stroke Motocross Bikes 1986 - 2006	2662
Yamaha YZ & WR 4-stroke Motocross Bikes (98 - 07)	2689
Yamaha 250 & 350 Twins (70 - 79)	0040
Yamaha XS250, 360 & 400 sohc Twins (75 - 84)	0378
Yamaha RD250 & 350LC Twins (80 - 82)	0803
Yamaha RD350 YPVS Twins (83 - 95)	1158
Yamaha RD400 Twin (75 - 79)	0333
Yamaha XT, TT & SR500 Singles (75 - 83)	0342
Yamaha XZ550 Vision V-Twins (82 - 85)	0821
Yamaha FJ, FZ, XJ & YX600 Radian (84 - 92)	2100
Yamaha XJ600S (Diversion, Seca II) & XJ600N Fours (92 - 03) ♦	2145
Yamaha YZF600R Thundercat & FZS600 Fazer (96 - 03) ♦	3702
Yamaha FZ-6 Fazer (04 - 07) ♦	4751
Yamaha YZF-R6 (99 - 02) ♦	3900
Yamaha YZF-R6 (03 - 05) ♦	4601
Yamaha 650 Twins (70 - 83)	0341
Yamaha XJ650 & 750 Fours (80 - 84)	0738
Yamaha XS750 & 850 Triples (76 - 85)	0340
Yamaha TDM850, TRX850 & XTZ750 (89 - 99) ◊ ♦	3540
Yamaha YZF750R & YZF1000R Thunderace (93 - 00) ♦	3720
Yamaha FZR600, 750 & 1000 Fours (87 - 96) ♦	2056
Yamaha XV (Virago) V-Twins (81 - 03) ♦	0802
Yamaha XVS650 & 1100 Drag Star/V-Star (97 - 05) ♦	4195
Yamaha XJ900F Fours (83 - 94) ♦	3239
Yamaha XJ900S Diversion (94 - 01) ♦	3739
Yamaha YZF-R1 (98 - 03) ♦	3754
Yamaha YZF-R1 (04 - 06) ♦	4605
Yamaha FZS1000 Fazer (01 - 05) ♦	4287
Yamaha FJ1100 & 1200 Fours (84 - 96) ♦	2057
Yamaha XJR1200 & 1300 (95 - 06) ♦	3981
Yamaha V-Max (85 - 03) ♦	4072

ATVs

Title	Book No
Honda ATC70, 90, 110, 185 & 200 (71 - 85)	0565
Honda Rancher, Recon & TRX250EX ATVs	2553
Honda TRX300 Shaft Drive ATVs (88 - 00)	2125
Honda TRX300EX, TRX400EX & TRX450R/ER ATVs (93 - 06)	2318
Kawasaki Bayou 220/250/300 & Prairie 300 ATVs (86 - 03)	2351
Polaris ATVs (85 - 97)	2302
Polaris ATVs (98 - 06)	2508
Yamaha YFS200 Blaster ATV (88 - 02)	2317
Yamaha YFB250 Timberwolf ATVs (92 - 00)	2217
Yamaha YFM350 & YFM400 (ER and Big Bear) ATVs (87 - 03)	2126
Yamaha Banshee and Warrior ATVs (87 - 03)	2314
Yamaha Kodiak and Grizzly ATVs (93 - 05)	2567
ATV Basics	10450

TECHBOOK SERIES

Title	Book No
Twist and Go (automatic transmission) Scooters Service and Repair Manual	4082
Motorcycle Basics TechBook (2nd Edition)	3515
Motorcycle Electrical TechBook (3rd Edition)	3471
Motorcycle Fuel Systems TechBook	3514
Motorcycle Maintenance TechBook	4071
Motorcycle Modifying	4272
Motorcycle Workshop Practice TechBook (2nd Edition)	3470

◊ = not available in the USA   ♦ = Superbike

The manuals on this page are available through good motorcycle dealers and accessory shops.
In case of difficulty, contact: **Haynes Publishing**
(UK) +44 1963 442030   (USA) +1 805 498 6703
(SV) +46 18 124016
(Australia/New Zealand) +61 3 9763 8100

MCL23.12/07

Preserving Our Motoring Heritage

< The Model J Duesenberg Derham Tourster. Only eight of these magnificent cars were ever built – this is the only example to be found outside the United States of America

Almost every car you've ever loved, loathed or desired is gathered under one roof at the Haynes Motor Museum. Over 300 immaculately presented cars and motorbikes represent every aspect of our motoring heritage, from elegant reminders of bygone days, such as the superb Model J Duesenberg to curiosities like the bug-eyed BMW Isetta. There are also many old friends and flames. Perhaps you remember the 1959 Ford Popular that you did your courting in? The magnificent 'Red Collection' is a spectacle of classic sports cars including AC, Alfa Romeo, Austin Healey, Ferrari, Lamborghini, Maserati, MG, Riley, Porsche and Triumph.

A Perfect Day Out

Each and every vehicle at the Haynes Motor Museum has played its part in the history and culture of Motoring. Today, they make a wonderful spectacle and a great day out for all the family. Bring the kids, bring Mum and Dad, but above all bring your camera to capture those golden memories for ever. You will also find an impressive array of motoring memorabilia, a comfortable 70 seat video cinema and one of the most extensive transport book shops in Britain. The Pit Stop Cafe serves everything from a cup of tea to wholesome, home-made meals or, if you prefer, you can enjoy the large picnic area nestled in the beautiful rural surroundings of Somerset.

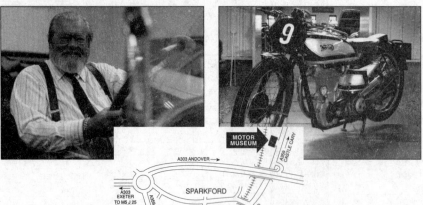

> John Haynes O.B.E., Founder and Chairman of the museum at the wheel of a Haynes Light 12.

< The 1936 490cc sohc-engined International Norton – well known for its racing success

The Museum is situated on the A359 Yeovil to Frome road at Sparkford, just off the A303 in Somerset. It is about 40 miles south of Bristol, and 25 minutes drive from the M5 intersection at Taunton.
Open 9.30am - 5.30pm (10.00am - 4.00pm Winter) 7 days a week, *except Christmas Day, Boxing Day and New Years Day*
Special rates available for schools, coach parties and outings Charitable Trust No. 292048